Object-Oriented Programming In Pascal

Object-Oriented Programming in Pascal

A Graphical Approach

D. Brookshire Conner Brown University

David Niguidula Brown University

Andries van Dam Brown University

Addison-Wesley Publishing Company • Reading, Massachusetts • Menlo Park, California • New York • Don Mills, Ontario • Workingham, England • Amsterdam Bonn • Sydney • Singapore • Tokyo • Madrid • San Juan • Milan • Paris

The cover shows a G. Rhoads/Rock Stream audiokinetic sculpture in Logan Airport in Boston. The sculpture is a complex system of ramps and elevators, constantly moving chrome balls through an intricate structure. Here, as in an object-oriented program, simple objects have been assembled into an artwork greater than the sum of its parts.

This book was reproduced from text and illustration files supplied by the authors.

Figure 2.1 reprinted with special permission of King Features Syndicates.

Sponsoring Editor: Lynne Doran Cote
Assistant Editor: Maite Suarez-Rivas
Production Supervisor: Juliet Silveri
Copyeditor/Proofreader: Joyce Grandy
Cover Design Supervisor: Eileen Hoff
Manufacturing Manager: Roy Logan

Library of Congress Cataloging-in-Publication Data

Conner, D. Brookshire.
Object-oriented programming in Pascal: a graphical approach / D. Brookshire Conner, David A. Niguidula, Andries van Dam.
p. cm.
ISBN 0-201-62883-X
1. Object-oriented programming (Computer science) 2. Pascal (Computer program language) I. Niguidula, David A. II. van Dam, Andries, 1938- . III. Title.
QA76.64.C638 1995
005. 13'3--dc20 94-48465
CIP

1 2 3 4 5 6 7 8 9 10-MA-9998979695

Preface

The book you are holding represents a new direction in introductory computer science instruction. For more than a decade, we've been hearing that object-oriented programming (OOP) is "the wave of the future" and that it has a central place in the computer science curriculum. Recently, the debate has moved from *whether* OOP belongs in the curriculum to *where* it belongs. Now, with this book, we present our answer: We think OOP should be taught at the beginning. We don't mean that OOP should be introduced sometime during the first course; OOP should be part of the very first chapter.

What's more, the premise of this book is that students need to see *all* of OOP at the beginning. Students then can write significant object-oriented programs using all of the OOP mechanisms, from inter-object communication via parameters and pointers, to inheritance, virtual methods, and polymorphism, before learning most features of the programming language, such as flow of control, arithmetic, or even base types. Then, as students learn more about the constructs of the language, they can use the tools of object-oriented design to create even more powerful, extensible programs.

The power of OOP, we have discovered, can be diluted if students do not see all of the machinery at the beginning, tempting as it might be to delay concepts such as pointers, virtual methods, and polymorphism. It has been our experience that students' programs become too convoluted because they must compensate for missing functionality. Our approach cultivates good object-oriented design habits from the start and puts OOP power to work as early as possible, to allow construction of programs of significant size and complexity.

For those of us who have been teaching structured (procedural) programming, teaching OOP at the start requires a significant shift in mindset. In teaching this new way ourselves, we have occasionally felt uncomfortable giving up "tried and true" pedagogy for this new approach. However, the payoff has been terrific. It's exciting to watch students design and build interactive paint programs less than a month into the course, then create a working arcade game (like Tetris) just halfway through a semester. It's satisfying to know that students go into later courses with a solid start in object-oriented design and programming.

We hope that you, too, find this approach exciting and worthwhile.

PARSING THE TITLE

Our title, *Object-Oriented Programming in Pascal: A Graphical Approach*, may not win any awards for brevity, but we do think it accurately reflects what is truly important and unique about this book. To elaborate, allow us to deconstruct our title.

Object-Oriented Programming

Object-oriented design and programming form the foundation of this book. In the first eight chapters (Part I) of the book, we devote our full attention to *all* the key concepts of OOP: defining objects and instances, sending messages, creating communication links, inheritance, virtual methods, and polymorphism. To make sure these concepts aren't just so many big words, we show how they play out in practice by examining complete Pascal programs. However, these programs do not require learning much Pascal syntax; essentially, all we need are the statements to declare classes, instances, and variables; message passing and parameters; a brief introduction to pointers; and assignment. In the rest of the book, we cover the traditional topics such as arithmetic, flow of control, and arrays, but always from an OOP point of view.

Throughout Part I, we also place a heavy emphasis on the design of programs. Knowing how to program is more than learning the syntax of a particular language; a good programmer is one who can take a specification and design a solution that will meet the user's needs. An object-oriented approach requires that we think about the program as a system of objects from the beginning of the design process.

We emphasize that the objects in the system should be designed for re-use. Although this concept may be a little more abstract, since we are forced to think about more than the task currently at hand, we think it pays off well. In the early chapters, we focus on the use (and re-use) of objects in existing libraries; later, we spend more time designing new objects that can be used in multiple programs.

Learning the technique of "systems thinking" requires practice with systems. Besides the numerous exercises (which we will describe in more detail shortly), we also provide examples of programs, where we start with a specification, walk through the design, and show the development of the code. Chapter 8, for example, walks through the development of a simple interactive paint program and ties together the ideas of OOP described in Part I.

Of course, we don't leave objects behind once we finish those chapters. Object-oriented design and programming techniques permeate the book.

Pascal

This text uses Pascal. Specifically, we have written all of the code using Borland Pascal for Windows. Borland provides extensive object libraries with all of its Pascal products. The Borland Pascal for Windows environment is quite friendly, with its debugging and help facilities that both novice and expert programmers can appreciate. As an abbreviation, we refer to the Pascal language and the object-oriented extensions as OOPas (for *Object-Oriented Pascal*).

Beyond the tools that come with Borland Pascal for Windows, we've also added our own library of objects for Windows called GP (for *Graphics Package*). These additional classes are not meant as a substitute for the complete package provided by Borland; rather, they are a basic set of graphic user interface (GUI) tools that provide a way to get started with object-oriented programming. GP has enough functionality that students can use it in advanced courses as well.

If you want to run the programs in this book, you need both Borland Pascal for Windows and the GP library. (Details on how to obtain GP appear a little later in this Preface.)

Some of you may be wondering why we didn't use another language; after all, Pascal is not inherently an object-oriented language. We spent a good deal of time examining C++, as well as more "purely" object-oriented languages such as Eiffel and Self. We believe C++ is too large, idiosyncratic, and unsafe for introductory students. It is all too possible for introductory students to get lost in the complexity and obscure run-time errors of C++, when we would rather that they focus on the basics of programming and design. It's been our experience that when we do teach C++ (in the fourth course in our computer science sequence), our OOPas-trained students transfer their knowledge quite well. Languages like Eiffel and Self hold a great deal of promise, but, at the moment, are not in common enough use.

A Graphical Approach

We kept the same subtitle as our earlier work, *Pascal on the Macintosh: A Graphical Approach* (Addison-Wesley, 1987), for the same reasons. First, interactive graphics programming has become even more crucial for today's computer professionals; the vast majority of programs written on all platforms have graphical user interfaces and the bulk of code in interactive programs lies in their GUIs. Indeed, the reason most of our examples involve various aspects of GUIs is that GUIs are the most common denominator of the types of programs students will write after they complete their studies, and GP gives them a solid foundation in this important area of software.

The graphical approach also reinforces our emphasis on objects. To learn how to use objects, students need a library, and it made sense for that library to have a focus. The library could focus on a specific discipline, such as engineering or music, but that would necessarily limit our examples to ideas from that discipline and would assume reader knowledge of that discipline. Rather, we chose graphics as the focus so that very little prior knowledge — essentially, just some basic ideas from high school algebra and geometry — was required for students to understand what the objects are and what they do.

We've also found that graphics is particularly attractive for students who are new to programming. It's easy for students to make the connections between objects in their programs and graphical objects that appear on the screen. The graphical user interface is a familiar paradigm for today's students, who are increasingly familiar with computers prior to taking the introductory course. Finally, graphics programs are easier to debug, provide more satisfying results, and are simply more fun than traditional number- and character-crunching programs.

The idea of "a graphical approach" also implies that we use graphics to teach programming concepts. You will see illustrations generously distributed throughout the book, especially to explain some of the more notoriously difficult concepts, such as recursion, linked lists, and object interrelationships.

FEATURES

The Graphics Package (GP) Library

When we began teaching our objects-first approach in 1993, we began with the hypothesis that students could learn OOP from the start only if they were given a set of interesting, building-block objects from which they could create programs. First, however, the students needed access to a set of objects that were powerful enough to build applications, yet could be understood, as we said earlier, with little background in any particular domain. The result is the Graphics Package (GP) library.

Parts of GP are explained in detail in the text; Appendix D also contains descriptions of the GP classes students will need to use. Rather than just read about GP, however, students can explore how it works by loading the library into Borland Pascal. With this software, students have access to basic graphics tools (such as lines, colors, and ovals) and graphical user interface widgets (such as buttons and sliders). In addition, GP contains tools for creating simple animations.

The software and the accompanying documentation are being distributed, free of charge, on the Internet. The software distribution site also contains all of the code for the examples in the book, so students can, for example, actually use the paint program described in Chapter 8 and see how GP (and OOPas) work.

To access the software from the Internet, use telnet or ftp to access `aw.com`. At the prompt, log in as `anonymous` and use your Internet address as the password. From there, you can change to the `conner.cs1.oop` directory with the command `cd conner.cs1.oop`. The `readme.txt` file in that directory contains more detailed instructions and descriptions of all the files you may want to download. Documentation as well as source code also are available via the World Wide Web at the following URL:

```
http://www.cs.brown.edu/software/gp/
```

Object Diagrams and Syntax Boxes

We've also adopted a convention for showing object classes, instances, and the relationships among them. The *object diagrams* seen throughout the text are based on the notation developed by James Rumbaugh and colleagues in *Object-Oriented Modeling and Design* (Prentice-Hall, 1991). These illustrations show not just the contents of each object, but how it works as a part of the program's system.

Important object classes, such as classes in GP, are described in their own *object boxes*. A list of object boxes in the main text appears after the Table of Contents.

Each new Pascal concept is summarized in a *syntax box* that describes the concept's purpose, syntax, and usage. We've found that these boxes are useful references, so you will find a list of syntax boxes after the Table of Contents.

Exercises for All Students

Each chapter concludes with a summary and exercises. We've included three types of exercises: *Understanding Concepts,* which are short-answer or discussion questions; *Coding Problems*, which ask the reader to write a section of a program, such as an object definition or a method; and *Programming Problems*, which are complete programming projects that can be completed using the concepts addressed thus far in the book and the object libraries. The topics of the problems come from many different disciplines and activities, and they should prove interesting to more than just computer science majors.

WHAT YOU'LL FIND INSIDE

This book is designed for introductory computer science courses and could be used over one or two semesters, or two or three quarters. We expect that a single semester course could cover at least all of Parts I and II, and the strings and array chapters in Part III. Courses that move at a brisker pace could add the sets and files chapters in Part III and/or the chapters of Part IV. We do not assume that every instructor will cover every chapter. Here, then, is a brief description of how the chapters are organized.

Part I: Objects

As we mentioned earlier, the first eight chapters focus on the primary concepts of object-oriented programming. All of the programs in this chapter are built using GP, or a special "Starter Unit" of objects assembled from several GP objects. We use the object classes of these libraries as building blocks for our programs, starting in Chapter 2. We do cover familiar Pascal territory: the PROGRAM statement; the mainline; declaring variables, procedures, and functions; and using parameters. In addition, we look at the syntax necessary for implementing object-oriented concepts, such as the declaration of objects in the TYPE section of a program, the use of key words such as CONSTRUCTOR and INHERITED, the declaration of links, associations (pointers) and of subclasses, and the use of units.

These chapters form the foundation for the rest of the book, and we strongly recommend that these chapters be covered in order so that students have all of the requisite machinery.

Part II: Syntax for Math and Flow of Control

The second part covers the fundamentals of standard Pascal. Here, we see the concepts that most books discuss at the beginning: numbers, constants, and flow of control. We also introduce recursion in this section of the book and discuss the common bugs that occur when using flow-of-control statements, as well as strategies and tools to use in debugging.

Taking advantage of our approach, we use examples in this section that rely on the graphics primitives of GP. We also have tried to put every concept in the book in the context of object-oriented programming. In this section, we discuss how the object-oriented tools described in Part I, such as polymorphism, can implicitly perform some of the same results as code explicitly written with flow-of-control statements such as CASE. The OOP tools also allow us to approach some traditional topics in new ways: For example, we can describe recursion as a specific case of sending messages from one instance to another. This use of recursion is revisited in the chapters on data structures.

Part III: Built-in Collections

The third part addresses some of the more advanced fundamentals of Pascal. We examine characters and strings and the accompanying string functions. We explore one- and two-dimensional arrays and discuss the way Pascal allows us to work with structures such as sets and files. As an example of using the string functions, we also begin exploring the ideas of grammars and parsing. This may provide introductory students with just a small peek at some of the topics they are likely to encounter in later computer science courses. (Some instructors may choose to skip the sections or chapters on parsing, sets, and files, since that material is not needed for subsequent chapters.)

Part IV: Data Structures

The final part deals with dynamic storage allocation and the data structures that rely on it. The order of our chapters is a little different from most books: We introduce stacks, queues, and then linked lists, followed by trees. We begin by showing how the stack data structure allows nodes to be added and removed (in a particular manner) from one end of a collection. Queues extend the idea by implementing the addition and removal of nodes using both ends. Linked lists go even further, allowing for insertion and deletion at any point in the list of nodes. Finally, trees add the ability to place nodes on branches.

All of these structures, however, are based on the notion that individual nodes within the list are objects, not just records. For this reason, you may find that our approach to inserting and removing nodes from these structures differs from what one sees in a procedural programming approach. By providing our nodes with the necessary methods to insert and delete, we maintain our OOP approach of cooperating objects and create structures that are more flexible (through polymorphism) than "traditional" dynamic data structures tend to be. Should you have time, the final chapter provides a brief introduction to the analysis of algorithms, as a bridge to upper-level courses.

FORMATTING AND NOTATIONS

A number of notations are used throughout the text. Code, whether in the text body or separated in the text, appears in `Courier`. New ideas initially appear in *italics*. Metavariables in code appear in ***`italicized Courier`***.

Class boxes are summaries of the classes used in the book. Each class box has two or three parts. The first part is the class's title, which also includes a brief description of the class's intended purpose. This is followed by a section describing the class's methods. This section does not necessarily list *all* of the methods available — just the ones relevant for the part of the book the class is being used in. Consult Appendix D for complete GP documentation. Finally, some class boxes will include a third section describing the class's instance variables. Most class boxes do not include this section, as it is not necessary to know the class's implementation in order to use it effectively.

Syntax boxes are summaries of Pascal instructions, and most of these boxes follow the same format. The *Purpose* section provides a brief overview of when the instruction is used. The *Syntax* section provides an example of the syntax itself. Parts of the syntax that are programmer-specified (as opposed to keywords) are enclosed in angle brackets and italicized. A section titled *Where* describes any limitations on the elements used in the syntax. The *Returns* section describes the values that a function may return. Finally, the *Usage* section describes the semantics of the syntax shown. You will also see that syntax boxes appear with a gray background.

ACKNOWLEDGMENTS

This project would not have been worthwhile — or even possible — without the input of students in our introductory class at Brown. Since 1992, students in Computer Science 15 (and its predecessor, Computer Science 11) have provided valuable feedback on the book, on GP, and on our entire approach to object-oriented programming and design. We thank them for their patience as we experimented on them and for their many constructive contributions.

Each year, a group of students become even more involved with the course as undergraduate teaching assistants. They truly are the engine that makes the course run. The TAs in 1992, 1993, and 1994 particularly helped a great deal with the preparation of this manuscript, from formatting earlier drafts to being the first respondents to the text. We'd like to acknowledge our appreciation for all of the TAs' help, and we'd like to particularly mention Dave Wadhwani, Aris Kavour, and Ed Bielawa, for countless summer hours spent over a hot word processor, and Gwen Shipley, Bidemi Carrol, Ron Palmon, and Ely Greenfield, for taking primary responsibility for helping to get the first drafts of the manuscript into a form that students could use.

We also want to thank two individuals who have gone far and above the call of duty. Robert Duvall has been of great assistance in our own transition from a procedural programming to an OOP approach in our class, being involved in discussions ranging from the choice of a language to the creation of assignments. He was deeply involved in developing the first version of GP (with Brook Conner, Ed Bielawa, and Ralph Ruiz) and has been very helpful in teaching the rest of our TAs to think "the OOP way."

Ralph Ruiz has been a crucial part of this book in each of its versions, from being a teaching assistant and then head teaching assistant for the course, to developing the version of GP that uses Windows, to sweating out the figures and code examples throughout the manuscript. Ralph has provided expertise, intelligence, and insight to this collective effort.

Our colleagues in the Brown Computer Science Department have encouraged our efforts in developing this introductory course and in designing a curriculum that emphasizes objects throughout our students' careers. Trina Avery, as always, has provided valuable assistance in the editing of this text, and Lori Agresti has done wonders to keep us all in constant communication. Mary-Kim Arnold also provided top-rate copyediting, spending many hours at each phase of the manuscript's development. As a student of the class at the same time, she was especially helpful at finding passages that while grammatically correct were completely baffling to the new student.

Addison-Wesley has made an important commitment to this new approach to introductory computer science, and we particularly appreciate the efforts of Lynne Doran Cote, Maite Suarez-Rivas, Peter Gordon, Juliet Silveri, and the editing, production, and marketing staffs. We also want to thank the reviewers who contributed their time and comments to help improve this work: Anthony Baxter (University of Kentucky), Kim Bruce (Williams College),

Leon Levine (University of California–Los Angeles), Don Retzlaff (University of North Texas), Janice T. Searleman (Clarkson University), and Allen Tucker (Bowdoin College). Pat Lewis provided valuable comments.

Our families have been most supportive throughout the development of this project, showing much patience, understanding, and affection, even when we fell into our "writing moods." Our warmest thank you's for tolerating us go to Mary-Kim, to Reina and Gregory (and Gregory's new brother or sister), to Debbie, and to all of our families and friends.

We hope you will provide your thoughts and reactions to this book and its approach; you can contact us via e-mail at `dbc@cs.brown.edu` (Brook Conner), `dan@cs.brown.edu` (David Niguidula), and `avd@cs.brown.edu` (Andy van Dam). Enjoy!

Providence, Rhode Island

D.B.C.
D.A.N.
A.v.D.

Contents

Figures

11. Choosing One of Many

12. Loops

13. Recursion

14. Bugs and Debugging

15. Letters and Strings

16. Arrays

23. Linked Lists **491**

24. Trees **525**

Class Boxes

Syntax Boxes

10. Making Choices 235

11. Choosing One of Many 261

12. Loops 277

15. Letters and Strings 337

16. Arrays 353

17. Sets 373

18. Parsing Strings 387

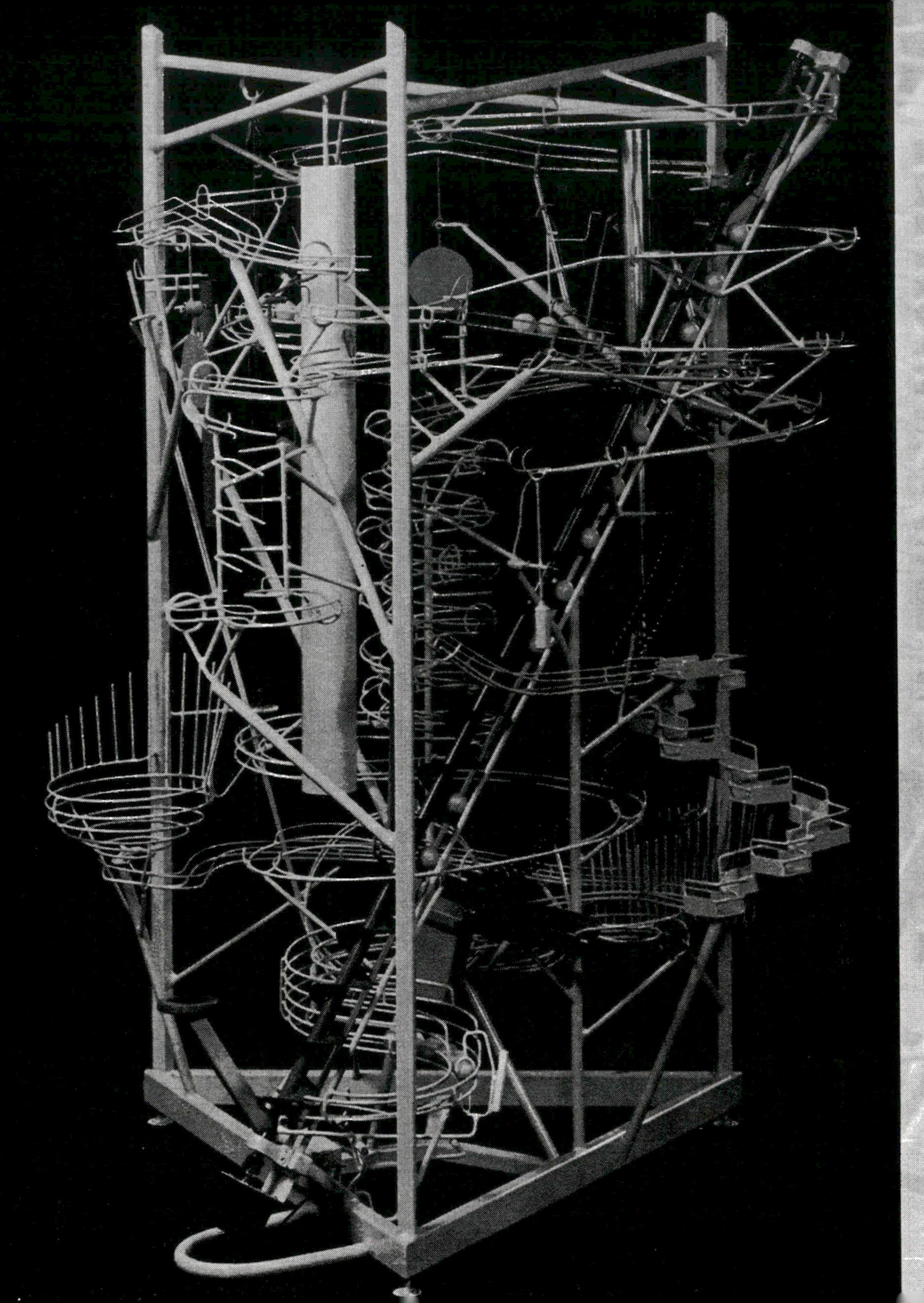

Part I

Objects

When we write programs, we are designing and implementing *systems*. In this book, we will be using *objects* as the fundamental building blocks of our systems. There are many different ways you can design systems, and many different ways you can implement these designs using computer programming. This book focuses on a particular style of design and programming, one centered on objects. Thus this book is about *object-oriented design* and *object-oriented programming*.

The book as a whole is divided into four parts. The first part describes the fundamentals of object-oriented design and object-oriented programming. In the first eight chapters, you will be learning how to use objects effectively and how to make high-quality objects of your own. In many ways, this is the most important part of the book. The remaining parts fill in some details and present some widely useful system designs. Thus if you have a complete and thorough understanding of this part of the book, the rest should be easy.

The second part of the book describes tools for developing the component parts of your own objects. If you've programmed before, you should find many of these tools familiar. The third part describes some basic ways to handle fixed-size collections of objects. The book finishes with some powerful ways to organize collections of objects, where the collections can grow and shrink in size over time.

We'll start Part I of the book with a description of a computer and how we will be using it. We'll also introduce you to the basic idea of a system. Starting in Chapter 2, you'll see how to use some objects that someone else has defined, and then, in Chapter 3, you'll learn how to make simple objects. Chapter 4 will show you some of the complexities of getting objects to talk to one another. You'll continue in the following chapter by exploring how to describe the relationships between objects in a system.

Chapter 6 will bring you to inheritance — the heart of object-oriented programming and what makes it truly different from other programming styles. That is the turning point, and where you will start building large, exciting programs. You'll build a complete paint program, starting in Chapter 6 and adding features to it in Chapters 7 and 8 as you learn how to design and build larger and more complex systems. At that point, you'll have completed our tour of objects.

1 Computers and Design: A Bird's-Eye View

1.1 WHAT WILL YOU LEARN IN THIS BOOK?

Let's start at the most natural place to begin: the end. You're finishing a programming project from the final chapter. Over the past few weeks, you have been putting your program together, piece by piece. You began with a vision of what you wanted your program to do and have turned that vision into a reality. Slowly, like an artist creating a sculpture, you have shaped your program; you have kept the overall vision in mind as you designed the pieces and worked on each detail.

Your program represents all the things you have learned since you started reading this book. You have considered the problem carefully and determined how the solution can be represented as a system of cooperating components called *objects*, each itself possibly composed of smaller objects. You have determined which objects you could reuse from other programs and which objects you needed to create just for your program. You have thought about your audience — the people who may use your completed program — and designed a program that is "user-friendly." In other words, you have used object-oriented design techniques to guide your creation.

Maybe you've written several thousand lines of Pascal, the programming language used in this book, but the task hasn't been overwhelming because your design is well structured and logical. You used a "divide and conquer" technique to break down the program into an organized set of objects. Your program is accompanied by *documentation* — text that explains how the whole system works and what each object does. The documentation was written so that you, or some other programmer, can reuse the objects later.

The program has benefited from your patience and your ingenuity. You needed patience to *debug* your design carefully — in other words, to fix the errors (or *bugs*) that inevitably appear — and to take the time to *test* your program in order to find the bugs and ensure that your objects behave as expected. Your ingenuity is evident in the design, since no two programmers design a program in quite the same way.

Now is the moment of truth. You show the program to a friend who is an experienced programmer or to an instructor. She first runs the program as if she were a naive computer user, then reads through your program listing, looking at how you have designed your objects. Next, she peruses your documentation. Finally, she looks at you and says, "Fantastic." You lean back in your chair, satisfied. After all, you have accomplished a major feat. You have learned what it takes to design and implement a program.

OK. Let's leap back to the present. You may be thinking, "I thought programming was just learning a language to type into a computer!" You may be imagining yourself sitting at a computer in the middle of the night, drowning in reams of computer paper filled with incomprehensible words like `XOR` and `Readln`, searching desperately for some elusive bug.

Programming doesn't have to be like that. The "trick" to solving a programming problem, whether it is your first academic assignment or a professional group project, is to have a good *design*. Although the specific terminology of programming is important, it is not as essential to building a working program as a complete and thorough design. This book discusses a design strategy that currently is being used at all levels of programming work — *object-oriented design*. This strategy makes it possible to organize programs as sets of objects that, when put together, model the real (or an imaginary) world. Objects and object-oriented design will be discussed in more detail later in this chapter.

The goal of programming is to make the computer do something useful, fun, or both for a particular user. Your boss might want to use the computer to chart financial growth; your brother or sister might want to play a computer game. As a programmer, you will be able to take a specification that is stated informally in a natural (human) language — English in our case — and from this specification create an appropriate design, develop the objects that comprise your design, write a program in a computer language, and finally deliver a program that meets the specification you were given.

The programming/problem-solving process we will use in this book is the same one used to create the computer applications that you encounter every day. We will discuss the fundamental techniques that are used by real-world programmers to develop application programs ranging from automatic teller machines to air traffic control systems to molecular modeling systems to computer games. As the book progresses, we will talk more specifically about many topics, including object-oriented design, the *syntax* (the formal punctuation, order, and rules for constructing statements in the language) of Pascal, and the use of computer graphics. However, the specifics are just the means to an end. The goal of programming is to make useful tools.

In fact, we won't see any of these details in this chapter. There are no programs to read or write here; just a bird's-eye view of computing, objects, and design.

1.2 COMPUTER TERMINOLOGY

Learning to use a computer is much like learning your way around a new city. At first, all the new sights can seem overwhelming, but soon things become familiar. Once you have learned how to get where you need to go, you can explore new areas. Similarly, even though you will be introduced to a great deal of material in these early chapters, the basics of programming soon will become second nature.

Hardware: Things You Can Touch

Let's begin with a brief tour of your computer. The physical parts of the machine are referred to collectively as its *hardware*. If you can touch it, it's hardware. So hardware includes the obvious parts of a computer, such as its *screen* (or *monitor*), *keyboard*, and *mouse*. All these components usually are connected to the back of a *box* (slang for "computer") by cables. You will see all these parts if you sit in front of your own computer, or, if it isn't handy, in Figure 1.1. When you type at the keyboard or manipulate the mouse, your actions are communicated to the main box. "What's inside the box?" you might ask.

Figure 1.1

The hardware of a computer

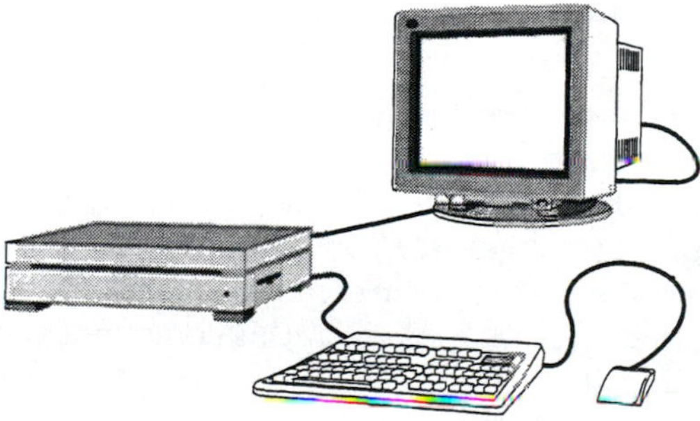

Just as the external hardware is made up of interconnected parts, if you were to open the box and look inside, you'd see that the internal hardware is divided into parts also connected to one another. The most important part is the *central processing unit* (or CPU for short). This is a computer chip, also known as a microprocessor, where much of the real work of the computer is performed. The CPU is connected to the other parts, including *memory*, where the CPU can store information it needs to retrieve quickly. Other internal components include various sorts of *disk drives*, including floppy drives, hard drives, and CD-ROM drives, which are different devices the CPU can use to store and retrieve information. The CPU performs this function by communicating with the drives, which typically are controlled by their own chips (though these specialized controllers often are quite simple). By communicating with other chips, the CPU can perform other functions, such as drawing pictures on the monitor, performing advanced mathematics, or talking to other computers over a network. Figure 1.2 shows a schematic of the various parts inside a computer.

Figure 1.2
A schematic of the parts inside a computer

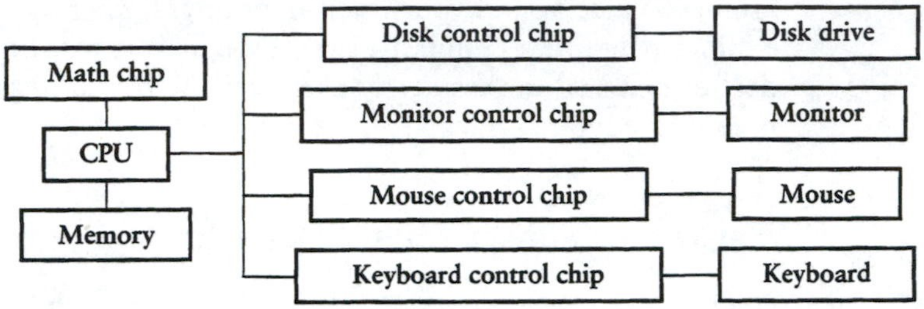

In essence, a computer is a collection of special-purpose parts, all working together. Each part does its own job: The disk drives store information, the monitor draws pictures, and the CPU oversees the entire activity. We're going to build programs that work in much the same way. Various parts of our programs will be specialized for various jobs. By cooperating, simple parts can be put together into more complex parts. But how and why do these simple parts cooperate?

Manipulating Information: What Computers Do

Computers are machines for manipulating information. That information could be poetry. It could be equations or mathematical surfaces or pictures or music. It could be alien space monsters in a video game. To manipulate all these kinds of information, the computer must have a way to describe it all. We've seen that computers are made up of specialized parts that communicate with one another. Let's take a look at this communication.

When people talk to one another, they use a language. When they want to save some information, they use that same language. For example, this book contains information about programming, and it is written in English. Computer parts, however, aren't smart enough to use a complicated and often ambiguous human language like English. Because each part is simple and specialized, computer parts use a simple and specialized language.

English uses an alphabet of twenty-six letters. Computer language also uses letters, but because computer parts are simple and specialized, computer language uses the simplest useful alphabet possible, consisting of only two letters. These letters typically are represented by the numerals "1" and "0," which correspond to "on" and "off," in the computer. This is just about the smallest alphabet you could use. Think about it — if you had an alphabet with only one letter, like "a," all the words in your language would be pretty boring. Your words would be things like "aaaa" or "a" or "aaaaaaaa." With two letters, things are still pretty boring, but at least you can make patterns: "101010" or "111011101110" or "001001001." We can call the computer's alphabet a *binary alphabet*, to refer to the two characters used. Since we use digits instead of letters in our alphabet, words in this language are made up of binary digits, more commonly known as *bits* (from *b*inary dig*it*).

As we have seen, bits can form patterns. Through these patterns, a computer can store descriptions and communicate the information the descriptions contain. Those descriptions could be words or sentences or even pictures. For example, consider a smiley face, represented as a series of bits, with zeros white and ones black, as shown in Figure 1.3.

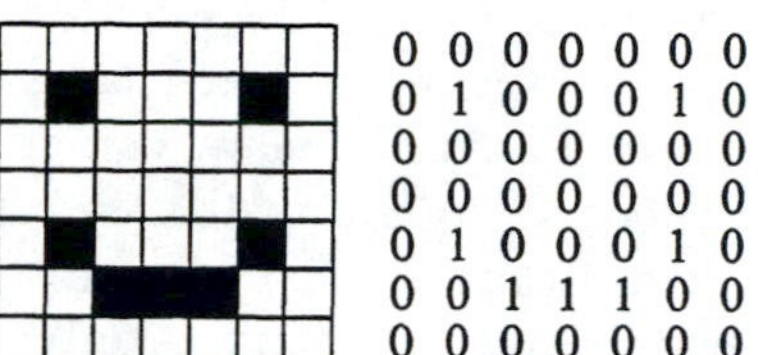

Figure 1.3

A smiley face in binary, with zeros white and ones black

One of the most amazing features about computers is that fundamentally all they use are patterns of ones and zeros, organized into ever more complex patterns. You may wonder exactly how a machine can "understand" these patterns and do so many things with them. Think back to the days of the Old West. To communicate between towns that were hundreds of miles apart, telegraph companies connected wires across the plains. Operators sent messages across these wires using Morse code — a system of electrical dots and dashes representing letters, numbers, and punctuation.

A computer also runs on electrical impulses. The CPU consists of many hundreds of thousands, even several million, simple electronic devices, each of them either on or off, corresponding to the two letters in the computer's "alphabet." This CPU equivalent of Morse code is called *machine code*. Machine code relays simple instructions and data to and from the CPU by using the equivalent of dots and dashes. Zeros represent CPU devices that are off, and ones represent devices that are on.

Single bits don't tell the CPU very much, so bits are grouped into larger units. For example, each character in English text (such as a single letter, digit, or punctuation mark) is stored in the machine's memory as a sequence of eight bits, or one *byte*, and instructions and data typically are stored in two, four, or eight consecutive bytes.[1]

Bits and bytes are what the computer uses to communicate among its many parts. The sequences of electrical impulses, organized in long patterns of on and off, are what make a computer work. What we'll examine next is how people can create and manipulate those sequences.

1. You will notice that many things in computer science come in units of 1, 2, 4, 8, 16, and other powers of 2. Often, this is because we can represent things in binary code: One bit can represent two values, two bits can represent 2^2 (four) values, three bits can represent 2^3 (eight) values, and so on.

Software: Things You Can't Touch

Now we know a bit about the computer's hardware and how the hardware's parts work together. But all this talk of *hard*ware might have you asking, "So then what is *soft*ware?" A simple answer is that if hardware is the parts of the computer you can touch, then software is the parts of the computer you can't touch. A better answer is that software is the patterns of bits stored in and manipulated by the hardware.

When the CPU retrieves information from memory, it receives a long and complex pattern of bits. The main job of the CPU is to interpret that pattern and perform actions based on that interpretation. It does this by associating different patterns with different actions. The sequence "11100000" is a code that might mean "add two numbers together," while "01011010" might mean "draw a line on the screen." As before, we can put these relatively simple patterns and interpretations together to make more complex patterns and interpretations, just like letters can be combined into words, then phrases, then sentences, then paragraphs, then chapters, then books. This is how software gets built — simple parts are combined into more complex parts.

For example, some software provides the CPU with instructions on how to communicate with the other parts of the hardware. This software usually is called the *operating system*, because it is a *system* of cooperating software parts telling the CPU how to *operate* the rest of the computer. The operating system, or OS for short, provides easier ways for other software to operate the computer. Word processing software uses the operating system to save files on the hard disk, rather than reproducing the complex patterns of controlling the hard disk itself. A video game is a piece of software that makes extensive use of the parts of the operating system that deal with drawing on the screen. Both word processing software and video games use the operating system to get information about the keyboard and the mouse. Other kinds of software make use of other parts of the operating system.

Programming is the art, craft, and engineering discipline of designing and building software. To program effectively, you will make extensive use of software that has been written by other programmers. Let's take a closer look at some other software now.

Writing Programs: Building Your Own Parts

When you create your own software, you write a *program*. Think of your program as a detailed and precise description of something you want to build. Computers are, in some sense, extremely stupid. They aren't very good at resolving ambiguity or incompleteness. Thus your program must be extremely precise and detailed.

If you used English to describe software, a computer wouldn't be able to understand it, because most English sentences, like sentences in all natural languages, contain ambiguities and incomplete thoughts. So, we need to use a *programming language* instead of a natural language like English. The particular language we will be using is called *Pascal.*

Pascal, like other programming languages and natural languages, uses a *grammar* — a set of rules that you must follow in order to be understood. The difference is that, in a natural language, if you hear someone use incorrect grammar, you usually can determine what the person meant anyway. In a programming language, however, if your grammar is incorrect, the computer has no idea what you may have meant. Again, this is because computers have no imagination; they are one hundred percent literal-minded.

A set of grammatical rules describes the *syntax* of a language. For example, English grammar includes the rule that most statements have a subject followed by a verb. We refer to grammatical mistakes in a program as *syntax errors*. Just one syntax error can keep an entire program from running. As in a good short story, every word in a program has a purpose; every punctuation mark and every formatting convention has a purpose as well. If you leave out or mix up any part of the description, the computer can't be sure it understands every single thing you're trying to describe.

A number of computer languages are available for writing programs. You may have heard of some of them: BASIC, C, C++, FORTRAN, COBOL, LISP. We are using Pascal as an introductory language for a number of reasons. First, it is a relatively simple and common language, used by students and professional programmers throughout the world for developing application programs. Versions of Pascal exist for most hardware *platforms* (personal computers, or PCs for short, workstations, mainframes, and other computers). Second, Pascal is powerful enough to develop any application, from databases to arcade games, and has enough structure to help beginning programmers implement their programs with relative ease. Finally, many modern versions of Pascal have "object-oriented extensions," which means that they include additional syntax for defining objects. Borland Pascal is just one such version of this language, and the one we will be using throughout this book. We'll also refer to Borland Pascal and its extensions as OOPas, short for "Object-Oriented Pascal."

So, OOPas is the computer language you will be using to build your programs. You can think of building programs in much the same way you would consider building any physical object, like a car, for example. To build a car, you have to choose different parts (such as engines and wheels and seats) and put them together in the right ways. Object-oriented programming is a lot like that. You're going to choose *objects* and put them together. Now, with a car, you can put things together using tools such as screwdrivers, wrenches, and welding equipment. You'll need tools to build programs, too, but your tools will be very different.

You will need tools that are themselves software in order to build more software, which is a little like using tools to build more tools. The first tool you will use is a *text editor*, which lets you enter and edit your lines of Pascal. It is similar to a word processor, but Borland Pascal's text editor has additional features to make programming easier. For example, Borland's text editor will allow you to highlight "reserved words" — words that have specific meaning in Pascal — and to format your code with indentation.[2]

Once you've used the text editor to describe your program, you have to ask the computer to try to understand that description. The computer must translate your description into machine code that the CPU then can execute. To do this, you will use a tool called a *compiler.* The compiler analyzes your description using the grammar of the programming language and translates it to the corresponding machine code. If the program is not grammatically correct, the compiler can't understand it and can't generate machine code.

We'll look at other pieces of software as we need them. Now, let's take a closer look at the basic ideas behind objects.

1.3 OBJECTS

We've talked a lot about "parts" — the parts of the hardware, the parts of software, and how some of these work together. We've also alluded to how things in the real world are made up of parts. A car's parts include an engine, wheels, and doors. The "object" in "object-oriented programming" corresponds most closely to a part in the real world.

An object simulates a real-world part. It is, however, only a simulation. When you describe an object in Pascal, the object meets that description exactly — no more and no less. Remember, computers are dumb. A computer can't figure out what you mean just because you call an object a "car." You have to tell the computer that cars need engines, and then you have to describe the engine and how to simulate how an engine works, or the simulated car won't run.

The need for explicit description may seem like a limitation, and it does make computer programming harder than many people think it should be. Most programs are extremely complicated and extremely detailed. Even if your program doesn't contain any syntax errors, it could have some incorrect details. As a result, the program doesn't behave quite the way you want it to. Such mistakes are called *bugs*. Bugs occur so frequently that we'll devote an entire chapter to them, and will deal with how to prevent them throughout the entire book.

Despite their need for detail and precision, computers still can simulate most anything you can think of, including other computers. This makes computers the most general-purpose tool ever invented. Hammers are general-purpose tools, too, and even can act a little like other tools. A hammer can simulate a screwdriver, but it does it very poorly. Trying to drive a screw by hitting it with a hammer can leave you with nothing but a broken screw. And try to make a hammer simulate a flashlight or an oven, and you won't get very far at all. Now this isn't to say that a computer can light up a dark room or

2. For further details, refer to your Borland Pascal manual.

bake a soufflé (at least, not without some extra hardware). What a computer can do is describe these processes and mimic them.

So, pick something out in the real world; let's choose a chair. Describing a chair to a computer is like describing a chair to someone who has never seen or used one before, say an alien space monster. Your first reaction probably would be to describe the chair's *attributes* — the color, size, location. Next, you might talk about what the chair is made of, what kind of parts it has, such as legs, seat, and back. However, to your alien space monster, this would not be sufficient. You also would need to describe what a chair can do or what it can be used for; we'll call these functions the chair's *behaviors*. Chairs can be sat upon. They can be moved around. Folding chairs can be folded up. All chairs can support some amount of weight. These aspects of a chair seem pretty obvious, because it is part of our assumptions of what the word "chair" means, but none of this is obvious to a space monster or a computer.

Remember that these associations we now make — a chair is something to sit on — were things we didn't start out knowing. Babies, for example, assume everything they encounter is food — the concept of "chair" as "something to sit on" has to be learned. Thus we come back to the need for lots of detail. Not only do we have to describe what a particular object can do, but we also have to describe the right way to do it. Most people know which end of a hammer to hold on to. Once again, computers don't.

We'll present more detail on what goes into a description of an object in Chapter 2, "Objects." Chapter 3, "Making Objects," will show you how to write your own descriptions.

1.4 ORGANIZING OBJECTS INTO SYSTEMS

You undoubtedly have studied systems in other fields. In biology, the term "system" is used to denote a group of interconnected parts, like the "circulatory system" or the "digestive system." In social studies, we look at systems like "the extended family" or "the democratic system of government." Here, as in those other fields, the system is the whole, made up of smaller parts — in this case, the program is the whole and the individual objects are the smaller parts. Unlike other fields, though, we'll be asking you not just to study existing systems but also to create them.

When you try to describe a single object in complete detail, you end up with quite a lot of information. If you try to describe many objects in complete detail, you end up with more information than any one person can understand. This property isn't specific to objects. It isn't even specific to computers. Any sufficiently complex system is too big for one person to understand completely. For example, doctors specialize in different parts of the body, because the body as a whole is too complicated for any one person to understand in exhaustive detail. So some doctors know more about the heart, and others know more about bones. And others are general practitioners and know quite a bit about everything, but not as much about a specific system as a specialist.

Hiding Unnecessary Information

Despite the fact that a general practitioner doesn't know all the finest details about the intricacies of the way your body works, she still can help you when you feel sick. Why? Simply because she doesn't need to know everything to know what is wrong. Your family doctor doesn't need to be a brain surgeon to give you the proverbial two aspirins for a headache.

Computer software works the same way. You don't need to be a programmer in order to use a word processor. When we design and build our own software systems, we'd like this same kind of thing to be true. It shouldn't be necessary to know everything about a piece of software in order to use it. We call this idea *encapsulation*.

When we describe an object, we describe everything about the object. But not all of this detail is important for using the object. A car has a hood over its engine, hiding the details of the engine from people who normally don't care about it (like the drivers). When we describe an object, we can place a "hood" over parts of the object, simply by describing those parts as being hidden. We will discuss making various parts of an object visible or invisible in Chapter 3.

The Parts Hierarchy

Hiding things isn't the only way to make a system easier to understand. Real-world systems are made up of smaller, simpler subsystems. The human body, for instance, is made up of many subsystems, including the muscular system, the skeletal system, the digestive system, the nervous system, and the circulatory system. Each of these systems is composed of still smaller systems. The circulatory system includes the heart, blood, and blood vessels. The blood vessels themselves are organized by function, with arteries taking blood away from the heart, capillaries distributing blood to cells that need it, and veins returning blood to the heart.

Software systems can be organized the same way. Objects can be made up of other objects. Much like taking stock parts and assembling them into cars, small, simple objects can be assembled into bigger, more complex objects. This idea often is called *software reuse*, because it enables descriptions of objects (software) to be used again and again. Indeed, software reuse is an important benefit of object-oriented design.

By organizing simple objects into complex objects, we create a *parts hierarchy*. The biggest, most complex objects form the top of this hierarchy, and the simplest ones form the bottom of this hierarchy. We will discuss making parts hierarchies in Chapter 3.

A Taxonomy of Objects

Another way to make a software system easier to understand is to describe how different parts are similar to one another. Zoologists describe how various animals are similar or different using a taxonomy. Lions and housecats are kinds of cats. Because both are kinds of cats, we know something about each of them — they both eat meat and pounce on their prey. The fact that both cats and dogs are kinds of mammals tells us how cats and dogs are similar: They both have hair and bear live young.

When you know something about mammals, learning about dogs involves learning only what is special about them. Likewise, learning about cats involves learning only what is special about cats, not the information about mammals that you already know. Knowing about mammals makes it easier to learn about cats. Indeed, learning about any new kind of mammal will be easier. We'll see how to apply this to our software in Chapter 6.

1.5 DESIGNING A SYSTEM

Throughout this book, you will be considered a designer of software systems. Your mission, should you choose to accept it, is to create individual software objects that you will combine to create a software system, which may be used as a subsystem of another software system. We've seen various ways in which systems can be broken down and described, but as we've said, in computer science, you don't just describe systems, you design new ones.

Let's suppose we wanted to create a new kind of bicycle. You can think of the bicycle as a system made of individual objects. (The bicycle itself is an object, as well.) First, we'd consider the specifications of the bicycle — what capabilities should it have? Should it be primarily for off-road or city use? Is it for one or two (or more) people? Second, we might analyze what we know about bicycles and refine our specifications accordingly. Third, we would design both the bicycle as a whole and its component parts. We might find many of the parts we need in a catalog. We also might find that we have to create some parts from scratch. After we have designed the bicycle, we'd go to the fourth step — assembling the bicycle. Finally, we would see whether our new bicycle matched our specifications by testing it in appropriate situations.

Developing a program is similar to the five steps of the bicycle scenario:

1. The *specification* of the system
2. The *analysis* of the specification
3. The *design* of the system
4. The *implementation* of the design
5. The *testing and debugging* of the implementation.

Let's look at each of these stages in detail.

Specifying the System

"What's this program for, anyway?" Before you start laying down hundreds or more of lines of Pascal code, it makes sense to know *why* you are writing the program. Typically, a program starts with a *system specification*, which is a natural-language description of the system. The specification might be trivial — "a program that can calculate the distance between two points on a grid" — or complex — "a simulation of rush-hour traffic in New York City."

The initial specifications for your programs may come from the exercises in this book. Often, you will receive a specification from someone who knows very little about computers and just has some task that a program might help. The specification minimally gives you a description of a system and who might use the program once it is complete.

Analyzing the System

From the specifications, you then can analyze the system. That is, you can ask questions about the system to see whether you understand it and have all the information you need to create it. For example, to calculate the distance between two points, you need to know things like, "What two points?" and "Should the distance be measured in miles or inches or what?" In particular, the analysis should provide a more detailed specification, leading to a better sense of how the system might break into different parts. Analysis should give you a sense of the system as a whole.

Designing the System

Once you understand the system as a whole, you can start to think about the component objects. For example, to design the "distance-between-two-points-on-a-map" system, you might create two objects to represent the points and a line object whose endpoints are defined by those two point objects.

What you are doing is following the strategy of *divide and conquer*. The system as a whole can be considered a single object, but most systems are far too complex to be dealt with all at once. Instead, you can divide the system "object" into component objects, making a parts hierarchy. Certain component objects might still be too big and might have to be divided further into smaller objects. For example, if you were thinking about writing a desktop publishing program, you might think about a "document" that consists of text and figures; the figures might consist of an illustration and a caption; the illustration might have lines and other graphic objects; and the line, as we just saw, would contain two individual points.

The heart of a good program is a good program design. We will be discussing some hints for creating an object design, such as a graphical notation for describing objects and their relationships. We'll also be looking at *pseudocode*, which is a way of describing tasks that is somewhere between

English statements and OOPas code and often is used in the design stage. The care you take at the design stage will save hours of aggravation during the implementation and debugging stages.

Implementing the Design

When you outline a term paper, you might not write in complete sentences. Similarly, when you design objects and their methods, you might not use the full OOPas syntax. So far, you haven't had to worry about the details of the programming language. During the design stage, you will concentrate on what the individual objects represent and how they connect to create the larger system. During the implementation phase, however, you will need to think about how to create the code in OOPas.

Recall that you will use an editor to enter your program. In addition, the OOPas compiler will tell you whether your program is syntactically correct. Another useful tool to help you implement your design is a proper programming *style*. A programming style is not a software tool but a set of conventions for naming components and for laying out the program, including indentation and spacing. Although these conventions are not required to make the program run, they do make the program much easier to read and to understand.[3] You can compare a programming style to a writing style — a paper might be written in either a formal or an informal style. Switching from a formal style to an informal one or vice versa within a single paper can be confusing and make your argument more difficult to follow.

You also will want to *document* your program — that is, provide English language comments with your code — so that you can keep track of what each object represents and what each part of the object does. Documentation might not seem necessary for small programs, but you should get into the habit of writing it. You will appreciate documentation as your programs grow in size and complexity.

Testing and Debugging the Program

A syntactically correct program is not the same as a working program or a complete system. If you have removed all the syntax errors, you can get your program to run. But does it do everything that it was supposed to? And does it do it all correctly?

You need to go back to the specifications and develop ways to test your program. Suppose you have written a program to print a calendar page for any month in history. You might consider the following tests — does it work for months with 30 and with 31 days? Does it handle February correctly? Does it handle leap years correctly? Does it give an appropriate message if the user

---

3. We will describe our stylistic conventions as we look at OOPas code examples.

misspells the name of a month or enters other input that the program doesn't understand?

As you go through your testing, you may notice bugs or errors in the program. *Debugging* is the process of removing those bugs. Some bugs are obvious; others are very subtle and only appear in particular cases. Finding bugs in a program can frustrate even the best programmers, and even the best programmers write imperfect code. So it shouldn't alarm you if the program you have entered doesn't perform exactly as you intended. Somewhere in the transition from your idea of what the program should do to the computer's execution of your compiled program, something was translated incorrectly. The best way to find bugs is to look at the description of each object in your program and carefully examine how the computer interprets that description. Take the time to find the bug before you enter a change in your program — even if that means walking away from your computer for a while. If you make haphazard changes in your program, you may introduce more bugs than you remove.

Although it is important to learn how to debug, the best way to get rid of bugs is not to create them in the first place. Careful specification, analysis, object design, and coding will help prevent bugs from occurring.

Finally, after all of your own testing and debugging, it's time for the true litmus test — giving the program to your intended users. There is a significant difference between "working" programs and "good" programs. A program that works gets the computer to solve the problem at hand, but a good program is one that remembers the human factor. Programs are written by people and are intended for people to use. The creativity you bring to solving problems, the clarity you provide to a design, and the consideration you bring to your program's users are what will make you a "good" programmer.

Summary

Programming is a craft and, like all crafts, it has a technical aspect and a design aspect. The technical aspect requires that you understand a programming language and its syntax. In this book, we will be studying an object-oriented extension to the language Pascal — Borland Pascal (which we will refer to as OOPas). The technical aspect also requires that you learn how to enter, run, and debug a program correctly.

It helps to understand, in a general way, what is going on inside the computer as you work. A computer is made up of many physical parts, called hardware, which, at the instructions of software, perform the various tasks of the computer. Even as technology advances and the latest and greatest devices and programs become available, the component parts of hardware and software still serve the same primary functions.

Although an understanding of the technical aspect of a programming language is necessary, it is not sufficient for learning how to program. Understanding the design aspect of programming is crucial. In this book, we will learn object-oriented design. This approach to programming means that we consider our software products as systems, which are made of independent component parts called objects. These objects each have defined characteristic attributes and behavior and can communicate with one another. The objects and their communication make up the system as a whole.

When you program, you are taking a specification defined by the potential user (or vendor) of the program and designing a system of objects to fulfill that specification. The process of program design uses skills that extend beyond programming and computer science to many other disciplines in which analysis and synthesis are used to create a "product," such as writing a paper, designing a mechanical or electronic system, or creating an econometric model. This book provides some specific hints and suggestions for creating a good program design, starting with the specification of the system and continuing through the phases of implementation and debugging. Ultimately, though, you will develop your own unique style of programming and use your own creativity and ingenuity to write software. This book will not teach you how to find the one right answer to programming problems, since there is no such thing. Rather, you will learn how to use the tools of the craft to shape your own software systems.

Exercises

There are three types of exercises in this book. The Understanding Concepts problems are designed to test your comprehension of the material in the chapter. Usually these questions require a short answer in prose. The Coding Exercises test a specific concept or concepts in programming or program design. Usually you are asked to write or modify a portion of a program. The Programming Problems are extensive problems that use concepts from the current chapter but also rely on your mastery of knowledge from previous chapters. These problems ask you to write entire programs, often using objects that are included in the object libraries we have made available on the Internet. See the Preface for information on how to obtain these libraries.

We will see Coding Exercises and Programming Problems in future chapters.

Understanding Concepts

1. Think about some things you have designed — research papers, science experiments, artistic creations, or household needs. How would you explain the design of those things to someone creating a design for the first time?

2. Compare the design process outlined in this chapter with the process you used to produce some other design you have created.

3. Which of the following are hardware and which are software?

   a. mouse
   b. machine code
   c. disk drive
   d. screen
   e. compiler
   f. memory chips
   g. operating system
   h. Borland Pascal

4. What is the key difference between a programming language like OOPas and machine code?

5. What does it mean to "divide and conquer" a problem?

6. Imagine that you have a robot that understands only four commands: "turn left," "turn right," turn around," and "go forward <distance>" where "distance" is any measure of distance (e.g., 3 miles, 10 steps, 50 meters). Tell your robot how to get from where you live to the grocery store.

7. Describe to a friend, who has never cooked before, how to prepare scrambled eggs, toast, and orange juice. (Assume you've attached labels to all the utensils in the kitchen.)

8. Describe the following systems to a layperson:

   a. How a federal bill becomes a law
   b. How a student registers for classes
   c. How a customer gets food at a restaurant

2

Understanding Objects

In Chapter 1, we saw an analogy between designing a program and designing a bicycle. When a bike racer creates her customized bicycle, she does not simply combine sets of components. She considers the task, the tools, and the catalog of standard parts she has available, and then outlines the job, before putting her winning bicycle together. Similarly, architects are responsible for determining what a client needs from a building, taking into account the site, the resources of materials, time, and money, and developing sketches, blueprints, and models before ground is ever broken. The same "top-down" process of design extends beyond the creation of physical objects. You can see this process in the design of artistic productions, from Broadway shows to corporate logos, and in the design of educational endeavors, from research papers to student seminars.

Like other engineers, artists, or educators, software engineers are responsible for the design and building of products that clients will use. Beginning in this chapter, we will give a description of how to solve programming problems and design object-oriented programs. Like the bicycle designer selecting parts from a catalog, we will start simply by selecting parts and putting them together in a complete solution. In later chapters, we'll see how to build our own parts.

By necessity, there will be a lot of new terminology in this chapter as we work through the words used to describe a computer program. As you will see, some terminology uses familiar English words in the standard sense, some in a more specialized computer-ese sense.

Keep in mind — especially if you are new to programming — that you are using a process of design that you probably have used successfully in projects in the past. Odds are, you have followed the same sequence of specifying a problem, analyzing it, designing a solution, implementing your solution, then testing that solution for correctness. The tools and terminology are different, but the processes are very similar.

2.1 WHAT ARE OBJECTS?

Objects are the building blocks of programs. Objects in a programming language are roughly equivalent to nouns in a natural language in that they represent some person, place, thing, or idea in the software system. Objects may represent tangible things in the real world, like "school," "city," or "automobile," or more abstract concepts like "meeting," "department," or "House of Representatives."

We can describe objects and systems in many different ways, much as we can describe things in the real world in many different ways. Our "real world" descriptions use written or spoken English. However, computers don't understand English. So, in the previous chapter, we introduced the idea of a programming language as a precise language for describing systems that a computer can understand. However, a programming language is in some ways too precise. The precision becomes encumbering. We need alternatives to English and programming languages for describing systems.

As the old saying goes, "A picture is worth a thousand words." Although this may not be true if the words were Hemingway's and the picture was a snapshot by your neighbor's three-year-old child, pictures often can help us gain an understanding of the overall design of a system. Figure 2.1 shows one of cartoonist Rube Goldberg's systems. Each component part has its own role, yet the system as a whole accomplishes a larger goal (in this case, closing a screen door). This system is successful because each object "communicates" with another to trigger the next action.

Figure 2.1 *Rube Goldberg cartoon showing component parts of a system*

When we build software systems, we would like them to be more practical (and less fragile) than Rube Goldberg's systems. But having this picture greatly aids our understanding of what the system is supposed to do, since a textual description of this system would be hopelessly confusing. Let's consider a more real-world example. Figure 2.2 shows one way to look at an automobile — as an electromechanical system with many individual components.

Figure 2.2
Components of an automobile

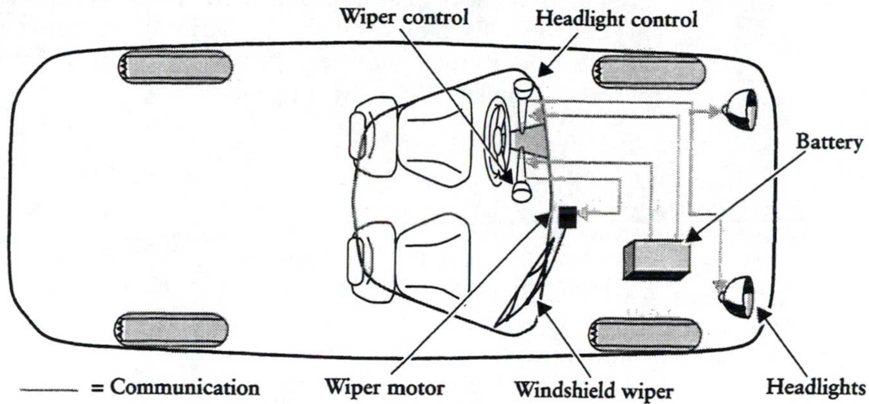

Such a schematic diagram helps greatly in understanding what the individual parts of the automobile are and how they work together (imagine explaining windshield wipers and how to control them to someone who had never seen them). A schematic diagram of our software systems will do the same.

We'll get to schematics of our objects in a moment. First, though, let's look a bit more at the basic aspects of objects. Objects in a software system are like the components of the automobile. Each object in a system has clearly defined *behaviors*, an *identity*, and a *state*.

An Object's Behaviors

An object's *behaviors* are its capabilities — that is, what the object is able to do. Each wiper, for example, moves from left to right (and back again) across the windshield in an arc. Most object-oriented programmers refer to behaviors as what the object "knows" how to do. In this case, we can say that a wiper "knows," for example, how to change speed in response to a signal or *message* from the wiper control switch. (This is where programming objects differ from real-world objects. The rubber and plastic that make up a wiper on your car don't "know" anything. However, in a computer program, we can define behaviors for every object so that it "knows" how to do things.) In Figure 2.2, we've marked some communication paths on which messages run between the components of the car. Using OOPas code, we will define the behaviors for an object.

An Object's Identity

Similar objects are differentiated by their *identity*. On a car, there are usually two windshield wipers, one on the left and one on the right. These wipers are independent; one might be broken while the other one is working. The wipers on one car also have a separate identity from the wipers on another car; each is a unique object. Identity may seem obvious, but it is important for our programming because identity means that *one object can change without affecting any other*. Each object is thus a complete, independent entity. For example, we can fix one wiper while leaving the other broken. In OOPas, we can distinguish two similar objects by their *identifiers*.

An Object's State

An object's *state* is a description of its properties and its parts. Consider, for example, the car's windshield wipers (itself an object). We can say that the wipers are "on" or "off." We can say that the speed of the wipers is "none," "intermittent," "low," or "high." We could think of the wipers as "working" or "broken," "clean" or "dirty," or describe any number of properties to identify any single wiper. All the relevant properties of an object combine to specify its *state*. The state of an object, then, describes the object *at a particular moment in time*.

We can describe many other things about the car using state. For example, the car's size and shape could be described by state. The car's color might be part of its state, even though cars rarely change color. We also can describe the car's components, such as its doors, and its contents, such as its passengers.

2.2 CLASSES AND INSTANCES

In object-oriented programming, we have terminology that lets us describe an object's behavior, identity, and state. Let's take each of these in turn.

We noted that there are (at least) two windshield wipers on any car. When referring to a *specific one*, we usually use its identifier (e.g., the left wiper). We can also talk about wipers in general. In object-oriented programming, an *object class* is a type or category of object and an *object instance* is a particular object. An object class might be "windshield wiper." An object instance might be identified as "the left wiper on the President's limousine." (For the rest of the book, we use "class" to mean "object class" and "instance" to mean "object instance.") Each instance thus has its own identity, which means that we can tell one instance to perform a behavior without affecting any other instance. We sometimes say that each instance is a unique *instantiation* of a class. Note that all instances of a class can perform the same behaviors.

It often helps to summarize information about a class in a diagram. We will use a notation throughout the book that is fairly common in object-oriented programming.[1] Figure 2.3 shows how our notation describes a simple car. The diagram shows the class name in boldface at the top. Next, the diagram shows the behaviors that instances of the class can perform, indicating only *what* an

1. Our notation is based on that in James Rumbaugh et al., *Object-Oriented Modeling and Design* (Englewood Cliffs, N.J.: Prentice-Hall, 1991).

object can do, not *how* it does it. We'll save the how for next chapter. Finally, the diagram shows the state (the parts and attributes) of instances of the class.

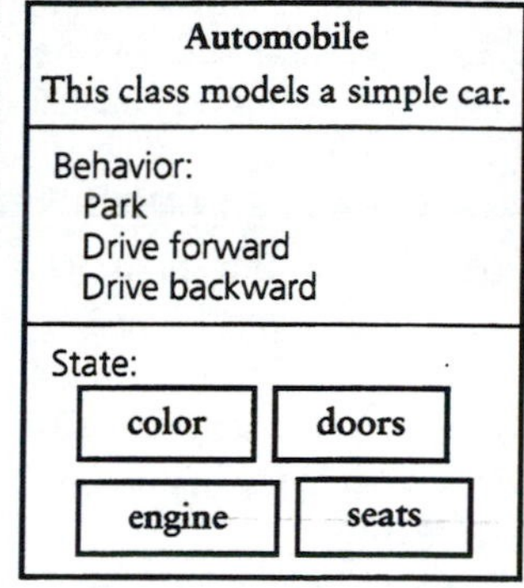

Figure 2.3 *Class diagram for a simple automobile*

2.3 A SIMPLE OBJECT

You've now had a first look at a number of terms we use for talking about objects — classes and instances, state, behavior, and identity. Let's consider a simple object that we can use to build a program.

Most application programs have a *graphical user interface* (GUI) used to control the application. Figure 2.4 shows some of the standard elements of a GUI — "pull-down" menus for choosing commands, windows in which the program's action takes place, and buttons to choose a tool or action.

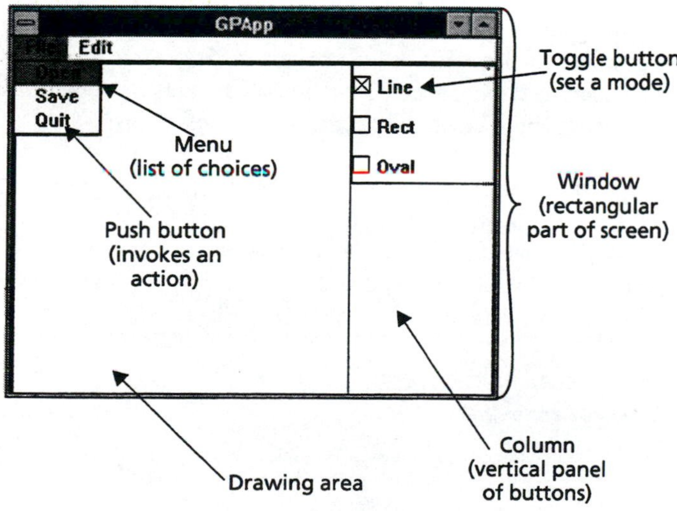

Figure 2.4 *Parts of a graphical user interface (GUI)*

You'll be building programs with graphical user interfaces throughout the book. You'll learn how to create programs with a GUI by using a collection of classes provided with this book. A collection of classes often is called a *class library*, since it contains many descriptions of objects, much as a real library contains many descriptions of real phenomena in the form of books. The library you will be using is called GP (for *Graphics Package*). All the GUI components shown in Figure 2.4 are defined as classes within the GP library. Chapter 7 will discuss the library in detail and show how to create a simple yet completely functional program for painting pictures.

Class libraries are much like parts catalogs. Just as you can go through a catalog deciding what parts to order to assemble into a car or a bicycle, you can go through a class library deciding what classes can be used to build bigger and more useful classes. GP is a rich library, containing most of the elements needed for any application using a GUI. You can't order a car (i.e., a complete application) from it, but you can order enough to make your own car, whether it is a compact little putt-putt or a Formula 1 race car. Let's start with a a simplified version of GP called `StarterUnit`. A ***unit*** is what OOPas calls libraries of object-class definitions that reside in a single file. We'll use this set of classes here and in Chapters 3 and 4. As it happens, this unit's classes were built with GP. Using material discussed later in the book, you'll know enough to build everything in `StarterUnit` yourself.

2.4 A SAMPLE PROGRAM

After all these preliminaries, we finally get to the moment that you've been waiting for — the unveiling of an actual OOPas program. The following is a complete, if not very useful, program. It creates a window and then waits for the user to click on the Quit button to make the window disappear and end the program. The entire program looks like this:[2]

```
{*********************************************************
Program: ShowAndQuit.
This program brings up a window with a single button labeled Quit.
When the user clicks on the Quit button, the program ends. Other
than that, the program does nothing.
*********************************************************}

PROGRAM ShowAndQuit;
USES StarterUnit;
```

2. This program, and all others whose code appears in this book, can be found on the Internet in a software distribution accompanying this book. See the preface for the address.

```
{*********************************************************
Mainline. The mainline first sends a message to the application to
initialize it, and then sends a message to run it.
**********************************************************}

VAR
   firstApp : SUSimpleApp; { main application }
BEGIN
   firstApp.Init; { initialize main application }
   firstApp.Run;
END. { Mainline }
```

In the next few sections we discuss what each line of this program does. When a user runs the program, a single window appears, as shown in Figure 2.5. On the right is a Quit button. The program waits for the user to move the pointer (using the mouse) over the Quit button, and click. Then the program ends. Anything else the user does for input (like typing at the keyboard or clicking elsewhere with the mouse) is ignored.

Figure 2.5

Main window created by SUSimpleApp

How does OOPas know to do this? The program is performing the behaviors defined for the `SUSimpleApp` class. Before we do a line-by-line analysis of the program, let's look at this class.

2.5 THE STARTER UNIT APPLICATION

When we look at the description of an object class we plan to use, we want to know the *purpose* of the class, or what the class is supposed to represent. We also want to know what behaviors instances of the class provide. We want to know exactly what we can do with instances of the class, and how to do it. This information often is called a class's *interface*. Note that this isn't the same kind of interface we saw in a GUI — a class's interface is used in a program, whereas a GUI is used by a person.

The interface also gives instances a way to communicate with one another. In object-oriented terminology, we say that one instance can *send a message* to another instance in order to get the recipient instance to perform the desired behavior. In the car example, the driver can turn a switch marked "wipers" to "on." This sends a "start the current flowing" message to the battery. The battery then would send electric current messages to the right and left wiper motors. The resulting action of the motors then causes the wipers to move by sending a "move" message to the wipers. When one instance sends a message to another, it identifies both the name of the intended recipient and the name of the method whose behavior the sender wants to invoke. A third component of the message, which we'll encounter later, is any data the instances need to exchange. We can say that we send a "sort" message to a list, and when the list receives the message, it responds by performing the appropriate behavior — sorting the list in, say, alphabetical order. We'll discuss sending messages in more detail in the next two chapters.

The first object class we will examine is called `SUSimpleApp`. The "SU" stands for "Starter Unit." By convention, the prefix of a class name indicates the unit or library in which the class definition resides. The "App" is short for "Application Framework." The "framework" is the object that provides the basic functionality of a program. For example, the program should be able to respond when the user presses a mouse button or a key on the keyboard.

`SUSimpleApp` provides us with behaviors that control the screen, keyboard, and mouse, hiding the complexity of controlling the hardware directly. For our purposes, `SUSimpleApp` will provide the application framework for our first program. `SUSimpleApp` can display the main window for a program on the screen.

However, `SUSimpleApp` is more than the window interface you see on the screen. It also has behavior to handle what is called the *input stream* — the mouse clicks and keyboard presses that take place when the user is using the GUI. A behavior called `Run` knows how to handle the input *events* in the input stream, such as when the user presses a key or clicks with the mouse. `Run` tells the appropriate button or menu or other GUI component to make that component perform the appropriate action. In an oversimplified way, the method `Run` handles input as shown in Figure 2.6.

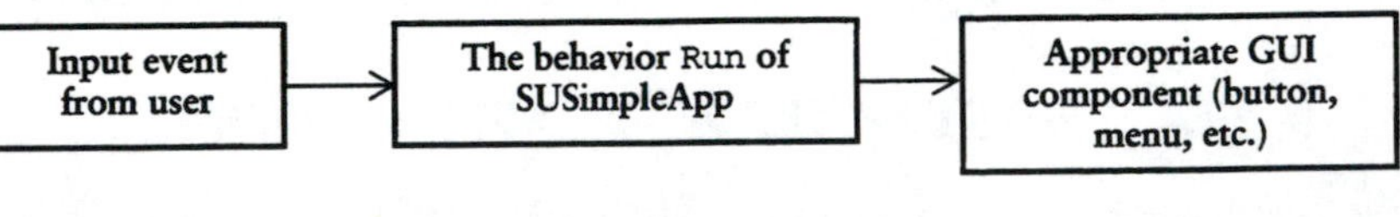

Figure 2.6 *Simplified view of SUSimpleApp's input handling*

Essentially, `Run` is an intermediary that responds to the mouse and keyboard, taking an input event as it occurs and passing it on to the GUI component designed to deal with it. From Figure 2.5, we see that `SUSimpleApp` has only one such component — a *button* marked "Quit." Buttons are areas of the screen that are sensitive to input from the user in the form of mouse clicks. When the user clicks on the Quit button, `Run` tells the button that it was clicked on. The Quit button knows that when it is clicked on, it should make the window disappear and cause the program to end. When the user clicks on any other area of the window or presses on any keyboard key, `Run` has no other GUI component to notify, so those events are ignored. `Run` is a very complex behavior, and we will be looking at it in increasing detail as the book progresses.

Besides `Run`, the `SUSimpleApp` class has one other behavior called `Init` (short for "initialization"). `Init`'s purpose is to establish the initial state of an instance. For example, sending the `Init` message to an instance of `SUSimpleApp` prepares the instance for receiving events from the mouse and keyboard.

Throughout the book, we will be describing a number of classes that have been *predefined* for you. Each time we come across a new class, we'll describe its purpose and methods with a *class description box* such as Class Box 2.1.

Class Box 2.1
SUSimpleApp

SUSimpleApp

`SUSimpleApp` controls the main window for an application. It defines the area of the screen that the program uses and handles events from the input stream.

Behaviors:

`Init;`

The `Init` behavior prepares the application to receive events from the input stream.

`Run;`

The `Run` behavior creates the window in which the program will run and handles events from the input stream. That is, it detects keyboard presses and mouse clicks and passes a message to the appropriate GUI component within the window. Since `SUSimpleApp` has just one component, the Quit button, `Run`'s effect is to wait for the user to click the Quit button and then leave the program.

If you have done any programming without using object-oriented techniques, you may be expecting an explanation of exactly how the methods of `SUSimpleApp`'s classes work. In object-oriented programming, though, we are not concerned about *how* classes that we use work, only with *what* they do, so we can use them to build our applications. The classes are "black boxes" that encapsulate — that is, hide — their inner workings from their users.

2.6 DOCUMENTATION

The first few lines of our sample program on page 24 are known as *comments*. OOPas ignores everything appearing inside curly brackets — `{OOPas ignores this statement}`. Whatever appears as a comment has no effect on the eventual running of the program.

So, you may be asking yourself why we would clutter our program with text that doesn't do anything. The one-word answer is *documentation*. Not only do we want a program that works; we want a program that can be read and understood by ourselves and by other programmers. (Readability is also why programmers have developed *stylistic* conventions for naming and layout, including capitalization and indentation of the code.) In debugging, the comments help us remember the goal of the overall program and of individual object classes and their methods. Later, when we create our own classes and make them available to other programmers, we can use comments to describe the capabilities of any class we've made.

Comments in a program are of two sorts — *block comments* and *inline comments*. The first few lines of our first program are a block comment that describes the purpose of the program and what the program will do. Later in the program, we see the inline comment "initialize main application." It is important to remember that the comments describe the program but don't affect its execution. We'll return to documentation later in the chapter.

2.7 THE *PROGRAM* AND *USES* STATEMENTS

OOPas, like most computer languages, has a small number of *reserved words* that have particular meaning in the language and cannot be used for any other purpose. These are listed in Appendix A and appear in capital letters in our sample programs. However, the reserved words provide OOPas with a very limited vocabulary. OOPas also lets us use *identifiers*, or names, in our program, as long as we tell OOPas what the identifiers represent.

Programs in any computer language are collections of instructions; each instruction is a bit like a sentence in a natural language. Instructions in OOPas can be divided into two broad categories — declarations and statements. *Declarations* are used to provide *names* for the parts of the program — object classes, instances, and so on. *Statements* are descriptions of *behaviors* we want various objects to perform. Together, declarations and statements make up a program. In OOPas, we typically put each instruction on a separate line. Comments are not considered instructions and often occupy many lines.

Let's look at the instructions of our sample program. The first line after the block comment is the *program declaration*. The line has three parts — the reserved word `PROGRAM`, the name `ShowAndQuit`, and a semicolon. (OOPas instructions are separated by semicolons.) OOPas allows names to be any combination of letters, numbers, and underscores, as long as the first character is a letter or an underscore. In this case, our identifier is `ShowAndQuit`, and the program declaration declares that `ShowAndQuit` is the name of our current program.

The program declaration is formally described in Syntax Box 2.1. (The parts of the syntax box are described in the Formatting and Notations section of the Preface.)

Syntax Box 2.1
PROGRAM

Purpose:

To declare the program.

Syntax:

```
PROGRAM <name>;
```

Where:

<name> is an identifier that is the name of the program.

Usage:

The *<name>* identifier may contain letters, digits, and the underscore symbol (_). *<name>* must begin with a letter or underscore and, like all identifiers, cannot be one of OOPas's reserved words. (See Appendix A.)

The `PROGRAM` statement is followed immediately by the `USES` statement. The `PROGRAM` statement is found at the beginning of all programs, whereas the `USES` statement is needed only when we are using classes that are defined in a separate unit. As it turns out, though, that is essentially all of the time, since we'll almost always be making new objects out of pre-existing objects from another library. The `USES` statement lists the units needed by the program at hand; its syntax is given in Syntax Box 2.2.

In our current program, we need only one unit. If we needed more than one, as we will later in the book, we would create a list and separate the individual units with commas, as in the following:

```
USES StarterUnit, GraphicsPackage;
```

The `USES` statement "imports" code that is defined in other files. When OOPas encounters this statement, it searches for the file where the `StarterUnit` is defined and loads the class and method definitions from that unit into memory. This allows the current program to use the classes defined in `StarterUnit`. Thus, because we're using the Starter Unit, we can make instances of any class defined in that unit. This is a simple form of code reuse — we are reusing some code that someone defined previously.

Syntax Box 2.2

USES

Purpose:

To indicate units that are needed by the current program.

Syntax:

```
USES <unit 1>, <unit 2>, ... <unit n>;
```

Where:

<unit 1>, *<unit 2>*, ... *<unit n>* are names of units.

Usage:

The effect of the `USES` statement is that all classes declared in the listed units are now available for use in the current file.

It is assumed that the units are in the same directory as the current program. While there is only one `USES` statement in any program, there is no upper limit on the number of units that can be listed in the `USES` statement.

We'll discuss units in more detail in Chapter 7, including how to define our own units.

2.8 DECLARING OBJECT INSTANCES

Following the `USES` statement and another block comment is the *declaration of local variables*. Such declarations begin with the reserved word `VAR`. The term "variable" in OOPas has essentially the same meaning as in algebra — it names and holds a value. In OOPas, we need to declare variables and classes before we can use them. These declarations are similar to the "cast of characters" list that appears at the beginning of a play, in that all the characters are named before any of the action takes place. In variable declarations, we list all the instances (i.e., characters) before any statements (i.e., actions) take place.

The variable declaration has three parts — a variable's name, a colon, and the variable's *type*. The type indicates what kind of instance the local variable will hold, i.e., the class of the instance. In our initial programs, the type will always be the name of an object class. (We will see other types starting in Chapter 9.)

In our sample program, the declaration `firstApp : SUSimpleApp;` indicates that the variable `firstApp` is an *instance* of the `SUSimpleApp` class. The variable declaration provides a name for an instance that will be used in the code that follows. The syntax of variable declarations in general is described in Syntax Box 2.3.

Syntax Box 2.3

Declaration of local variables

Purpose:

To declare identifiers of variables used in a method.

Syntax:

```
VAR
   <variable identifier> : <data type>;
```

Where:

<variable identifier> is the name of the variable. The name can begin with a letter or an underscore (_).

<data type> is the type of data that *<variable identifier>* holds. When we are declaring instances, *<data type>* is a class name.

Usage:

The names listed in a `VAR` section identify instances that can be used in the current method. In this chapter, the only method we have seen is the mainline. As always, extra blank spaces (or no blanks at all) are fine.

2.9 THE MAINLINE

Recall that any object-oriented program is a system comprised of components called objects.The words "system" and "program" are synonyms, and while the system is made of objects, the "system" as a whole is also an object. The "system object" has a single special behavior that runs the system, called the *mainline*. The mainline appears at the end of a program, and its purpose is to declare instances of a small number of objects and tell those objects which behaviors to perform to get the system going.

The reserved words `BEGIN` and `END` "bracket" multiple statements into a single compound statement called a *block*. The `BEGIN` is not followed by any punctuation. The `END` of the mainline is followed by a period, indicating the end of the program. We usually add a comment indicating that the `END` is for the mainline.

2.10 SENDING A MESSAGE TO AN INSTANCE

So, what are the specific statements within the `BEGIN/END` brackets? The mainline of our program tells the `firstApp` instance declared as a local variable to perform its two behaviors, one after the other. Telling an object to perform one of its behaviors is called *sending a message* to that instance. So the mainline first sends the message `Init` to `firstApp`, then sends the message `Run` to the `firstApp` instance. We saw earlier that the `Init` message tells the instance to establish its initial state. After that, the `Run` message tells the instance to handle the user's input (specifically, to wait for a click on the Quit button).

```
BEGIN
  firstApp.Init; { initialize main application }
  firstApp.Run;
END. { Mainline }
```

Let's look at the syntax of these statements. We have the name `firstApp`, followed by a period and the method name `Init` and a semicolon. When OOPas encounters this statement, it "decodes" it, one part at a time. First, it looks at the name `firstApp`. Since this isn't an OOPas reserved word, OOPas has to figure out what kind of object `firstApp` is. From the `VAR` variable declaration above, OOPas determines that `firstApp` is an instance of the `SUSimpleApp` class. The period signals a particular method of an object.[3] In this case, the message is sent by the mainline to its `firstApp` instance of the `SUSimpleApp` class telling it to execute its `Init` behavior. Again, the mainline doesn't need to worry about how this behavior works, only what it does, which is build the instance. Syntax Box 2.4 summarizes this syntax.

Syntax Box 2.4

Sending a message to an instance

Purpose:

To tell an instance to perform a behavior.

Syntax:

```
<instance name>.<method name>;
```

Where:

<instance name> is the name of an instance that has already been declared.

<method name> is the name of a method defined for *<instance name>*'s class.

Usage:

This statement can appear within any `BEGIN/END` pair where *<instance name>* is declared as a variable. Its effect is to send the *<method name>* message to *<instance name>*. The next statement is not executed until *<instance name>* has completed the behavior defined in *<method name>*.

3. Computer scientists often refer to periods as "dots." Thus this particular syntax sometimes is called *dot notation*.

The preceding paragraph is a description of what OOPas does mechanically. When we read programs, though, we can think of these statements as messages sent from the mainline to an instance (in this case, `firstApp`). In the statement `firstApp.Init;` the mainline — the system object — is telling its `firstApp` instance to establish its initial state.

Statements of a `BEGIN/END` block are executed one at a time. Our mainline begins by sending the `Init` message. The mainline waits until the `firstApp` instance has completed its `Init` behavior; then it sends the `Run` message. OOPas keeps track of the statement being executed at any given time and moves to the next statement in the sequence only when the previous statement has been executed.

The order in which statements appear is important. The statements of the mainline are executed from top to bottom — or more precisely, from `BEGIN` to `END`. Reversing the order of the two statements in this program will not work; the `Run` method cannot be executed properly until an `Init` message is sent.

Summary

The object-oriented technique for building programs starts with some fundamental building blocks that were described in this chapter. Because objects in a program are conceptual, we began by defining some terms that let us describe objects.

All objects have behaviors, state, and a unique identity. An object's behaviors are what the object "knows" how to do. Objects are named by an identifier.

The term "object" can be used to denote either an object class or an object instance. In this book, though, we will use "object" to refer to instances. Classes are categories; instances are particular objects. We can refer to a category like "car" or to a particular object like "the 1991 Chevy that I drove in high school." In a program, we define a class, then create instances of it to use in the program.

The objects in a program are part of a system. The individual object instances are all independent, but they can communicate by sending messages to one another. This communication among instances allows the system to achieve a goal that is more than the sum of the individual instances' behaviors.

You were introduced to a library of objects in the `StarterUnit`. When developing object-oriented programs, you can choose to be "appropriately lazy" — that is, you can rely on objects that others have already defined for you. We used a simple application object that provided a GUI (graphical user interface), then created a mainline that asked the simple application to set its initial state and then wait for the user to click on a Quit button. This sample program demonstrated how to

- Declare a program (the `PROGRAM` declaration).
- Use previously defined units (the `USES` statement).
- Declare instances of objects as variables (the `VAR` declarations).
- Create the boundaries of a mainline (the `BEGIN/END` brackets).
- Use the "dot notation" for sending a message to an object.
- Make our program more readable by adding documentation.

When we have a complete program, with statements in the correct order and appropriate documentation, we can tell OOPas to compile and execute the program. The statements are executed one by one, and the result should be a system that exhibits the behavior defined in the original problem specification.

We've now seen the core of object-oriented programming. If the details of OOPas syntax seem a bit overwhelming right now, don't worry; it will become familiar. When writing your programs, concentrate on their design. What do I want my program to do? What are the component objects? You may want to think about real-world systems and their component parts. It is also important to look at things from the other direction: Consider the parts you have. Can they be put together to create the system? Object-oriented programming means taking a different look at the world and thinking about how you can model a system on the computer — much as, years ago, you modeled the world with your toys and blocks.

Exercises

Understanding Concepts

1. Describe how the components of the following systems work (in a layperson's terms):

   a. a piano key making a sound
   b. a manual can opener
   c. an adjustable monkey wrench
   d. a stapler.

2. Describe attributes and behaviors of the following real-world objects:

   a. a pet goldfish
   b. a bicycle
   c. a wind-up toy
   d. precipitation (only snow and rain)

3. Describe the component objects of the following systems, and list attributes and behaviors of the components:

   a. an aquarium
   b. a stereo
   c. a marching band
   d. an office building

4. Look at any existing Windows programs, such as those in the "Accessories" group that comes with Windows. What components are common to all? That is, what do you expect to see when you open a Windows application?

5. Explain what each of the following mean to Borland Pascal:

   ```
   { }
   ;
   PROGRAM
   USES
   newName: SUApp;
   ```

6. Which of the following are allowed as identifiers?

   a. Third
   b. 3rd
   c. third
   d. Program3

7. If comments do not affect a program's execution, why do we include them?

8. Which of the following are attributes of objects, and which are behaviors?
   a. a person's name
   b. a person's place of birth
   c. a person's occupation
   d. how a person communicates
   e. a person's ability to walk

Coding Exercises

1. Try switching the lines `firstApp.Init` and `firstApp.Run` in the sample program code at the end of Section 2.4 on page 25. What happens? Why?
2. Suppose that we changed the `VAR` declaration in the code at the end of section 2.4 on page 25 to

```
VAR
  currentApp: SUSimpleApp; { main application }
```

   What else would need to change?
3. Show how you can change the name of the program from `ShowAndQuit` to `ShowAndStop`. Does anything else have to change?
4. What happens if you leave out the `USES` statement? Does the program compile? Does it work correctly?
5. What happens if you leave out the `VAR` statement? Do you get a compiler (syntax) error or a run-time error (one that occurs as you run the program)?

3 Making Objects

3.1 CREATING A SYSTEM

In Chapter 2, we walked through our first simple but complete program. However, the program didn't do anything very useful. We used a previously defined class, and we didn't create any new classes. Let's turn now to a system that's a little more interesting and explore the tools we need to create it.

Suppose we were given the following specification for a program:

This program should draw a house like the one in Figure 3.1.

Figure 3.1
Desired output of program

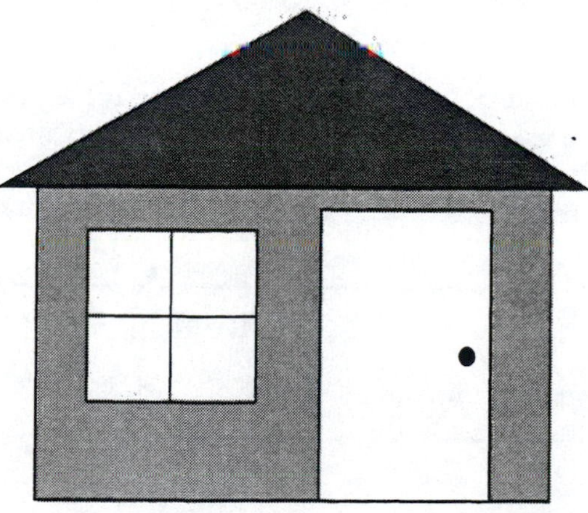

This sounds simple enough. With pen and paper, we could draw this house with little effort. But how do we get a program to do this?

Remember that when we write programs, we are creating software *models*. You probably have had some experience building models. Maybe, as a child, you built simple models of houses from blocks, or sand castles using buckets. Maybe, later, you designed more sophisticated models such as scenery for a play, or tracks for miniature cars or trains. To create a reasonable model, you have to consider what you're trying to model and represent only its salient features (state and behavior). In other words, we're not after a faithful replication in all possible detail — just those details that are relevant to the model.

Our model house is quite simple, but there are details that you might not consider at first. In this case, we note that the house shows one wall, the door, the roof, and a window. In addition, we might want to take note of how various parts of the house are arranged in the figure.

When we consider the detail, it is often useful to reword the original description of the program into a more formal *specification*. In object-oriented design, the specification should describe the system that the program models. (Note that a specification talks more about what the program *is* than what it *does*.) In this case, our "system" is a model of a simple house. So our specification is:

This program should model a house that, when drawn, shows one wall, a door, a window, and a roof. The house should look like the one in Figure 3.1.

The parts of a house can be the objects of our system. It usually helps to make a list of the objects we will need in our system. A good place to start is a list of nouns, often extracted from the original specification of the problem. In our current problem, the list of nouns is pretty straightforward:

program	wall	window
house	door	roof

This list of nouns can be the primary set of object classes for the program. At this point, it is useful to know which object classes already have been defined by others and which of our own we might reuse. We know from Chapter 2, for example, that the `SUSimpleApp` class already is defined in `StarterUnit`. In

Class Box 3.1
SURoof

SURoof

`SURoof` represents the roof of a house.

Behaviors:

`Init;`

This behavior establishes the initial position of the roof. It does not, however, draw the roof.

`Draw;` This behavior draws the roof on the screen.

our programs, "program" and "application" are pretty much synonyms, so an instance of the `SUSimpleApp` class can be used to represent the word *program* in our list.

`StarterUnit` also has some other classes defined for drawing houses, as described in Class Boxes 3.1–3.4. These boxes might seem repetitive, and we will see in Chapter 6 how we can "factor out" commonality into classes that are similar. For now, though, you should remember that each class is independent.

Class Box 3.2
SUWindow

SUWindow

`SUWindow` represents a window of a house.

Behaviors:

`Init;`

This behavior establishes the initial position of the wall. It does not, however, draw the window.

`Draw;` This behavior draws the wall on the screen.

Class Box 3.3
SUDoor

SUDoor

`SUDoor` represents a door of a house.

Behaviors:

`Init;`

This behavior establishes the initial position of the door. It does not, however, draw the door.

`Draw;` This behavior draws the door on the screen.

Class Box 3.4
SUWall

SUWall

`SUWall` represents a wall of a house.

Behaviors:

`Init;`

This behavior establishes the initial position of the wall. It does not, however, draw the wall.

`Draw;` This behavior draws the wall on the screen.

The `SUWall` class could have a behavior called `Show` rather than `Draw`. It is best not to assume that what is defined for one class will be defined for any other class, though it is a good idea to be consistent about names you choose for your own programs.

3.2 DESIGNING YOUR OWN OBJECT

Only one class from our list — house — is not defined in `StarterUnit`, so we must define it. To finish our program, we need to design a new class for the house that we'll call `HOUSESimpleHouse`. (By convention, classes have a prefix indicating what unit or program they came from; thus all of the `StarterUnit` classes start with "SU" and the single class defined for our current program starts with "HOUSE.")

To design an object, we have to think about how we describe its state and behaviors. The first aspects of the object's state that we will look at are the component parts — in the case of our house, a window, roof, door, and wall. The other aspects of the object's state are its properties, but the specification of our house doesn't include any properties for the house as a whole. In object-oriented terminology, we say that the house *contains* one instance of the `SUWindow` class, one instance of the `SUDoor` class, and so on.

We also need to think about the class's behaviors. We know that `HOUSESimpleHouse`, like all classes, needs a behavior to establish its initial state. We'll call the behavior `Init`. We also know, from what we want the program to do, that we need a way to draw the house, which we'll call `Draw`.

Let's look at a diagram summarizing this information. Figure 3.2 shows how our notation describes the `HOUSESimpleHouse` class. Notice that it has all the components we described. It provides two behaviors to create and draw the house and describes all the parts of the house, including their classes.

Figure 3.2

Class diagram for the HOUSESimple-House

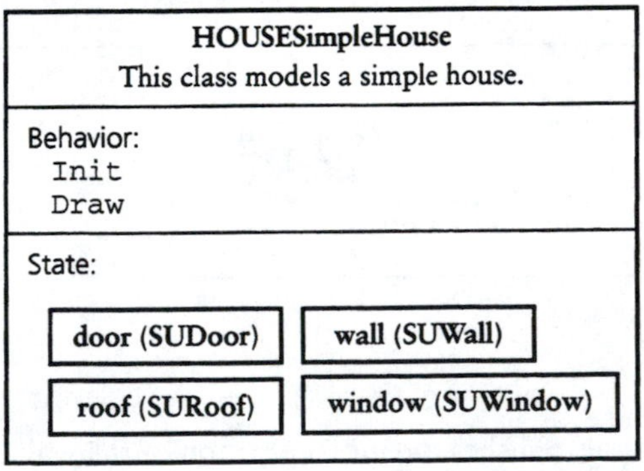

HOUSESimpleHouse This class models a simple house.

Behavior:
`Init`
`Draw`

State: door (SUDoor) — wall (SUWall) roof (SURoof) — window (SUWindow)

3.3 VIEWS OF AN OBJECT

So far we have talked about individual object classes and instances. Let's return to how the system of objects works together. When you learn to drive a car, you learn how to operate all of the controls and signals that are right in front of you in the driver's seat. You learn that when you turn the steering wheel, or press a pedal, or flip a switch, some action takes place. As a driver, you need to know that when you shift the transmission to "reverse," the car will be ready to move backward. You don't need to know exactly how moving the gear shift makes this happen; you just need to know that moving the shift to "R" will have the desired effect on which way the car moves.

The gear shift is a part of the car's *interface* — the part of the car that you as the driver can operate. The mechanism used by a particular car to shift to reverse is called the *implementation*. The same part of an interface might have any number of implementations, depending on the particular object. If you get in any car with an automatic transmission and move the gear shift to "R," you will be ready to move in reverse.

Similarly, object instances in an object-oriented program have an interface and an implementation. The interface is the "public view" of the object, and the implementation is the "private view." Typically, the interface consists of the names of behaviors and comments to the programmer describing how to use those behaviors. The implementation contains the Pascal statements that actually perform the behavior. We've already used the interface of an object in the `ShowAndQuit` program in Chapter 2. You weren't concerned with how the `firstApp` responded to the `Run` message; you just knew that it would work, the same way you know that a car will work when you turn the ignition.

Object-oriented programmers describe the separation of implementation and interface by saying objects are *encapsulated*. An individual object is like a capsule, or "black box," whose internal workings are hidden from view. As Figure 3.3 shows, the private implementation is hidden from the object's user; only the designer of the object needs to know how it actually works.

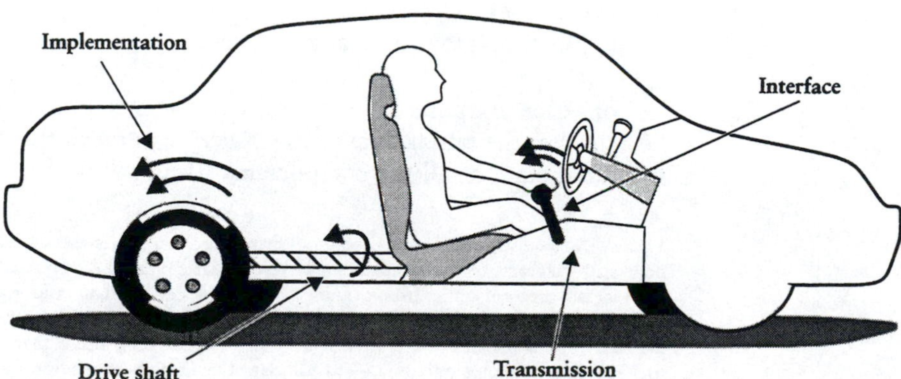

Figure 3.3
Shifting to reverse: the interface and implementation

One advantage of separating the interface from the implementation is that it allows programs to be maintained more easily. Suppose we have written a program using an object that holds a list of names and has a behavior to put the names in alphabetical order. Now suppose we discover a faster way to sort the names in the list. We can change the implementation of the sorting behavior and, as long as we keep the same interface and the sorting behavior keeps the same overall behavior, we don't have to change any other object in the entire system.

3.4 DEVELOPING PSEUDOCODE

Once we have summarized the overall behaviors of a class, we need to consider specifically how to code those behaviors.

Individual behaviors describe tasks that need to be done. Since a task may be complex, we must practice "divide and conquer." By breaking each task into subtasks, and subtasks into sub-subtasks, we simplify the subtasks at the lowest level so that they can be coded in a single or a few OOPas statements. We also need to translate each behavior from English to OOPas. The intermediate steps, which are lists of the behavior's subtasks, are written in abbreviated English sentences that can look more and more like OOPas as the behavior is broken down into individual statements. The task lists written before one gets down to the level of OOPas code are known as *pseudocode*.[1]

The pseudocode of each behavior should start with a statement of the behavior's purpose. (Although the purposes of the behaviors in your first programs may seem obvious, writing them down is a good habit to establish for your later programs, where the purpose may not be as simple to state.) We can state the purposes of our behaviors as follows:

Class: HOUSESimpleHouse
Behavior: Init
  Purpose: Establishes the initial state of the house
Behavior: Draw
  Purpose: Draws the house on the screen

From each purpose, we can break down the behavior into smaller tasks. "Establishes the initial state of the house" can mean that we should establish the initial state of all the components. Thus we need to send an "initialize"

1. Those of you who have used procedural programming may have been taught to use pseudocode or flow chart diagrams to begin the design of your program. In object-oriented design, our initial breakdown of the problem comes from defining object classes rather than tasks and subtasks. Thus we don't need to develop pseudocode until later in the design process. By the time we get to this point, the individual behaviors of the classes are usually fairly small tasks. This means that it will take fewer layers of pseudocode — perhaps only one — to translate the English description of the behavior into OOPas statements.

message to each component. Similarly, to break down the task "draws the house on the screen," we can say that we will send a message to each of the house's components, telling them to draw themselves on the screen. Thus our pseudocode can be refined as follows:

```
Class: HOUSESimpleHouse
Behavior: Init
   Purpose: Establishes the initial state of the house
   Pseudocode:
      Send initialize message to wall
      Send initialize message to door
      Send initialize message to window
      Send initialize message to roof

Behavior: Draw
   Purpose: Draws the house on the screen
   Pseudocode:
      Send draw message to wall
      Send draw message to door
      Send draw message to window
      Send draw message to roof
```

After each stage of pseudocoding, we should see whether we know how to translate our tasks as stated to OOPas statements. If we do, we can stop pseudocoding. For each task that still seems too big to be tackled by a few OOPas statements, we will need to refine the pseudocode further. Each line of pseudocode above, however, corresponds to a behavior provided by one of the classes for the parts of the house, so our pseudocode is detailed enough. We will translate it into OOPas in a moment.

3.5 CLASSES AND INSTANCES REVISITED

Recall from Chapter 2 that each class defines what is common among its instances. An object class is a bit like a rubber stamp in that it defines what the object will look like. The imprints made by a particular rubber stamp all look exactly the same, but each has its own identity and can be represented by a unique identifier. In Figure 3.4, the stamps all look the same, but they can be identified by their unique location. In a sense the class is a template or mold for producing specific instances of the generic class. These specific instances, though, each will be unique. To define a class, we have to define its properties and behaviors. The properties and parts of an object are stored as values of *instance variables*; together, the instance variables define the state of an object. A rubber stamp, for example, provides each imprint with a color determined by what ink was used with the stamp. We might define "position" and "color" as instance variables. Each instance will have not only its own location but also its own color, as in Figure 3.5 — one could be black, and two could be light grey. Thus, the class definition (the stamp) describes the existence of instance variables; each instance might have a different value for those instance variables.

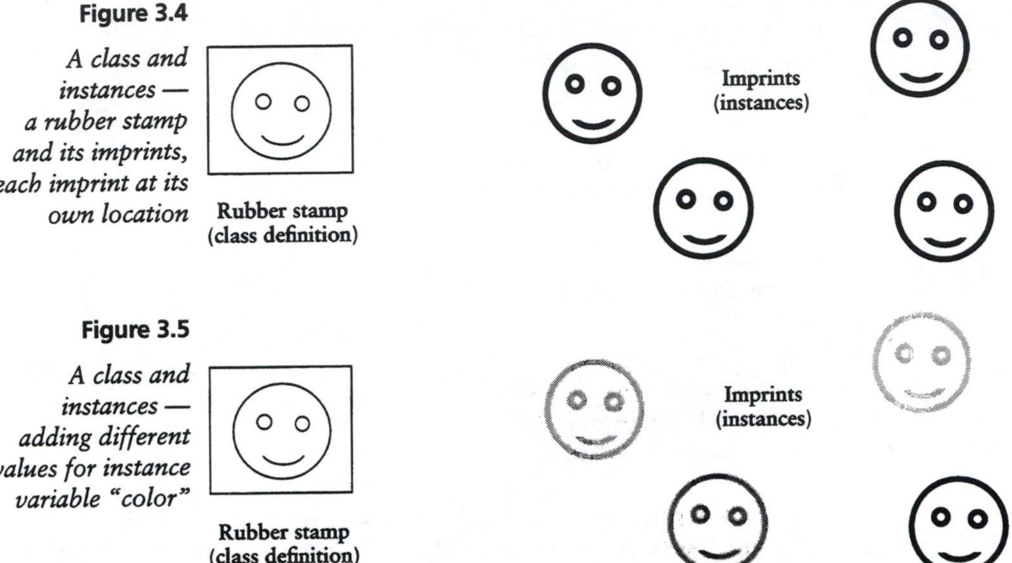

Figure 3.4 *A class and instances — a rubber stamp and its imprints, each imprint at its own location*

Figure 3.5 *A class and instances — adding different values for instance variable "color"*

In a class definition that describes windshield wipers, we might have instance variables to store data that indicate whether a wiper is on or off, what its current speed is, the last time it was cleaned, and whether it is broken. The instance variables also can describe properties that don't change frequently (if at all) over time, but differentiate one instance from another, such as an object's color or the components that comprise the object. In a class definition that models a car's body, we might have instance variables named "vehicleIdentificationNumber," "numberOfDoors," "typeOfTransmission," and "mainColor." A vehicle's identification number never would change, but its color could change occasionally if the car is painted. Whether or not the values of an instance variable change frequently, each instance will have different data values for the instance variables. For example, one instance might have a color "red" and another a color "blue," but all instances have the same *types* of data values within them (a color). When we define the class's instance variables, we need to determine what types of data are necessary to describe an instance's state. To extend an analogy we made earlier, if the object classes and instances are roughly equivalent to nouns in a language, instance variables used as attributes are like adjectives, as in the sentence, "I drive a red, two-door Ford Mustang."

Instance variables also can be used for *containment*. When one object contains another, as when a car contains an engine, an instance variable can be used to hold the contained object. Note that the difference between an instance variable being used to contain another object and an instance variable being used as an attribute is not always clear. For example, should we model a four-door car by using an instance variable holding the information that the car has *four* doors as opposed to two, three, or five? Or should we model the car by observing that a door is quite clearly a part of the car, and thus each door should be an instance variable representing this relationship? In one case, the car contains four instances of the class `Door`. In the other, the car merely contains the number "4," indicating that the car has four doors. As in all cases of design, there isn't one right answer. Depending on exactly what features of the car were most important, we might choose either approach, or even both. For selling the car, it might be enough to know that the car has four doors. But for repairing the car, it would probably be useful to have a physical description of the door as well (e.g., if the door was dented in an accident). It all depends on what we want to *model*.

If instance variables are analogous to adjectives or parts, then behaviors are like the verbs of an object-oriented program. The behaviors of object classes are defined in *methods*. Since they correspond to behaviors, methods are used to respond to messages sent to the object. The methods can change the current state of the instance or communicate with a different object instance (such as a contained instance). Thus we might say that a wiper has a "WipeIntermittently" method that allows it to wipe the windshield, wait a set amount of time, and wipe again. It might also have a "ChangeSpeed" method that lets it get faster or slower, or an "IndicateWhenBroken" method that signals a light on the dashboard to light up when the wiper motor is broken.

3.6 DECLARING AN OBJECT CLASS

As we saw earlier, OOPas requires that everything be declared before it can be used. Let's look, then, at a class declaration — specifically, the declaration of our `HOUSESimpleHouse` class.

```
TYPE
  HOUSESimpleHouse = OBJECT { displays a house }
    CONSTRUCTOR  Init;
    PROCEDURE    Draw;
  PRIVATE
    wall         : SUWall;          { the front wall }
    door         : SUDoor;          { the front door }
    window       : SUWindow;        { window next to door }
    roof         : SURoof;          { the roof of the house }
  END;
```

Overall, the OOPas syntax for declaring an object class is very similar to the diagram in Figure 3.2. The class has a section for the name, a section for the public interface, and a section for the private parts of the class.

Let's look at each part of the declaration. The reserved word TYPE is similar to the reserved word VAR we saw in the previous chapter. TYPE is used to indicate the beginning of the class declarations, rather than the beginning of variable declarations for which VAR was used. TYPE declarations appear at the beginning of a program (typically right after the PROGRAM and USES statements), so that the declarations are available throughout the rest of the program. (We'll get back to the order of declarations toward the end of this chapter.)

The line `HOUSESimpleHouse = OBJECT` declares that the identifier `HOUSESimpleHouse` is an object class. (It is unfortunate that OOPas uses OBJECT in its syntax; we would prefer the word CLASS. It is important to remember that the word OBJECT in the TYPE declarations is used to declare object classes, not instances.) By convention, we capitalize the first letter of the class name following the unit prefix and the first letter of all subsequent words (the second "S" and "H" in "HOUSESimpleHouse").

Everything appearing after the declaration of the class name and before PRIVATE is part of the class's public interface. The reserved word PRIVATE indicates which part of the declaration is to be available only within the current class. The word PRIVATE can be followed by any number of instance variable declarations.

The preceding example defines two methods in the public section:

```
CONSTRUCTOR Init;
PROCEDURE Draw;
```

The identifiers `Init` and `Draw` are the names of the methods we chose earlier. In the definition, we also have to declare what type of method each is. The reserved words CONSTRUCTOR and PROCEDURE indicate the method type. We'll look at the use of these reserved words in detail in just a moment.

The PRIVATE section of `HOUSESimpleHouse` has four instance variables:

```
wall        : SUWall;          { the front wall }
door        : SUDoor;          { the front door }
window      : SUWindow;        { window next to door }
roof        : SURoof;          { the roof of the house }
```

The declaration of these instance variables is syntactically the same as the declaration of the `firstApp` variable in our program in Chapter 2. The identifier is followed by a colon, a type name (a class name for now), and a semicolon. The key distinction between instance variables and the local variables we saw in the mainline before is that instance variables are defined (after PRIVATE) for a class and are accessible to all methods in the class, whereas the other variables are defined (after VAR) for the method only. This means that the mainline can send the `Init` message to an instance of `HOUSESimpleHouse`, because `Init` is public. But the mainline can't access the private instance variables of `HOUSESimpleHouse`. Conversely, an instance of `HOUSESimpleHouse` can't access local variables defined for the mainline, such as an instance of `SUSimpleApp`.

Both local variables and instance variables hold instances. The difference is where the variables are defined, not what they can hold. Local variables are defined locally, within a method. Instance variables are defined within a class, meaning each instance contains its own copy.

This difference in place of definition leads to a difference in *accessibility*, often called *scope* in computer science (a concept we will revisit in Chapter 4). Instance variables model things that can change about an object. Hence any behavior of an instance ight need to examine and possibly modify instance variables, so all methods have access to the instance variables and thus can look at or modify them.

Another way to look at the distinction between a local variable and an instance variable is to consider the variable's *lifetime*. Instance variables hold objects that exist for as long as the instance they are contained in exists. Local variables hold objects that exist only during a response to a particular message. If the same message is sent again, the local variables in the method will hold different objects from the last time the method was used.

The object class declaration is a description of all of the parts of the class. It's important to declare your classes carefully. Syntax Box 3.1 summarizes the syntax for declaring an object class. The order in which methods and instance variables are listed in a class declaration is not important. However, the order of statements within a `BEGIN/END` block is important, as we shall see.

3.7 DEFINING OBJECT METHODS

The class declaration gives a template to describe the class. What we need to do now is translate our pseudocode into OOPas code, turning our abstract behaviors into concrete methods.

Defining the code for methods is similar to defining the code for a mainline. For example, here is the code for our class's `Init` method:

```
{*******************************************************
The Init method establishes the initial state of the house by
initializing all of its components.
*********************************************************}

CONSTRUCTOR HOUSESimpleHouse.Init;
BEGIN
  wall.Init;
  door.Init;
  window.Init;
  roof.Init;
END;
```

Syntax Box 3.1

Declaring an object class

Purpose:

Declares an object class as a data type.

Syntax:

```
<class name> = OBJECT
  CONSTRUCTOR <constructor name>;
  PROCEDURE <method name 1>;
  ...
  PROCEDURE <method name m>;
PRIVATE
  <instance variable 1> : <data type>;
  ...
  <instance variable n> : <data type>;
END;
```

Where:

<class name> is an identifier that names the class. By convention, class names that appear begin with the name of the unit or program in which they are defined (for example, all classes defined in the GP unit start with GP, as in `GPMenu` and `GPPushButton`).

The methods defined in the public section of a class are available for use by other classes. `PRIVATE` marks the private sections of a class.

<method name i> are the names of the methods. They can be sent as messages to this object by other objects. The method header in this definition must match the header where the method's behavior is specified in the code. Note that there can be any number of methods. The declaration must include a constructor. The constructor is always a public method.

<instance variable i> are the names of the data stored within the class. *<data type>* is the type of data that each instance variable can hold. This may be the name of a class previously defined in this program or in the units listed in the `USES` statement. It may also be a base type (see Chapter 9).

Usage:

The class declaration appears in the `TYPE` section of the program. The class must be declared before any of its instances. Further, *<class name>* can be declared only once in a given program.

The method starts with a block comment. This comment should contain the purpose that we outlined in the pseudocode and describe the overall behavior of the method.

Following the block comment is the *method header*. In this example, the reserved word `CONSTRUCTOR` is followed by the class name, a period, the method name, and a semicolon. Note that we always use the *class* — not an instance — identifier in the method name, because this method is defined for all instances of HOUSESimpleHouse.

As with the mainline, the statements constituting the body of the method are wrapped in BEGIN/END brackets. In this case, though, the END is followed by a semicolon. (END is followed by a period, rather than a semicolon, only in the mainline.)

Now, within the BEGIN/END brackets, we can send messages to the instance variables declared for the class. In this case, the first line after the BEGIN sends an Init message to the wall instance.

At first glance, it might seem that we are violating the rule that we have to declare something before we can use it, since we did not declare wall within the block of the HOUSESimpleHouse.Init method. However, the header HOUSESimpleHouse.Init indicates that this method is part of the definition of HOUSESimpleHouse, which means that all the instance variables and methods of HOUSESimpleHouse can be accessed within this method. Thus we can use the private instance variable wall within the method.

The statement wall.Init; instructs OOPas to send a message to the wall instance to initialize itself. When OOPas sees this statement, it determines that wall is an instance of SUWall, so it executes the method defined as SUWall.Init. When OOPas comes to the door.Init; statement, it executes the method defined as SUDoor.Init. Each of these initialization methods does something different (even though they are all called Init), because they were defined differently in their respective classes within StarterUnit. We don't know what they do, nor do we *need* to know!

It's worth noting that the header of the method (CONSTRUCTOR HOUSESimpleHouse.Init;) uses the class name, while the statements within the method use instance names. The header of the method merely is describing a behavior that is true for all instances of a class. The statements, though, are actions that particular instances contained within an instance of the class are to perform.

To summarize, the HOUSESimpleHouse.Init method sends four messages telling the four instance variables to initialize themselves. Note that each message refers to a different method because each instance variable is of a different class. When all of the Init messages have been sent, the method ends.

In this case, the code for the Draw method is very similar to the constructor. If you were writing this code from the pseudocode, you could start by writing the block comment and the header of the class as follows:

```
{*********************************************************
The Draw method draws the house on the screen.
**********************************************************}

PROCEDURE HOUSESimpleHouse.Draw;
BEGIN
  ...
END;
```

The syntax for this method is similar to the constructor; the only difference is that the reserved word CONSTRUCTOR is replaced by the reserved word PRO-

CEDURE. The reserved word PROCEDURE is used for "regular" methods, while the word CONSTRUCTOR is used only for the method that establishes the initial state of an instance. Establishing the initial state of an object is so important and so common that OOPas provides the special keyword CONSTRUCTOR just for that. Every class we define will have a constructor. Some classes can build instances in several ways, so those classes will have several constructors, though only one particular constructor will be used for any one instance.

Within the BEGIN/END brackets, we need to write the code that performs the tasks defined in the pseudocode. The first line of the pseudocode says, "Send draw message to wall." We can translate this into the statement wall.Draw. (We can verify the name of the method by looking at Figure 3.2 for SUWall.) Each of the other lines of pseudocode also indicates that we should send draw messages, so we can translate the pseudocode into the following procedure:

```
PROCEDURE HOUSESimpleHouse.Draw;
BEGIN
  wall.Draw;
  door.Draw;
  window.Draw;
  roof.Draw;
END;
```

We said earlier that the method headers must match the method names listed in the class declaration. If we change the name of a method, we must change it in two places — the class declaration and in the method header.

You may wonder about the apparent duplication between the method declaration in the public section and the definition of the method. Remember that other objects make use only of the class declaration — its interface — which gives us and OOPas no information about the implementation of each method. The implementation of a class consists of the definitions of its methods. Figure 3.6 shows how the method appears in both the interface and implementation, and Syntax Box 3.2 details the syntax of method definitions. In the method declaration, the class name is not stated before the method name, since the class is already named because the method declaration occurs within the class declaration. The method definition *does* include the class name to allow the programmer to define methods in any order, using the prefixed class name to help identify the method being defined.

3.8 COMPLETING THE PROGRAM

We've defined the HOUSESimpleHouse, but that class is just a part of a larger system. To complete the program, we need to create a mainline. The mainline essentially is the constructor for the system object.

Figure 3.6

Relationship between method header and class declaration

Interface (or declaration)

```
TYPE
  HOUSESimpleHouse = OBJECT
    CONSTRUCTOR Init;
    PROCEDURE Draw;
  PRIVATE
  ...
  END;
...
PROCEDURE HOUSESimpleHouse.Draw;
BEGIN
  wall.Draw;
  door.Draw;
  window.Draw;
  roof.Draw;
END; { HOUSESimpleHouse.Draw }
```

Correspondence

Implementation (or definition)

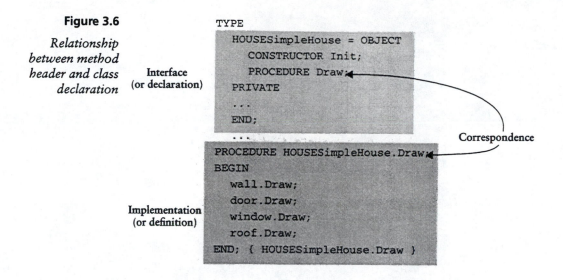

The `SUSimpleApp` used earlier can provide the application framework for drawing our house. This framework provides a window on the screen in which the house can be drawn and a Quit button to indicate when we are done looking at the house.

We can think of the "system object" as containing two instances — an instance of `SUSimpleApp` and an instance of `HOUSESimpleHouse`. Now, let's think for a moment about what we want the system to do.

We want to initialize both of our instances, and then we want the house to appear. Finally, we want to wait for the user to press the Quit button. This suggests that our pseudocode should look like this:

Class: <system>
Method: Mainline
  Purpose: To get the system going
  Pseudocode:
    Send Initialize message to application framework
    Send Initialize message to house
    Send Draw message to house
    Send Run message to application framework

The order of tasks is important. We cannot tell the application to `Run` before we send the `Draw` message, because the user would have to click the Quit button, which would make the window disappear before the house ever appears. If the window has disappeared, then we can't see the results of `Draw`.

At this point, we can code the mainline. First, we need to declare the instances we will use; these will appear in the `VAR` section of the mainline. The mainline, however, has no predefined instance variables, so we need to declare the local variables. Then we will send messages to those instances.

Syntax Box 3.2

Defining a method

Purpose:

To define a behavior for a class.

Syntax:

```
PROCEDURE <class name>.<method name>;
VAR
   <variable 1> : <data type>;
...
   <variable n> : <data type>;

BEGIN
   <statement 1>;
...
   <statement m>
END;
```

Where:

<class name> is the name of a class previously declared in this program.

<method name> is the name of the method. This name must also appear in the class declaration (i.e., the `TYPE` section).

*<variable i>*s are local variables required by the method. (In this chapter, they are used only in the mainline.)

*<data type i>*s are the types of each variable.

*<statement i>*s are the OOPas statements. Note that the statements are separated by semicolons. A semicolon is optional after the last statement.

Usage:

The method header names a block of statements. These statements, when executed in order, define a behavior for the class. Duplicate method names are not allowed within the same class (although a method in another class within the program might have the same name).

`BEGIN` and `END` surround all the statements in the procedure body. Note that `END` is followed by a semicolon. This semicolon denotes the end of a block of statements.

There are three variations of the `PROCEDURE`:

- The `CONSTRUCTOR` is a procedure that establishes the initial state for an object. Syntactically, it is identical to the procedure declaration except that the reserved word `PROCEDURE` is replaced by `CONSTRUCTOR`.
- The mainline is a procedure that is called when the program begins. It does not have a `PROCEDURE` header; it is assumed to be the `BEGIN/END` block at the end of the program. The mainline's `END` is followed by a period instead of a semicolon.
- A `FUNCTION` is a method that returns a value. It is described in Chapter 5.

```
{*****************************************************
The mainline gets the system going. The instances are initialized.
Then the house is sent a message to draw itself. Finally, the
application waits for the user to indicate when to quit.
*****************************************************}

VAR
  mainHouse    : HOUSESimpleHouse;{ house instance }
  mainApplication: SUSimpleApp; { window where drawing occurs }
BEGIN
  mainApplication.Init;
  mainHouse.Init;
  mainHouse.Draw;
  mainApplication.Run;
END.
```

The program's overall purpose should be explained in a comment at the top of the program. This *block comment* should explain the larger goal of the system and include some of the details of the program's development — your name, the last time you revised it, and any modifications you've made to earlier versions. A summary of the uses of documentation appears in Syntax Box 3.3.

Syntax Box 3.3

Comments

Purpose:

To describe in natural language what the code is doing.

Syntax:

```
{ <text of comment> }
```

Usage:

Anything between comment brackets is ignored by the OOPas compiler. Comments are crucial:

1. At the top of the program. It should contain:
   - the program name
   - your name
   - the date of last revision
   - a description of the program: its major structure and breakdown.
2. At the top of each method, including the mainline. It should contain:
   - the class name and the method name
   - the purpose of the method
   - any complex or interesting points about the procedure, such as error conditions or special cases that may or may not be handled by the method.
3. In the definition of a class or variable of any sort.

Figure 3.7

The program schematic

Program Header

```
PROGRAM <program name>;
USES <unit 1>, ..., <unit n>;
```

Class Declarations

```
TYPE
  { class block comment }
  <class name 1> = OBJECT
    CONSTRUCTOR <constructor name>;
    PROCEDURE <method name 1>;
    ...
    PROCEDURE <method name m>;
  PRIVATE
    <instance variable 1> : <data type>;
    ...
    <instance variable v> : <data type>;
  END; { <class name 1> }

  { class block comment }
  <class name 2> = OBJECT
    CONSTRUCTOR <constructor name>;
    PROCEDURE <method name 1>;
    ...
    PROCEDURE <method name m>;
  PRIVATE
    <instance variable 1> : <data type>;
    ...
    <instance variable n> : <data type>;
  END; { <class name 2> }
...
```

Method Definitions

```
{ procedure block comment }
CONSTRUCTOR <class name 1>.<method name 1>;
VAR
  { variables, if any, that are local to this method }
BEGIN
  ...
END; { <class name 1>.<method name 1> }
...
{ procedure block comment }
PROCEDURE <class name 2>.<method m>;
  ...
END; { <class name 2>.<method name m> }
...
```

Mainline

```
{ Mainline }
VAR
  { variables, if any, that are local to the mainline }
BEGIN
  ...
END. { Mainline }
```

3.9 THE PROGRAM SCHEMATIC

We've written all the parts of the program. Now we need to put them in order. As Figure 3.7 shows, there are four sections of the program — the program header, the class declarations, the method definitions, and the mainline. Study this program carefully; your own programs will be modeled on it. Though we haven't declared and defined more than one object class, the schematic allows for multiple object classes. You can see the schematic fleshed out in the complete program that follows:

```
{*********************************************************
David Niguidula; Program: House; July 1994. This program draws a
house with a door, wall, window, and roof. The program then waits
for the user to click on the Quit button.
**********************************************************}

PROGRAM House;
USES StarterUnit;
TYPE
  HOUSESimpleHouse = OBJECT { represents a house }
    CONSTRUCTOR  Init;
    PROCEDURE    Draw;
  PRIVATE
wall        : SUWall;           { the front wall }
door        : SUDoor;           { the front door }
window      : SUWindow;         { window next to door }
roof        : SURoof;           { the roof of the house }
  END;

{*********************************************************
Methods for HOUSESimpleHouse
**********************************************************}


{*********************************************************
The Init method establishes the initial state of the house by
initializing all of its components.
**********************************************************}

CONSTRUCTOR HOUSESimpleHouse.Init;
BEGIN
  wall.Init;
  door.Init;
  window.Init;
  roof.Init;
END;
```

```
{*********************************************************
The Draw method draws the house on the screen.
*********************************************************}

PROCEDURE HOUSESimpleHouse.Draw;
BEGIN
  wall.Draw;
  door.Draw;
  window.Draw;
  roof.Draw;
END;

{*********************************************************
The mainline gets the system going. First, the instances are
initialized. Then, the house is sent a message to draw itself.
Finally, the application waits for the user to indicate when she is
ready to quit.
*********************************************************}

VAR
  mainHouse        : HOUSESimpleHouse;{ house instance }
  mainApplication  : SUSimpleApp;     { window where drawing and
              action will take place }
BEGIN
  mainApplication.Init;
  mainHouse.Init;
  mainHouse.Draw;
  mainApplication.Run;
END.
```

Summary

An object has two parts — a declaration and a definition. The declaration (or interface) includes the methods (the concrete implementations of the abstract behaviors) that are available to other objects. It also includes a list of the private parts of the object. The definition (or implementation) is the set of the actual bodies of all the methods provided by the object — the statements between BEGIN/END pairs that describe what the method actually does. We say that objects are encapsulated because their implementation is internal. That is, the interface may tell us *what* behavior an object can perform, but exactly *how* that object performs that behavior is known only to the person who wrote the object.

The objects in a program are part of a system. All individual object instances are independent, but they can communicate by sending messages to each other. This communication among instances allows the system to achieve a goal that is more than the sum of the individual instances' behaviors.

In this chapter's program, we went through the initial stages of object-oriented design. From a problem specification, we identified a set of classes and looked at the classes that already had been defined through the class description boxes.

Then, we designed the one class — a house — that previously had not been defined.

Designing a class means considering what data are needed to describe the class's state and what methods are needed to describe the class's behavior. The instance variables of a class can be instances of other component classes (in our example, an instance of the `SUDoor` class was an instance variable in the `HOUSESimple-House`).

The methods of a class can be described using pseudocode. After we have identified the purpose of a behavior, we can break it down into individual tasks. If need be, we can break down those tasks into smaller ones. Eventually (and usually quite quickly), we reach a point where the tasks can be translated into OOPas code.

During the design stage, it is often useful to designate classes with a class diagram. The notation used throughout the book shows which parts of a class are public and which are private and defines the names of the instance variables and methods.

From the design, we can write the code for a class. The class declaration goes in the `TYPE` section of a program and, like the object diagrams, shows which instance variables and methods are public and which are private. The methods of a class are defined as procedures. One special procedure, the constructor, establishes the initial state of an object instance.

When we have a complete program, in the correct order and with appropriate documentation, we can tell OOPas to compile and execute the program. The statements are executed one by one and should result in a system that exhibits the behavior defined in the original problem specification.

In Chapter 2, we looked at the core of object-oriented programming. In this chapter, we learned how to build that core. We learned how to build our own objects.

Exercises

Understanding Concepts

1. Choose a play from a library, and pick a scene. Suppose you were asked to build the set for this play. What objects would you need for the scene? (One relatively simple set: Thorton Wilder's *Our Town.*)

2. Write a specification for a program that allows two players to play tic-tac-toe.

3. Draw an object diagram for the `SURoof` class.

4. Describe the difference between an instance and an instance variable.

5. Describe the difference between an instance variable and a local variable.

6. Describe the interface of a mechanical device, such as:

   a. video cassette recorder
   b. a dishwasher
   c. a stereo
   d. an automatic teller machine

7. Write, in pseudocode terms, how to make a peanut butter and jelly sandwich.

8. Can we put the code of the `HOUSESimpleHouse.Draw` method ahead of the code for `HOUSESimpleHouse.Init` in the file? Why or why not?

Coding Exercises

1. Suppose we change the declaration

   ```
   mainHouse: HOUSESimpleHouse;
   ```

   in the code in Section 3.9 to the declaration

   ```
   sample: HOUSESimpleHouse;
   ```

   What else in the code would have to change?

2. In the same code, suppose we changed the `HOUSESimpleHouse` declaration to

   ```
   HOUSESimpleHouse = OBJECT
     CONSTRUCTOR Init;
     PROCEDURE DrawWholeHouse;
   PRIVATE
     frontWall: SUWall;
     frontDoor: SUDoor;
     mainWindow: SUWindow;
     newRoof: SURoof;
   END;
   ```

   How would the rest of the code change?

3. Modify the code in Section 3.9 so that a second house instance, called `secondHouse` is declared in the mainline and that the new house (as well as `mainHouse`) is initialized and drawn.

4. `SU` contains an additional class called `SUShutter`. This class has an `Init` method to initialize the shutters and a `Draw` method to draw the shutters. Modify the code in Section 3.9 so that the house also contains an instance variable of class `SUShutter`.

Programming Problems

The Starter Unit contains other classes, which are described ahead of each set of problems:

SUEyes

Purpose: Represents two eyes of a face

Methods:

```
Init;    { Establish the position of the eyes }
Draw;    { Draw the eyes }
```

SUNose

Purpose: Represents the nose of a face

Methods:

```
Init;     { Establish the position of the nose }
Draw;     { Draw the nose }
```

SUSmile

Purpose: Represents the smile of a face

Methods:

```
Init;     { Establish the position of the mouth }
Draw;     { Draw the smile }
```

SUFrown

Purpose: Represents the frown of a face

Methods:

```
Init;     { Establish the position of the mouth }
Draw;     { Draw the frown }
```

1. Write a program that creates a Face object, and draw it so it has a smile.

2. Modify the program from Programming Problem 1, but draw it with a frown.

SUArms

Purpose: Represents the two arms of a stick figure

Methods:

```
Init;          { Establish the position of the arms }
DrawAtSide;    { Draw the arms at the side }
DrawInAir;     { Draw the arms in the air }
Erase;         { Erase the current drawing of the arms }
```

SULegs

Purpose: Represents the two legs of a stick figure

Methods:

```
Init;            { Establish the position of the legs }
DrawStanding;    { Draw the legs in a standing position }
DrawJumping;     { Draw the legs jumping in the air }
Erase;           { Erase the current drawing of the legs }
```

SUBody

Purpose: Represents the body of a stick figure

Methods:

```
Init;     { Establish the position of the body }
Draw;     { Draw the body }
Erase;    { Erase the body }
```

3. Using the preceding methods, write a program to show a frowning stick figure that is standing with arms at its side.

4. Write a program to show a smiling stick figure that is jumping with arms in the air.

5. Write a program that shows the figure standing, then jumping, then standing, then jumping. (The figure should be erased between movements.)

SUFish

Purpose: Represents a goldfish

Methods:

```
Init;        { Initialize the goldfish at a random position }
StartLeft;   { Establish the goldfish's position on the left side of the screen }
StartRight;  { Establish the goldfish's position on the right side of the screen }
DrawStill;   { Draw the goldfish in its current position }
SwimLeft;    { Swim from its current position to the left side of the screen }
SwimRight;   { Swim from its current position to the right side of the screen }
```

SUShark

Purpose: Represents a shark

Methods:

```
Init;        { Initialize the shark at a random position }
StartLeft;   { Establish the shark's position on the left side of the screen }
StartRight;  { Establish the shark's position on the right side of the screen }
DrawStill;   { Draw the shark in its current position }
SwimLeft;    { Swim from its current position to the left side of the screen }
SwimRight;   { Swim from its current position to the right side of the screen }
```

6. Write a program that shows two goldfish starting from opposite ends of the screen and swimming toward each other.

7. Write a program that shows a goldfish swimming across the screen, followed by a shark traveling in the same direction. (Note that the goldfish will swim all the way across before the shark starts.)

8. Expand Programming Problem 7 so that after the shark reaches the same side as the goldfish, both the goldfish and the shark swim back in the opposite direction.

4

Sending Messages

Chapters 2 and 3 described object classes and instances. Although each instance has a unique identity — its own set of private instance variables and methods that determine its state and behavior — instances need to communicate with one another to make a system work.

Instances communicate with one another by sending messages. We can send messages to an instance to have that instance perform some behavior. In Chapter 3, we saw that the mainline sent messages to an instance of the house, and the house in turn sent messages to tell the instances of the wall, door, window, and roof to initialize and draw themselves. In this chapter, we will elaborate on that communication process. We will examine *parameters*, which are pieces of information that make a message more specific. We'll also learn a bit more about graphics along the way.

4.1 REVISING THE HOUSE

In Chapter 3, we looked at a complete program that drew a house. Whenever we ran the program, it was always the same house.

Let's add a little more flexibility to this house. Suppose we are developing a new program to describe a street of houses, which in turn might be used for a housing subdivision. For each house, we want to specify its color and position on the screen. Each house is painted in two colors — a main color for the wall and roof and a trim color for the window and door (Figure 4.1).

Note that colors in the figures are shown as shades of gray. You can run this program (and see the real colors) on your computer, using the software available on the Internet (see the preface).

To develop this program, we can begin with a specification. Then we'll analyze this specification to design and implement the objects we will need:

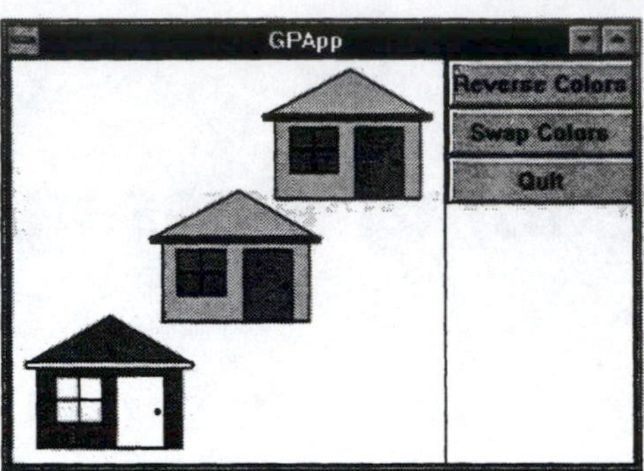

Figure 4.1
Painted houses

This application is a model of a street. The street has three houses; each house has a wall, a door, a window, and a roof. One color is used to paint the wall and the main part of the roof, and a second color is used to paint the door, the window, and the trim of the roof.

The program asks the user to select the position and colors for each house. The colors are selected from a vertical panel that pops up on the screen. Once the houses are drawn, the user can do one of three things:

- *Exchange the main and trim colors of a house. The user first clicks on a house. When the "Reverse Colors" button is clicked, the main and trim colors are exchanged.*
- *Swap the colors of two houses. The user clicks on the "Swap Colors" button and then chooses two houses. The main and trim colors of one house are exchanged with the main and trim colors of the other house.*
- *Quit the program. The user clicks on a "Quit" button to end the program.*

In this chapter we will revise the house class from the last chapter, using some new methods from the `SUWindow`, `SUWall`, `SUDoor`, and `SURoof` classes. Also, we'll develop the methods for a class we'll call `StApp` that respond to the "Reverse Colors" and "Swap Colors" buttons. We'll call the program "Street" and use `St` as the first part of the class name.

To get started, let's look at how to use the new graphic elements that we need to design this program — colors and points. We'll start implementing our program specification in Section 4.3, after we've looked at colors and points.

4.2 COLORS AND POINTS

As mentioned in Chapter 3, this book provides a library of objects called *GP* (*Graphics Package*). We can access the contents of GP in the same way that we added the classes of the `StarterUnit` in Chapter 3. When we include the unit name — `GraphicsPackage` — in the `USES` statement at the top of our code, all the classes and instances defined in GP are available in our program.

We'll be looking at the object classes defined in GP throughout the book. For now, let's just see how GP lets us work with colors and points. In GP, colors are represented by a class called `GPColor`, described in Class Box 4.1. A particular instance can be a particular color, like red or purple or even mauve.

Class Box 4.1
GPColor

GPColor

This class describes a color. Particular instances represent particular colors.

Constructors:

`InitAsRed;` Make this instance represent red.

`InitAsOrange;` Make this instance represent orange.

`InitAsYellow;` Make this instance represent yellow.

`InitAsGreen;` Make this instance represent green.

`InitAsBlue;` Make this instance represent blue.

`InitAsPurple;` Make this instance represent purple.

`InitAsBlack;` Make this instance represent black.

`InitAsWhite;` Make this instance represent white.

Methods:

Similar methods exist, allowing instances to be changed to represent another color. The names of these methods are `ChangeToRed`, `Change-ToOrange`, and so on. (See Appendix D for details.)

We now can begin to define a new class to represent a colored house, `StHouse`. Since we said that we want the house to have a main color and a trim color, we can begin by providing the following class declaration with two instance variables:

```
StHouse = OBJECT
  { Public methods will go here. }
PRIVATE
  mainColor,                          { for walls and roof }
  trimColor     : GPColor;            { for window and door }
END; { StHouse }
```

Here we have created two instance variables of the class `GPColor`. The comma separating the instance variables is just a shorthand, so we needn't type the class name on every line. Thus the preceding declaration produces the same result as the following declaration:

```
StHouse = OBJECT
  { Public methods will go here. }
PRIVATE
  mainColor       : GPColor;          { for walls and roof }
  trimColor       : GPColor;          { for window and door }
END;
```

(Note that we use boldface type to indicate altered or new code.)

We also said that we want to store information about a house's position. If, for example, we wanted to keep track of the center of the house, we could store this position using another class defined in GP, called `GPPoint` and described in Class Box 4.2. Instances of `GPPoint` contain information about a single position on a drawing area, such as the top left corner of a drawing area. We're going to use an instance of `GPPoint` for the center of the house.

Class Box 4.2

GPPoint

GPPoint

An instance of `GPPoint` represents a single location within a drawing area.

Constructor:

`Init;`

The point will be the center of the drawing area. `GPPoint` has many other methods that will be shown later.

Our declaration now looks like this:

```
StHouse = OBJECT
  { Public methods will go here. }
PRIVATE
  mainColor,                          { color of main parts }
  trimColor       : GPColor;          { color of trim }
  center          : GPPoint;          { center of the house }
  { More instance variables will be added here shortly. }
END;
```

4.3 SENDING MESSAGES WITH PARAMETERS

Methods, as stated earlier, are the means for sending messages to instances. Let's consider how we send messages in the real world. If passed a note from someone that said, "See me!" you probably would have a general sense of what action to take, but you would need more information — like where and when. If passed a note from your instructor that said, "See me after class in my office," and another note from a friend that said, "See me at noon outside the cafeteria," you would go to different places at different times. In both cases, you would act on "See me," but the specific time and place would be different. When we want to send a message and provide particular information, we use *parameters*. Parameters in a programming language are like the location and time, in that they give more specificity to a message.

Let's look at some methods from the `StarterUnit` that use parameters. The methods of the house component classes we saw in Chapter 3 always drew a wall, door, roof, or window in the same place and with the same color. Additional methods are defined for these classes in the `StarterUnit`. These methods are `InitWithColorAndCenter` and `Erase`. Class Boxes 4.3–4.6 summarize these object classes and their methods. In each of the classes' `InitWithColorAndCenter` methods, we see that they all use parameters. The parameters are pieces of information that the methods need in order to do their work.

Class Box 4.3
SUWall

SUWall

Instances of this class represent a painted wall of a house.

Methods:

`InitWithColorAndCenter(color : GPColor; center: GPPoint);`

Initialize the wall's color and position. `color` is an instance of `GPColor` representing the color that the wall should be painted. `center` is an instance of `GPPoint` representing the center of the house. `InitWithColorAndCenter` calculates the position of the wall based on this point.

`Draw;` Draw the wall in its current position.

`Erase;` Erase the wall from its current position.

Using instances of these classes, we can detail our `StHouse` class as follows:

```
StHouse= OBJECT
{ Public methods will go here. }
PRIVATE
  mainColor,                           { color of walls, roof }
  trimColor     : GPColor;             { color of window, door }
  center        : GPPoint;             { center point of house }
  colorWall     : SUWall;              { front wall of house }
  colorWindow   : SUWindow;            { window of house }
  colorDoor     : SUDoor;              { front door of house }
  colorRoof     : SURoof;              { roof of house }
END; { StHouse }
```

Class Box 4.4
SUWindow

SUWindow

Instances of this class represent a painted window of a house.

Methods:

`InitWithColorAndCenter(color : GPColor; center: GPPoint);`

Initialize the window's color and position. `color` is the color that the window should be painted. `center` is the center of the house. `InitWithColorAndCenter` positions the window based on this point.

`Draw;` Draw the window in its current position.

`Erase;` Erase the window from its current position.

Class Box 4.5
SUDoor

SUDoor

Instances of this class represent a painted door of a house.

Methods:

`InitWithColorAndCenter(color : GPColor; center: GPPoint);`

Initialize the door's color and position. `color` is the color that the door should be painted. `center` is the center of the house. `InitWithColorAndCenter` positions the door based on this point.

`Draw;` Draw the door in its current position.

`Erase;` Erase the door from its current position.

Class Box 4.6
SURoof

SURoof

Instances of this class represent a painted roof of a house.

Methods:

`InitWithColorAndCenter(mainColor : GPColor; trimColor : GPColor; center: GPPoint);`

Initialize the roof's colors and position. `mainColor` and `trimColor` are the colors that the roof should be painted. `center` is the center of the house. `InitWithColorAndCenter` positions the roof based on this point.

`Draw;` Draw the roof in its current position.

`Erase;` Erase the roof from its current position.

In this case, an instance of the `SUWall` can be initialized by sending an `InitWithColorAndCenter` message, but the class description in Class Box 4.3 tells us we must provide two parameters to make the message more specific, because the wall needs to know its color, and the wall needs to know the house's center, so that it (the wall) can determine its own position. Thus when we send a message to the `InitWithColorAndCenter` method, we have to specify both pieces of information. The following code fragment shows how we might send this initialization message to a color wall instance:

```
{*****************************************************
This method establishes the initial state of house.
*******************************************************}

CONSTRUCTOR StHouse.Init;
BEGIN
  { initialize instance variables }
  mainColor.InitAsYellow;
  trimColor.InitAsGreen;
  center.Init;
  { initialize components }
  colorWall.InitWithColorAndCenter(mainColor, center);
  { More messages will go here. }
END; { StHouse.Init }
```

In this code fragment, we begin by constructing the instance variables `mainColor`, `trimColor`, and `center`. The instance variables `mainColor` and `trimColor` are constructed as before. The instance variable `center` receives its value from a constructor defined for the class `GPPoint` called `Init`. Then we send a message to `colorWall` (its constructor). The message says that the wall should be initialized using the color stored in `mainColor` and the point stored in `center`. We thus affect the initial state of the instance `colorWall` — it is (in this case) the color yellow and is positioned so that the center of the house is at the random point held by `center`. It is crucial to note that we are sending the *values* held by `mainColor` and `center` — not the instance variables themselves. OOPas copies the values of the instance variables and sends them to the constructor. The method `colorWall.InitWithColorAndCenter` has no idea that the values it receives as part of the `Init` message are copied from instance variables called `mainColor` and `center`, since all it cares about are the values of the color and the point.

Syntactically, sending a message with parameters begins the same way as sending any other message: We specify the instance (`colorWall`) and follow it with a period and the method name (`InitWithColorAndCenter`). After the method name, we list the parameters in parentheses and separate them by commas. A semicolon follows the closing parenthesis that indicates the end of the parameter list:

```
colorWall.InitWithColorAndCenter(mainColor, center);
```

The order of the parameters *must* match their order in the definition of the method. We saw in Class Box 4.3 that the `InitWithColorAndCenter` method of the `SUWall` takes the color parameter first and the point parameter second. The statement `colorWall.InitWithColorAndCenter(mainColor, center);` is not the same as `colorWall.InitWithColorAndCenter(center, mainColor);`. For the code to compile, a statement that sends a message with parameters has to provide the correct number of parameters, each of the type the recipient expects. Thus `colorWall.InitWithColorAndCenter(center, mainColor);` will not compile, because the types of the parameters don't match the types expected by `SUWall.InitWithColorAndCenter`. The variable `center` is not a `GPColor`, and the variable `mainColor` is not a `GPPoint`.

Let's finish the rest of the `HouseClass.Init` method.

```
{*******************************************************
This method establishes the initial state of house. It sets the
house's main color to be yellow and its trim color to be green.
*******************************************************}

CONSTRUCTOR StHouse.Init;
BEGIN
  mainColor.InitAsYellow;
  trimColor.InitAsGreen;
  center.Init;
  colorWall.InitWithColorAndCenter(mainColor, center);
  colorWindow.InitWithColorAndCenter(trimColor, center);
  colorDoor.InitWithColorAndCenter(trimColor, center);
  colorRoof.InitWithColorAndCenter(mainColor, trimColor, center);
END; { StHouse.Init }
```

The final statement, `colorRoof.InitWithColorAndCenter`, requires two `GPColor` parameters and one `GPPoint` parameter. From the compiler's perspective, it doesn't matter whether we send `trimColor` first and `mainColor` second, or vice versa — OOPas checks only that the first and second parameters are of type `GPColor`. Switching the order of the parameters, however, makes a big difference to the result of the program. Class Box 4.6 says that the first parameter to the `InitWithColorAndCenter` method of `SURoof` is the main color and that the second is the trim. If you were to reverse the order of the parameters in `colorRoof.InitWithColorAndCenters`, you would get a green roof with yellow trim, rather than the yellow roof with green trim that you set out to create.

Whenever you use parameters, the number, order, and types of parameters must be correct for OOPas to compile the code. The names of the parameters do not have any bearing on whether the code is correct — the names are just placeholders for their values. Thus it is up to you to make sure that the parameters match the description found in the class description box. You must ensure that the parameters you pass have not only the correct type, but also the correct *meaning*, something the compiler cannot check.

4.4 ASSIGNMENT

The assignment statement in OOPas performs the basic operation of storing information in a variable. For example, we can make the main color of the house the same as the trim color using the following assignment statement:

```
mainColor := trimColor;
```

The *assignment operator* (:=, often read as "gets") tells OOPas to store a value. Its syntax is described in Syntax Box 4.1. OOPas assigns values to variables from right to left. That is, the statement begins by evaluating the expression on the right. The term *expression* in computer science has essentially the same meaning as in algebra — it is a combination of terms and operators that results in a value. Here the expression is a single variable. We'll see other kinds of expressions later on. In this case, the value of `trimColor` is stored in `mainColor`.

Syntax Box 4.1
Assignment

Purpose:

To assign a value to a variable.

Syntax:

```
<variable name> := <expression>;
```

Where:

<variable name> is a variable or parameter.

<expression> is a variable, function, parameter, or constant — or any combination of them, with operators and parentheses — that evaluates to the same type as *<variable name>*.

Usage:

The *<expression>* on the right is evaluated. If *<expression>* has multiple parts, as in a chain of arithmetic operations, then it is evaluated according to the hierarchy of operations.

The final result of *<expression>* is stored in *<variable name>*.

(Functions are explained in Chapter 5. Constants and arithmetic expressions are explained in Chapter 9.)

Similarly, we could use the following statement to store the main color in the variable `trimColor`:

```
trimColor := mainColor;
```

In these examples, note that both sides of an assignment statement evaluate to the same data type. Because the variables `mainColor` and `trimColor` are both values of type `GPColor`, the variable on the left side of the assignment statement must also be of type `GPColor`.

We cannot mix data types, however. If, for example, you put an instance of `GPPoint` on one side of an assignment statement and an instance of `GPColor` on the other, the compiler would give you an error message like this:

```
trimColor := center;
ERROR: Type mismatch
```

Also remember that assignments move from right to left. This means that the item to the left of the assignment operator must be a variable, not a method. Thus the following statement also generates a compiler error:

```
trimColor.InitAsBlue := InitAsColor;
ERROR: constructor InitAsBlue found where variable required
```

When a value is assigned to a variable, any old values of that variable are replaced by the new value. Consider the following set of statements:

```
{ Presume blue and black are declared as instances of GPColor. }
blue.InitAsBlue;
black.InitAsBlack;
{ 1. } mainColor := blue;
{ 2. } trimColor := black;
{ 3. } mainColor := trimColor;
```

In the first statement, `mainColor` is set to the color blue. In the second statement, `trimColor` is set to the color black. In the third statement, OOPas takes the value of `trimColor` (black) and assigns it to `mainColor`. Now, `mainColor` is also black; there is no record of the fact that `mainColor` was previously blue. The latest assignment statement is the one that matters; any reference to `mainColor` after this block of three statements will refer to the color black.

Using assignment, we now can write a method that reverses the trim color and the main color of a house:

```
PROCEDURE StHouse.ReverseColors;
VAR
  temporaryColor : GPColor;

BEGIN
  temporaryColor.Init;
  temporaryColor := mainColor;
  mainColor := trimColor;
  trimColor := temporaryColor
END;
```

Notice that we need a local variable, `temporaryColor`, to hold the value of `mainColor` after we've assigned `trimColor` to it . We *still* need to initialize this local variable, even though we're about to assign to it. Assignment in OOPas works only on variables that hold valid instances.

Variables hold only a single value at a time. Once we've assigned the value of `trimColor` to `mainColor`, the old value of `mainColor` is no longer available from `mainColor`. Because we have previously saved the value of `mainColor` in `temporaryColor`, however, we can assign the value of `temporaryColor` (which is the same as the value that used to be stored in `mainColor`) to `trimColor`.

The local variable `temporaryColor` is a "temporary variable." In other words, it holds a value necessary to swap the colors. When we assign `trimColor` to `mainColor`, we wipe out any previous value of the house's main color. As a general rule, when we want to swap two values, we can use the following pseudocode:

```
Assign value of first variable to "temporary" variable
Assign value of second variable to first variable
Assign value of "temporary" variable to second variable
```

This swapping technique is used widely in computer science and is diagrammed in Figure 4.2. Note that swapping two values requires three variables — we cannot simply exchange the two values, since they must be stored in some variable at all times and only one assignment is performed at a time.

Figure 4.2 *Swapping*

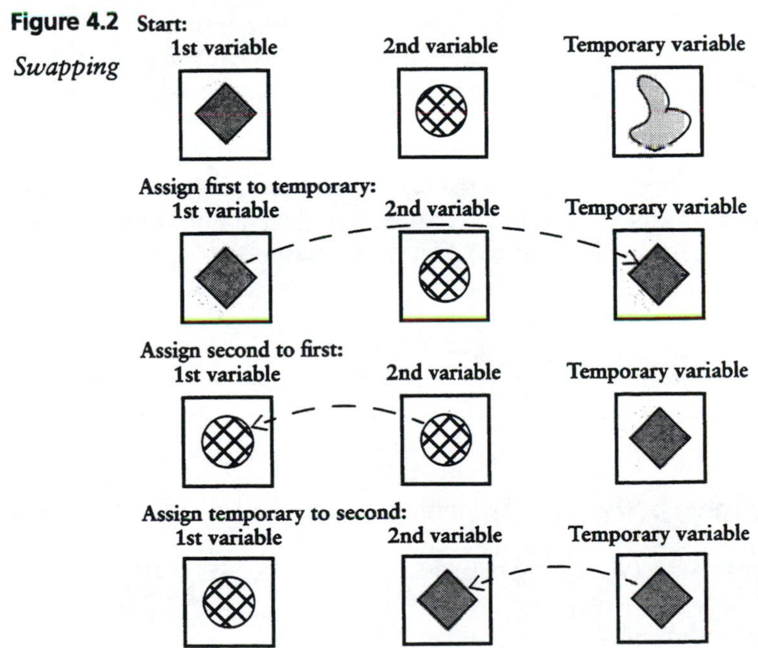

4.5 VALUE PARAMETERS

The constructor we defined in Section 4.3 will initialize a house so that its main color is always yellow, its trim color is always green, and its center is always at a random point. This isn't good enough, though, for our `Street` program, since we want the *user* to choose the colors and the point. (Specifically, the `StApp` class is to retrieve this information from the user, then send it to an instance of `StHouse`.) The user might pick blue and white for the first house, and red and green for the second. The `StHouse` cannot control what the user picks; rather it receives the colors from another method that obtained the colors from the user. Therefore we need to provide a new version of the constructor that *receives* the main color, trim color, and point as parameters.

There are two kinds of parameters: *value parameters* and *variable parameters*. Since we're interested in the *value* of the color picked by the user, we're going to use value parameters. Later in the chapter, in Section 4.7, we'll learn about variable parameters.

Methods with a Single Parameter

Before we being our study of value parameters, let's define two simpler methods, `SetMainColor` and `SetTrimColor`, which will let us change the colors of the house after it has been created. These methods will take a single parameter to indicate what the new color should be. To declare a method that accepts parameters, we must formally declare the parameters as part of the procedure or constructor heading in both the class declaration and the method definition. The method needs to know the names and the data types of the parameters it is receiving. This is the same information that we need to declare an instance variable or a local variable, and the parameters in a procedure heading look much like a list of variable declarations:

```
StHouse = OBJECT
   ...
   PROCEDURE SetMainColor(newMainColor : GPColor);
   PROCEDURE SetTrimColor(newTrimColor : GPColor);
   ...
```

As always, the method definition is quite similar to the declaration:

```
PROCEDURE StHouse.SetMainColor(newMainColor : GPColor);
BEGIN
   mainColor := newMainColor;
   wall.SetColor(mainColor);
   roof.SetMainColor(mainColor)
END;
```

```
PROCEDURE StHouse.SetTrimColor(newTrimColor : GPColor);
BEGIN
  trimColor := newTrimColor;
  window.SetColor(trimColor);
  door.SetColor(trimColor);
  roof.SetTrimColor(trimColor)
END;
```

Notice that once we have defined the parameter in the method header, we can use it as if it were a local variable. In this case, we used it on the right-hand side of an assignment statement. Like a local variable, though, parameters aren't accessible outside of the method.

Methods with Multiple Parameters

Now we will add a constructor that takes three parameters, so that we can construct a house with different colors and its own location. Our new version of `StHouse` then looks like this:[1]

```
TYPE
  StHouse = OBJECT
    CONSTRUCTOR  Init;
    CONSTRUCTOR  InitWithColorsAndCenter(
      newMain         : GPColor;            { color for house }
      newTrim         : GPColor;            { color for trim }
      newCtr          : GPPoint             { pos for house }
      );
    PROCEDURE    SetMainColor(newMainColor : GPColor);
    PROCEDURE    SetTrimColor(newTrimColor : GPColor);
    PROCEDURE    ReverseColors;
    { Other public methods will go here. }

  PRIVATE
    mainColor,                        { for walls and roof }
    trimColor   : GPColor;            { for window and door }
    center      : GPPoint;            { center point of house }
    colorWall   : SUWall;             { front wall }
    colorWindow : SUWindow;           { window on front side }
    colorDoor   : SUDoor;             { front door }
    colorRoof   : SURoof;             { roof }
  END; { StHouse }
```

And here is our new constructor, `StHouse.InitWithColorsAndCenter`:

1. Note that we format the parameter list so that we have space for "glossary comments," one per parameter.

```
{**********************************************************
This method establishes the initial state of the house. First, the
colors of the house and its position are set. Then, each of the
other components of the house are initialized.
**********************************************************}

CONSTRUCTOR StHouse.InitWithColorsAndCenter (
      newMain         : GPColor;               { color for main }
      newTrim         : GPColor;               { color for trim }
      newCtr          : GPPoint                { pos for house }
      );
BEGIN
  mainColor.Init;
  trimColor.Init;
  center.Init;

  { Store the information in the instance variables. }
  mainColor := newMain;
  trimColor := newTrim;
  center := newCtr;

  { Initialize the components of the house. }
  colorWall.InitWithColorAndCenter(mainColor, center);
  colorWindow.InitWithColorAndCenter(trimColor, center);
  colorDoor.InitWithColorAndCenter(trimColor, center);
  colorRoof.InitWithColorAndCenter(mainColor, trimColor, center);
END; { StHouse.Init }
```

The syntax of a method definition with multiple parameters is similar, but not identical, to a variable declaration list. The name of the parameter is followed by its data type. The parameters are separated by semicolons and enclosed in parentheses. A semicolon follows the closing parenthesis and separates the method header from the rest of the method definition. This final semicolon also means that we don't need a semicolon after the final parameter's data type. (In this case, `newCtr: GPPoint` is not followed by a semicolon, because it is the last parameter.) Like variables, parameters with the same data type can be separated by commas. The complete syntax is summarized in Syntax Box 4.2. The equivalent method heading shown here

```
CONSTRUCTOR StHouse.InitWithColorsAndCenter (
      newMain,                                 { color for main }
      newTrim         : GPColor;               { color for trim }
      newCtr          : GPPoint);              { pos for house }
```

also declares that `newMain` and `newTrim` are of the data type `GPColor`.

In the `BEGIN/END` block of our constructor, we still begin by setting the values of the instance variables `mainColor`, `trimColor`, and `center`. The assignment statement `mainColor := newMain;` is valid because `mainColor` is a

Syntax Box 4.2

Method definition with value parameters

Purpose:

To define the method name and its formal parameters.

Syntax:

```
PROCEDURE <class name>.<method name>(<parameter list>);
(or)
CONSTRUCTOR <class name>.<method name>(<parameter list>);
```

Where:

The reserved word PROCEDURE or CONSTRUCTOR is used to indicate the type of method. *<class name>* is the name of an object class. *<method name>* is an identifier indicating the name of this method. (By convention, we capitalize the first letter of *<method name>*).

<parameter list> is the list of parameters received by the method. It has the following structure:

```
<parameter sublist 1>: <parameter type 1>;
<parameter sublist 2>: <parameter type 2>;
...
<parameter sublist n>: <parameter type n>
```

Where:

<parameter sublist 1>, . . . , *<parameter sublist n>* are lists of one or more parameter names (called formal parameters). Individual parameters in each sublist are separated by commas.

<parameter type 1>, . . . , *<parameter type n>* are the corresponding data types of each parameter sublist.

Usage:

The method name is considered a "message" that instances of *<class name>* can receive. The parameters qualify that message and allow data to be received by *<method name>*.

The declarations of parameters are similar to declarations of instance variables and local variables: a list of identifiers (the *<parameter sublist>*s) is followed by a colon and a data type. Semicolons are used to separate the declarations of parameter sublists. The last parameter sublist is an exception. A right parenthesis is placed before the semicolon. Note there is no semicolon after *<method name>*.

Within the BEGIN/END brackets, the method treats parameters as if they were local or instance variables.

There need not be a parameter list for every method declaration. If the method takes no parameters, no parameter list is necessary (see Syntax Box 3.2).

The method heading, with the parameter list, must also appear in the object class's definition in the program's TYPE section.

variable of type `GPColor` and because `newMain` contains a value that is also of type `GPColor`. It doesn't matter (syntactically) whether `newMain` is declared as a parameter, a local variable, or an instance variable. All that the assignment statement needs to verify is that `newMain` is of the correct type.

However, the meaning of this constructor is different from the simpler constructor `Init`. Any `InitWithColorsAndCenter` message sent to `StHouse` will contain the information about the main and trim colors and the center point. Essentially, we have made the message more specific. The first version without parameters said "initialize," whereas the new version says, "initialize with the following colors and point on the screen."

In essence, the parameters serve as *placeholders*. That is, we know that when the `StHouse.InitWithColorsAndCenter` message is sent, `InitWithColorsAndCenter` will receive additional information. We don't know exactly what that information will be, so we use the parameters to "hold the place" where the information will come in. The names `newMain`, `newTrim`, and `newCtr` will be the method's local names that will hold the "real" color and point values when a message is received. Writing the method in terms of these placeholders makes it generic, capable of processing arbitrary values sent to it. These generic placeholders are called *formal* parameters, and the "real" values sent to the formal parameters are called *actual* parameters.

4.6 FORMAL AND ACTUAL PARAMETERS

We saw earlier in the chapter how to send parameters to a predefined method. Sending parameters to a method that you have defined yourself works the same way. First, you would type the name of the instance name and the method, followed by a list of parameters in parentheses. Suppose for purposes of illustration we had a sample class that sent an `InitWithColorsAndCenter` message to `StHouse`. The code for a method might look like this:

```
PROCEDURE SampleClass.Test;
VAR
  sampleHouse      : StHouse; { sample house }
  primaryColor     : GPColor; { main color of house }
  secondaryColor   : GPColor; { trim color of house }
  location         : GPPoint; { location of house }
BEGIN
  primaryColor.InitAsBlue;
  secondaryColor.InitAsRed;
  location.Init;
  sampleHouse.InitWithColorsAndCenter(primaryColor,
            secondaryColor, location);
END; { SampleClass.Test }
```

The variables used to name the values passed by the sending method (here `primaryColor`, `secondaryColor`, `location`) are known as *actual* parameters. The parameters used to receive these values in the recipient method (i.e., the placeholders) are known as *formal* parameters (here `newMain`, `newTrim`, and `newCtr`, as shown in the method's declaration). The actual parameter identifiers typically are not the same as the formal parameter identifiers. The method that sends a message (in this case, `SampleClass.Test`) never needs to know the names of the formal parameters, since the sender needs to know only the type of each parameter and the order in which they are declared. Conversely, `StHouse.InitWithColorsAndCenter` doesn't need to know the names of the actual parameters, since the method is defined without knowing who will use it. Thus the sender and the receiver are isolated from each other, and the sender only knows the types of the method's parameters, not the names.

As we saw earlier, parameters are sent, in order, from sender to receiver. There is a *one-to-one correspondence* between formal and actual parameters. In this example, OOPas copies the value of the first actual parameter (`primaryColor`) into the first formal parameter declared in the heading of `StHouse.InitWithColorsAndCenter` (that is, `newMain`). Similarly, OOPas copies the value of the second actual parameter (`secondaryColor`) into the formal parameter `newTrim` and the value of the third actual parameter (`location`) into the formal parameter `newCtr`.

The passing of parameters takes place before anything else is done in the method. This means that every formal parameter receives a value from the sender of the message before any of the statements in its `BEGIN`/`END` block are executed.

The details of sending a message with parameters are summarized in Syntax Box 4.3.

4.7 VARIABLE PARAMETERS

You may wonder how we are going to swap the colors of two houses. Our `ReverseColors` method can reverse the color of only the single house to which the message `ReverseColors` is sent. We'll need *variable parameters* to be able to pass two arbitrary houses as parameters. When we used parameters before, we were interested only in the values being provided. Now, we wish to *change* the instances being passed as parameters. The instances are thus *variable*, using the word "variable" as an adjective, not as a noun.

The specification states that the user can click on a button and swap the colors of two houses. When the user clicks on the "Swap Colors" button, the button sends a message asking the user to select two houses. Then, the button sends `StApp` a `SwapColors` message, telling it what houses should have their colors swapped. Let's look at this `SwapColors` method in greater depth.

We call our houses `house1` and `house2`. Each house has a different main color and trim color and we want to exchange the colors of `house1` with the

Syntax Box 4.3
Sending parameters

Purpose:

To send a message with parameters.

Syntax:

```
<instance name>.<method name>(<parameter 1>, <parameter 2>,
                              ..., <parameter n>);
```

Where:

<instance name> is the name of an instance.

<method name> is the name of a method that belongs to the instance's class.

<parameter 1>, *<parameter 2>*, . . ., *<parameter n>* are the actual parameters.

Usage:

The actual parameters sent by this statement must have the same data types as the formal parameters declared in the corresponding method header. That is, if the first parameter received by a method is an instance of `GPPoint`, *<parameter 1>* must also be an instance of `GPPoint`.

The parameters are separated by commas. The value of the first parameter listed in the message is received by the first parameter listed in the method heading, and so on, with a one-to-one correspondence. This implies that there must be the same number and type of actual and formal parameters.

If the sending method expects a value parameter, the corresponding actual parameter may be a variable, constant, or expression (constants and expressions are explained in Chapter 9). If the sending method expects a variable parameter, the actual parameter must be a local or instance variable.

colors of `house2`. Essentially, we want to swap the colors as in `ReverseColors`, except from one house to another.

A Single Variable Parameter

To exchange the house colors, we need to be able to ask a house what its trim color is and what its main color is. We can use variable parameters for this task. We can write two methods, `GetMainColor` and `GetTrimColor`, to provide the main color and the trim color to any object that asks for them:

```
StHouse = OBJECT
   ...
   PROCEDURE GetMainColor(VAR col : GPColor);
   PROCEDURE GetTrimColor(VAR col : GPColor);
   ...
END;
```

These methods look a lot like SetMainColor and SetTrimColor, except that we see the familiar keyword, VAR, being used in a different place. The method definitions look similar too:

```
PROCEDURE StHouse.GetMainColor (VAR col : GPColor);
BEGIN
  col := mainColor
END;

PROCEDURE StHouse.GetTrimColor (VAR col : GPColor);
BEGIN
  col := trimColor
END;
```

The big difference we see here (besides the addition of the VAR keyword) is that the parameter is on the left-hand side of the assignment, not the right-hand side. We are assigning the main color (or the trim color) to the parameter, not the other way around. The actual parameter given to this method will be changed to contain the main color of the house. The VAR reserved word is a marker, telling us that this parameter is a variable parameter (as opposed to the value parameters we saw before) and can be used to change the actual parameter in this fashion.

With two kinds of parameters — value and variable — you may wonder how you can determine which kind to use in any given situation. Consider the instance that is sending the message. Does it need a changed version of the parameter it is sending? Is the instance sending a message to get a value back? If so, then the parameter should be variable. If the sender simply is trying to tell the recipient to do something, then the parameter should be a value parameter. In practice, value parameters are far more common than variable parameters. You can think of the formal variable parameter as "taking on the identity" of an actual parameter, while the formal value parameter just takes on the value of an actual parameter.

Multiple Variable Parameters

Now that we can obtain the colors of the house, we can return to SwapColors. Remember that SwapColors is supposed to take two houses and exchange their colors. We use variable parameters when we want to change actual parameters, like the houses we will give to the SwapColors method. We use value parameters when we don't want to change the actual parameters. With VAR parameters, the changes will be made to the actual parameters of the sending method. Value parameters are copies of the actual parameters. Thus any changes made to value parameters will be made to the copies, not to the actual parameters. To change the colors of two houses, we must use variable parameters.

We now have two pairs of terms describing parameters: value and variable and formal and actual. *Value* and *variable* distinguish between two different kinds of parameter mechanisms, and *formal* and *actual* describe two parts of a single mechanism. With a value parameter, the actual parameter is copied into the formal parameter, so changes to the formal parameter do not affect the actual parameter. With a variable parameter, however, the formal parameter refers to the actual parameter. Any changes to the formal parameter affect the actual parameter.

Let's return to our method to swap the colors of two houses. Using our swapping technique twice, once for the main color and once for the trim color, we can write the pseudocode as follows:

StApp.SwapColors

Purpose:
  Swap the colors of two houses
Pseudocode:
  Erase the houses

  { swap main colors }
  Assign main color of house 1 to "temporary" variable
  Assign main color of house 2 to main color of house 1
  Assign "temporary" variable to main color of house 2

  { swap trim colors }
  Assign trim color of house 1 to "temporary" variable
  Assign trim color of house 2 to trim color of house 1
  Assign "temporary" variable to trim color of house 2

  { show the houses in their new colors }
  Draw the houses

Each of the preceding lines of pseudocode is fairly straightforward. We can code the statements as follows:

```
{**********************************************************
This method swaps the main and trim colors of two houses.
**********************************************************}

PROCEDURE StApp.SwapColors(
        VAR house1      : StHouse;                  { first house }
        VAR house2      : StHouse);                 { second house }
VAR
   tempColor1, tempColor2 : GPColor;

BEGIN
   house1.Erase;
   house2.Erase;
```

```
   { Swap the main colors. }
   house1.GetMainColor(tempColor1); { house1's main to temp }
   house2.GetMainColor(tempColor2); { house2's main to house1 }
   house1.SetMainColor(tempColor2);
   house2.SetMainColor(tempColor1); { temp to house2 }

   { Swap the trim colors. }
   house1.GetTrimColor(tempColor1); { house1's trim to temp }
   house2.GetTrimColor(tempColor2); { house2's trim to house1 }
   house1.SetTrimColor(tempColor2);
   house2.SetTrimColor(tempColor1); { temp to house2 }

   { Draw houses with new colors. }
   house1.Draw;
   house2.Draw;
END; { StApp.SwapColors }
```

In the method heading, we see that `SwapColors` takes two parameters, `house1` and `house2`. The parameters are preceded by the reserved word `VAR`, indicating that `house1` and `house2` are *variable parameters*. (Note that the keyword `VAR` can denote both the variable parameters and the local variables of a method. When `VAR` occurs inside a parameter list, it indicates variable parameters, but when `VAR` comes before the `BEGIN/END` block, it indicates local variables.)

Suppose we sent a `SwapHouse` message using the following code fragment:

```
{*******************************************************
A test method to swap the colors of two houses.
********************************************************}

PROCEDURE SampleClass.TestSwap;
VAR
   comicStreet : StApp;
   calvinHouse : StHouse;
   susieHouse  : StHouse;

BEGIN
  ...
  comicStreet.SwapColors(calvinHouse, susieHouse);
  ...
END; { SampleClass.TestSwap }
```

Let's see what happens when the `SwapColors` message is sent to `comicStreet`. As with all messages with parameters, a one-to-one correspondence is established. The first actual parameter (`calvinHouse`) corresponds to the first formal parameter (`house1`) and the second actual parameter (`susieHouse`) corresponds to the second formal parameter (`house2`). Then, `SwapColors` method executes its statements. When we use variable parameters, the formal parameter is effectively just a synonym for the actual parameter. Thus each reference to `house1` in `SwapColors` refers to the same instance as `calvinHouse` in `SampleClass.TestSwap`. Because `house1` and `house2` are defined as variable parameters, when the method ends, the changes to `house1` are saved in `calvinHouse` and the changes to `house2` are saved in `susieHouse`. If we had skipped the `VAR` in the declaration and made `house1` and `house2` value parameters, the colors would still be switched on the screen (since we redrew the houses after swapping the colors), but the changes would not have been saved in `SampleClass`'s instance variables.

As we have seen, sending a message with variable parameters looks no different from sending a message with value parameters. It is what happens to the actual parameters that makes the semantic difference.

The positions of the `VAR` and the semicolons in a method header's parameter list determine which parameters are variable and which are value. In the method heading, the `VAR` indicator is in effect until a semicolon is found. We could, for example, rewrite the header of `StApp.SwapColors` as follows:

```
PROCEDURE StApp.SwapColors(
        VAR house1,                          { swap this }
        house2      : StHouse);              { ... with this }
```

In this case, we have declared both `house1` and `house2` as variable parameters. Some other examples of parameter lists are given in Figure 4.3. Syntax Box 4.4 summarizes the use of variable parameters.

Figure 4.3

Value and variable parameters

Parameter list	Meaning
`(parm1, parm2 : GPColor);`	**Both *parm1* and *parm2* are value parameters.**
`(parm1 : GPColor;` `VAR parm2 : GPColor);`	***parm1* is a value parameter. *parm2* is a variable parameter.**
`(VAR parm1 : GPColor;` `parm2 : GPColor);`	***parm1* is a variable parameter. *parm2* is a value parameter.**
`(VAR parm1, parm2 : GPColor);`	**Both *parm1* and *parm2* are variable parameters.**

Four points worth checking when you are passing parameters are listed in Syntax Box 4.5. Checking these points will help minimize debugging time.

4.8 CONVENTIONS

When declaring methods with parameters, we follow some conventions for naming methods and using documentation. We include comments about what each parameter does — documentation. This *glossary* of parameters is especially helpful for other programmers who use your class. These users do not

Syntax Box 4.4

Variable parameters

Purpose:

To declare parameters that will be changed during the method.

Syntax:

```
VAR <parameter sublist>: <parameter type>;
```

Where:

<parameter sublist> is the list of variable parameters. Individual parameters in the sublist are separated by commas.

<parameter type> is the data type of all of the parameters in the list.

The entire notation above appears in the method heading, defined in Syntax Box 4.2.

Usage:

When VAR appears in front of a parameter list, it indicates that changes made to the formal parameters in the list should be applied to the corresponding actual parameters. This means that when the method has completed executing its statements, the parameters sent to the method contain any changes that are made during the method. The changes are not saved for value parameters.

Except for the keyword VAR, the declaration of parameters is exactly the same as the declaration of methods with value parameters.

Syntax Box 4.5

Checklist for parameter passing

Checklist for Parameters:

1. Are the numbers of actual and formal parameters the same?
2. Does the type of each formal parameter match the declared type of its corresponding actual parameter?
3. Are the values passed as parameters in the correct order?
4. Are only parameters that will be changed passed as variable parameters?

need to see the actual workings of your method, but they do need to know what parameters must be sent and what changes (if any) they undergo in your method. There is no need to know the actual identifier of a parameter, since only its type is of interest to the programmer who wants to use the method. However, knowing these identifiers may help explain what the parameter does, if the name is a good reminder of what the parameter does (i.e., if the name is suitably mnemonic).

Many object-oriented programmers use methods that start with "Set" and "Get." We used them in defining our StHouse class. The "Set" methods do nothing but change the state of an instance, typically by changing the value of one of the instance variables. The "Get" methods, which often use VAR parameters, simply retrieve a value from an instance. In our examples, we had methods that set and get the colors and the center of the house. Some programmers fall into the bad habit of writing a set and get method for each of the instance variables in a class. This is not a good idea because it exposes too much of a class. Remember, someone who wants to use your class shouldn't necessarily need to gain access to every part of that class. It doesn't make sense, for example, to allow other users to gain access to the wall or the roof in our `StHouse`. Using set and get methods sparingly will help ensure that your instances stay encapsulated.

4.9 WHEN TO USE PARAMETERS AND VARIABLES

We've now examined the three kinds of data a method can use — parameters, instance variables, and local variables. Inside the `BEGIN/END` block, they all behave in the same way: They represent instances whose contents we can store, retrieve, and update. So, how do we know when to use which?

The answer depends on what we want to do with these data *outside* of the current method. Figure 4.4 shows where each type of data exists and is accessible. A particular kind of variable is accessible only from inside a box, not from the outside. This property is called the *scope* of the local variable, instance variable, or parameter.

Figure 4.4

Scope of instance variables, local variables, and parameters

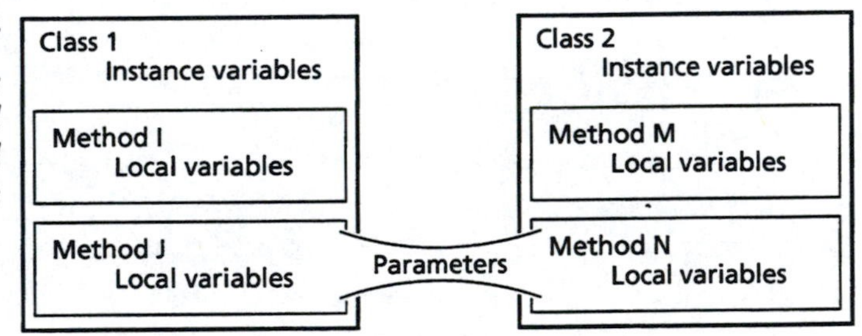

Local variables, the most confined in scope, can be used only in the method in which they are declared. Thus in Figure 4.4 they are shown inside the box corresponding to an individual method. One common use of a local variable is the "temporary" variable that we used in swapping values. We don't need to hang on to that temporary variable once the swap is complete, so we can declare it as a local variable. It's important to note that local variables are completely wiped out after the method's END.

Instance variables have a wider scope than local variables and are available for all the methods of a class.[2] Notice that they are inside the outermost box.

2. Those with programming experience will note that instance variables are "global" to all the methods in the class. The class's designer must ensure an instance variable's state remains correct at all times.

Think of an instance variable as a property or attribute of the class. It should help to describe an instance's current state. All the instance variables of a class should be initialized in that class's constructor. In this way, we can ensure that if any other method uses the instance variable, it will have a valid value. If the data describe something about the class that you want to make available to all of the class's methods, then you should use an instance variable. Since the instance variables are available to all methods, you, as a class designer, must be sure that the state of the instance is consistent at all times, given that you have no control over the order in which class methods will be requested by other methods.

Note that the distinction between local variables and instance variables is not what they can hold — all kinds of variables hold instances. Rather, the words *local* and *instance* refer to where the variable itself is located and therefore who has access to it. Instance variables are inside of an instance and are available to anything inside that instance; local variables are inside a method and are available only to other things inside that method.

Parameters are a crucial part of the communication link between methods. Since parameters are part of the method's interface, to determine whether an object should be a parameter, ask yourself, "Will these data be provided by some other class?" If so, you can then determine whether the parameter should be a value or variable parameter by asking, "Will the other class want to have its actual parameter modified by the receiver?"

The distinction among local variables, instance variables, and parameters may seem subtle. The key to understanding these differences is to focus on the purpose of the method and the description of the class. For a class, keep in mind what it is supposed to model and you will have an easier time determining whether a piece of data describes its state (and thus should be an instance variable). For a method, remember the method's purpose, and you will have an easier time determining what data are needed temporarily to perform this method's behavior (and should be local variables) and what data must be provided by or returned to some other method (and thus should be a parameter).

Summary

In this chapter, we have looked at many ways that objects communicate with each other. We started with the assignment statement, a key to storing information. It allows us to copy the information from an expression to a variable.

Communication occurs through the relay of messages from one instance to another. We can use parameters to qualify the messages we send. When we send a message with parameters, we have to make sure that we are sending the correct number of parameters and that each parameter is of the correct type. The interface of a class will tell us what types are expected, and in what order.

Parameters are declared in the heading of a method. They resemble variable declarations in that they have identifiers, require a data type, and should have a glossary definition. Within the `BEGIN/END` block of a method, the parameters can be treated like any other variable.

There are two types of parameters — value parameters and variable parameters. Both are declared in the heading of a method. In the case of a *value* parameter, the corresponding formal parameter in the receiver's method receives a copy of the actual parameter's value. In the case of VAR parameters, the corresponding formal parameter takes on the identity of the actual parameter — it is a "pseudonym." Thus any changes to it are in fact changes to the actual parameter. Syntactically, the parameter list begins with VAR when variable parameters are used.

Exercises

Understanding Concepts

1. Can you determine, by examining a method from BEGIN to END, which identifiers are declared as parameters, which are local variables, and which are instance variables?
2. When the OOPas compiler compares an actual and a formal parameter list, what must correspond in the two lists?
3. In the following procedure declarations, identify which are value parameters and which are variable parameters:

```
PROCEDURE Sample.First(VAR color1, color2: GPColor; point1:
            GPPoint);
PROCEDURE Sample.Second(VAR color1: GPColor; point1: GPPoint;
            color3: GPColor);
PROCEDURE Sample.Third(color1: GPColor; VAR point1: GPPoint; VAR
            color2: GPColor);
PROCEDURE Sample.Fourth(VAR color1: GPColor; point1: GPPoint;
            VAR color2, color3: GPColor; point2: GPPoint);
PROCEDURE Sample.Fifth(color1: GPColor; point1: GPPoint);
```

Coding Exercises

As needed, classes from StarterUnit will be defined before the coding exercises and programming problems. You will see the interface to the class as it appears in StarterUnit's TYPE declarations (but without the PRIVATE section). Use the following classes for Exercises 1 and 2:

```
{ SUPattern defines a pattern of alternating blocks. }
SUPattern = OBJECT
  { Init establishes the colors of the pattern. }
  CONSTRUCTOR Init(firstColor, secondColor: GPColor);
  { FillScreen draws the entire screen in the pattern colors. }
  PROCEDURE FillScreen;
PRIVATE
     ...
END;
```

```
{**********************************************************
The mainline establishes the pattern as alternating red and blue
squares, fills the screen, and tells the application to run.
***********************************************************}

VAR
   curApp      : SUApplication;    { application object }
   curPat      : SUPattern;        { pattern to fill screen }
   firstCol,
   secondCol   : GPColors;         { colors used in pattern }
BEGIN
   curApp.Init;
   firstCol.InitAsBlue;
   secondCol.InitAsRed;
   curPat.Init(firstCol, secondCol);
   curPat.FillScreen;
   curApp.Run;
END.
```

1. What is the effect if we change the fourth line of the mainline as follows?

   ```
   curPat.Init(secondCol, firstCol);
   ```

2. How could you change the code so that the pattern consisted of alternating green and yellow?

3. Suppose that the header of `StHouse.Init` in Section 4.5 is changed to:

   ```
   CONSTRUCTOR StHouse.Init(
      newTrim   : GPColor; { color for trim }
      newMain   : GPColor; { color for rest }
      newCtr    : GPPoint);{ point for center }
   ```

   What else would have to change in the method?

Programming Problems

Let's expand on the Aquarium components of Chapter 3.

```
SUFish
   { Includes all methods defined in Chapter 3, plus: }
   PROCEDURE   GetPoint    ( VAR pt : GPPoint);
      { fish's current pos }
   PROCEDURE   MoveToward  (pt: GPPoint);
      { move fish toward pt }
   PROCEDURE   MoveFrom    (pt: GPPoint);
      { move fish away from pt }
```

```
SUShark
   { Includes all methods defined in Chapter 3, plus: }
   PROCEDURE   GetPoint    (VAR pt : GPPoint);
     { shark's current pos }
   PROCEDURE   MoveToward  (pt: GPPoint);
     { move shark toward pt }
   PROCEDURE   MoveFrom    (pt: GPPoint);
     { move shark away from pt }

SUPlant
   CONSTRUCTOR   Init;
     { establishes random position for plant }
   PROCEDURE     Draw;
     { draws the plant in the aquarium }
   PROCEDURE     GetPoint  ( VAR pt : GPPoint);
     { plant's position }
```

1. Write a program with a goldfish and a plant. From its initial position, the goldfish should make three moves toward the plant.

2. Write a program with a goldfish and a shark. After they are initialized, the goldfish and shark should alternate moving. The goldfish should move away from the shark's current position, and the shark should move toward the goldfish's current position. Both the shark and the goldfish should make three moves.

3. Write a program with a goldfish, a shark, and a plant. After initialization, the goldfish should move toward the plant, and the shark should move toward the goldfish. Again, the shark and goldfish should alternate moves, and each should make three moves.

4. Write a program with three goldfish, a shark, and a plant. After initialization, all four animals should move in the following sequence: shark, goldfish 1, goldfish 2, goldfish 3. During the first sequence, the shark should move toward goldfish 1, goldfish 1 should move away from the shark, and goldfish 2 and 3 should move toward the plant. During the next sequence, the shark should move toward goldfish 2, goldfish 2 should move away from the shark, and goldfish 1 and 3 should move toward the plant. During the final sequence, the shark should move toward goldfish 3, goldfish 3 should move away from the shark, and goldfish 1 and 2 should move toward the plant.

Use these methods for Programming Problems 5 and 6. Let's extend the stick figure classes from Chapter 3 by adding the following methods:

```
SUEyes
   PROCEDURE   SetColor (newColor: GPColor);
     { This method sets the color of the eyes }
   PROCEDURE   GetColor (VAR theColor : GPColor);
     { Retrieves color of eyes }
```

```
SUArms
  PROCEDURE   SetShirtColor (newColor: GPColor);
    { This method draws a shirt in the specified color }
```

5. Modify Programming Problem 2 of Chapter 3 so that it draws a person with a frown and red eyes.

6. Modify Programming Problem 5 of Chapter 3 so that the stick figure has eyes and a shirt with the same color.

Use the following methods for Problems 7–9.

```
SUDesk
{ Purpose: Represents a desk in a dorm room. }
  CONSTRUCTOR    Init;
    { This method establishes the position of the desk. }
  PROCEDURE      SetColor    (newColor: GPColor);
    { Establish color of the desk when drawn filled. }
  PROCEDURE      GetColor    (VAR theColor : GPColor);
    { This method retrieves the color of the desk }
  PROCEDURE      DrawOutline;
    { Draws the outline of the desk }
  PROCEDURE      DrawFilled;
    { Draws the desk in the given color }

SUChair, SUBed, SUDoor
  { All have same methods as SUDesk }
```

7. Write a program that draws all the components of the dorm room (desk, chair, bed, and door) in outline form.

8. Write a program that coordinates by color. Get the color of the door, then set the rest of the furniture to that color. Finally, draw each piece as filled.

9. Write a program that draws two of the pieces in outline form and two as filled. The filled pieces should have different colors.

5

Associations

5.1 A NEW KIND OF OBJECT RELATIONSHIP

So far, we have seen two different kinds of object relationships. First, we've seen the *class–instance* relationship, which allows us to create separate instances (each with its own state and identity, but with identical behaviors) from a single class. Second, we've seen the *containment* relationship, where an instance of one class is an instance variable inside another class.

In this chapter, we will examine a third kind of object relationship known as association. *Association* describes a relationship in which an instance variable of one class is *linked* to an instance of another class. That is, one object should be able to send messages to another object without containing it. Associations are the most common type of relationship in many systems. If you think of all of the objects with which you interact on a daily basis, you "contain" very few of them, but you send messages of some kind to almost all of them. Consider a VCR. Using a remote, you can send messages to a VCR, telling it to play or rewind. Clearly, you do not contain a VCR, though you might be associated with one (perhaps quite closely).

5.2 ASSOCIATIONS AND LINKS

We can think of a link as a description of a relationship between two objects. We can describe many human relationships in daily life as links. For example, "a student is linked to a school, " "an athlete is linked to a team," and "a person is linked to a family."

In each case, we have used "is linked to" to represent a more specific relationship: "A student studies at a school," "an athlete belongs to a team," "a person is related to a family." You may note that, grammatically, we are linking two nouns — subject and object — with a verb phrase. Note that the relationship is not symmetric; you can't exchange the nouns using the same verb.

Reconsider your VCR. The remote control for your VCR can be considered a link between you and your VCR. You can use the link to send messages to the VCR — play, rewind, and so on — but the VCR can't send messages to you, at least not using the remote. Like the remote, links allow messages to be sent one way. If you want messages sent the other way, you need another link going the other way. A VCR can send messages to you by using a display on its front panel, indicating such things as it is currently rewinding a tape or that the time is precisely 12:00.

A link thus goes from one object to another. Just as we describe a category of objects using a class, we describe a category of links using an association. Whereas a link may state that "Jane's VCR remote is used to send messages to Jane's VCR," an association describing that link would indicate that "VCR remotes are used to send messages to VCRs." Thus links are between instances and associations are between classes.

Classes can, of course, participate in any number of associations, and links *to* a specific instance can originate in any number of instances of the same or of different classes. Since we're using them to send messages, the particular links in a system are closely related to the particular messages being sent by objects. Messages are passed from sender to receiver (or recipient) instance, while links go from source to destination instance. A link thus serves as a one-way pipeline for messages from a source/sender instance to its destination/receiver instance.

5.3 AN EXAMPLE: TELEPHONES

Let's consider what an association looks like in OOPas. Suppose we wanted to improve on our house model from Chapter 4 by adding a telephone, so that the residents can make phone calls. We'll start by realizing that we need a phone jack for our house and that we'll have to hook up the phone jack to the telephone lines. In the case of our house, let's suppose that there's a telephone pole nearby that we'd like to include in our picture of a house, so the phone jack will be connected to the telephone pole.

As it happens, our `StarterUnit` has a number of classes we can use for this situation. There's both a `SUTelephonePole` and a `SUTelephoneWallJack`. `SUTelephonePole` is described in Class Box 5.1, and `SUTelephoneJack` is described in Class Box 5.2. Like the walls, doors, and windows we saw before, we can draw both telephone poles and telephone jacks. However, we see there are also methods to attach new phone jacks to telephone poles. We also see a method in `SUTelephoneWallJack` to allow a phone jack to send or receive calls. In a moment, after hooking up the phone jack, we'll hook up a phone and make use of these methods.

Class Box 5.1
SUTelephonePole

SUTelephonePole

This class models a simple telephone pole.

Methods:

`Init;` Construct the telephone pole.

Class Box 5.2
SUTelephoneWall-Jack

SUTelephoneWallJack

This class models a simple modular phone jack.

Methods:

`Init(thePole : SUTelephonePoleAsn);` Construct the telephone pole.

`GetPoleLink(VAR myPoleLink: SUTelephonePoleAsn);`
Retrieve a link to the jack's telephone pole, using a `VAR` parameter.

`GetPoleLinkFunc : SUTelephonePoleAsn;`
Retrieve a link to the jack's telephone pole, using a function.

`CallOperator;` Connect to the telephone operator via the telephone pole.

`PlugIn(phone:SUTelephoneAsn);`
Hook up a phone to the wall jack. Calls coming in via the jack will ring the phone.

Instance Variables:

`poleLink : SUTelephonePoleAsn;` A link to a telephone pole.

But first, let's look at where we should place the jack and the pole and how they should be connected. The phone jack should be inside the house, since we want to plug a phone into it later. Thus our revised house class will contain an instance of the wall jack. Neither the house nor the phone jack contains the telephone pole. Most houses don't contain telephone poles, and phone jacks are much too small to physically contain a telephone pole. Furthermore, most telephone poles are used by more than one house and more than one phone jack and we can't have one instance contained within many other instances, since that would be like having one thing simultaneously in two boxes that didn't contain each other.

Figure 5.1 is an instance diagram of links between instances. Links are represented by arrows labeled with the association connecting an instance variable in the "source" instance with a "destination" instance. Note that whereas we used rectangles with square corners to represent classes (as in Figure 4.4), we use rectangles with rounded corners to represent instances of classes. When we have an instance, we put its class in parentheses. Similarly, when we draw a link, we note its type by placing the association in parentheses. Here, the destination instances are *outside* the source instance. The link `poleLink` is a link of the type `SUTelephonePoleAsn`; `SUTelephonePoleAsn`, in turn, is a type that associates an instance of any class to an instance of `SUTelephonePole`.

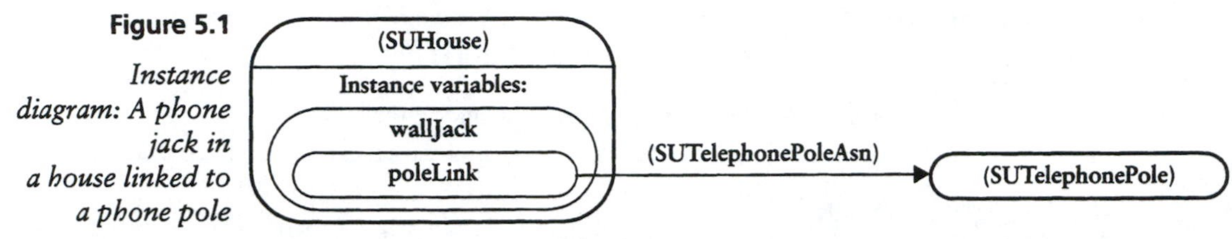

Figure 5.1 *Instance diagram: A phone jack in a house linked to a phone pole*

5.4 DECLARING ASSOCIATIONS AND LINKS

In the syntax of OOPas, the declaration of an association lies outside any class definition, because it describes a relationship to a class. The syntax is quite simple: The name of the association type is followed by an equals sign, a caret (^), and the name of a class. We often place association declarations before class declarations, for reasons that will be clearer when we talk about linked lists in Chapter 23. By convention, we end the association name with suffix `Asn` and start it with the class name (as in `Pole` and `PoleAsn`).

Once we have declared the association type, we can use it to create links in any other class declarations. Thus part of the declaration for `SUTelephoneWallJack` looks like this:

```
{ The association declaration for SUTelephonePoleAsn }
SUTelephonePoleAsn = ^SUTelephonePole;
{ A class that uses that association to describe links }
SUTelephoneWallJack = OBJECT
  CONSTRUCTOR Init(newPoleLink:SUTelephonePoleAsn);
  ...
PRIVATE
  poleLink: SUTelephonePoleAsn;
  ...
END; { CLASS WallJack}
```

We've discussed associations as relationships between two classes and links as specific instances of associations from a source instance to a destination instance. OOPas syntax declares an association type only in terms of the destination class. For example, `SUTelephonePoleAsn = ^SUTelephonePole;` declares that links of type `SUTelephonePoleAsn` will have an instance of a `SUTelephonePole` as a destination. The source class is determined by use. An instance variable within a class definition, such as `poleLink` in the `SUTelephoneWallJack` class, or a local variable or parameter, will determine the source of the link, because whatever has the link will act as the source.

The syntax for declaring association types and instance variables that are links is summarized in Syntax Box 5.1.

Syntax Box 5.1

Declaration of association types and link variables

Purpose:

The type defines an association to a class; the variable declaration establishes an instance variable for a link in a class definition.

Syntax:

```
TYPE
  <association identifier> = ^<class name 1>;
  <class name 2> = OBJECT
    ...
    <link variable> : <association identifier>;
    ...
  END;
```

Where:

<association identifier> is any legal OOPas identifier; by convention, we use the suffix "Asn".

^ is the caret sign.

<class name 1> is a class to which the association will refer.

<class name 2> is a class name.

<link variable> is an instance variable defined in either the public or private sections of *<class name 2>*; by convention, we use the suffix "Link".

Usage:

Associations are used when an instance of *<class name 2>* needs to call methods of an instance of *<class name 1>*, but should not contain the instance of *<class name 1>*. Instances of *<class name 1>* could contain instances of *<class name 2>*, however.

Within the methods of *<class name 2>*, the syntax

```
<instance variable name>^.<method name>
```

can be used to call a method of *<class name 1>*.

When you want to refer to the link variable by itself in a statement, use *<link name>*. When you want to refer to the instance of *<class name 1>*, use *<instance variable name>* followed by the caret.

5.5 PASSING AND ASSIGNING LINKS

Let's take a look at how we're going to use this phone jack. Remember, it's going to be a part of our house, so it will be an instance variable. Now, we can write a new version of our house class to include the phone jack. Let's call this new class HouseWithPhone. We will use the SU classes we've seen earlier. To keep our example brief and focused on the new parts, we won't specify different colors and positions for the house:

```
HouseWithPhone = OBJECT { represents a house }
    CONSTRUCTOR Init(newPoleLink : SUTelephonePoleAsn);
    PROCEDURE Draw;
  PRIVATE
phonejack    : SUTelephoneWallJack;
wall         : SUWall;              { front wall }
door         : SUDoor;              { front door }
window       : SUWindow;            { window next to door }
roof         : SURoof;              { roof of house }
  END; { house }
```

This new class is very similar to the old one. We have duplicated everything from the old house class in this new house class.

Let's look more closely at the new parts. First, we'll consider the constructor. As before, we'll construct the door, the window, the wall, and the roof. Now, we'll construct the phone jack as well, for which we'll need a link to the pole. Thus the new constructor takes a `SUTelephonePoleAsn` as a parameter and passes it to the wall jack's constructor:

```
CONSTRUCTOR HouseWithPhone.Init(newPoleLink : SUTelephonePoleAsn);
BEGIN
  phonejack.Init(newPoleLink);
  wall.Init;
  door.Init;
  window.Init;
  roof.Init;
END;
```

That was pretty straightforward. We simply passed the link to the pole on to the part of the house that really needed it, namely the wall jack. The same thing happens with a real phone line running from a pole to a house. Once inside the house (i.e., once passed into the constructor method), the phone line goes to exactly where it needs to connect, namely the wall jack.

Now let's look inside the phone jack to see what its constructor does.

```
CONSTRUCTOR SUTelephoneWallJack.Init(
      newPoleLink : SUTelephonePoleAsn);
BEGIN
  poleLink := newPoleLink;
END;
```

Here, we simply assign the link `newPoleLink` to the instance variable `poleLink`. Earlier, in Chapter 4, we used assignment on *instances*. Now we're using it on *links to instances*. Assigning an instance to a variable means that the variable contains a copy of the instance being assigned. Thus changes to the copy stored in the variable won't affect the original instance that had been assigned to that variable. However, when we assign a link to a variable, it is that link that is copied, not the instance. Therefore, as many links as are needed can be made to any one object.

5.6 USING A LINK TO SEND A MESSAGE TO THE DESTINATION

Now that we have a phone jack, we can make phone calls. As you might expect, this works by sending messages along the link we've established. We can't yet receive phone calls, because links are one way. We've established a link from the wall jack to the telephone pole, but not the other way. We'll fix this in the next section.

But first, let's place a phone call to the operator. `SUTelephoneWallJack` has a method, `callOperator`, that we can use to do this (as shown in Class Box 5.2). Since our house has a wall jack as an instance variable, we can place a call simply by sending the `callOperator` message to the wall jack:

```
phonejack.callOperator;
```

Of course, we'd really like to do this from a telephone object. For the moment, however, we're more interested in modeling the fact that the objects are connected (i.e., using associations and links) rather than the objects themselves, so our house isn't bothering with the details of a telephone yet. Those details aren't important to *this* model. Other unimportant details include the fact that phone wires are actually physical objects. If we were interested in modeling the wires themselves (rather than the connections they provide), we might make the wires objects. Wire objects still would need associations though, since a wire clearly doesn't contain either of the things at its ends.

Now, `callOperator` isn't anything new. It's simply sending a message, as we saw in Chapter 2. But how does `callOperator` itself work? As it happens, a wall jack simply forwards calls to the phone system, and the first stop on the way to the phone system is the telephone pole. `SUTelephonePole` has a `callOperator` method of its own, so the wall jack simply can call the telephone pole's `callOperator` method. However, we can't just send a message, because thus far we've only sent messages from an instance to an instance variable it contained and the wall jack doesn't have a pole as an instance variable. The wall jack has a *link to a pole.*

We need some new syntax to handle this situation. Sending a message along a link looks almost exactly like sending a message to an instance directly. The difference is in the use of a caret (^):

```
PROCEDURE SUTelephoneWallJack.callOperator;
BEGIN
  poleLink^.CallOperator;
END;
```

Since `poleLink` is a link to an instance, not an instance itself, we have to place the caret before the period when we send the `CallOperator` message. You can remember that you need a caret because the association type declaration, `PoleAsn = ^Pole;`, also uses a caret. Except for the caret, using the method of a "linked to" instance is no different from using the method of a "contained" instance. We can interpret the statement `poleLink^.callOperator` as "send a `CallOperator` message to the instance to which `poleLink` is linked." Thus a link is a handle or an indirect name of an instance.

5.7 ESTABLISHING LINKS

We've said that `poleLink` is linked to instances of `SUTelephonePole`. We see that the formal parameter `newPoleLink` receives a link that is sent as an actual parameter. But how did the link get established? Let's look at our mainline. Here, the mainline from Chapter 3 has been modified to create a telephone pole and attach it to the house:

```
{*****************************************************
Mainline
*****************************************************}

VAR
  telephonePole    : SUTelephonePole;    { pole to link to }
  mainHouse        : HouseWithPhone;     { house instance }
  mainApplication  : SUSimpleApp;        { application }
BEGIN
  mainApplication.Init;
  telephonePole.Init;
  mainHouse.Init(@telephonePole);
  mainHouse.Draw;
  mainApplication.Run;
END. { Mainline }
```

Here, we see how a link gets attached to a real instance. Let's focus on the boldfaced line, since it is the most important one for links. This line initializes our new house class. The operator `@` is a special symbol that can be read as "link to." This operator returns a link to its parameter, so the statement `mainHouse.Init(@telephonePole);` says that we should pass the "link to `telephonePole`" to the `Init` method. The `@` operator can be used in front of any instance. In essence, the `@` operator is the inverse of the `^`; `@telephonePole` can be read as "the link to `telephonePole`" and `poleLink^` can be read as "the instance to which `poleLink` is linked."

We can use `@` as we would any link. For example, we can use it on the right-hand side of an assignment.The syntax of `@` is covered in Syntax Box 5.2.

Syntax Box 5.2

Creating a link to an instance

Purpose:

To create a link to an instance.

Syntax:

```
<link variable> := @<instance name>;
```

Where:

<link variable> is a link that is of a type that associates to *<class name>*.

<instance name> is an instance of the same *<class name>*.

Usage:

This assignment is used when a link variable is to be linked to a particular instance. Note that the "at sign" appears on the right side of the assignment.

5.8 LINKS TO CONTAINERS

We have seen a number of examples of an instance of one class containing an instance of another class. For example, in Chapter 3, we saw that the house contained the window, door, roof, and wall. Representing the wall's containment in the house was very straightforward. We simply listed an instance variable of `SUWall` in the class definition of `HouseWithPhone`, and this meant that each instance of `HouseWithPhone` would contain an instance of `SUWall`. The `HouseWithPhone` methods, then, could send messages to the instance of `SUWall`, for example, to initialize or draw the wall.

What if we want to send messages in the opposite direction — from the wall to the house? The wall does not contain the house. You may ask, "Why can't the contained instance (the wall) send a message to its container (the house)?" The reason is that the contained class couldn't name all of its possible container classes since they aren't known at compile time — any class defined later on could contain instances of a previously defined class. OOPas does not have a way of syntactically indicating the relationship from the wall to the house. Instead, we create an association between contained and container, the wall class and the house class. The relationship between contained class and its container class thus is implemented as a link between their instances.

In Chapter 4, we saw that the `House` contained instance variables called `mainColor` and `trimColor` that stored the colors of the house. The instances of `SUWall` and other house components received this information as parameters in `InitWithColorAndCenter`.

In that program, which did not use associations, each time that we changed the main or trim color of the house, we had to send a message to the house components to change their colors. The `SetMainColor` and `SetTrimColor` methods looked like this:

```
{************************************************************
This method sets the main color of the house.
************************************************************}

PROCEDURE StHouse.SetMainColor(main: GPColor);
BEGIN
  mainColor := main;
  wall.SetColor(mainColor);
  roof.SetColor(mainColor)
END; { House.SetMainColor }

{************************************************************
This method sets the trim color of the house.
************************************************************}

PROCEDURE StHouse.SetTrimColor(trim: GPColor);
BEGIN
  trimColor := trim;
  window.SetColor(trimColor);
  door.SetColor(trimColor)
END; { House.SetTrimColor }
```

This code works perfectly well. But what happens if we want to change the house in some way? Suppose, for example, that we had more than one window or needed more than one wall. For every component we add to the house, we would need to add another statement to `SetMainColor` or `SetTrimColor` that sets the additional component's color.

Alternatively, we could have the house components, when it was time to draw, retrieve their colors from the house instead of having the house set the colors for them. This makes the components more self-sufficient. (In Chapter 4, we defined `GetTrimColor` and `GetMainColor` procedures for the `House`.) To use these methods, we need a link from each component to the house.

Let's consider, then, what the `SUWall` class might look like. Rather than storing the color itself, the wall uses its link to the house to retrieve the house's main color using `GetMainColor`. We could change the constructor and class definition accordingly, as shown in the following code:

```
StHouseAsn = ^StHouse;
SUWall = OBJECT
  CONSTRUCTOR Init(newLink: HouseAsn);
  PROCEDURE Draw;
  PROCEDURE Erase;
PRIVATE
  houseLink: StHouseAsn;
END; { CLASS SUWall }

{********************************************************
The constructor establishes the link to the house.
*********************************************************}

CONSTRUCTOR SUWall.Init(newLink: StHouseAsn);
BEGIN
  houseLink := newLink;
END;
```

Now, `houseLink` will retain the link to the house, and through that link, we can send messages to the house. This means that the wall's `Draw` method can send a message to the house as follows:

```
{********************************************************
This method draws the wall.
*********************************************************}

PROCEDURE SUWall.Draw;
VAR
  currentColor : GPColor; { color used to draw wall }
BEGIN
  houseLink^.GetMainColor(currentColor);
  { Messages to draw the wall appear here. }
END;
```

Since the responsibility for getting the color now lies with the house component, `House` simply needs to store a change in color; it does not need to send `SetColor` messages to the components.

```
{********************************************************
This method sets the main color of the house.
*********************************************************}

PROCEDURE StHouse.SetMainColor(newMainColor : GPColor);
BEGIN
  mainColor := newMainColor;
END;
```

What's important to note here is the different means of communication between the two objects. The house, which contains the wall, simply sends messages to the wall. The wall, however, needs a link to the house in order to send it messages. In both cases, a name was needed to identify the receiver of a message. With containment, the name provides direct access to the contained instance. With a link, the name provides indirect access to the container, requiring a caret before a message can be sent.

Now let's take yet another look at containment.

5.9 IMPLEMENTING CONTAINMENT USING LINKS

We've been slowly working through relationships between objects in these first few chapters. These relationships have a lot in common. In particular, links to objects often can serve as a way of implementing containment when instance variables wouldn't be convenient. One very important such case is when the object to be contained can't be constructed by the container.

With a real house, this occurs often. Look around your own house and ask yourself, "How many of the objects here were built here?" Some things, like walls, windows, and fireplaces, were built right there on site. Other things, however, like a TV or an oven, were built somewhere else, probably at a factory, and were brought to the house. The house still contains them, but the house's construction doesn't include construction of these parts. Let's continue with our telephone example. We've got a wall jack, and now we need a telephone to plug into the jack. `SUTelephone` is a class provided by `SimpleUnit` that we can use for this, and is described in Class Box 5.3.

Class Box 5.3
SUTelephone

SUTelephone

This class models a simple telephone.

Methods:

`Init;` Construct the telephone.

`Ring;` Ring the phone.

`CallOperator;`

Call the operator, using any phone jack into which this phone is plugged.

`ConnectToJack(jackLink: SUTelephoneWallJackAsn);`

Connect the phone to the passed jack.

Most wall jacks are installed when a house is built, but most telephones are not. Thus we're going to make a link to a telephone built somewhere else, even though the house itself contains the phone. Before we look at the code for this link, let's consider why we can't use regular containment to model the phone. Remember that the constructor for the house constructed every single part of the house:

```
CONSTRUCTOR House.Init(pole: SUTelephonePoleAsn);
BEGIN
   phonejack.Init(pole);
   wall.Init;
   door.Init;
   window.Init;
   roof.Init;
END;
```

If we simply made the phone an instance variable, its constructor would have to be called inside the constructor for the house. But we don't want to build the phone inside the house — we want to build the phone somewhere else and then install it in the house, just like we would do it in the real world.

Since we can't use a regular instance variable, we'll use a link. But this leads us the question of what to do with the link in the constructor for the house. We could pass to the constructor the link to the phone, but we'd like to be able to build the phone after building the house (in case we don't have a buyer for the house right away, for example). The solution to this problem is provided by the *null link* or *null pointer.*[1] OOPas provides a reserved word that represents a link that isn't linked to any object at all. This reserved word is `NIL`. Now, when we construct our house, we can use `NIL` for the link to the phone and assign a link that points to an actual phone instance later. Here's what our constructor looks like now:

```
CONSTRUCTOR House.Init(pole: SUTelephonePoleAsn);
BEGIN
   phoneJack.Init(pole);
   phoneLink := NIL;
   wall.Init;
   door.Init;
   window.Init;
   roof.Init;
END; { House.Init }
```

We can now add a method that installs the phone by assigning a suitable link to `phoneLink`. We'll also hook the phone up to our wall jack by passing the wall jack a link to the phone. This way, when we use the phone, calls can get passed along to the phone system. Here's the installation method:

1. Links often are called "pointers." Link is a design concept, and pointer is an implementation concept.

```
PROCEDURE House.InstallPhone(newPhoneLink : SUTelephoneAsn);
BEGIN
  phoneLink := newPhoneLink;
  phoneJack.plugIn(phoneLink);
END;
```

5.10 USING FUNCTIONS

Now suppose that someone from the telephone repair company comes to our house and needs to know into which telephone pole our phone jack is plugged. `SUTelephoneWallJack` could define a procedure that takes one `VAR` parameter of type `SUTelephonePoleAsn`, as follows:

```
PROCEDURE SUTelephoneWallJack.GetPoleLink(
      VAR myPoleLink : SUTelephonePoleAsn);
BEGIN
  myPoleLink := poleLink { provide a link to telephone pole }
END;
```

As an alternative, we can use a *function*. When we use a procedure that takes a `VAR` parameter, we need a place to store the result, such as another variable. This is inconvenient if we're planning on simply passing the `VAR` parameter as an actual parameter to another procedure call. A function is a method that can be used in place of a variable. Let's compare use of a `VAR` parameter with use of a function. First, look at the use of a `VAR` parameter:

```
PROCEDURE Sample.UsingVar;
VAR
  tempLink : SUTelephonePoleAsn;
BEGIN
  wallJack.GetPoleLink(tempLink); { sends VAR parameter }
  repairPerson.ClimbPole(tempLink)
END;
```

Notice that we first had to retrieve a link to the pole, then tell the repairperson to climb it. Now look at the function version:

```
PROCEDURE Sample.UsingFunction;
VAR
  tempLink : SUTelephonePoleAsn;
BEGIN
  tempLink := wallJack.GetPoleLinkFunc; { uses function }
  repairPerson.ClimbPole(tempLink)
END;
```

GetPoleLinkFunc is the function defined as a member of SUTelephoneWall-Jack that returns a link to a telephone pole. If a procedure is like telling an object to perform some behavior, then a function is a method that asks an object for something. In this case, we're asking the wallJack to give us its link to the telephone pole.

However, functions can be used as expressions. We've used a function as an expression on the right-hand side of an assignment, but we can also use expressions (including functions) to pass values on to value parameters. We could use the function where we used the temp variable before and rewrite this method even more succinctly as follows:

```
PROCEDURE Sample.UsingFunctionAsExpression;
BEGIN
  repairPerson.ClimbPole(wallJack.GetPoleLinkFunc)
END;
```

Note that we didn't need the temporary variable.

However, you can't use a function with a VAR parameter, since a VAR parameter makes changes to what is passed to it. Hence, an actual variable needs to be passed to a VAR parameter so that it has a place to store those changes.

5.11 DEFINING YOUR OWN FUNCTIONS

To understand how to write our own functions, we'll examine how the function GetPoleLinkFunc is defined. Compare the procedure GetPoleLink from the previous section to the function GetPoleLinkFunc:

```
PROCEDURE SUTelephoneWallJack.GetPoleLink(
        VAR myPoleLink : SUTelephonePoleAsn);
BEGIN
  myPoleLink := poleLink { if poleLink is the link the wall jack
                uses to talk to the pole }
END;

FUNCTION SUTelephoneWallJack.GetPoleLinkFunc : SUTelephonePoleAsn;
BEGIN
  GetPoleLinkFunc := myPole
END;
```

There are two differences between the method headings of functions and those of procedures. First, the reserved word PROCEDURE is replaced by the reserved word FUNCTION. Second, the method heading ends with a colon and a data type (in this example, the type SUTelephonePoleAsn) indicating what type of value is returned.

Our function is very simple. Its single statement is an assignment statement. The left side of the assignment statement, unlike the assignments we saw earlier, contains the name of the method instead of a variable name. This special assignment statement indicates what value should be returned by the function.

Syntax Box 5.3 indicates the details of a function declaration. Note that functions can receive parameters just like any other method. You should also note that in OOPas you cannot return an instance with a function, only a link to an instance.

5.12 VARIABLE LIFETIMES

Before we finish this chapter, we should address one last important topic when dealing with links. Now that you've seen links that don't link to anything, you might wonder what happens if you try to send a message to the instance to which this link is linked? What happens if you send the message `phoneLink^.callOperator;` before installing the phone?

The answer is that our program stops working. We've followed a link to an object that isn't there. In this situation, the computer doesn't know what to do and simply stops the program. This effect often is called a *crash*. When designing and implementing a program, it is an excellent idea to guard against such situations. These bugs may make the program unusable. For example, suppose we tried to call the operator in the house's constructor. We would never be able to construct a house, because it always would crash the program.

Unfortunately, setting a pointer to `NIL`, as we did before installing our telephone, isn't the only way to produce a link that doesn't link to an actual object (also known as a *bad pointer*). An object has a particular *lifetime*, depending on where it was constructed. If an object gets to the end of its lifetime, links pointing to it will now point to something that is no longer an object. The link won't actually be `NIL`, but instead will point to where the object used to be.

What will happen when you send a message along such a link? Before, when the link was explicitly `NIL`, the computer could tell right away that something wasn't right. The program crashed as soon as the message was sent. Now, however, the computer may not be able to tell immediately. In fact, the computer may try to execute the object's methods. It may proceed for a while, until it finds something strange enough that it can't make sense of it, at which point the program will crash. These bugs are especially hard to track down.

To prevent these bugs, it is very important to keep in mind how long the objects to which you link are going to last. As we said, an object's lifetime depends on how it was constructed. Objects constructed as instance variables of other objects last as long as the object in which they are contained. That is, the wall of our house instance doesn't last any longer than the house itself, nor does it spontaneously collapse while the house is still standing. So if you make a link to an object's instance variable, make sure the object that contains that

Syntax Box 5.3

Function declaration

Purpose:

To declare a function name and its formal parameters.

Syntax:

```
FUNCTION <class name>.<function name>(<parameter list>)
        : <return type>;
FUNCTION <class name>.<function name> : <return type>;
```

Where:

<class name> is the name of an object class.

<function name> is an identifier indicating the name of this function. (By convention, we capitalize the first letter of *<function name>*.)

<parameter list> is the list of parameters received by the function. It has the following structure:

```
<parameter sublist 1> : <parameter type 1>; ...
<parameter sublist n> : <parameter type n>
```

Where:

<parameter sublist 1> . . . <parameter sublist n> are lists of one or more parameter names (called formal parameters). Individual parameters in each sublist are separated by commas.

<parameter type 1> . . . <parameter type n> are the corresponding data types of each parameter sublist.

Usage:

Since functions are used to return a single value, usually only value parameters are sent to them. To return more than one value, use VAR parameters.

Note that if the function takes no parameters, the parameter list is omitted.

When a function message is sent, it must be returned to a place (such as an assignment statement or a parameter list) where a value of *<return type>* will be used.

To return a value, the body of the function must include a statement that assigns the value to the function name:

```
<function name> := <return value>;
```

Where:

<function name> is the same as the *<function name>* above.

<return value> is any variable, constant, or expression that evaluates to the *<return type>* of the function.

By convention, this statement is the last one in the body of the function.

The function heading, with the parameter list, must also appear in the object class's definition in the program's TYPE section.

variable will last long enough. Remember, both local variables and parameters last only as long as the method itself, so you should almost never make a link to them. The one exception is local variables in the mainline, which last as long as the program does, so you know that links to them can be made safely.

Summary

In this chapter, we looked at a powerful kind of relationship among objects. This relationship is known as an association. A class can have an instance variable that is a link to another instance without having to contain the instance. We use links when we want to retrieve information from another instance, not contain that instance. (For example, a car does not contain the road on which it drives, but it reacts to situations on the road, such as bumps and turns.) We will use links extensively throughout the remainder of the book.

We create a special type for associations. In the `TYPE` declarations, we use the syntax *`<association name>`* `= ^`*`<class name>`*. Thus we can use *`<association name>`* as the type of instance variables of any class that are used as links to instances of the association class. From there, we need two special operators. The caret (`^`) follows a link variable. For example, if we have an association called `SampleHouseAsn`, which is associated with `House`, and a link to an instance of the house called `sampleHouseLink` (of type `SampleHouseAsn`), we can send any of the messages defined in `HouseClass` by using `sampleHouseLink^.`*`<method name>`*. We also can create a link by assigning the result of the `@` operator (such as `@sampleHouse`) to a variable of type `sampleHouseAsn`.

When instance A contains instance B as an instance variable, instance A can send messages to instance B by using its name. The converse is not true. To send a message from B (the contained object) to A (the containing object), an association must be defined for A's class and a link of that type to be used as an instance variable in B's class.

We also can use associations to model containment in situations where instance variables are inadequate. In particular, if we wish to construct the contained instances made in a location outside of the constructor for the container, we can do so, passing a link to the new object on to the container. We used this technique to model a telephone in our house. The telephone was built elsewhere, and when the house was ready for occupancy, the phone was installed. To handle explicitly links that were not yet linked to instances — such as the phone link before the phone was installed — we made use of the `NIL` pointer.

We briefly looked at functions, a kind of method that returns a value. This value can be used in the place of variables that are passed to value parameters, or in the place of variables that are used on the right-hand side of an assignment.

If associations are misused, they can cause program crashes. When designing and implementing your programs, be sure that the links your code follows actually point to real instances, not to objects whose lifetimes have expired.

Exercises

Understanding Concepts

1. Describe the differences among the class–instance, containment, and association relationships.
2. What is the difference between an association and a link?
3. When is the ^ sign used? When is the @ sign used?
4. What does a NIL link represent?
5. What are the lifetimes of

   a. local variables
   b. variable parameters
   c. value parameters
   d. instance variables.

Coding Exercises

Suppose we have the following TYPE:

```
TYPE
   SUTelephoneWallJackAsn = ^SUTelephoneWallJack;
```

and the following variables:

```
myJack: SUTelephoneWallJack;
secondJack: SUTelephoneWallJack;
aJackLink: SUTelephoneWallJackAsn;
poleLink: SUTelephonePoleAsn;
```

1. Initialize both myJack and secondJack, using poleLink as the parameter.
2. Initialize aJackLink so that it links to secondJack.
3. Send a CallOperator message to both myJack and aJackLink.
4. Write a method that retrieves the pole associated with myJack. Write it once using GetPoleLink and a second time using GetPoleLinkFunc. Use the link to initialize secondJack.
5. Get the pole associated with aJackLink and use it to initialize myJack. Do this once using GetPoleLink, and a second time using the GetPoleLinkFunc function instead.
6. Suppose we wanted to install a second phone in the house using the code in Section 5.9. How do you modify the code in this section?
7. Suppose that we changed the interface of the method StApp.ReverseColors of Chapter 4 to

   ```
   PROCEDURE StApp.ReverseColors(houseLink: StHouseAsn);
   ```

   What in the body of the method would have to change?

8. Modify the `StApp.SwapColors` method of Chapter 4 by replacing `house1` and `house2` in the parameter list with links of the type `StHouseAsn`. What else in the body of the method has to change?

Programming Problems

The following components represent a grid, like a checkerboard, and the squares within the grid. We can create a path through the grid, which starts at the bottom left corner and moves toward the top right corner. The `SUGrid.NextSquare` function will determine a "random walk" — that is, it will determine randomly what the next square in a path should be from any given square in the grid.

```
SUSquareAsn = ^SUSquare;
SUSquare = OBJECT    { represents a square on a grid }
  CONSTRUCTOR Init; { constructed by the SUCheckerboard }
  PROCEDURE AddColor(newColor: GPColor);
    { set square's color; a square can have multiple colors by
             using AddColor repeatedly with different colors }
  PROCEDURE Display; { shows the square }

SUGrid = OBJECT
  CONSTRUCTOR Init;     { initializes the grid of 8 x 8 squares }
  PROCEDURE ShowAll;    { displays all the squares }
  FUNCTION FirstSquare: SUSquareAsn;
    { returns the first square in a path }
  FUNCTION NextSquare(curSq: SUSquareAsn): SUSquareAsn;
    { returns next free square in a path from current square }
```

1. Write a program that shows one random walk through the grid.
2. Write a program that shows two random walks through the grid. Each path should be a different color and the program should alternate the moves between the paths.

Among the 500 channels on your new cable system are the "Black and White Channel," which shows a half hour of black, followed by a half hour of white all day, and the "Color Channel" which shows a half hour of red, followed by a half hour of blue, then a half hour of green.

Assume that you have the following two (partial) class definitions:

```
Channel = OBJECT
  CONSTRUCTOR Init(Show800, Show830, Show900, Show930: GPColor);
    { colors shown on the channel at 8:00, 8:30, 9:00, and 9:30 }
  PROCEDURE Get800;
  PROCEDURE Get830;
  PROCEDURE Get900;
  PROCEDURE Get930;

Television = OBJECT
  ...
  PROCEDURE DisplayShow;
```

Also, the `StarterUnit` contains a class called `SUDisplay` with the following interface:

```
SUDisplay = OBJECT
   CONSTRUCTOR Init;
   PROCEDURE FillSolid(solidColor: GPColor);
      { displays one color filling screen }
   PROCEDURE FillSplit(topColor, btmColor: GPColor);
      { displays two colors, one filling the top half, the other in
               the bottom half }
   PROCEDURE Pause;    { freezes the display for about 5 seconds }
```

3. Complete the class definitions and write a program so that `Television.DisplayShow` shows what is on the Black and White channel at 8:30.

4. Modify the program in Programming Problem 6 so that `Television.DisplayShow` shows what is on the Color channel at 9:00.

5. Add a method to Programming Problem 6 called `Television.DisplayBoth` that shows a split screen, with what is appearing on the Black and White channel at 8:00 on top, and what is appearing on the Color channel at 8:00 on the bottom.

6. Modify `Television.DisplayBoth` in Programming Problem 8 so that it shows what is on both channels at 8:00, pauses, and then shows what is on both channels at 8:30, pauses, and so on, until it has shown what is on in all four time slots on both channels.

6 Inheritance and Virtual Methods

Inheritance, the last relationship among objects that we will examine, lets us model *categories* of objects. It is often useful to talk about categories: We may want to refer to the properties of "shapes" rather than "circles" and "squares," or "birds" rather than "sparrows" and "orioles." The inheritance relationship allows us to "factor out" properties and behaviors that are common among a group of classes and to define them just once in a single class that describes the common aspects of the group of classes. We can then create specialized classes that inherit the "factored" properties and behaviors and that add further properties and behaviors.

Inheritance relationships, along with association and containment relationships, help to model more of the interaction among objects and help make our systems more understandable. They also can save a tremendous amount of work by letting us reuse existing code to retain particular behaviors and make only incremental additions to define new behaviors.

Because it adds so much to our descriptive abilities, and because what it adds provides so much in terms of code reuse and the ability to make incremental improvements in a system, inheritance is usually seen as the most powerful aspect of object-oriented programming. Most computer scientists feel that without inheritance, there is no object-oriented programming.

We've been talking about various ways of describing objects. Let's begin our discussion of inheritance by looking at what inheritance adds to our descriptive abilities.

6.1 INHERITANCE

We are constantly trying to organize information by putting it in categories. We organize both informally, by separating many pieces of paper into piles, or formally, by creating a taxonomy of species. In these schemes, we put things together that have something in common — a pile of bills; the animals that only eat plants. Inheritance lets us describe these categories.

Inheritance as Specialization

With inheritance, we can take all the similar aspects of a set of classes and put them into a single, shared class. The rest of this chapter will explore how classes inherit methods and instance variables from other classes. Let's consider some classes describing animals, shown in Figure 6.1.

Figure 6.1

Inheritance hierarchy

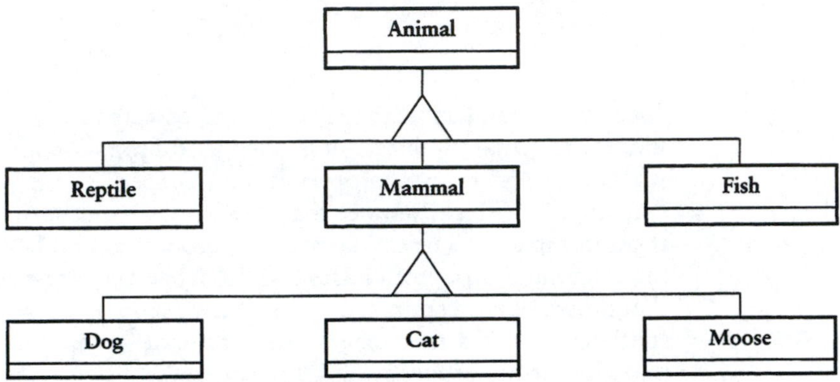

Figure 6.1 shows a *tree* representation of a set of classes in which each class is a specialization of the class above it. Reading from the bottom, we see that "dog," "cat," and "moose" are kinds of "mammals," which in turn are kinds of "animals." We refer to the topmost item, "animal," as the *root* of the tree and to the items at the end of a path through the tree ("reptile" or "moose") as the *leaves* of the tree. An inheritance relationship is represented by a triangle on the line connecting the classes. In our notation, the superclass will usually be above the subclasses in the diagram; the triangle always "points at" the superclass. We'll use tree structures regularly to represent class hierarchies.

"Mammal" is a kind of "animal." "Moose" is a kind of "mammal." This type of relationship is known as an "is-a" (or, sometimes, "is-a-kind-of") relationship. Note that "is-a" goes in one direction only, in the same way that the triangle used in the diagram points in one direction only: While every cat "is-a" mammal, not every mammal "is-a" cat.

In object-oriented language, we call "animal" a *superclass* and "mammal" a *subclass*. A single class can be both a superclass and a subclass. Here, "mammal" is a subclass of "animal" and is also the superclass of "moose." (You will sometimes hear the terms "base class" and "derived class" or "ancestor class" and "descendant class" used in place of "superclass" and "subclass," respectively.)

Inheritance as Generalization

As another example of inheritance, let's consider the house components from Chapter 3. Each had a `Draw` method. In Chapter 4, we saw that all the house components had other methods in common, such as `Erase`. Some house components had a single color, available through the two methods `SetColor` and `GetColor`, and others had both a trim color and a main color, available through `SetMainColor`, `GetMainColor`, `SetTrimColor`, and `GetTrimColor`.

As an alternative to thinking of subclasses as specializations of a superclass, a superclass can be considered a *generalization* of subclasses. For example, we can identify the methods that house components have in common. A superclass holding all of those methods is a generalization of the house component classes. What kinds of generalizations can we identify? All house components can `Draw` themselves and `Erase` themselves. We can call a class with these two methods defined ("factored out") a `SUHouseComponent`. Some house components are plain, having only one color. Others, like the roof, have trim modeled with two colors. We can make one generalization for plain components that provides `SetColor` and `GetColor` methods. This generalization, called `SUPlainComponent`, clearly "is-a" `SUHouseComponent`. A second generalization, `SUTrimmedComponent`, models all kinds of house components that have both a main color and a trim color.

Figure 6.2 shows these generalizations, along with the house components we've already seen. Note that any one specific component (such as `SUWall`) inherits from a more general component and thus "is-a" more general component, as shown by inheritance relationships.

Figure 6.2

Inheritance as generalization: House components

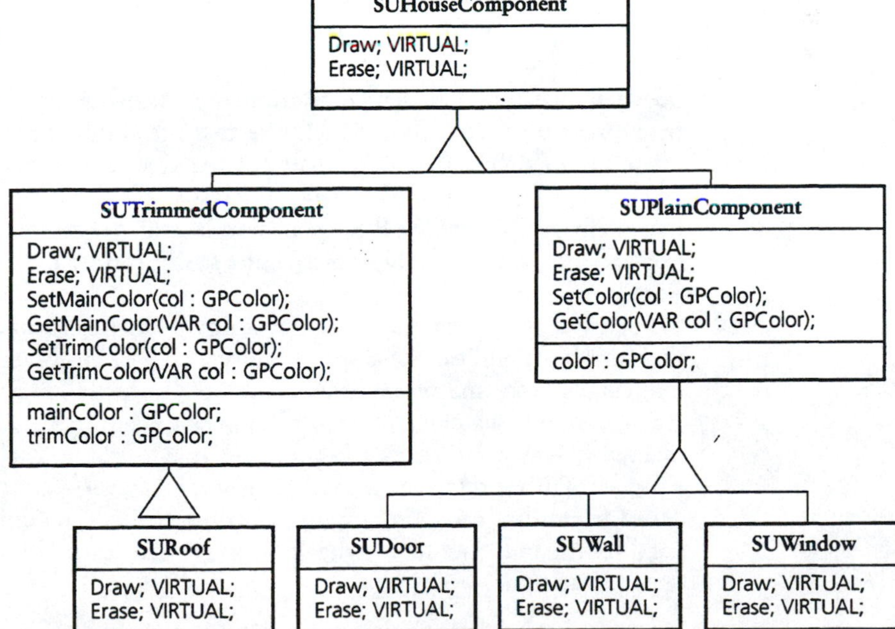

Each Subclass Can Do Things in Its Own Way

In fact, this isn't the whole story. Methods like `SetColor` and `GetColor` are simple: `SetColor` stores the passed parameter in the instance variable `color`, and `GetColor` stores the instance variable `color` in the passed parameter (we can't use a function for this since functions can't return instances). Methods like `Draw` and `Erase` are different, though. Each house component needs to draw something different, and though all house components can draw themselves, each draws differently. Each house component thus needs a different definition of `Draw`.

Similarly, animals also have behaviors that are defined differently for each kind of animal. All animals eat, but each kind of animal eats in a different way. Some animals graze, some hunt, and others scavenge.

When implementing these kinds of varying behaviors in OOPas, we call them *virtual methods*, to distinguish them from the kinds of methods we've seen before. A virtual method can be defined differently by each subclass. Notice that each kind of house component in Figure 6.2 has its own `Draw` and `Erase` method and that each one is labeled `VIRTUAL`. We'll return to the reserved word `VIRTUAL` momentarily.

The house component classes from `StarterUnit` are subclasses of `SUPlainComponent` and `SUTrimmedComponent`. Some of the exercises at the end of this chapter use other house components that are other subclasses of `SUHouseComponent`. Since we already know the methods provided by the base classes, learning the derived classes is fairly easy.

6.2 INHERITANCE IN OOPAS

So what does the inheritance relationship mean? A subclass *inherits* all the properties of its superclass. Much like real-life children genetically inherit the attributes of their parents, the instance variables and methods defined for the superclass are also defined for the subclass. Let's implement our animal class hierarchy in OOPas. We'll keep it simple and use it primarily as a way to explore the syntax of inheritance, before using inheritance in a real application.

First, we need a class to represent animals. In this simple example, all animals are born and eat, sleep, play, and watch TV. However, each kind of animal eats, sleeps, and plays differently, though they all watch TV in the same way (by simply watching whatever happens to be on). For example, a dog eats meat, whereas a moose eats berries and foliage. Thus `Eat`, `Sleep`, `Play`, and `WatchTV` will be the four behaviors of our class `Animal` (with a constructor called `Born`), but each kind of animal will *redefine* (or, equivalently, *override*) `Eat`, `Sleep`, and `Play` to do what that particular kind of animal does, leaving `WatchTV` alone.

Let's look at the class `Animal` first.

```
Animal = OBJECT
   CONSTRUCTOR     BeBorn;
   PROCEDURE       Eat;        VIRTUAL;
   PROCEDURE       Sleep;      VIRTUAL;
   PROCEDURE       Play;       VIRTUAL;
   PROCEDURE       WatchTV;
END;
```

Since this is a generic animal, we have no instance variables (and thus no need for the keyword `PRIVATE`). We don't yet know what kind of subparts or attributes our animal will have. It could be a moose with fur, four legs, and antlers, or it could be a centipede with a hard shell and a hundred legs, or it could be a fish with scales and no legs at all.

Let's look at the pseudocode for the `WatchTV` method:

Animal.WatchTV
All animals watch TV the same way — they watch whatever happens to be on.

There isn't anything especially interesting about this method, so we won't look at its definition in more detail. We will, however, show how different kinds of animals use it in just a moment.

The VIRTUAL Keyword

There is something different about this class definition, though: The `Eat`, `Sleep`, and `Play` methods are followed by a new reserved word, `VIRTUAL`. The reserved word `VIRTUAL` indicates a virtual method. Our method declaration

```
PROCEDURE Eat; VIRTUAL;
```

says that all animals can eat but that specific kinds of animals might eat in different ways. Notice that `WatchTV` isn't marked as a virtual method, because all animals watch TV by simply watching what happens to be on.

Let's look at the definition of these virtual methods.

```
PROCEDURE Animal.Eat;
BEGIN
END;

PROCEDURE Animal.Sleep;
BEGIN
END;
```

```
PROCEDURE Animal.Play;
BEGIN
END;
```

A virtual method in the class `Animal` is an empty shell; it is said to be defined *in interface only.* A virtual method forces all of the subclasses to respond to the same message with the same interface. While the method `Animal.Eat` doesn't do anything, it *is* part of the definition. All subclasses of the class `Animal` now are defined to have a method called `Eat`. All animals know how to eat. When we define a new kind of animal, we will also describe how that animal `Eat`s. The keyword `VIRTUAL` itself is described in Syntax Box 6.1.

Syntax Box 6.1

VIRTUAL

Purpose:

To designate a method as a virtual method.

Syntax:

```
PROCEDURE <method name>(<parameter list>); VIRTUAL;
```

or

```
FUNCTION <method name>(<parameter list>)
        : <return type>; VIRTUAL;
```

Where:

<method name> is the name of the method.

<parameter list> is the required list of parameters.

<return type> is the type of data returned by a function.

Usage:

A virtual method must be defined in both the superclass and a subclass. The *<method name>*, *<parameter list>*, and *<return type>* in both the superclass and the subclass must be identical. The body of the superclass's virtual method, however, may just be an empty shell.

The reserved word `VIRTUAL` must appear in the method heading.

Multiple subclasses may redefine (or override) a superclass's virtual method. The particular method called is determined by OOPas at run time, according to the class of the instance receiving the corresponding message.

Let's define our constructor as well:

```
CONSTRUCTOR Animal.BeBorn;
BEGIN
END;
```

Once again, we see that there is nothing within the BEGIN/END pair. Like Eat, Sleep, and Play, there isn't any particular thing that all instances of Animal will do for this method. However, we always need a constructor for an object. The constructor is used by the OOPas compiler to set up virtual methods, even if nothing else happens in the constructor. Thus, if you don't define a constructor, virtual methods will not behave correctly.

Now that our generic Animal has been described, we can describe more specific kinds of animals.

Defining a Subclass

The next class we define is Mammal. There are four things we'd like to model about mammals: First, a mammal "is-a" animal; second, mammals have hair; third, mammal young are born alive, and so begin breathing when first born; and fourth, mammals nurse their young.

```
Mammal = OBJECT(Animal)
   CONSTRUCTOR     BeBorn;
   PROCEDURE       Nurse;
PRIVATE
   PROCEDURE       BeginBreathing;
   myHair : Hair;
END;
```

Let's look at the first line of the class definition. The reserved word OBJECT is followed by the name of another class in parentheses. This is the part of the class definition that models the fact that a mammal "is-a" animal. This notation indicates to OOPas that Mammal is a subclass of Animal. Our Mammal has all of the instance variables and methods we've listed here, as well as all of the methods (and instance variables, if there were any) of the class Animal. Thus our Mammal can watch TV. Our Mammal also knows that it should be able to Eat, Sleep, and Play, though these virtual methods have not been defined. More specific kinds of Mammal will provide definitions. Syntax Box 6.2 describes the syntax for indicating that one class is a subclass of another.

Let's take a look at the other parts of the subclass definition. We can add instance variables in a subclass. We've added an instance variable myHair to model the fact that mammals have hair (we aren't modeling the hair itself, so we will not go into the details of the class Hair). We also can add methods in a subclass. Here, we have added two methods, BeginBreathing and Nurse. BeginBreathing will be used to indicate that a baby mammal starts to breathe when it is born. The method Nurse models the fact that mammals can nurse their young. Notice that BeginBreathing is declared in the PRIVATE section of the class definition. BeginBreathing isn't a message that other objects ought to be able to send to mammals, since it is something the mammal does only as part of being born.

Syntax Box 6.2

Defining a subclass

Purpose:

To indicate that a class is the subclass of another class.

Syntax:

```
TYPE
   <class name> = OBJECT (<superclass name>)
     { methods and instance variables defined here }
   END;
```

Where:

<class name> is the name of the class being defined.

<superclass name> is the name of the class being inherited from.

Usage:

The effect of placing *<superclass name>* in the definition of *<class name>* is that *<class name>* inherits all of the methods and instance variables defined in *<superclass name>*. Thus the methods and instance variables defined for *<class name>* need be only those things needed to specialize the class.

<superclass name> may also inherit methods and instance variables; if so, *<class name>* inherits everything that *<superclass name>* inherits.

Defining the Constructor

Let's define some of these methods. We won't bother with `Nurse` or `Breathe`, since they are both normal methods. Our constructor, however, is different.

All constructors for derived classes construct instances in two stages. The first stage performs the constructor for the superclass; the second stage constructs the instance variables added by the subclass.

A schematic of a derived class in Figure 6.3 shows the members of the class in two groups. The first group is those members (both instance variables and methods) that were defined by the superclass, while the second is those members that were defined by the subclass. Both groups need to be initialized.

Thus the superclass portion can provide members for the subclass to use, but the superclass needs to initialize these members first. Initialization is performed by the constructor, and every class needs a constructor — even base classes like `Animal`. Hence, we always initialize the superclass things first. In our case, this means setting up the virtual methods `Eat`, `Sleep`, and `Play` (done by OOPas as part of the constructor `Animal.BeBorn`).[1] Then, we can initialize the new things provided by the subclass.

1. Because of how virtual methods are implemented by OOPas, they must be initialized. The OOPas compiler knows to do this as part of an object's constructor, but can't do it without a constructor. Thus you must always define a constructor for a class with virtual methods.

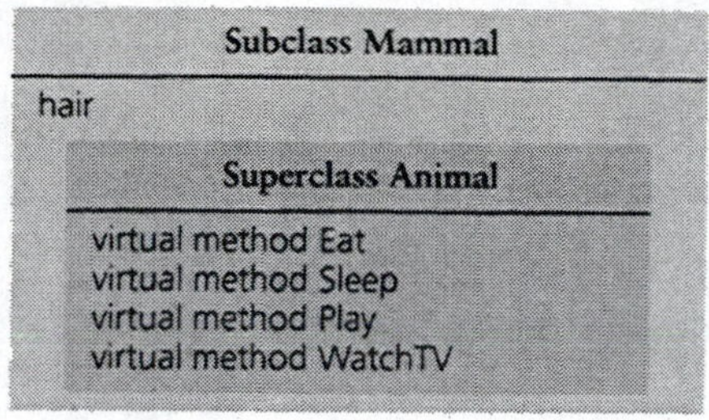

Figure 6.3

A derived class in two parts: Superclass portion and subclass portion

Up to this point, when sending messages we have used the syntax

```
<instance name>.<method name>;
```

which sends a message to the appropriate instance. We can't use this syntax to initialize the superclass part of the mammal instance, since we don't know the name of the instance being constructed. We do know the name of the method. However, it is the same as the method we're currently using. Even if we had an instance to send the `BeBorn` message to, we wouldn't want to, because we're already in `Mammal.BeBorn`. We want to be able to invoke `Animal.BeBorn` for the current instance, the one executing `Mammal.BeBorn`.

A new reserved word, `INHERITED`, lets us do this. By using `INHERITED` along with the name of the constructor we want to use, we can use the superclass's constructor to initialize the superclass parts of the instance, even though the constructors have the same name. Thus

```
INHERITED BeBorn;
```

invokes the constructor `Animal.BeBorn` on the superclass portion of the current instance, setting up the virtual methods `Eat`, `Sleep`, and `Play`. You can expect to find an invocation of the inherited constructor as the first line of any constructor for any subclass. The syntax for `INHERITED` is described in Syntax Box 6.3.

Keeping this in mind, let's examine the constructor for the class `Mammal`:

```
CONSTRUCTOR Mammal.BeBorn;
BEGIN
   { Construct the superclass part of the instance. }
   INHERITED BeBorn;
   { Construct the subclass part of the instance. }
   myHair.Init;               { Mammals have hair. }
   self.BeginBreathing;       { Mammals breathe when first born. }
END;
```

We now can initialize the state of our animal that is specific to the class `Mammal`. Of course, we need to initialize the mammal's hair. We can do this by calling its constructor:

Syntax Box 6.3

INHERITED

Purpose:

To indicate that a subclass is sending a message that is defined in a superclass and has the same name as the method currently being executed.

Syntax:

```
INHERITED <method name>(<parameter list>);
```

Where:

<method name> is the name of the method defined in the superclass.

<parameter list> are the parameters required for the method.

Usage:

The `INHERITED` reserved word is used when a subclass's method wants to use a method defined in a superclass. When OOPas encounters this word, it searches for *<method name>* in the current class's immediate superclass. If the method is not found there, OOPas moves to the next superclass in the hierarchy. OOPas continues to move up the hierarchy until the method name is found and then calls that method.

`INHERITED` is used only when *<method name>* has the same method name as the method in which the statement is found; for example, if an `Init` method wants to send an `Init` message defined in a superclass, `INHERITED` should be used. It can be used for any method, though it is most commonly used for constructors.

```
myHair.Init;
```

We also need to make the new mammal start breathing. We can do this using our private method `Breathe`. However, as with the constructor `BeBorn`, we don't know the name of the instance to which we want to send the message. We don't want to use `INHERITED`, though, because the class `Animal` doesn't define a method `BeginBreathing`. OOPas provides a new keyword, `self`, that always refers to the current instance. So we can send a message to the current instance as follows:

```
self.BeginBreathing;
```

The keyword `self` is described in Syntax Box 6.4.

Sending a message to oneself is so common that OOPas makes `self` optional, so that you don't have to specify any instance name. When OOPas does not see an instance name, it presumes that a message is being sent to the current instance, to `self`. Using this fact, we could rewrite our constructor as follows:

Syntax Box 6.4

Self

Purpose:

To refer to the current instance.

Syntax:

```
self.<some message>; { Send a message to this instance. }
@self                { Provide a link to this instance. }
```

Where:

<some message> is any message that could be sent to the current instance.

Usage:

Whenever it is necessary to refer to the current instance, either to send a message to it or to make a link to it, use the keyword `self`.

The current instance is the instance that received a message to which a method is responding. `Self` has no meaning in the mainline, because the mainline does not respond to messages.

If a message name appears in a method with no instance, it is assumed that the message has an implicit `self` — and the current instance should send the message to itself.

```
CONSTRUCTOR Mammal.BeBorn;
BEGIN
   { Construct the superclass part of the instance. }
   INHERITED BeBorn;
   { Construct the subclass part of the instance. }
   myHair.Init;                  { Mammals have hair. }
   BeginBreathing;               { Mammals breathe when born. }
END;
```

Redefining Virtual Methods

`Mammal` is too generic to do anything differently for the virtual methods `Eat`, `Sleep`, and `Play`. After all, each kind of `Mammal` will `Eat`, `Sleep`, and `Play` in its own special way. Thus `Mammal` didn't provide any definition for these methods at all. We can still tell a `Mammal` to `Eat`, but it will use the definition of `Eat` inherited from `Animal`, which means it will do nothing.

Let's look at a class that does have a different way of eating and sleeping — a `Cat`. As the diagram in Figure 6.1 shows, a `Cat` "is-a" `Mammal`. As we know from the real world, a `Cat` eats, sleeps, and plays in its own special way. In particular, a `Cat` will not behave the same as a `Dog`.

```
Cat = OBJECT(Mammal)
   CONSTRUCTOR     BeBorn;
   PROCEDURE       Eat;        VIRTUAL;
   PROCEDURE       Sleep;      VIRTUAL;
   PROCEDURE       Play;       VIRTUAL;
PRIVATE
   PROCEDURE       Stalk;
   PROCEDURE       Pounce;
   PROCEDURE       KillPrey;
   PROCEDURE       Catnap;
   myWhiskers     : Whiskers;
   myPaws         : Paws;
END;
```

Once again, some instance variables have been added to our class. Cats have whiskers and paws, and our class definition reflects this (as with `Hair`, we haven't actually provided the details of `Whiskers` and `Paws`, because they aren't crucial to the example). We also see some new private methods that provide our cat with suitably catlike behavior. We use these private methods to provide the new definitions (or *re*definitions if you prefer) of `Eat`, `Sleep`, and `Play` for cats:

```
PROCEDURE Cat.Eat;
BEGIN
   Stalk;
   Pounce;
   KillPrey
END;

PROCEDURE Cat.Sleep;
BEGIN
   Catnap
END;

PROCEDURE Cat.Play;
BEGIN
   Pounce;
   Pounce
END;
```

Now we see that cats eat, sleep, and play differently from mammals (and from animals). A `Cat` eats by using the methods `Stalk`, `Pounce`, and `KillPrey` to stalk, pounce upon, and kill whatever it wants to eat. Similarly, a cat sleeps by taking a `Catnap`. Finally, cats play by pouncing randomly around a couple of times. For many animals (cats included), play is a way to practice hunting techniques. Cats pounce when playing to practice the pouncing they do when hunting. Our class `Cat` models this by using the same private method `Pounce` to implement the two behaviors `Eat` and `Play`.

A quick class definition for another class from Figure 6.1, `Moose`, demonstrates how another class might redefine `Eat` and `Sleep` in its own way:

```
Moose = OBJECT(Mammal)
  CONSTRUCTOR     BeBorn;
  PROCEDURE       Eat;        VIRTUAL;
  PROCEDURE       Sleep;      VIRTUAL;
  PROCEDURE       Play;       VIRTUAL;
PRIVATE
  PROCEDURE       EatBerriesAndLeaves;
  PROCEDURE       SleepInTheWoods;
  PROCEDURE       ButtHeads;
  myAntlers      : Antlers;
END;
```

We can now say that a moose sleeps in the woods, eats berries and leaves, and plays by butting heads:

```
PROCEDURE Moose.Eat;
BEGIN
  EatBerriesAndLeaves
END;

PROCEDURE Moose.Sleep;
BEGIN
  SleepInTheWoods
END;

PROCEDURE Moose.Play;
BEGIN
  ButtHeads
END;
```

The class `Moose` redefined the method `Eat` to eat berries and leaves, and the class `Cat` redefined `Eat` to stalk, pounce, and finally kill its prey.

6.3 POLYMORPHISM

But how do we use redefined methods? When using inheritance, remember, we are saying that an instance of one class "is-a" instance of another class as well. So any messages that can be sent to instances of the superclass can also be sent to any instance of any subclass. This opens the door for extensibility, because we can add as many subclasses as we want at any time. Old code that used the superclass can do new things by using new subclasses, as we'll now see.

Virtual Methods Used Via a Link

Because an instance of a subclass "is-a" instance of the superclass as well, we can send an actual parameter to a method that is a link to a subclass when the formal parameter is declared as a link to a superclass. Consider this sample method, which takes an animal through its day:

```
PROCEDURE Simulation.OneDay( animalLink : AnimalAsn );
BEGIN
   animalLink^.Eat;            { Get breakfast. }
   animalLink^.Play;           { Have some fun. }
   animalLink^.Sleep;          { Nap. }
   animalLink^.WatchTV;        { Watch the news. }
   animalLink^.Eat;            { Get dinner. }
   animalLink^.Sleep;          { Go to bed. }
END;
```

The method `WatchTV` is not virtual. Hence, no matter what kind of animal is pointed to by `animalLink`, `WatchTV` behaves the same. This is of course exactly the behavior we wanted, since we said that all animals `WatchTV` in the same way. But the other methods, `Eat`, `Sleep`, and `Play`, are virtual. We want different kinds of animals to do the different things we described above: A `Cat` should `Pounce` and a `Moose` should `ButtHeads`.

The magic of virtual methods is that they do the right thing. If your formal parameter is declared as a link to an instance of `Animal` and you provide a link to an instance of `Cat` as your actual parameter, `Eat`, `Sleep`, and `Play` will behave as for a `Cat`, not as for an `Animal`. The animal will stalk, pounce, then kill to eat, catnap to sleep, and pounce a couple of times to play. Had a link to an instance of a `Moose` been used as the actual parameter, then the animal would spend its day eating berries and leaves, sleeping in the woods, and playfully butting heads.

The animal is said to be *polymorphic*, that is, of many forms. It might be a cat, a moose, a dog, a reptile, a fish, or any other subclass of `Animal`. This ability of associations to a base class to hold links to instances of a subclass even extends to subclasses that haven't been defined yet. We're free to add more subclasses to an inheritance hierarchy at a later point, so that an old method that expects a link to an instance of `Animal` can later receive a link to an instance of a kind of `Animal` that didn't exist when the method was defined, such as a `MartianSpaceMonster`. A `MartianSpaceMonster` might thus spend its day eating people, sleeping in a flying saucer, and playfully destroying the Earth, even though `Simulation.OneDay` is completely unaware of the existence of a `MartianSpaceMonster`. For that matter, `Simulation.OneDay` doesn't even need to know about the existence of a `Cat`. All `Simulation.OneDay` needs to know about is the class `Animal`.

Polymorphism thus makes possible a unique kind of code reuse. Without polymorphism, we could write new code that uses old classes. With polymorphism, *old* code can use *new* classes. We don't need to debug the old code — it already has been debugged. Thus we get even more productivity out of work we may have done years ago.

Polymorphism is probably the most powerful mechanism of object-oriented programming. As such, we'll come back to it again and again, both within this chapter and throughout the rest of the book.

A note of caution: When we send parameters, we can send a *link* to a subclass as a link to a superclass, but we *cannot* send an *instance* of a subclass as an instance of a superclass. Why? Because when we send an instance as a parameter, we have to copy it. If the method to which we are sending it expects an instance of the superclass, however, it will have set aside only enough space in memory for the superclass: A subclass might be bigger. Thus we would get an error message if we had sent an instance of `Cat` as a parameter where an instance of `Mammal` was expected. Links work because a link to anything is always the same size in memory, but what the link connects to can be any size.

Determining Which Method Gets Used

When using polymorphism, it is important to have a clear understanding of which methods will be used in which situations. Let's take a closer look at `Simulation.OneDay`. Suppose a link to a `Cat` was passed as an actual parameter for `animalLink`. The instance is shown in Figure 6.4, along with the `Animal` hierarchy and where each virtual method was defined.

Figure 6.4

A link to a Cat used as a link to an Animal

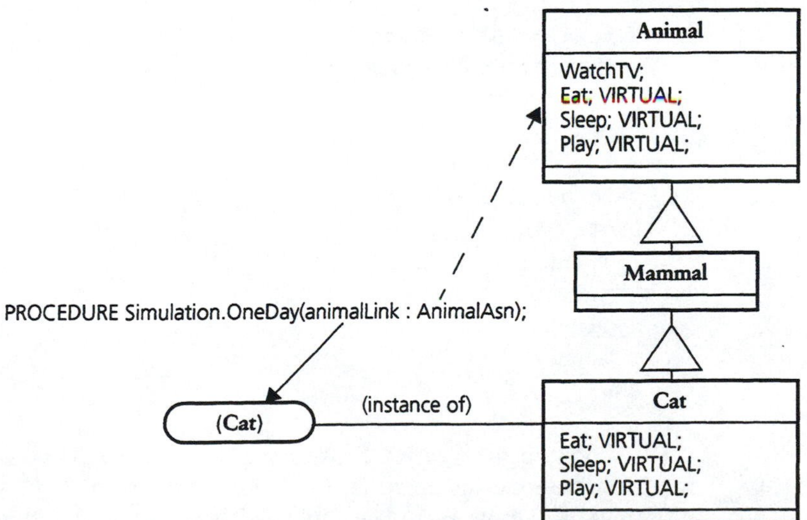

OOPas determines which method definition to use for a virtual method by following the link to the instance, then going from the instance to its actual class. If a definition isn't provided by that class, OOPas looks for a definition in the superclass. If a definition isn't found there, OOPas keeps looking in the superclass's superclass, moving up the inheritance tree until it either finds a definition or reaches a "root" class with no superclass (in which case, the method has no definition, and thus there's an error in the program). So the first definition of `Eat` that OOPas finds is `Cat.Eat`, even though `AnimalAsn` expects to point to an instance of `Animal` (as represented by the dashed line).

This process of determining which method to use is applied to virtual methods only. If a method is not virtual, like `WatchTV`, OOPas uses a much simpler procedure to determine which definition to use. OOPas uses the type named in the association (`Animal` in these examples) to find a method definition. Had `Mammal` or `Cat` tried to provide an alternate definition of `WatchTV`, it would not have been used in `Simulation.OneDay`. OOPas would use the definition provided by `Animal`, the type pointed to by `AnimalAsn`.

Thus, within a method, you can always tell which nonvirtual method will get used: the one defined for the class named in the association, which of course may be inherited (although `WatchTV` is not — if `Simulation.OneDay` was defined as receiving a `MammalAsn`, `WatchTV` *would* be inherited). It is not necessary to know what instance a link points to when working with nonvirtual methods. Nonvirtual methods are thus said to be *statically bound*, because the dynamic execution of the program does not affect which method is used. Conversely, virtual methods are *dynamically bound*, because the dynamic behavior of the program (the actual link passed to a method) affects the choice of methods.

Now let's consider a new kind of animal, a `Kitten`. A `Kitten` clearly "is-a" `Cat`. Further, a `Kitten` will `Eat` and `Sleep` the same way a `Cat` does. However, a `Kitten` is more energetic and playful than a `Cat`, so a `Kitten` will `Pounce` more to `Play`:

```
Kitten = OBJECT(Cat)
  CONSTRUCTOR     BeBorn;
  PROCEDURE       Play; VIRTUAL;
END;

PROCEDURE Kitten.Play;
BEGIN
  Pounce;
  Pounce;
  Pounce;
  Pounce
END;
```

Looking at Figure 6.5, we see a link to a `Kitten` being used in `Simulation.OneDay` as `animalLink`. Which definition of `Play` is used? OOPas follows the link, then goes to the class `Kitten`, finding `Kitten.Play`. Now consider `Eat` or `Sleep`. OOPas follows the link again, continuing to the class, but `Kitten` doesn't define `Eat` or `Sleep`. OOPas thus continues on to `Cat`, `Kitten`'s superclass, and finds definitions for `Eat` and `Sleep` there.

Figure 6.5

A link to a Kitten used as a link to an Animal

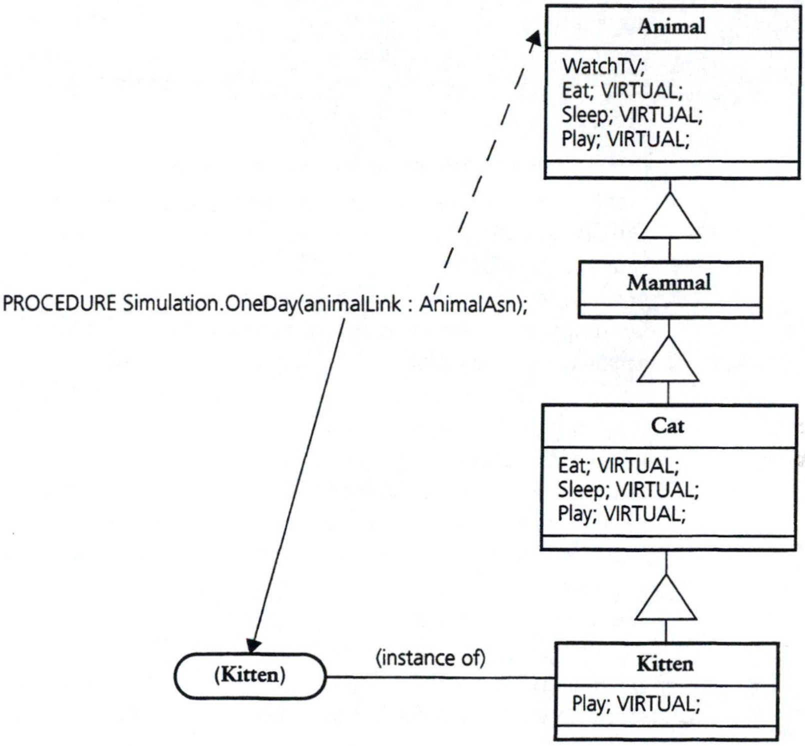

6.4 AN EXAMPLE: A SIMPLE PAINT PROGRAM

An interactive paint program is rather large and complex with many different parts, many recognizable from other software you've used. By using inheritance and polymorphism, we'll keep the workload quite manageable, even with lots of different parts. Rather than define an entire interactive application from scratch, we can use the GP package, which provides us with a generic interactive application. Using inheritance, we can redefine selected parts of GP classes, much as we redefined `Eat`, `Sleep`, and `Play` for our animals.

Let's look at an example of an interactive graphical application: a paint program. The application's purpose is quite simple: It should allow a user to draw in a drawing area. We specify the problem as follows:

This application represents a simple paint program. The user can use the mouse like a pencil to draw lines in the application's canvas. The application also should provide a quit button that stops the program when pressed, and a clear button that clears the canvas when pressed.

Let's look at the nouns in this specification:

application	pencil	program
paint program	line	clear button
user	canvas	painting
mouse	quit button	

(Note that we have listed more than just the nouns: We have used adjectives to identify nouns when necessary, such as "quit button" and "paint program.") We can quickly eliminate *user* and *mouse* as potential classes, since they represent things that are outside of our software system. Additionally, *paint program* seems to refer to the entire program, as do *application* and *program*. Combining these nouns into a single class we'll call `SPApp` (for "simple paint application"), we will have a subclass of `GPApplication`.

We are left with six potential classes: `SPApp`, *line*, *canvas*, *pencil*, *clear button*, and *quit button*. Right now, we'll focus on designing these six classes. In Chapters 7 and 8, we'll extend our simple drawing program with colors and more drawing controls. Therefore, as we design these six classes, we'll try to keep our design as flexible as possible, so that we can reuse our object classes.

At this point in the program development, we can consider two additional sources of inspiration. First, we can examine a sketch of the interface (Figure 6.6), to see how the graphical user interface (GUI) is organized.[2] For example, we note that the screen is subdivided into a main drawing area on the left and the region for the quit and clear buttons on the right. Our interface shows the program after a few lines have been drawn in the main drawing area (that is, in the canvas). Second, it is worth looking at classes that have been defined already in libraries. Let's start with the GP library. All the classes in the GP library are described in Appendix D and in documentation available on the Internet (see the Preface).

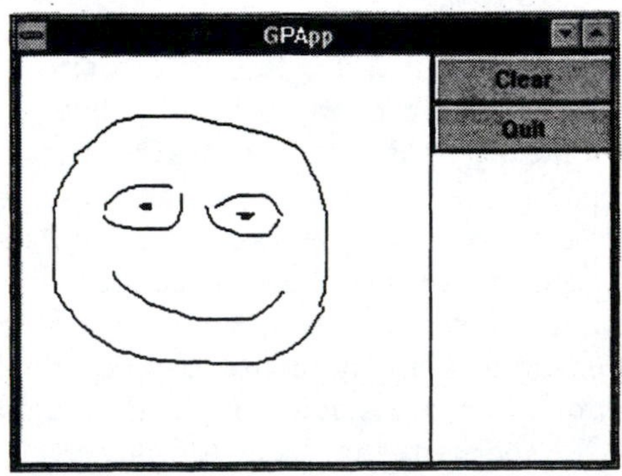

Figure 6.6 *Interface of the simple paint program*

2. The graphical objects in a GUI, such as buttons, menus and sliders, often are called *widgets*.

6.5 MAKING A NEW SUBCLASS OF A GP CLASS

GP is a taxonomy of elements used to create GUIs. GP defines standard GUI components — menus, buttons, drawing areas, and rows and columns of other components; as well as drawing primitives — lines, rectangles, points, and colors. You have used all of these classes before but without access to the details.

The class `GPApplication`, as described in Class Box 6.1, can contain all of the application's GUI components. We will define `SPApp` as a subclass of `GPApplication`. The class `SUSimpleApp` used in earlier chapters is itself a subclass of `GPApplication`. In fact, you should see two familiar methods, `Init` and `Run`, indicating that `SUSimpleApp` "is-a" `GPApplication`, since they have some behavior in common. Before, we provided you with a class containing all the GUI components you needed (which was simply a "quit" button). Now you get to implement your own class, which will have different abilities.

Class Box 6.1
GPApplication

GPApplication
= OBJECT (GPManager)

This manager is used as the main window of a program.

Methods:

`Init;` Construct the application, creating a window for the GUI.

`Run;`

Wait for actions by the user and forward them to the appropriate GUI component. This method runs until some GUI component calls the `Quit` method.

`Quit;` Cause the `Run` method to stop running.

We note from Figure 6.6 that the application contains a main drawing area and a column of buttons. Correspondingly, we can designate instance variables that represent the drawing area and the column. GP has a class called `GPDrawingArea` to represent drawing areas (see Class Box 6.2).

GP distinguishes between components that can contain other GUI components on the screen and those that cannot. The former are known as *managers* and are represented by the class `GPManager`. The application is an example of a manager; in fact, `GPApplication` is a subclass of `GPManager` — see Figure 6.7. The drawing area and buttons are examples of components that cannot contain other GUI components; they are not subclasses of `GPManager` and so don't appear in Figure 6.7. We won't be using the class `GPManager` directly, but we will use its subclasses and its affiliated association type, `GPManagerAsn`.

Class Box 6.2

GPDrawingArea

GPDrawingArea

This class provides an area in which things can be drawn.

Methods:

```
Init(managerLink: GPManagerAsn);
```

Construct the drawing area. `managerLink` should point to the GP object that contains the drawing area on the screen.

```
Clear(color : GPColor);
```

Erase any drawing done in this drawing area. The drawing area is completely erased and set to the color passed as `color`.

Figure 6.7

Base manager classes of GP. Some classes have been left out for clarity.

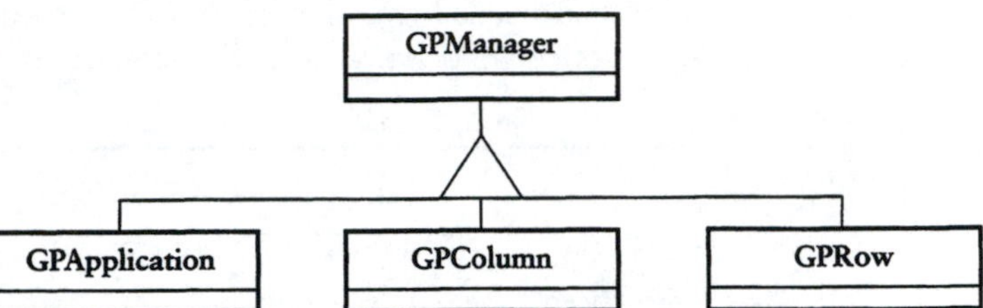

Let's look at one of the subclasses of `GPManager`, `GPColumn` (also shown in Figure 6.7). The class `GPColumn` arranges any components it contains into a column. That's all it does. In fact, as seen in Class Box 6.3, it doesn't even have any methods besides a constructor. A similar class, `GPRow`, acts just like `GPColumn` except that it arranges the components it contains in a row instead of a column. We'll stick with columns in our examples.

Class Box 6.3

GPColumn

GPColumn

= OBJECT (GPManager)

This manager organizes all the GUI components it contains in a column.

Methods:

```
Init( containerLink : GPManagerAsn )
```

Construct the column. This constructor takes a link to the manager that contains it.

Note that each part of the GUI occupies a region of the screen. You can look at any point of the screen and decide what part of the user interface is there. In effect, the method `Run` that we used with `SUSimpleApp`, which also is used by `GPApplication`, does the same thing. When the user clicks with the mouse, `Run` determines what particular part of the GUI the user clicked on based on the cursor's location on the screen. The `Run` method then sends a message to that part of the GUI that was clicked on by the user. Some parts of the GUI, such as buttons, perform very specific actions in response to `Run`'s messages. Other parts, like managers, don't do anything in response to `Run`'s messages.

Making a New Kind of Button

Let's see how to create a specialized subclass ourselves by considering the paint program. First, we need a quit button.

Buttons are provided by a class in GP called a `GPPushButton`, described in Class Box 6.4. The purpose of the `GPPushButton` class is to provide a button on the screen that the user can click, but, as defined in the class, the button does nothing. What we're going to do is build a new kind of button, one that extends `GPPushButton` in one very specific way: When the user clicks on it, our new button will do something — specifically, the button will quit the application.

Class Box 6.4
GPPushButton

GPPushButton

This class provides a button the user can click on to perform an action.

Methods:

`Init(managerLink: GPManagerAsn);`

Construct the button. It will be contained on the screen within the manager pointed to by the passed link.

`SetName(newName : string);`

Make the button's name be the passed `string`. The button will display this `string`. A `string` is a sequence of characters, and will be discussed further in Chapter 15.

`Activate; VIRTUAL;`

Do nothing. The method is called when the user clicks on the button. Subclasses of `GPPushButton` are expected to redefine this method.

The quit button clearly should have the behavior described for `GPPushButton` instances: the ability to be clicked by the user. This means the quit button "is-a" push button and will inherit from the `GPPushButton` class. We then can create a class diagram for our new class, called `SPQuitButton`, that is derived from `GPPushButton`, as shown in Figure 6.8. `SPQuitButton` inherits all the methods and instance variables defined in `GPPushButton`. Thus an instance of `SPQuitButton` can receive a `SetName` message, even though it is defined by `GPPushButton`.

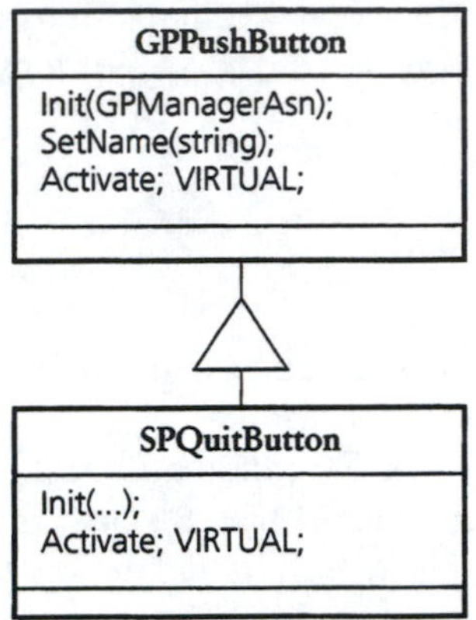

Figure 6.8 *Class diagram with inheritance*

The button needs to tell the application to quit. In general, each button we make will need to send messages to an object that the button doesn't contain (as this button does not contain the application). We will call the object to which a button sends a message the button's *target*. In this case, the quit button needs a link of type `GPApplicationAsn` to point to its target application, as indicated by the arrow in Figure 6.9. (You'll notice in Appendix D that most of the GP classes have affiliated association types.) The quit button's constructor will have a parameter for the link to the application.

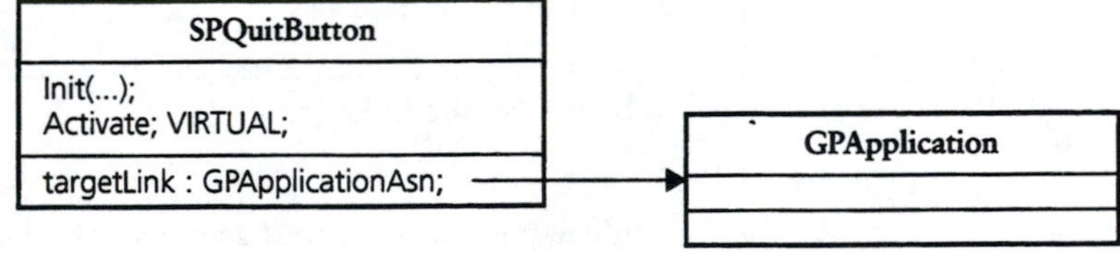

Figure 6.9 *SPQuitButton has a link to GPApplication.*

Now, how do we translate our new class into OOPas code? The class definition for this subclass is very similar to other class definitions:

```
SPQuitButton = OBJECT (GPPushButton)
  CONSTRUCTOR Init (
      containerLink    : GPManagerAsn;          { what contains me }
      newTargetLink    : GPApplicationAsn);     { app to quit }
  PROCEDURE Activate; VIRTUAL;
PRIVATE
  targetLink    : GPApplicationAsn;
END;
```

The Button's Constructor

The first method we should implement for our button is, of course, the constructor, since we can't do anything with an instance until we've constructed it. The following pseudocode describes the tasks we need the `Init` method to accomplish:

SPQuitButton.Init
Purpose: Establish the initial state of the quit button
Pseudocode:
 Establish the position of the button inside its container
 Store the target to which the button will send messages
 Name the button on the screen

We mentioned earlier that the second parameter of the `Init` method is the target object; this means that we can translate the line "store the target to which the button will send messages" by using an assignment statement:

```
{*******************************************************
This method establishes the initial state of the quit button.
********************************************************}
CONSTRUCTOR SPQuitButton.Init(
        containerLink    : GPManagerAsn;           { who contains me }
        newTargetLink    : GPApplicationAsn);      { link to target }
BEGIN
   { Establish the position of the button inside its container. }
   ...
   { Store the target of the button's actions. }
   targetLink := newTargetLink;
   { Name the button on the screen. }
   ...
END;
```

Note that our button is quite general. It can be contained in any sort of `GPManager` and can tell any application to quit simply by passing different links to the constructor.

How do we code the other two lines of pseudocode? We see in the class description box for `GPPushButton` that there are methods that perform these actions: `GPPushButton.Init` establishes the position for the button and `GPPushButton.SetName` establishes the name to be used in the button. So, all we have to do is send those messages.

Since our constructor already is called `Init`, we can use the keyword `INHERITED` to access the constructor `Init` of our superclass, `GPPushButton`. We said that we wanted to send the `SetName` message defined in `GPPushButton`. Here we can just type the name of the message (using the implicit `self`, as described in Syntax Box 6.4), as in the following code:

```
{*********************************************************
This method establishes the initial state of the Quit button.
*********************************************************}

CONSTRUCTOR SPQuitButton.Init(
        containerLink    : GPManagerAsn;           { who contains me }
        newTargetLink    : GPApplicationAsn);      { link to app }
BEGIN
   { Establish the position of the button inside its container. }
   INHERITED Init(containerLink);
   { Store the target of the button's actions. }
   targetLink := newTargetLink;
   { Name the button on the screen. }
   SetName('Quit');
END; { SPQuitButton.Init }
```

Now let's consider what happens to the parameters when an `Init` message is sent to the instance. We're going to make use of polymorphism, as described in Section 6.3. Let's send an `Init` message to the `quitButton` instance as follows:

```
PROCEDURE SampleClass.SampleMethod (
        aColumnLink      : GPColumnAsn;            { link to column }
        anAppLink        : GPApplicationAsn);      { link to app }
VAR
   quitButton  : SPQuitButton;  { example quit button }
BEGIN
   ...
   quitButton.Init(aColumnLink, anAppLink);
   ...
END; { SampleClass.SampleMethod }
```

When the `Init` message is sent, OOPas looks for the definition of `SPQuitButton.Init` and sends that message. As we see in the class definition, the `Init` method takes two parameters. The header of the class definition says that the *formal* parameters are, in order, of types `GPManagerAsn` and `GPApplicationAsn`. However, the first *actual* parameter in the preceding code is of the type `GPColumnAsn`. You might think that this would cause an error message because the types do not match. But remember that polymorphism lets us use a link to an instance of the subclass wherever a link to an instance of the superclass is expected. We see from the subclass hierarchy in this example that `GPColumn` inherits from `GPManager` (or, to use the "is-a" language from Section 6.1, `GPColumn` "is-a" `GPManager`). Thus a link to the subclass `GPColumn` can be sent as a parameter where a link to the superclass `GPManager` is expected.

Defining a Virtual Method for the Button

`GPPushButton` has a method, `Activate`, that is called when a button is clicked so that some action is performed. However, there is no way in which `GPPushButton` can know what action should be performed; that has to be defined in the subclasses. If we were to look at the code for `GPPushButton.Activate`, we would see the following:

```
PROCEDURE GPPushButton.Activate;
BEGIN
END;
```

Like the class `Animal` and its methods `Eat` and `Sleep`, the virtual method doesn't do anything. Let's define our quit button's `Activate` method. We know that when a quit button is pressed, the application should quit. The GP documentation shows that `GPApplication` has a method, `Quit`, that quits the application. The quit button itself is defined as follows:

```
SPQuitButton = OBJECT (GPPushButton)
  CONSTRUCTOR Init (
       containerLink    : GPManagerAsn;
       newTargetLink    : GPApplicationAsn);
  PROCEDURE Activate; VIRTUAL;
PRIVATE
  targetLink: GPApplicationAsn;
END;
```

Note that this class redefines the `Activate` method. The new `Activate` method will simply send the `Quit` message to the application.

```
{*******************************************************
The Activate method quits the application.
*******************************************************}
PROCEDURE SPQuitButton.Activate;
BEGIN
  targetLink^.Quit
END;
```

Note that even though `Activate` is defined in the superclass, we have to list it in the subclass declaration. This is true for any virtual method we redefine in a class: We need to include every method for which we provide code in the corresponding class definition.

Now that we've seen how to create a quit button, let's see how to define a clear button. Looking at Class Box 6.2, we see that `GPDrawingArea` provides a `Clear` method. Our clear button thus links to a `GPDrawingArea` instance and provides an `Activate` method that sends the `Clear` message rather than the

`Quit` message. Even though both `SPQuitButton` and `SPClearButton` override the same `Activate` virtual method provided by `GPPushButton`, the button instances do the right thing in response to the user's click: The clear button clears, and the quit button quits.

Let's take a look at the code for the clear button. Notice how the crucial parts are different from the quit button. Although the class definition looks essentially the same, the definition of the `Activate` method is different.

```
SPClearButton = OBJECT (GPPushButton)
  CONSTRUCTOR Init (
       containerLink    : GPManagerAsn;
       newTargetLink    : GPDrawingAreaAsn);
  PROCEDURE Activate; VIRTUAL;
PRIVATE
  targetLink     : GPDrawingAreaAsn; { Clear this. }
END;

CONSTRUCTOR SPClearButton.Init (
       containerLink    : GPManagerAsn;
       newTargetLink    : GPDrawingAreaAsn);
BEGIN
  INHERITED Init(containerLink);
  targetLink := newTargetLink;
  SetName('Clear')
END;

PROCEDURE SPClearButton.Activate;
VAR
  color        : GPColor; { color to clear drawing with }
BEGIN
  color.InitAsWhite;
  targetLink^.Clear(color)
END;
```

Both `SPQuitButton` and `SPClearButton` are classes describing buttons. We've seen how virtual methods provide the parts of those buttons that differ from the more generic `GPPushButton`, in that they do something when clicked on by the user. We can use virtual methods to describe how other parts of the GUI respond to user actions. Let's look at a more complex example now.

6.6 DEFINING AN INTERACTOR

As mentioned in earlier chapters, we use the `Run` method of our `StarterUnit` application classes to handle the input stream. The `Run` method receives input from the mouse and the keyboard and sends a message to the appropriate GUI component. If the user clicks on a button, for example, the `Activate` message is sent to that button. A drawing area, however, will need to handle more than just a mouse click; it needs to know how to respond to mouse movements or double clicks or input from the keyboard in an application-specific way.

GP includes a set of classes called *interactors* that provide methods for handling different kinds of input. We can associate with a drawing area an interactor that specifies how that drawing area should react to inputs received by `Run`. When `Run` sends messages to a drawing area indicating that the user has taken some action, the drawing area forwards the messages to any suitable interactors with which it is associated. By changing the interactor associated with a drawing area, we can change how the drawing area responds to user actions, a capability which we will use in Chapter 7.

The use of interactors is thus another example of polymorphism. By adding new kinds of interactors, we can extend our program, as we'll see in Chapter 8. Old objects, such as `GPDrawingArea`, can use new kinds of interactors in the same way as they used old kinds of interactors.

Let's look at one specific example defined as `GPMouseInteractor`. We know that `GPApplication.Run` can handle mouse input; `GPMouseInteractor` has virtual methods corresponding to messages sent by `Run` when `Run` receives input from the mouse inside a drawing area. The drawing area can forward these messages to an interactor, which responds using its virtual methods. `GPMouseInteractor` is shown in Class Box 6.5.

Class Box 6.5

GPMouse-Interactor

GPMouseInteractor

This class is used to respond to user actions in a drawing area. These actions include pressing and releasing the mouse button, and incremental movements by the mouse.

Methods:

`Init(...);` Establish the initial state of the interactor.

`ButtonDown(pt : GPPoint); VIRTUAL;`

The behavior when the mouse button is first pressed.

`ButtonMotion(pt : GPPoint); VIRTUAL;`

The behavior when the mouse is moved while the button is pressed.

`ButtonUp(pt : GPPoint); VIRTUAL;`

The behavior when the mouse button is released.

The `ButtonDown`, `ButtonMotion`, and `ButtonUp` methods are defined as virtual in `GPMouseInteractor`. A superclass with at least one empty virtual method is said to be an *abstract* class. `Animal` and `Mammal` were both abstract, since neither provided nonempty definitions of `Eat`, `Sleep`, or `Play`. Because (at least) one of the methods has no defined behavior, it makes little sense to create an instance of that class. We create instances of the *concrete* subclasses defined from that abstract class. `Cat` was a concrete class. Most of the graphic user interface classes defined in GP are abstract, and the subclasses that we write will redefine one or more behaviors of an abstract class. Thus we don't want to use an instance of `GPMouseInteractor` in our program, but rather to create a subclass from which we can make instances.

In our subclass, we need to redefine the behaviors of `ButtonDown`, `ButtonMotion`, and `ButtonUp`. We know from the parameter list of `GPMouseInteractor` that each of these methods receives the current location of the mouse as a parameter (remember that a virtual method defines a particular interface, including a particular parameter list). In our program, when the user clicks in the drawing area, we want a path to begin drawing. While the user holds down the mouse button, the path should follow the mouse movements. When the user lets the mouse button go, the path should end.

The path will be made using an instance of the `GPLine` class shown in Class Box 6.6. This class has methods called `SetStart` and `SetEnd` that establish the endpoints of the line; we can change the endpoints of our line and keep redrawing the line as it changes.

Class Box 6.6

GPLine

GPLine

This represents a straight line segment with two end points. It can be drawn in a drawing area.

Methods:

`Init;`

Establish the initial state of the line. Its start and end points are both the origin, (0, 0).

`SetStart (startPt : GPPoint);`

Tell the line to use the passed point as its start point.

`SetEnd(endPt : GPPoint);`

Tell the line to use the passed point as its end point.

`Draw( daLink : GPDrawingAreaAsn);`

Draw the line in the passed drawing area. The line is drawn from its start point to its end point. It asks the drawing area for a color to draw in.

```
DrawWithStyle( daLink : GPDrawingAreaAsn;
          style : GPDrawingStyleAsn);
```

Draw the line in the passed drawing area. The line is drawn from its start point to its end point. The line is drawn according to the passed style.

Let's think about the pseudocode for our new concrete interactor class. We'll begin by naming the class `SPPencilInteractor`, since it represents a "pencil" tool that draws pencillike lines in the sketchpad. We know the class will inherit the methods defined in Class Box 6.5. In addition, it will need two instance variables.

First, a concrete interactor needs a target for its actions — that is, we should know what is to be affected by the mouse click. In this case, users clicking in the drawing area should see results in the drawing area. Note that an interactor could just as easily affect some other part of the application — it needn't do anything to the drawing area from which it is receiving messages. We should then have an instance variable we'll call `targetLink` that will be a link to an instance of `GPDrawingArea`, which we last saw in Class Box 6.2. Our second instance variable is needed to keep track of the current line; we'll use an instance of `GPLine`. Our class is diagrammed in Figure 6.10.

Figure 6.10
SPPencilInteractor

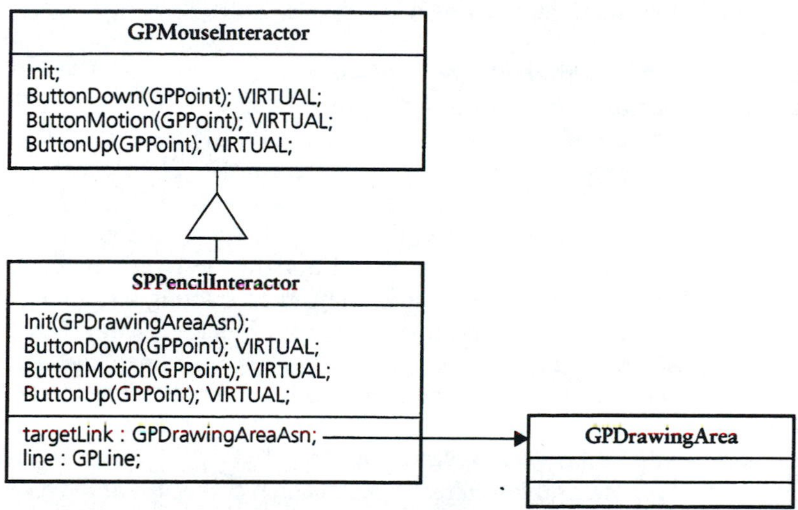

Now, let's consider what should happen in each of the methods indicated in the diagram. The method to initialize the class just needs to initialize the parts of the object. As before, we make sure to call `INHERITED Init`. This should always be done when implementing a new subclass. Your constructor will thus have two parts: initializing the superclass (thus initializing all instance variables and virtual methods provided by the superclass) and initializing any new instance variables and virtual methods defined by the subclass.

SPPencilInteractor.Init

Purpose: Establish the initial state of the interactor

Pseudocode:

```
Send inherited Init message
Store target drawing area link
Send init message to line
```

We see that the `Init` method needs to initialize the two instance variables: the link to the drawing area and the line. Which of these will be parameters to `Init`? Let's review why they are instance variables. We can choose instance variables, local variables, or parameters; to make the decision, let's return to the definitions at the end of Chapter 5. The target drawing area is not a part of the `SPPencilInteractor`, but it needs to be associated with it. The link to the drawing area will be created in another method, and that method therefore needs to send the link as a parameter to the constructor so it can be stored in `targetLink`. The line, however, need not be determined outside this method and can be just an instance variable.

Let's move on to the virtual methods inherited from `GPMouseInteractor`. One nice thing about using a virtual method is that the interface is easy to determine; we just copy the interface of the superclass's method. This is what we do for `ButtonDown`, `ButtonMotion`, and `ButtonUp`.

The `ButtonDown` method should begin a line when the user first clicks the mouse in the drawing area.

SPPencilInteractor.ButtonDown
Purpose: Begin a line at the current point
Pseudocode:
  Send a message to the line to start at the current point

As the mouse moves, the user wants to see the line she has drawn so far. The `ButtonMotion` method should update the screen by drawing a line from the initial point to the current point, then starting a new line at the current point. Mouse movements are detected very quickly so that each new line may be very short. While the user is drawing a series of lines, the effect on the screen is a more or less continuous curve following the mouse's movements.

SPPencilInteractor.ButtonMotion
Purpose: End the current line and begin a new line at the given point
Pseudocode:
  Send a message to the line to end at the current point
  Draw the current line
  Send a message to the line to start at the current point

Finally, when the user releases the mouse button, the last endpoint and line should be drawn.

SPPencilInteractor.ButtonUp
Purpose: End the current line
Pseudocode:
  Send a message to the line to end at the current point
  Draw the current line

As we shall see in the next two chapters, there are other behaviors to be defined for mouse clicks, movements, and releases. Separate subclasses of

GPMouseInteractor can be used to create the other behaviors — all they have to do is override the virtual methods ButtonDown, ButtonMotion, and ButtonUp, as we did for our pencil. We will see an example of this kind of polymorphism in Chapter 8.

We still need to link our new interactor with a drawing area. GPDrawingArea contains a method called AddInteractor that links an instance of GPDrawingArea to an instance of an interactor. Suppose we have created an instance of the SPPencilInteractor called pencil. We can send an AddInteractor message with a link to pencil as a parameter. This will complete the link to pencil from our instance of GPDrawingArea, as seen in the example program in the next section. Note that the drawing area needs a link to the pencil interactor even though the pencil interactor already has a link to the drawing area. The method Run will send messages indicating user actions to the drawing area, not to the interactor, because the drawing area is a region of the screen and the interactor is not (recall that Run sends messages to the appropriate region of the screen). Therefore, the drawing area must forward those messages to our interactor. To do that, it needs a link to our interactor, since otherwise it wouldn't know to which instance to send the messages.

6.7 EXAMPLE PROGRAM

What follows is the paint program. It uses the same code for the SPQuitButton and SPClearButton that we saw earlier in the chapter. The program also uses the code for SPPencilInteractor derived from our pseudocode. This code also includes a definition for a class, SPButtonColumn, which contains the clear and quit button. This class is simply a subclass of GPColumn with instance variables for the buttons. The last class, SPApp, contains the column, the drawing area, and an instance of the pencil interactor, which is given to the drawing area as part of the constructor for the application.

This is the first nontrivial program in this book. It makes use of all the important features of object-oriented programming, including polymorphism, code reuse, and a top-down design based on objects. While the complete program may seem daunting, it is an extremely good idea to read it from beginning to end several times. Compile it, then run it. Study how it behaves and use that knowledge to increase your understanding of the program itself.

Just as you learn writing prose by both writing yourself and reading other people's writing, you learn programming by both programming yourself and studying other people's programs. Studying this program and understanding the relationships between its many objects may take time, but it is time well spent. Understanding the objects in this program will make it that much easier to build objects in your own programs.

```
{**********************************************************
The paint program. Name: Rafael R. Ruiz 9/25/94
**********************************************************}

PROGRAM Painter;
USES GPApplicationUnit, GPDAreaUnit, GPButtonUnit, GPManagerUnit,
          GPColorUnit, GPInteractorUnit, GPShapesUnit;
TYPE

{**********************************************************
This class is the drawing interactor. It draws a series of small
lines connected at their endpoints to approximate a smooth curve.
**********************************************************}

SPPencilInteractor = OBJECT (GPMouseInteractor)
  CONSTRUCTOR    Init         (newTargetLink : GPDrawingAreaAsn);
  PROCEDURE      ButtonDown   (pt : GPPoint); VIRTUAL;
  PROCEDURE      ButtonMotion (pt : GPPoint); VIRTUAL;
  PROCEDURE      ButtonUp     (pt : GPPoint); VIRTUAL;

PRIVATE
  targetLink    : GPDrawingAreaAsn;{ drawing area to be drawn in }
  line          : GPLine;         { used to draw lines }
END;

{**********************************************************
This class is the quit button inside of an action panel.
**********************************************************}

SPQuitButton = OBJECT (GPPushButton)
  CONSTRUCTOR Init (
      containerLink    : GPManagerAsn;
      newTargetLink    : GPApplicationAsn);
  PROCEDURE Activate; VIRTUAL;
PRIVATE
  targetLink    : GPApplicationAsn; { the link to the application
           needed to quit the program }
END;

{**********************************************************
This button clears the drawing.
**********************************************************}

SPClearButton = OBJECT (GPPushButton)
  CONSTRUCTOR Init (
      containerLink    : GPManagerAsn;
      newTargetLink    : GPDrawingAreaAsn);
  PROCEDURE Activate; VIRTUAL;
PRIVATE
  targetLink    : GPDrawingAreaAsn; { what this button clears }
END;
```

```
{*********************************************************
This class is the container for the Quit and Clear buttons.
*********************************************************}

SPButtonColumn = OBJECT (GPColumn)
  CONSTRUCTOR Init (
      containerLink    : GPApplicationAsn;     { Quit this. }
      drawingAreaLink  : GPDrawingAreaAsn);    { Clear this. }
PRIVATE
  clearButton      : SPClearButton;    { Clear drawing area. }
  quitButton       : SPQuitButton;     { Quit the application. }
END;

{*********************************************************
This class represents the window (and its contents) in which the
program executes and an interactor.
*********************************************************}

SPApp = OBJECT (GPApplication)
  CONSTRUCTOR Init;
PRIVATE
  canvas           : GPDrawingArea;    { the drawing area }
  column           : SPButtonColumn;   { panel of push buttons }
  pencil           : SPPencilInteractor; { the drawing interactor }
END;

{*********************************************************
This is the end of the TYPE section. No more class definitions
appear after this point in the program. The next section of the
program contains all the definitions of the methods for the
classes that were described above.
*********************************************************}

{*********************************************************
Methods for SPPencilInteractor
*********************************************************}

{*********************************************************
This method is the interactor's constructor. It sets up the link to
the drawing area and the initial state of the line.
*********************************************************}

CONSTRUCTOR SPPencilInteractor.Init(newTargetLink :
           GPDrawingAreaAsn);
BEGIN
  INHERITED Init;
  targetLink := newTargetLink;
  line.Init;
END;
```

```
{*********************************************************
This method responds to mouse presses in the drawing area. It
prepares to draw the first line.
*********************************************************}

PROCEDURE SPPencilInteractor.ButtonDown (pt : GPPoint);
BEGIN
  line.SetStart(pt);
END;

{*********************************************************
This method responds to mouse movement with the mouse button down
in the drawing area. It completes the previous line, draws it, and
prepares the next line to be drawn.
*********************************************************}

PROCEDURE SPPencilInteractor.ButtonMotion (pt : GPPoint);
BEGIN
  line.SetEnd(pt);
  line.Draw(targetLink);
  line.SetStart(pt);
END;

{*********************************************************
This method responds to mouse releases in the drawing area. It
completes and draws the previous line (which is also the final line
to be drawn).
*********************************************************}

PROCEDURE SPPencilInteractor.ButtonUp (pt : GPPoint);
BEGIN
  line.SetEnd(pt);
  line.Draw(targetLink);
END;

{*********************************************************
Methods for SPButtonColumn
*********************************************************}


{*********************************************************
The column's constructor initializes the buttons.
*********************************************************}

CONSTRUCTOR SPButtonColumn.Init (
      containerLink    : GPApplicationAsn;
      drawingAreaLink  : GPDrawingAreaAsn);
BEGIN
  INHERITED Init(containerLink);
  clearButton.Init(@self, drawingAreaLink);
  quitButton.Init(@self, containerLink);
END;
```

```
{*********************************************************
Methods for SPQuitButton
**********************************************************}

{*********************************************************
The quit button's constructor sets the button's name and link to
the application.
**********************************************************}

CONSTRUCTOR SPQuitButton.Init (
       containerLink    : GPManagerAsn;
       newTargetLink    : GPApplicationAsn);
BEGIN
   INHERITED Init(containerLink);
   targetLink := newTargetLink;
   SetName('Quit');
END;

{*********************************************************
This method responds to mouse presses when the cursor is on the
quit button. It stops the program by sending a Quit message to the
application.
**********************************************************}

PROCEDURE SPQuitButton.Activate;
BEGIN
  targetLink^.Quit;
END;

{*********************************************************
Methods for SPClearButton
**********************************************************}


{*********************************************************
This method is the clear button's constructor. It sets the
button's name and link to the drawing area.
**********************************************************}

CONSTRUCTOR SPClearButton.Init (
       containerLink    : GPManagerAsn;
       newTargetLink    : GPDrawingAreaAsn);
BEGIN
   INHERITED Init(containerLink);
   targetLink := newTargetLink;
   SetName('Clear');
END;
```

```
{**********************************************************
This method responds to mouse presses on the clear button. It
clears the drawing area.
**********************************************************}

PROCEDURE SPClearButton.Activate;
VAR
  color : GPColor;
BEGIN
  color.InitAsWhite;
  targetLink^.Clear(color);
END;



{**********************************************************
Methods for SPApp
**********************************************************}

{**********************************************************
This method constructs the drawing area, button column, and pencil
interactor. Most link to the app, hence the @ self parameter.
**********************************************************}

CONSTRUCTOR SPApp.Init;
BEGIN
  INHERITED Init;
  canvas.Init(@self);          { On screen, canvas is inside me. }
  column.Init(@self, @canvas); { On screen, column is inside me. }
  pencil.Init(@canvas);        { The pencil draws on the canvas. }
  canvas.AddInteractor(@pencil); { Canvas sends msgs to pencil. }
END;

{**********************************************************
The program's mainline sets up the app and starts it running.
**********************************************************}

VAR
  paintApp : SPApp;
BEGIN
  paintApp.Init;
  paintApp.Run;
END.
```

Summary

In this chapter we explored a relationship among classes called inheritance, which is the hallmark of object-oriented programming. It is often useful to arrange classes into an "is-a" hierarchy, where one class, the subclass, inherits all of the properties of another, the superclass. The subclass is typically specialized by providing additional instance variables or methods that are unique to the subclass. Inheritance is defined by placing the name of a superclass in parentheses after the word `OBJECT` in the subclass definition.

Inheritance allows a single definition of instance variables or methods in a superclass to be used in all of its subclasses (and in their subclasses). Rather than write out the same code for each subclass, we can define it once and be done with it. Libraries such as GP take advantage of this feature. The common elements of, say, a button are "factored out" and defined in the class `GPPushButton`. The subclasses inherit those common elements and presumably add more specialized information.

An instance of a subclass can use any of the methods in the superclass. But how does OOPas know when to use an inherited method? When OOPas compiles a message sent to an instance, it first searches the instance's class definition for the method. If that search is unsuccessful, OOPas then moves to the superclass to see whether the method is defined there. If that search is unsuccessful, OOPas continues to move up through superclasses until it either finds the method or runs out of superclasses to search when even the root class doesn't have it.

A variation on that theme happens when we want to send an inherited message from *inside* a subclass. When a subclass's method wants to use a message definition defined in one of the superclasses from within a method *with the same name*, it precedes the method call with the reserved word `INHERITED`. OOPas follows the procedure for finding the method described in the last paragraph, but begins at the current class's immediate superclass. This is often used in creating constructors. Each class must have its own constructor, but a subclass's constructor will often want to include the behavior defined in the superclass's constructor. (Unlike other methods, the constructor of a subclass typically has the same name (`Init`, for example) as its superclass, but need not have the same parameter list.)

We next examined virtual methods, which greatly enhance the power of inheritance. These are methods that are typically declared in the superclass in the interface only; the definition of the body of the method is an empty `BEGIN/END` block. Virtual methods force all of a class's subclasses to have a method with a particular name (and parameter list), but each subclass can define the behavior for that method. An example is the `Activate` method for `GPPushButton`. All buttons should perform an action when the button is pressed. The virtual method guarantees that the action will be defined in a method called `Activate` but allows the subclasses to define the behavior individually.

A link to a subclass may be sent as a parameter to a link to a superclass, but an instance of a subclass cannot be sent as a parameter to a superclass. This is useful when we want to define a method and use methods of a general superclass but are not sure which subclass will be sending the method. This extremely important technique is called polymorphism. Other examples of polymorphism will be shown in later chapters.

When a message is sent to an instance via a link, polymorphism is being used. OOPas determines which virtual method to use in response to a message in this situation by looking in the instance's actual class, then searching parent classes for the method. With nonvirtual methods, OOPas first looks not in the instance's actual class but in the class named by the association describing the link. Virtual methods thus use dynamic binding (at run time), with the method used (or bound) determined by the dynamic behavior of the program (what link was passed). Non-virtual methods use static binding (at compile time), with the method used determined by the static description of the program (the class named in the association).

You can think of virtual methods as important placeholders. A virtual method is a method that needs to appear in all subclasses with the same name, but whose particular behavior will be defined in the subclass. The superclass's virtual method is often just an empty shell, and the subclass must override the method fully.

This completes our coverage of the basic concepts of object-oriented programming. The next two chapters will strengthen your understanding of these concepts by using them in new and more complex situations.

Exercises

Understanding Concepts

1. Draw an inheritance hierarchy such as depicted in Figure 6.1 for the following:
   a. Animals: birds (eagles, penguins) and fish (carp, cod)
   b. Digits 0–9: odd and even numbers
   c. Digits 0–9: those that can be drawn just with straight lines, those that can be drawn just with curves, and those that are a combination of straight lines and curves
2. Why do we have to create a separate class for `SPQuitButton` (as opposed to making it just an instance of `GPPushButton`)?
3. When do you use the reserved word `INHERITED`? When do you use `VIRTUAL`? Can you use them together?
4. What is a virtual method?

Coding Exercises

1. Create a class definition (and appropriate methods) for a "Clear and Quit" button that first clears and then quits the application.
2. Modify the `House` program from earlier chapters so that it draws the house when a button is pushed.
3. Rewrite the interface for the `SUShark` and `SUFish` classes in the exercises in Chapter 3 and Chapter 4, using a superclass called `SUSeaCreature`.
4. Given what you wrote in Coding Exercise 3, does it make sense for `SUPlant` to be a subclass of `SUSeaCreature`? Why or why not?

Programming Problems

1. Add to the Aquarium exercises from Chapter 4 by allowing the user to press a button on the screen to move the shark or the goldfish.
2. Modify the Random Walk program from Chapter 5 by allowing the user to press a button on the screen to indicate which path should move next. (That is, a button labeled "path 1" should show the next step along path 1.)
3. Modify the Random Walk program so that the user can choose the color for the paths.
4. Modify the Television program from Chapter 5 so that the user can select a channel and a time and see the appropriate display.
5. Modify the Diagrams program from Chapter 5 so that the user can select the foreground and background colors from a set of color buttons.
6. Write a program with three buttons, each of which draws a different house. The houses may use any of the SU classes seen previously as well as the following classes:

```
SUOvalWindow = OBJECT(SUPlainComponent) { an oval window }
  CONSTRUCTOR Init;  { establishes start position for window }
  PROCEDURE Draw;    { draws the window }

SUWindowWithShade = OBJECT(SUPlainComponent) { a window with a
           shade }
  CONSTRUCTOR Init;  { establishes start position for window }
  PROCEDURE Draw;    { draws the window }

SUDoubleDoor = OBJECT(SUTrimmedComponent) { double front door }
  CONSTRUCTOR Init;  { establishes start position for door }
  PROCEDURE Draw;    { draws the window }

SUFlatRoof = OBJECT(SUPlainComponent) { represents plain roof }
  CONSTRUCTOR Init;  { establishes start position for door }
  PROCEDURE Draw;    { draws the window }

SUChimney = OBJECT(SUPlainComponent) { represents a chimney }
  CONSTRUCTOR Init;  { establishes start position for door }
  PROCEDURE Draw;    { draws the window }
```

7. Extend the stick figure program from Chapter 3 by designing a face class that can accommodate a frown or a smile.
8. Extend the stick figure program from Chapter 3 so that when the user presses a button on the screen, it shows the figure jumping or standing.

7

Designing Individual Objects

Good design is a crucial part of a well-crafted program. The best way to learn design is by doing, so this text won't dictate any hard and fast principles of good design. Instead, you'll see the design decisions that went into the construction of some programs and you'll be encouraged to use these kinds of decisions as starting points for your own designs.

One of the most important rules of thumb for good design is an idea we've already seen — divide and conquer. Each of the programs we've seen thus far first was divided into smaller, more manageable chunks, in order to arrive at a clearer, more understandable design.

In this chapter, we will extend the capabilities of our paint program from Chapter 6. Another good rule of thumb is to design and implement systems that can be modified easily, since needs often change over time. A program that is easily modified supports *extensibility*, one of the key features of object-oriented programs.

We will walk through the design of one program in its entirety, from the problem specification to the development of OOPas code. Here, we'll be reusing many of the GUI components developed in Chapter 6. As you read this chapter, keep in mind the higher-level concepts of object-oriented design and consider how these ideas may apply to the design of other programs. Then read the code at the end of the chapter carefully, to gain a better understanding of how the GUI components of GP work. (We'll be using these components in all future exercises and examples.)

7.1 SPECIFYING THE PROBLEM

We now want to add color to our paint program from Chapter 6. The program specification would look something like this:

This application represents a simple paint program. The user can use the mouse like a pencil to draw lines in the application's drawing area. The application also should provide a group of two buttons: a quit button that stops the program and a clear button that clears the drawing. A second group of buttons allows choice of a paint color.

For most graphical programs, it makes sense to draw a picture of the program's user interface. In this case, the user might see something like Figure 7.1.

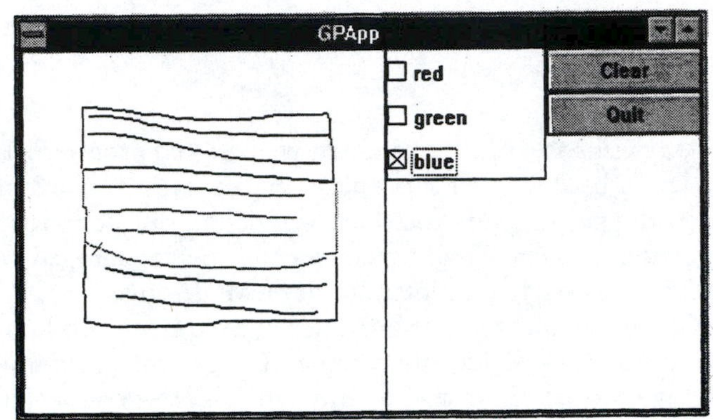

Figure 7.1

A simple paint program

The picture helps us to make some choices. Consider the assumptions made in designing the user interface. Often, you might assume that things should be in a certain place or have a certain "look and feel" because other programs have done similar things that way. When designing the program itself and its many objects, you might make the same kind of assumptions. Here, for example, we might assume that the user should be able to draw squiggly lines in a manner as similar as possible to the manner they are drawn in other paint programs. Recognizing these assumptions is a simple form of analysis, since it helps us realize what sorts of details were left out of the specification.

Thus, when thinking about these choices, your first and most important task is to understand the problem specification. A complicated and well-executed program that fails to meet the initial specifications is inadequate. The program must do what it is intended to do.

7.2 COMPARING HIERARCHIES

Let's reconsider the picture of our new colorful paint program in Figure 7.1. Remember that our paint program in Chapter 6 contained a drawing area and a column, and the column itself contained two buttons: the clear button and the quit button.

A Containment Hierarchy

Note that we use "containment" in the preceding paragraph in two different though related senses. First, a button is contained *geometrically* within its column, but, second, that same button is contained as an instance variable *within the class definition* of the column. These two related senses of containment are illustrated in Figures 7.2 and 7.3. Figure 7.3 shows the containment hierarchy, with the canvas, the color column, and the button column contained within the application. The lines with diamonds on the ends serve to indicate containment: the instance closest to the diamond contains the other instance. We can also use nested boxes to show containment, as in Figure 7.4. In this case, our figure has many similarities to our picture: Our picture can help us decide containment relationships. Note that Figures 7.3 and 7.4 provide essentially the same information but in different forms.

Figure 7.2

Graphical containment on the screen

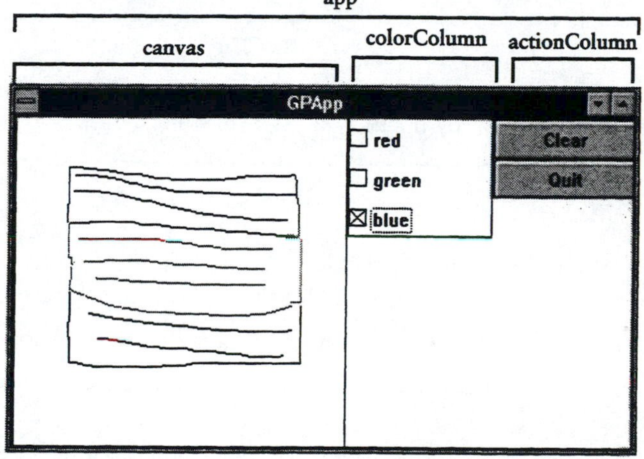

Figure 7.3

Containment of instance variables in the paint program

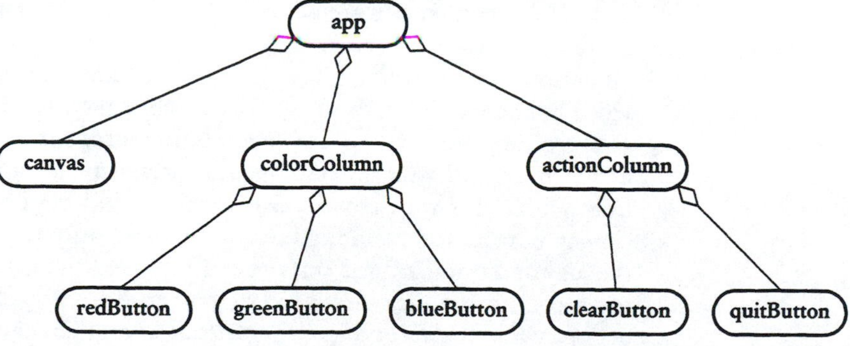

We'll discuss the various GP components throughout this chapter. For now, it's important simply to understand that the application contains the columns and drawing area, and the columns in turn contain buttons.

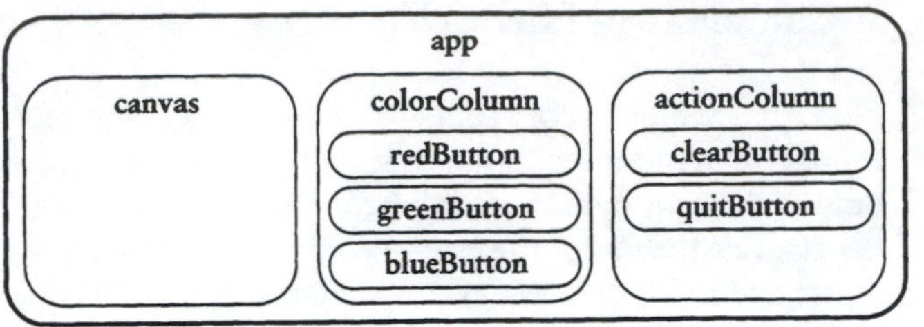

Figure 7.4

Nested boxes showing containment in the paint program

An Inheritance Hierarchy

Let's take a detailed look at how different kinds of buttons are defined in GP. A button, in general, is a rectangular area of the screen. When a mouse click is detected inside the button's area, some action is taken. Some methods describing the behavior of the class `GPButton` are given in Class Box 7.1.

Class Box 7.1

GPButton

> **GPButton**
>
> This is an abstract class modeling a button — a region on the screen that can be pressed on by the user to perform some action.
>
> ---
>
> **Methods:**
>
> `Init;` Initialize the button.
>
> `SetName(name:string);` Set the name of the button to the string.
>
> `Activate; VIRTUAL;` A method called when the button has been pressed.

We saw parts of the `GPButton` class, namely `SetName` and `Activate`, when we studied the class `GPPushButton` in Section 6.5. `GPPushButton`'s `SetName` and `Activate` methods are actually methods of `GPButton` — `GPPushButton` is a subclass of `GPButton`. The class `GPButton` defines characteristics common to all buttons. In particular, all buttons have a name and perform an action (provided by the virtual method `Activate`) when the user presses them.

There are two sorts of buttons. Some buttons, when pressed, perform an action once and when pressed again, perform the same action again. A car horn works this way. Now consider the second kind of button, an air-conditioning button, for example. Press the air-conditioning button in your car and the air conditioning turns on; press it a second time, and the air conditioning turns *off*, not on. The first kind of button is a *push button* and performs an action, while the second is a *toggle button* and changes a state. The quit and clear buttons were push buttons.

GP defines two subclasses of `GPButton` to handle these two kinds of buttons. `GPPushButton`, which we've already seen, and `GPToggleButton` inherit all of the properties of `GPButton` — they both have a `SetName` method to set the name they display and an `Activate` method to perform an action when pressed. Toggle buttons, however, have a second virtual method, `DeActivate`, that is used the second time they are pushed. Like an air-conditioner button, click once and the button turns on, calling `Activate`. Click a second time and it turns off, calling `DeActivate`. Figure 7.5 shows the relationship among these classes. We'll use a collection of toggle buttons working together to change the current painting color (which is part of the paint program's state).

Figure 7.5

Class diagram with inheritance

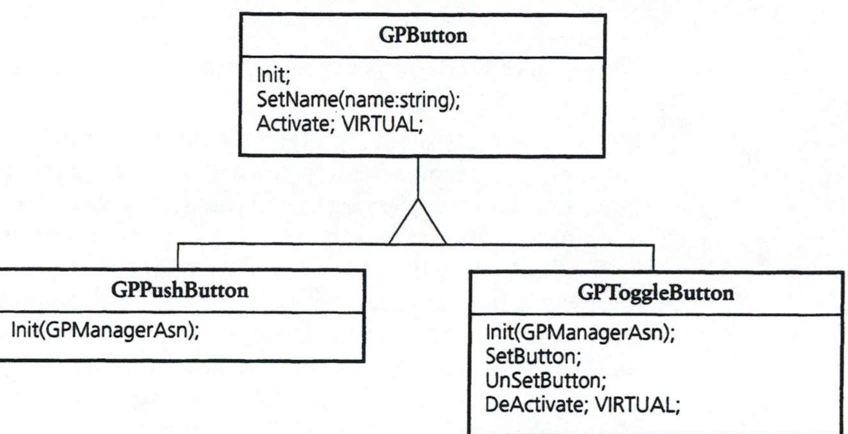

The subclasses are more specific forms of the superclass. The `GPToggleButton` class, for example, has the additional method `SetButton` to change its state to checked (so that a small "x" appears next to the button's name); another method, `UnSetButton`, changes the button's state to unchecked (so that there is no "x"). These two nonvirtual methods call the corresponding virtual methods, `Activate` and `DeActivate`. The methods `SetButton` and `UnSetButton` are known only to instances of `GPToggleButton` — not to instances of `GPButton` or `GPPushButton`.

7.3 COLOR BUTTONS

In Chapter 6, we derived a subclass from `GPPushButton` in order to build buttons that quit the application or cleared the drawing area. We're going to do something similar to build our color buttons, but this time we'll derive a subclass from `GPToggleButton`.

To see why we're using toggle buttons instead of push buttons for our color buttons, let's look at the behaviors of the buttons we're trying to build. The clear button performs an action — it erases the drawing when the user presses it. Like a push button on a telephone that beeps when pressed, clear buttons (and `GPPushButtons` in general) don't act unless being pressed. Compare this behavior to that of a light switch — when you press a light switch, it changes state, so as to affect the light it is connected to *after* it has been pressed. Our color buttons perform the same way: When a color button is pressed, its color becomes the current drawing color and this change remains in effect, even after the button has been pressed. We can make this visually apparent using an "x" (or checkmark) that remains next to a toggle button when it has been set. `GPToggleButtons` provide this kind of behavior, so we derive our color button from `GPToggleButton` rather than `GPPushButton`.

When to Derive a New Subclass

Program designs should always be *minimal but sufficient*. They should be no more complex than necessary, since a complex design is harder to build, maintain, and improve. Keeping this in mind, let's check the design of our clear and quit buttons for pointers in designing our color buttons.

We built the clear button and the quit button as two subclasses from `GPPushButton`, because each button had a different behavior. Although they both sent a message when activated, they sent different messages to different objects. Now, as a preliminary design, we could follow the same pattern for our color buttons. After all, they do different things. One button sets the drawing's current color to red. Another sets it to green. A third sets it to blue. Just as we did with the clear and quit buttons, we could have one subclass for each button on the screen. A class hierarchy for this sort of design is shown in Figure 7.6.

Figure 7.6

Tentative class diagram with a subclass per color

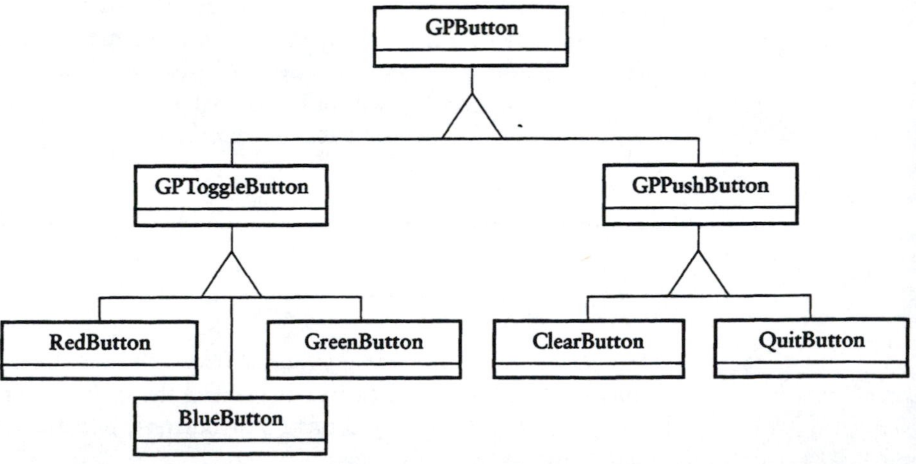

Although a red button clearly "is-a" toggle button (and similarly for all the other color buttons), and a red button is not a green button (and similarly for all the other pairs of colors), all the color buttons have something in common: They are all color buttons. Any particular color button "is-a" color button! A "color button" is a *generalization* of the red button, the green button, and the blue button.

At this point, we should reconsider our design a bit to determine exactly what the three color buttons have in common. Once we have done that, we can declare a class `ColorButton` that provides exactly what the color buttons have in common. Going back to the specification, we see that the color buttons all should let a user choose a color in which to paint. So each button can correspond to a particular color and pressing a particular button can choose that color. This is the common functionality we can put into the `ColorButton` class. We can provide the color as an instance variable of type `GPColor`. The color must be given to a drawing area, so `ColorButton` also will be associated with a `GPDrawingArea`. Finally, we can implement the virtual method `ColorButton.Activate` by sending a message to the drawing area, telling it to use the color as the current drawing color.

Having done that, we can see that there isn't much left for the tentative classes `RedButton`, `GreenButton`, and `BlueButton` to do — they merely correspond to particular colors. Further, `ColorButton` needs a color passed into its constructor, because it can't make the color simply out of nothing. So, instead of having subclasses for each color, we can construct three different instances of `ColorButton`, passing three different colors. Our design now has fewer classes and is simpler and easier to understand. Figure 7.7 shows a new class diagram reflecting this simpler alternative. Now, when more colors become available, and we thus need more color buttons, we can create more instances of the `ColorButton` class, rather than adding more classes.

Figure 7.7

Class diagram with one subclass for color buttons

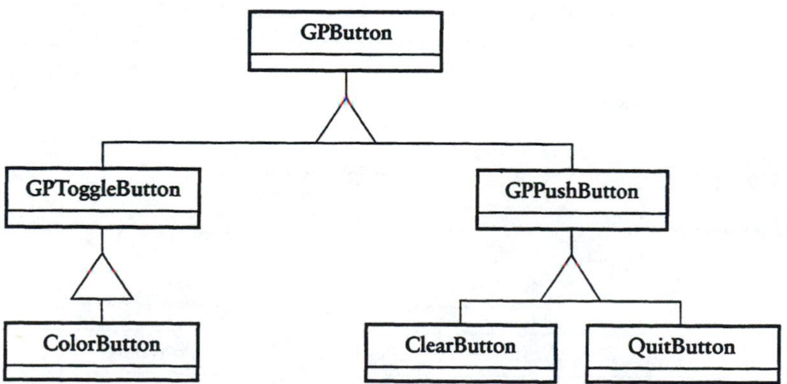

When trying to decide whether a new subclass is necessary, consider whether it behaves differently from existing subclasses. The clear button was a good choice for a subclass because it behaved differently from the quit button. The red, green, and blue buttons were not good subclasses, because they all behaved in the same way. The differences lay in the objects they used (each used a different color), not in behavior.

7.4 BUILDING COLUMNS OF BUTTONS

Let's now consider how one or more buttons are assembled into managers. Recall from Section 6.5 that managers are simply kinds of GUI components that can hold other components on the screen.

When a color is chosen, it should remain the active color until another is chosen. We want our color buttons to behave like station selection buttons on a radio: You can listen to only one radio station at a time, and you can draw in only one color at a time.

From the brief summary in Figure 7.8 of the different managers available (an elaboration of Figure 6.7), we see that `GPRadioColumn` is the class we're looking for. It contains toggle buttons and is designed so that only one of the toggles can be set at a time, like the buttons on a radio. We'll create a class called `SPColorColumn`, a subclass of `GPRadioColumn` to hold color buttons.

Let's examine how toggle buttons work when contained in a `GPRadioColumn`. When the user selects a toggle button, it sends a message to the `GPRadioColumn` instance containing it, saying that it has been set. `GPRadioColumn` first resets the previously selected button by sending it an `UnSetButton` message. The nonvirtual `UnSetButton` changes the button's state, then calls the virtual `DeActivate` message. Then the `GPRadioColumn` instance sends a `SetButton` message to the just selected button, which then sends itself an `Activate` message. Thus `GPRadioColumn` ensures that only one of its buttons is set at any time. Since changing the state of a button with `SetButton` or `UnSetButton` is different from the button's response to the change provided by the methods `Activate` or `DeActivate`, subclasses of `GPToggleButton` can change the response without having to keep track of the button's state — keeping track of the state thus can be reused.

Figure 7.8

GPManager subclasses

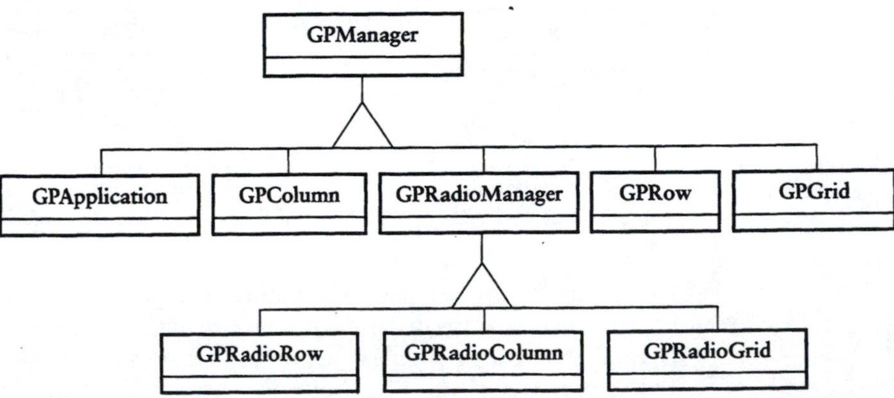

Other than its behavior with toggle buttons, `GPRadioColumn` is just like `GPColumn` — it organizes all of its buttons into a column. There are also managers called `GPRow` and `GPRadioRow` that work just like `GPColumn` and `GPRadi-`

oColumn, except that they organize their buttons into rows instead of columns. There are also two classes, GPGrid and GPRadioGrid, that organize their buttons into grid formations. For now, though, we'll stick with columns.

Defining the Color Column Class

GP defines classes for buttons and columns, but we need to specialize those classes for our own purposes. In the next section, we examine how to create our own subclasses of buttons. Now, let's define subclasses of the columns. As an example, consider SPColorColumn, our subclass of GPRadioColumn for the paint program. It contains three color buttons — the instance variables redButton, greenButton, and blueButton are instances of SPColorButton.

The SPColorColumn needs a constructor. The constructor, in turn, should initialize the color buttons. We can write the initial part of the code as follows:

```
{*******************************************************
This class contains the color buttons. It is a tool column and thus
allows only one toggle button to be pressed at a time.
*********************************************************}
SPColorColumn = OBJECT (GPRadioColumn)
  CONSTRUCTOR Init (
      containerLink    : GPManagerAsn;
      targetLink       : GPDrawingAreaAsn);
PRIVATE
  redButton       : SPColorButton;   { the button for red }
  greenButton     : SPColorButton;   { the button for green }
  blueButton      : SPColorButton;   { the button for blue }
END;
```

Let's look at our constructor now. It takes two parameters: a link to the application containing the column and a target link to the drawing area. The color buttons will use the target link themselves to set the drawing color.

```
CONSTRUCTOR SPColorColumn.Init (
      containerLink    : GPManagerAsn;
      targetLink       : GPDrawingAreaAsn);
VAR
  red, green, blue : GPColor;
BEGIN
  INHERITED Init(containerLink);
  red.InitAsRed;
  green.InitAsGreen;
  blue.InitAsBlue;
```

```
   redButton.Init(...);
   greenButton.Init(...);
   blueButton.Init(...);

   redButton.SetButton;
END;
```

The constructor begins by sending the superclass's constructor message. (If we had not included that line, we would have failed to initialize the components of the `SPColorColumn` instance that are inherited.) Then it initializes the colors it will give to the buttons and initializes the buttons. Finally, it sets one button (the red one) to provide a default painting color.

Defining the Color Button Class

How many parameters does the constructor `SPColorButton.Init` need? First, the button needs to send messages to the radio column, so it needs a link to a radio column (remember that the column contains the button, and so can send messages to it, but the contained button needs a link to its container). Second, the button also needs to tell the drawing area to use a different color, so it needs a link to a drawing area. The third thing the button needs is a color. All of these will be parameters to the constructor. For the second and third parameters, we can pass along the `targetLink` parameter to the `INHERITED Init` of `GPToggleButton` and also the appropriate color. But what about the first parameter?

We need to send the contained button a link to a color column containing it. But this is done inside the method that initializes the color column. Therefore we want to refer to the very color column instance that the method is initializing, which is, of course, unknown at the time the classes are compiled. We again use `self` (last described in Syntax Box 6.4) to refer to the current instance. Thus we can use the following code:

```
redButton.Init(@self, targetLink, red);
greenButton.Init(@self, targetLink, green);
blueButton.Init(@self, targetLink, blue);
```

Here, the first parameter, `@self`, can be read as "a link to myself," that is, as "a link to the current color column." You can think of the reserved word `self` as a placeholder for a particular instance.

We now know enough to write down the entire class definition for `SPColorButton`. It has the constructor we were just discussing, as well as an `Activate` method. We won't need a `DeActivate`, since a drawing area can have only one color to draw in, so setting the color using `Activate` will be sufficient. The class definition follows. By this point, you should be fairly comfortable with it, so we won't discuss every line.

```
SPColorButton = OBJECT (GPToggleButton)
  CONSTRUCTOR Init (
      containerLink    : GPManagerAsn;
      newTargetLink    : GPDrawingAreaAsn;
      newColor         : GPColor);
  PROCEDURE Activate; VIRTUAL;
PRIVATE
  targetLink     : GPDrawingAreaAsn;{ Tell this the color. }
  color          : GPColor;         { Select this color. }
END;
```

The constructor is straightforward — it calls `INHERITED Init`, initializes the link to the drawing area, sets its own name to be the name of the color, and initializes and sets its color:

```
CONSTRUCTOR SPColorButton.Init (
      containerLink    : GPManagerAsn;
      newTargetLink    : GPDrawingAreaAsn;
      newColor         : GPColor);
BEGIN
  INHERITED Init(containerLink);
  targetLink := newTargetLink;
  color.InitAsWhite;
  color := newColor;
  SetName(color.GetName);
END;
```

Notice that the name of the button is set to the name of the color using the function `color.GetName`, which returns a `string`. Like a link, functions can also return a `string`. We will examine strings in more detail in Chapter 15.

The `Activate` method asks the drawing area for a *drawing style*. This is an object that describes how drawing is performed in the drawing area — in particular, what color is used. The drawing area returns a link, which we store in a local variable. We then send a message to the instance pointed to by that link, telling it to change the color it is using. When shapes are drawn, they will ask the drawing area for the style, using the style to pick a color.

```
PROCEDURE SPColorButton.Activate;
VAR
  drawingStyleLink : GPDrawingStyleAsn;
BEGIN
  drawingStyleLink := targetLink^.GetDrawingStyle;
  drawingStyleLink^.SetDrawingForeground(color);
END;
```

7.5 GROUPING CLASSES INTO UNITS

In Section 2.7, we defined the USES statement, which lists the units that our program uses. Units are convenient ways of grouping related classes together, and our program is getting large enough that we'll need to organize all our classes in this way. We've been organizing our classes in this text by talking about the color buttons in one section and the clear and quit buttons in another. By placing these classes in different units, we can give our program a similar organization.

Let's look at the color buttons and color column that we've just described. These classes are closely related. The color buttons are created by and contained in the color column: Without the color buttons, we don't need the color column. Similarly, a single color button is pretty useless: We need to be able to choose among several colors, and a single button only selects a single color.

So a unit for the color buttons and their column makes sense. We'll call it ColSel, short for "color selection." Since each unit goes in its own separate file, unit names should be valid file names as well as valid Pascal identifiers.

A unit uses the new syntax summarized in Syntax Box 7.1. Units have two parts, an interface and an implementation. The *interface* is analogous to the public parts of objects — it is what everyone else can use in the unit. The *implementation* is thus like the private part — no one outside the unit can use it directly. We simply list the classes in a TYPE section in the interface part and define the methods of those classes in the implementation part.

Let's see what this looks like for our color buttons and color column. In the following code, notice that we're prefixing the classes with the letters "CS" to correspond to the name of the unit, instead of the letters "SP," which we used when they were defined in the "Simple Paint" program. We use these prefixes because class names have to be unique, even if they're in different units. If you had two classes named Orange, one in a unit called Citrus and another in a unit called Color, and your USES statement included both Color and Citrus, OOPas would not know which Orange to use. We prevent that ambiguity by prefixing our class names with the name of the unit they're in.

```
UNIT ColSel;
INTERFACE
USES GPButtonUnit, GPDAreaUnit, GPColorUnit, GPManagerUnit,
            GPApplicationUnit, GPDStyleUnit;
TYPE

  CSColorButton = OBJECT (GPToggleButton)
    CONSTRUCTOR Init (
      containerLink    : GPManagerAsn;
      newTargetLink    : GPDrawingAreaAsn;
      newColor         : GPColor);
    PROCEDURE Activate; VIRTUAL;
```

Syntax Box 7.1

UNIT

Purpose:

To declare a unit.

Syntax:

```
UNIT <name>;
INTERFACE
<Class declarations>
IMPLEMENTATION
<Method definitions>
END;
```

Where:

<name> is an identifier that is the name of the unit.

<Class declarations> is a set of classes provided by the unit.

<Method definitions> is the set of definitions of all the methods provided by the classes listed in the interface.

Usage:

The *<name>* identifier may contain digits but must begin with a letter, and it cannot be one of Pascal's reserved words. (See Appendix A.)

```
  PRIVATE
    targetLink           : GPDrawingAreaAsn;{ Tell this the color. }
    color                : GPColor;         { Select this color. }
  END;

  CSColorColumn = OBJECT (GPRadioColumn)
    CONSTRUCTOR Init (
      containerLink      : GPApplicationAsn;
      targetLink         : GPDrawingAreaAsn);
  PRIVATE
    redButton            : CSColorButton;
    greenButton          : CSColorButton;
    blueButton           : CSColorButton;
  END;

IMPLEMENTATION

CONSTRUCTOR CSColorButton.Init (
      containerLink      : GPManagerAsn;
      newTargetLink      : GPDrawingAreaAsn;
      newColor           : GPColor);
BEGIN
  INHERITED Init(containerLink);
```

```
  targetLink := newTargetLink;
  color.InitAsWhite;
  color := newColor;
  SetName(color.GetName);
END;

PROCEDURE CSColorButton.Activate;
VAR
  drawingStyleLink : GPDrawingStyleAsn;
BEGIN
  drawingStyleLink := targetLink^.GetDrawingStyle;
  drawingStyleLink^.SetDrawingForeground(color);
END;

CONSTRUCTOR CSColorColumn.Init (
        containerLink     : GPApplicationAsn;
        targetLink        : GPDrawingAreaAsn);
VAR
  red, green, blue : GPColor;

BEGIN
  INHERITED Init(containerLink);

  red.InitAsRed;
  green.InitAsGreen;
  blue.InitAsBlue;

  redButton.Init(@self, targetLink, red);
  greenButton.Init(@self, targetLink, green);
  blueButton.Init(@self, targetLink, blue);

  { Red is the default color used when the program starts up. }
  redButton.SetButton;
END; { CSColorColumn.Init }

END. { This is the end of UNIT ColSel. Note that there was no BEGIN
              to match this END. }
```

The code hasn't changed. It is simply in a more manageable chunk. Rather than trying to understand the entire program at once, we can look at the parts that work together closely. We know that there is a clear button and a quit button, but these aren't crucial to understanding how the color buttons and color column work together. The `ColSel` unit thus doesn't include them.

Of course, we can define other units for other parts of our drawing application. Another unit is needed for the clear and quit buttons, along with their column. Although these don't work together as closely as the color buttons and the color column, the column makes little sense without the buttons and the buttons themselves both operate on the whole painting (or application). We'll create a unit for these buttons, called `AppCom`, short for "Application Commands":

```
UNIT AppCom;
INTERFACE
USES GPButtonUnit, GPApplicationUnit, GPManagerUnit, GPDAreaUnit,
           GPColorUnit;
TYPE
  ACQuitButton = OBJECT (GPPushButton)
    CONSTRUCTOR Init (
      containerLink    : GPManagerAsn;
      newTargetLink    : GPApplicationAsn);
    PROCEDURE Activate; VIRTUAL;
  PRIVATE
    targetLink : GPApplicationAsn; { Tell this to quit. }
  END;

  ACClearButton = OBJECT (GPPushButton)
    CONSTRUCTOR Init (
      containerLink    : GPManagerAsn;
      newTargetLink    : GPDrawingAreaAsn);
    PROCEDURE Activate; VIRTUAL;
  PRIVATE
    targetLink : GPDrawingAreaAsn; { what this button clears }
  END;

  ACActionColumn = OBJECT (GPColumn)
    CONSTRUCTOR Init (
      containerLink    : GPApplicationAsn;
      drawingAreaLink  : GPDrawingAreaAsn);
  PRIVATE
    clearButton        : ACClearButton;
    quitButton         : ACQuitButton;
  END;

IMPLEMENTATION

CONSTRUCTOR ACActionColumn.Init (
      containerLink    : GPApplicationAsn;
      drawingAreaLink  : GPDrawingAreaAsn);
BEGIN
  INHERITED Init(containerLink);
  clearButton.Init(@self, drawingAreaLink);
  quitButton.Init(@self, containerLink);
END; { ACActionColumn.Init }
```

```
CONSTRUCTOR ACQuitButton.Init (
      containerLink    : GPManagerAsn;
      newTargetLink    : GPApplicationAsn);
BEGIN
  INHERITED Init(containerLink);
  targetLink := newTargetLink;
  SetName('Quit');
END; { ACQuitButton.Init }

PROCEDURE ACQuitButton.Activate;
BEGIN
  targetLink^.Quit;
END; { ACQuitButton.Activate }

CONSTRUCTOR ACClearButton.Init (
      containerLink    : GPManagerAsn;
      newTargetLink    : GPDrawingAreaAsn);
BEGIN
  INHERITED Init(containerLink);
  targetLink := newTargetLink;
  SetName('Clear');
END; { ACClearButton.Init }

PROCEDURE ACClearButton.Activate;
VAR
  color       :GPColor; { color to clear drawing with }
BEGIN
  color.InitAsWhite;
  targetLink^.Clear(color);
END; { ACClearButton.Activate }

END. { UNIT AppCom }
```

Finally, we can make a unit just for our pencil tool. In doing this, we're allowing for future inclusion of other interactors and buttons to control them, as discussed in Chapter 8. We'll call our unit "Paint":

```
UNIT Paint;
INTERFACE
USES GPDAreaUnit, GPInteractorUnit, GPShapesUnit;
TYPE

  PPencilInteractor = OBJECT (GPDrawingInteractor)
    CONSTRUCTOR Init       (newTargetLink : GPDrawingAreaAsn);
    PROCEDURE   ButtonDown (startPt : GPPoint);VIRTUAL;
    PROCEDURE   ButtonMotion(movePt : GPPoint); VIRTUAL;
    PROCEDURE   ButtonUp   (endPt : GPPoint);  VIRTUAL;
```

```
   PRIVATE
     targetLink         : GPDrawingAreaAsn;{ draw in this }
     line               : GPLine;          { used to draw lines }
   END; { CLASS PPencilInteractor }

IMPLEMENTATION

CONSTRUCTOR PPencilInteractor.Init(
      newTargetLink : GPDrawingAreaAsn);
BEGIN
   INHERITED Init;
   targetLink := newTargetLink;
   line.Init;
END; { SPPencilInteractor.Init }

PROCEDURE PPencilInteractor.ButtonDown(startPt : GPPoint);
BEGIN
   line.SetStart(startPt);
END; { PPencilInteractor.ButtonDown}

PROCEDURE PPencilInteractor.ButtonMotion(movePt : GPPoint);
BEGIN
   line.SetEnd(movePt);
   line.Draw(targetLink);
   line.SetStart(movePt);
END; { PPencilInteractor.ButtonMotion}

PROCEDURE PPencilInteractor.ButtonUp(endPt : GPPoint);
BEGIN
   line.SetEnd(endPt);
   line.Draw(targetLink);
END; { PPencilInteractor.ButtonUp }

END. { UNIT Paint }
```

7.6 EXAMPLE PROGRAM

As a result of all the units we made in Section 7.5, our complete program has become extremely simple. We use the units we've already defined, create an application, and run it:

```
PROGRAM SimplePaint;
USES GPApplicationUnit, GPDAreaUnit, ColSel, AppCom, Paint;
```

```
TYPE
  SPApp = OBJECT (GPApplication)
    CONSTRUCTOR Init;
  PRIVATE
    canvas          : GPDrawingArea;     { the drawing area }
    colorColumn     : CSColorColumn;     { column of color btns }
    actionColumn    : ACActionColumn;    { column for quit btn }
    pencil          : PPencilInteractor;{ drawing interactor }
  END;

CONSTRUCTOR SPApp.Init;
BEGIN
  INHERITED Init;
  canvas.Init(@self);
  colorColumn.Init(@self, @canvas);
  actionColumn.Init(@self, @canvas);
  pencil.Init(@canvas);
  canvas.AddInteractor(@pencil);
END; { SPApp.Init }

VAR
  paintApp : SPApp;
BEGIN
  paintApp.Init;
  paintApp.Run;
END. { Mainline }
```

Summary

In this chapter, we looked at some principles of design. First, we designed for extensibility, by building a design that could be modified easily to respond to changing needs. Also, we analyzed the relationships between objects to help clarify the design. We looked at a containment hierarchy, in which instances of one class (such as a column) contained instances of another class (such as another column), which could in turn contain instances of yet another class (such as buttons). Another hierarchy we considered was an inheritance hierarchy that modeled "is-a" relationships between objects.

We wanted to keep our design minimal but sufficient. A program should do just what it needs to, in the simplest manner possible. An overly complex program is harder to write, harder to debug, and harder to understand.

We also looked at the principle of generalization. We saw that the color buttons had many features in common and generalized the individual color buttons into a color button class that provided these common features. Exploiting generalization can reduce repetition in design and implementation.

Finally, we looked at using units to organize our programs. Units contain a set of related classes as well as their implementations. A unit presents related classes together, in one file, making it easier to see how classes that work together closely perform their tasks.

Exercises

Understanding Concepts

1. What is the difference between a containment and an inheritance hierarchy?
2. Diagram the containment and inheritance hierarchies in any of the programming problems in Chapter 6.
3. Describe how to extend the paint program to include another kind of interactor.
4. What is the difference between a file that begins with `UNIT` and one that begins with `PROGRAM`?
5. What behaviors are inherited by `GPToggleButton` from `GPButton`? by `GPPushButton` from `GPButton`?
6. What behaviors of `GPToggleButton` and `GPPushButton` are not inherited from `GPButton`?
7. Why is the `Activate` method defined in `GPButton`?

Coding Exercises

1. Modify the paint program to add a yellow button.
2. Modify the paint program so that when the user chooses a particular button, the pencil draws in a color chosen at random.
3. Modify the body parts program of Chapter 3 by creating a unit for different kinds of faces (smiling, frowning, or with different color eyes).
4. Building classes from the `SUArms` and `SULegs` classes, create a unit for different kinds of bodies (jumping, standing, wearing different colored shirts).
5. Divide the Television program from Programming Problem 4 in Chapter 6 so that one unit has the buttons and the other has the display information.

Programming Problems

1. Modify the House program from earlier chapters so that the user can see one of three different kinds of house, depending on her choice of one of three buttons.
2. Modify the House program so that the user can choose a color from a set of buttons for the house's main color.

3. Modify the House program to have a "main color" button and a "trim color" button as well as a set of color buttons. The main color and trim color buttons are toggles; if the user chooses the main color button, then a color, then the main color of the house is set to that color, and similarly for the trim color.

4. Write a program using the Face and Body units from the coding exercises so that the user can choose a face and a body from a menu and see the resulting stick figure.

5. `StarterUnit` has an interactor called `SUContinuousPencil` that differs from the `SPPencilInteractor` in that it draws on its own; that is, it makes a random pattern without the user moving the mouse. Write a program in which the user uses a button to choose a color. Two more buttons allow the user to "start" or "stop" the continuous pencil. The class definition is as follows (instance variables are omitted, since you will simply instantiate this class):

```
SUContinuousPencil = OBJECT
  CONSTRUCTOR    Init(targetLink : GPDrawingAreaAsn);
  PROCEDURE      Start;       { Make pencil start drawing. }
  PROCEDURE      Stop;        { Make it stop. }
PRIVATE
  { instance vars here }
END;
```

8

Designing a System of Objects

8.1 THE PROCESS OF MAKING A PROGRAM

In Chapter 7, we focused on designing and building a single class: a color button. We made several instances of it, but we still had only a single class to design. Continuing with our paint program, we're going to add new kinds of painting tools, such as the ability to draw straight lines and rectangles. These tools, along with the buttons to control them, comprise a system of related objects. This chapter is about designing systems of objects, a harder task than designing a single object.

You'll learn new principles of design in this chapter, and you should look at this chapter as another step on the road to learning the art of designing computer programs. As you read the example programs, pay close attention to how they were designed; the process of design is more important than the design itself.

Five Steps for Building a System of Objects

Merely understanding a complex system is hard enough. We are faced with the even harder task of designing and implementing such a system. This chapter works through an example of this difficult problem.

Now, that may make the design task sound very difficult. It is not as bad as all that. We learned some important design principles in Chapter 7. By applying them to our new, bigger problem, we'll make quite a lot of progress. However, we'll find some new principles useful as well. In general, we'll follow a sequence of five steps: *specification*, *analysis*, *design*, *implementation*, and *debugging*.

1. *Specification* is the process of determining what your system should be able to do. Usually, you, the programmer, will do this in concert with a *client*, someone who wants to use the software you intend to build.
2. *Analysis* is the process of understanding your specification. This may seem obvious: if you were involved in specifying it, surely you understand it. However, it is easy to need something without understanding how to get it. Consider the need for a car. Knowing that you need a car won't get you very far if you don't understand the problems of obtaining one (finding a dealer, picking the right model, and financing it) and of owning one (filling it with gas, keeping it well maintained, and paying for any insurance).
3. *Design* is the process of describing a system meeting the specification. We can choose and describe the various parts that make up a complex system using knowledge gained during the analysis phase.
4. *Implementation* is the process of turning a system description into a real system. If a system has been designed well, turning the design into an actual workable implementation is often quite straightforward.
5. *Debugging* is the process of identifying the mistakes (or bugs) you made in the previous four steps. Finding bugs necessitates repeating that step and continuing from there. For example, realizing that the designed parts of the system don't actually provide all the capabilities needed is a mistake in the design phase. The system needs to be redesigned, then reimplemented, then debugged again. Obviously, debugging is not so much a step of its own as an ongoing process. The earlier bugs are caught, the better.

These five steps and their order are themselves design principles. Following them in order when building your own programs is an extremely good idea. We'll cover all of them in this chapter. Debugging is so important that we return to it in a chapter of its own, Chapter 14.

From Individual Objects to Systems of Objects

While Chapter 7 focused on good ways to design classes or subclasses of objects, such as the principle of a minimal but sufficient design, the preceding five steps describe a process targeted at designing systems of objects rather than individual objects. Indeed, keeping the idea of a system in mind is one of the principles we're going to look at.

Just because we're looking at a system, though, doesn't mean that design principles we learned in previous chapters don't apply. We're going to revisit a couple of earlier ideas, polymorphism and extensibility, and see how they work when applied to a large system of objects.

Another important principle we'll use is *event-driven programming*; we've been using this principle to build our user interfaces but haven't talked about it in any detail yet. But before we look at all of these principles, we need to start at the beginning — a specification for a program to build.

8.2 THE SPECIFICATION: A COMPLETE PAINT PROGRAM

Let's begin by specifying our revised paint program. Most paint programs let you paint with a variety of tools. You can use a pencil tool, like the one we implemented in Chapter 6, but often you can also use tools for drawing straight lines, rectangles, or ovals. In this chapter, we're going to add a line tool and a rectangle tool to our paint program, leaving additional tools as exercises. Let's look at a brief specification for this program:

This application is a simple paint program. The user can use the mouse to paint various shapes in a canvas, including scribbly lines, straight lines, and rectangles. A set of buttons controls what kind of shape the mouse paints. Another set of buttons lets the user pick a color to draw in. Two more buttons let the user clear the painting and end the program.

In Chapter 7, the color buttons were placed in a radio column to ensure that only one color was selected at a time. The objects we will build in this chapter are related to one another in more complex ways, and many different classes are responsible for many different parts of the application's behavior.

We thus have a system of cooperating objects. Each one is small and relatively easy to understand, but of little use by itself. By putting them together, however, we get more than the sum of the parts. But before we try to put these parts together, we need to understand our specification better.

8.3 ANALYZING THE PROBLEM

We've said it before and we'll say it again: You can't write a program if you don't know what you want it to do. Before you build a house, you have to know how big it will be, so that the foundation will be the right size. But to know how big the house will be, you have to know how many people will live in it, so that you can be sure that the house has enough room. This isn't to say that you can't add a new wing to the house if it needs more room — extensibility is important, too. The point is that a good design can save you an unbelievable amount of work.

Often people try to build a program without a careful design, and, like a house with no design, often the result doesn't do everything it should. Invariably, fixing the deficiency takes far longer than doing it right would have. Even worse, the deficiency is usually fixed without a plan as well, meaning the "fixed" program is likely to have new shortcomings and bugs. This becomes a vicious circle of introducing new bugs as fast as old bugs are fixed.

Why don't people get it right the first time? This question is a reasonable one. The answer invariably is that not enough effort was put into the early stages: specification, analysis, and design. Before designing, we always begin with a specification of the problem. But how can we tell when a specification has enough detail for a good design? We *analyze* the problem to see whether we have enough information to start devising a solution.

Of course, analysis is rarely perfect. We may think carefully and design our house with what we believe to be enough bathrooms, only to have a much larger family move in than we had expected. Suddenly, the house needs more bathrooms — not because our design was flawed. Instead, demands exceeded our expectations. A well-designed house would simplify the addition of new bathrooms, for example, by having sufficient plumbing. By analogy, a well-designed program is designed to be *extensible*.

Unfortunately, too, an analysis can sometimes be completely wrong. We may have to go back to the drawing boards and reanalyze our problem completely. This happens most often when we don't understand the problem quite as well as we think we do. Usually, the mistakes we made in the first analysis can help us get the second (or subsequent) analysis of the problem right.

Storyboards

One useful tool for analyzing problems that use a GUI is a *storyboard*. A simple storyboard for a cartoon is shown in Figure 8.1. Moviemakers and cartoonists use storyboards as visual summaries of movies or cartoons. A storyboard for a movie consists of one or more pictures for each scene, perhaps with text describing what is going on in each picture. A slow-moving scene, like a panoramic view of scenery, might need only a single picture to give an idea of the real scene in the movie. An action-packed scene, like a gunfight or a car chase, however, might need many pictures to convey enough information about what will happen in the real movie scene.

Figure 8.1

A sample storyboard for a cartoon

A storyboard for a program works in much the same way. We create a series of "screen shots," representing what the user sees at important points in the program. The big difference between this kind of storyboard and one for a cartoon is that computer programs are *interactive*. Unlike the cartoon you watch from start to finish, computer programs pause and ask for some kind of input to complete their tasks. Thus a storyboard needs to indicate where a user is expected to provide input. Typically, a computer storyboard contains a series of sample screen shots with annotations indicating what's happening in the picture and what the system does in different situations.

Let's create a storyboard for our paint program. Again, we won't worry about OOPas details at this point; we're just looking at the problem from the user's point of view. As we develop the storyboard, we will find out where we have to make decisions that are not in the problem specification.

You may be familiar with painting programs, but even programs you know are worth analyzing with fresh eyes. Let's consider, for example, what happens when the user paints a line and then a rectangle. In our earlier painting program, we decided to put the buttons on the right and the canvas on the left. The specification suggested that we have three groups of buttons: the line, rectangle, and pencil buttons to select painting tools; the color buttons to select colors; and the clear and quit buttons to perform particular actions.

We expect that one of the painting tool buttons is selected automatically when the program starts up. If none of the tools were selected, nothing would happen when the user clicked in the drawing area, because the program wouldn't know which painting tool to use. (It's important to note when you expect nothing to occur; computer scientists often refer to this kind of event as a *no-operation*, or *no-op* for short.) In general, though, the user will select a tool button, not the program. The fact that a tool button is selected when the program starts up is a *special case*, something to watch for when designing a program.

So, let's say the line button is selected. We don't want to worry about the special case of when the program starts, so we'll presume the user selected the line button. What should happen? The first action might be to select and click on the button — that is, to indicate that the line button is the one in use, so that the user knows that she is drawing lines (visually indicated with a cross next to that button). At this point, though, no lines appear in the drawing area. (See Figure 8.2.)

Figure 8.2

Storyboard frame: Clicking on the line button

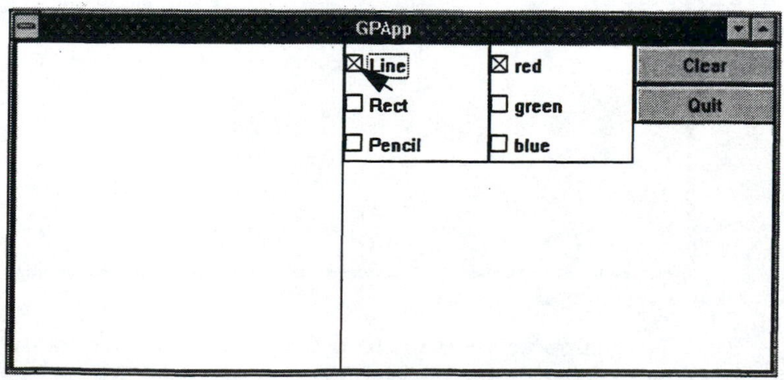

Now, we can use the conventions used in other paint programs. To draw a line, the user should click in the drawing area at the place where the first endpoint of the line should be.

Then, what happens? We can paint a line using a *rubberband* technique. Suppose you hold down one end of a rubberband with one hand, creating a fixed point. If you move the other end with your free hand, you define a line that can be stretched or contracted, depending on how you move that other end. In many painting programs, the movement of the mouse simulates the rubberband. If we hold the mouse button down after clicking on the initial endpoint, the application should draw a line following the mouse movements. Figure 8.3 shows that the user has moved the mouse toward the top and to the right from an initial point.

Figure 8.3

Storyboard frame: Creating the line using a rubberband

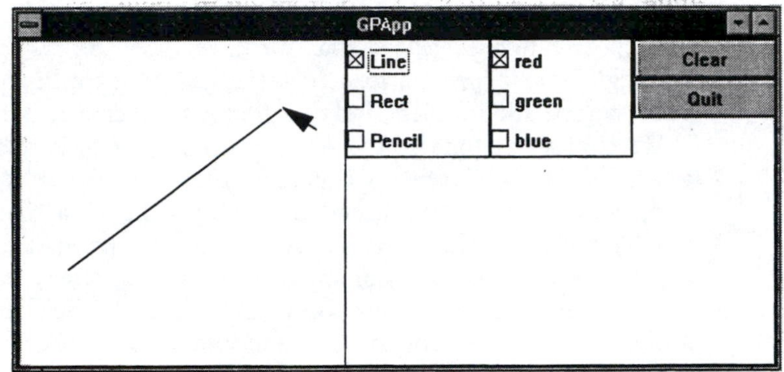

The line will move around as long as we keep the mouse button down; releasing it establishes the position of the second endpoint. Note that in Figure 8.4, we have moved the mouse somewhat from its position in Figure 8.3, but we no longer have any trace of that older position.

Figure 8.4

Storyboard frame: Completing the line

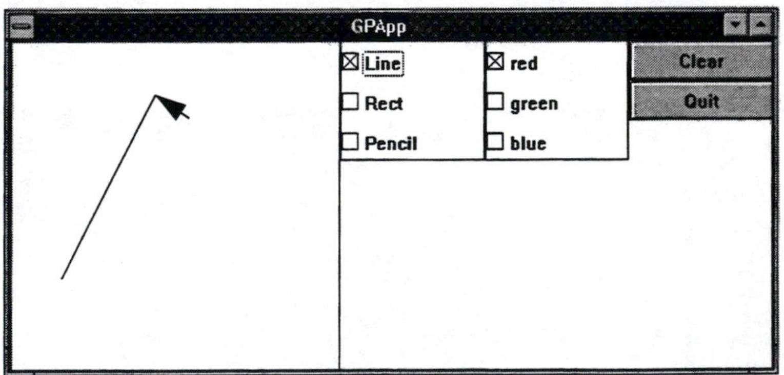

Now suppose we want to draw a rectangle. We follow the same process. First the user should click on the button, then click on one corner of the rectangle. Let's again use the rubberband technique for drawing the rectangle; as the user holds the mouse button down, the rectangle grows, extending from the first point to the point indicated by the mouse's current position. Suppose, while the user has the mouse button down, it overlaps the line as shown in Figure 8.5.

Figure 8.5

Storyboard frame: Using rubberbanding to draw a rectangle

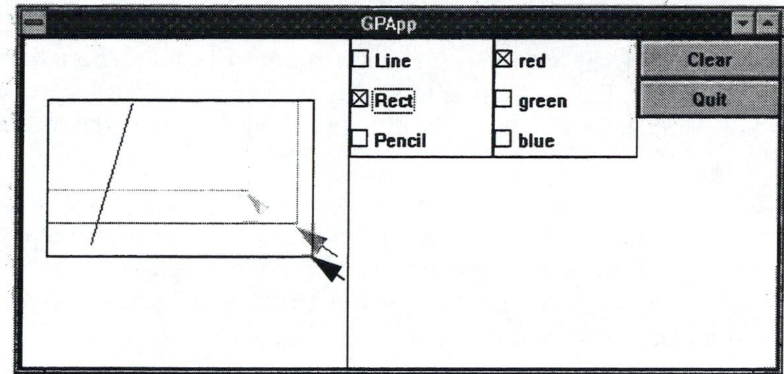

As we move the rectangle around, its old position disappears and its new position is drawn. Imagine, though, that the user moved the mouse to overlap the line already in the drawing area. The line should remain intact, no matter where the rectangle goes. How will we make this happen? We don't have to figure that out right now — at this point, we just have to know that as we rubberband a shape, the existing shapes in the drawing area should not be affected.

Finally, if the user selects the pencil tool, we can use the `PencilInteractor` defined in Chapter 6 to draw a line that traces the mouse's movements.

Domain Analysis

We can develop the storyboard further for the other actions that the user might take, analyzing the *domain* of the program. This process is sometimes known as *domain analysis* — analyzing the program from the perspective of people who might use it. For a paint program, the domain is pretty general: Any user of a computer should be able to use this application. However, if we are developing a program for musicians that draws different notes and rests on a staff, we would probably want to think about how musicians compose music and what kinds of notations are necessary. The key to user-centered design is to know your user. As you develop your storyboard, keep your audience in mind — the user may be an expert in some subject domain but a novice when it comes to computers. Your analysis of the problem should take into account the domain *and* the user's expected computing skills.

Let's consider what happens when the user clicks on any of the other buttons. We can make the following observations:

- The user should be able to use a familiar way of choosing colors, such as the color column used in Chapter 7.
- The user should be able to switch freely between the line tool, the rectangle tool, and the pencil tool using radio buttons to ensure that only one mode is active at a time.
- In the interest of extensibility, we should be able to add more tools later that can be used in a similar way — although today's user might be satisfied with this simple paint program, tomorrow's user might need more capabilities. Extensibility entails simplifying the future addition of tool buttons and interactors. In particular, we'd like to use the pencil interactor from Chapter 6.
- When the user clicks on the clear button, all the painting in the canvas should simply disappear. For now, to keep things really simple, we won't ask the user to confirm whether she wants to clear the canvas, though asking for a confirmation is a "user-friendly" practice and makes the program more pleasant to use.
- When the user clicks on the quit button, the program should just stop. Again, to keep things simple, we won't ask for a confirmation.
- If the user draws a shape and releases the button outside the canvas, the shape should be cut off at the border of the canvas (see Figure 8.6).

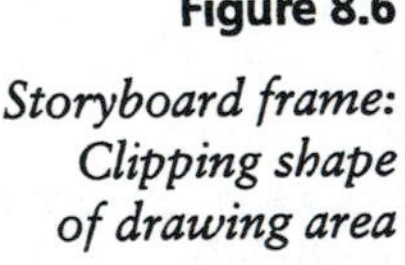

Figure 8.6

Storyboard frame: Clipping shape of drawing area

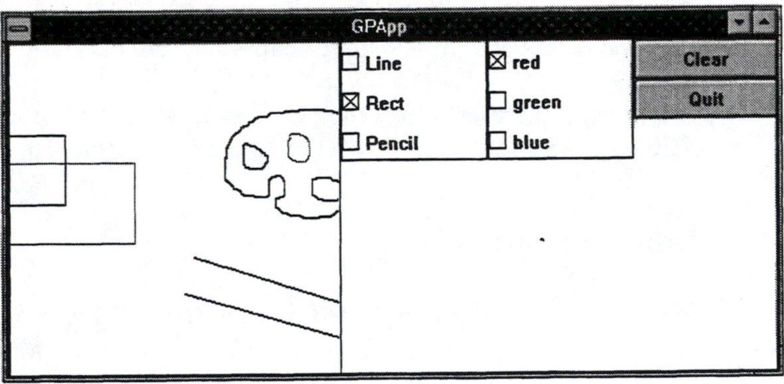

These are all answers to the question, "What else do we know about the program?" The storyboard thus helps us to think about the program's specification. Drawing a storyboard and then trying to write down what we learn from it about the application from the storyboard helps us take into account what the user has said about the program in the specification and what we think needs to happen.

Our analysis has given us a greater understanding of the system, enabling this more detailed specification:

This application is a simple paint program. The user can use the mouse to paint various shapes in a canvas, including scribbly lines, straight lines, and rectangles. A set of mutually exclusive buttons controls what kind of shape the mouse paints, that is, what mode the program is in. Another set of mutually exclusive buttons lets the user select a color in which to paint. Two more buttons let the user clear the canvas and end the program.

The canvas is to the left and the various buttons are arranged in columns to the right. One column contains three buttons that set a painting mode:

- *When choosing the line button, the user can create a line on the canvas using a rubberband technique: She holds the mouse button down and "stretches out" the line.*
- *When choosing the rectangle button, the user can create a rectangle in the canvas using a rubberband technique.*
- *When choosing the pencil button, the user can paint a line in the canvas, as if a pencil were following the mouse.*

A color column, containing a set of color buttons, lets the user choose the single color in which the currently selected tool will paint.

The other column contains two buttons that perform actions:

- *When the user chooses the clear button, the drawing area will be cleared.*
- *When the user chooses the quit button, the application will end.*

Our more detailed specification leaves us much better prepared to design our system.

8.4 DESIGNING THE CLASSES

Our analysis has given us a significantly more detailed specification of our program. At this time, we're ready to begin the next phase of developing a program: designing it.

The initial phase of the design process will consist of three steps. The first step is identifying possible classes; second is describing the classes's purposes; and the third step is identifying and describing the relationships among the classes. Having done that, we'll be ready to move on and begin writing pseudocode for the classes' methods.

Picking Out Possible Classes

We begin designing by looking at the specification, using its nouns to provide us with a list of potential classes. Picking out the nouns in the preceding specification gives us this list:

application	set of buttons	rectangle
paint program	color	pencil button
user	columns	pencil
mouse	column to set mode	color column
shapes	painting mode	color button
canvas	line button	other column
scribbly lines	line	actions
straight lines	rubberband technique	clear button
rectangles	rectangle button	quit button

We know that we can eliminate some of these nouns. Clearly, *application* and *paint program* refer to the same thing. *User* and *mouse* are things with which the application will interact, but are not part of the application itself. *Buttons* is redundant, since we have already listed all the individual kinds of buttons. All the different shapes appear twice as well. Finally, *actions* refers to something the user does, not something the application needs to worry about.

The list of nouns, remember, is just the starting point. Indeed, some object-oriented programmers believe the list of nouns can be misleading, since specifications are rarely written carefully enough to take into account all possible classes. For example, we know from Chapter 7 that there are different types of columns: A radio column is used to contain buttons that set modes, whereas an ordinary column is used to contain buttons that perform one-shot actions. Thus we don't really want to represent *painting mode* as a class; rather, the phrase "one column contains three buttons that set a painting mode" can be represented by a subclass of `GPRadioColumn`.

In addition, although we might feel that some nouns don't make good classes in this situation, in other situations the same nouns might make excellent classes. For example, if we had an undo button that could undo the last user action, making *actions* correspond to a class would work quite well. In fact, later in the book, we will make an undo button and will use class `Action` to do it.

We also have a notion of a currently selected tool or painting mode. However, we already know that a `GPDrawingArea` has an association with an interactor in order to send messages to it. Thus the canvas links to our currently selected interactor, since that is the interactor the user will draw with.

Our notion of a currently selected painting color is handled similarly. The drawing area has a link to a single style, which contains information on the color to paint in. Selecting different buttons tells the drawing style to use different colors.

Our list of classes then reduces to the following:

application	rubberband technique	color button
shapes	rectangle button	other column
canvas	rectangle	clear button
column to set mode	pencil button	quit button
line button	pencil	
line	color column	

Using Predefined Classes

The next step in our analysis is to find out what work has already been done. We can consider which classes we need to define and which are already defined for us in a library (or unit). Reusing objects that have already been defined can save us a great deal of work.

Libraries are a crucial element of object-oriented programming. Cognitive scientists have studied how experts in various fields solve problems. By and large, they look at a problem and ask themselves, "What problem does this resemble?" Consciously or not, experts think about the repertoire of problems they have solved in the past; they try to find approaches and strategies that have been successful in the past and might be appropriate for the current problem. Programming libraries represent the expertise of others. GP, in particular, allows us to build programs using graphic classes that have already been created. From our list of nouns, the GP documentation, and the classes we implemented in units in Chapter 7, we can extract a list of predefined classes we can use to implement the nouns from our description:

This noun	is implemented by this class
line	`GPLine`
rectangle	`GPFramedRect`
canvas	`GPDrawingArea`
color button	`CSColorButton`
color column	`CSColorColumn`
pencil	`PPencilInteractor`
action column	`ACActionColumn`
clear button	`ACClearButton`
quit button	`ACQuitButton`

Note that we're using one new class: `GPFramedRect`. This class is a subclass of `GPShape`, just like `GPLine`. It draws a hollow rectangle, whereas `GPFilledRect` draws a filled rectangle (a solid rectangle drawn in the current color). You can send the `Draw` message to instances of `GPFramedRect`, just as you can to `GPLine`. `Draw` is a virtual method provided by `GPShape`, so `GPLine.Draw` draws lines and `GPFramedRect.Draw` draws rectangles.

Often when we look for predefined classes, we also determine that we need additional behaviors to fulfill the specification. This is where we have to create our own subclasses from the original classes. For example, we know that `GPColumn` is an abstract class; we want to create our own subclass for our own column because we want it to include our particular buttons. Similarly, we know that we will want to create our own specialized subclass of `GPApplication`. We thus can handle some more nouns on our list:

This noun will be a class	subclassed from this class
application	`GPApplication`
column to set mode	`GPColumn`

We also have to decide which GP class might be most appropriate when there are a variety of very similar classes in GP. Consider, for example, the use of buttons in this program. Although GP has no predefined class for "Line button," we know it has classes for toggle buttons and push buttons. We know, then, that the button classes in our list will be subclasses of one of the existing GP classes — but are they subclasses of `GPToggleButton` or `GPPushButton`? As we saw in Section 7.3, toggle buttons are used to set a mode and push buttons are used to perform a one-shot action. Since we want to set modes with the shape buttons (that is, only one of the line, rectangle, and pencil buttons should be active at any time), the *line button, rectangle button,* and *pencil button* should be subclasses of `GPToggleButton`:

This noun will be a class	subclassed from this class
line button	`GPToggleButton`
rectangle button	`GPToggleButton`
pencil button	`GPToggleButton`

There is one noun left on our list: *rubberband technique*. The rubberband technique will provide the stretchable lines that can be drawn over the picture without erasing what is already there. To implement the rubberband technique, we use another subclass of `GPShape` called `GPRubberShape` (shown in detail in Class Box 8.1). This class, in turn, has three subclasses, as shown in Figure 8.7.

An instance of a rubber shape class is drawn with the rubberband technique we saw in the storyboard in Figures 8.2 through 8.6. In fact, `GPRubberShape` is a subclass of `GPShape`: Whereas a `GPShape` is a generic kind of shape, a `GPRubberShape` is a `GPShape` that is drawn using a rubberband technique.

The rubber shape classes thus have three methods that "stretch" the rubberband. The `StartDraw` method begins the drawing of a shape — essentially, it holds down one end of the rubberband at the point chosen by the user. The "regular" `Draw` method (inherited and redefined from `GPShape`) executes while the rubberband is being stretched; it erases the shape from its previous position and redraws it from the original point to the current position. The `FinishDraw` method is used when the rubberband is "released," that is, when the user releases the mouse button after stretching out the shape. Thus we'll use instances of subclasses of `GPRubberShape` instead of subclasses of `GPShape` like `GPLine` and `GPFramedRect`.

However, we found in Chapter 6 that `GPLine` was not enough to translate a user's mouse movements into a line: We needed a `PencilInteractor` class as well to translate the user's actions into messages to a shape. Similarly, we'll need to associate our drawing area with an interactor that knows what messages to send to rubber shapes. Notice that one class of interactor can potentially draw any kind of `GPRubberShape` by using a link. As Class Box 8.1 shows, `GPRubberShape` defines all the methods needed to draw any kind of rubber shape. Thus by using an association to a `GPRubberShape`, multiple instances of one class of interactor can rubberband any kind of `GPRubberShape` by linking each instance to a different kind of `GPRubberShape`, exploit-

Class Box 8.1

GPRubberShape

GPRubberShape

= OBJECT (GPShape)

This class represents a shape drawn using the rubberband technique. The shape can be drawn, then its position changed, and the shape drawn in a new place. The old drawing of the shape is erased without disturbing the rest of the drawing area.

Methods:

`Init;`

Establish the initial state of the shape. Its start and end points are both the origin.

`SetTopLeft(startPt : GPPoint);`

Tell the shape to use the passed point as its top left point.

`SetBottomRight(endPt : GPPoint);`

Tell the shape to use the passed point as its bottom right point.

`StartDraw(daLink : GPDrawingAreaAsn);`

The first time the shape is drawn in a particular draw and erase sequence, use this method. This method does not erase the previously drawn shape.

`Draw(daLink : GPDrawingAreaAsn);`

Draw the shape in the passed drawing area. The shape goes from its start point to its end point. The shape drawn by the previous call to `Draw` is erased.

`FinishDraw(daLink : GPDrawingAreaAsn);`

The last time a shape is drawn in a particular draw and erase sequence, use this method. This method draws the final shape so that it is not erased.

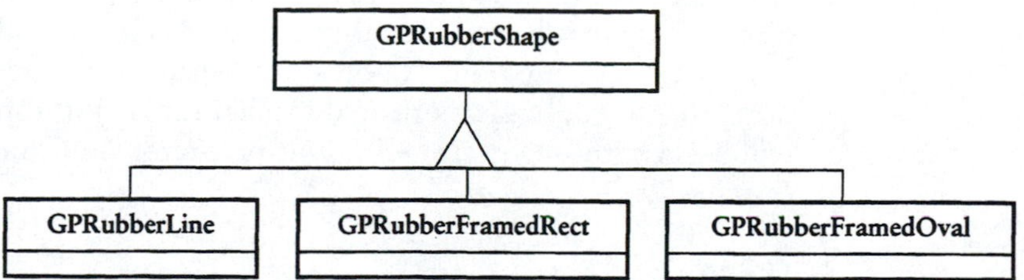

Figure 8.7

Rubber shape hierarchy

ing polymorphism. Thus each tool button will correspond to a different instance, but some of these instances may be instances of the same class. Now we can give this class a name; we'll call it a "rubberband interactor" and make it a subclass of `GPMouseInteractor`.

In Chapter 6, we provided the drawing area with a link to the pencil interactor using the method `AddInteractor`. This was done just once as part of the constructor for the application. In this program, however, we have multiple interactors, so which ones we use in the drawing area will depend on which mode the user has set: Is the mouse painting lines, rectangles, or squiggly lines? This is where the three tool button classes come in. When the user clicks on a tool button, the tool button will provide the drawing area with a link to an interactor, while the program is running. This is similar to the way the color buttons worked in Chapter 7. Whenever the user clicked on a color button, that button gave its color to the drawing area.

There is a difference though. Although it always has only one color to draw in, a drawing area can have any number of interactors. Thus we'll need to use `GPToggleButton`'s `DeActivate` method. When one button is clicked on, the button corresponding to the previous mode will have its `DeActivate` method called. While `Activate` calls `AddInteractor`, `DeActivate` calls `RemoveInteractor`, ensuring that only one interactor will be used at any one time.

It's not unusual for most (or in this case, all) classes to be related to one of the predefined classes. In fact, that is part of the point of GP — to define the skeleton of programs that use a graphical user interface, so that programmers can use the classes or create subclasses to flesh out the details of a particular application and let GP do most of the work of implementing the GUI. The GUI is often the biggest and most complex part of modern applications, so getting help from a library like GP can be a big advantage. Of course, libraries help build all kinds of software, not just graphical software, so using a library can help no matter what you are trying to build. Thus when creating your own programs, it is worthwhile to study how your classes might fit in with existing ones.

Establishing the Purposes of the Classes

The next step is to name and define each of the classes we need to develop. Often the best place to start is to define the purpose of each class. Of course, we don't have to define the predefined classes. In this case, we are designing classes that are subclasses of other classes, as already indicated.

Let's call our program "CoolPaint," since we're building a paint program using lots of cool object-oriented mechanisms. Our application's classes thus will begin with the letters "CP." Our program will define one class, the application:

CPApp
This is the main window of the program. All the actions and painting occur here.

The rest of the classes will be defined in units. In particular, the various drawing tools will be added to the `Paint` unit from Chapter 7. Therefore, we can use these same paint tools in another program, employing the `USES` statement to access the class definitions. Since they are in the `Paint` unit, the class names all start with "P."

The first class we'll describe is the column containing the buttons for setting the painting mode. We need a short, descriptive name, though. In paint programs, each possible mode is often called a "tool," so setting the line-painting mode would be called "selecting the line tool." Thus we can think of our column of mode-setting buttons as a column of tool buttons, or, in other words, a tool column:

PToolColumn
This column is the set of buttons that sets the drawing mode for the drawing area.

Now, of course, we need the buttons themselves, as well as the interactor they will use.

PLineButton, PRectButton, PPencilButton
These buttons let the user set a painting mode. Each button corresponds to a different mode. The line button corresponds to a mode in which the mouse is used to create lines, the rectangle button to a mode for creating rectangles, and the pencil button to a mode for creating scribbly lines.

When activated, each button provides the drawing area with a link to a corresponding interactor. When deactivated, each button asks the drawing area to stop sending messages to that interactor.

PRubberbandInteractor
This type of interactor responds to the user's mouse input to rubberband lines or rectangles.

At this point we should be thinking of the classes as independent entities. The purpose of each class should be unique (although, of course, there are likely to be relationships among classes). If you find that two of your classes have the same purpose, you may want to think about the relationship among those classes — might one be a subclass of the other? contain the other? be associated with the other? Or might it make sense to create two instances of the same class?

The purpose of each class should also be complete. When possible, try to use language from the original specification. Ideally, you should be able to hand a class description to another programmer and have the class she writes work in your system. At the very least, another programmer ought to be able to understand from your class purposes what the class is supposed to do. Don't fall into the temptation of saying, "Well, *I* know what this class is supposed to do, so I don't have to write it down." Even the simplest programs can have a dozen classes, and keeping them straight with clear purpose statements will be a great help in implementing and debugging your program.

Establishing Relationships

With the purposes established, we can think about the relationships, instance variables, and methods of the classes. When you reach this point in developing your own programs, you can take one of two approaches: You may want to either think about the relationships *among* a set of classes or think about the details *within* a single class.[1] Either approach is valid, and in developing any program you may go back and forth between the relationships and the internals of a class.

In this case, let's start with the relationships among the classes. We have seen three kinds of relationships: inheritance, containment, and association. We already saw the inheritance relationships when we worked on our lists of nouns at the beginning of this section. We chose various GP classes as ones from which to subclass.

Now, let's consider associations among the objects. We ask ourselves the question, "Where does an instance of one class have a relationship with another?" Let's think about what the toggle buttons in our program need to do. When the user chooses the line button, the program should let the user draw a line in the drawing area. (This is clear from the purpose statements we wrote earlier.) Thus the buttons on the tool column — and for the same reason, the clear button — should be associated with the drawing area, as in Chapter 6.

Additionally, we see from our storyboard that when the user clicks on the line button, the mouse in the drawing area should use a rubberband technique to draw a line. This means that the line button (as well as the two other tool buttons) needs to provide the drawing with a link to an interactor from the button's method `Activate` using the drawing area's method `AddInteractor`. The tool button previously set will use its `DeActivate` method to tell the drawing area to stop using the previous interactor by using the drawing area's `RemoveInteractor` method. Thus the line, rectangle, pencil, and clear buttons should be associated with the drawing area in order to send the drawing area messages about interactors. This link will be an instance variable we'll call `targetLink`.

Recall that the rubberband interactor has a link to a rubber shape when it is constructed to make use of polymorphism. The object that constructs that interactor will have to provide the link to the shape. But what should contain (and thus construct) the interactor?

In Chapter 6, the application contained the pencil interactor and gave that interactor to the drawing area. However, in that program, the drawing area didn't switch between multiple interactors. Since the buttons will be telling the drawing area to use one of many interactors, each button should contain the interactor it gives to the drawing area.

Since a button contains an interactor, it will need to construct it. This means that the button needs access to the rubber shape as well, and the simplest way

1. This can be viewed as a choice between a *breadth-first* design, where we get a sense of many classes before designing any completely, and a *depth-first* design, where we concentrate on one at a time.

to provide this access is for the button to contain the shape. Figure 8.8 shows these relationships among classes. Both the line button and the rectangle button contain a rubberband interactor and a rubber shape. Note that the pencil button doesn't need an instance of `GPLine` — the `GPPencilInteractor` already contains a line.

Figure 8.8

Associations between buttons and other classes

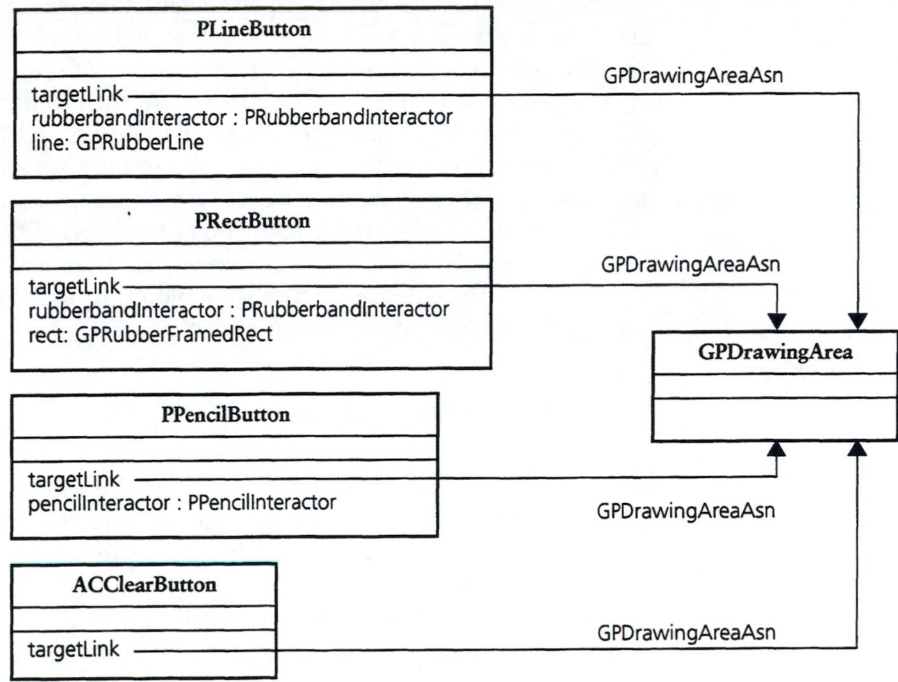

8.5 DO WHAT YOU'RE TOLD: EVENT-DRIVEN PROGRAMMING

At this point, we've done a fair amount of breadth-first design toward meeting our original specification, having applied our analysis to help make decisions in the design process. We're pretty clear about where we're going, having identified the classes we're planning to instantiate.

Let's continue with some depth-first design by looking at one class in detail, `PRubberbandInteractor`. We implemented a single interactor in Chapter 6. However, our current program will use two different classes of interactors — `PPencilInteractor` and `PRubberbandInteractor` — and will use three different instances, one of the pencil interactor and two of the rubberband interactor (one instance for each mode).

Thus we will have several instances of interactors in this program. Each tool button will use `AddInteractor` and `RemoveInteractor` to tell the drawing area to which interactor and at what time it should send messages. Thus two distinct operations are occurring: a button telling the drawing area what interactor to use and the drawing area telling an interactor what actions the user performed. We're going to begin with the second operation, examining the interactors themselves, leaving the buttons and their workings until Section 8.6.

Notice that all the buttons, all the interactors, and the drawing area do something in response to the user's actions. GP uses a concept called *event-driven programming* wherein objects don't do anything until told to. Objects respond to events. In our case, events include such things as the user clicking on a button or moving the mouse in the drawing area. However, the concept of event-driven programming is not limited to user interface programming. In the real world, when something happens, something else takes some action. If a fire alarm sounds (something happening, an event), a fire truck will respond (an object responds to that event). If we wished to model such a situation, the fire alarm could produce events corresponding to sounding an alarm. A fire truck object would respond to that event.

Control-Flow Diagrams

For a better understanding of `PRubberbandInteractor`, let's take a closer look at how the objects communicate with one another. In particular, which object is in control of which other objects? How does this control change over time? This is often called the *flow of control*. Let's look at what happens when the drawing area responds to a user's actions, as seen in the flow-of-control diagram in Figure 8.9. The drawing area sends messages (received from the method `Run`) to the interactor whenever the user clicks and moves the mouse within the drawing area.

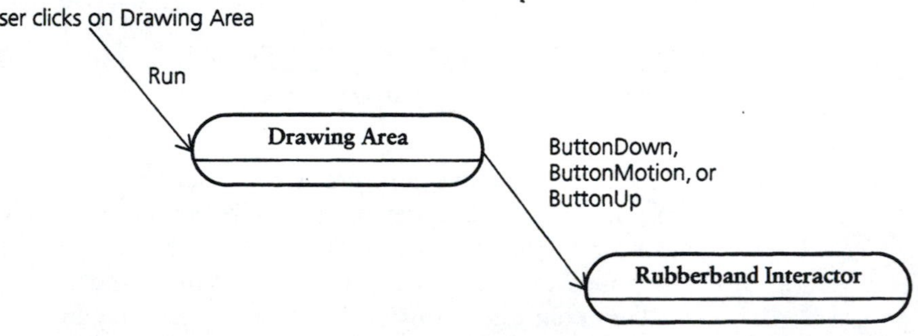

Figure 8.9 *The drawing area controlling the current interactor*

Arrows between instances show messages sent between instances; the messages names appear beside the arrows. Notice that the arrowheads are open-ended, to distinguish them from the solid arrows used for links and associations. (Note that since flow-of-control diagrams describe when and where messages are sent, anything connected by arrows in such a diagram must also be associated and/or contained in a class diagram.)

Let's fill in the details of this flow-of-control diagram. When the user clicks the mouse button, the `Run` method of our application determines which GUI component contained the mouse click. If the mouse was clicked in the drawing area, `Run` sends a message to the drawing area. The drawing area responds by sending a message to its current interactor. (The drawing area previously became linked to an interactor by an `AddInteractor` method, which we will see in a moment.) In Figure 8.9, our interactor is an instance of the class we are going to define as `PRubberbandInteractor`.

How did the drawing area become linked to a particular interactor in the first place? When the user clicked on a tool button, that button gave the drawing area a link to an interactor using the `AddInteractor` message. We can draw a flow-of-control diagram for this situation as well (shown in Figure 8.10). In this case, the user clicked on the line button (as determined by the method `Run`), which then sent the message `AddInteractor` to the drawing area, passing a link to an interactor suitable for rubberbanding lines.

Figure 8.10

Flow of control when clicking on the line button

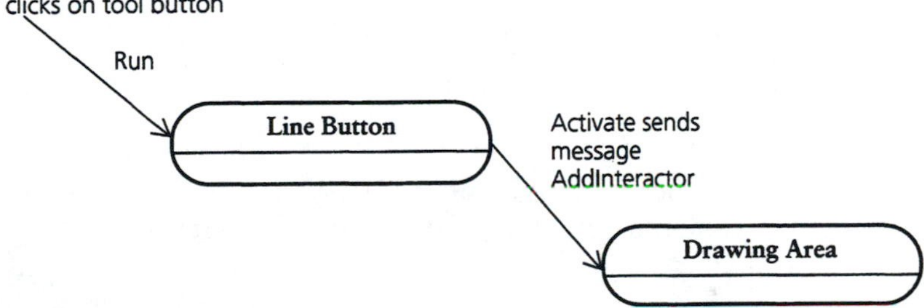

The interactor contains the methods that actually respond to the mouse actions, and these methods, in turn, tell a rubber shape how to move around. Figure 8.11 expands Figure 8.9 with this additional detail. Note that this figure includes some containment because the line button contains both a `PRubberbandInteractor` and a `GPRubberLine`.

At this time, `Run` probably seems like a good deal of mysterious magic. Rest assured, in the coming chapters you'll learn more than enough to understand how the `Run` method works. For the moment, you just should be aware that you're using event-driven programming and that the `Run` method is smart enough to figure out what method to call when an event occurs.

Designing the Methods

So, knowing that the `Run` method will call the right virtual methods, let's build the virtual methods we want it to call. The superclass `GPMouseInteractor`, which we will specialize to define `PRubberbandInteractor`, has three virtual methods that handle mouse events, as we saw in Chapter 6: `ButtonDown` is

Figure 8.11

Messages being sent to the correct user interface object

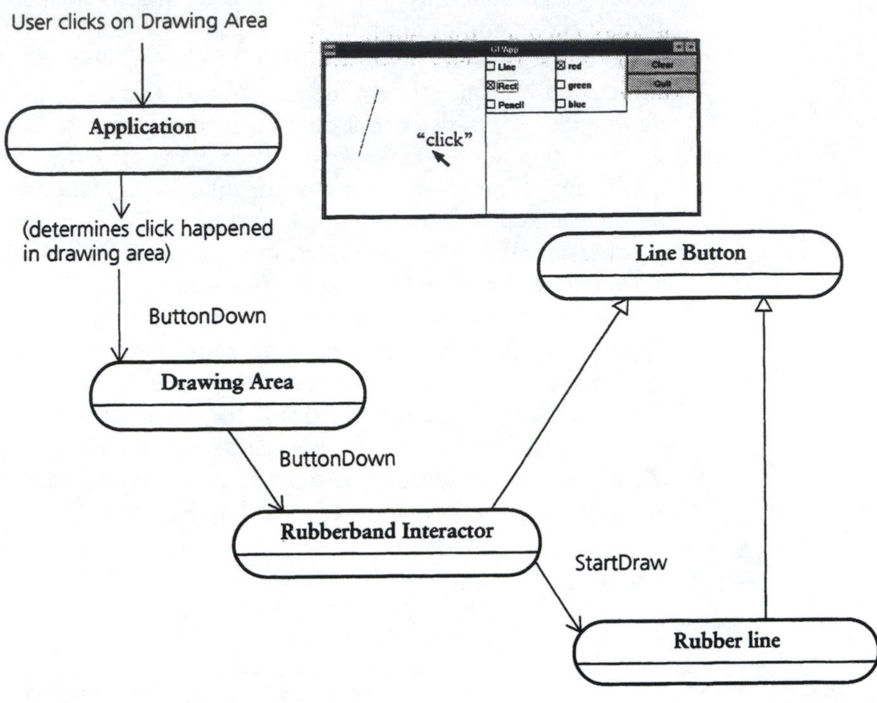

called when the mouse button is pressed, `ButtonMotion` is called while the mouse is moving, and `ButtonUp` is called when the mouse is released.

Note, however, that the `ButtonDown`, `ButtonMotion`, and `ButtonUp` methods are only the first stage of the response to the input events detected in the drawing area. You can see this in Figure 8.11 by noting that these methods send messages themselves, messages that are thus also part of the response to the initial event.

We also know we need an `Init` method for `PRubberbandInteractor`. Now we can make a list of methods for the class, along with their purposes (which, incidentally, can later be used in the block comments of the code).

Class: PRubberbandInteractor
Inherits from: GPMouseInteractor

Instance Variables:
To be filled in

Methods:
Init(targetLink : GPDrawingAreaAsn; newShapeLink : GPRubberShapeAsn);
This method initializes the interactor.

ButtonDown(startPt: GPPoint); VIRTUAL;
This method sends messages to the rubber shape to establish the top left and initial bottom right points of the shape and draw itself.

ButtonMotion(currentPt: GPPoint); VIRTUAL;
This method sends messages to the rubber shape as motion is detected in the drawing area. It sends messages to the rubber shape to change the bottom right point of the shape and to draw itself.

ButtonUp(endPt: GPPoint); VIRTUAL;
This method sends messages to the rubber shape to complete the shape. It sends messages to change the bottom right point and to draw itself.

With these purposes in mind, let's develop the more detailed pseudocode for the individual methods. For each method, we ask ourselves, "How will an instance of this class perform this behavior?"

Designing the Instance Variables

Let's figure out what instance variables our rubberband interactor needs. To be able to rubberband different kinds of shapes, we said in the last section, each button should contain a different instance of the `PRubberbandInteractor`, each handling a different kind of shape. Clearly, the interactor will need access to the shape. Since the interactor needs to handle any kind of rubber shape, we need to use a link to `GPRubberShape`, rather than containing an instance as an instance variable. We'll also need to know which drawing area will be the target of the rubberband interactor, because the interactor will expect to draw the shape in a drawing area.

Where will the link to the shape come from? In general, from whatever object sends a message to construct the interactor. We know, in this case, that the rubber shapes are contained within the buttons. Since the link thus comes from outside the class, it needs to be sent as a parameter. Now we ask, "Will this link be needed by other methods?" As we take a quick look at the purposes of the three methods that respond to the user's actions, we see that they all need to send messages to the rubber shape. Thus the link needs to be an instance variable.

We don't know what kind of shape we will receive; since `Init` may be sent a rectangle or a line or another rubber shape, we will declare the formal parameter to receive a link to an instance of the superclass `GPRubberShape`. (Polymorphism, as discussed in Chapter 6, makes this possible.)

Pseudocoding

We now have some idea of what the class `PRubberbandInteractor` needs by way of methods and instance variables, so we can start to write the pseudocode for the class. Let's begin with the class's instance variables:

Class: PRubberbandInteractor

Instance Variables:

```
targetLink  : GPDrawingAreaAsn    { where to draw }
shapeLink   : GPRubberShapeAsn;   { shape to rubberband }
```

Now we have actual names for the instance variables to use in the pseudocode for the individual methods. The first method to pseudocode is often the constructor, because it is so crucial to establishing what the object is. So here's our pseudocode for the constructor:

PRubberbandInteractor.Init(newTargetLink: GPDrawingAreaAsn;
newShapeLink: GPShapeAsn);

This method initializes this interactor, establishing its links

Pseudocode:

Send inherited Init message
Store newTargetLink in instance variable targetLink
Store newShapeLink in instance variable shapeLink

Let's move on to the `ButtonDown`, `ButtonMotion`, and `ButtonUp` methods. We know from the interface of `GPMouseInteractor` (see Class Box 6.5) that each of these inherited methods will receive the next point as a parameter of type `GPPoint`.

As we saw in the storyboard, when we rubberband a shape, we want to draw a temporary shape from the initial point to a current point; if the user moves the mouse, that old shape should disappear and a new shape should be drawn from the initial point to the new current point. We saw in Class Box 8.1 that `GPRubberShape` uses three methods to draw a rubber shape: `StartDraw`, `Draw`, and `FinishDraw`. These methods will be useful as we develop the `ButtonDown`, `ButtonMotion`, and `ButtonUp` methods of the rubberband interactor.

We also know that each of the methods that draw the shape interactively will receive a point as a parameter, since this parameter is listed in the class box for `GPMouseInteractor`. The `ButtonDown` method should fix that initial point. We'll make that point one endpoint of the shape; we know from our class descriptions that `GPRubberShape` has a method to store the first point of a shape, so we'll call the method `SetTopLeft`. We also know that we want to show the initial position, sending the `StartDraw` message to the shape pointed to by `shapeLink`. To send that message, though, we need to establish both endpoints of the shape. Thus we need to set both the top left and bottom right points of the shape, using the point received as a parameter.

ButtonDown (startPt: GPPoint);

Begins the drawing of a shape

Pseudocode:

Send SetTopLeft message to shapeLink's instance with startPt as a parameter
Send SetBottomRight message to shapeLink's instance with startPt as a parameter
Send StartDraw message to shapeLink's instance

Now, the `ButtonMotion` method also should receive a point — specifically, the point that the user currently is indicating. What we want to do is draw a shape from the initial point to the current point and erase the old shape from the screen. The `Draw` method of the rubber shape classes will take care of the erasing and drawing for us. All we need to do is establish the second endpoint of the shape. This can be expressed in pseudocode as follows:

ButtonMotion(movePt: GPPoint);
 Draws the shape as it is stretched
Pseudocode:
 Send SetBottomRight message to shapeLink's instance with movePt as a parameter
 Send Draw message to shapeLink's instance

Finally, we come to the `ButtonUp` method. In this case, when the user releases the button, the current point becomes the second endpoint of the line, and the final line should be drawn. This means that the `ButtonUp` pseudocode is quite similar to the `ButtonMotion` pseudocode:

ButtonUp(endPt : GPPoint);
 Completes the drawing of a shape
Pseudocode:
 Send SetBottomRight message to shapeLink's instance with endPt as a parameter
 Send FinishDraw message to shapeLink's instance

We're now done with the `PRubberbandInteractor` class. The pseudocode is detailed enough that it's easy to write down the code:

```
PRubberbandInteractor = OBJECT (GPMouseInteractor)
  CONSTRUCTOR     Init(
        newTargetLink    : GPDrawingAreaAsn;
        newShapeLink     : PRubberShapeAsn);
  PROCEDURE       ButtonDown (startPt : GPPoint); VIRTUAL;
  PROCEDURE       ButtonMotion (movePt : GPPoint); VIRTUAL;
  PROCEDURE       ButtonUp   (endPt : GPPoint); VIRTUAL;
PRIVATE
  targetLink      : GPDrawingAreaAsn;
  shapeLink       : GPRubberShapeAsn;
END;

CONSTRUCTOR PRubberbandInteractor.Init (
        newTargetLink    : GPDrawingAreaAsn;
        newShapeLink     : GPRubberShapeAsn);
BEGIN
  INHERITED Init;
  targetLink := newTargetLink;
  shapeLink := newShapeLink
END;
```

```
PROCEDURE PRubberbandInteractor.ButtonDown (startPt : GPPoint);
BEGIN
  shapeLink^.SetTopLeft(startPt);
  shapeLink^.SetBottomRight(startPt);
  shapeLink^.StartDraw(targetLink);
END;

PROCEDURE PRubberbandInteractor.ButtonMotion (movePt : GPPoint);
BEGIN
  shapeLink^.SetBottomRight(movePt);
  shapeLink^.Draw(targetLink);
END;

PROCEDURE PRubberbandInteractor.ButtonUp (endPt : GPPoint);
BEGIN
  shapeLink^.SetBottomRight(endPt);
  shapeLink^.FinishDraw(targetLink); { Draw new shape. }
END;
```

8.6 HOW THE OBJECTS WORK TOGETHER: A SYSTEM

Let's look at how some of our classes work together before we continue with the implementation of our program. When we built our pencil tool in Chapter 6, the application's constructor sent the drawing area the message `AddInteractor`, telling it to use the pencil interactor to respond to user input. This means that a drawing area is associated with an interactor. But in that program, there was only one interactor. We're still going to use `AddInteractor`, but it will be sent from a button's `Activate` message, thus dynamically changing the drawing area's link to an interactor. Adding this dynamically changing link to our class diagram from Figure 8.8, we can see the changing link in Figure 8.12.

At this point, we have a preliminary design for the buttons: Each one contains an instance of an interactor, and each one uses `AddInteractor` when sent the message `Activate`, and `RemoveInteractor` when sent the message `DeActivate`. We can pseudocode the line button as follows:

PLineButton
targetLink: GPDrawingAreaAsn
myInteractor: PRubberbandInteractor;
myLine : GPRubberLine

PLineButton.Activate
    targetLink^.AddInteractor(@myInteractor)

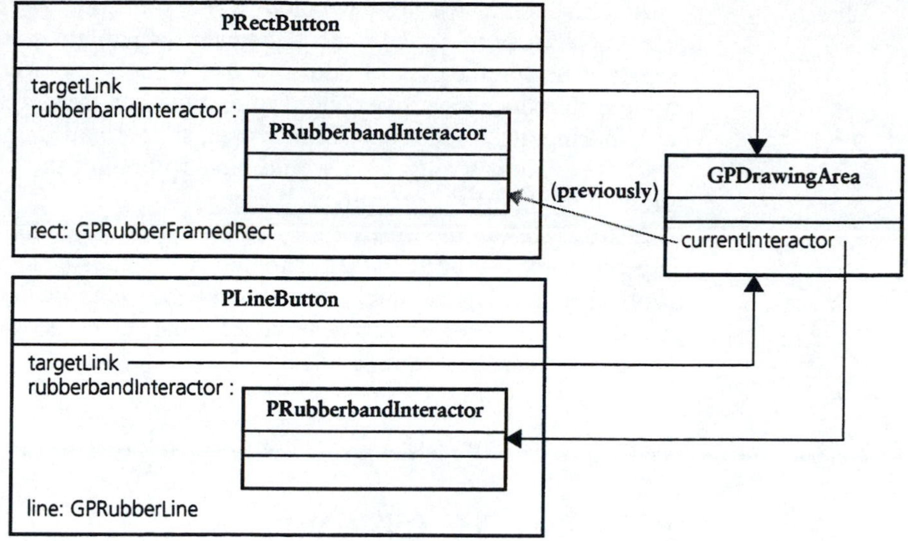

Figure 8.12 *Chained associations*

```
PLineButton.DeActivate
    targetLink^.RemoveInteractor(@myInteractor)
```

The rectangle button is similar:

```
PRectButton
targetLink: GPDrawingAreaAsn
myInteractor: PRubberbandInteractor;
myRect : GPRubberFramedRect

PLineButton.Activate
    targetLink^.AddInteractor(@myInteractor)

PLineButton.DeActivate
    targetLink^.RemoveInteractor(@myInteractor)
```

Finally, the pencil button is also quite similar:

```
PPencilButton
targetLink: GPDrawingAreaAsn
myInteractor: PPencilInteractor;

PLineButton.Activate
    targetLink^.AddInteractor(@myInteractor)

PLineButton.DeActivate
    targetLink^.RemoveInteractor(@myInteractor)
```

At this point, we simply could write the code — our pseudocode is extremely close to actual code. However, you might notice a good deal of repetitiveness in the pseudocode. One of the goals of object-oriented programming is to reduce repetitive code. Typing the same thing again and again is not only boring, it's error prone. Even worse, suppose all the times you wrote the code, you had it wrong! You would have to find all the places you typed the same thing, fixing the error in each case.

Instead, we can use inheritance, factoring out the common code into a new superclass for our buttons. This superclass will thus be a generalization of the tool buttons. In fact, much as we noticed in Chapter 7 that color buttons could be represented using a general `ColorButton` class, we'll now see how we can use a general `ToolButton` class.

8.7 REFINING THE DESIGN

Our tool buttons have several things in common. First, they all have some common instance variables; for example, they all need a link to a drawing area. Second, they all contain some sort of interactor. The words "some sort" serve as a clue in this case. A generic tool button needs to contain some kind of interactor, but we're not sure what kind. Keeping in mind that a link can sometimes serve to model containment (as discussed in Section 5.9), we will see how to use a link to `GPMouseInteractor` to "contain" one instance of any kind of interactor (either a `PPencilInteractor` or a `PRubberbandInteractor`). Finally, the buttons have some behavior in common: They all add and remove their interactor in the same method. Let's look at this last aspect.

Look at the flow of control when the user clicks on the rectangle tool button, as shown in Figure 8.13. Clicking on the rectangle tool tells the drawing area what the new interactor should be, by sending the `AddInteractor` message. `AddInteractor` takes a `GPMouseInteractorAsn` as a parameter, so a link to the rectangle button's interactor will work just fine. We can ensure that the drawing area has only one interactor associated with it by sending a `RemoveInteractor` message. This message can be sent when a button is sent a `DeActivate` message by the radio column containing the button.

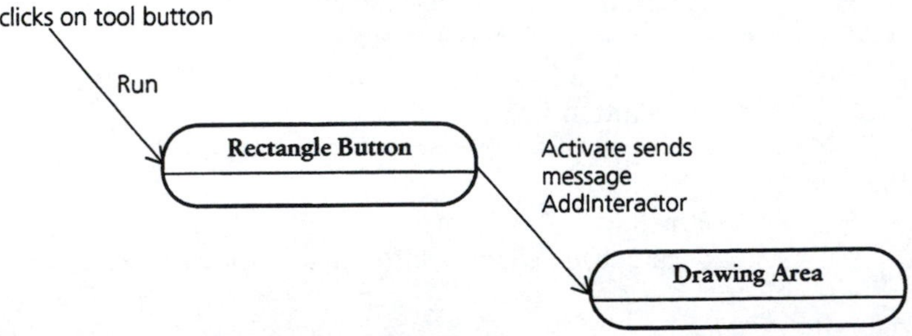

Figure 8.13 *Flow of control when clicking on the rectangle button*

Now compare what happens when the user clicks on the line tool. The flow-of-control diagram is shown in Figure 8.10. Notice that Figures 8.13 and 8.10 differ in only one way: which instance sends the message `AddInteractor` (but the message being sent is the same). This corresponds to the similarity we saw in the pseudocode in Section 8.6.

Designing Generic Superclasses

As Figure 8.8 shows, the tool buttons (including the pencil button) are similar in their instance variables as well as their behavior. But these similarities are not uniform: All tool buttons give an interactor to a drawing area when clicked, but only tools for rubberbanding have a `PRubberbandInteractor` as an instance variable, though all tool buttons contain an instance of a subclass of `GPMouseInteractor`. This suggests two separate generalizations. The first generalization captures the fact that all tool buttons do the same thing when clicked: They install an interactor in their target drawing area (implying that they contain or are associated with some kind of interactor). The second generalization captures the fact that all tool buttons for rubberbanding build and contain a `PRubberbandInteractor`. Let's look at a class diagram that shows these generalizations. Figure 8.14 shows that tool buttons are kinds of toggle buttons and that "rubber tool buttons" are kinds of tool buttons. `PToolButton` contains the commonality among the different kinds of tool buttons.

Figure 8.14 *Two generalizations: Tool buttons and rubber tool buttons*

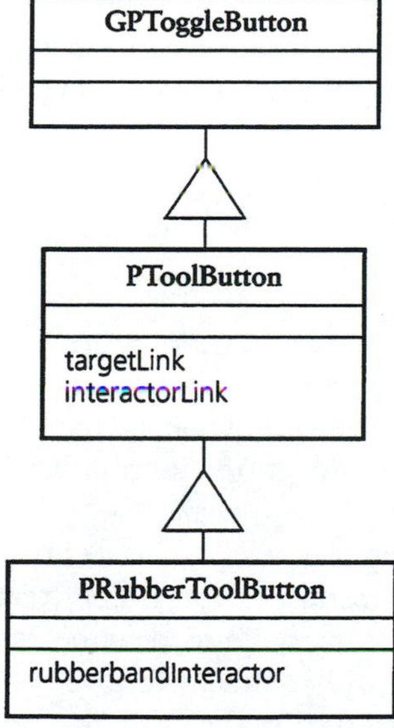

Notice that `PToolButton` has a link to an interactor. It needs a link, because part of its purpose is to tell a drawing area to use a particular interactor. In Section 5.9, we examined how links could be used as containment, when what was to be contained couldn't be constructed by the container. This is exactly the case here: The tool button must be able to give an interactor to the drawing area, so it either must contain the interactor or be associated with it. The tool button can't contain the interactor, because different subclasses of `PToolButton` will make different interactors, making it impossible for `PToolButton` to construct the right kind of interactor. Thus `PToolButton` is associated with an interactor that is passed to it in its constructor (see Figure 8.15).

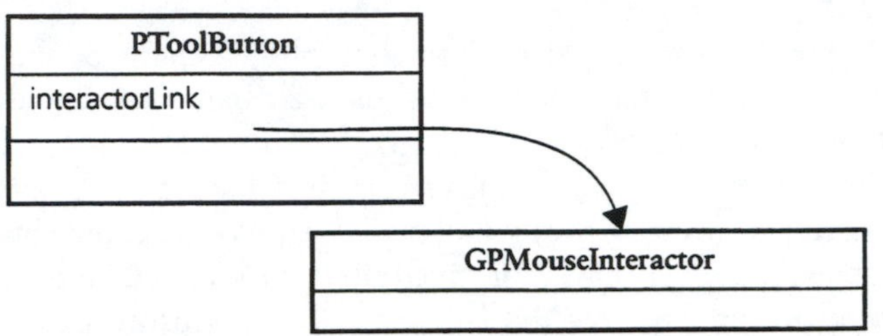

Figure 8.15 *PToolButton is associated with a GPMouseInteractor.*

But what class should contain that interactor? Let's consider all possible classes that might contain the interactor. We've already established that `PToolButton` can't contain the interactor — it is too generic to know what kind of interactor to construct. Perhaps the column that will contain the button could contain the interactor. This solution doesn't feel quite right: The interactor is very closely associated with the button, and putting the interactor in the column is a clumsy separation of objects that belong together. Similarly, putting the interactor inside other classes just increases the separation between the button and the interactor. So, we're back to square one: The interactor should be contained in the button, but the button is too generic to contain the interactor.

Designing Specific Subclasses

However, a derived class of `PToolButton` can be more specific. In particular, the class `PRubberToolButton` is specific enough to contain a `PRubberbandInteractor`. Since `PRubberToolButton` knows it is a tool button for rubberband interactors, it is reasonable for it to contain an actual instance of `PRubberbandInteractor`.

Now let's complete our class diagram with subclasses for the individual tool buttons. We have three particular kinds of tools: line, rectangle, and pencil. Clearly, the line and rectangle buttons have to be subclassed from `PRubberToolButton`. They will create the rubber shapes to give to our rubberbanding interactor so that it has the right kind of shape. Now we're left with the pencil tool button, which we can subclass from `PToolButton`, since, like `PRubberToolButton`, it knows what kind of interactor to construct. Figure 8.16 shows these additional subclasses (for brevity, we omit the instance variables shown in Figure 8.14).

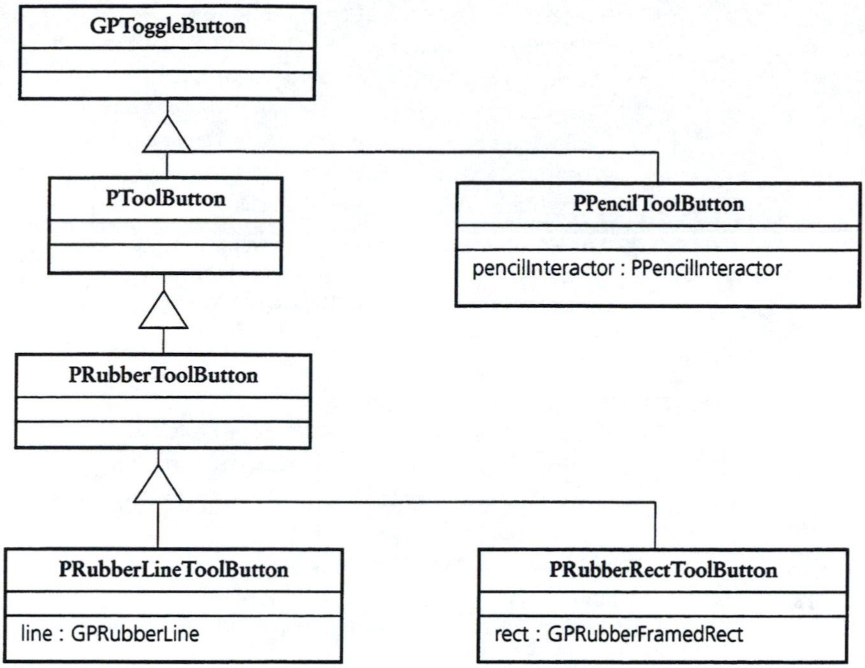

Figure 8.16

Subclasses of PToolButton and PRubber-ToolButton

At this point, we've established all the relationships among the classes. It turns out that all of our new classes are related to some other class, either to one that we have created or to a predefined GP class. This is often but not always the case; programs in which one class stands independently of the others are perfectly okay. The way to determine whether you are done with your relationships is to look at every class to make sure you have considered all the possible association, inheritance, and containment relationships it might need.

8.8 IMPLEMENTING THE CLASSES

We've now gone through the design phase, having considered carefully the classes and the relationships among them. All our classes have a clear purpose, and all their methods have been pseudocoded. At this point, writing the code should be straightforward. We're ready for the next phase: implementation.

All these classes are going into the `Paint` unit, so they're prefixed with a "P." First, we look at our tool button. It is subclassed from `GPToggleButton` and takes three parameters in its constructor: the column that contains it, the drawing area for its interactor, and the interactor itself. It then defines two calls, `Activate` and `DeActivate`, which add and remove the interactor.

```
PToolButton = OBJECT (GPToggleButton)
  CONSTRUCTOR    Init       (
      containerLink     : GPManagerAsn;
      newTargetLink     : GPDrawingAreaAsn;
      newInteractorLink : GPMouseInteractorAsn);
    PROCEDURE Activate;    VIRTUAL;
    PROCEDURE DeActivate;  VIRTUAL;
  PRIVATE
    targetLink        : GPDrawingAreaAsn;
    interactorLink    : GPMouseInteractorAsn;
  END;

CONSTRUCTOR PToolButton.Init (
      containerLink     : GPManagerAsn;
      newTargetLink     : GPDrawingAreaAsn;
      newInteractorLink : GPMouseInteractorAsn);
BEGIN
  INHERITED Init(containerLink);
  targetLink := newTargetLink;
  interactorLink := newInteractorLink;
END;

PROCEDURE PToolButton.Activate;
BEGIN
  targetLink^.AddInteractor(interactorLink);
END;

PROCEDURE PToolButton.DeActivate;
BEGIN
  targetLink^.RemoveInteractor(interactorLink);
END;
```

`PToolButton` uses its interactor in a polymorphic way: The tool button doesn't care exactly which interactor it has, just that it has an interactor, leaving us free to reuse the methods. Subclasses of `PToolButton` can pass any kind of interactor they want.

Next, let's write down our rubber tool button. Let's start with its constructor. It will need to do two things: construct the rubberband interactor, and send an inherited constructor message to its superclass. We know the tool button makes use of `PRubberbandInteractor`. We haven't defined that class yet, but we do know we will need to construct the interactor here. The rubberband interactor will need two pieces of information to be constructed, as discussed in Section 8.3: a link to the drawing area it will draw in, and a link to a `GPRubberShape`, the shape it is drawing. If we define `targetLink` as the drawing area link and `shapeLink` as the link to the rubber shape, we can construct `rubberbandInteractor` as follows:

```
rubberbandInteractor.Init(targetLink, shapeLink);
```

Now we can send a message to `PToolButton` (this class's superclass) to complete the construction. That is, we'll send an `INHERITED Init` message. From the code we've defined, we know that `PToolButton.Init` takes three parameters: a link to a container, a link to a drawing area, and a link to an interactor. If we state that the link to the container and the link to the drawing area are passed to `PRubberToolButton.Init` as parameters `containerLink` and `newTargetLink`, then we can set up the `Init` message as follows:

```
INHERITED Init(containerLink, newTargetLink, @rubberbandInteractor);
```

Our subclasses of `PToolButton` don't need to redefine `Activate` and `DeActivate`. The subclass has to ensure that `PToolButton` receives the correct interactor in the `Init` message, so that `Activate` and `DeActivate` send messages to the correct interactor via `interactorLink`.

The rubber tool button's constructor still takes three parameters, but the third is a link to a `GPRubberShape`, not to an interactor. The rubber tool button constructs its own interactor using the link to the shape. It then passes its interactor to the constructor for its base class, `PToolButton`.

```
PRubberToolButton = OBJECT (CPToolButton)
  CONSTRUCTOR Init (
      containerLink    : GPManagerAsn;
      newTargetLink    : GPDrawingAreaAsn;
      shapeLink        : GPRubberShapeAsn);
PRIVATE
  rubberbandInteractor : PRubberbandInteractor;
END;

CONSTRUCTOR PRubberToolButton.Init(
      containerLink    : GPManagerAsn;
      newTargetLink    : GPDrawingAreaAsn;
      shapeLink        : GPRubberShapeAsn);
BEGIN
  rubberbandInteractor.Init(newTargetLink, shapeLink);
  INHERITED Init(containerLink, newTargetLink,
            @rubberbandInteractor);
END;
```

Now we can build our tool buttons. They are fairly simple: They merely create an interactor or a rubber shape and pass it to the inherited constructor:

```
PRectButton = OBJECT (PRubberToolButton)
  CONSTRUCTOR Init (
      containerLink    : GPRadioColumnAsn;
      newTargetLink : GPDrawingAreaAsn);
```

```
  PRIVATE
    rect : GPRubberFramedRect;
  END;

CONSTRUCTOR PRectButton.Init (
      containerLink    : GPRadioColumnAsn;
      newTargetLink    : GPDrawingAreaAsn);
BEGIN
  rect.Init;
  INHERITED Init(containerLink, newTargetLink, @rect);
  SetName('Rect')
END;

PLineButton = OBJECT (PRubberToolButton)
  CONSTRUCTOR Init (
      containerLink    : GPRadioColumnAsn;
      newTargetLink    : GPDrawingAreaAsn);
PRIVATE
  line : GPRubberLine;
END;

CONSTRUCTOR PLineButton.Init (
      containerLink    : GPRadioColumnAsn;
      newTargetLink    : GPDrawingAreaAsn);
BEGIN
  line.Init;
  INHERITED Init(containerLink, newTargetLink, @line);
  SetName('Line')
END;

PPencilButton = OBJECT (PToolButton)
  CONSTRUCTOR Init (
      containerLink    : GPRadioColumnAsn;
      newTargetLink    : GPDrawingAreaAsn);
PRIVATE
  pencil : PPencilInteractor;
END;

CONSTRUCTOR PPencilButton.Init (
      containerLink    : GPRadioColumnAsn;
      newTargetLink    : GPDrawingAreaAsn);
BEGIN
  pencil.Init(newTargetLink);
  INHERITED Init(containerLink, newTargetLink, @pencil);
  SetName('Pencil')
END;
```

Finally, we can make a tool column that contains all of these buttons.

```
PToolColumn = OBJECT (GPToolColumn)
  CONSTRUCTOR Init (
       containerLink    : GPApplicationAsn;
       targetLink       : GPDrawingAreaAsn);
PRIVATE
  line : PLineButton;
  rect : PRectButton;
  pencil : PPencilButton;
END;

CONSTRUCTOR PToolColumn.Init (
  containerLink : GPApplicationAsn;
  targetLink    : GPDrawingAreaAsn);
BEGIN
  INHERITED Init(containerLink);
  line.Init(@self, targetLink);
  rect.Init(@self, targetLink);
  pencil.Init(@self, targetLink)
END;
```

As stated at the start of this chapter, if we've done a good job on design, implementation is straightforward. Classes in class diagrams became classes in OOPas. Links show up as instance variables whose type is an association type. And contained objects show up as plain old instance variables.

8.9 IMPROVING THE DESIGN TO PROVIDE MORE EXTENSIBILITY

We now essentially have finished with the difficult classes comprising our paint program. We still must assemble the pieces: placing all the buttons and columns in a completed application, then instantiating and running that application from our mainline. But before we do that, let's spend some time on the last phase of building a program: debugging. As it happens, there aren't any bugs per se, but there is an improvement we can make to the design. Since we're modifying our design, we will have to reimplement a few classes.

Compare our pencil interactor and our rubberband interactor in Figure 8.17. Notice that they both have a link to a target drawing area. So we've found another place to apply the principle of generalization: We'll make a new class representing drawing interactors that have to be associated with a drawing area. Let's call this class a `PDrawingToolInteractor`, because it captures a common part of all our drawing tools, namely, that they need a place to draw. Figure 8.18 shows the new class hierarchy for our interactors. Now, when we want to add a new kind of drawing tool, such as a spray can or eraser, we can subclass from `PDrawingToolInteractor` and we'll have the association with the drawing area already.

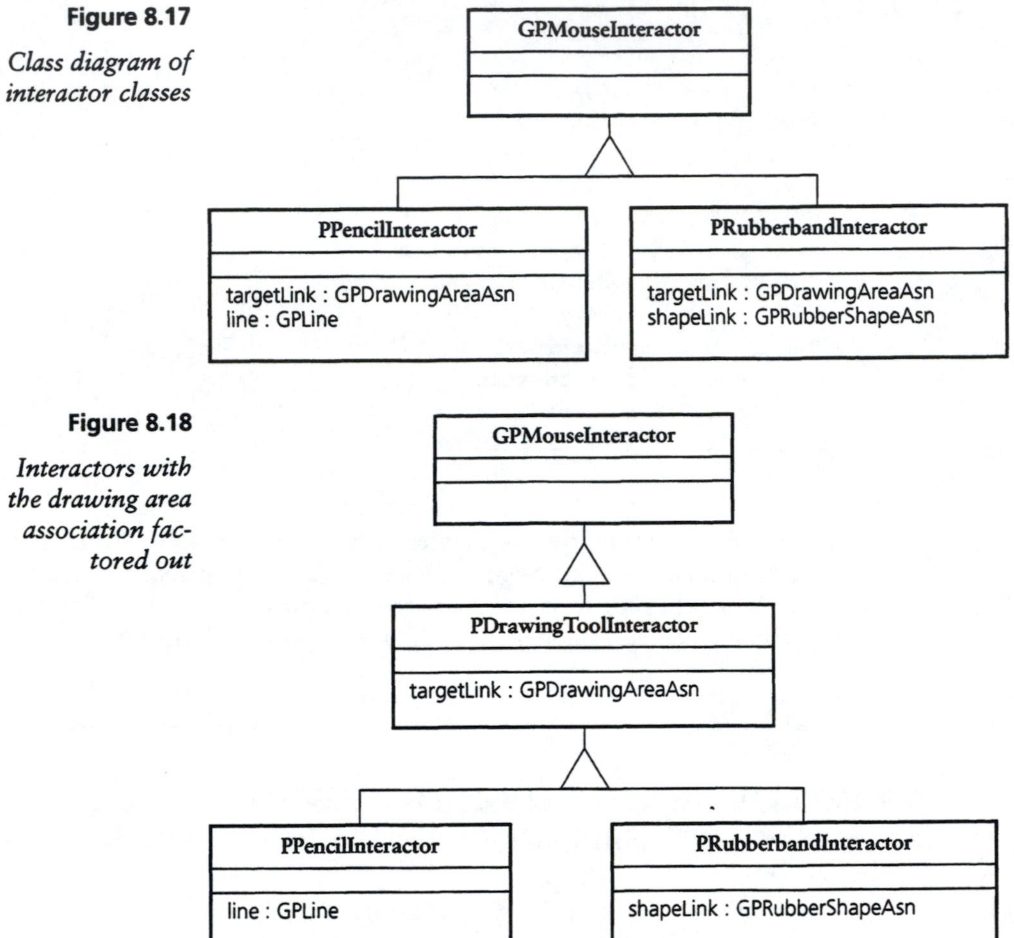

Figure 8.17 *Class diagram of interactor classes*

Figure 8.18 *Interactors with the drawing area association factored out*

Notice that we have to modify the pencil interactor and the rubberband interactor. Modifying code you've already written and debugged is dangerous, since you always risk introducing new bugs into it. If this is code you've already spent a lot of time debugging, it's especially painful.

A good way to prevent redoing old code is to plan for *extensibility*. One of the biggest advantages of object-oriented programming is that it is designed to make programs easily extensible. In fact, inheritance and subclassing are what make extensible code relatively easy to write.

In earlier chapters, we didn't build in extensibility as well as we might have, in order to simplify the code. Now, knowing better, we can redo `PPencil-`

Interactor and PRubberbandInteractor. As we will see, the changes aren't big. In fact, only the class declaration and the constructor change at all. We won't add any new methods or change any other methods we've already written (hence we won't show them again here). This is good — it means we won't have to change any other classes that use either of these two classes, so our changes affect only a small part of the program. In general, this is the best you can hope for when changing old code: that the changes don't require lots of other changes elsewhere as well.

First, we write our new class, PDrawingToolInteractor:

```
PDrawingToolInteractor = OBJECT (GPMouseInteractor)
  CONSTRUCTOR Init(newTargetLink : GPDrawingAreaAsn);
PRIVATE
  targetLink : GPDrawingAreaAsn;
END;

CONSTRUCTOR PDrawingToolInteractor.Init (
        newTargetLink    : GPDrawingAreaAsn);
BEGIN
  INHERITED Init;
  targetLink := newTargetLink
END;
```

That was easy enough. Now all we need to do is change our two interactor classes to be inherited from this new class, then remove their target link instance variable (since they inherit one now) and make the necessary changes to their constructors:

```
PRubberbandInteractor = OBJECT (PDrawingToolInteractor)
  CONSTRUCTOR    Init        (
        newTargetLink    : GPDrawingAreaAsn;
        newShapeLink     : GPRubberShapeAsn);
  PROCEDURE      ButtonDown (startPt : GPPoint); VIRTUAL;
  PROCEDURE      ButtonMotion(movePt : GPPoint); VIRTUAL;
  PROCEDURE      ButtonUp   (endPt : GPPoint); VIRTUAL;
PRIVATE
  shapeLink : GPRubberShapeAsn;
END;

CONSTRUCTOR PRubberbandInteractor.Init (
        newTargetLink    : GPDrawingAreaAsn;
        newShapeLink     : GPRubberShapeAsn);
BEGIN
  INHERITED Init( newTargetLink );
  shapeLink := newShapeLink;
END;
```

```
PPencilInteractor = OBJECT (PDrawingToolInteractor)
   CONSTRUCTOR      Init       (targetLink : GPDrawingAreaAsn );
   PROCEDURE        ButtonDown (startPt : GPPoint); VIRTUAL;
   PROCEDURE        ButtonMotion(movePt : GPPoint); VIRTUAL;
   PROCEDURE        ButtonUp   (endPt : GPPoint); VIRTUAL;
PRIVATE
   line : GPLine;
END;

CONSTRUCTOR PPencilInteractor.Init (newTargetLink :
             GPDrawingAreaAsn);
BEGIN
   INHERITED Init (newTargetLink);
   line.Init;
END;
```

The importance of extensibility and its close cousin, reuse, can't be overemphasized. Design for them early and often. The best time to provide for extensibility is in the design stage, when you're still only drawing class diagrams: It's much easier to redo a drawing than a program.

The programs in this chapter and in Chapter 7 have reused code over and over again, by using a simple USES statement. The code we now have is flexible and easily modified, allowing more colors, more drawing tools, and more ways to make a painting. The exercises at the end of the chapter will let you try this for yourself, adding such things as an oval tool, an eraser, and a paintbrush.

8.10 THE APPLICATION

There is only a single class left to implement — the entire application. It assembles the various columns we have made in the various units. Since it USES many predefined units, you should find it rather straightforward.

```
{**********************************************************
Program COOLPAINT              Name: Brook Conner
9/12/94
**********************************************************}

PROGRAM CoolPaint;
USES GPApplicationUnit, AppCom, Paint, ColSel, GPDAreaUnit;
TYPE
```

```
{**********************************************************
This class represents the canvas and the control columns.
***********************************************************}

CPApp = OBJECT (GPApplication)
  CONSTRUCTOR Init;

PRIVATE
  canvas          : GPDrawingArea;
  tools           : PToolColumn;
  colors          : CSColorColumn;
  actions         : ACActionColumn;
END;

{**********************************************************
This method tells the drawing area and columns to initialize
themselves.
***********************************************************}

CONSTRUCTOR CPApp.Init;
BEGIN
  INHERITED Init;
  canvas.Init(@self);
  tools.Init(@self, @canvas);
  colors.Init(@self, @canvas);
  actions.Init(@self, @canvas)
END;

{**********************************************************
This method tells the application to initialize itself and run.
***********************************************************}

VAR
  coolApp : CPApp;
BEGIN
  coolApp.Init;
  coolApp.Run;
END.
```

Summary

This chapter concludes the first part of this book, which discusses objects, how to design them, and how to put them together. The book began by presenting the concept of a system of objects working together to get a job done. We've come back to that here, working through design principles for building systems of co-operating objects. It took us eight chapters to get here, but now we have some very powerful tools in our toolbox: Our program in this chapter was a fairly complete painting program, which you can extend easily.

The first tool discussed in this chapter was, in many senses, the most important and powerful tool of all: a series of steps to follow when building any program. The first step is to specify exactly what your customer wants you to build. The second step is to analyze the customer's specification rigorously, learning as much as you can about what is to be built. Armed with this analysis, you can proceed to the third step: designing your program. With a complete design, the fourth step of implementing your program should come easily. Finally, your program will need some debugging. People make mistakes, and debugging is the process of removing the mistakes in your program that have been made during any of the four previous steps.

Following these steps, we first produced a specification for a paint program. This program was similar to the ones in Chapters 6 and 7 but added the ability to switch among several drawing tools. To make the drawing tools work, we designed and implemented a system of cooperating objects, including buttons to control the tools, the tools themselves, and the drawing area the tools drew in.

A thorough understanding and analysis of what you want to build can save you hours, even weeks, of grief when you actually build it. We looked at several aspects of analysis, including storyboarding of a system's expected behavior and a careful examination of its intended domain of use. This analysis provided a much more detailed specification of our paint program.

We then proceeded to design our objects. We picked objects by using the nouns in our specification as a starting point. We were able to make use of preexisting objects. This was a great help, since if someone else already has figured out how to handle a large part of a problem, coping with the rest of it can often be quite easy. Armed with complete implemented objects, we looked at how all the objects in the system related to each other.

We then moved on to look at the very idea of a system of cooperating objects. In such a system, many objects send messages to many others, and this can be a source of complexity in the design. So we looked at control-flow diagrams, which show which objects send which messages to which other objects. Control-flow diagrams indicate not only what objects are talking to what other objects, but what they are saying. Such diagrams are thus a useful tool for refining the design of a system. Objects that say the same thing are good candidates for generalization: making a new class that just handles the particular messages being sent to other objects.

Along the way, we found many examples of polymorphism. The generalizations we made in response to our work with control flow naturally took good advantage of polymorphism, as they didn't care exactly what objects they were talking to, just that they would be understood. For example, `PToolButton` was unconcerned about what kind of interactor it was adding to the drawing area — all it needed to do was add an interactor. Subclasses could thus polymorphically provide different interactors, changing and customizing the behavior of the base class. The rubber tool subclass could install a rubberbander and the pencil tool subclass could install a pencil interactor.

Another idea we investigated was event-driven programming. As we filled in the details of the flow diagram for our tool buttons, their interactors, and the drawing area, we saw that the situation was actually quite complex. Thinking in terms of event-driven programming allowed us to stop worrying about exactly when our buttons and interactors were called, letting us focus on the more important aspects of the design.

Throughout the chapter, we implemented various objects as their designs became complete. In a good object-oriented design, parts of the design can be implemented before other parts of the design are complete. The breakdown of a program into different parts makes this possible.

Finally, we came back to the idea of extensibility, finding a minor problem in our design that made extensibility a little harder than it had to be. With some simple modifications, we were able to generalize our interactors. Extensibility simplifies any addition of new capabilities to the program that we may not have considered when first designing it. In fact, some of the exercises work on just this point: adding new capabilities to the already existing program. Happy designing!

Exercises

Understanding Concepts

1. Draw a storyboard describing how a particular gadget works, such as a camera, a stove, or a car.
2. List some of the events in your life that make you do something and what those events make you do.
3. List some real-world systems that are designed to be extensible. Briefly explain how to extend them and what in their design makes this extensibility possible.

Coding Exercises

1. Make a new tool for drawing ovals. You will need to subclass from `PRubberToolButton`. Then subclass from `PToolColumn`, adding the button for your new tool to a new column. Modify `CPControlColumn` to contain your new tool column.

2. Make a paintbrush tool that draws a particular shape whenever the mouse is moved while the button is down. You will need to subclass from `PDrawingToolInteractor`, drawing the paintbrush's shape in each of the virtual methods `Buttondown`, `ButtonMotion`, and `ButtonUp`. Then subclass from `PToolColumn`, adding the button for your new tool to a new column. Modify `CPControlColumn` to contain your new tool column.

3. Make an eraser tool that erases the part of the drawing area dragged over by the mouse while the button is down. How could you implement this as a special kind of paintbrush? Could the paintbrush and the eraser tool be implemented as subclasses of another, more general class? Once you have implemented your eraser, add it to the tool column.

Programming Problems

1. Make a column that lets the user select one of a number of predefined shapes. Modify the paintbrush tool from Coding Problem 2, or make a new one, letting the column of shapes determine the shape the paintbrush draws. Add the new paintbrush tool to the controls for the paint program. Make a menu called "Brush Shapes" to contain the brush shape column. The House part classes (`SUWall`, `SUDoor`, `SUWindow`, `SURoof`) each have a method called

   ```
   DrawInRect(targetLink : GPDrawingAreaAsn;
              surroundRect : GPRubberRect);
   ```

   in which `surroundRect` is a rubber rectangle in which the entire house can be drawn.

   Modify the House program to add a New House button. When that button is clicked, the user should drag out a rubberbanded rectangle, and a house should be drawn in that rectangle.

2. Extend the program in Programming Problem 1 by allowing the user to choose a different kind of house to appear in that rectangle.

3. Extend the House program by allowing the user to select the main or trim colors of a house before it is drawn. (That is, whatever colors the user has last selected for the main and trim colors should be used when the user chooses New House.)

4. Modify the Dorm room program (using the `SUDormDoor`, `SUBed`, `SUDesk`, and `SUChair` classes) so that the user can click on a button and see that piece of furniture appear.

5. Extend the Dorm room program by allowing the user to drag out a rectangle in which the furniture should appear. Each of the SU classes has a method called `DrawInRect(targetLink : GPDrawingAreaAsn; surroundRect: GPRubberRect)` in which `surroundRect` is a rubber rectangle in which the particular piece of furniture should be drawn.

6. Extend the Dorm program further by providing a button to choose a color for all furniture drawn from that point on.

7. Extend the Dorm program by allowing the user to choose one of a set of color buttons, or a button marked "Outline." If a color button is chosen, all furniture should be drawn in that color. If the outline button is chosen, all furniture should be drawn in outline form.

8. Write a variation of the paint program in this chapter that lets the user show layouts of desktop publishing pages. The user should be able to drag out three kinds of shapes. A blank rectangle indicates a headline; a rectangle with a single diagonal line represents a piece of text; a rectangle with both diagonals drawn in an X represents a photo or graphic item. (Note that GP allows you to retrieve the corner points of a rectangle; see the GP documentation for details.)

Part II

Syntax for Math and Flow of Control

Part I of this book was a description of the object-oriented approach to programming. Using predefined objects from GP and other libraries, we have created interesting programs using relatively few lines of OOPas code.

What we have discussed so far is the foundation of an object-oriented program. Beginning with the next chapter, Chapter 9, we start learning about the parts of OOPas that are not concerned with objects. First, we will examine how we can use OOPas to work with numbers. Next, Chapter 10 and Chapter 11 will address how objects decide among alternative actions to perform. We'll move on in the next chapter to look at how an object can perform similar actions repeatedly. In Chapter 13, we'll examine a powerful technique called *recursion*, where an object sends messages to itself. We'll finish this part of the book with some useful information on debugging in Chapter 14.

This part of the book is perhaps the most syntax-intensive: Every chapter except Chapter 14 introduces new syntax. There's syntax for arithmetic, for performing actions repeatedly (also known as *looping*), and for making various kinds of decisions. Objects can describe almost everything, including abstractions like numbers, decisions, and loops. If we had a problem description that included those nouns, we'd be quite justified in identifying those nouns as good candidates for objects. However, the syntax in this part is not supported for objects.

Why all this extra syntax? The answer is that Borland Pascal, like many other object-oriented programming languages, is what is known as a *hybrid* programming language. Pascal was originally a *procedural* programming language, with no support for objects. Therefore, the original Pascal provided special syntax for such things as arithmetic, decisions, and loops. Borland Pascal simply added more syntax to provide objects. There was no reason to take out the syntax that was already there.

The special syntax that provides for arithmetic, decisions, and loops is useful, even with objects. Many applications perform arithmetic, make decisions, or do the same thing over and over — indeed, these actions were some of the first tasks computers were used to perform. So let's take a look at this extremely useful material.

9

Adding It Up

Originally, the manipulation of numbers was the primary use for computers. After all, the name of the machine comes from its ability to compute at high speed. Although many computer applications today still do a great deal of *number crunching*, an increasing number of programs use numeric manipulation simply as a step toward accomplishing a larger goal. For example, mathematics is the key to creating computer graphic images.

We'll be working a great deal with numbers, but we won't be getting into high-level mathematics. A little algebra and geometry from your high school days are all you will need. We'll be concentrating on using arithmetic to create simple drawings. We'll also examine how numbers are input by a user and output on the screen.

9.1 INTEGERS AND OPERATORS

Let's start with the simplest calculations OOPas can perform — arithmetic operations involving whole numbers. Whole numbers, when used in a statement, are called *literal integer constants* and are identical to the integers found in algebra. In OOPas, an *integer* is defined as any number in the set of negative and positive natural numbers and zero. Unlike algebra, though, the set of integers in OOPas does not extend infinitely. In our OOPas, the range of integers extends from –2,147,483,648 to +2,147,483,647. (These numbers are the largest that can be handled by 32 bits of memory.)

OOPas uses a set of *integer operators* similar to those used in arithmetic. For example, addition in OOPas is represented by a + sign. However, not all the OOPas operators are written exactly like their algebraic counterparts — the multiplication sign is an asterisk (e.g., `2*2`) rather than a cross (e.g., 2 × 2).

An *arithmetic expression* is defined as a sequence of constants, variables, operators, arithmetic functions, and parenthesized subexpressions that can be evaluated to a single value. An example is

```
hourlyRate * numDaysWorked
```

A more complex example is

```
hourlyRate * (daysWorked - daysOff) * 8
```

OOPas evaluates this expression by first subtracting `daysOff` from `daysWorked`, then multiplying the result by `hourlyRate` and multiplying this result by 8.

As in algebraic expressions, certain operators used in expressions in OOPas have higher priority than others and are performed first. These priorities are summarized in Syntax Box 9.1. As in algebra, you can alter these priorities by using parentheses. If no parentheses are present, a chain of operations of the same priority is evaluated from left to right.

Syntax Box 9.1

Integer operators

The Three High-Priority Operators:

`*`	Multiplication	written as *`<operand1>`*`*`*`<operand2>`*, computes the product of the two operands.
`div`	Division	written as *`<operand1>`* `div` *`<operand2>`*, computes the integer quotient of *`<operand1>`* divided by *`<operand2>`*, ignoring the remainder. For instance, `6 div 4 = 1` and `-11 div 3 = -3`.
`mod`	Modulo	written *`<operand1>`* `mod` *`<operand2>`*, computes the integer remainder of *`<operand1>`* `div` *`<operand2>`*. For example, `6 mod 4 = 2` and `-11 mod 3 = -2`.

The Two Low-Priority Operators:

`+`	Addition	written as *`<operand1>`* `+` *`<operand2>`*, adds the two operands.
`-`	Subtraction	written as *`<operand1>`* `-` *`<operand2>`*, subtracts the second operand from the first.

Where:

`<operand>` is any arithmetic expression.

OOPas evaluates an expression by combining operands with their operators. This language uses three rules for evaluation:

1. Expressions in parentheses are evaluated first, starting at the innermost level.
2. Within an expression, higher-priority operators take precedence.
3. Otherwise, evaluation takes place from left to right.

As an example, 2 + 4 * 5 evaluates to 22, because * has a higher priority than +. But the expression (2 + 4) * 5 evaluates to 30. The first sequence uses normal operator priorities, whereas the second performs the addition within the parentheses before the multiplication.

9.2 DECLARING INTEGERS

We've seen that every identifier must be declared before OOPas can use it. The variable declarations we've seen have been of the form `frontDoor: SUDoor;` where `SUDoor` is a class and `frontDoor` is an instance.

Declaring integer variables uses the same syntax: identifier, a colon, data type, and a semicolon, as in `numOfDays: integer;`. In this case, the data type is the word `integer`. Unlike the declarations we have seen previously, `integer` is not a class — it is one of OOPas's *base types*. Variables of base types differ from instances of classes in that variables of base types have no methods associated with them.

Base types can be used anywhere that we have seen class names or association names. For example, we could create a class using integers as follows:

```
TYPE
  REGISTRARCourse = OBJECT { represents single course on campus }
    CONSTRUCTOR Init(...; roomNumber: integer; ...);
    FUNCTION GetEnrollment:integer;
    ...
  PRIVATE
    numStudents: integer; { students enrolled in class }
    ...
  END;
```

9.3 ASSIGNING INTEGERS

Technically, a variable is the name of a piece of computer memory used in your program. Computer memory is analogous to a large set (many millions) of individually numbered post office boxes. Some of these boxes contain data values; others contain machine code instructions. OOPas reserves the necessary locations in memory to store a program's variables in the same way that a postmaster can reserve a post office box to store your mail. Unlike a post office box, however, a memory location can hold only one item. In Figure 9.1, the variable `length` has the value 12. In the case of an instance of a class, a block of memory is reserved to contain the instance variables and a connection to information describing what virtual methods to use for this instance.

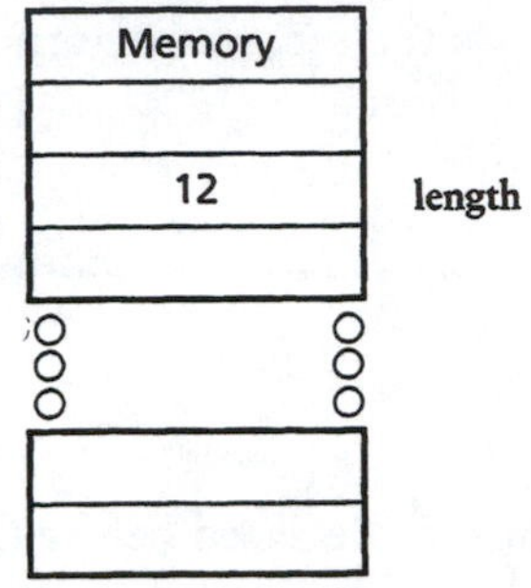

Figure 9.1 *The variable length found in memory*

The computer can look at the contents of any individual memory location without changing them. It also can change the contents of a memory location by writing new information over the old information. These two operations are similar to playing back and recording over the contents of a cassette tape.

We looked at how to declare a variable as an integer, but the declaration simply reserves a space in memory. The declaration itself does not affect the contents of the memory location. Previous programs may have used the same places in memory that OOPas has now reserved for your declarations. The values in these locations are leftover, or *garbage,* values and the program should replace them with new values. (With instances, we have used constructors to establish the instance's initial state, but base types do not have methods.) You can give a new value to a variable through assignment.

When we looked at assignment statements, we saw that OOPas assigns values to variables in two steps. First, the expression on the right of the assignment operator (:=) is evaluated. Then that result is placed in the variable on the left of the assignment operator. Let's look at some examples:

```
(1) sumVehicles  := 0;
(2) sumVehicles  := numberCars + numberBuses;
(3) totalPeople  := numInSection * 2 + teachingAssts;
```

In (1), `sumVehicles` is assigned the value 0. In (2), if `numberCars` = 5 and `numberBuses` = 4, then the expression on the right evaluates to 9 and `sumVehicles` is assigned the single value 9. In (3), if `numInSection` = 125 and `teachingAssts` = 15, then the right side evaluates to 125 * 2 + 15, or 250 + 15. The result, 265, is assigned to `totalPeople`.

OOPas variables can be used in the same way as algebraic variables — with one exception. You may want to give a variable a new value that depends on its old value. For example, to decrease `workDays` by the number of `sickDays` and store the result in `workDays`, you would type:

```
workDays := workDays - sickDays;
```

Figure 9.2 shows OOPas's two-step evaluation of the preceding statement. The expression on the right is evaluated first. Thus if `workDays` is 250 and `sickDays` is 6, the expression on the right evaluates to 244. The evaluated expression, when assigned to the variable on the left, replaces this variable's old value. Thus `workDays` is assigned 244, replacing the old value of 250.

Figure 9.2 *Evaluation of assignment statement*

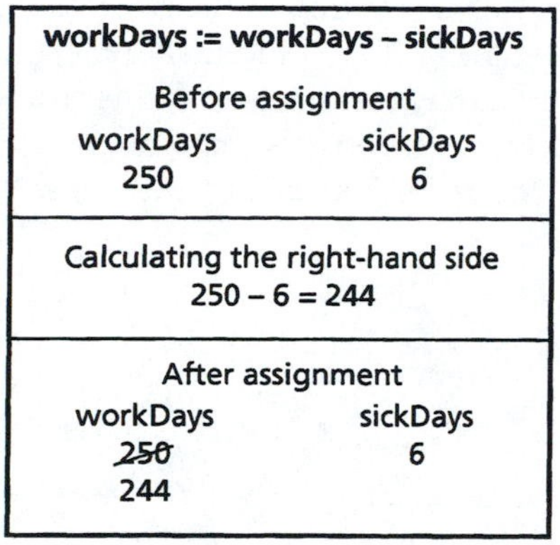

workDays := workDays – sickDays	
Before assignment	
workDays	sickDays
250	6
Calculating the right-hand side	
250 – 6 = 244	
After assignment	
workDays	sickDays
~~250~~	6
244	

The OOPas statement `workDays := workDays - sickDays` is quite different from the algebraic equation *workDays* = *workDays* – *sickDays*. The fundamental difference between the *imperative* assignment symbol of an OOPas statement and the *declarative* equals sign in an algebraic equation is that the OOPas `:=` operator "assigns," while the = sign of algebra declares that one side "is equal to" the other but *performs no action*. Note that the header of a class declaration is consistent in its use of = as a declaration:

```
REGISTRARCourse = OBJECT
```

9.4 REAL NUMBERS

The set of integers is not sufficient for our numeric needs: We need a way to represent numbers with fractional parts, or *real numbers*. Real numbers, also called *reals*, are often represented in *exponential* or *scientific notation*. This means that the number is written as a base value (the *mantissa*) multiplied by an integer power of 10 (the *exponent*). For example:

372.4 is written as 3.724e+02,

2,345,200 is written as 2.3452e+06,
.053 is written as 5.3e–02.

Here, the *e* signifies exponentiation; the sign and the last two digits indicate a power of 10. The expression "e+02" means 10 raised to the second power, and "e–02" means 10 raised to the negative second power (the mantissa divided by 100). Thus 3.724e+02 is the same as 3.724×10^2.

All the arithmetic operators used for integers can be used for reals except for the division and modulo operators. The `DIV` operator used with integers is replaced by the `/` operator, which signifies division in the conventional sense. The quotient of a division problem using the `/` operation must be stored in a real variable because OOPas represents the result of any `/` operation not as an integer, but as a real (e.g., `6/3` is stored as the real `2.0e0`, not as the integer `2`). In addition, because memory is finite, infinitely repeating decimals are cut off after eight digits. For example, the result of `5/3` is stored as `1.66666667`. The `mod` function, which returns the integer remainder of a division of two integers, has no meaning for reals. Syntax Box 9.2 summarizes the priorities of operators for reals.

Syntax Box 9.2
Real operators

Operators for Reals in Priority Order:

1. Multiplication (*) and division (/)
2. Addition (+) and subtraction (–)

Note: The integer operators `div` and `mod` do not work with reals.

Real numbers are represented in OOPas with the data type `real`. OOPas has a much larger range of representation for real data than for integer data, extending from approximately -10^{38} to 10^{38}. The smallest positive number that can be represented by a real expression is approximately 10^{-324}.

Real variables are declared in the same way as other data types. For example, the following declaration declares `lastCheckNum` as an `integer`, and `amountLastDep` and `balance` as `real` variables.The order of declarations is irrelevant.

```
TYPE
  CheckingAccount = OBJECT
    ...
  PRIVATE
    lastCheckNum: integer; { last check number to be processed }
    amountLastDep, { amount of last deposit }
    balance: real: { account balance }
  END;
```

9.5 ARITHMETIC FUNCTIONS

We often want to perform some mathematical functions beyond the normal arithmetic operators. For example, we may need to find squares and square roots, or use trigonometric functions like *sine* and *cosine*. To perform these and other common mathematical computations, we can use OOPas's *predefined functions*.

These functions are similar to those found in mathematics. Just as you can write

$$y = \sqrt{x}$$

in algebra, you can write the OOPas assignment statement

```
answer := Sqrt(num);
```

Again, the difference between algebra and OOPas is that the algebraic equals sign equates, while OOPas's `:=` symbol assigns. We say that OOPas evaluates the `Sqrt` function and *returns* a value. In this case, if `num` is 9.0, `Sqrt` returns the value 3.0 and OOPas assigns 3.0 to `answer`.

Syntax Box 9.3 shows the predefined functions for calculating squares and square roots.

Syntax Box 9.3

Sqr and Sqrt functions

Syntax:

```
Sqr(<expression>)
Sqrt(<expression>)
```

Where:

<expression> evaluates to a number of type `real`.

Returns:

`Sqr` returns an `integer` if *<expression>* evaluates to an `integer`; it returns a `real` if *<expression>* evaluates to a `real`. `Sqrt` always returns a `real`.

Usage:

Both `Sqr` and `Sqrt` begin by evaluating *<expression>*. When *<expression>* has been reduced to a single value, `Sqr` multiplies it by itself and `Sqrt` takes the square root.

If *<expression>* evaluates to a negative number, `Sqrt` halts the program.

As we saw in Chapter 5, the value returned by a function or expression must be stored somewhere. Thus the lines

```
Sqr (side);
Sqrt (horiz1 - vert1);
```

produce syntax errors, since no variables have been provided to store the results. You can place the returned value in a variable using an assignment statement:

```
areaOfSquare := Sqr(side);
partialSolution := Sqrt(horiz1 - vert1);
```

Arithmetic expressions also may be used as parameters. We could represent the mathematical expression

$$c = \sqrt{a^2 + b^2}$$

(the Pythagorean theorem) as the following:

```
c:= Sqrt(Sqr(a) + Sqr(b));
```

Note the parameter to `Sqrt` is itself an arithmetic expression.

In summary, arithmetic expressions can take a number of forms. They can be a literal constant (`cardsReceived := 5;`), a variable (`cardsReceived := numberKids;`), a predefined function (`cardsReceived := Sqr(avgKids);`), or a combination of any of these (`cardsReceived := spouse + 2 * marriedKids + singleKids + numKids * Sqr(avgNumGrandKids);`). Any of these expressions can be used on the right-hand side of the assignment statement or as parameters. A complete list of predefined functions appears in Appendix B.

9.6 CONSTANTS

Variables are used when values are assigned or changed in a program. Suppose, however, that we have a certain value that will not change during the course of an entire program. By giving that value a name, like a variable, you avoid having to write it out each time. This also enables you to keep the value constant throughout the program, making it impossible for the value to be changed by assignment. OOPas allows you to name a *symbolic constant*, or *constant* for short, which holds an unchangeable value.

Constants are declared using syntax similar to that for variables. The declarations are listed under the heading `CONST`. The constant identifier is followed by an equals sign (not a colon) and then the constant value.

```
CONST
  scale = 10; { number of feet that one pixel represents }
```

Constants usually appear immediately after the `USES` statements. When placed there, the constants can be used by the mainline or by any method within the constant's file. Their syntax is described in Syntax Box 9.4.

Syntax Box 9.4

The CONST declaration

Syntax:

```
CONST
  <constant name> = <constant value>;
```

Where:

<constant name> is an identifier that adheres to the naming rules and conventions of variables.

<constant value> is any numeric or literal string value.

Usage:

Any number of constants may be defined; they are defined before the `BEGIN` of the procedure or program where they are used.

Constants typically appear at the top of the file, immediately after the `PROGRAM` and `USES` or `UNIT` statement. In this position, the constant can be used throughout the rest of the program or unit. No two constants within the same program may have the same name.

Note: The equals sign in the definition is an equate sign to signify declaration, not an assignment symbol.

In the following program excerpts, we use a constant for the speed of light. Variables are used in the methods where they are declared, but the constant `LightSpeed` is "global" to all methods and therefore can be used in both the method `Einstein.Relativity` and in the mainline.

```
PROGRAM Physics;
CONST
  LightSpeed = 186281; { speed of light in miles/second }
  ...

TYPE
  ...

FUNCTION Einstein.Relativity(mass: real) : real;
BEGIN
  Relativity := mass * Sqr(LightSpeed);
END; { Relativity }
  ...
```

```
{ Mainline }
VAR
  earthDist   : real;  { current distance from sun to earth }
  travelTime  : real;  { time for light to travel sun to earth }
BEGIN
  ...
  { earthDist gets value somewhere in here. }
  travelTime := earthDist / LightSpeed;
       { Calculate time in seconds. }
  ...
END. { Physics }
```

Constants also are useful for values that will not change for many runs of the program, even though they represent a value that in real life is updated occasionally. Suppose an accountant wants to write a program to monitor the amount of money spent on taxes. Now, without a constant, she could keep typing the tax rate wherever it was needed in the program. But what if the tax rate was changed by the government? Then the accountant would have to go back and change every occurrence of the old tax rate to the new number.

Constants provide an alternative. Our accountant can declare the following constant:

```
CONST
  TaxRate = 30.0;     { tax rate in percent}
```

Instead of using "30.0" throughout the program, she can use `TaxRate`. Now, if the government changes the tax rate in the future, all she has to do is change this one line in the program.

Note that our `TaxRate` constant has a brief glossary comment, explaining what it is. Constants, like variables, should be documented with a glossary entry.

There are two types of constants in OOPas. We've just looked at symbolic constants — identifiers that are given a value once in the `CONST` section and maintain that value throughout the program. A literal constant is a value that appears anywhere in the body of a method. For example, in the assignment statement `radius := diameter/2;` the "2" is a literal constant.

9.7 AN EXAMPLE: A FINANCIAL CALCULATOR

Now, let's create a program that utilizes the concepts we've seen in this chapter. Our specification is as follows:

This program represents a simple financial calculator. It computes the total value of a savings account based on a constant interest rate, after a certain number of months have passed. The user can select the amount to deposit and the number of months. A slider shows the total value of the account. A Quit button allows the user to exit the program.

The nouns in this specification are:

financial calculator	total value	savings account
amount to deposit	interest rate	number of months
slider	quit button	program

We can use a subclass of `GPApplication` as our "program," and use our `ACQuitButton` class (from Chapter 7) for the quit button. We'll call the application `FCApplication`, for "Financial Calculator Application," and we'll put the code in a "FinCalc" unit. The application will hold the quit button, as well as the calculator itself. We can see a picture of this financial calculator in Figure 9.3.

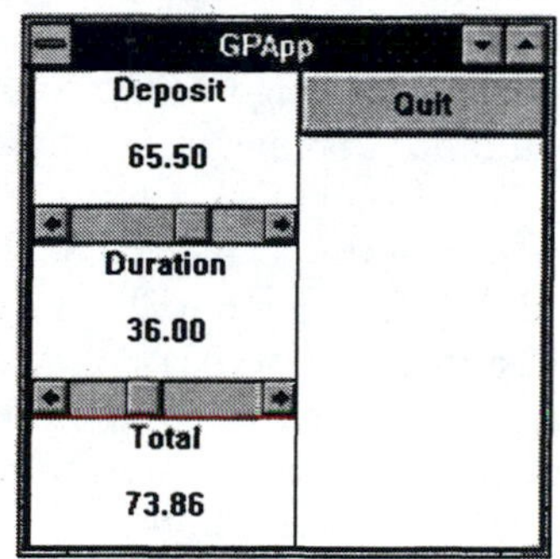

Figure 9.3 *The financial calculator application*

We now need a class to model a savings account. It will have a total value, an amount to deposit, an interest rate, and a time period in months. The financial calculator class will be used by the savings account to compute the total value from the amount deposited, the interest rate, and the number of months.

We'll use "sliders" to show the total value of the account, as well as to allow the user to specify the other quantities. A slider has a knob the user can drag back and forth to specify a numeric value. The knob (or "thumb") also can be positioned by the program, to tell the user a particular numeric value. There are several GP classes that provide sliders of various sorts. Figure 9.4 shows the class hierarchy for GP sliders. The class `GPSlider` provides a generic kind of slider, whereas `GPIntSlider` and `GPRealSlider` provide sliders with specifically `integer` and `real` values, respectively. We see several familiar methods for `GPSlider`, such as `SetName`, which behaves like the corresponding methods for `GPButton`. The virtual method `ValueChanged` is called whenever the user changes the value of the slider.

We will be using the subclasses. The class `GPRealSlider` redefines `ValueChanged` to call `RealValue`, passing the current value of the slider as a `real`.

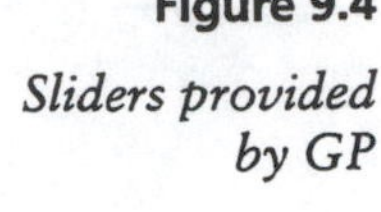

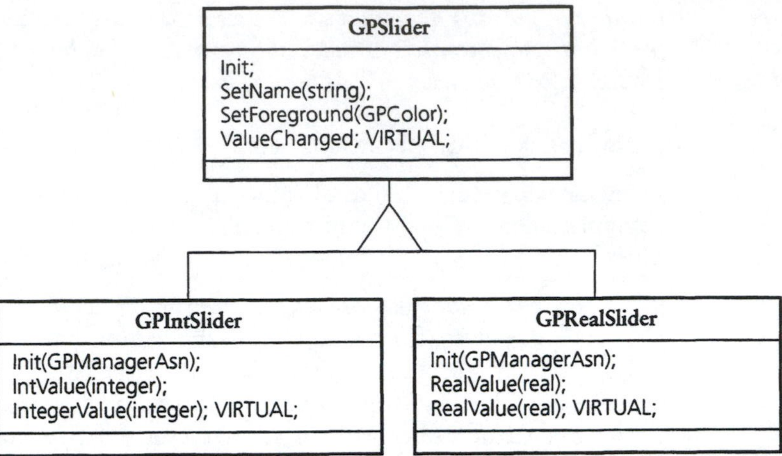

`GPIntSlider` and `IntValue` behave similarly. Thus we'll redefine `RealValue`, not `ValueChanged`, for our financial calculator.

So we can have one slider subclass for each of the total value, the initial value, the interest rate, and the number of months. The sliders for initial value and duration will update the savings account object with the new value. The savings account then will know to use the financial calculator to recompute the total value. Notice that the sliders for both initial value and duration need to talk to the savings account. Thus they'll all be derived from a subclass of `GPRealSlider` that contains an association to our savings account class, `FCSavingsAcct`. Let's write down these classes, starting with `FCAcctInfo-Slider`, the base class for initial value, and duration:

```
FCSavingsAcctAsn = ^FCSavingsAcct;
FCFinancialCalculatorAsn = ^FCFinancialCalculator;
FCAcctInfoSlider = OBJECT( GPRealSlider )
  CONSTRUCTOR Init(
      acct              : FCSavingsAcctAsn;
      calc              : FCFinancialCalculatorAsn );
PRIVATE
  myAcctLink     : FCSavingsAcctAsn;
  myCalculatorLink : FCFinancialCalculatorAsn;
  myTitle, myValue : GPLabel;
END;
...
```

The class `FCAcctInfoSlider` has four instance variables. One is a link to the savings account that this slider describes. Another is a link to the calculator that will determine the total value of the account. The other two instance variables are instances of the class `GPLabel`, which the slider will use to display its numerical value as well as to identify itself on the screen.

```
FCSavingsAcct = OBJECT( GPColumn )
  CONSTRUCTOR Init( parent : GPManagerAsn );
  PROCEDURE Update;
PRIVATE
  initialDeposit : FCDepositSlider;
  duration       : FCDurationSlider;
  myTitle, totalValue : GPLabel;
  calculator     : FCFinancialCalculator;
END;
```

The `FCDepositSlider` and the `FCDurationSlider` simply will inform the `FCFinancialCalculator` of any new values, then tell the `FCSavingsAcct` to `Update` itself. First, let's look at interest and the calculator itself. Presuming that the interest rate won't change on our savings account, we'll use a constant:

```
CONST
  interestRate = 4.00; { four percent interest on savings }
```

Now let's take a look at the real heart of this program — the financial calculator itself. It provides methods to set the different attributes of the account, and has a function, `TotalValue`, which returns the total value of the account.

```
FCFinancialCalculator = OBJECT
  CONSTRUCTOR      Init;        { All values are taken to be zero. }
  PROCEDURE        SetInitialDeposit( dep : real );
  PROCEDURE        SetDuration( dur : real );
  FUNCTION         TotalValue : real;
PRIVATE
  deposit, duration : real;
END;
```

Of course, the most important part of this object is the method `TotalValue`. Let's figure out the computations that have to be done by this method. First, we must take our interest rate, which is in percent over a year, and calculate the interest earned in a single month. We can do this by converting the percent to a decimal by dividing by a hundred, then dividing again by twelve (the number of months in a year) to figure out the interest earned per month as a decimal. We'll call this the `decimalInterest`.

The interest earned after one month is the `decimalInterest` times the initial deposit. The total value of the account is the initial deposit plus that product. We could get the same result by adding the `decimalInterest` to 1, then multiplying by the initial deposit. Now we can figure out the total value for any month quite easily. To get the total for the next month, we can take the total for any month and multiply it again by the `decimalInterest` plus 1. Let's call the `decimalInterest` plus 1 the `oneMonthTotal`. We simply can start with the initial deposit and get the total for a given duration by multiplying the initial deposit by the `oneMonthTotal` repeatedly, as many times as the length of the duration.

The arithmetic function `Pow` from the unit `GPUtil` will do this, by raising a number to any power. We raise the `oneMonthTotal` to the number of months and multiply the result by the initial deposit:

```
FUNCTION FCFinancialCalculator.TotalValue : real;
VAR
  decimalInterest : real;
  oneMonthTotal : real;
BEGIN
  decimalInterest := (interestRate / 100) / 12;
  oneMonthTotal := decimalInterest + 1;
  TotalValue := deposit * Pow(oneMonthTotal, duration)
END;
```

We'll finish off by providing the sliders and the other missing methods, such as `FCSavingsAcct.Update`:

```
TYPE
  FCDepositSlider = OBJECT( FCAcctInfoSlider )
    CONSTRUCTOR Init(acctLink : FCSavingsAcctAsn;
             calcLink : FCFinancialCalculatorAsn);
    PROCEDURE RealValue( newValue : real ); VIRTUAL;
  END;

  FCDurationSlider = OBJECT( FCAcctInfoSlider )
    CONSTRUCTOR Init(acctLink : FCSavingsAcctAsn;
             calcLink : FCFinancialCalculatorAsn );
    PROCEDURE RealValue(newValue : real); VIRTUAL;
  END;

CONSTRUCTOR FCDepositSlider.Init(acctLink : FCSavingsAcctAsn;
             calcLink : FCFinancialCalculatorAsn );
BEGIN
  INHERITED Init(acctLink, calcLink);
  myTitle.SetName('Deposit');
  myValue.SetNameWithReal(0.0)
END;

PROCEDURE FCDepositSlider.RealValue(newValue : real);
BEGIN
  myValue.SetNameWithReal(newValue);
  myCalculatorLink^.SetInitialDeposit(newValue);
  myAcctLink^.Update
END;
```

```
CONSTRUCTOR FCDurationSlider.Init(
        acctLink          : FCSavingsAcctAsn;
        calcLink          : FCFinancialCalculatorAsn );
BEGIN
   INHERITED Init(acctLink, calcLink);
   myTitle.SetName('Duration');
   myValue.SetNameWithReal(0.0)
END;

PROCEDURE FCDurationSlider.RealValue(newValue : real);
BEGIN
   myValue.SetNameWithReal(newValue);
   myCalculatorLink^.SetDuration( newValue );
   myAcctLink^.Update
END;

PROCEDURE FCSavingsAcct.Update;
BEGIN
   totalValue.SetNameWithReal(calculator.TotalValue)
END;
```

The remainder of the methods and classes (such as the application, USES statements, and the mainline) can be found on the Internet — see the Preface for details.

Summary

In this chapter, we began our examination of OOPas's "base types." Base types, as opposed to classes we have defined in our program's TYPE declarations, do not include methods; they are simply types that store data.

We looked at how OOPas handles numbers. It uses two base types — integer and real — to handle "whole numbers" and "real numbers," respectively. We looked at the arithmetic operators and at arithmetic functions, such as `Sqr` and `Sqrt`. We also looked a little more closely at how OOPas handles variable declarations and assignment statements by manipulating a location in memory. (This allows a statement like `total := total - amtLost;` to make sense in OOPas.)

When we work with numbers, it is often convenient to use constants. Literal constants are the numbers that might appear in a single statement, such as the "2" in the assignment statement `area := base * height / 2;`. Symbolic constants are identifiers that are equated with a particular value. These constants are declared after the PROGRAM and USES statement, which means they may be used throughout the file where they are declared.

Exercises

Understanding Concepts

1. What is the result when OOPas evaluates each of the following expressions?

   a. 5 + 7 * 938 mod 6 b. 4.5 /3 + 12
   c. 16 div 3 d. pi * 15

2. What is the difference between the algebraic expression $i = i + 1$ and the assignment statement `i := i + 1;` ?

3. If the variable on the left side of an assignment statement is of type `integer`, do all of the variables on the right side also have to be of type `integer`? Is this also true for `reals`?

4. Consider these two functions:

```
FUNCTION Exercise.A( VAR example : integer);
BEGIN
   example := example + 1;
   A := example
END;
FUNCTION Exercise.B( example : integer );
BEGIN
   example := example + 1;
   B := example
END;
```

   Now consider this method:

```
PROCEDURE Exercise.UseOfAAndB;
VAR
   orang, utan : integer;
BEGIN
   orang := 1;
   utan := 1;
   orang := A( orang );
   utan := B( utan )
END;
```

   What are the values in `orang` and `utan` at the end of executing this method? Explain the resulting values.

5. How do base types differ from objects?

Coding Problems

1. Write a function called `Temperature.Convert`. Assume `Temperature` is a class with an instance variable called `degreesF` that represents a temperature in degrees Fahrenheit. The `Convert` function should return the equivalent of `degreesF` in degrees Celsius. (The formula is $C = 5/9(F–32)$.)

2. Create a class called `Angle`. Its constructor should receive the degree of an angle. The class should have a method called `Draw` that takes an instance of a `GPPoint` as a parameter. The `Draw` method should draw the angle on the screen (e.g., if the angle is 90°, a right angle should appear on the screen).

3. Create a class called `Triangle`. Its constructor should receive an instance of `GPPoint` as a parameter. The class needs a `Draw` method, which will draw an equilateral triangle from the point selected.

4. Create a class called `Star`. Its constructor should receive an instance of `GPPoint` as a parameter; this is the center of the star. The class's `Draw` method should draw a five-point star around the center.

5. For the example program in Section 9.7, replace the three lines of expressions performed in the method `FCFinancialCalculator.TotalValue` with a single expression. You no longer should need any local variables. In addition, rewrite the same method with no more than one operator or function call per statement, storing all intermediate results in local variables. In both cases, verify that `TotalValue` still provides the same answers.

6. In the example in Section 9.7, make the interest rate adjustable from a slider controlled by the user. You should remove the constant declaration and add the interest rate to the `FCFinancialCalculator` class. Make any necessary changes to the computations performed by the `FCFinancialCalculator`.

Programming Problems

1. Make a class that displays the Revolutionary War U.S. flag (with 13 stars). You may want to use the `Star` object described in Coding Problem 4.

2. Create a program where one of several flags can be displayed. The user should be able to choose a flag to display from a set of buttons, then see that flag on the screen. You may want to use different country, state, or local flags.

3. Create an on-screen calculator that adds, subtracts, multiplies, and divides integers. You should have buttons for the digits 0 through 9, the addition, subtraction, multiplication, and division operations, a "clear" button, and an equals sign button.

4. In algebra, you learned that any line can be defined as $y = mx + b$, where m is the slope of the line and b is the y-intercept. Write a program that obtains the slope and a y-intercept from two sliders and draws the corresponding line on a set of axes.

5. Write a program that shows the departure and arrival times of a train. Using sliders, the user should enter the departure time and the time the train takes to reach its destination. The output should be two clock faces (i.e., "analog" clocks, with minute and hour hands), one showing the departure and one showing the arrival.

6. Add different kinds of interest calculations to the example in Section 9.7. Toggle buttons, like the tool buttons used in the paint program in Chapter 8, should let the user choose which interest calculation is used. You should provide the monthly calculation from the example, as well as daily, weekly, annual, and continuous calculation of interest. The different financial calculators should be subclassed from a more generic financial calculator to make use of polymorphism.

10

Making Choices

You face hundreds of decisions each day. As your alarm clock rings each morning, you ask yourself, "Should I get up and get dressed or sleep till noon?" When it is sunny outside, you ask yourself, "Should I go for a walk or stay inside and work?" And every few paragraphs or so, you wonder, "Should I keep reading this OOPas book or find something more interesting to do?" Situations like these, with exactly two options, provide *binary choices*.

Binary choices are an integral part of computer science. You have seen that a computer's basic circuits are turned on or off to represent one or zero. In this chapter, you will see that OOPas also "understands" the concept of true and false.

Typically, we use binary choices when we want OOPas to determine whether a comparison is true or false. For example, we might ask, "Assuming `balance` is an integer variable, is `balance` greater than zero?"

When we formulate a question that has a true or false answer, we can use that answer in one of two ways. OOPas has the data type `boolean` to store answers to true/false questions. In addition, a program's *flow of control* can be altered depending on the binary result of a comparison.

First we need to define the term "flow of control." We first encountered flow diagrams in Chapter 8, and now we'll look at them in some detail. A program's flow of control is the order in which its statements are executed. A trivial program without methods is called a *straight-line* program. That is, all the statements in its mainline are executed sequentially from top to bottom (or more precisely, from `BEGIN` to `END`). With procedures and functions, however, the flow of control is altered. When a procedure or function is invoked, the flow of control moves, or *branches*, to the `BEGIN` of the designated procedure and branches back upon completion. This chapter looks at another type of flow of control: the *conditional branch* to a different part of a program. That is, we see that OOPas can perform one task if a condition is true, another if it is false.

10.1 EVALUATING CONDITIONS

OOPas's simplest true/false decision is the comparison of two base type variables. In Chapter 9, we saw that numbers and strings can be represented as constants, variables, or expressions. The expressions `2+2`, `3 DIV sides`, and `((maxLen + 8.3) * size) + 9` are all legal expressions, assuming that `sides`, `maxLen`, and `size` all are declared appropriately as variables and that `sides` is an integer. OOPas requires that both sides of a comparison must be essentially the same base type. That is, OOPas *cannot* compare a `real` to a `string`, because it treats each data type differently. However, OOPas *can* compare a `real` to an *integer*, as it knows how to convert from one to the other.

Comparing Numbers

Comparisons often are used as parts of statements in OOPas; later in this chapter, we will discuss how to use them in decision-making code. We look now at how OOPas evaluates conditions, at how it decides whether a comparison is true or false. Let's look at a typical comparison:

```
(totalMarbles - marblesLost) > 50
```

To evaluate this condition, OOPas works from left to right, except that parenthesized expressions are evaluated first. Thus OOPas finds the value of `totalMarbles` and subtracts the value of `marblesLost`; then it compares the result of the subtraction to 50. For example, if `totalMarbles` is 60 and `marblesLost` is 16, the result is 44. The comparison can then be rewritten as `44 > 50`. Since 44 is not greater than 50, the condition `(totalMarbles - marblesLost) > 50` evaluates to the condition `false`.

OOPas determines whether a statement is `true` or `false` in the same way that you would calculate such statements. Some examples follow; note that when two symbols appear, such as "<=", the expression can be read as "less than or equal to."

This expression	evaluates to
`3 > 4`	`false`
`Trunc(10.4 + 1.5) < 13.0`	`true`
`0 >= 100`	`false`
`100 <= 100`	`true`
`6.7 <> 20/3`	`true`
`3 + 8 = 33 DIV 3`	`true`

Syntax Box 10.1 summarizes the boolean operators.

Syntax Box 10.1

Boolean expressions

Syntax:

`<expression1> <operator> <expression2>`

Where:

<expression1> and *<expression2>* are represented by constants, variables, or any combination of parenthesized subexpressions.

<operator> is a legal OOPas comparison operator (listed below).

Usage:

The expressions can be integers, reals, or any other data type, but the expressions on either side of the operator must be of the same type.

Comparisons are expressions, not complete OOPas statements. A comparison yields `true` or `false`, which must be used in the context of a complete OOPas statement.

The legal comparison operators are:

<>	not equal to
>	greater than
<	less than
<=	less than or equal to
>=	greater than or equal to
=	equal to

Note the difference between the = (equals) operator (used in logical comparisons and in defining constants, classes, and associations) and the := (assignment) operator (used for assigning values to variables).

Comparing Links

Sometimes, it is useful not just to compare base types, but to compare links. It doesn't make sense for one link to be "less than" or "greater than" another, but we can determine whether one link is "equal to" or "not equal to" another.

In a comparison of links, both sides of the comparison must link to the same class. Suppose that we have classes called `AppleClass` and `OrangeClass` that both are subclasses of `FruitClass`. We also have corresponding associations defined as `AppleAsn`, `OrangeAsn`, and `FruitAsn`.

The only comparison we can make is between two links of the same association. We cannot compare a link of type `AppleAsn` to a link of type `OrangeAsn`, and we cannot compare a link of type `AppleAsn` to a link of type `FruitAsn`.

In addition, we cannot compare instances. Any comparison that contains an instance of a class (as opposed to a link) will not compile; thus we cannot compare an instance of `AppleClass` to an instance of `OrangeClass`.

Now, given the one thing we can compare — links to the same class — it helps to consider what constitutes two links being "equal." Two links are equal when they are linked to the same instance. In Figure 10.1, we see that `orangeLink1` and `orangeLink2` are links to the same instance of `OrangeClass`; thus the comparison `orangeLink1 = orangeLink2` is `true`. We also see that `appleLink1` and `appleLink2` are links to different instances of `AppleClass`; thus the comparison `appleLink1 = appleLink2` is `false`.

Figure 10.1
Comparing links

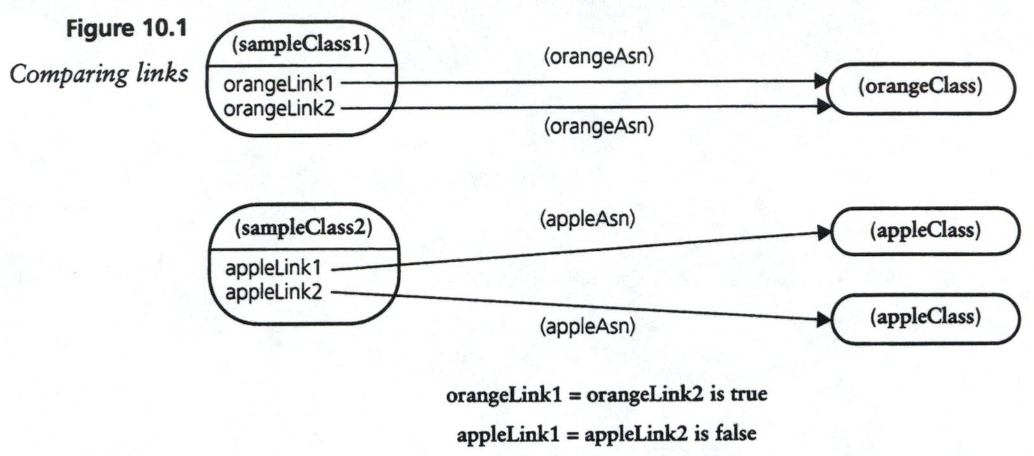

10.2 IF-THEN

How can we use these comparisons? We often state that we will or will not do something depending on some condition. If the traffic light is green, then we can continue to drive. If there is nothing in the refrigerator, then it's time to go shopping. If you've been working on a program for too long, then you should do something else for a while. Each of these sentences takes the form "If *<condition>*, then *<thing to do>*." OOPas has an `IF-THEN` statement that works in the same way.

For this chapter, we will use an instance of a class called `GPTextArea`. Instances of `GPTextArea` represent a section of the drawing area reserved for messages to the user. It can hold a single line of text and its position within a drawing area is initialized in its constructor. This class contains a method, `SetText`, that will display a string in the text area. It also contains a method, `AddText`, that connects a string to the string already showing in the text area. Figure 10.2 shows an example of a text area.

Suppose we were developing a system to reserve airline tickets. Our airline has a discounted fare for children under 13. In the following code, we assume that we have a passenger class that contains an `age` instance variable, which is an integer, and a `msgLink` instance variable, which is a link to a `GPTextArea`.

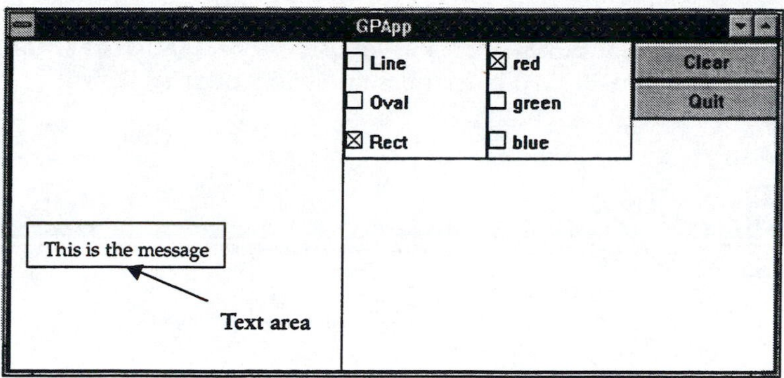

Figure 10.2 *An example of a text area*

By using an IF statement, we can determine whether the passenger should get the discounted fare:

```
{ This method determines the fare for an airline passenger. }
PROCEDURE PassengerClass.DetermineFare;
BEGIN
   ...
   { age of passenger retrieved from user here }
   ...
   IF age < 13 THEN
      msgLink^.SetText('Eligible for child''s discount.');
   ...
END;
```

The IF statement alters the flow of control. The statement consists of four parts: the reserved word IF, a condition, the reserved word THEN, and a statement or block of statements. The IF *<condition>* THEN construct cannot exist on its own; the statement or block of statements after the THEN is a part of the IF statement. Thus no semicolon appears after the THEN.

To show how the IF statement works, let's walk through the preceding code. First, the method (in the section represented by the ellipsis) asks the user to enter the age of the passenger, and this value is stored in `age`. Suppose the user types in 27. When OOPas comes to the IF statement, it compares `age` to 13. Because 27 < 13 is `false`, the `SetText` message is not sent.

Now, let's try this again using 4 as the value of `age`. The IF statement compares `age` to 13. The comparison (4 < 13) is now `true` and therefore the statement following the THEN (the `SetText` message) is performed. Thus the line "Eligible for child's discount" appears in the text area. (Note the use of a double apostrophe in `child''s`: two apostrophes appear as one in the output.)

When OOPas encounters an IF statement, it evaluates the condition between the IF and the THEN. If the condition evaluates to `true`, the corresponding statement (the `SetText` message in the preceding example) is executed. Otherwise OOPas skips the corresponding statement and moves on to the next statement in the program. This sequence is illustrated in Figure 10.3.

In the flow-of-control diagrams in this chapter and the next, the diamond-shaped boxes represent decisions (and thus have more than one exit). Syntax Box 10.2 describes the syntax of `IF` statements.

Figure 10.3

Flow of control of an IF-THEN statement

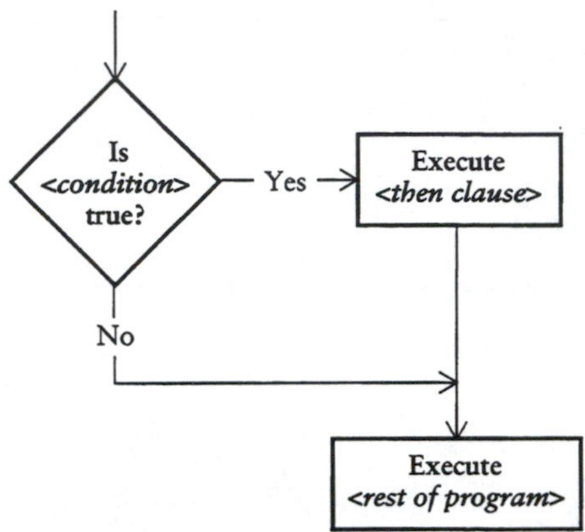


```
IF <condition> THEN
   <then clause>;
<rest of program>
```

Syntax Box 10.2

IF-THEN

Syntax:

```
IF <condition> THEN
   <statement>;
```

Where:

<condition> is any expression that evaluates to true or false.

<statement> is any legal OOPas statement. If more than one statement is to follow, then `BEGIN/END` brackets must surround the conditional code as shown below.

```
IF <condition> THEN
   BEGIN
      <statements> ;{ conditional code }
   END; { if }
```

Usage:

First *<condition>* is evaluated. When *<condition>* evaluates to `true`, *<statement>* is executed. When *<condition>* evaluates to `false`, execution continues with the statement after the conditional code.

Note that the entire conditional block is treated as a single statement, since there is no semicolon after the `THEN`.

Any statement can be part of an `IF` block, including another `IF-THEN` statement. Suppose, for instance, that the airline offers a special "Kid's Meal" to kids over the age of 2. We could generate another message for this situation by placing another `IF` statement inside the first `IF` statement, as follows:

```
PROCEDURE PassengerClass.DetermineFare;
BEGIN
   { age of passenger retrieved from user here }
   IF age < 13 THEN
      BEGIN
         msgLink^.SetText('Eligible for child''s discount.');
         IF age > 2 THEN
            msgLink^.SetText('Eligible for Kid''s Meal.');
      END;
END;
```

Note that in this code, there is more than one statement that should be executed if the condition is `true`. The block of statements that are conditional on the `IF` statement are surrounded by a `BEGIN` and `END`. As with method definitions, the `BEGIN` does not take a semicolon, but the `END` does.

In this case, one of the statements inside the `IF`'s block is another `IF` statement. Placing one conditional statement inside another is called *nesting*. There is no limit to the levels of nesting possible; we could add any number of `IF` statements inside the `IF`.

In the preceding example, the nested `IF` statement is executed only if the outer `IF` statement (`IF age < 13 THEN`) is `true`. Suppose we forgot the `BEGIN/END` brackets:

```
PROCEDURE PassengerClass.DetermineFare;
BEGIN
   { age of passenger retrieved from user }
   IF age < 13 THEN
      msgLink^.SetText('Eligible for child''s discount.');
      IF age > 2 THEN
         msgLink^.SetText('Eligible for Kid''s Meal.');
END;
```

If we run the second version and the user sets the value of `age` to 19, the user will see the message:

```
Eligible for Kid's Meal.
```

While there are 19-year-olds who probably would appreciate a Kid's Meal, it is not what the designers intended. This error results from not nesting the second `IF`. Only one statement after a `THEN` is executed, but a `BEGIN/END` block counts as only one statement, no matter how many statements it may actually contain. Thus in the second example the second `IF` condition is checked regardless of whether `age` is less than 13, because it is counted as the *second* statement after the `THEN`. Note that the indentation has nothing to do with the actual nesting of an `IF-THEN` statement: only being contained inside a `BEGIN/END` block will nest an `IF-THEN` statement.

10.3 IF-THEN-ELSE

Sometimes you may want to do one thing if a condition is `true` and something else if that condition is `false`. OOPas uses syntax resembling English with the `IF` *<condition>* `THEN` *<statement>* `ELSE` *<statement>* construct.

The `IF-THEN-ELSE` statement allows execution of one of two mutually exclusive blocks of statements — either the `THEN` block or the `ELSE` block. As in the normal `IF-THEN` statement, a boolean condition is evaluated. Again, if the condition is `true`, the statement block (or *clause*) following the `THEN` is executed, and flow of control goes on to the rest of the program. If the condition is `false`, however, the flow of control does not move immediately to the rest of the program, but instead goes to the statement following the `ELSE`. After the `ELSE` block is executed, flow of control goes to the first statement outside the `IF-THEN-ELSE` block. Figure 10.4 illustrates this process. Since the condition must be `true` or `false`, the `THEN` block and the `ELSE` block cannot both be executed. Either the `THEN` block or the `ELSE` block will be executed. See Syntax Box 10.3 for the syntax of an `IF-THEN-ELSE` statement.

Figure 10.4 *Flow of control of an IF-THEN-ELSE statement*

Is <condition> true?
Yes
No
Execute <then clause>
Execute <else clause>
Execute <rest of program>

```
IF <condition> THEN
   <then clause>
ELSE
   <else clause>;
<rest of program>
```

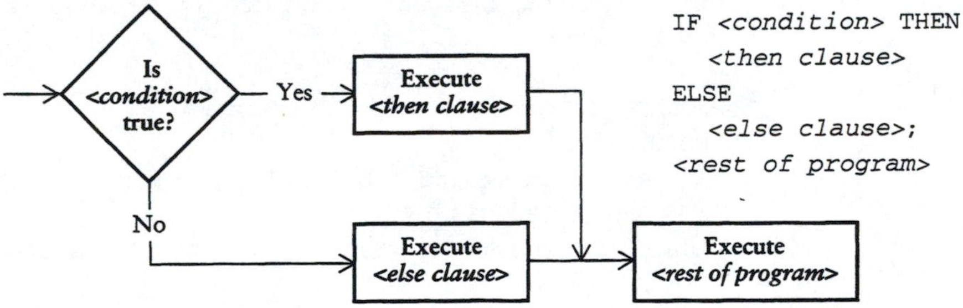

As an example, let's walk through the following code. We'll assume again that `age` is declared as an integer, that `msgLink` is an instance of `GPText-AreaAsn`, and that both are instance variables of `PassengerClass`; we'll also assume that a second link (of type `GPTextAreaAsn`), called `msgLink2`, is also an instance variable of `PassengerClass`.

```
PROCEDURE PassengerClass.DetermineFare;
BEGIN
  { age of passenger retrieved from user }
  IF age < 13 THEN
     msgLink^.SetText('Eligible for child''s discount.')
  ELSE
     msgLink^.SetText('Passenger pays adult fare.');
  msgLink2^.SetText('Calculating amount of fare...');
END;
```

Syntax Box 10.3
IF-THEN-ELSE

Syntax:

```
IF <condition> THEN
  <statement> { Note: no semicolon before else }
ELSE
  <statement>;
```

Where:

<condition> is any expression that evaluates to true or false.

<statement> is any legal OOPas statement. If more than one statement is used, then the statement block must be surrounded by `BEGIN/END` brackets.

Usage:

The *<condition>* after the word `IF` is evaluated. When the condition evaluates to `true`, the clause following the `THEN` is executed. When the condition evaluates to `false`, the clause following the `ELSE` is executed.

The `IF-THEN-ELSE` statement is treated by the compiler as a single statement. Thus semicolons appear only at the end of the entire construct, and not after the `THEN` or the `ELSE`.

As in the example in Section 10.2, the code assumes that the user has provided an age. Suppose the user enters 17. The next statement is an `IF` statement and OOPas evaluates the condition after the word `IF`. Since 17 < 13 is `false`, the statement after the `IF` is not executed.

However, this `IF` statement also has an `ELSE` clause, performed when the condition in the `IF` statement is `false`. Since `age < 13` is `false`, the `ELSE` clause is executed, producing the message:

```
Passenger pays adult fare.
```

Now the final `SetText` message is sent to the instance linked to `msgLink2`. The result is that the user will see the following messages in order:

```
Passenger pays adult fare.
Calculating amount of fare...
```

Now, let's look at the same code when the user types in 8. When the `IF` statement is encountered, the condition is `true`, and the first `SetText` statement displays:

```
Eligible for child's discount.
```

Remember that the `IF` and `ELSE` clauses are actually part of one larger compound statement. Having executed the `IF` block, OOPas ignores the `ELSE` clause and goes to the final `SetText` message to `msgLink2`, with the result of the following messages in order:

```
Eligible for child's discount.
Calculating amount of fare...
```

An `IF-THEN-ELSE` statement is *not* the same as two `IF-THEN` statements with opposing conditions. Suppose an employee decided to raise all employees' salaries such that those making under $7/hour would get an increase of $1/hour and all others would get a 10% increase in their salaries. The following code fragment is supposed to handle both cases, but it illustrates a problem that can arise from using disjoint `IF` statements instead of an `ELSE` clause:

```
IF hourlyWage <= 7.00 THEN
  hourlyWage := hourlyWage + 1.00; { increase by $1/hour }
IF hourlyWage > 7.00 THEN
  hourlyWage := hourlyWage * 1.10; { increase by 10% }
```

Suppose `hourlyWage` = 6.50. The program starts by comparing `hourlyWage` to 7.00. Since 6.50 < 7.00 is `true` and the first assignment statement is executed, `hourlyWage` goes from 6.50 to 7.50.

Now, OOPas continues to the next statement, which is another `IF` statement. OOPas calculates the condition `hourlyWage` > 7.00. Since `hourlyWage` is now 7.50, the comparison 7.50 > 7.00 is `true`, and the second assignment statement is also executed: 10% is added to `hourlyWage`, so that it now holds the value 8.25. This means that this person's `hourlyWage` has increased twice — from 6.50 to 7.50, and again from 7.50 to 8.25.

While this would certainly make certain employees quite happy, this double increase is not what was intended. The following code fragment produces the correct result:

```
IF hourlyWage <= 7.00 THEN
  hourlyWage := hourlyWage + 1.00{ increase by $1/hour }
ELSE
  hourlyWage := hourlyWage * 1.10; { increase by 10% }
```

Now if `hourlyWage` is 6.50, the first assignment statement is performed as shown. However, the `ELSE` clause is not performed, because the `IF` clause has already been executed. Thus `hourlyWage` is increased only once.

It is important to remember that `IF-THEN-ELSE` and opposing `IF-THEN`s are not necessarily identical. Always make sure that the `IF` statement you use gives you the desired result. To check, hand simulate your code carefully and test each possible condition.

10.4 USING BOOLEANS

As we have seen, OOPas can evaluate a condition, test whether it is `true` or `false`, and act upon that result in an `IF-THEN-ELSE` statement. Every condition that can be evaluated to either `true` or `false` is called a *boolean* condition, after the mathematician George Boole (1815–1864). OOPas also can store a `true` or `false` condition in a variable called a boolean variable. Declaring boolean variables is analogous to declaring a variable of type `integer` or `real`. The following declares a boolean variable called `negative`:

```
VAR
  negative: boolean;{ indicates whether a number is negative }
```

Boolean variables are much more restrictive than the other types of variables we have seen; they can have only one of the two values `true` or `false`. To give `negative` a value, we can assign a boolean constant to it:

```
negative := true;
```

or we can give it the value of a boolean expression:

```
negative := Sin(theta) < 0.5;
```

Although you may not have encountered boolean logic before, the preceding statement shouldn't seem foreign to you. You know that an assignment statement begins by evaluating the expression on the right. In this case, the expression is evaluated by finding the result of `Sin(theta)` (where `theta` is some variable), comparing the result to 0.5, and assigning the result of the comparison to `negative`. If `Sin(theta)` returns 0.13, then the assignment simplifies to `negative := 0.13 < 0.5`. Since this comparison evaluates to `true`, `negative` is assigned the value `true`.

Boolean variables are often used in place of the condition in `IF` statements, as in the following code fragment:

```
negative := (number < 0);
IF negative = true THEN
  msgLink^.SetText('Your number is less than zero.');
```

This code fragment simply breaks the line `IF (number < 0) THEN` into two parts: First the condition is evaluated and stored in `negative`, then the result of the comparison is checked by the `IF` statement. You might wonder why we would bother to store the results of a test in a boolean variable, when we could use the single condition `IF (number < 0) THEN`. We use this variable when we need the results of the test in multiple places but only wish to perform the test once. The variable in this situation often is called a *flag*.

As a final point, consider the IF statement

```
IF negative = true THEN
```

OOPas allows us to write this condition more compactly as

```
IF negative THEN
```

The THEN clause following this condition is executed only if negative evaluates to true. In other words, the = true syntax is optional.

10.5 LOGICAL OPERATORS

You now know how to establish and evaluate conditions and how to use them to determine flow of control. Up to this point, these conditions have been fairly simple. For greater flexibility, OOPas also allows the programmer to test for multiple or opposing conditions. OOPas uses three logic operators — NOT, OR, and AND — all of which are similar to their English equivalents.

NOT

NOT specifies the opposite of a given boolean condition. For example:

```
CheckingAccount = OBJECT
   ...
   PROCEDURE Transaction;
PRIVATE
   overdrawn : boolean;      { whether balance goes below 0 }
   balance,                  { amount of money in checking acct }
   withdrawal : real;        { amount taken out of account }
   slider : GPRealSlider;    { slider to display balance }
   ...
END;

PROCEDURE CheckingAccount.Transaction;
BEGIN
   ...
   balance := balance - withdrawal;
   overdrawn := (balance < 0);
   IF NOT overdrawn THEN
      slider.SetValue(balance);
   ...
END; { Transaction}
```

The line IF NOT overdrawn THEN is the equivalent of IF overdrawn = false THEN. The IF NOT version has the advantage of being easier to understand, however, since IF NOT overdrawn THEN is closer to everyday English than IF overdrawn = false THEN.

We can summarize the effect of NOT in the table shown in Syntax Box 10.4. This type of table, called a *truth table*, is used often in logic theory. It shows all of the possible combinations of a logical operator. (In the case of NOT, there are only two situations.)

Syntax Box 10.4

Truth table for NOT

<expression>	NOT *<expression>*
false	true
true	false

OR

Suppose a bank charges a customer $3.00 if she has less than $400.00 in her account during the month or if she writes more than 12 checks in that month. The code fragment to determine whether to apply this charge (assuming numChecks is a local variable) might look like this:

```
IF (balance < 400.00) OR (numChecks > 12) THEN
  balance := balance - 3.00;      { Deduct service charge. }
```

The statement balance := balance - 3.00 is executed only if at least one of the conditions (balance < 400.00) and (numChecks > 12) is true. In other words, if either or both of the boolean conditions are true, then the entire expression evaluates to true. If both conditions are false, the entire expression evaluates to false.

Suppose balance = 500.00 and numChecks = 14. The expression (balance < 400.00) is false, since 500.00 < 400.00 is false. On the other hand, (numChecks > 12) is true in this case, since 14 > 12 is true. Thus the entire boolean condition evaluates to (false) OR (true). Since at least one of the expressions evaluated with the OR operator is true, the entire expression evaluates to true and the assignment statement is executed.

Syntax Box 10.5 is a truth table of all the possible combinations of two boolean expressions and the value that results from combining them with OR.

Syntax Box 10.5

Truth table for OR

<expression1>	*<expression2>*	*<expression1>* OR *<expression2>*
true	true	true
true	false	true
false	true	true
false	false	false

AND

Suppose the same bank gives toasters to new customers who deposit more than $250.00. If the bank checks its accounts once a month, a new customer is one whose account is 31 or fewer days old, as in the following:

```
IF (numDays <= 31) AND (balance > 250.00) THEN
  SendToaster;
```

AND evaluates to `true` only when both expressions are `true`; otherwise, AND evaluates to `false`. Thus the procedure `SendToaster` is called only if both `numDays <= 31` and `balance > 250.00` evaluate to `true`. Syntax Box 10.6 show the truth table for AND.

Syntax Box 10.6

Truth table for AND

<expression1>	*<expression2>*	*<expression1>* **AND** *<expression2>*
`true`	`true`	`true`
`true`	`false`	`false`
`false`	`true`	`false`
`false`	`false`	`false`

Priorities and Long Expressions

In the same way that multiplication takes priority over addition, boolean operators have different priorities, as listed in Syntax Box 10.7. However, comparisons between numbers, such as < and >, have a lower priority than the boolean operators. Thus, we use parentheses often, as in this expression:

Syntax Box 10.7

Priorities of boolean operators

Precedence:

1. NOT (highest)
2. AND
3. OR (lowest)

Use parentheses to change the order of evaluation.

```
IF (numDays <= 31) AND (balance > 250.00) THEN
```

Boolean operators can be chained together, just as arithmetic expressions can contain more than one arithmetic operator. Suppose we had the following conditions to set the coordinates for a particular instance of `GPPoint`:

```
PROCEDURE SampleClass.SampleMethod ( threshold : integer );
VAR
   horiz, vert: integer;
   newPt: GPPoint;
BEGIN
   ...
   IF (threshold > 2) AND (NOT (horiz = vert) OR (vert >= 0) ) THEN
     newPt.SetCoords (horiz, vert);
   ...
END;
```

The boldfaced expression looks fairly complicated, but you can evaluate it without much difficulty as long as you start with the innermost expression and work outward. Say that both `horiz` and `vert` are 10. You begin evaluating the large expression with the innermost expression: `vert >= 0`. Since `vert = 10, vert >= 0` is `true`. Using substitution, you can rewrite the expression as follows:

```
IF (threshold > 2) AND (NOT (horiz = vert) OR (true)) THEN ...
```

Now you can evaluate `(NOT (horiz = vert) OR (true))`. Since both `horiz` and `vert` are 10, `horiz = vert` is `true`, and `NOT (horiz = vert)` is then `false`. `(false OR true)` evaluates to `true`. Now the expression looks like this:

```
IF (threshold > 2) AND true THEN ...
```

If `threshold` is `3`, then the expression becomes `true AND true` and evaluates to `true`. This in turn makes the entire expression `true`, and the `SetCoords` message is sent. If `threshold` is `2`, the entire expression is `false` and the statement is not executed.

When you use the AND and OR operators, *both* conditions are evaluated, even though it isn't always necessary (if one of the conditions of an AND is `false`, the whole expression must be `false`). You must consider how OOPas evaluates the condition to ensure that the evaluation will not cause an error.

Consider the statement:

```
IF (num <> 0.0) AND (total / num > 1.0) THEN ....
```

This causes a problem when `num` = 0. In this case, the first condition is `false`, so the whole boolean expression is `false`, no matter what the value of `total` is. Still, OOPas always evaluates both sides of an AND operator. When `total/num` is evaluated, OOPas tries to divide the value of `total` by the value of `num` — which is 0. Since division by 0 is illegal, a run-time error occurs. Run-time errors usually *bomb* or *crash* the program, meaning that execution stops abruptly. In contrast, the following code avoids the error situation:

```
IF (num <> 0.0) THEN
  IF (total/num > 1.0) THEN ...
```

10.6 USING LOGICAL OPERATIONS

Now that we have looked at complex boolean expressions, we'd like to make use of those expressions without having to retype them. There are two ways to do this. The first, and easiest, is to simply store the value of an expression in a *boolean variable*. The second way is to make use of a *boolean function*.

Assignment

The results of boolean operations can be stored in boolean variables, as we saw in Section 10.4. We simply use the type name `boolean` instead of `integer` or `real` and use assignment statements as we have in previous examples.

Let's reconsider our bank that awards toasters to new accounts. We can rewrite the example using a boolean variable as:

```
PROCEDURE CheckingAccount.DetermineIfWinner;
VAR
  numDays: integer;{ number of days account has been open }
  awardWinner: boolean;{ indicates whether customer wins toaster }
BEGIN
  ...
  awardWinner := (numDays <=31) AND (balance > 250.00);
  IF awardWinner THEN
    SendToaster;
  ...
END; { procedure }
```

After sending the toaster to the winner, the bank might be interested in keeping track of how many people have been receiving toasters. We could do this by adding the necessary code to the `THEN` part (making the `THEN` part nested in a `BEGIN/END` block in the process):

```
IF awardWinner THEN
  BEGIN
    SendToaster;
    myBank^.AcctReceivedAToaster(@self)
  END;
```

But suppose we wished to do something to all accounts, such as accumulate interest, before notifying the bank as a whole that this account had received a toaster? We could duplicate the code we needed, then place it in an ELSE clause:

```
IF awardWinner THEN
   BEGIN
      SendToaster;
      AccumulateInterest;
      myBank^.AcctReceivedAToaster(@this)
   END
ELSE
   AccumulateInterest;
```

The problem with this code, of course, occurs when we need to add more things to do to any account, after sending a toaster but before notifying the bank. We have two places we need to make changes, making it very easy to forget the changes in one place. Instead of using an ELSE clause, we can reuse our boolean variable in a separate IF statement:

```
IF awardWinner THEN
   SendToaster;
AccumulateInterest;
IF awardWinner THEN
   myBank^.AcctReceivedAToaster(@this)
```

Boolean Functions

The biggest shortcoming of boolean variables is when you want to re-evaluate the same expression with different values. Continuing with our checking account example, suppose some other part of the bank wished to find out whether a particular account was an award winner. One way we could implement this would be by copying the expression that determines award winners to another part of the program:

```
IF (currentAcct.Age <=31) AND (currentAcct.Balance > 250.00) THEN
   { Aha! An award winner } ....
```

But suppose the bank changes its policy of who should receive toasters and who should not? Perhaps the bank management feels the bank has been giving out too many toasters. If we had copied the expression for an award winner to many other places, we'd have to find all those places and change them. It would be easy to miss one expression, producing a bug, where one part of the program thought an account had received a toaster and another part hadn't.

We can write boolean functions for objects to handle this problem. If everybody uses the object's boolean function, then changing the boolean expression involves merely changing the function itself, once, rather than changing the expression everywhere it appears. Let's see this for our toasters:

```
FUNCTION CheckingAccount.IsAwardWinner : boolean;
BEGIN
  IsAwardWinner := (numDays <=31) AND (balance > 250.00)
END;
```

We can now use this function to get a value for our `awardWinner` variable:

```
PROCEDURE CheckingAccount.DetermineIfWinner;
VAR
  numDays: integer;{ number of days account has been open }
  awardWinner: boolean;{ indicates whether customer wins toaster }
BEGIN
  ...
  awardWinner := IsAwardWinner;
  IF awardWinner THEN
    SendToaster;
  ...
END; { DetermineIfWinner }
```

Even better, instead of assigning the return value of this function to a local variable, we could instead simply use the return value as a boolean expression:

```
IF IsAwardWinner THEN
  SendToaster;
```

Like arithmetic functions, which can be used anywhere an arithmetic function is valid, boolean functions can be used anywhere a boolean expression can. Boolean functions can be extremely useful. In fact, they can be used to compare instances for equality (or other conditions). Let's look at a boolean function defined for instances of `GPPoint` that checks to see whether two points are equal (`x` and `y` are instance variables that hold the coordinates):

```
FUNCTION GPPoint.Equal(pt: GPPoint) : boolean;
BEGIN
  Equal := (x = pt.GetX) AND (y = pt.GetY)
END;
```

We can use this `Equal` function in places that we'd like to use `=` for two points. You can define similar methods for other classes.

10.7 IF-THEN-ELSE IF

Suppose we want to expand our earlier airline example and offer different kinds of discounts, say, to those over 65. We are adding another condition to our earlier sequence (all we did before was see whether `age` is less than 13). To do this, we can use an extended sequence of `IF-THEN-ELSE` statements. Figure 10.5 shows the flow of control in the `IF-THEN-ELSE IF` statement.

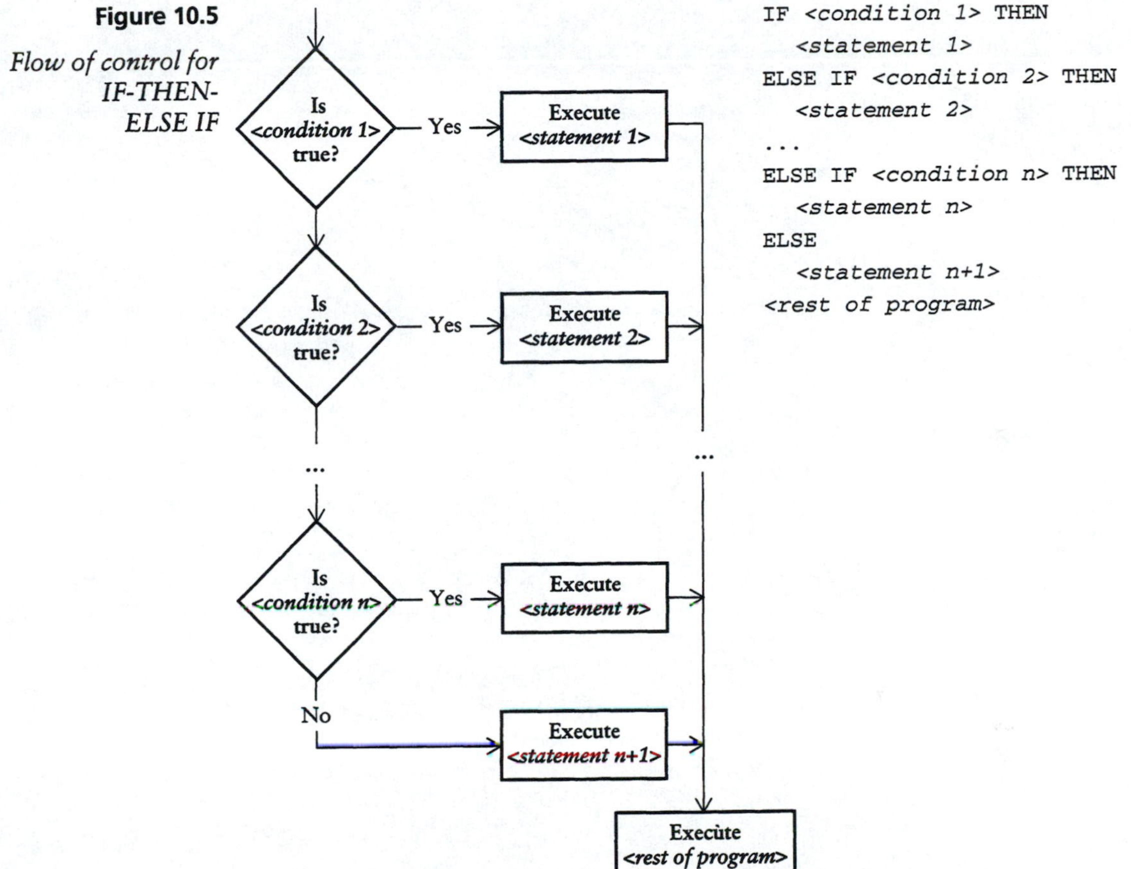

Figure 10.5
Flow of control for IF-THEN-ELSE IF

When OOPas encounters an `IF-THEN-ELSE IF` construct, it evaluates the boolean condition after the first `IF`. If this condition is `true`, the corresponding code is executed and flow of control moves to the next statement after the `IF-THEN-ELSE IF` construct. If the first condition is `false`, OOPas looks at the next boolean condition. Again, if this condition is `true`, the appropriate code is interpreted and executed; otherwise, the next boolean condition is evaluated. The conditions are checked, one at a time and from top to bottom, until one evaluates to `true`. Thus for *<statement 3>* to be executed, boolean conditions 1 and 2 must have been `false` and boolean condition 3 must be `true`.

The `IF-THEN-ELSE IF` construct can contain a final `ELSE`. If none of the other conditional code blocks are executed, the final `ELSE`'s block is performed. The complete syntax of an `IF-THEN-ELSE IF` construct is described in Syntax Box 10.8.

Syntax Box 10.8

IF-THEN-ELSE IF

Syntax:

```
IF <condition 1> THEN
   <statement 1>
ELSE IF <condition 2> THEN
   <statement 2>
...
ELSE IF <condition n> THEN
   <statement n>
ELSE
   <statement>;
```

Where:

<condition 1>, *<condition 2>*, . . . , *<condition n>* are expressions that evaluate to `true` or `false`.

<statement> is any legal OOPas statement. If more than one statement is used, the statement block must be surrounded by `BEGIN/END` brackets.

Usage:

<condition 1> is evaluated first. If it evaluates to `true`, then *<statement 1>* is executed. The rest of the `IF-THEN-ELSE IF` construct is ignored. If *<condition 1>* is `false`, then *<condition 2>* is checked; if *<condition 2>* is `false`, *<condition 3>* is checked. This process continues until a condition evaluates to `true`. At this point, the statement following the associated `IF` or `ELSE IF` is executed. If none of the conditions evaluate to `true`, the statement following the final `ELSE` is executed.

The `IF-THEN-ELSE IF` statement is treated by OOPas as a single statement. Semicolons must be used only at the end of the entire construct, not after the `THEN` or the `ELSE`.

The final `ELSE` and its associated *<statement>* are optional.

Let's return to the airline example. If we want to add another condition for discounts for passengers over 65, we can revise the code as follows:

```
PROCEDURE PassengerClass.DetermineFare;
BEGIN
   { age of passenger retrieved from user here ... }
   IF age < 13 THEN
      msgLink^.SetText('Eligible for child''s discount.')
   ELSE IF age > 65 THEN
      msgLink^.SetText('Eligible for senior discount.')
   ELSE
      msgLink^.SetText('Passenger pays regular fare.');
   { rest of method ... }
END;
```

With the `IF-THEN-ELSE IF` construct, OOPas checks each condition and executes the first statement associated with a `true` condition. Suppose the user enters the age 72. OOPas performs the comparisons in order; thus its first check is the expression `age < 13`. Since this is `false`, OOPas skips to the next `ELSE IF` and evaluates the condition `age > 65`. Since this is `true`, it sends the `SetText` message with the parameter "Eligible for senior discount." Now that one condition has been found to be `true`, all future conditions (none here) are ignored, and OOPas can skip to the statement following the final `ELSE` or `ELSE IF` statement.

Summary

In this chapter we saw how OOPas works with the concept of `true` or `false`. For example, you can ask OOPas to tell us whether `number < 0` is a true statement. Any of six operators (<, >, =, <=, >=, <>) can be used to compare two expressions. The expressions must be of the same base type — `integer` or `real` — or they must be links to instances of the same class. In the latter case, we don't really want to know whether one link is "less than" or "greater than" another; instead, we say that one link is equal to another if both link to the same instance.

Information on whether a comparison is `true` or `false` can be used to alter a program's flow of control. You can designate a block of statements and tell OOPas to execute it only if a particular condition is `true`. The `IF-THEN` statement tests the condition and tells OOPas whether the block should be executed. The more general `IF-THEN-ELSE` statement tells OOPas to perform one block if a condition is `true` and to perform another block if the condition is `false`.

The results of comparisons can be stored in boolean variables, which may contain only the values `true` or `false`. A boolean variable is declared in the same manner as a numeric or graphic variable. Booleans also can receive values in assignment statements.

OOPas provides three *logical operators* for creating more complex boolean expressions. The `NOT` operator inverts the value of a boolean expression. The `AND` operator looks at two boolean expressions and returns `true` if and only if both are `true`. The `OR` operator also looks at two boolean expressions but returns `true` if either or both are `true`. Complex boolean expressions can be computed by *boolean functions*, which return a boolean value. The return value of a boolean function can be used wherever a boolean expression can be used.

Exercises

Understanding Concepts

1. Write a conditional statement that prints the absolute value of the number stored in the `real` variable `distance`.

2. In the following code, assume that `year` is an `integer` variable. Which values of year will cause the `PrintRegularYear` message to be sent?

```
IF year MOD 100 = 0 THEN
  IF YEAR MOD 400 <> 0 THEN
    PrintLeapYear
  ELSE IF year MOD 4 = 0 THEN
    PrintLeapYear
ELSE
  PrintRegularYear
```

3. Rewrite the following method, using as few statements as possible:

```
Cola = OBJECT
  CONSTRUCTOR Init(newPrice, newSize: real);
  FUNCTION GetPricePerLiter: real;
  PROCEDURE OutputPricePerLiter; { displays cost per liter }
PRIVATE
  price,    { price of container of cola }
  size: real; { size of cola container, in liters }
END;

Grocery = OBJECT
  CONSTRUCTOR Init;
  PROCEDURE ComparePrices;
  PROCEDURE ShowMessage(message: string); { outputs a string }
PRIVATE
  redCola, blueCola: Cola;
END;

PROCEDURE Grocery.ComparePrices;
BEGIN
  IF redCola.GetPricePerLiter > blueCola.GetPricePerLiter THEN
    BEGIN
      redCola.OutputPricePerLiter;
      blueCola.OutputPricePerLiter;
      ShowMessage('Red Cola is the better buy.');
    END

  ELSE IF redCola.GetPricePerLiter < blueCola.GetPricePerLiter
        THEN
    BEGIN
      redCola.OutputPricePerLiter;
      blueCola.OutputPricePerLiter;
      ShowMessage('Blue Cola is the better buy.');
    END

  ELSE IF redCola.GetPricePerLiter = blueCola.GetPricePerLiter
        THEN
    BEGIN
      redCola.OutputPricePerLiter;
      blueCola.OutputPricePerLiter;
      ShowMessage('Neither cola is the better buy.');
    END;
END; { method }
```

4. What is the bug in the following code? How can it be corrected?

```
FUNCTION Worker.CalculateWeeklyPay(numHours:real) : real;
VAR
  wages: real;{ wages earned this week }
  overTimeHours: real;    { num of hours worked overtime }
BEGIN
  wages := numHours * hourlyWage;
  IF numHours > 40 THEN
    { Calculate overtime pay — 1 1/2 times normal pay. }
    overTimeHours := numHours - 40;
    wages := wages + (overTimeHours * hourlyWage * 3/2);
  CalculateWeeklyPay := real;
END;
```

5. A store that normally sells blank videotapes for $3.95 each gives discounts for large orders. The store gives a 10% discount if you buy 10–19 tapes, a 25% discount if you buy 20–29 tapes, and a 33% discount if you buy 30 or more tapes. The following code is supposed to output the cost, depending on the value of numToBuy. What is wrong with the code? How can it be debugged?

```
CONST
  tapePrice = 3.95;{ full cost of one videotape }

{ returns full cost of purchase given number of tapes to buy }
FUNCTION Exercise.PurchaseTapes(numToBuy: integer) : real;
VAR
  cost,{ total cost }
  discount: real; { % off for large order }
BEGIN
  IF numToBuy > 10 THEN
    discount := .10
  ELSE IF numToBuy > 20 THEN
    discount := .25

  ELSE IF numToBuy > 30 THEN
    discount := .33
  ELSE
    discount := 0.0; { no discount }
  cost := price * numToBuy;
  cost := cost - (discount * cost);
  PurchaseTapes := cost;
END;
```

6. Consider this function:

```
FUNCTION Exercise.Sample ( val : integer ) : boolean;
BEGIN
  Sample := val >= 1;
END;
```

Then consider the two procedures `Silly` and `Sillier`:

```
PROCEDURE Exercise.Silly;
VAR
  value : integer;
  sampleVar : boolean;
BEGIN
  value := 1;
  sampleVar := value >= 1;
  IF sampleVar THEN
    value := value - 1;
  IF sampleVar THEN
    value := value - 1;
END;

PROCEDURE Exercise.Sillier;
VAR
  value : integer;
BEGIN
  value := 1;
  IF Sample(value) THEN
    value := value - 1;
  IF Sample(value) THEN
    value := value - 1;
END;
```

What, if any, differences are there in the value of the local variable `value` when the two procedures reach their ends? Explain.

Coding Problems

1. In a certain figure skating competition, three judges rate performances on a scale of 1.0 to 6.0, with 6.0 being the best. Scores are given to the nearest tenth of a point. The lowest of the three scores is ignored, and a skater's final score is the average of the other two judges' ratings. Write a function that accepts three judges' scores as parameters and returns the skater's final score.

2. All of the composite (nonprime) numbers are multiples of 2, 3, 5, or 7 (except, of course, 2, 3, 5, and 7). Write a method that receives an integer between 2 and 100 as a parameter and sends the message Prime or Composite, depending on the number.

3. Write a method that takes four parameters that represent the horizontal and vertical coordinates of two points. The method should output a line of text, indicating whether the first point is to the northeast, north, northwest, west, southwest, south, southeast, or east of the second point, or if the coordinates represent the same point.

4. In the game of fizz-fuzz, players count off the numbers from 1 to 100. When a player's number contains a 7 or is divisible by 7, the player should not count the number but instead should say "fizz." If the player's number contains a 7 *and* is divisible by 7, the player should say "fizz-fuzz." Write a method that dis-

plays the number, "fizz," or "fizz-fuzz" in a text area, depending on the contents of an `integer` parameter called `playerNum`.

5. Write a method that, given today's date, generates tomorrow's date. Don't forget to take leap years into account.

6. Make a new kind of financial calculator like the one used in Chapter 9 by modeling a savings account with a variable interest rate based on the current value of the account. Savings accounts with less than $100 should be assessed a service charge of $3 each month. Accounts with between $100 and $500 in them should earn no interest, but not be charged a fee. Accounts with more than $500 but less than $2000 should earn 2% interest. Accounts with more than $2000 should earn 5% interest.

Programming Problems

1. Write a program that shows the arrival and departure times of a flight. The user should indicate the direction, distance, and departure time of the flight. You can assume that a plane flies at 600 miles per hour, and that each 1000 miles in an east–west direction indicates a change in time zone.

2. Extend the Aquarium example (last seen in Programming Problem 1 in Chapter 6). If a shark sees a fish (that is, if the shark, heading in its current direction, will swim into the fish), it heads toward the fish. If a fish sees a shark, it heads away from the shark. If the fish sees a plant, it heads toward the plant.

3. Write another extension of the Aquarium example: This time, assume the edges of the screen are the limits of where the fish and shark can swim. If a fish or shark reach a limit, it should change direction.

4. Extend the banking examples in this chapter and in Chapter 9 by providing both checking accounts and savings accounts. Both kinds of accounts should allow withdrawals and deposits. Savings accounts should earn interest either using the method described in Coding Problem 6 or using a fixed daily rate of 1.5% (see Programming Problem 6 in Chapter 9). Checking accounts should allow the user to write checks, which cost $2.95 per check. Finally, it should be possible to transfer funds from one account to the other.

   In all cases, the account's methods should check whether there is sufficient funds to perform the operation. If there isn't, an informative message should be displayed and the transaction should not be processed.

5. Write a program that clips lines outside a certain area. First, ask the user to specify a rectangular area as the clipping area. Then, ask the user to choose two endpoints of a line. Your program should draw only the part of the line that is the clipping area. (*Hint:* First divide the possibilities according to how many endpoints are inside the area. Then consider how lines intersect.)

6. Write a variation of Programming Problem 5. After selecting an "outside clip" tool, the user can drag out a rectangle. Subsequent drawing by a rubberbanding straight-line tool should draw only the part of the line inside the rectangle

drawn by the outside clip tool, clipping all parts of the line (and only those parts of the line) outside the rectangle. Your program should draw only the part of the line that is the clipping area. Only one clipping rectangle need be active at a time: If the user draws another one, it replaces the previously drawn clipping rectangle. (See the previous exercise for a hint.)

7. Extend Programming Problem 6 by providing an "inside clip" tool. In this case, only those parts of the line drawn *outside* the clip rectangle should be drawn, clipping all parts inside the clipping rectangle. As before, only one clipping rectangle need be active at a time.

8. Implement clippable rectangles, ovals, and pencils, allowing for either inside clipping rectangles or outside clipping rectangles, based on whichever of Programming Problem 6 or Programming Problem 7 you implemented. If you did both, choose one.

11

Choosing One of Many

In Chapter 10, we saw how to choose one of two alternatives using an IF-THEN statement. Using a series of IF-THEN-ELSE IF statements, we could choose from a series of possibilities. Choosing exactly one alternative out of many is fairly common, though, and OOPas provides an additional construct specialized for that purpose, as opposed to the more general IF-THEN-ELSE IF. In this chapter, we'll study CASE statements, which execute one statement out of many, depending on the value of a variable.

11.1 ENUMERATED TYPES

The variable we use in a CASE statement to select one statement from many statements can be an integer. However, numbers aren't always good descriptions of things in the real world. When we're building a program to model something, for instance, we want the program itself to be a good model. Let's consider modeling something we've all encountered at one time or another: butterflies. Looking at Figure 11.1, we see a picture of the life cycle of a butterfly. Butterflies live in stages, starting as eggs and hatching into caterpillars (more technically, the larva stage). After a while, a caterpillar cocoons itself into a pupa, from which an adult butterfly emerges.

We could model each of these four stages (egg, caterpillar, pupa, adult) with a different class. Certainly, the behaviors of each of the four stages differ greatly. For example, only adult butterflies have wings and can fly. However, a different class for each stage would mean having different instances for different stages. If we wanted to model the life of a single butterfly, that wouldn't be what we want. We would want a single instance that changes over time.

For such situations, we can use enumerated types. An *enumerated type* consists of a fixed number of named values, in our case, the different stages of the life cycle of a butterfly. We can define an enumerated value in the TYPE section

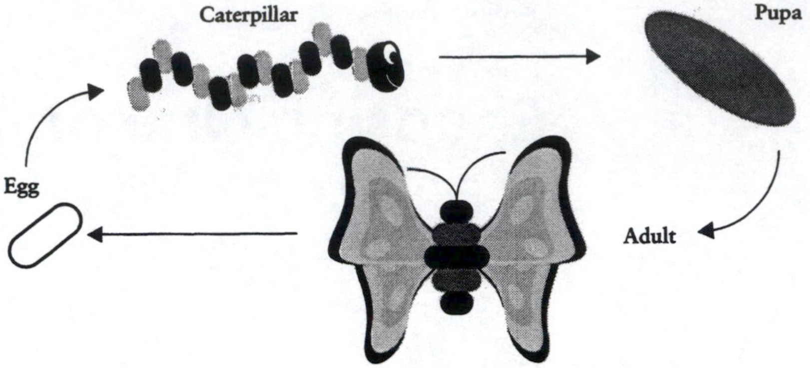

Figure 11.1

Stages in a butterfly's life cycle

Caterpillar
Pupa
Egg
Adult

by providing a name for the enumerated type as a whole and listing all of the possible values:

```
TYPE
  ButterflyLifeCycleStage = ( Egg, Caterpillar, Pupa, Adult );
```

Making Variables from an Enumerated Type

Now that we've declared an enumerated type, we can declare local and instance variables whose type is `ButterflyLifeCycleStage`. For instance, we can make a `Butterfly` class. We'll give the class an instance variable for the stage the butterfly is in (adding methods and instance variables as we go).

```
Butterfly = OBJECT
  CONSTRUCTOR Init; { Lay a butterfly egg. }
PRIVATE
  stage : ButterflyLifeCycleStage;
END;
```

Now, when we construct an instance of `Butterfly`, we can initialize the butterfly's life cycle to a value of the enumerated type. In our case, we want to use `Egg`, because that's how all butterflies start out:

```
CONSTRUCTOR Butterfly.Init;
BEGIN
  stage := Egg
END;
```

Assignment of an enumerated type works just as you might expect. A variable of an enumerated type can be on the left-hand side of an assignment operator as long as the right-hand side is an expression that evaluates to a value of the same enumerated type. Of course, any of the named values of an enumerated type are valid expressions (just as integer literals such as `1` and `42` are valid integer expressions).

In fact, there's a special enumerated type we made extensive use of in Chapter 10, but we didn't tell you it was an enumerated type: `boolean`. `boolean` is an enumerated type with only two values:

```
TYPE
  boolean = ( false, true );
```

OOPas automatically includes this definition; for this reason, we didn't provide it earlier.

Comparing Variables of Enumerated Types

Now let's suppose we want our butterfly class to have a `Fly` method. Of course, only adult butterflies can fly. It would be nice if the `Butterfly` class could have a `Fly` method only for those instances whose `stage` is `Adult`. However, we cannot define a method that exists only when an instance variable has a particular value, and we've already decided that having different classes wouldn't work — we want one instance to be our butterfly changing its life cycle stage over time.

So what can we do? We can use an `IF` statement inside the `Fly` method, performing the actions of flying (such as fluttering the butterfly's wings) only when the `stage` is `Adult`:

```
PROCEDURE Butterfly.Fly;
BEGIN
  IF stage = Adult THEN
    FlutterWings { Do what it takes to fly. }
END;
```

All the boolean operators we saw in Chapter 10 can be used both on variables of enumerated type and on the values themselves. In the `Fly` method, we checked whether the butterfly was of the correct stage to fly. Similarly, we can determine whether the butterfly had been hatched yet, simply by seeing whether its stage was past the `Egg` stage. In `Fly`, we simply tested for equality. Now, we'll make use of the order of the values in the enumeration:

```
FUNCTION Butterfly.HasBeenHatched : boolean;
BEGIN
  IF stage > Egg THEN
    HasBeenHatched := true
  ELSE
    HasBeenHatched := false
END;
```

The order of the values of an enumerated type is determined by the order in which we listed them in the definition of the type. Thus it's quite important that we enumerated the stages of a butterfly's life cycle in order from youngest to oldest. Thus comparisons using < or > are based on age. Had we listed the values in the opposite order, a comparison like `stage > Egg` would never be `true`.

Two special functions make use of this order: `Succ` and `Pred`. The function `Succ` takes a value of an enumerated type and returns the next value (or successor, hence the name) of the enumerated type. Thus `Succ(Egg)` returns `Caterpillar`. There is no successor for the last value in an enumerated type, so `Succ(Adult)` will produce an error from OOPas. The function `Pred`, as you might guess, produces the previous value (or predecessor) of the enumerated type. So `Pred(Adult)` returns `Pupa`, and, predictably, `Pred(Egg)` is an error.

We can use `Succ` to define a `Metamorphose` method for our butterfly. Since `Succ` fails if we apply it to the last value of an enumeration, we'll have to do something special if the butterfly is an `Adult`. In this case, we'll make the `Metamorphose` method a boolean function. It will return `true` if the butterfly successfully metamorphoses. If it is an `Adult`, then `Metamorphose` will return `false`.

```
FUNCTION Butterfly.Metamorphose : boolean;
BEGIN
  IF stage < Adult THEN
    BEGIN
      stage := Succ(stage);
      Metamorphose := true
    END
  ELSE
    Metamorphose := false
END;
```

11.2 CASE

Suppose we wished to do something different for each stage in the life cycle of a butterfly? For example, let's consider how to implement a butterfly's `Eat` method. Eggs clearly don't eat anything, nor do pupae. Caterpillars eat various kinds of leaves, and adult butterflies eat nectar from flowers. We could represent these differences with a series of `IF-THEN-ELSE` statements, but there is a better way.

The `CASE` construct allows us to choose from more than two mutually exclusive choices. The `CASE` statement is something like a vending machine. Coin-operated machines have simple mechanisms to figure out how many of each coin have been inserted (see Figure 11.2). Coins that are deposited fall onto a ramp with slots for each different type of coin. When a coin hits the

Figure 11.2

Vending machine operation

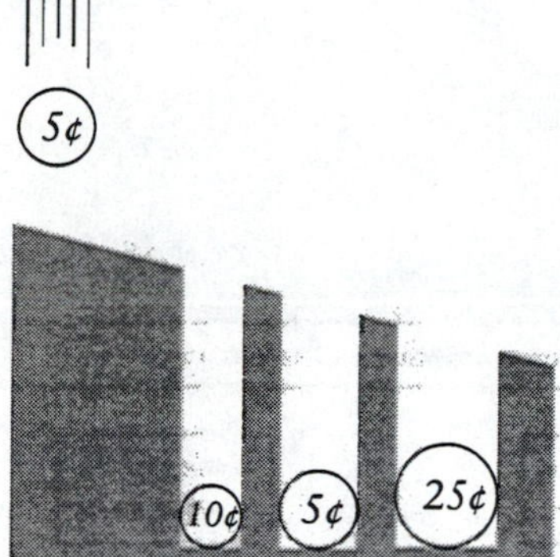

ramp, it rolls down until it reaches a slot in which it fits and then falls into that slot.

Enumerated types, integers, and characters are *ordinal types* — the values come in a particular order (remember `Succ` and `Pred`) and so can be counted. A `CASE` statement contains a variable or expression called a *selector*, which must be of an ordinal type. The selector is followed by the word `OF` and a list of possible values.

The `CASE` statement's selector is like the coin in the vending machine: OOPas matches the value in the selector to one of the values in the `CASE` statement's list. Each value is associated with a statement, and flow of control moves to the statement or block associated with the selector's value. Just as the coin can fall in only one hole of the vending machine, only one value in the list can be matched by the selector. After execution of the appropriate statement list, the flow of control moves to the `CASE` statement's `END`. This process is illustrated in Figure 11.3 and detailed in Syntax Box 11.1.

Let's look at an example by returning to our butterfly's eating habits. Recall that we said that eggs don't eat anything. Caterpillars eat leaves. Pupae don't eat, and adult butterflies eat nectar. Presuming we have methods for the specific eating actions, our method looks like this:

```
PROCEDURE Butterfly.Eat;
BEGIN
  CASE stage OF
    Egg:
      DoNothing;
    Caterpillar:
      EatLeaves;
    Pupa:
      DoNothing;
    Adult:
      EatNectar
  END
END;
```

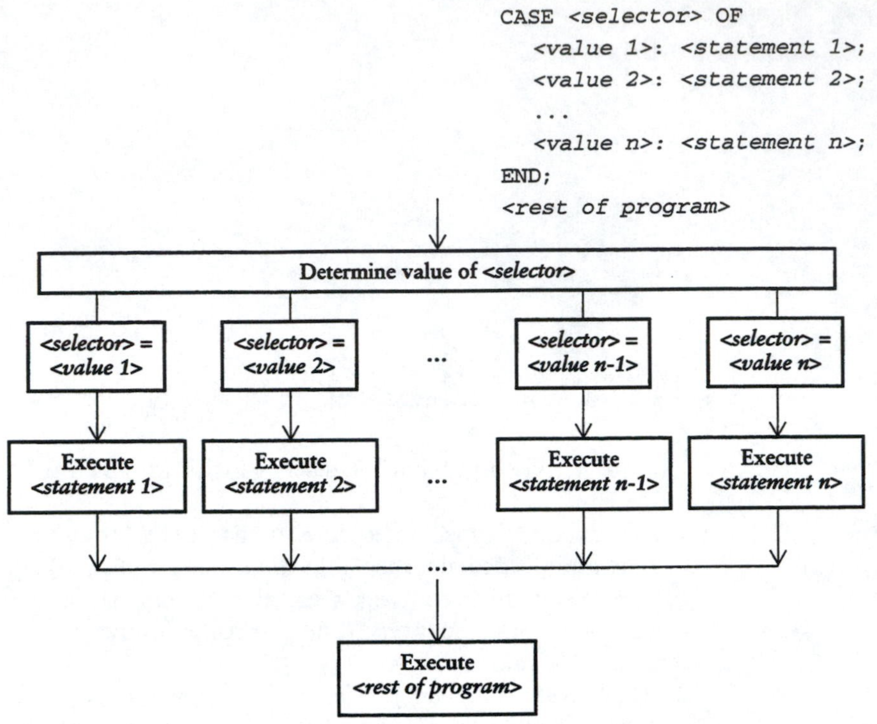

Figure 11.3

Flow of control of a CASE statement

Note that each item in the CASE statement's list is associated with a single statement. Suppose we wanted to make our model of butterflies eating more detailed. Before a caterpillar can eat leaves, it has to find some. In that case, we'd want multiple statements associated with a single item.

```
PROCEDURE Butterfly.Eat;
BEGIN
  CASE stage OF
    Egg:
      DoNothing;
    Caterpillar:
      BEGIN
        FindLeaves;
        EatLeaves
      END;
    Pupa:
      DoNothing;
    Adult:
      EatNectar
  END
END;
```

Syntax Box 11.1

CASE

Purpose:

To execute one of any number of mutually exclusive blocks of statements, depending on the value of an expression.

Syntax:

```
CASE <selector> OF
   <value 1> :    <statement 1> ;
   <value 2> :    <statement 2> ;
   ...
   <value n> :    <statement n> ;
   ELSE           <statement n+1> ;
END;  { CASE }
```

Where:

<selector> is an expression of ordinal type such as `integer`, `char`, or an enumerated type. *<value 1>*, *<value 2>*, . . . , *<value n>* are single integers or characters, or groups of integers or characters separated by commas. *<statement 1>*, *<statement 2>*, . . . , *<statement n>*, *<statement n+1>* are legal OOPas statements. If more than one statement is used, the statements must be surrounded by `BEGIN`/`END` brackets.

Usage:

The *<selector>* is evaluated. If one of the values *<value 1>*, *<value 2>*, . . . , *<value n>* matches *<selector>*, then the corresponding *<statement>* is executed. If the *<selector>* does not match any of the values, then *<statement n+1>* (following the `ELSE`) is executed.

Only one of the statements in the `CASE` construct is performed.

Note that the `END;` of the `CASE` construct does not have a corresponding `BEGIN`. The `ELSE` clause is optional.

The preceding code demonstrates that, just as we saw in `IF` statements, we can group multiple statements inside a `BEGIN`/`END` pair and use the resulting compound statement where we expected a single statement.

This code might seem a little tedious to type, especially since there are really only three different results — both eggs and pupae do nothing to eat. We can combine selectors in a `CASE` statement when they result in the same action. For example, we can condense our `Eat` method simply by combining values into three lists: stages that do nothing to eat, stages that eat leaves, and stages that eat nectar. It just happened that two of the lists had only one item, but with a greater range of values in a `CASE` statement, that might not be the situation. The items within each list are separated by commas. The method that follows does exactly the same thing as the previous version; it's just shorter.

```
PROCEDURE Butterfly.Eat;
BEGIN
   CASE stage OF
      Egg, Pupa:
         DoNothing;
      Caterpillar:
         BEGIN
            FindLeaves;
            EatLeaves
         END;
      Adult:
         EatNectar
   END
END;
```

If the value of the variable does not match any of the available options, a problem arises with the CASE construct. Unlike the IF statement, which simply continues execution on the first line after the statement, an "unmatched" CASE statement can cause a run-time error. To avoid this situation, many versions of OOPas (including ours) provide the ELSE option. For example, suppose that you want to categorize students according to how long they've been in school. We can categorize students who don't fit into one of the four expected categories as "Special" students, as in the following code:

```
TYPE
   StudentYear = (Frosh, Soph, Jr, Sr, Special);
   Student = OBJECT
      ...
      FUNCTION GetYear : StudentYear;
   PRIVATE
      ...
      duration : integer; { semesters student has been in school }
   END;
FUNCTION Student.GetYear : StudentYear;
VAR
   category: StudentYear;
BEGIN
   CASE duration OF
      6, 7 : category := Sr;
      4, 5 : category := Jr;
      2, 3 : category := Soph;
      0, 1 : category := Frosh;
   ELSE
      category := Special;
   END;
   GetYear := category;
END; { GetYear }
```

Again, only one statement within the CASE statement is executed, but now the ELSE guarantees that every possible value of duration is covered.

The IF-THEN-ELSE IF construct is preferable to a CASE statement in two situations. Since the values of the CASE statement's selector must be of an ordinal type, we must use IF-THEN-ELSE IF whenever the decision is to be based on boolean conditions of any sort. The CASE statement also falls short when the multiple possibilities are not based on a single value, for example, when you might use an AND or OR boolean expression.

11.3 AVOIDING CASE WITH POLYMORPHISM

It's very tempting to use CASE statements in a variety of circumstances. For example, it might make sense to rewrite our paint program from Chapter 8, believing that it is easier to select an interactor using a CASE statement. That is, we might use a class like this:

```
TYPE
  ToolButtonKind = ( Line, Rect, Pencil );
  ToolButtonUsingCase = OBJECT(GPToggleButton)
    CONSTRUCTOR Init(containerLink:GPManagerAsn;
              newKind : ToolButtonKind;
              newTargetLink:GPDrawingAreaAsn);
    PROCEDURE Activate; VIRTUAL;
    PROCEDURE DeActivate; VIRTUAL;
  PRIVATE
    kindOfButton : ToolButtonKind;
    targetLink : GPDrawingAreaAsn;
    lineInteractor : PRubberLineInteractor;
    rectInteractor : PRubberRectInteractor;
    pencilInteractor : PRubberPencilInteractor;
END;

CONSTRUCTOR ToolButtonUsingCase.Init(
      containerLink    : GPManagerAsn;
      newKind : ToolButtonKind;
      newTargetLink    : GPDrawingAreaAsn);
BEGIN
  INHERITED Init(containerLink);
  kindOfButton := newKind;
  targetLink := newTargetLink;
  lineInteractor.Init(targetLink);
  rectInteractor.Init(targetLink);
  pencilInteractor.Init(targetLink);
END;
```

```
PROCEDURE ToolButtonUsingCase.Activate;
BEGIN
   CASE kindOfButton OF
      Line: targetLink^.AddInteractor( @lineInteractor );
      Rect: targetLink^.AddInteractor( @rectInteractor );
      Pencil: targetLink^.AddInteractor( @pencilInteractor );
   END
END;

PROCEDURE ToolButtonUsingCase.DeActivate;
BEGIN
   CASE kindOfButton OF
      Line: targetLink^.RemoveInteractor( @lineInteractor );
      Rect: targetLink^.RemoveInteractor( @rectInteractor );
      Pencil: targetLink^.RemoveInteractor( @pencilInteractor );
   END
END;
```

The problem with this approach comes in the long term. What happens when we want to add a new shape button to our program? We would have to backtrack and modify the code in which the `CASE` statements reside (the `Activate` and `DeActivate` methods), as well as the enumerated type describing the kinds of buttons. With multiple `CASE` statements (e.g., other places where different things are done depending on what kind of tool is in use), we would have to update each and every `CASE` statement. This doesn't seem like a big problem for our paint program, but this program was quite small. In large programs, it can be quite easy to forget to correct just one `CASE` statement, introducing a bug in your program.

Because such mistakes are so likely, revising code is a bad idea. With object-oriented programming, instead, we can introduce functionality by adding subclasses, as we did in some exercises in Chapter 8. In this way, we generate new code for subclasses and needn't touch code that we already have completed.

If you have a `CASE` statement in your pseudocode or code, you may want to think about generating subclasses. Compare the preceding `CASE` statement to how our paint program actually was implemented using polymorphism:

```
PROCEDURE PToolButton.Activate;
BEGIN
   targetLink^.AddInteractor(interactorLink);
END;

PROCEDURE PToolButton.DeActivate;
BEGIN
   targetLink^.RemoveInteractor(interactorLink);
END;
```

```
CONSTRUCTOR PRubberToolButton.Init(
      containerLink    : GPManagerAsn;
      targetLink       : GPDrawingAreaAsn;
      shape            : GPRubberShapeAsn);
BEGIN
  rubberbandInteractor.Init(targetLink, shape);
  INHERITED Init(containerLink, targetLink,
            @rubberbandInteractor);
END;

CONSTRUCTOR PRectButton.Init (
      containerLink    : GPRadioColumnAsn;
      targetLink       : GPDrawingAreaAsn);
BEGIN
  rect.Init;
  INHERITED Init(containerLink, targetLink, @rect);
END;

CONSTRUCTOR PLineButton.Init (
      containerLink    : GPRadioColumnAsn;
      targetLink       : GPDrawingAreaAsn);
BEGIN
  line.Init;
  INHERITED Init(containerLink, targetLink, @line);
END;

CONSTRUCTOR PPencilButton.Init (
      containerLink    : GPRadioColumnAsn;
      targetLink       : GPDrawingAreaAsn);
BEGIN
  pencil.Init(targetLink);
  INHERITED Init(containerLink, targetLink, @pencil);
END;
```

This code is certainly longer, requiring five classes instead of one, so at first you might think this code is worse. So why is this code better? The reason is polymorphism. If we want to add a new kind of tool, say an oval-drawing tool, we simply make a new subclass:

```
TYPE
  POvalButton = OBJECT(PRubberToolButton)
    CONSTRUCTOR Init(
      containerLink : GPRadioColumnAsn;
      targetLink : GPDrawingAreaAsn);
  PRIVATE
    oval : GPRubberFramedOval;
  END;
```

```
CONSTRUCTOR POvalButton.Init(
      containerLink : GPRadioColumnAsn;
      targetLink : GPDrawingAreaAsn);
BEGIN
  oval.Init;
  INHERITED Init(containerLink, targetLink, @oval);
END;
```

It doesn't matter whether we have defined five subclasses of `PToolButton` or twenty-five. We still needn't modify the parts of the interface we've already built. Compare this to the situation discussed earlier when we used a `CASE` statement: We had to correct the `CASE` statement every time we added a new button. Thus the advantage to using polymorphism is that we can expand the functionality of our programs as much as we want, without having to modify code we've already written.

Summary

In this chapter, we looked at statements that expand our capabilities to make choices beyond simple `true` or `false` decisions. The `CASE` statement chooses among blocks of code for execution, depending on the value of a selector, which must be an ordinal type. The type `integer` is ordinal, as are enumerated types, which we first saw in this chapter.

An enumerated type consists of an ordered list of values. Once declared in the `TYPE` section of a program or unit, an enumerated type can be used wherever any other type can be used — for local variables, instance variables, or parameters. Enumerated types can be compared for equality and for hierarchy. Special functions `Succ` and `Pred` take a value of an enumerated type and return the successor and predecessor of that value.

To use the `CASE` statement, you have to know all the possible values of the selector and specify the code associated with each value. If the selector's value is not associated with any code, OOPas halts program execution. Adding a "none of the above" case with the `OTHERWISE` clause avoids this problem. If you find you need a `CASE` statement, it might be a signal for you to rethink your design; often, using subclasses and polymorphism in place of `CASE` statements can make your code more expandable and recyclable for the long term.

`CASE` statements are insufficient when we are not dealing with ordinal types (such as `real` or instances of classes), or when the different conditions are not mutually exclusive. These situations require the use of the most general `IF-THEN-ELSE IF` construct.

Many situations that might seem like a good place to use a `CASE` statement can be handled more efficiently by using polymorphism. Using polymorphism in place of a `CASE` statement makes a system more easily extensible, since adding new functionality to a `CASE` statement means rewriting it, which could introduce new bugs in old code. Adding new functionality using polymorphism does not entail this risk, since it simply involves adding a new class without modifying old code.

Exercises

Understanding Concepts

1. What is wrong with the following declaration?

```
TYPE
  cardType = (Ace, 2..10, Jack, Queen, King);
```

2. Why isn't `real` an ordinal type?

3. If `curStage` is a variable of the enumerated type `ButterflyLifeCycleStage` described in Section 11.1, what does `Pred(Succ(curStage))` return?

4. When do `Pred` and `Succ` return error messages?

5. Assume that `place` is an integer variable and contains a value from 1 to 5. Write a `CASE` statement that prints one of the following, depending on the value of place: 1st, 2nd, 3rd, 4th, 5th.

6. Assume `myCoin` is an instance variable of the class `Coin` and that `GetValue` returns the value of the coin. Also assume that `msgLink` is a link to a message area. What's wrong with the following code? How can you fix it?

```
PROCEDURE Finances.PrintCoinValue(myCoin: Coin;
  msgLink: GPTextAreaAsn);

BEGIN
  msgLink^.SetText('Your coin has the face of ');
  CASE myCoin.GetValue OF
    1.00: msgLink^.AddText('Susan B. Anthony.');
    0.50: msgLink^.AddText('John F. Kennedy.');
    0.25: msgLink^.AddText('George Washington.');
    0.10: msgLink^.AddText('F.D. Roosevelt.');
    0.05: msgLink^.AddText('Thomas Jefferson.');
    0.01: msgLink^.AddText('Abraham Lincoln.');

    OTHERWISE
    msgLink^.AddText('no one I know.');
  END; { CASE }
END;
```

7. What would you have to do to eliminate the `CASE` statement from the `Finances.PrintCoinValue` method from Exercise 6?

8. Explain how you might use subclassing, rather than enumerated types, for the butterfly example. What are some of the problems with your design? How might you fix them?

Coding Problems

```
TYPE
  Days = (Sun, Mon, Tue, Wed, Thur, Fri, Sat);
  Months = (Jan, Feb, Mar, Apr, May, Jun, Jul, Aug, Sep, Oct, Nov,
            Dec);

  Date = OBJECT
    { methods here }
  PRIVATE
    day: Days;
    month, date, year: integer;
END;
```

1. Write a function called `Date.NextDay` that returns the day of the week after the current day. (Obviously, if the current day is `Sat`, then the next day is `Sun`.)

2. Write a function called `Date.GetMonth` that returns the value of the enumerated type `Months` corresponding to the integer (1 to 12) stored in the instance variable `month`.

3. Write a function called `Date.SetMonth` that receives a value of the enumerated type `Months` as a parameter and sets the instance variable `month` to the corresponding integer from 1 to 12.

4. Chess masters sometimes determine that it is worth sacrificing a piece if one can capture a more powerful piece. The pieces, in ascending order of importance, are pawn, knight, bishop, rook, queen, king. Write a function that compares a white piece and a black piece and determines which player (if either) gains from the exchange (i.e., which player captures the more powerful piece).

5. Suppose you have the following enumerated types:

   ```
   TYPE
     Pres = (Ford, Carter, Reagan, Bush, Clinton);
     VP = (Rockefeller, Mondale, BushVP, Quayle, Gore);
   ```

   Write a method that accepts a parameter of type `Pres` and returns the corresponding entry in the `VP` list.

Programming Problems

1. Write a program that, when given a number from 1 to 1000, displays the equivalent in Roman numerals.

2. Write a program that determines the day of the week for a given date.

3. Write a program that asks the user to indicate a number from 1 to 6 and then outputs the way in which that number is represented on a die.

4. Write a program that shows the phases of the moon. The user should indicate the dates of two consecutive full moons. Assume that the visible portion of the moon changes on a constant basis, from full, to new, and back to full. The pro-

gram should ask the user to indicate a date, then show the area of the moon that is visible that day.

5. The game of MasterMind™ involves two players. One creates a code of four pegs using six colors (Black, White, Red, Yellow, Blue, Green). The other player then has 12 guesses to determine the code. The guesser presents a possible 4-peg code. The codemaker responds with another code: a filled circle for each peg of the correct color in the correct place, a framed circle for each peg of the correct color in the wrong place. For example, if the code is Blue-Yellow-Blue-Green, the following are possible guesses and responses:

Yellow-Yellow-Yellow-Yellow	1 FILLED
Blue-Yellow-Green-Blue	2 FILLED, 2 FRAMED
Red-Blue-White-Green	1 FILLED, 1 FRAMED
Blue-Blue-Red-Black	1 FILLED, 1 FRAMED
Black-Blue-White-Red	1 FRAMED

Write a program in which the user plays against the computer. (You can choose which role the computer will play, codemaker or guesser.)

12

Loops

You probably have realized by now that a computer can't do anything that a person can't do by hand. Ironically, one advantage of the computer is that it *can't* think — it doesn't "mind" doing the mundane jobs that people *could* do but would rather avoid. Among the most mundane tasks are those that must be performed over and over again. This chapter discusses *loops* — programming constructs that repeat blocks of statements.

Now we will look at three new statements — `FOR`, `REPEAT-UNTIL`, and `WHILE` — which allow us to repeat blocks of code. Like the `IF-THEN` and `CASE` statements, loops affect the order in which statements are executed.

There are two broad categories of loops. Loops in the first category repeat a set of statements a predetermined *number* of times. Loops in the second category repeat a set of statements an unknown number of times, stopping when a specified *condition* is met. The first kind of loop is known as a *definite loop*, since the number of repetitions is known ahead of time, and the second kind is an *indefinite loop*.

12.1 DEFINITE LOOPS

The library GP contains the `GPLine` and `GPFilledRect` classes, which have `Draw` methods. Let's take a closer look at how those `Draw` methods output their shapes using loops.

Drawing a line is a matter of connecting a series of pixels, which are illuminated individually. For the purposes of this example, we'll simplify the technical details and assume that the `Draw` methods have a local variable, called `curPt`, that is an instance of `GPPoint`. Also, we'll assume that `GPPoint` has a `SetCoords` method to set the point's coordinates and a `Draw` method to illuminate a single pixel at the point's coordinates.

To draw a line, `GPLine.Draw` takes the endpoints specified by its `startPt` and `endPt` instance variables (of type `GPPoint`) and illuminates all the pixels in between. Let's keep things simple and draw a horizontal line from (0, 10) to (100, 10). In this case, `Draw` must illuminate 101 pixels. Without using loops, `Draw` would need 202 separate statements to draw the 101 pixels:

```
curPt.SetCoords(0, 10);
curPt.Draw;
curPt.SetCoords(1, 10);
curPt.Draw;
curPt.SetCoords(2, 10);
curPt.Draw;

   ...

curPt.SetCoords(99, 10);
curPt.Draw;
curPt.SetCoords(100, 10);
curPt.Draw;
```

Such repetition is unnecessarily tedious, even for a computer.

How do we use a loop construct to eliminate the repetition? First, we'll note that in this special case of drawing a horizontal line, the vertical coordinate never changes. To figure out which pixels to draw, `GPLine.Draw` must start at `startPt`'s coordinates and illuminate pixels, one at a time, until it reaches the `endPt`. For a horizontal line, we easily can calculate how many pixels must be drawn, by taking the difference between `endPt`'s horizontal coordinate and `startPt`'s horizontal coordinate. Since we can determine exactly how many pixels must be drawn on the line, we can use a *definite* loop, which in OOPas is the `FOR` statement.

The `FOR` loop has four parts: an *upper* and a *lower limit*, which are integer expressions that indicate how many times the loop should be executed; a *loop counter* or *index*, which is an integer variable that keeps track of which execution of the loop is currently in progress; and a *loop body*, which is the statement to be repeated. Figure 12.1 illustrates how these parts work.

A `FOR` loop first gives the loop counter an initial value, or a lower limit. OOPas then compares the loop counter to the loop's upper limit until the loop counter's value exceeds the upper limit, at which point the loop exits. Before then, however, the statements that make up the loop body are executed. After each loop body execution, the counter is incremented (increased by 1), and the loop's *exit condition* (in Figure 12.1, "Is *<counter>* greater than *<upper limit>*?") is tested again.

In the horizontal line example, we now can see how to draw the line with a `FOR` statement:

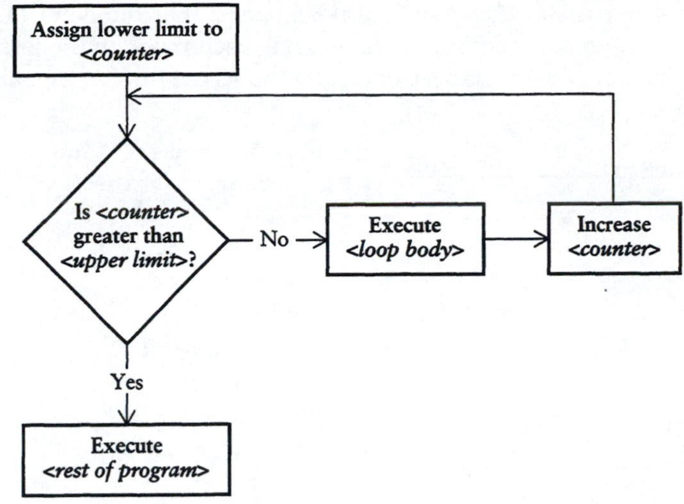

Figure 12.1 *Flow of control of a FOR loop*

```
PROCEDURE GPLine.DrawHorizontalLine(targetLink:GPDrawingAreaAsn);
VAR
  curPt: GPPoint;
  curHoriz, curVert, leftHoriz, rightHoriz: integer;
BEGIN
  curPoint.Init;
  leftHoriz := startPt.GetX; rightHoriz := endPt.GetX;
  curVert := startPt.GetY;
  FOR curHoriz := leftHoriz TO rightHoriz DO
    BEGIN
      curPt.SetCoords(curHoriz, curVert);
      curPt.Draw(targetLink)
    END; { FOR }
END; { GPLine.DrawHorizontalLine }
```

The first time through the loop, the loop counter `curHoriz` receives the value `leftHoriz`. Then, `curPt` is sent a `SetCoords` message to set the pixel at (`curHoriz`, `curVert`). After the loop body in the `BEGIN/END` block is executed, the flow of control returns to the top of the loop and `curHoriz` is incremented. Each pass through the loop increments `curHoriz` by one until it reaches the value of `rightHoriz`. (Remember that `curVert` stays the same throughout the execution of the loop.)

For the line from (0, 10) to (100, 10), this means that, in a preceding code fragment not shown here, `startPt` has been set to (0, 10) and similarly that `endPt` has been set to (100, 10). When the loop is encountered, `curHoriz` is initialized to have the same value as `leftHoriz` (0). Then, since `curHoriz` (0) is less than `rightHoriz` (100), the body of the loop is executed and the point (`curHoriz`, `curVert`), or (0, 10), is illuminated.

When the bottom of the loop is reached, flow of control returns to the top of the loop. `curHoriz` is incremented by one and now has the value 1. `cur-`

Horiz is still less than `rightHoriz`, and thus the point (1, 10) is illuminated. This process continues, illuminating each point on the line. Figure 12.2 shows the code, the variable values, and the screen just before painting pixel (5, 10).

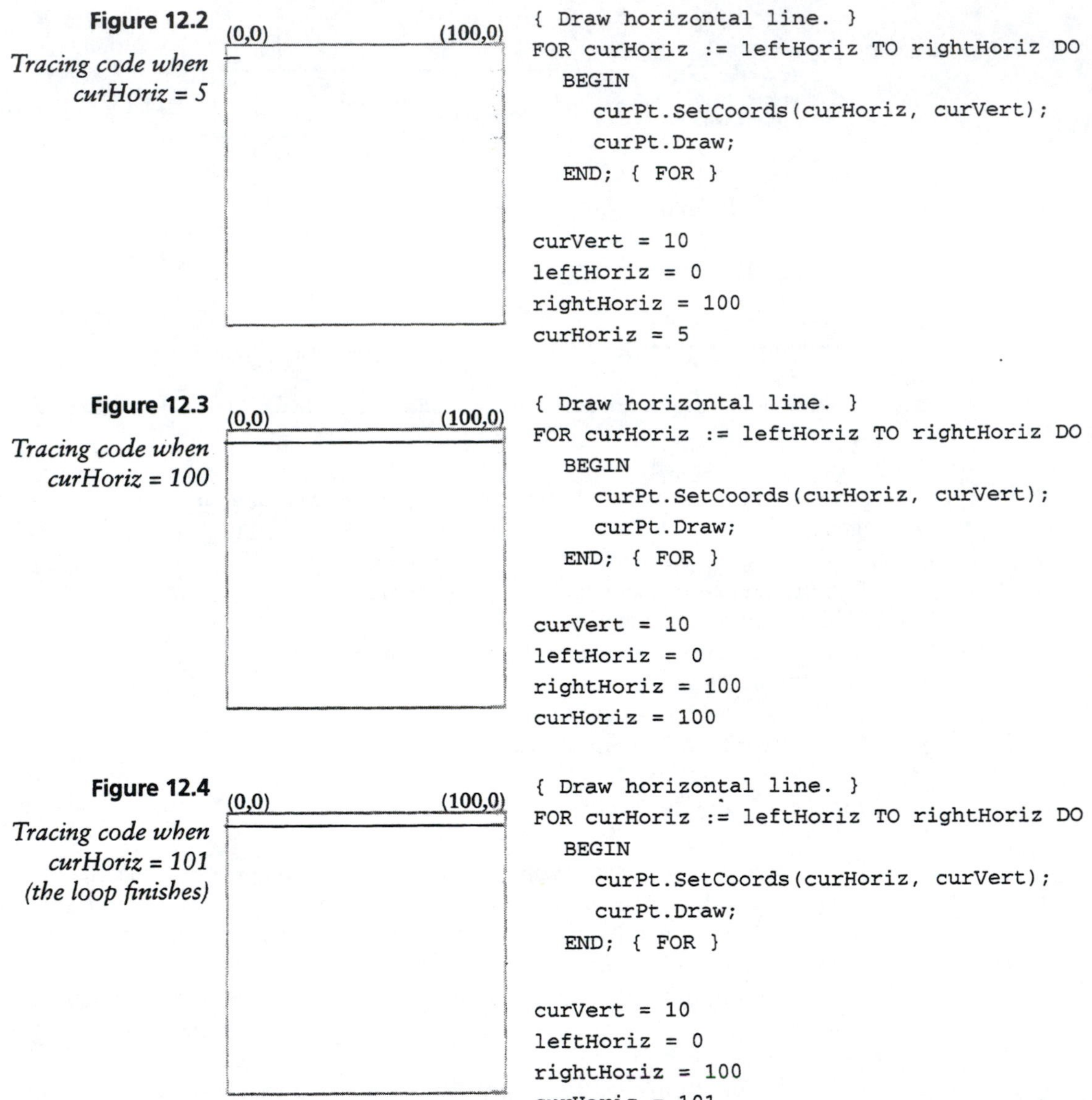
(0,0)
(100,0)
{ Draw horizontal line. }
FOR curHoriz := leftHoriz TO rightHoriz DO
BEGIN
curPt.SetCoords(curHoriz, curVert);
curPt.Draw;
END; { FOR }
curVert = 10
leftHoriz = 0
rightHoriz = 100
curHoriz = 5
(0,0)
(100,0)
{ Draw horizontal line. }
FOR curHoriz := leftHoriz TO rightHoriz DO
BEGIN
curPt.SetCoords(curHoriz, curVert);
curPt.Draw;
END; { FOR }
curVert = 10
leftHoriz = 0
rightHoriz = 100
curHoriz = 100
(0,0)
(100,0)
{ Draw horizontal line. }
FOR curHoriz := leftHoriz TO rightHoriz DO
BEGIN
curPt.SetCoords(curHoriz, curVert);
curPt.Draw;
END; { FOR }
curVert = 10
leftHoriz = 0
rightHoriz = 100
curHoriz = 101

Figure 12.2 *Tracing code when curHoriz = 5*

Figure 12.3 *Tracing code when curHoriz = 100*

Figure 12.4 *Tracing code when curHoriz = 101 (the loop finishes)*

The loop continues and eventually `curHoriz` is set to 100. Because `cur-Horiz` still is not greater than `rightHoriz`, the loop is executed (see Figure 12.3). After (100, 10) is illuminated, however, flow returns to the top of the loop and `curHoriz` would increase to 101. Now that the loop counter is greater than the upper limit, the loop stops executing and the flow of control moves to the first statement after the loop body. In Figure 12.4, execution is about to leave the loop. The variable `curHoriz` would be assigned the value 101 if the loop continued. When the loop is done, though, `curHoriz` will maintain the value 100. Syntax Box 12.1 shows the general format of the `FOR` loop.

Syntax Box 12.1
FOR loop

Purpose:

To repeat a block of code a predetermined number of times.

Syntax:

```
FOR <counter> := <lower limit> TO <upper limit> DO
   <statement>;     { body of loop }
```

Where:

<counter> is a variable of an ordinal type, such as `integer` or an enumerated type. Another ordinal type, `char`, will be presented in Chapter 15.

The value of *<counter>* can be used in an expression but cannot be changed with an assignment statement in the body of the loop.

<lower limit> and *<upper limit>* are constants, variables, or expressions that evaluate to the same type as *<counter>*.

<statement> is any legal OOPas statement. If more than one statement is to be repeated, `BEGIN/END` brackets must surround the repeated code:

```
FOR <counter> := <lower limit> TO <upper limit> DO
BEGIN
   <statements>;{ body of loop }
END;
```

Usage:

The `FOR` loop executes the statements in the body of the loop as many times as specified by the upper and lower limits.

When the `FOR` statement is first encountered, *<counter>* is assigned the value of *<lower limit>*. That value then is compared to *<upper limit>*. As long as *<counter>* is less than or equal to *<upper limit>*, the statements in the body of the loop are executed. When the last statement in the body of the loop is performed, the flow of control returns to the `FOR` line. Then *<counter>* is increased by one and again compared to *<upper limit>*. When *<counter>* is greater than *<upper limit>*, the flow of control exits the loop and moves to the statement immediately following the last statement in the loop body.

If *<lower limit>* is greater than *<upper limit>*, the loop body is not executed.

As in other flow-of-control statements, the entire block of a `FOR` loop is actually one statement. No semicolon appears after the `DO` on the top line. This implies that the loop body is part of the `FOR` statement; the `FOR` line cannot stand alone.

12.2 NESTED LOOPS

Any legal OOPas statement can be placed in the body of a loop, including other loops. Putting flow-of-control statements inside other flow-of-control statements is a common programming technique and is another example of *nesting* that we saw in Chapter 10 with the nested `IF-THEN` statement.

The method `GPPoint.Draw` draws a shape in zero dimensions; by using one `FOR` loop, the horizontal line code we just saw can draw a shape in one dimension. A rectangle in two dimensions can be drawn by nesting two loops. Assume for the moment that we need to write the code for `GPFilled-Rect.Draw` from scratch. First let's think about what we want to do — draw a filled rectangular area — and then let's figure out how to implement it.

The box drawn by `GPFilledRect.Draw` is filled in by drawing a sequence of closely spaced horizontal lines. This differs from drawing a single straight line, in that neither the horizontal nor the vertical coordinate is held constant. What we want to do is put the vertical coordinate at its lowest value, draw a horizontal line, increase the vertical coordinate by one, draw another horizontal line, and continue until the vertical coordinate reaches its upper limit. This process can be performed by a `FOR` loop. We can create the following pseudocode for this method:

```
FOR each vertical coordinate DO
   Draw a horizontal line
```

We said previously that pseudocode should contain very little programming language syntax, yet here we see the notation *FOR each . . . DO*. Flow-of-control constructs are the major exception to our "no OOPas in the pseudocode" rule. Using the reserved words `FOR`, `DO`, `IF`, `THEN`, `ELSE`, `CASE` (and, as we shall see, `WHILE`, `REPEAT`, and `UNTIL`) in the pseudocode forces us to group blocks of tasks into loops or conditional branches. In the pseudocode examples, reserved words are in uppercase.

We implement "Draw a horizontal line," using this code:

```
FOR curHoriz := leftHoriz TO rightHoriz DO
   BEGIN
      curPt.SetCoords(curHoriz, curVert);
      curPt.Draw;
   END; { FOR }
```

This loop draws a horizontal line at a vertical value of `curVert`.

To code the line "FOR each vertical coordinate DO," we need three variables — a counter, the loop's lower limit, and the loop's upper limit. The variables must be of type `integer`. If we create local variables `curVert`, `topVert`, and `bottomVert`, the pseudocode can be translated into:

```
FOR curVert := topVert TO bottomVert DO
```

Thus the finished method looks like this:

```
PROCEDURE GPFilledRect.Draw;
VAR
  leftHoriz, rightHoriz: integer;  { x-coords of endpoints }
  topVert, bottomVert: integer;    { y-coords of endpoints }
  curHoriz, curVert: integer;      { coords of pt to draw }
  curPt: GPPoint;                  { point to draw }

BEGIN

  leftHoriz := startPt.GetX;
  topVert := startPt.GetY;
  rightHoriz := endPt.GetX;
  bottomVert := endPt.GetY;

  FOR curVert := topVert TO bottomVert DO
    BEGIN
      FOR curHoriz := leftHoriz TO rightHoriz DO
        BEGIN
          curPt.SetCoords(curHoriz, curVert);
          curPt.Draw;
        END; { FOR curHoriz }
    END; { FOR curVert }

END; { GPFilledRect.Draw }
```

Let's trace the code segment when we send the following messages:

```
VAR
  newRect: GPFilledRect;
  newStart, newEnd: GPPoint;

BEGIN
  newStart.InitWithCoords(10, 10);
  newEnd.InitWithCoords(100, 100);
  newRect.InitWithPoints(newStart, newEnd);
  newRect.Draw;
END;
```

In the assignment statements, we set `topVert` to 10, `bottomVert` to 100, `leftHoriz` to 10, and `rightHoriz` to 100. In the fragment in Figure 12.5, `curVert` begins at (10).

The flow of control moves to the next statement, which is the *inner* FOR loop. The variable `curHoriz` is assigned the value of `leftHoriz` (10). At this point (see Figure 12.6), the pixel at (`curHoriz, curVert`) — (10, 10) — is illuminated.

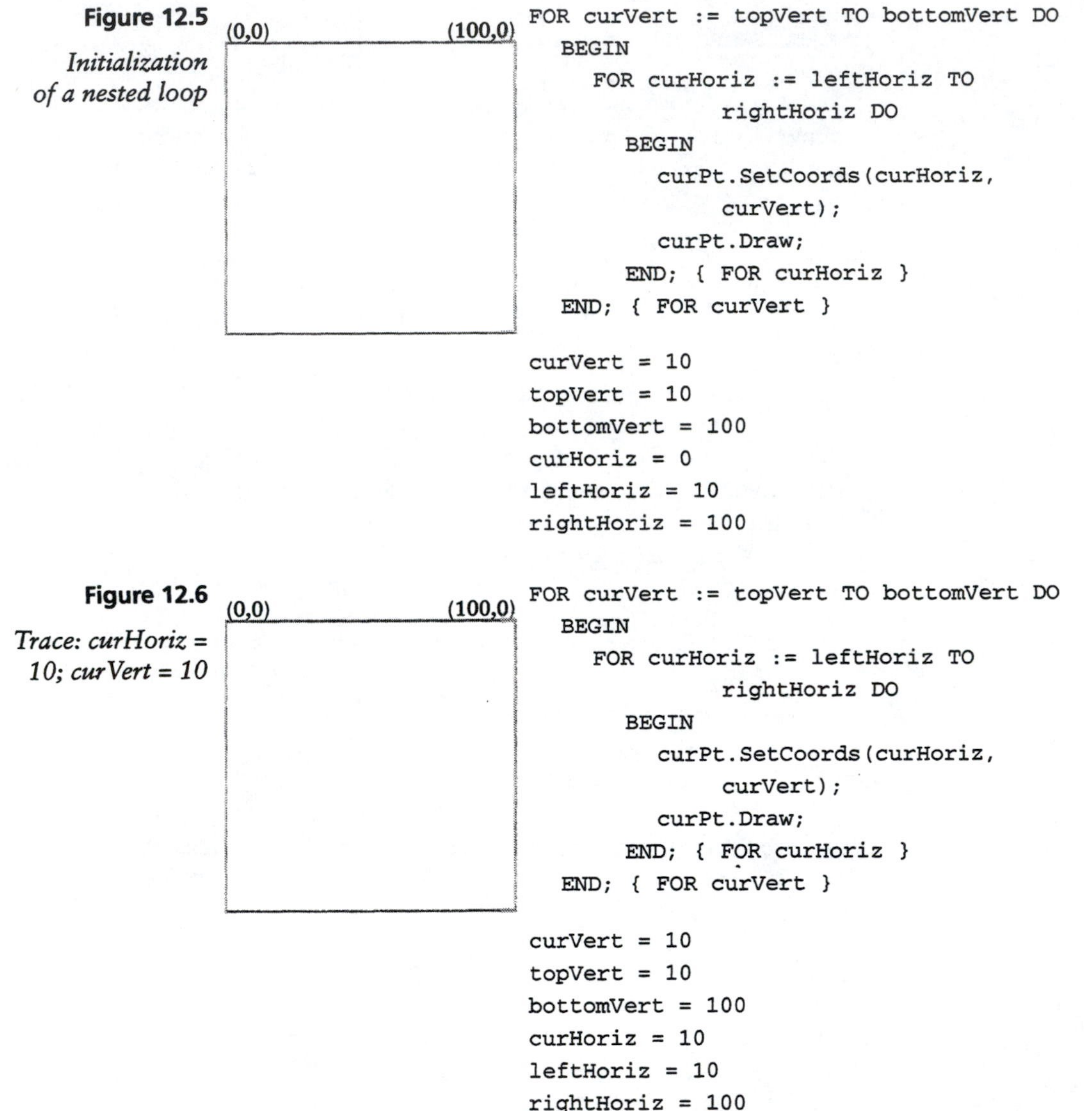
(0,0)
(100,0)
FOR curVert := topVert TO bottomVert DO
  BEGIN
    FOR curHoriz := leftHoriz TO
            rightHoriz DO
      BEGIN
        curPt.SetCoords(curHoriz,
            curVert);
        curPt.Draw;
      END; { FOR curHoriz }
  END; { FOR curVert }
curVert = 10
topVert = 10
bottomVert = 100
curHoriz = 0
leftHoriz = 10
rightHoriz = 100
(0,0)
(100,0)
FOR curVert := topVert TO bottomVert DO
  BEGIN
    FOR curHoriz := leftHoriz TO
            rightHoriz DO
      BEGIN
        curPt.SetCoords(curHoriz,
            curVert);
        curPt.Draw;
      END; { FOR curHoriz }
  END; { FOR curVert }
curVert = 10
topVert = 10
bottomVert = 100
curHoriz = 10
leftHoriz = 10
rightHoriz = 100

Figure 12.5 *Initialization of a nested loop*

Figure 12.6 *Trace: curHoriz = 10; curVert = 10*

Flow of control then returns to the top of the inner loop; `curVert` keeps the same value, but `curHoriz` is incremented to 11. For the moment, `curVert`'s value is frozen at 10.

The inner loop continues execution (`curHoriz` continues to increase by 1), and a horizontal line is drawn at `curVert` = 10 (see Figure 12.7).

Now `curHoriz` would be incremented to the value 101. Since this is greater than `rightHoriz`, the flow of control exits the loop and goes to the statement

Figure 12.7

Trace: curHoriz = 100; curVert = 10

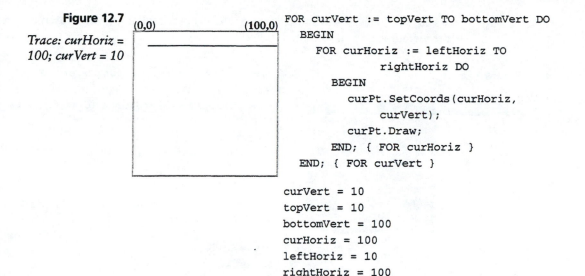

(0,0) (100,0)

```
FOR curVert := topVert TO bottomVert DO
  BEGIN
    FOR curHoriz := leftHoriz TO
            rightHoriz DO
      BEGIN
        curPt.SetCoords(curHoriz,
            curVert);
        curPt.Draw;
      END; { FOR curHoriz }
  END; { FOR curVert }
```

```
curVert = 10
topVert = 10
bottomVert = 100
curHoriz = 100
leftHoriz = 10
rightHoriz = 100
```

immediately following the loop end. In other words, the inner loop's `SetCoords` and `Draw` messages are skipped and flow of control moves to the outer `END`; bracket. This signals the end of the outer loop body's execution, and flow of control moves to the top of the outer, or `curVert`, loop statement.

`curVert` is now increased by one, and the inner `FOR` loop starts from the beginning again, drawing a line where `curVert` = 11. Again, `curHoriz` starts at `leftHoriz` (10) and goes to `rightHoriz` (100) (see Figure 12.8).

Figure 12.8

Trace: curHoriz = 50; curVert = 11

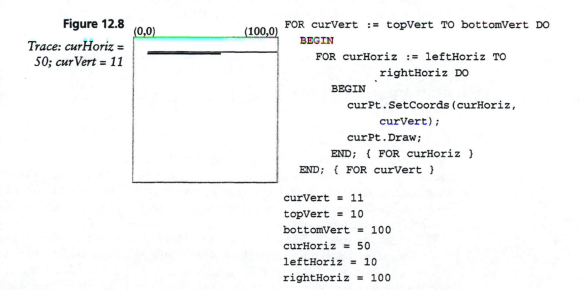

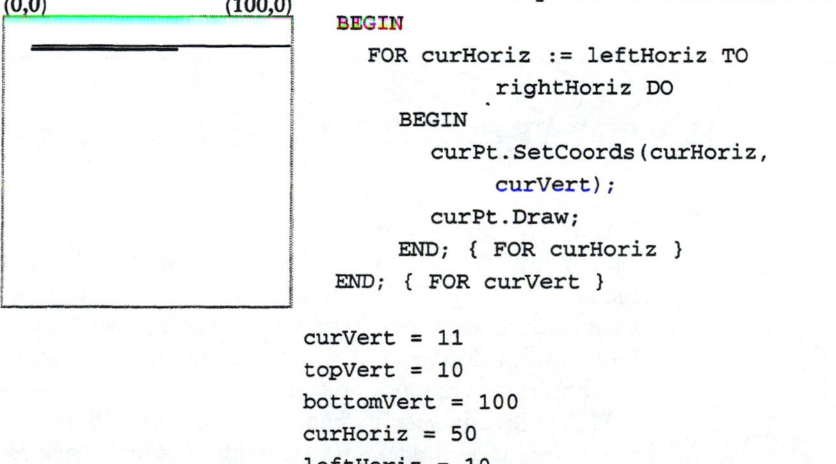


```
FOR curVert := topVert TO bottomVert DO
  BEGIN
    FOR curHoriz := leftHoriz TO
            rightHoriz DO
      BEGIN
        curPt.SetCoords(curHoriz,
            curVert);
        curPt.Draw;
      END; { FOR curHoriz }
  END; { FOR curVert }
```

```
curVert = 11
topVert = 10
bottomVert = 100
curHoriz = 50
leftHoriz = 10
rightHoriz = 100
```

Only when the inner loop is completed does the outer loop counter increase. The outer loop stops after a horizontal line is drawn where `curVert`

= 100. Figure 12.9 shows the trace of the program when the last statement of the rectangle code is executed.

Figure 12.9

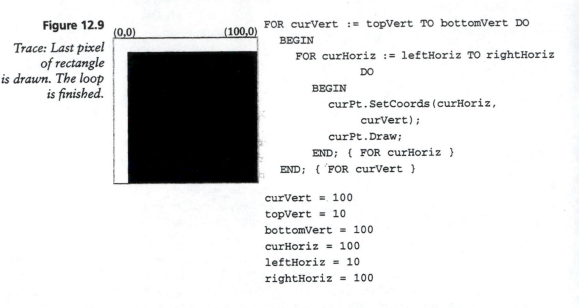

Trace: Last pixel of rectangle is drawn. The loop is finished.


```
FOR curVert := topVert TO bottomVert DO
  BEGIN
    FOR curHoriz := leftHoriz TO rightHoriz
            DO
      BEGIN
        curPt.SetCoords(curHoriz,
            curVert);
        curPt.Draw;
      END; { FOR curHoriz }
  END; { FOR curVert }

curVert = 100
topVert = 10
bottomVert = 100
curHoriz = 100
leftHoriz = 10
rightHoriz = 100
```

In practice, it would be too time consuming to trace 100 iterations of a FOR loop, let alone two nested loops. Usually, when testing your code, you can restrict testing to the first and last time through the loop (called the *boundary conditions*) and a typical "in-between" case. If all three tests provide correct results, the loop probably works correctly under all conditions.

12.3 REPEAT-UNTIL LOOPS

The REPEAT-UNTIL construct is one of OOPas's two *indefinite loop* statements. When using definite FOR loops, you must state, before you enter the loop, exactly how many times the loop will execute; the upper and lower limits of the loop counter are determined before the FOR loop begins execution. In contrast, with an indefinite loop, you do not know when you are going to exit the loop until the loop already has been entered. Some action or assignment inside the loop causes the loop to stop executing.

We've already seen examples of indefinite loops in use, though the loops themselves were hidden inside a method. Think back to the Run method of the GPApplication class. Looking at a sample interface in Figure 12.10, recall that the Run message, sent to an instance of GPApplication, caused the application to wait until the user did something, like click on a button or draw in the drawing area, then respond to the user's action, then wait again. This happened repeatedly, until the user clicked on the quit button.

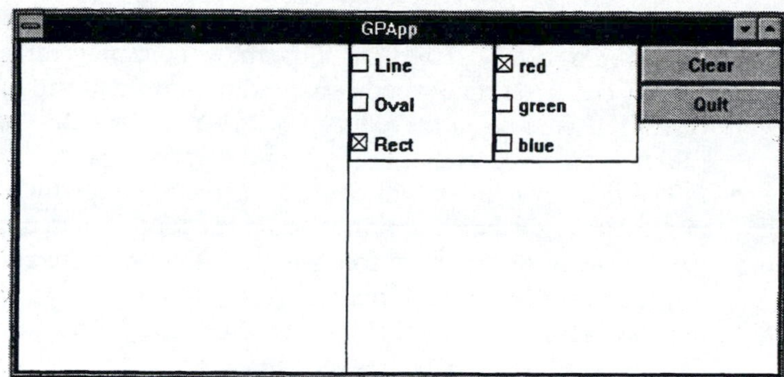

Figure 12.10

A paint program. The Run method makes use of indefinite loops.

A REPEAT-UNTIL loop follows the same pattern: A set of actions is repeated until a certain condition is satisfied. The Run method, which is implemented as a REPEAT-UNTIL loop, follows the same pattern. The actions repeated are waiting for and responding to a user's actions. The condition that becomes true to end the loop is whether the user clicks on the quit button. Let's take a look at one way the Run method could be implemented.

```
PROCEDURE GPApplication.Run;
VAR
  event : GPEvent; { An Event models a user's action. }
BEGIN
  REPEAT
    WaitForNext(event);
    RespondTo(event)
  UNTIL quitWasHit { set to true by the Quit method }
END;
```

We begin with the reserved word REPEAT. When OOPas sees REPEAT, it recognizes that it is beginning a loop but it needn't take any specific action. The REPEAT simply serves as a marker, indicating the beginning of the loop, much as TYPE marks the beginning of the object definitions.

Following the REPEAT are the statements that make up the loop's body. The loop's body starts right after the REPEAT and ends at the reserved word UNTIL. In our case, there are two statements in the loop body. The first, WaitForNext(event), waits for the next action performed by the user. The parameter event is a VAR parameter and is filled in with a description of the user's action by the WaitForNext method. Armed with that description, OOPas proceeds to the next statement, RespondTo(event), which examines the event and determines which object should respond to it. Both methods are private methods of GPApplication. For example, if the event describes the user clicking down on the quit button, RespondTo tells the quit button to respond to a click, which it does with its Activate message:

```
PROCEDURE ACQuitButton.Activate;
BEGIN
  targetLink^.Quit
END;
```

At the bottom of the loop is the `UNTIL` statement, where we find the boolean condition `UNTIL quitWasHit.` Like the conditional statements in Chapter 10, OOPas can determine whether a condition evaluates to `true` or `false`. In this case, OOPas looks at the value of `quitWasHit`, which is initialized to `false` in the constructor of `GPApplication` and is set to `true` by `GPApplication.Quit`.

The flow of control will depend on the value of the exit condition in the `UNTIL` clause. If the condition is `true`, the loop is exited, and the flow of control moves to line of code following the `UNTIL`. If the condition is `false`, the flow of control returns to the top of the loop — that is, the statement following the `REPEAT`. Figure 12.11 shows how the loop's flow of control works. Syntax Box 12.2 summarizes the syntax for a `REPEAT-UNTIL` loop.

Figure 12.11

Flow of control for REPEAT loop

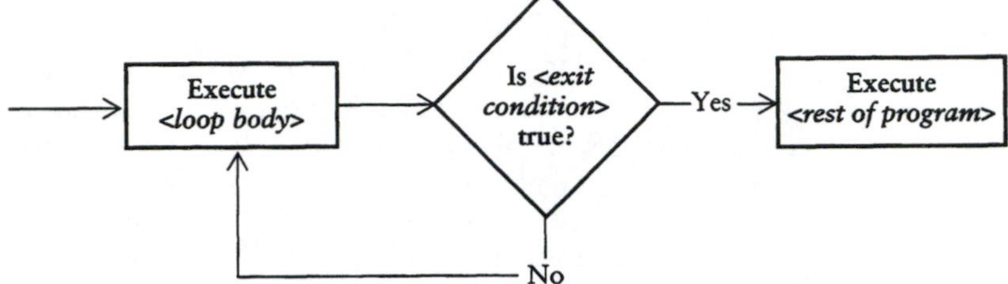

Syntax Box 12.2

REPEAT-UNTIL loop

Purpose:

To repeat a block of code until a condition is true.

Syntax:

```
REPEAT
   <statements>;{ body of loop }
UNTIL <exit condition>;
```

Where:

<exit condition> is a variable or expression that evaluates to a boolean.

<statements> are any number of legal OOPas statements, but unlike the case of other flow of control statements, it is not necessary to surround the loop body with `BEGIN/END` brackets.

Usage:

The body of the loop always is executed at least once. The condition is tested after all the statements in the body have been executed. If *<exit condition>* evaluates to `false`, the flow of control returns to the `REPEAT` statement. If *<exit condition>* evaluates to `true`, the flow of control continues at the statement following the `UNTIL`.

At some time, *<exit condition>* must be set to true in the body of the loop. If *<exit condition>* remains `false`, the loop never exits.

To make sure that the loop exits, we need to make sure that at least one of the statements inside the loop body affects the exit condition. (Here, we know that `quitWasHit` will be set to `true` when the user presses the quit button.)

The primary difference between this loop and the `FOR` loops we saw earlier is that we don't know how many times we will execute the loop. The exit condition of the loop is not based on a counter, as in the `FOR` loop; it is based on the value of a boolean condition.

12.4 WHILE LOOPS

OOPas has another type of indefinite loop construct, a `WHILE` loop. For the most part, `WHILE` loops can be used in the same situations as `REPEAT` loops. The main difference between the two is that the exit condition for a `WHILE` loop is checked at the top of the loop and that of the `REPEAT` loop is checked at the bottom. Thus the body of a `REPEAT` loop is *always* executed at least once and the body of a `WHILE` loop may be bypassed altogether.

It is easy to confuse the use of the boolean condition in the `WHILE` and `REPEAT` loops — a `WHILE` loop exits when the condition is `false`, and an `UNTIL` loop exits when the condition is `true`. Thus the `WHILE` loop's condition can be restated as "continue to loop if `true`," as opposed to the `REPEAT`'s "exit loop if `true`" condition. Still, both conditions are referred to as "exit conditions." Figure 12.12 shows the flow of control for the `WHILE` loop.

Figure 12.12

Flow of control for WHILE loop

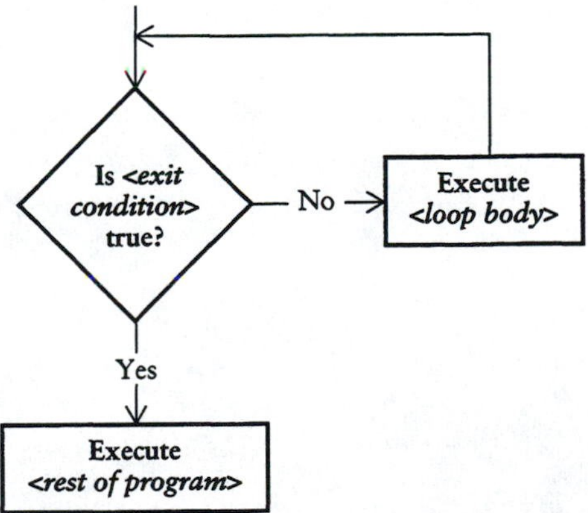

To demonstrate the use of `WHILE` loops, let's consider the fish and shark examples used in Programming Problem 2 in Chapter 10. One of the fish's methods was `SUFish.SwimLeft`, which would make the fish swim until it reached the left side of the drawing area. If the fish was already at the left side, it wouldn't move. To get to the left side, it moves a little bit each time until it gets there.

`SUFish.SwimLeft` is implemented using a `WHILE` loop. The loop checks whether the fish is at the left side of the drawing area and, if not, moves the fish to the left one pixel. It keeps moving the fish until the left side of the screen is reached:

```
PROCEDURE SUFish.SwimLeft;
VAR
  currentPosition : GPPoint; { holds current position of fish}
BEGIN
  GetPoint(currentPosition); { Fish asks self for current pos. }
  WHILE currentPosition.GetX > 0 DO { Left edge has x-coord 0. }
    BEGIN
      currentPosition.SetX(currentPosition.GetX - 1);
      Erase;
      MoveToward(currentPosition);
      Draw
    END { WHILE }
END;
```

Syntax Box 12.3

WHILE loop

Purpose:

To repeat blocks of code while a condition is true.

Syntax:

```
WHILE <exit condition> DO
  <statement>;      { body of loop }
```

Where:

<exit condition> is a variable or expression that evaluates to a boolean.

<statement> is any legal OOPas statement. If more than one statement is to be repeated, `BEGIN/END` brackets must surround the repeated code:

```
WHILE <exit condition> DO
  BEGIN
    <statements>;    { body of loop }
  END;
```

Usage:

<exit condition> is tested before the body of the loop is executed. If *<exit condition>* is `true`, the body is executed; thus the "exit" condition is really a "continue looping" condition. When the entire loop body has been executed, the flow of control returns to the top of the `WHILE` loop. *<exit condition>* is then checked again. When *<exit condition>* is `false`, the flow of control continues at the statement after the end of the loop.

Note that *<exit condition>* must be set to `false` in the body of the loop. If *<exit condition>* always remains `true`, the `WHILE` loop will never exit.

Unlike the REPEAT loop we saw in Section 12.3, we notice that we have to initialize any variables we may need inside the loop before we start the loop. In particular, we need to get a value for the currentPosition local variable. Once that is done, we can run the loop.

We begin with another reserved word — WHILE — followed by a boolean expression, and finally the reserved word DO. As long as the boolean expression is true, the statement following the DO will be executed. OOPas expects only a single statement. Since we want to perform several actions, we group them inside a BEGIN/END compound statement. In our case, as long as the *x*-coordinate of the fish's position is greater than the *x*-coordinate of the left edge of the drawing area (which is zero), then we will want to move the fish.

To move the fish, we first decrement the *x*-coordinate of the fish. Then, using the Erase method, we erase it and tell it what its new position is using its own MoveToward method. Finally, we draw the fish in its new position.

Upon completion of these steps, the loop starts again. Now, we've moved one pixel closer to the edge of the drawing area. Note that if we started the fish at the left edge of the screen (with its *x*-coordinate 0), the exit condition would be false from the very start. The fish wouldn't move at all.

Syntax Box 12.3 discusses the syntax of WHILE loops.

12.5 LOOP VARIATIONS

The loops discussed thus far are the simplest that OOPas provides. Although these are the loops most commonly used, two variations — backward FOR loops and indefinite loops with multiple exits — can be handy in special cases.

Backward *FOR* Loops

OOPas allows FOR loops to count backward by the use of the keyword DOWNTO. The syntax for such loops is almost identical to the regular FOR loop, except that *<lower limit>* TO *<upper limit>* is replaced by *<upper limit>* DOWNTO *<lower limit>*. When the loop starts, the counter is initialized to *<upper limit>*. Then, each time flow of control returns to the top of the loop, the counter decreases by 1. The loop exits when the counter is less than *<lower limit>* (see Syntax Box 12.4).

Indefinite Loops with More Than One Exit

We introduced the logical operators AND, OR, and NOT in discussing IF statements. Since the exit conditions on REPEAT and WHILE loops are boolean conditions, we can use any boolean expression after the UNTIL or between the

Syntax Box 12.4

Backward FOR loop

Purpose:

To repeat a block of code a predetermined number of times.

Syntax:

```
FOR <counter>:= <upper limit> DOWNTO <lower limit> DO
   <statement>;    { body of loop }
```

Where:

<counter>, *<lower limit>*, and *<upper limit>* are defined as in Syntax Box 12.1 (FOR Loop).

<statement> is any legal OOPas statement. If more than one statement is to be repeated, BEGIN/END brackets must surround the repeated code:

```
FOR <counter> := <upper limit> DOWNTO <lower limit> DO
  BEGIN
    <statements>;{ body of loop }
  END;
```

Usage:

The backward FOR loop executes the statements in the body of the loop as many times as specified by the upper and lower limits.

When the FOR statement is first encountered, *<counter>* is assigned the value of *<upper limit>*. That value then is compared to *<lower limit>*. As long as *<counter>* is greater than or equal to *<lower limit>*, the statements in the body of the loop are executed. When the last statement in the body of the loop is performed, the flow of control returns to the FOR line. Then *<counter>* is decreased by one and again compared to *<lower limit>*. When *<counter>* is less than *<lower limit>*, the flow of control exits the loop.

If *<upper limit>* is less than *<lower limit>*, the loop body is not executed.

WHILE and the DO, including using logical operators. Thus indefinite loops can have multiple exit conditions.

Consider our SUFish. Suppose we want the fish to swim to the left as long as there isn't another fish in the way. We can change the boolean expression in the WHILE loop from this:

```
WHILE currentPosition.GetX > 0 DO
```

to this:

```
WHILE (currentPosition.GetX > 0) AND
              (NOT OtherFishAt(currentPosition)) DO
```

thus providing two exits for the loop: (1) when the fish gets to the left edge of the screen and (2) when there is already a fish at the current position. In either case, the flow of control continues to the line immediately following the end of the loop. However, if the loop exits when another fish is in the way, we might want the fish to turn around. You therefore need to place an `IF-THEN` statement immediately after the end of the loop:

```
WHILE (currentPosition.GetX > 0) AND
            (NOT OtherFishAt(currentPosition)) DO
BEGIN
  ...
END;
IF OtherFishAt(currentPosition) THEN TurnAround;
```

Whenever a loop has more than one exit condition, the code immediately following the loop should include an `IF-THEN` or a `CASE` statement to determine which exit condition is true, and respond accordingly.

Summary

In this chapter we looked at different types of loops. Loops are either definite or indefinite and are used to repeat blocks of code.

The definite loop in OOPas is known as a `FOR` loop and allows code to be executed a known number of times. OOPas provides two forms of indefinite loops: the `REPEAT-UNTIL` loop and the `WHILE` loop. Both types use a boolean (exit) condition to signal the end of the loop's execution. Though the two loops are similar, they are not interchangeable; the body of a `REPEAT` loop always is executed at least once, but the body of a `WHILE` loop may not be executed at all.

Exercises

Understanding Concepts

1. A definite loop consists of three parts: an initialization of the loop counter, a way to change the counter, and an exit condition. How are these parts indicated in a `FOR` loop?

2. What is the difference between a `WHILE` and a `REPEAT` loop?

3. Explain how to implement a `FOR` loop using a `REPEAT` loop or a `WHILE` loop.

4. Assume `GetCostOfNextItem` is a function that returns the cost of something in a grocery store. The following code is supposed to loop until it finds a cost of 0. What's wrong with this code?

```
cost := GetCostOfNextItem;
WHILE cost <> 0 DO
  total := total + cost;
  cost := GetCostOfNextItem;
```

5. The following code is supposed to calculate `base` to the `exponent` power. What is wrong here? How can it be fixed?

```
FUNCTION RaiseToPower(base, exponent: integer): integer;
VAR
  result: integer;
  curPower: integer;
BEGIN
  result := base;
  FOR curPower := 1 TO exponent DO
    result := result * base;
  RaiseToPower := result;
END;
```

6. If an exit condition in a `WHILE` or `REPEAT` loop is a double exit, why might you need an `IF` statement to follow it?

Coding Problems

1. Write a method that tells how to distribute change. Given an amount less than $1.00, the method should indicate how many quarters, dimes, nickels, and pennies are needed (using the highest-valued coins possible).
2. Write a method that draws a chessboard (an 8×8 grid, with alternating black and white squares).
3. Write a method that displays all the prime numbers between 2 and 100.
4. Write a method that, given an integer between 3 and 10, draws an equilateral polygon with the specified number of sides.
5. Suppose we had a class called `ThreeDPoint` that allowed us to specify a point using three dimensions. Its constructor (`Init`) takes three integers as parameters, corresponding to coordinates along the *x*-, *y*-, and *z*-axes, and its `Draw` method maps the three-dimensional point onto the two-dimensional screen. Modify the code in Section 12.2 so that it draws a cube in three dimensions.
6. Suppose your screen represents a still pond. Ask the user to pick a point to represent a stone being thrown into the water. Simulate the ripples of water that surround the stone. When the stone hits the water, circular waves should start appearing, centered where the stone hit. A new wave begins every 1/5 of a second, and its radius increases by three pixels each 1/10 of a second. Simulate the wave movements for 30 seconds (assume that one iteration of your method's loop takes 1/10 of a second to execute).

Programming Problems

1. Develop a music layout program. The user should be able to choose a type of note (whole, half, quarter, eighth), and a location on a staff, and that note is added to the end of the score. Assume here that measures are four beats long, and for the sake of simplicity, your program should allow the user to enter only complete measures. For example, if a measure begins with a dotted half-note (three beats), the user should only be allowed to add notes that are less than or equal to one beat.

2. Modify the paint program from Chapter 8 by adding a polygon button. The user enters a number of sides, and a polygon with that many sides is added to the painting.

3. Write a program that draws the pattern of stars on the U.S. flag. The pattern consists of five rows of six stars alternating with four rows of five stars.

4. As an extension of the last program, allow the user to choose from different time periods, and show the U.S. flag from that time period.

5. In the atomic shell model, the nucleus of an atom is surrounded by orbits, or shells, of electrons. The shells fill, starting at the shell closest to the nucleus; one shell must be filled before an electron can reside in the next shell. The innermost shell holds 2 electrons; the next shells (in order, going away from the nucleus) hold 8, 8, and 18 electrons. Write a program that asks the user to enter an atomic number from 1 to 36 (corresponding to the number of electrons) and draws a model of the shells.

6. Write a program that draws a clock with an hour, minute, and a second hand. Your program should ask the user for the current time and then display that time. After the time is shown, your program should execute a loop that moves the hands. Each iteration of the loop should correspond to one second (even though the loop will take less than one second to execute). Show the clock movements for an hour (3600 iterations of the loop).

7. Extend the aquarium program, by allowing the shark and fish to move in turn (using rules from Programming Problem 2 in Chapter 10) until the shark eats the fish or until the shark leaves the scene.

8. Extend the financial calculator from Chapter 9 by showing a line graph that represents the value of the investment over time.

13 Recursion

In Chapter 12, we looked at the various loops we can use to perform the same task over and over again. In this chapter, we will be looking at a different approach to performing a repetitive task — a technique called *recursion*. When we used a loop, we sent the same message over and over again, thus performing many tasks. In recursion, we can get a method to do more work by having the method send the same message it is responding to.

Think back to a classic book from your childhood. In Dr. Seuss's *The Cat in the Hat Comes Back*,[1] the Cat in the Hat needs to clean up a spot. But he decides that the task is too big to do by himself. So he lifts his hat and out pops Little Cat A, who is a smaller version of the Cat in the Hat. Little Cat A looks at the spot and decides that they need even more help with this task. The smaller cat lifts his hat, and another even smaller cat is there. Little Cat A says,

> This is Little Cat B.
> And I keep him about,
> And when I need help,
> Then I let him come out.

Each cat has a little replica of himself under his hat — and the littler cats come out to help the bigger cats. Ultimately, Little Cat Z appears and cleans the spot. When the job is finished, the cats, one by one, return to their hats.

Recursion works in much the same manner as the cats. Starting with a large Cat in the Hat, the same task (or cat) is performed in a progressively smaller size. Eventually, the task is small enough to be trivial, and all the cats hop back into their hats.

Of course, recursion isn't something used only by cats — it is used in many mathematical definitions as well. For example, a function called *factorial* often is defined recursively. The function factorial, written $n!$, is the number of

1. Dr. Seuss, *The Cat in the Hat Comes Back* (New York: Beginner Books, 1958).

ways you can arrange *n* things in a row. You can arrange one thing in a row one way. You can arrange two things in a row two ways — twice as many ways as you could arrange one thing. You can arrange three things in a row in six different ways — three times as many ways as you could arrange two things. This pattern continues. In general, you can arrange *n* things in a row in *n* times as many ways as you could arrange $n - 1$ things. Thus *n*! is defined in terms of a smaller version of itself: $(n - 1)!n$, a pattern identifying this definition as being *recursive*.

13.1 SENDING THE SAME MESSAGE TO YOURSELF

As an example, suppose we want to be able to draw a spiral. Rather than using actual curves, we'll model a spiral with short lines, just as we modeled a continuous pencil line with short lines, last seen in Chapter 8. The specification of a spiral follows:

The spiral starts at a particular point. The spiral is made of successively shorter lines, each line at an angle to the previous one. The difference in length and angle can be specified, as well as the length of the longest line segment (the first one). The spiral can be drawn in a particular drawing area.

By picking out the nouns, we can get a list of the parts of our spiral object:

spiral	line	difference in angle
particular point	angle	length of longest line
shorter lines	difference in length	particular drawing area

"Spiral," of course, is just the object we're designing. "Difference in length," "difference in angle," "length of longest line," and "particular drawing area" all describe attributes of the spiral. The rest of the nouns describe things that are used to build the spiral, such as "shorter lines" and "particular point." Class Box 13.1 summarizes these attributes and the two methods our spiral will have, the constructor and a method to draw the spiral.

Using the arithmetic we learned in Chapter 9, we could use some trigonometry to figure out how to draw lines at various angles. Instead, we'll use a new class, described in Class Box 13.2, called `GPTurtle`. A real-life turtle knows where it is and what direction it is facing. Our turtle also knows this, but it also carries a pen, drawing a line behind it as it moves around the screen. If you have used the Logo programming language, the turtle will be familiar to you. Since our turtle is a class, it is easy to have as many turtles as desired by simply making new instances. Now, we can draw a spiral using a turtle by telling it repeatedly to go `Forward` and to `Turn`.

Class Box 13.1
Spiral

Spiral

A spiral drawn in a window.

Methods:

```
Init(newTargetLink : GPDrawingAreaAsn; newStart : GPPoint;
        newAngleIncr : real; newLengthIncr : integer);
```

The constructor. Takes parameters for the drawing area to draw in, start point, and increments for both angle and length.

```
Draw
```

Draw the spiral.

Instance Variables:

`startPosition : GPPoint;` where the spiral starts.

`targetLink : GPDrawingAreaAsn;` drawing area the spiral draws in.

`angleIncrement : real;` the angle between successive line segments.

`lengthIncrement : integer;` the difference in length between lines.

Class Box 13.2
GPTurtle

GPTurtle

A turtle can move around the screen, leaving a trail wherever it goes.

Methods:

```
Init(targetLink : GPDrawingAreaAsn);
```

The constructor. Takes a drawing area for the turtle to "live" in. The turtle starts in the center of the drawing area.

```
DrawForward(lineLength : integer);
```

Move the turtle `lineLength` pixels forward, drawing a line from the old position to the new position.

```
Turn(angle : real);
```

Turn the turtle to the left. `angle` is in degrees.

```
MoveTo(position : GPPoint);
```

Move the turtle to `position`. No line is drawn.

Armed with our turtle and the description of the spiral we want to make, we now can write down the class declaration and the constructor. Both are straightforward, though the class we implement will be a bit different from the one described in Class Box 13.1. In particular, we'll change some of the instance variables, although the interface to the class won't change.

```
Spiral = OBJECT
  CONSTRUCTOR Init(
       targetLink       : GPDrawingAreaAsn;
       newStart         : GPPoint;
       newAngleIncr     : real;
       newLengthIncr    : integer);
  PROCEDURE Draw(length : integer);

PRIVATE
  turtle        : GPTurtle;
  startPosition : GPPoint;
  angleIncrement : real;
  lengthIncrement : integer;
END;
```

Notice that Class Box 13.1 included an attribute to link to the drawing area. Since the turtle will be performing the drawing, and it has its own link to the drawing area, we don't need the drawing area link as an attribute in the class `Spiral`. The constructor still takes this link as a parameter. The link simply is passed on to the turtle directly:

```
CONSTRUCTOR Spiral.Init(
       targetLink       : GPDrawingAreaAsn;
       newStart         : GPPoint;
       newAngleIncr     : real;
       newLengthIncr    : integer);
BEGIN
  turtle.Init(targetLink);
  turtle.MoveTo(newStart);
  startPosition := newStart;
  angleIncrement := newAngleIncr;
  lengthIncrement := newLengthIncr
END;
```

Sending One Message

We're now ready to do the real work of defining our `Spiral` class: implementing the `Draw` method. As a way to get started, let's think carefully about the construction of a spiral. Clearly, the first step, seen in Figure 13.1, is to move the turtle forward and turn it a bit. What's next? Well, we still have to draw the rest of the spiral, but this task is the same as drawing a new, smaller spiral at the position and angle where the turtle left off. The only difference is that now we want to draw it with a smaller initial side. So we can rephrase our original task of "draw a spiral" as "draw a line and then draw a smaller spiral." How do we draw a smaller spiral? We start by drawing a line with the turtle, then turning it, as seen in Figure 13.2. Once we've done that, we simply draw a smaller spiral. We draw spirals by drawing one line, then drawing a smaller spiral. All we have to figure out now is when to stop drawing smaller spirals.

Figure 13.1

The first step in drawing the spiral: The turtle moves forward and turns.

Figure 13.2

Continuing the spiral: Drawing smaller lines as the turtle turns

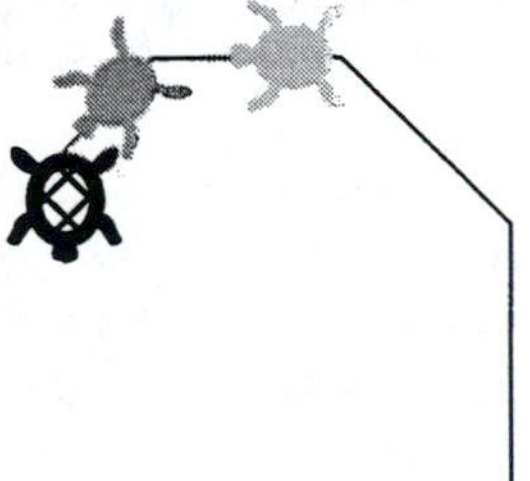

Stopping is actually not that tricky. We simply use an `IF-THEN` statement to check the length of the line we are about to draw. If the line is short enough, we don't need to draw a smaller spiral. How short is short enough? If the length is less than or equal to zero, we don't need to bother to draw the line.

Now, we're ready to implement the `Draw` method. We simply check that the length isn't too short. If so, we draw a line and turn the turtle, then draw a smaller spiral:

```
PROCEDURE Spiral.Draw( length : integer );
BEGIN
   IF length > 0 THEN
      BEGIN
         turtle.DrawForward( length );
         turtle.Turn( angleIncrement );
         Draw( length - lengthIncrement )
      END
END;
```

The key to this method, and the very part that makes it recursive, is the line of code that says

```
Draw( length - lengthIncrement )
```

Inside the `Draw` method, we're sending the `Draw` message *again*. This may seem a little funny at first, but there's really nothing unusual going on. A method can send any message we want to any instance to which the method has access. One of the instances a method has access to is `self`, so an instance can send a message to itself. We've even seen methods send messages with the same name as the method, way back in Chapter 6.

The difference there was that we used the `INHERITED` keyword so that the instance receiving the message (`Init`, in that case) would respond with its parent's method rather than with the method that was sending the message. Since we're not using `INHERITED`, the instance responds to the `Draw` message with the same `Draw` method that sent the message in the first place. Recursion thus always starts with an instance sending the same message, but using that message to handle a smaller version of the original task (such as drawing a smaller spiral). Recursion must eventually "bottom out" by reaching a point where no further messages are sent (in our spiral, when the `length` is less than zero so nothing is drawn at all).

Each time a method is used to respond to a message, a copy of the method is created to hold the parameters and local variables the method uses. This copy is called an *activation* of the method. Each activation exists for exactly as long as it takes to run the code in the method, performing each statement in the method in turn. So consider an activation for our `Draw` method, which holds one value, the `length` parameter, and one `IF-THEN` statement. The `IF-THEN` statement itself contains three message sends. The first tells the turtle to draw, and the second tells the turtle to turn. Each of these message sends creates activations corresponding to the turtle's methods. Finally, the last message is the recursive `Draw`, which creates a second activation for the `Draw` method, as shown in Figure 13.3. Let `length` start at 3, and let `lengthIncrement` be 2 (this will be a very small spiral).

We can see that the second activation has its own copy of the parameter `length`. The second copy's `length` has a different value, without affecting the first copy's value. Each message send makes a new activation. In Figure 13.4, we see a final activation being created for the recursive `Draw` in Figure 13.3. Now, `length` is –1, and the first test in the `IF` statement fails. No more activations are created. Notice that the activation where `length` is 3 waits for the other activations to finish. Had we started with `length` being 103, we would have had 50 more activations waiting in a row.

Activations are created even for nonrecursive methods, but we've been able to ignore activations until now. However, remember from Section 5.12 that you cannot make a link to a local variable, because finishing a method destroys the activation. Since the actual space for the local variable is contained in the activation, what you would have linked to is destroyed. Thus the link lasts longer than what it links to.

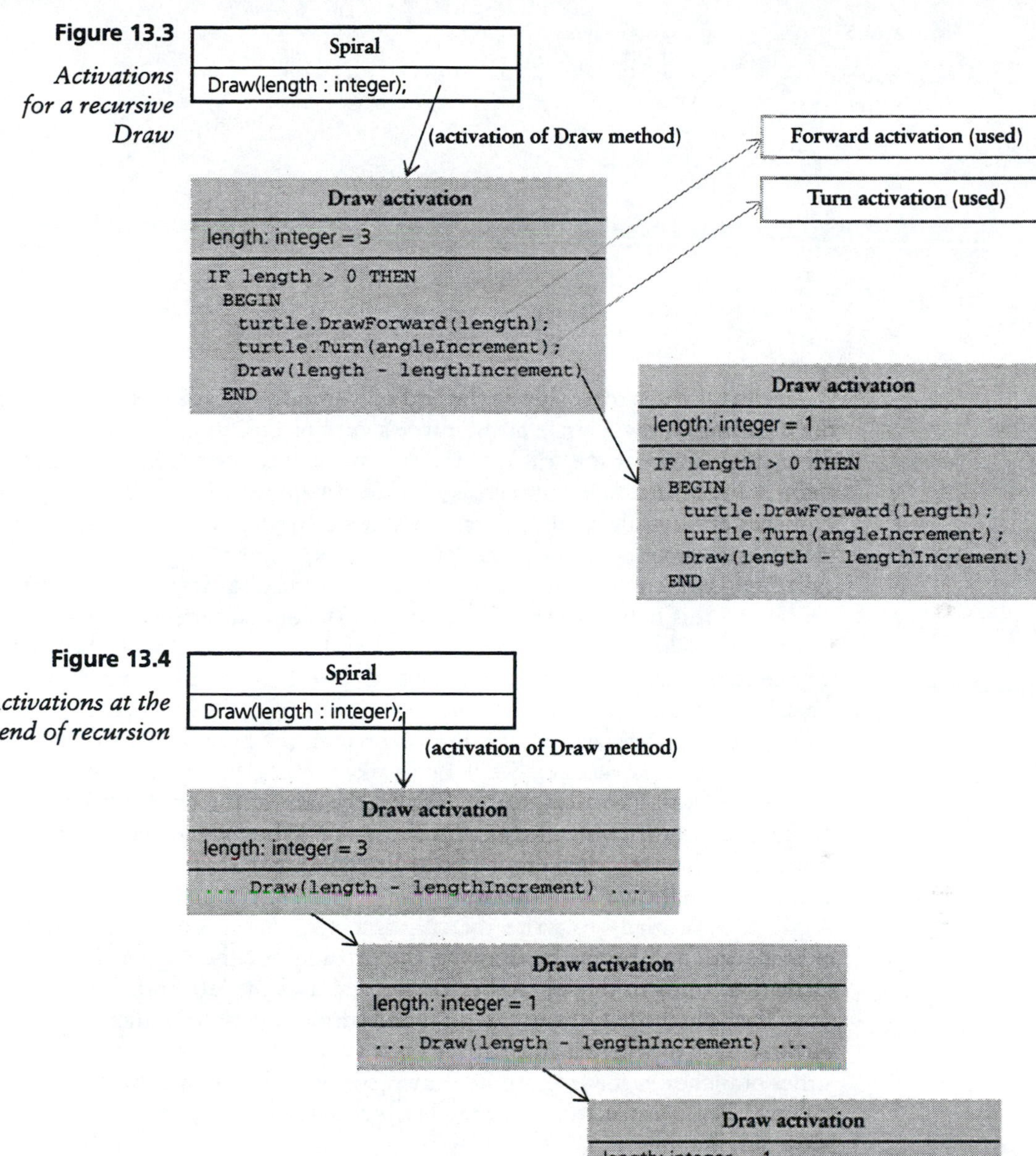

Figure 13.3 *Activations for a recursive Draw*

Figure 13.4 *Activations at the end of recursion*

Sending Many Messages

Our spiral was fun, but suppose we'd like to draw a tree instead. Figure 13.5 shows a picture of the kind of tree we'd like to draw. Take a close look at the leftmost branch. It looks a lot like the spiral we just built, except for the leaf at the end and all the other branches sprouting off of it.

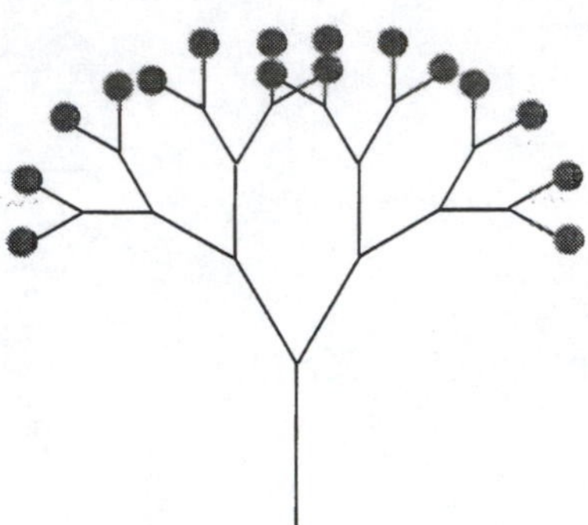

Figure 13.5
A recursively drawn tree

The leaf is easy to provide at the end of a spiral. Instead of simply stopping the drawing, draw a circle at the turtle's current position. The branches are a bit trickier. Start at the trunk of the tree by comparing the left branch to the right branch. The right branch is a rotated copy of the left branch — both branches are simply smaller trees. We saw this pattern in the spiral: The complex object is composed of smaller, simpler versions of itself. This property, called *self-similarity*, is one of the principal features of fractals (including the spiral and this tree).[2] The tree is recursive. The only difference is that we now have two smaller copies to make, instead of the one we had with the spiral.

The constructor for our tree is essentially the same as the constructor for the spiral. We make the turtle, then save various parameters of the tree, such as how much shorter each branch should be than the previous one (which we'll call the `branchIncrement`). We'll also make the angle to turn for each branch an instance variable called `angle`. Finally, the size of the smallest branch will be an instance variable called `smallestBranch`. When we reach a point in the recursion when we would draw a branch smaller than that, we'll stop drawing branches and draw a leaf instead.

We're now ready to write the `Draw` method. It takes a single parameter, `branchSize`, and begins by drawing the "trunk" of the current branch. The turtle then turns to the left and recursively draws the left branch in a smaller size. Then the turtle turns to the right and draws the right branch. Finally, the turtle returns to where it started. This last step is especially important, so that other branches in the tree can be drawn correctly. The complete `Draw` method follows. The constructor and the class declaration can be found in the software distribution.

```
PROCEDURE Tree.Draw( branchSize : integer );
BEGIN
  IF branchSize > smallestBranch THEN
```

2. For more on self-similarity and fractals, including a more mathematical treatment of the examples in this chapter, see Benoit Mandelbrot, *The Fractal Geometry of Nature* (New York: Harper & Row, 1987).

```
            BEGIN
               { Draw the trunk. }
               turtle.DrawForward( branchSize );

               { Draw the left branch. }
               turtle.Turn( angle );
               Draw( branchSize - branchIncrement );

               { Draw the right branch. }
               turtle.Turn( -2.0 * angle );
               Draw( branchSize - branchIncrement );

               { Put the turtle back where we started. }
               turtle.Turn ( angle );
               turtle.DrawForward( -branchSize )
            END
         ELSE
            DrawLeaf { Draw circle at turtle's pos, ending recursion.}
      END;
```

As before, each method invocation creates an activation. Whereas each activation of `Spiral.Draw` only created a single recursive activation, `Tree.Draw` creates two recursive activations. Thus a picture of the activations for `Tree.Draw` looks like the tree itself (as shown in Figure 13.6). Each activation is numbered in the order in which it is created.

Figure 13.6

Activations for Tree.Draw

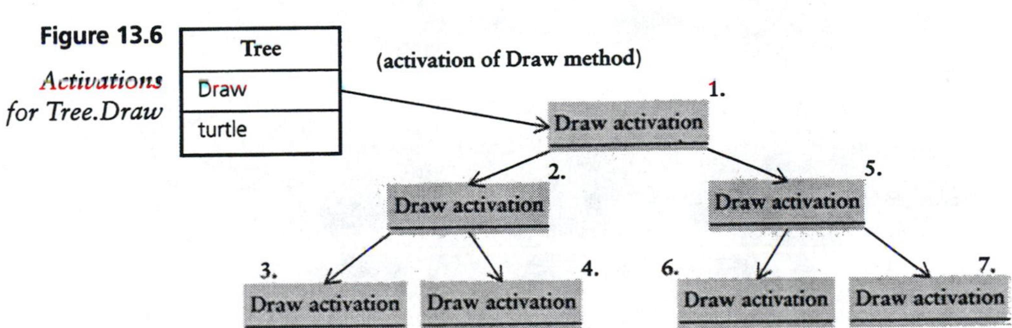

Note that all of the activations share the single instance variable `turtle`. This explains why each time we draw a branch, we position the turtle to return it to its starting position. For example, after activation 2 has executed activation 3, the turtle needs to be correctly positioned for activation 4. Similarly, activation 6 must return the turtle so that activation 5 can then invoke activation 7 correctly. Finally, after activation 1 has executed activation 2 (which executed 3 and 4), the turtle has to be in the correct position to execute activation 5 (which will in turn execute activations 6 and 7).

13.2 SENDING A MESSAGE TO ANOTHER OBJECT

Now let's try something a bit more complex. Instead of recursively sending a message to itself, the object we'll build now will make new objects and send messages to them. Before, one object sent many messages to itself. Both the spiral and the tree recursively sent itself a `Draw` message. However, we could just as easily build objects that send messages not to themselves but to other instances of the same class. These objects could send messages to yet other instances in turn. These objects could be either contained or linked to. In this chapter, the objects will be contained in activations as local variables. We will see examples of recursion across links in later chapters, such as Chapters 18, 23, and 24. For now, though, we'll stick with our fractals.

Our new design will be a bit like a snowflake, only four-sided instead of six-sided. We start with a square and replace each quarter of the square with a T-shaped figure. In each quarter, the T is rotated a quarter turn. Figure 13.7 shows the initial square being replaced by four T-shaped blocks (using shading to make the replacement clear) and the resulting design. Figure 13.8 shows the result of replacing each of the sixteen squares in Figure 13.7 (four per T-shaped block) with four T-shaped blocks, and the resulting figure. We stop when the T-shaped blocks get so small we couldn't see them on the screen.

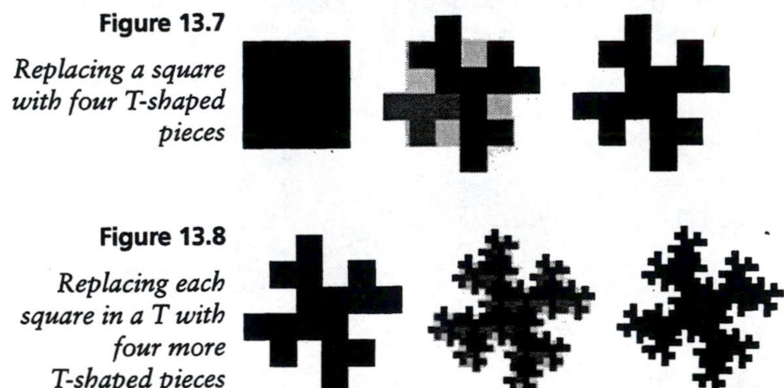

Figure 13.7 *Replacing a square with four T-shaped pieces*

Figure 13.8 *Replacing each square in a T with four more T-shaped pieces*

Let's describe our square snowflake. The self-similarity of this fractal should be apparent, and we'll keep an eye out for how this is reflected in the specification.

This object is a square snowflake. It is formed by starting with a single square "seed." The seed is replaced with a pattern of four T-shaped designs, each at a different orientation, and each composed of four squares one-sixteenth the size of the original square. Each of the four squares in a T-shaped design is itself a new seed, being replaced by four new T-shaped blocks. If a seed is sufficiently small, it is drawn as a single dot.

This provides us with a short list of nouns to pick out our classes:

square snowflake	square seed	pattern
T-shaped design	orientation	dot

The square snowflake will be our primary class. Because of the recursive nature of our snowflake, the seed square is itself a square snowflake, so it doesn't need a different class. T-shaped design is another obvious class. Dot is good, but we needn't write our own class for it; instead, we can use `GPPoint`, a class that contains a `GPPoint` but also knows how to `Draw` itself. "Pattern" and "orientation" are our only remaining nouns, and as it happens, we don't actually need a separate class for the *pattern* of T-shaped designs, because the `SquareSnowflake` class will create four instances of `TShapedDesign`, implicitly creating a pattern. Exploiting self-similarity, each `TShapedDesign` will produce more square seeds.

Now, we only have to deal with "orientation." Orientation is an attribute of `TShapedDesign` — each instance of the design has one of four orientations. We could implement this class in many different ways. We could make an enumerated type for the orientation and use `CASE` statements to handle the different ways shapes can be oriented. However, future modifications of our snowflake would require changing all those `CASE` statements.

Instead, we'll make `TShapedDesign` a base class and derive four different classes from it — one for each different orientation. This strategy gives us the advantage of being able to make asymmetrical snowflakes, simply by making a different subclass of `TShapedDesign`. Taking a cue from what T-shaped designs do in the specification, we'll call the base class `ReplacementPart`.

We now have a pretty good idea of what our various classes need. We'll start with `SquareSnowflake`, which has two points that describe the starting square. When told to `Draw` itself, it needs a drawing area in which to draw.

```
SquareSnowflake = OBJECT
  CONSTRUCTOR Init( point1, point2 : GPPoint );
  PROCEDURE Draw( targetLink : GPDrawingAreaAsn );
PRIVATE
  corner1, corner2 : GPPoint;
END;
```

Now we can define `ReplacementPart`. Like `SquareSnowflake`, the constructor will take two points and drawing will require a drawing area. Since this is a base class, the `Draw` method is virtual.

```
ReplacementPart = OBJECT
  CONSTRUCTOR Init( point1, point2 : GPPoint );
  PROCEDURE Draw( targetLink : GPDrawingAreaAsn ); VIRTUAL;
PRIVATE
  corner1, corner2 : GPPoint;
END;
```

Finally, we have the class definitions for the four kinds of replacement parts. We'll call these `TUpperLeft`, `TUpperRight`, `TLowerRight`, and `TLowerLeft`. Each one has four instances of `SquareSnowflake`, although each class will call the snowflakes different things, since they are in different positions. Because the four class definitions are essentially the same, we'll only show one here:

```
TUpperLeft = OBJECT( ReplacementPart )
  CONSTRUCTOR Init( point1, point2 : GPPoint );
  PROCEDURE Draw( targetLink : GPDrawingAreaAsn ); VIRTUAL;
PRIVATE
  trunk, top, middle, bottom : SquareSnowflake;
END;
```

The constructors for a `SquareSnowflake` and a `ReplacementPart` are trivial: They store the two points. Let's begin instead with the `Draw` method for a `SquareSnowflake`. When we draw the snowflake, either the snowflake will be so small we can draw it as a single dot, or we will draw the snowflake by drawing the four T-shaped designs. If the two corners of the snowflake are the same, then the snowflake is small enough to draw as a point.

```
PROCEDURE SquareSnowflake.Draw ( targetLink : GPDrawingAreaAsn )
VAR
  point : GPPoint;
  ul : TUpperLeft;
  ur : TUpperRight;
  lr : TLowerRight;
  ll : TLowerLeft

BEGIN
  IF NOT corner1.Equal(corner2) THEN
    BEGIN
      ul.Init( corner1, corner2 );
      ur.Init( corner1, corner2 );
      lr.Init( corner1, corner2 );
      ll.Init( corner1, corner2 );
      ul.Draw( targetLink );
      ur.Draw( targetLink );
      lr.Draw( targetLink );
      ll.Draw( targetLink )
    END

  ELSE
    BEGIN
      point.InitWithCoords( corner1.GetX, corner1.GetY );
      point.Draw( targetLink )
    END
END; { Draw }
```

Now let's consider the constructor for `TUpperLeft`. To create the four snowflakes, the constructor needs to calculate the corner points for each snowflake. Figure 13.9 diagrams an instance of `TUpperLeft`, showing where the snowflakes appear, what the passed points are, and which points need to be calculated.

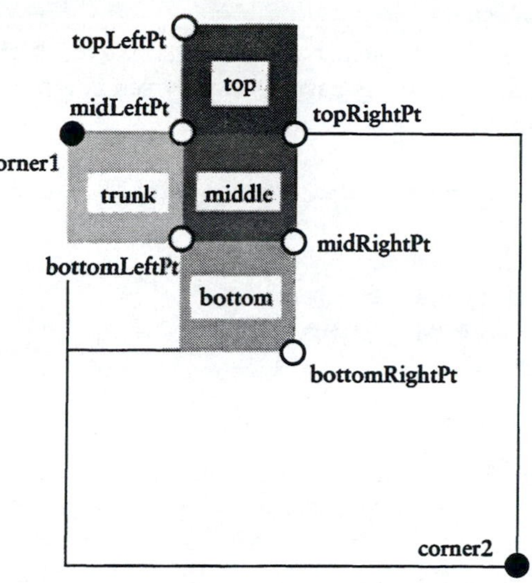

Figure 13.9

The instance variables used by a T-shaped piece

```
CONSTRUCTOR TUpperLeft.Init ( point1, point2 : GPPoint )
VAR
  topLeftPt, midLeftPt, topRightPt, bottomLeftPt, midRightPt,
            bottomRightPt : GPPoint;
  rightEdgeX, leftEdgeX, lowerMiddleY: integer;

BEGIN
  INHERITED Init( point1, point2 );

  { Create all the points. }
  rightEdgeX := (corner1.GetX + corner2.GetX) DIV 2;
  leftEdgeX := (corner1.GetX + rightEdgeX) DIV 2;
  bottomRightPt.InitWithCoords(rightEdgeX, (corner1.GetY +
            corner2.GetY) DIV 2);
  lowerMiddleY := (corner1.GetY + bottomRightPt.GetY) DIV 2;
  midLeftPt.InitWithCoords( leftEdgeX, corner1.GetY );
  topRightPt.InitWithCoords( rightEdgeX, corner1.GetY );
  bottomLeftPt.InitWithCoords( leftEdgeX, lowerMiddleY );
  midRightPt.InitWithCoords( rightEdgeX, lowerMiddleY );
  topLeftPt.InitWithCoords( leftEdgeX, corner1.GetY +
            (corner1.GetY - lowerMiddleY) );
```

```
  { Now create the four snowflakes. }
  trunk.Init( corner1, bottomLeftPt );
  bottom.Init( bottomLeftPt, bottomRightPt );
  middle.Init( midLeftPt, midRightPt );
  top.Init( topLeftPt, topRightPt )
END;
```

That was a bit complex, but the worst is over. Now all we have left is the `Draw` method. This one is easy: It simply sends a `Draw` message on to each of the four instances of `SquareSnowflake`:

```
PROCEDURE TUpperLeft.Draw( targetLink : GPDrawingAreaAsn );
BEGIN
  trunk.Draw( targetLink );
  top.Draw( targetLink );
  middle.Draw( targetLink );
  bottom.Draw( targetLink )
END;
```

When we drew a tree or a spiral in Section 13.1, there was only one instance. In this example of recursion, each recursive step sends another message to a *different* instance, rather than to the same instance. A snowflake makes four new T-shaped designs as local variables. These T-shaped designs contain *new* snowflakes as instance variables. The original snowflake then sends each T-shaped design a `Draw` message. A T-shaped design responds to `Draw` by sending `Draw` to each of its new snowflakes. Eventually, when `Draw` is sent to snowflakes that are so small that they are a single dot on the screen, the recursion ends.

Thus the T-shaped designs are created solely within the activation of `SquareSnowflake.Draw`, as shown in Figure 13.10. The T-shaped parts are effectively contained within the activation (as shown by the diamond-ended containment lines). Each T-shaped part contains four `SquareSnowflakes`, telling them all to `Draw` (as shown by the four additional activations of `Draw`).

Figure 13.10

Activations in a SquareSnowflake and various replacement parts

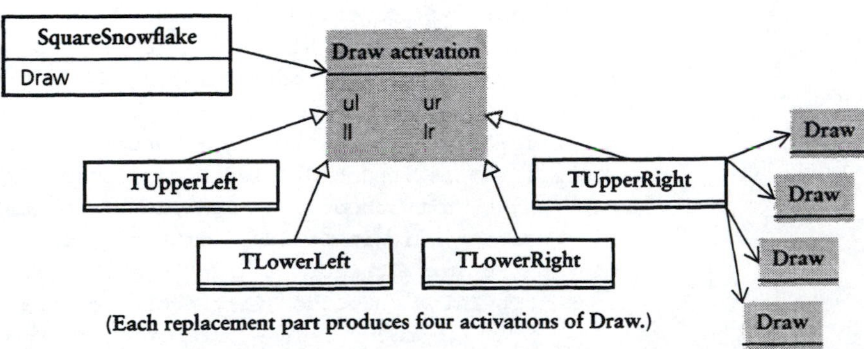

13.3 LOOPS AND RECURSION: COMPUTATIONAL EQUIVALENCE

Recursion is an extremely powerful tool and it takes a while to recognize which problems lend themselves to a recursive solution. Furthermore, recursion isn't strictly necessary, because anything that can be done with recursion also can be done with a loop. As an example, let's rewrite `Spiral.Draw` from Section 13.1 using a `WHILE` loop. A method that uses loops instead of recursion is said to be *iterative*, in contrast to a method that uses recursion and is *recursive*. Hence we call this new method `DrawIteratively`:

```
PROCEDURE Spiral.DrawIteratively ( length : integer );
BEGIN
  WHILE length > 0 DO
    BEGIN
      turtle.DrawForward( length );
      turtle.Turn( angleIncrement );
      length := length - lengthDecrement
    END {WHILE}
END;
```

So why learn recursion? We could just as well ask why learn loops, because anything that can be done with a loop also can be done with recursion. Let's look at `GPApplication.Run` from Section 12.3 again:

```
PROCEDURE GPApplication.Run;
VAR
  event : GPEvent; { A GPEvent models a user's action. }

BEGIN
  REPEAT
    WaitForNext(event);
    RespondTo(event)
  UNTIL quitWasHit
END;
```

A recursive form of this method looks like this:

```
PROCEDURE GPApplication.RunRecursively;
VAR
  event : GPEvent;
BEGIN
  IF NOT quitWasHit THEN
```

```
    BEGIN
      WaitForNext(event);
      RespondTo(event);
      RunRecursively
    END
END;
```

Recursion and loops are computationally equivalent in terms of the kinds of things they can compute. However, loops and recursion are each more suited to describing different things. For example, although it is easy to describe the spiral with a loop, it is much more cumbersome to describe the tree with a loop, much less the square snowflake. Similarly, drawing horizontal lines a pixel at a time as we did in Section 12.1 can be done recursively, but we may not want to think of drawing a line as drawing a dot and then drawing a line one unit shorter (although we certainly could). So deciding when to use recursion and when to use loops is simply a matter of which way of describing things seems more appropriate to the specific object.

Again, it takes experience to learn to recognize which problems are best done recursively and which are best done iteratively. We will come back to recursion repeatedly, in Chapters 18, 23, and 24.[3]

Summary

In this chapter, we examined the idea of recursion — a way of performing a task by performing smaller versions of that task, until a task becomes so small as to be trivial.

One example of recursion was drawing a spiral by drawing a single line and then drawing a smaller spiral. This process involved drawing a line, then performing a single smaller version of the overall task (drawing a spiral). With a little more work, we drew a tree by drawing a line and performing *two* smaller versions of the overall task. More complex tasks might involve performing many smaller versions of the overall task.

Spirals and trees involved only a single instance sending messages to itself. We examined another example where an instance made more instances, sending messages to them. These instances then made smaller versions of the first instance, thereby performing recursion. Recursion thus can happen across a system of objects and not merely within a single object.

We concluded by examining the expressive power of loops versus recursion. Loops and recursion are equivalent in computational power: Anything computable by a loop can be computed by recursion and vice versa. However, some problems are more naturally recursive (such as drawing trees) and other problems are more naturally iterative (such as counting things). Whether to use recursion or

3. Programmers familiar with procedural programming may be surprised to find so much recursion. When used with virtual methods and polymorphism, recursion is quite natural and extremely powerful, as we will see in these later chapters.

iteration in a particular situation is a design decision that should be based on the situation being modeled.

Exercises

Understanding Concepts

1. Identify where the recursive methods in this chapter bottom out.
2. Why is it important that recursive methods bottom out?
3. Why aren't `INHERITED` calls considered recursive?

Exercises 4 through 6 refer to the following function. It calculates balance and interest for a certain number of days. Interest is compounded daily.

```
CONST
  intRate = 0.05;{ current annual interest rate }
TYPE
  Account = OBJECT
    CONSTRUCTOR Init(newBalance: real);
    FUNCTION Compound(days: integer): real;
      { calculates balance and interest for certain number of
        days }
  PRIVATE
    balance: real;  { balance in the account }
  END;

FUNCTION Account.Compound(days: integer): real; { bal in acct }
VAR
  todayBal: real;{ current balance }
BEGIN
  IF days = 0 THEN
    Compound := balance
  ELSE
    BEGIN
      todayBal := Compound(days-1);
      todayBal := todayBal * (1 + intRate/365);
      Compound := todayBal;
    END
END;
```

4. If balance is set to 100, what does `Account.Compound(4)` return? (This is the new balance on $100 stored in the bank for 4 days.)
5. What is the bottom-out condition of the recursion?
6. Rewrite this code using iteration instead of recursion.

7. The following is a recursive implementation of a common Pascal function. What does it do?

```
{ Restriction: num1 >= num2 }
FUNCTION Arithmetic.LongWay(num1, num2: integer): integer;
BEGIN
  IF num1 < num2 THEN
    LongWay := 0
  ELSE
    LongWay := LongWay(num1 - num2, num2) + 1;
END;
```

Coding Problems

1. Change the order of the `Draw` message sends in `SquareSnowflake.Draw` so that the order is lower left, lower right, upper right, upper left. Does this ordering make a difference in the intermediate results? in the final result of the program?

2. Write a recursive function that raises a number to an integer power.

3. The greatest common denominator (GCD) of two positive integers `num1` and `num2` is defined by the following pseudocode. Implement it as a method.

```
IF num2 = 0 THEN
  GCD = num1
ELSE
  GCD = greatest common denominator of num2 and (num1 mod num2)
```

4. Implement the following multiplication algorithm using recursion: Start with two numbers *a* and *b* where *a* > *b*. Create pairs of numbers, halving *a* (ignore fractional parts) while doubling *b*. Continue this operation until the halving yields 1. To find the product *a* * *b*, add all the doubled numbers that correspond to odd numbers in the halving operation. For example, 18 times 51 is calculated as follows:

```
51   25   12   6    3    1
18   36   72   144  288  576
```

The product is: 18 + 36 + 288 + 576 = 918.

5. Modify the change-making method of Coding Problem 1 in Chapter 12 to make it recursive.

Programming Problems

1. Write a program to draw a design according to the following definition. Start with a square in the center of the drawing area; let's say it is *X* pixels wide. Next, draw four squares that are each *X*/2 pixels wide and centered at the corner of the larger square. Continue drawing squares at the corners of the new squares until the recursion moves to draw a square less than two pixels wide.

2. Write a program that selects a number from 1 to 1000 according to this definition. Start at the halfway point (500). Select, randomly, whether to choose the current number or to select a number higher or lower. If higher, go halfway between 500 and 1000; if lower, go halfway between 0 and 500. Repeat this process until one number is selected.

3. Write a program that draws a black and white screen. Split the screen in half, choose one of the halves at random, and paint it black. Split the other half in half, choose one of those halves (quarters), and paint it white. Continue splitting and alternating colors until the area of the screen being drawn is less than 4 pixels wide.

4. Write a program that recursively draws marks on a straight line. First, the line should be drawn. Then, a mark should be drawn that indicates where the line splits in half. Then, marks should be drawn that indicate where the line splits into four pieces. This process should continue until 16 evenly spaced marks are drawn on the line.

14

Bugs and Debugging

Mistakes in a program are called *bugs*. Why "bugs"? The legend is that back when computers were the size of buildings but had the computational power of today's digital watch, some programmers discovered an error in their program and couldn't figure out what it was. Eventually, deep inside the computer, someone found the problem — an insect was stuck inside the computer and had caused a short circuit of a component. When the insect was removed, the programmers remarked, "It was just a bug."

Now, whether or not that story is true, bugs can be quite serious problems. A bug in a banking program can mean mistakes in funds allocation. A bug in some of the software controlling a space shuttle can be fatal. A bug in our paint program from Part I means we can't paint pretty pictures. So, we'll spend this chapter familiarizing you with common bugs and the kind of "bug repellent" you can use against them.

14.1 BUGS THAT PREVENT A PROGRAM FROM RUNNING

Some bugs prevent you from running your program. In a sense, these are the safest and easiest kinds of bugs to handle because, if the program can't run, no one can use it inadvertently. These bugs are relatively easy to fix.

Compile-Time Bugs

The easiest bugs to locate and fix are *syntax errors*. OOPas's syntax rules are extremely precise. Whenever there is a syntax error, OOPas tells you two things: what is wrong and where the problem is. Unfortunately, OOPas can't fix the problem. Consider the following code fragment, which illustrates a common syntax error you probably have encountered in your programming by now:

```
BEGIN
  ...
  anObject.Run
  anotherObject.MakeNoise;
  ...
END;
```

OOPas will tell you that there's an error in the boldfaced line: It found `anotherObject` when it expected a semicolon. To fix the problem, you would put a semicolon on the line *before* the boldfaced line, but the syntax of OOPas doesn't care which line the semicolon is on, just that it is there. Thus OOPas can't do better than saying, "Somewhere before this point, there is an error."

Common syntax errors including missing punctuation (like the semicolon in the preceding code) or, alternatively, extra punctuation where it doesn't belong:

```
anObject..Run;
```

Other common syntax errors include extra or missing comment braces, which could cause OOPas to ignore some code. The following code inadvertently comments out code:

```
anObject.Run; { This comment continues to include the next line
anobject.MakeNoise; { Never gets called -- this is a comment. }
```

Missing, extra, or incorrect keywords are also easy syntax errors to make, such as forgetting the `THEN` in an `IF-THEN`; putting in an extra `END` at the end of a method; putting a semicolon after a `THEN`, `ELSE`, or `DO`; or using `DO` in place of `OF` in a `CASE` statement. Another common keyword-related mistake is to give a variable or a class the same name as a keyword, such as calling an object that models a mathematical function "`Function`."

Arithmetic is fertile ground for syntax errors, particularly in complicated expressions — it's easy to include an extra operator, or leave out a parenthesis.

Getting the types wrong also happens frequently. In Chapter 9, we pointed out one easy way to do this by trying to assign a `real` to an `integer` or vice versa. Passing parameters of the wrong type (or even mistakenly reordering the parameters of the right type) is something we saw in Chapter 4. Finally, Chapter 5 showed us how to determine whether the types of associations are compatible for assignment.

The last common mistake that the compiler may catch is simple: misspellings. If an object or method isn't referred to by its exact name, the compiler doesn't know what to do. It will think the misspelled object or method is an object or method that was never declared.

Run-Time Bugs

Run-time bugs are more serious than compile-time bugs. Rather than being errors caught by the compiler and fixed by the programmer before the program actually is used, run-time errors, as their name suggests, are caught only when the program is run.

There are three common kinds of run-time errors, only two of which you are likely to encounter in the exercises and programs in this book. The first, and most likely, follows a `nil` link (also known as a `nil` pointer, and first mentioned in Chapter 5). If you try to call a method or access an instance variable through a link, and the link is `nil`, what happens? Your program stops — it *crashes*. If this happens when you run your program within Borland's code development environment, the debugger (described later in Section 14.4) will show you where in your program you attempted to use a `nil` pointer. However, if you are using your program in another environment, your program simply dies.

The second kind of run-time error is an *arithmetic exception*. By far, the most common form of this is *divide by zero*. Other arithmetic exceptions include similar mathematically undefined situations, such as taking the square root of a negative number or finding the tangent of $\pi/2$. A kind of arithmetic exception unique to computers occurs when numbers get too big. Back in Section 9.1, we learned that an `integer` in OOPas can only be so big (or so small if negative). So what happens if, for example, we add two really large `integers`? Let's add 2,147,483,000 to itself; it is just a bit smaller than the largest number OOPas can handle. Or, if you prefer, let's multiply this number by 2. This is an example of another form of arithmetic exception, often called *overflow* because the number is too large to hold in the amount of space OOPas sets aside for an integer. Because of the way arithmetic is implemented in a computer, the result in such a situation usually is that the number "wraps around" and continues counting from the smallest negative number.

The third kind of error is one you can't do much about. Fortunately, it isn't really your fault, either. Consider what happens when the *hardware* of the computer doesn't work quite right. Clearly, your software has little hope of working correctly in this case, though sometimes your software can detect when this happens and try to do something else. A similar situation occurs when the operating system encounters some sort of problem. Both hardware and operating system failures are extremely rare, though.

14.2 PROGRAMS THAT MISBEHAVE

In a sense, syntax errors and arithmetic exceptions are the easy bugs to fix. When they happen, you know something has gone wrong, and you usually know exactly what it was. The hardest programs to fix are the ones that simply do not do what you want them to. Computers can do only what you tell them to; they cannot know what you mean.

Uninitialized Variables

One of the things that programmers often mean to say but often forget to put in their program explicitly is initialization. Uninitialized variables can cause a program to behave quite unpredictably. Why? Because an uninitialized variable essentially contains nothing but random junk. OOPas can't tell the difference between random junk and a viable object — if the program says there's an instance at a particular place in the computer's memory, then there must be an instance there. But if the instance hasn't been initialized, what actually is in that memory is whatever was in that memory the last time it was used.

By forgetting to call the instance's constructor, you've produced an instance that hasn't been initialized. For links and built-in types like `integer` and `real`, there are no constructors. Instead, you should make sure you assign a valid value to these variables before you use them, whether you're dealing with a local variable or an instance variable. If the constructor hasn't been called or the variable hasn't been assigned, the instance is junk. The only kind of instance you don't call the constructor for is a parameter, since parameters are being passed to a method by some other object that should have constructed it properly.

So if you've called the constructor, the instance is fine, right? But what happens if the constructor doesn't do what it is supposed to? In particular, the constructor might not initialize a particular instance variable. Or worse, the constructor of a derived class might not include a call to the base class's `INHERITED` constructor, in which case all of the base class's instance variables would not be constructed correctly.

The important concept is that every variable should be properly initialized. If you point to any variable in your program, you should be able to identify where it was initialized.

Semantic Errors

Of course, forgetting to initialize a variable isn't the only way to make a mistake. For example, you might have added two numbers when you meant to subtract them. This may seem like a silly mistake. After all, everyone knows the difference between addition and subtraction, right? Programmers mistakenly add or subtract not because they don't know the difference but because they may be unsure of which one to use. This mistake is unlikely in a small program, but a large program can be an extremely complex system, so complex that no one person can possibly understand it all. In this setting, it is all too easy to make a mistake about what to do.

Such mistakes aren't limited to arithmetic, of course. They are just as likely to arise when programmers use one method of an object when they should have used another method, or perhaps another object entirely. Perhaps the programmer told an object to erase something that actually needed to be drawn instead. Or perhaps, in trying to `Draw` an object, the programmer used a method called `Show`, rightfully thinking that `Show` is a pretty reasonable name for a method to display an object. But if the object is modeling a theater, the `Show` method could have quite a different effect.

Carefully translating pseudocode and design diagrams into code is the best way to prevent this kind of problem.

Design Errors

The worst kind of errant program is not one that omits an initialization, or sends an incorrect message. The worst kind is one in which the *design* is flawed. Every statement could be correct, but if the program's design doesn't meet its specification, the correctness of individual statements is worthless. A design should be minimal, but it also needs to be *sufficient*. The best way to prevent design errors is to construct a complete and thorough design.

14.3 COMMON FLOW-OF-CONTROL ERRORS

In this section, we'll look at some of the ways that compound statements can go wrong, producing run-time, semantic errors. Statements such as `IF-THEN`, `CASE`, and `REPEAT-UNTIL` and recursive messages can alter dramatically what a program does. If a program behaves in ways the programmer did not intend, the results can be serious.

Improperly Nested Conditionals

In Chapter 10, we saw an easy way to make a mistake when using an `IF-THEN` statement: leaving out a `BEGIN-END` pair. The same kind of mistake can be made with `CASE` statements. Nested conditional statements can be especially tricky to get right: A misplaced `END` (and not necessarily a missing one) can cause serious problems. Keeping your indentation consistent can help prevent these problems. Also, keeping your methods short can help — a short method with less flow of control is easier to understand and thus easier to get right.

Infinite Loops and Unending Recursion

Nesting conditionals can be complicated, but with loops or recursion, you can make mistakes easily without any nesting. The first problem we're going to look at is a loop or recursion that never ends, an *infinite loop*.

Regardless of which loop you use, you always should hand simulate carefully to see that the loop behaves correctly at the boundary conditions (the entrance and the exit of the loop or the start or end of the recursion) and in a typical situation in between. You also should hand simulate naively to make sure that the loop iterates the correct number of times. Although this eliminates many mistakes, some loop errors still occur frequently.

An infinite loop occurs when the loop's exit condition is not satisfied or a recursive message sends only nonrecursive messages. For example, the following loop never will exit:

```
VAR
  point : GPPoint;

BEGIN
  oddnum := 1;
  point.InitWithCoords(0, 10);
  WHILE oddnum <> 100 DO
    BEGIN
      point.SetX(oddnum);
      point.Draw(targetLink); { targetLink : drawing area }
      oddnum := oddnum + 2;
    END; { while }
END;
```

At first glance, it appears that this loop will draw dots for the odd numbers between 1 and 100. However, the exit condition `oddnum <> 100` will never become `false`. Look at the hand simulation of the preceding code fragment in Figure 9.13. Each time through the loop, `oddnum` increases by 2. Eventually it gets the value 99, and a dot will be drawn at coordinates (99, 10) (see Figure 14.1). Then `oddnum` increases by 2 and receives the value 101 (see Figure 14.2). The condition `oddNum <> 100` is still `true`. It never gets the value 100, and thus the condition of the `WHILE` loop is never `false`. The loop continues to execute indefinitely. To fix the program, change the exit condition of the loop to either `oddnum <= 100` or `oddnum < 101`.

Figure 14.1

Infinite loop: oddNum = 99

```
oddnum := 1;
WHILE oddnum <> 100 DO
  BEGIN
    point.SetX(oddnum);
    point.Draw(targetLink);
    oddnum := oddnum + 2;
  END; { while }
```

```
Watches
oddNum = 99
```

99th dot

Figure 14.2

Infinite loop: oddNum = 101

```
oddnum := 1;
WHILE oddnum <> 100 DO
  BEGIN
    point.SetX(oddnum);
    point.Draw(targetLink);
    oddnum := oddnum + 2;
  END; { while }
```

```
Watches
oddNum = 101
```

101st dot

● ● ● ● ● ● ●

Let's consider a slight modification of our `Spiral` object from Chapter 13. Suppose the method `Draw` was implemented like this:

```
PROCEDURE Spiral.Draw(length : integer);
BEGIN
  IF NOT length = 0 THEN
    BEGIN
      turtle.DrawForward(length);
      turtle.Turn(angleIncrement);
      Draw(length - lengthIncrement)
    END
END;
```

Now suppose our `lengthIncrement` was 2, and we started with a `length` of 3 (or any odd length). Eventually, we'd get to a call to `Draw` where `length` was 1. The next call to `Draw` would receive a `length` of 1 - `lengthIncrement`, or –1 . Since the boolean expression `NOT length = 0` is `true`, we continue to draw, even though the `length` is becoming more and more negative. In fact, the drawing will never end, because the `length` never will equal zero. After a little bit, the spiral will be so large, it will be completely off the screen.

Loops That Don't Start

A `WHILE` loop exit condition that is set to `false` before the `WHILE` is encountered prevents execution of the loop. The same kind of error can occur in a recursive call when no recursive message is sent. Loops or recursion that are entered incorrectly can be as serious as loops that never exit. When you hand simulate pseudocode, make sure that your entering condition is correct.

The following example is intended to draw dots for all odd numbers less than 2, followed by all odd numbers less than 3, and so on up to all odd numbers less than 100:

```
continue := true;
point.InitWithCoords(0,0);
FOR current := 2 TO 100 DO
   BEGIN
      point.SetY(current);
      oddnum := 1;
      WHILE continue DO
         BEGIN
            point.SetX(oddnum);
            point.Draw(targetLink);
            oddnum := oddnum + 2;
            IF oddnum > current THEN
               continue := false;
         END; { WHILE }
   END; { FOR }
```

The first time through the loop, `current` starts at 2 and `oddnum` is set to 1. Because the `WHILE` condition is `true`, the inner loop is entered and a dot is drawn at coordinates (1, 2). The variable `oddnum` is then increased by 2 and assigned the value 3. Because the `IF` condition is `true` (3 > 2), `continue` is set to `false`. When the `WHILE` condition is checked, the condition is `false` and the loop body is skipped. The flow of control goes to the `END;` of the `FOR` loop and then back to the `FOR` line, where `current` is increased to 3. `oddnum` is reset to 1, but `continue` is still `false`, so the inner `WHILE` loop will not be entered again.

To fix this loop, we move the line that initializes `continue` — that is, `continue := true;` — between the lines `oddnum := 1;` and `WHILE continue DO`.

Forgetting to include `BEGIN/END` brackets can also cause problems. The following code won't draw anything:

```
oddnum := 1;
WHILE oddnum <= 100 DO
     point.SetX(oddnum);
     point.Draw(targetLink);
     oddnum := oddnum + 2;
```

This program also will be caught in an infinite loop, since the body of the loop consists of one statement (`point.SetX(oddnum)`); OOPas ignores the indentation. Remember, if no `BEGIN/END` brackets are found in a `FOR` or `WHILE` loop, OOPas assumes that the loop body is one line long. In this case, `oddnum` is never incremented, and the code just sets the *x*-coordinate of the point.

Off-by-One Errors

An *off-by-one* error occurs when a loop or recursion executes one too many or one too few times. The following code fragment, which is intended to add the odd integers from 1 to `number`, demonstrates this problem:

```
{ value of number set here by user }
...
sum := 0;
count := 1;
WHILE (count < number) DO
   BEGIN
     sum := sum + count;
     count := count + 2
   END; { WHILE }
```

This loop will produce an incorrect result if `number` is odd. In that case, the loop actually is computing the sum of the odd integers from `1` to `(number - 2)`, instead of from `1` to `number`. The `WHILE` condition should have been written as

```
WHILE (count <= number) DO
```

Conditions similar to off-by-one errors can occur with `FOR` loops. Look at the code fragment:

```
limit := 0;
FOR distance := 1 TO limit DO
   { body of loop }
```

The body of this loop is not executed, because the first value of `distance` (1) is not less than or equal to the value of `limit` (0).

For the same reason, the following loop body is executed only once:

```
limit := 1;
FOR distance := 1 TO limit DO
   { body of loop }
```

The difficult thing about off-by-one errors is that they rarely generate error messages — they just generate incorrect answers. Worse, you may not recognize that the results are incorrect. An error of this kind can be difficult to detect once a program has proceeded to the testing stage.

How can you avoid off-by-one errors? A good set of test cases with known answers is a tremendous help. You may not always have such test cases handy, however. As soon as you write a loop, you should perform three tests (two of which we have already seen). First, be sure that the loop will not be entered when you don't want it to (say, in special cases such as when the input differs from expected). Second, test the exit conditions to see that the loop will be exited when it should be and not until then. Finally, examine the conditions for the first and last cycles of the loop to be certain they are executed properly. This final testing of the loop's boundary conditions often eliminates off-by-one errors.

14.4 DEBUGGING TOOLS

It is essentially impossible to keep track of everything in a complex computer program without some kind of help. The best kind of help in understanding the program is a clear, well-documented design. The better the design, the more the program models what it is intended to model, the easier it will be to figure out what any one piece of the program is meant to do.

Of course, this isn't always enough. Thus most programming environments, Borland Pascal's included, provide a set of tools to help find and remove bugs. These tools range from simple browsers that let you examine the structure of a large program in different ways to debuggers that let you walk through a program one step at a time, seeing exactly what the program is doing at every step.

Browsing

The first tool we'll look at is called a *browser*. The browser can be used to examine your object classes, your units, and local variables belonging to the mainline (which the browser calls globals). This tool can help you keep track of a large program. It also can point out errors in the program's organization: If the browser shows you all the classes in a particular unit, you may realize that the list of classes just doesn't make much sense — perhaps some of the classes should be in another unit, or perhaps this unit needs other classes that it neither USES nor defines.

The browser is used the most to examine classes. When you start browsing objects, the browser window comes up, showing a class diagram of every class in your program, including the ones in GP. Unless you have a large screen, you will need to use the scrollbars to see a different part of the class diagram. Your Borland Pascal manual can tell you how to configure the browser so that it doesn't display all the classes in GP.

When using the browser, you can examine classes more closely simply by clicking on the representation. If looking at a class, you can click on it and see all of its methods. Clicking on a method will show you its code. A button at the top of the browser lets you go back to the previous view.

The Debugger

The *debugger* is an extremely powerful tool. It allows you to examine a program step by step and see exactly where the mistake is.

By stepping or tracing, you can watch statements execute. If you *step* through code, you watch your messages transmit within a single method. You keep looking at the body of one method, and the debugger executes one line at a time. When you *trace*, however, you don't continue looking at a single method. Each time a message is sent, you follow the message until you are looking at the body of the method that was used to respond to the message. Your next step or trace will occur at that point. The debugger also can tell you exactly where run-time errors occur, highlighting the expression that produced the error.

Watching variables is as easy as telling the debugger which ones to watch. The debugger displays the variables' values at all times in a window. Each time you step or trace, these values might change, but the window always will show their current values. You even can modify the values of some kinds of variables (built-in types). You can use this tool if you know that the value of a particular variable is wrong and want to check for further bugs in the program by putting in the correct value for the variable.

Stepping, tracing, and watching are of somewhat limited use in large programs, like most of those you build with GP. Why? Because GP itself is so complex that if you tried to step through it to find problems in your own code, you would get lost quite quickly. Objects you define as subclasses of GP often have their methods called as a result of a great deal of computation by GP (which handles the hard work of such things as keeping track of where the mouse is at all times, what the keyboard is doing, and what other windows on the screen are doing). Thus, if you tried a combination of tracing and stepping, starting from the `Run` method in your mainline, you might never find your code. Fortunately, tools are available in the debugger to alleviate this problem.

The Activation Viewer

The first tool in the debugger displays the activations. The activations are displayed top to bottom, with the one being evaluated at the top. Activations waiting for another activation to finish are lower down and the mainline is at the bottom. When the mainline sends a message, an activation is created from the method responding to that message and that activation goes on top of the display. When that method calls another method, the new activation goes on top. Whenever a method is finished, its activation gets removed from the top. Note that only the activation on top can be removed — methods lower down are waiting for methods higher up to perform some computation.

At any point in your stepping or tracing, you can open the view of the current activations. By showing you all the methods in use, this view will help you answer questions like, "Which method called the one we're currently looking at?" and "Which method called that one?" You can follow the activations all the way back to the mainline, which is always the bottom; if the mainline isn't waiting for another method, the program isn't running.

The view of the activations also shows the values of local variables and parameters used by the current methods. This is especially helpful for debugging recursive methods, which sometimes create a whole series of otherwise identical activations (since one method is waiting for the results of a "smaller" version of itself). By checking the values of local variables and parameters, you can make sure that a recursive method is progressing correctly, with each smaller method actually getting smaller and by the correct increment.

Finally, the view of the activations can be used to control exactly where you would like to step or trace next. When stepping or tracing, you can choose what activation you want to be in simply by selecting it in the view. Stepping or tracing proceeds at that point after finishing whatever methods are necessary to get there.

Breakpoints

The view of the activations is best for understanding where you are and how you got there. It is quite useful when a run-time error occurs unexpectedly, for example — the view of the activations shows you exactly what the program was doing when the error occurred. However, the view of the activations doesn't help you get where you want to be.

Breakpoints help you get where you want to be. A breakpoint is like a mark in your program. Whenever the program gets to the mark, it stops and tells the debugger where it is. If you suspect a bug in a particular method, simply place a breakpoint there and run the program. When it gets to that point, the program will "break." You then can start stepping or tracing at that point, using the activations view to understand how you got there.

Using breakpoints is the most effective way to debug a large program. They allow you to avoid the tedium of stepping through the entire program and instead focus on a particular area and squash your bugs.

14.5 DEBUGGING STRATEGIES

Debugging, like programming, is a skill learned best by practice, and it doesn't consist solely of using specialized tools. Here, we will suggest some guidelines to structure your debugging. There are no known rules for how to debug, only guidelines.

Debugging in Pieces

The first suggestion is to implement your program in small workable chunks. In so doing, you also will be able to debug in more manageable pieces. Trying to write a substantial program in one fell swoop and then trying to get all of the bugs out is one of the surest known recipes for disaster in programming.

Slow and steady wins the race in the long run, and the long run is what we're after. The best way to implement your program is not in leaps and bounds but in small steps. Instead of implementing every class at once, implement them one at a time. After implementing each one, test it: Make sure that little step is a sure one.

Using Stubs and Drivers

"But wait," you blurt, "how can I test one single class when it depends on so many others in order to work properly?" This question is very astute, and if you're asking it, you've got a good handle on the big problems of design. The troubling answer is that you can't implement classes independently. They may depend on one another intrinsically in order to function correctly.

So is there a clever answer? Yes, there is: Go ahead and implement the other objects, but only as much as needed by what you're *really* testing. This technique is called using *stubs* and *drivers*. Stubs and drivers are incomplete implementations of the classes in your program that serve as placeholders, implementations that provide the necessary interface but not the necessary behavior. Stubs and drivers are used until the other objects have been implemented, at which point the stubs and drivers are superfluous.

A stub (or stubbed class) is a class with nothing but public methods and empty method bodies. This kind of class definition has the minimal functionality to behave like a real useful object. You now can use the stubbed class to test other parts of the program. If necessary, you can slowly add more detail to a stubbed object, making it perform more and more of the tasks the complete object will need to perform.

Whereas stubs are minimal objects that can be *used* by the object you're really testing, drivers are minimal *users* of the object you are testing. Often, a driver is a separate program, a small application that instantiates the object to be tested and tries out all of its methods. A driver is an excellent way to thoroughly test a small part of the overall system. For example, the method `Simulation.OneDay` in Section 6.3 is a simple driver for the `Animal` class. It makes use of all of `Animal`'s methods, thus ensuring that they behave correctly.

A Complete Specification

Testing a program thoroughly and incrementally by using stubs and drivers where necessary is a good idea, but the best defense against bugs is not to introduce them in the first place. The best way to avoid introducing bugs is to have a thoroughly complete design of your program before you begin coding. And the best start to having a complete design is to have a complete specification.

A specification should include everything that a program can do, from its most basic actions to its handling of strange error conditions. If the specification you are given isn't complete, finish it yourself. It will make your design that much easier.

That doesn't mean you should slack off on the program design just because you have a detailed specification. A specification is no more a working program than a design is. So flesh out that specification with a detailed design. By getting the design right, you will have eliminated many bugs before they have a chance to be implemented.

Summary

Bugs come in a wide variety. The easiest bugs to find and remove are compile-time bugs, including syntax errors such as misspellings and bad punctuation. The OOPas compiler tells you where the syntax is incorrect, allowing you to use an editor to fix the problem.

Run-time errors are problems with the semantics of the program. OOPas doesn't know how to deal with a run-time error, and often it will crash. Usually, crashes aren't as bad as they sound, because the debugger can tell you exactly what the program was doing at the time of the crash.

One common problem is uninitialized objects. Other common mistakes arise from using the wrong semantics, including using the wrong method of an object and using the wrong expression in a message or arithmetic expression. Mistaken semantics also can be produced by misplaced nesting constructs in conditionals.

Loops and recursion are powerful programming tools, but often they are the cause of serious programming bugs: Infinite loops, off-by-one errors, and incorrectly entered or exited loops easily can occur. The best way to catch such bugs is to hand simulate the pseudocode and OOPas code naively, especially for the entry and exit boundary conditions.

The Borland Pascal programming environment provides many tools to help find and prevent these bugs. The browser is one such tool that can help understand complex programs. The debugger can help find (and thus eliminate) bugs by letting the programmer step through code as it executes. Breakpoints can help get to a relevant point of program execution, and the activation view can help the programmer understand what that point of execution is in context.

Despite these tools, the best way to fix bugs is to prevent them. Preventing bugs is best accomplished by careful implementation. An incremental implementation, making use of stubs and drivers, can help ensure that various classes perform as advertised. Even more important is a thorough design of the program being implemented.

Exercises

Understanding Concepts

1. Browse through the classes of GP. What classes inherit from other classes? Why? What classes don't inherit from other classes, and why?

2. What is the difference between a compile-time bug and a run-time bug? Is this the same difference as that between syntactic and semantic errors?

3. Why should you fix compiler errors in the order they appear?

4. Where, generally, does it make sense to put breakpoints?
5. How can you decide which variables you want to watch?
6. Take a coding exercise or a short programming problem from an earlier chapter, and keep a journal of how you approach the problem. What design strategies did you use? Note when you found bugs, whether in the design, the pseudocode, or the coding stages of developing the program, and your thinking process for finding the bugs.
7. Find a partner and exchange "buggy" programs. That is, take one of your working programs from an earlier chapter and deliberately add bugs to it, and ask your partner to do the same. Then, exchange programs, and see whether you can debug your partner's code.

Coding Problems

Each coding problem in this chapter consists of a method with a bug in it. Find the bugs, describe them, then fix them.

1. The `GCD` function returns the greatest common divisor of two integers using Euclid's method:

```
FUNCTION Arith.GCD(num1, num2: integer): integer;
VAR
   temp: integer;             { used for swapping }
   newNum2: integer;     { temporary holder of new smaller num }
BEGIN
  { Make sure that num2 is the smaller. }
  IF num1 < num2 THEN
    BEGIN
      temp := num1;
      num1 := num2;
      num2 := temp
    END;
  WHILE num2 > 0 DO
    BEGIN
      newNum2 := num1 mod num2;
      num1 := num2;
      num2 := newNum2
    END;
  GCD := num1
END; { GCD }
```

2. This method draws a polygon. `GetNextPoint` retrieves the next point around the polygon's perimeter; this method draws a line from point to point, ending when `GetNextPoint` returns the first point of the polygon.

```
PROCEDURE Polygon.Draw;
VAR
  firstPt, { first point in the polygon }
  curPt, nextPt: GPPoint; { current and next point in polygon }
  curLine: GPLine; { line to draw in polygon }
BEGIN
  firstPt := GetNextPoint;
  curPt := firstPt;
  REPEAT
    nextPt := GetNextPoint;
    curLine.SetEndPoints(curPt, nextPt);
    curLine.Draw;
    curPt := nextPt;
  UNTIL (nextPt.GetX = firstPt.GetX) AND (nextPt.GetY =
           firstPt.GetY)
END;
```

3. The following method returns a link to the midpoint of a line. Note that `end1` and `end2` are defined as instance variables of type `GPPoint` inside of `LineClass`.

```
FUNCTION LineClass.MidPoint: GPAPointAsn;
VAR
  middle: GPPoint;
  midX, midY: integer;
BEGIN
  midX := (GetX(end1) + GetX(end2)) div 2;
  midY := (GetY(end1) + GetY(end2)) div 2;
  middle.SetCoords(midX, midY);
  MidPoint := @middle;
END;
```

4. This method calculates the number of ways that a number of people can be arranged at a table. If there are *n* guests, the total number of arrangements is *n*!, or n * (*n* – 1) * (*n* – 2) . . . * 3 * 2 * 1. This method calculates the number of arrangements for groups ranging from 2 to 10 guests.

```
PROCEDURE Party.FindArrangements;
VAR
  numGuests, { number of guests to seat }
  curGuest, { current guest in loop }
  arrange: integer; { number of arrangements }
BEGIN
  arrange := 1;
  FOR numGuests := 2 TO 10 DO
    BEGIN
      FOR curGuest := 1 TO numGuests DO
        arrange := arrange * curGuest;
```

```
            PrintMessage(numGuests, arrange)
            { PrintMessage is a method of the Party class that prints
                  the number of arrangements corresponding to a
                  particular number of guests. }
        END
    END;
```

Programming Problems

1. A restaurant has 10 tables for 2, 15 tables for 4, 5 tables for 6, and 1 table for 10. Write a program that divides the potential customers equally among 6 waiters and waitresses.

2. Create a linoleum tile pattern. First, create the pattern within a square area, then repeat it so it fills the screen (as shown in Figure 14.3).

Figure 14.3

Repeating a pattern to fill the screen

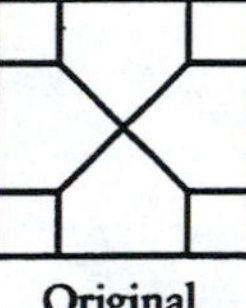

Original

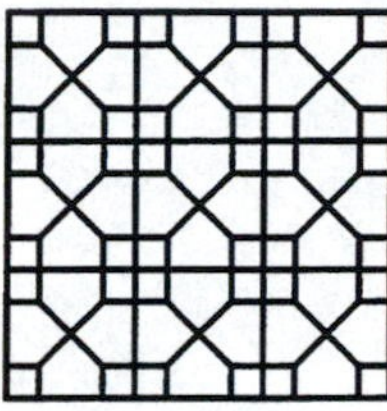

Repeated pattern

3. Modify the Aquarium example (last seen in Programming Problem 7 in Chapter 12) so that no two creatures (goldfish, shark, plant) can occupy the same space at the same time.

4. Design a four-function calculator for integers. The user should be able to click buttons on the screen and add, subtract, multiply, and divide integers.

5. A pool is one meter square. A lily pad in the pool is one centimeter square. The lily pad will double in size every day. Create a simulation showing the growth of the lily pad. Stop either when 30 days have gone by or when the pool is filled. (Extension: Once you have written the program, consider your repeating mechanism. Do you use recursion, a loop, or some combination? Can you rewrite the program using a different mechanism for repeating?)

Part 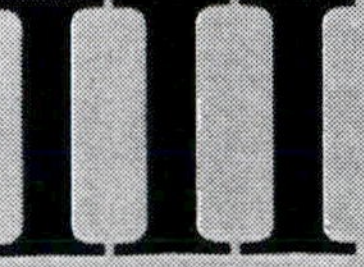

Built-in Collections

Now that we've seen all the ways we can define classes and give them useful behaviors, we need a way to group and arrange large numbers of instances. When you look around you, many of the objects you see appear in great profusion, organized in regular patterns. For example, we've talked about modeling chairs. But how about modeling a movie theater? We can model the individual chair in a theater, but a theater usually will have hundreds of chairs. That same movie theater will have movie-goers. We can model an individual movie-goer, but movie-goers often stand in line, and if the movie is popular, the line can be quite long.

Both a movie theater and a line of movie-goers are *collections* of other kinds of objects. The theater is a collection of seats, along with some individual things like the screen and the projector. The line is a collection of movie-goers, which may have its own additional attributes such as the movie the line is for. The theater doesn't change in size — it was built with a certain number of seats, and it always will have that number of seats. The size of the line, however, is dynamic: Just before a popular movie starts, the line might be quite long, but if the line is for an obscure movie, it will be quite short.

The remainder of the book will deal with collections of various kinds. This part is focusing on *fixed-size collections*, such as the movie theater. Part IV of the book will deal with *dynamic-size collections*, such as the line of movie-goers.

The fixed-size collections we will be dealing with make use of new OOPas syntax to describe the collections. They include some very specialized collections, such as strings, discussed in Chapter 15. Strings are sequences of characters. We've seen strings briefly before and now we'll learn a great deal more about using them. Arrays, discussed in Chapter 16, are a much more general form of collection. Arrays are collections of instances of any one type, one after the other. Strings are much like arrays of letters, but real arrays can contain numbers, or colors, or something else entirely. Chapter 17 discusses sets, which you may remember from introductory math classes. Unlike arrays and strings, the elements in sets don't have any particular order. For instance, members of a club don't have any intrinsic order — they are just members.

Chapter 18 will return to strings, examining parsing — some powerful ways to work with strings. OOPas uses parsing to understand the syntax of your programs. This chapter will explore the techniques used to do this.

This part will conclude with Chapter 19, covering files. Files aren't actually fixed in size, but they do use special syntax, so we've included them in this part. Files are like arrays of arbitrary data, stored on a computer's disks. Unlike arrays, we can add data to them (which is what makes them of arbitrary size). Like arrays, though, the contents of a file are ordered strictly. Files are very useful for storing information from your program for later use, perhaps by another program or by your program being run a second time.

15

Letters and Strings

Every day, you see many uses of computers that save time and help people. In addition to these proper uses of computers, you undoubtedly also have seen some abuses. Let's look at one example: computerized junk mail. Before the advent of computer-based text processing, everybody got the same advertising flyers. These days, though, computers are used to "personalize" a company's ad. Instead of the following:

> You are eligible to receive a special discount on a build-it-yourself yacht. You have the chance to become the envy of your entire town when you bring your new yacht down the street.

mailing houses now can generate a "personalized" letter such as this:

> You, Ralph R. Ruiz, are eligible to receive a special discount on a do-it-yourself yacht. Mr. Ruiz, you have the chance to become the envy of Cranston, RI, when you bring your new yacht down World Drive.

Such "individualized" mass mailings are possible because character string variables for items such as the name, address, and town of the recipient can be placed in the form letter and replaced with specific values from a file of such data. In this chapter, we discuss how to program such a mailing, and how we use OOPas to store and manipulate single characters and character strings to do this.

15.1 CHARACTER TYPES

Previously, we have used *string literals* to provide text that the user interface can display, such as the text "Quit" on a button. OOPas also provides a base type for storing single letters, symbols, and blanks in variables. Any single character that can be typed on the keyboard can be represented in a variable declared as a `char`. A partial list of the set of legal `char` values follows (the full list appears in Appendix C):

'A', 'B', . . . , 'Z', 'a', 'b', . . . , 'z', '1', '2', . . . , '9', '0', '!', '@', ';', '(', ')', . . .

char Literals, Variables, and Constants

Like integers, reals, and strings, characters can be used in your programs by simply using a *literal*. Like string literals, `char` literals are written with single quotation marks around them to distinguish them from identifiers. The only difference between `char` literals and `string` literals is that `char` literals have only one character between the quotation marks.

We can use the `char` typename anywhere we can use any other typename: to declare parameters, local or instance variables, or function return values. Syntax Box 15.1 describes the use of the `char` type.

Syntax Box 15.1

Declaration of a char variable

Purpose:

To declare a character variable.

Syntax:

```
VAR
   <identifier> : char;
```

Where:

<identifier> names a local variable, instance variable, or parameter.

Usage:

A variable of the base type `char` contains a single character.

Characters are implemented as integers with a limited range. Each character corresponds to a particular small integer. Different computer systems could use different correspondences. An 'a' on one system might be represented by 97 (which it is in OOPas) and be represented by some completely different integer on another system. Most computers, though, including the PCs on which OOPas runs, use the ASCII (American Standard Code for Information Interchange) encoding, described in Appendix C.

Much as you can declare symbolic constants for numbers like `integer` and `real`, you can declare symbolic constants of type `char`. You simply use a `char` literal as the right-hand side of a `CONST` declaration:

```
CONST
   Slash = '/';
```

Using *char* Variables

Any character, whether a letter, number, symbol, or blank, can be compared to any other character using the integers that correspond to them.The order of characters, known as the *collating sequence,* determines which characters are less than or greater than others. For example, the number sign (#) is represented in ASCII as the number 35. Order in the collating sequence corresponds to alphabetic order. When OOPas compares characters, it compares their numeric values. Thus the number sign (#) is less than the dollar sign ($), because the representation of the number sign (35) is less than that of the dollar sign (36). When OOPas compares two characters, it is really comparing the values of their corresponding ASCII codes. In effect, character comparisons are evaluated by first converting the characters to their integer ASCII values and treating the comparison as a regular integer comparison, following all the rules we discussed in Chapter 10. Of course, this all happens internally; you needn't concern yourself with this level of detail when programming in OOPas.

The following is a list of some of the legal character comparisons in OOPas:

```
'a' = 'a'          'a' <= 'c'
'a' < 'b'          'b' >= 'b'
'A' < 'a'          'B' > 'A'
'a' <> '+'         '3' < 'a'
'a' > ' '          '3' > '2'
```

All these comparisons evaluate to `true` when used in boolean expressions.

Of course, we can use variables or functions returning `char` values instead of the literal characters used in those comparisons. Comparisons like them can be used wherever a `boolean` variable is expected, such as the condition for an `IF-THEN` statement, when assigning to a `boolean` variable, or when checking the termination of a loop.

Because the comparisons are based directly on the characters' ASCII values, we could use the `Ord` function to make the comparison. In fact, a comparison of the `Ord` of two-character variables is always the same as a comparison of the variables themselves, so we rarely will use `Ord` in this manner.

Characters are not used very often by themselves; the base type `string` is far more common, as sequences of characters (strings) are more common than individual characters. However, we will find uses for single characters in Chapter 18, when we will walk through a string, looking at each character in turn.

One large distinction between the `char` base type and the `string` base type is that `char` is an ordinal type; that is, all the values for characters can be counted, but all the possible values for strings cannot.[1] This means that a `char` variable can be used as the selector in a `CASE` statement, for example, in specialized applications, such as parsing, which we will get to in Chapter 18.

---

1. Technically speaking, the number of possible strings is finite because computers limit the size of strings. But, within OOPas, the number of possible strings makes it impractical to refer to it as an ordinal type.

15.2 STRINGS

Instead of using single characters, we usually use a sequence of characters called a *string*. OOPas provides a built-in type called `string` that implements sequences of characters. As a built-in type, `string` can be used much as any other built-in type. Let's see how to use them now.

String Literals

Our brief exposure to a string in the Chapter 6 example program was limited to using a string to make a name for a push button. To set the name of a button, we send a `SetName` message to a subclass of `GPButton`. That message is defined to take one parameter: a string representing the name of the button. Thus an instance called `QuitButton` could have its name set as follows:

```
QuitButton.SetName('Quit');
```

In this case, we have used a *literal string* — that is, the string `'Quit'` literally appears in the program (as opposed to being stored in a variable or symbolic constant). Literal strings appear in OOPas programs in between apostrophes (in this case, `'Quit'`).

A string can contain any sequence of letters, numbers, spaces, and symbols. Let's look at some examples of literal strings:

```
(1) 'What is your name?'
(2) 'Please input a number between 5 and 7: '
(3) 'Aren''t computers fun?'
(4) ''
(5) ' '
```

Strings (1) and (2) show that a string can be any combination of letters, symbols, numbers, and blank spaces. String (3) shows a special case: the two apostrophes in `Aren''t` are necessary to represent a single apostrophe (rather than the end of the string). String (4) is the *null,* or *empty,* string because it contains no characters. On the other hand, if string (5) is the parameter to a method, a single blank space is passed. A blank is not the same thing as a null string, because a blank takes up a space in the string like any other character.

String Variables

The identifier `string` is a base type in OOPas, just as `integer`, `real`, and `char` are base types. String variables receive values the same way as other variables do. Syntax Box 15.2 describes using the string type name to declare variables.

For example, we can declare and then use a string in an assignment statement as follows:

```
VAR
 name: string;
BEGIN
 ...
 name := 'Robert C. Duvall';
 ...
END;
```

This example assigns a literal string to a variable and thus uses apostrophes. The apostrophes do not count as part of the string itself, but the spaces between the words do count. Thus, in this example, `name` receives a 16-character string. (Don't forget that the period and spaces also count as characters.) In OOPas, a string variable may contain up to 254 characters.

Syntax Box 15.2

Declaring a string variable

Purpose:

To declare a string variable.

Syntax:

```
VAR
   <identifier>: string;
```

Where:

<identifier> is a variable identifier. This identifier must begin with a letter and cannot be any of the keywords listed in Appendix A.

Usage:

When a `string` is declared, it initially holds a garbage value of length 0.

We can access any particular character in a `string` by *indexing* a `string`. Using special syntax (described in Syntax Box 15.3), we can use an `integer` to get a `char` at the position corresponding to the value of the `integer`. You can refer to an individual character in a string by its index. The characters in a string are numbered from left to right, starting with 1. To refer to an individual character, use the notation `<string var>[<position>]` . For example, if the string variable `name` holds `'Edward Mark Bielawa'`, then `name[1]` holds the character `'E'`, `name[7]` holds a blank character, and `name[19]` holds the character `'a'`. However, we cannot refer to `name[20]` or any position greater than the entire length of the string because a run-time error would result. You can use any character within a string as if it were a variable of type `char`.

Syntax Box 15.3

Indexing a string

Purpose:

To obtain a particular `char` in a string.

Syntax:

```
<string> [ <integer> ]
```

Where:

<string> is a `string` variable or constant and the index *<integer>* is an `integer` variable, literal, or constant.

Usage:

This expression returns the `char` at position *<integer>* in the *<string>*.

This is an expression of type `char`, and can be used anywhere a `char` is expected.

GP contains a class called `GPText` that allows us to output strings to the drawing area. `GPText` is a subclass of `GPShape`. The constructor `Init` takes a parameter that is a link to a drawing area and indicates where the string should be drawn. `GPText` contains a `SetCoords` method to establish the point in the drawing area where the text should appear. `GPText` contains a method called `SetString`, which receives the string that should be drawn as a parameter. Finally, `GPText` also has a method called `Draw`. This method draws the string on the screen, where its bottom left will begin at the location stored as the position. Thus if we want to place the string 'Robert C. Duvall' in the bottom left corner of the screen, we can use the following code:

```
VAR
  name: GPText;

BEGIN
  name.Init;
  name.SetCoords(0, 0);
  name.SetString('Robert C. Duvall'); { Set string to draw. }
  name.Draw(newDrawingAreaLink); { Draw string in position. }
END;
```

Output of text in the drawing area requires that we store the `string` inside an instance of `GPText`. After the instance knows where it should begin drawing and what `string` it should draw, we can draw the text using the `Draw` method.

The `SetString` method requires a `string` parameter. The actual parameter needn't be only a literal `string`; it can be a `string` variable as well. We can modify our last block of code slightly by adding a `string` variable:

```
VAR
  name: GPText;
  nameString: string; { string version of text }

BEGIN
  name.Init;
  name.SetCoords(0, 0);
  nameString := 'Robert C. Duvall';
  name.SetString(nameString); { Set string to draw. }
  name.Draw; { Draw string in position. }
END;
```

We can use any string "expression" as an actual parameter to `SetString`. This includes literal `strings` and `string` variables; it also includes the results of functions that return `strings`, as we shall see in Section 15.4.

15.3 COMPARING STRINGS

String comparison is very similar to numeric comparison. Remember, the term "string" is short for "character string." In comparing two strings, OOPas begins by comparing the first characters of the strings. If they are identical, OOPas then compares the second characters, and continues searching until it finds characters in corresponding positions that are not identical. At that point, it compares the characters just as it would compare two variables of type `char`, using their ASCII code.

The following are `true` string comparisons. Notice that they correspond to English alphabetic ordering:

```
(1) 'able' < 'baker'
(2) 'RED' >= 'BLUE'
(3) 'Woo' > 'Wolf'
(4) 'red' > 'RED'
(5) ' number' < 'number'
(6) '#$@*!' = '#$@*!'
(7) 'lamp' < 'lamppost'
```

The first three examples should be obvious to you. The comparisons stop after the first character in `(1)` and `(2)` because the `'a'` in `'able'` is less than the `'b'` in `'baker'` and the `'R'` in `'RED'` is greater than or equal to the `'B'` in `'BLUE'`. In example `(3)`, the first two characters of each string are identical. However, OOPas will not claim that two strings are equal until all of the characters have been compared. When OOPas compares the third characters (that is, the second `'o'` in `'Woo'` and the `'l'` in `'Wolf'`), it finds that the character on the left is greater than the corresponding character on the right; therefore the string on the left is greater than the string on the right.

Examples `(4)` and `(5)` again stop after the first character, but for less obvious reasons than in `(1)` and `(2)`. In both `(4)` and `(5)`, OOPas checks the numeric representations of the first character and determines that the `'r'` of `'red'` is greater than the `'R'` of `'RED'` and that the leading blank space in `' number'` is less than the `'n'` in `'number'`.

In example `(6)`, OOPas compares all characters of both strings. Since all five characters in both strings are identical, the entire strings must be equal.

In the final comparison, the first four characters of `'lamp'` and `'lamppost'` are identical. When OOPas tries to compare the fifth character of both strings, it notices that the string on the left does not have a fifth character. Since nothing remains of the left string, a null character (represented in the ASCII code as a 0) is compared to the fifth character of `'lamppost'`. Since the representation of the null character is less than that of any other character, the string on the left is less than the string on the right.

15.4 STRING FUNCTIONS

Just as OOPas supplies us with arithmetic functions, like `Sqr` and `Sqrt`, OOPas supplies us with string functions that allow us to manipulate strings. One of the simplest is `Length`, which simply returns how many characters are in a string. Others we will look at include `Copy`, which duplicates part of the string, and `Concat`, which glues two strings together into a new string, concatenating them. We'll look at other string functions in Chapter 18.

Length

A string's length is defined as the number of characters held by the string. The length is not necessarily the same as its maximum allowable length (254 characters); rather, it is the number of characters that it has received as a result of some assignment.

To determine the length of a string, we can use the `Length` function, which returns an integer value indicating the length of the string. The null string returns the smallest value — it has a length of 0. Since a string variable can hold up to 254 characters, the greatest value returned by `Length` is 254. We can see some examples in Syntax Box 15.4.

Copy

To copy an entire string, we can assign that string to a `string` variable to hold the copy. To copy only a small part of the `string`, however, we can't use a

Syntax Box 15.4

Length

Purpose:

To find the length of a string.

Syntax:

```
Length( <string> )
```

Where:

<*string*> is a literal or variable string. It can also be a string expression, meaning that it can contain any function that returns a string.

Returns:

An `integer` between 0 and 254.

Usage:

`Length` finds the number of characters in a `string`. For example:

- `Length('Apt #A3')` returns 7,
- `Length('Jane Wang')` returns 9,
- `Length(' ')` returns 1,
- and `Length('')` returns 0.

simple assignment. Instead, we can use the `Copy` function, which copies a particular part of a source `string` to a "destination" `string` and returns a part of a string. To use the `Copy` function, we have to specify the total string, the position at which to start, and the length of the string to copy.

Let's look at a brief example.

```
VAR
  name, firstName, lastName : string;

BEGIN
  name := 'Jane Jetson';
  firstName := Copy(name, 1, 4);
  lastName := Copy(name, Length(firstName) + 2,
              Length(name) - (Length(firstName) + 1));
  ...
END;
```

In this code, we begin by giving `name` the value `'Jane Jetson'`. We then use `Copy` to copy the first four characters out of `name` and into `firstName`; thus `firstName` receives the value `'Jane'`. `Copy` has no effect on the variable `name`; the variable still holds the value `'Jane Jetson'` even though the first name has been copied into another variable.

The second call to `Copy` uses nested functions. Again, `name` is used as the source string. The copying begins at the position `Length(firstName) + 2`, which evaluates to 6 (we added one to account for the space, and added one again, to start copying beyond the space). The number of characters is found by evaluating the expression `Length(name) - (Length(firstName) + 1)`. The function `Length(name)` returns the value 11 and `Length(firstName) + 1` is 5, so the expression evaluates to 11 – 5, or 6 (we added one to the length of the `firstName` to account for the space). Thus, OOPas starts at position 6 and copies the next 6 characters, as shown in Figure 15.1.

Figure 15.1 *Process used by Copy function*

```
Copy(name, Length(firstName) + 2,
     Length(name) - (Length(firstName) + 1))
```

Length(firstName) + 2 → Copied portion (positions 6–11)

1	2	3	4	5	6	7	8	9	10	11
J	a	n	e		J	e	t	s	o	n

Length(name) = 11

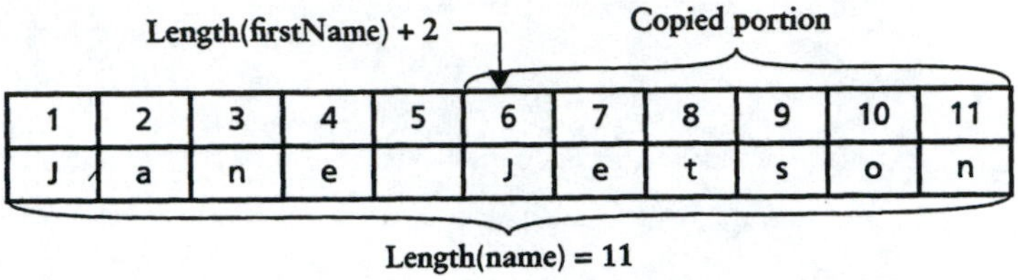

Syntax Box 15.5 shows the use of `Copy`.

Concatenation

After copying parts of strings using `Copy`, we might want to put them back together. OOPas allows us to *concatenate*, or join two strings with a string function called `Concat`.

Suppose we extended our preceding code example, and "glued" the first and last names back together using `Concat`.

```
VAR
  name, firstName, lastName, newName : string;
BEGIN
  name := 'Jane Jetson';
  firstName := Copy(name, 1, 4);
  lastName := Copy(name, Length(firstName) + 2,
              Length(name) - (Length(firstName) + 1));
  newName := Concat(firstName, lastName);
END;
```

Note that the `Concat` method takes two strings as parameters. The function returns the string stored in the first instance followed immediately by the string stored in the second instance. In this case, the function returns `'Jane'` immediately followed by `'Jetson'` — that is, after this method, `newName` will contain the string `'JaneJetson'`.

Syntax Box 15.5

Copy

Purpose:

To copy part of a string.

Syntax:

`Copy(<source>, <start>, <num chars>)`

Where:

<source> is a literal or variable `string`. It also can be a `string` expression, meaning that it can contain any function that returns a `string`.

<start> and *<num chars>* are both `integer` expressions.

Returns:

A `string`.

Usage:

`Copy` copies *<num chars>* characters from the string *<source>* beginning at position *<start>*.

If *<num chars>* is less than or equal to zero, a null string is returned.

If *<start>* is less than 1, `Copy` still begins at position 1. If *<start>+<num chars>* is greater than the length of the `string`, then `Copy` copies only the characters up to the end of the `string`.

For example, if we have the assignment statement:

```
name := 'Rafael Ruiz';
```

we get the following results from `Copy`:

- `Copy(name, 6, 4)` returns `'l Ru'`
- `Copy(name, 1, 4)` returns `'Rafa'`
- `Copy(name, 4, 0)` returns `''` (the null string)
- `Copy(name, 8, 15)` returns `'Ruiz'`

Notice that `Concat` runs the strings together; it does not place spaces between the various components. If we want spaces, we have to specify them. The easiest way to solve this problem is to nest calls to `Concat`, adding in a literal string `' '`:

```
newName := Concat(firstName, Concat(' ', lastName));
```

This fragment will produce the result `'Jane Jetson'` because of the extra space in the literal string in the nested call to `Concat`. Note that we could switch the order of the calls to `Concat` and get the same results:

```
newName := Concat( Concat( firstName, ' '), lastName);
```

It's not unusual to concatenate several strings like this. For example, the following code fragment concatenates sevenstrings into one:

```
VAR
  wholeName: string;
BEGIN
  wholeName := Concat('Mary', Concat('-', Concat('Kim',
      Concat(' ', Concat('Arnold', Concat(' ', 'Conner'))))));
  ...
END;
```

The result is that `wholeName` will contain the string

```
'Mary-Kim Arnold Conner'
```

In this fragment, `wholeName` is assigned the value of a `Concat` message. The second parameter, though, is also a `Concat` function that concatenates a hyphen and the remainder of the name, which is itself a concatenation. This chaining of concatenation proceeds, adding names and spaces, until finally a space and the last name is added. Although we could just type one literal string in this example, suppose we got some of the strings from parameters or instance variables, as in this simple class for a person's name:

```
TYPE
  PersonName = OBJECT
    CONSTRUCTOR Init(newFirst, newMiddle, newLast : string );
    FUNCTION WholeName : string;
  PRIVATE
    first, middle, last : string;
  END;

CONSTRUCTOR PersonName.Init(newFirst, newMiddle, newLast:string);
BEGIN
  first := newFirst;
  middle := newMiddle;
  last := newLast
END;

FUNCTION PersonName.WholeName : string;
BEGIN
  WholeName := Concat( first, Concat(' ', Concat( middle,
           Concat( ' ', last))))
END;
```

The syntax for `Concat` is summarized in Syntax Box 15.6.

Syntax Box 15.6

Concat

Purpose:

To join two strings.

Syntax:

```
Concat(<str 1>, <str 2>)
```

Where:

<str 1>, *<str 2>* are literal or variable `strings`. Each `string` can also be a `string` expression, meaning that it can contain any function that returns a `string`.

Returns:

A `string`.

Usage:

`Concat` begins by finding the end of *<str 1>*. The first character of *<str 2>* is then attached to the end of *<str 1>*.

`Concat('now', 'here')` returns `'nowhere'`. If the concatenated `string` is longer than 254 characters, all the overflow characters will be truncated.

Summary

The world is not made of just numbers; we need to read and write text as well. The `string` base type is defined in OOPas to handle strings of characters. Just as we have literal numeric constants, we can have literal strings of characters; just as we can have variables of type `integer`, we can have variables of type `string`.

In this chapter, we looked at variables of two base types: `char` and `string`. For the most part, variables of type `char` and `string` are like variables of the other base types in the way they are declared or set by assignment. To use a char or `string` literal in your program, you must mark the literal text with apostrophes. A symbolic constant also can receive a `char` or `string` value as long as the text appears inside apostrophes.

Comparisons can be performed on characters, because each character is stored with a unique representation as a small integer. The correspondence between integers and characters is called the ASCII collating sequence. One character is less than another if the ASCII value of the first character is less than the ASCII value of the second. String comparisons are performed by comparing characters in corresponding positions in the two strings, one at a time. When OOPas finds that a character in one string is not equal to the character in the corresponding position in the other string, it can say that one string is less than or greater than the other. Thus OOPas can determine that two strings are equal only by comparing all the characters in both strings and finding that each set of corresponding characters are equal.

Since OOPas provides a `string` data type, `char` variables are not used very often. Since `char` is an ordinal type, `char` variables can be used as the selector in a `CASE` statement.

Strings can contain up to 254 characters and behave slightly differently from the other atomic data types. If you try to assign a `string` literal of more than 254 characters to a `string` variable, the characters beyond position 254 will be ignored by OOPas. Except for this size consideration, though, strings of any length can be manipulated in the same way.

You also can refer to any individual character in a string simply by giving the name of the string variable and the position of the character in the string. The first character in any string is at position 1, the character immediately to its right is at position 2, and so on.

OOPas provides a number of predefined functions and procedures for manipulating string expressions. The `Length` function returns the current number of characters (not the maximum length) of a string. The `Copy` function returns a specified section of a string, and the `Concat` function returns a new string composed of two other strings "glued" together, one after the other. All these functions can be used on string variables of any declared length.

Exercises

Understanding Concepts

1. When is a `char` type more appropriate than a `string`?

2. Declare a constant called `pop` that contains an apostrophe.

3. What is the difference between the assignment statements `start := true;` and `start := 'true';`?

4. Which of the string functions discussed in this chapter return `integers`? Which return `strings`?

5. Which of the following comparisons return `true`? Which return `false`?

```
'a' < 'A'
'*' > ' *'
'LESS' < 'GREATER'
' U S A ' = 'USA'
'DeStefano' >= 'Desmond'
'' > ' '
```

6. Given the two statements `alpha := 'pizza';` and `beta := 'zapped';`, what is returned by the following code?

```
Length(alpha)
Length(beta[3])
Concat(alpha, alpha)
Copy(alpha, 3, 2)
Concat( Copy(alpha 3, 2), Copy(beta, 3, 4) )
```

Coding Problems

For problems that require input from the user, refer to the GP documentation in Appendix D, specifically the classes `GPPromptDialog`, `GPIntDialog`, `GPRealDialog`, `GPBooleanDialog`, and `GPStringDialog`.

1. Write a method that accepts three strings as `VAR` parameters and returns them in alphabetical order.

2. On a telephone, letters are associated with digits as follows:

2	A	B	C
3	D	E	F
4	G	H	I
5	J	K	L
6	M	N	O
7	P	R	S
8	T	U	V
9	W	X	Y

   Write a method that, when given a string of any length, translates the letters to the corresponding telephone digits. Generate an error message if the string contains letters (Q and Z) that cannot be translated.

3. Write a method that does the reverse of Coding Problem 2: Given a 7-digit string, find the corresponding phone number.

4. Write a method that takes a string representing a name in the form <*first name*> <*space*> <*last name*> and returns a `string` in the form <*last name*> <*comma*> <*space*> <*first name*>. Thus 'Rafael Ruiz' becomes 'Ruiz, Rafael'.

5. Write an object that displays a string on a diagonal line. It should be able to start the diagonal at a `GPPoint` passed to it. The diagonal should go down and to the right at a 45 degree angle. Each character should be progressively farther down the line. The distance between each character should be passed to the object as well.

Programming Problems

1. Add a Text button to the paint program from Chapter 8. When choosing the Text button, the user selects a point in the drawing area and a prompt dialog pops up. The user enters the desired text. When the user presses "OK," the desired text is drawn in the drawing area at the position selected.

2. Implement the game Hangman. The computer should pick a random word from a preprogrammed list of words. The user then picks individual letters. If the letter picked is in the word, the computer draws the word with all the correct characters that have been guessed so far (using an underscore "_" for letters that have not been guessed). If the user guesses wrong, then the computer adds another body part to a hanging figure. If the body is completed before the word is, the computer wins. Otherwise, the user wins.

3. Create a marquee on your screen. Ask the user to enter a `string`. Then, move the `string` across the screen from right to left.

4. Write a program that shows a bar graph. The user should enter three values and three labels (for example, if the graph shows ice cream that is sold on a given day, the user might enter Chocolate, 50; Vanilla, 100; Strawberry, 20). The program should use the values to draw bars of different heights and the user's labels to label the bar graph.

5. Write a program that draws comic balloons. The user should enter text, then a balloon such as those seen in the comics should appear around the text. The size of the balloon should vary with the length of the text.

16

Arrays

Atomic data types contain only one piece of data. Examples of atomic data types are `integers`, `reals`, `booleans`, enumerated types, and `chars`.

Objects, on the other hand, contain many pieces of data — as many instance variables as needed. Objects are an example of a *composite data type*. A composite data type is a collection of data items that are logically related and are stored under one name. Objects thus are a very general kind of composite data type, since they contain methods as well as data. In this chapter, we will see a simple composite data structure that has no methods — the *array*. We'll be looking at how arrays can be used to store a collection of data, such as a sequence of numbers or a list of cities.

16.1 ARRAYS OF BASE TYPES

Let's begin by exploring how we can use a simple array. We'll examine the structure of an array of integers, but the way we work with arrays of `integers` generalizes to arrays of other base types, such as `strings` or `reals`, and to arrays of instances or links.

The Fibonacci series is a famous mathematical sequence. The sequence begins with a zero and a one. The following numbers in the sequence are found by adding the previous two numbers. Thus the third number is the sum of the first and second numbers ($1 = 1 + 0$); the fourth number is the sum of the second and third numbers; and so on. The beginning of the sequence looks like this:

0 1 1 2 3 5 8 13 21 34 55 89

Let's say that we want to be able to store the first 20 numbers of a sequence. Using what we already know about variables, we could call our class `FibSequence` and declare 20 different instance variables, one for each `integer`. The following is just a portion of the instance variable declarations we would need:

```
TYPE
  FibSequence = OBJECT
    CONSTRUCTOR Init;
    { other methods here }
  PRIVATE
    firstNum,                 { first # in sequence }
    secondNum,                { second # in sequence }
    thirdNum,                 { third # in sequence }
    fourthNum,                { fourth # in sequence }
    fifthNum,                 { fifth # in sequence }
    ...
    twentiethNum: integer;    { twentieth # in sequence }
  END;
```

This code may look like it gets the job done, but it really is not effective. For instance, how would you display the 20 Fibonacci numbers in this sequence in an instance of `GPText`? You could write a 20-line method, but what would happen when you wanted to display 21 Fibonacci numbers? You'd have to rewrite the method. Imagine if you wanted to display 121 Fibonacci numbers. This kind of code simply isn't general enough. It is useful for a single application, but we'd much rather have objects that we can *reuse*.

What we need is a way of grouping related variables together under a single name. OOPas uses a convention that you probably will remember from high school math: *subscripted variables*. In math, several points on a curve might be called P_1, P_2, P_3, and so on. Similarly, mathematical notation allows us to refer to the Fibonacci numbers as Fib_1, Fib_2, Fib_3, and so on. We can do the same thing in OOPas. But since subscripts cannot be typed into a line of text, we put the "subscript" in square brackets after the *array* variable (e.g., `fib[1]`, `fib[2]`, `fib[3]`, . . .). This is the same notation that we have used to refer to any single character in a `string`. Indeed, a `string` typically is implemented in OOPas as an array of characters.

Like an object, an array is a compound data type that stores a predetermined number of data items under a single name. Unlike the object, all the data must be of the same type and used for the same purpose. Also, array elements are named by subscripts, and instance variables in an object are named by their identifiers. Using arrays makes programs easier to read and write, since all items in a collection can be identified by a single subscripted name instead of separate variable names.

Before we learn how to use an array, it may be helpful to visualize the data structure. Figure 16.1 shows the array `fib`. This array name applies to each of the 20 elements, or positions, in the array. Each element has its own subscripted name and is separated from all other elements. We can work with the contents of each position without worrying about any of the other elements.

Figure 16.1

An array of 20 elements

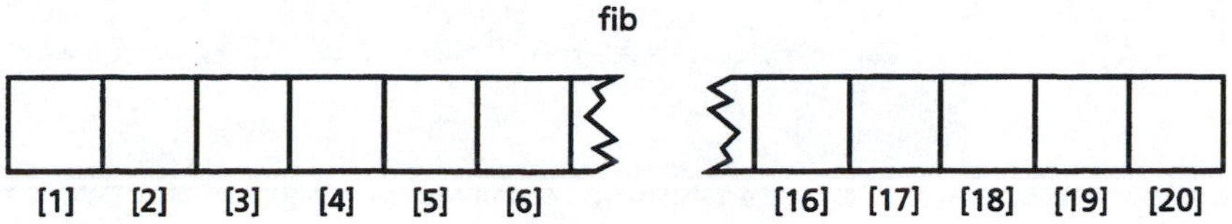

fib

[1]	[2]	[3]	[4]	[5]	[6]	...	[16]	[17]	[18]	[19]	[20]

16.2 DECLARING ARRAYS

Using an array solves the problem of declaring 20 different instance variables. In the previous example, we stored all 20 integers in one data structure and used that as a single instance variable instead of keeping track of 20 separate items. So how do we tell OOPas that we want to use an array?

Declaring an array is not very different from declaring ordinary atomic variables, except that we must specify how many elements the array will have. Each element in an array is numbered, and all the elements must be enumerated in an increasing sequence; that is, we can number the elements from 1 to 1000, from 0 to 1, or from 63 to 847. Negative numbers also can be used in the array's enumeration. For example, we can number the elements from –100 to –1 or from –50 to +50. We also can use `char` types, such as 'a' to 'z', to number the elements. However, we cannot skip any values in specifying the array; that is, we cannot have an array whose four elements are numbered 2, 4, 6, and 8. Thus, to tell OOPas about an array, we need to specify the *lower and upper bounds* of the array's *range*. OOPas then will be able to determine the size of the array.

Specifying the range tells OOPas *how many* positions to reserve, but we cannot leave it at that. Imagine going to a grocery store and asking for "a dozen." After giving you a quizzical look, the grocer would ask, "a dozen what?" It makes a difference whether you are ordering a dozen mangoes or a dozen watermelons. Arrays can be used to collect any type of data, as long as all the elements in the array are of the same type. Thus we need to specify the data type as well as the range of the array's elements. Let's look at an example of an array declaration:

```
CONST
  MAXELEMENTS = 20;{ max number of elements in the list }
TYPE
  numSequenceType = ARRAY[1..MAXELEMENTS] OF integer;
```

```
FibSequence = OBJECT
  CONSTRUCTOR Init;
  { Other methods go here. }
PRIVATE
  fib: numSequenceType;{ sequence of Fibonacci #'s }
END;
```

Declaring an instance variable as an array is a two-part process. First, we define the general type of array. The type `numSequenceType` is not an object, but merely a template for a declaration we will use later. Whenever the OOPas compiler sees `numSequenceType`, it will know that the program means an array of 20 integers. OOPas requires that a type name — that is, the item on the right side of a colon in the declaration of an instance variable, local variable, or parameter declaration — be a single identifier. Thus OOPas requires that we create a type definition for every type of array we will need.

Now, let's consider the parts of the definition of `numSequenceType`. The right side of the = sign begins with the keyword ARRAY, indicating that the variable is an array. The range then is specified in square brackets. The first and last elements are separated by two periods, which are the equivalent of ellipses (. . .) in English. Following the range is the keyword OF and the data type of all elements (in this case, `integer`). Thus `fib` is an array with 20 elements, numbered from 1 to 20, where each element is an `integer`.

In the preceding example, the size of the array can be changed easily by changing the value of MAXELEMENTS. We can use constant identifiers in the ranges of arrays as long as they are declared in the CONST declaration section. However, we cannot use variables in ranges. Arrays always hold the same number of elements throughout the course of the program. Thus arrays can be used only when the amount of data to be stored is known before execution of the program. If the exact size of the array is unknown when the program is written, you must plan for the worst case by setting up an array large enough to handle the maximum amount of data the program could encounter. Although it is acceptable to leave part of the array unused, your program will have an out of bounds error (discussed later in the chapter) if it tries to store more data in an array than there are declared elements. This syntax is summarized in Syntax Box 16.1.

16.3 USING ARRAYS

Let's develop some methods for our Fibonacci sequence that will show how we can use arrays. We begin by initializing the sequence. The `Init` method places the Fibonacci values in the 20 elements of the array. In previous constructors, we simply initialized each of the instance variables. Here, we might say the same thing:

Syntax Box 16.1

Declaring an array

Purpose:

To declare a variable of an array type.

Syntax:

```
TYPE
   <array type> = ARRAY[ <lower bound>..<upper bound> ]
          OF <elem type>;
```

Where:

<array type> is any legal identifier.

<lower bound>..<upper bound> gives the range of the array. *<lower bound>* and *<upper bound>* must be ordinal type constants (integers, characters, enumerated types). *<upper bound>* must be greater than *<lower bound>* .

<elem type> is the data type of each individual element in the array. This type may be any predefined type or any class or other type declared in the program's `TYPE` declarations.

Usage:

The range of the array (*<lower bound>..<upper bound>*) says two things about the array: the number of subdivisions in the array and the legal values of the subscript or index to the array.

The range includes both the lower bound and the upper bound. If you define an array with a range from 1 to 5, you have 5 elements. If you declare it from 0 to 5, you have 6 elements.

Class: FibSequence
Method: Init
Purpose: Initializes the elements of the sequence

So, how do we work with the elements of a sequence? We know that each element is an integer, and we want to assign that `integer` the next number in the sequence. The first number in the sequence is 0, the second number is 1, and all of the other numbers depend on the previous two numbers. One possibility is to use a `FOR` loop, advancing through all the elements and assigning the value of each `integer`. Let's revise the pseudocode to show the loop:

FibSequence.Init
Purpose: Initializes the elements of the sequence
Pseudocode:

    Initialize first element to 0
    Initialize second element to 1
    FOR each remaining element in the list DO
        Initialize element n to sum of element n-1 and element n-2

Let's look now at how we can translate this pseudocode into OOPas code. To do so, we have to know how to gain access to any individual item in the array. Any integer value in the range, including negative numbers, can be used as a *subscript*, or *index*, in the array. The array name `fib` in our example is followed by an index value in square brackets, for example, `fib[12]` to specify the 12th element. Each index value identifies a single element in the array. Index values can be integer-valued expressions. It is important to note that the subscripts of an array as specified by the range bear no relation to the actual information stored in the array. The index values in OOPas, like subscripts in math, merely provide a method of referring to one item when many items have the same collective name.

In the first line of the pseudocode, we want to assign the integer 0 to the first array element of the `fib` array. In OOPas, all compound variables are denoted starting with the group name on the left. Thus we begin by telling OOPas that we want to work with `fib`, then we specify the particular element within the array. This is done by enclosing the *array index* (in this case, the integer 0) in square brackets as follows:

```
fib[1]
```

An array variable complete with a subscript number refers to a single element and therefore can be used in OOPas statements just as any other atomic variable might be. Thus `fib[1]` refers to an integer, and we can assign a value to the integer with a standard assignment statement:

```
fib[1] := 0;
```

Figure 16.2 illustrates the results of this assignment statement.

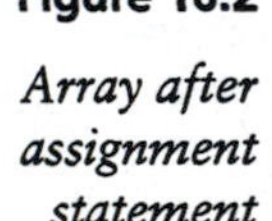
Figure 16.2
Array after assignment statement

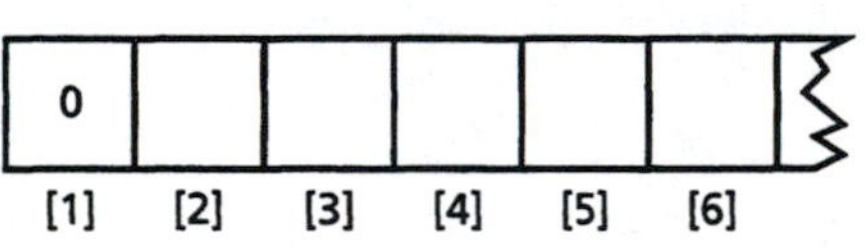

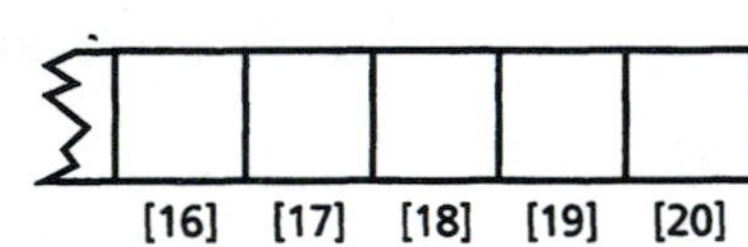

Thus we can begin our method with two assignment statements as follows:

```
PROCEDURE FibSequence.Init;
BEGIN
{ Assign initial values. }
   fib[1] := 0;
   fib[2] := 1;
   ...
END;
```

As Figure 16.3 shows, the first assignment statement places the value 0 in the first position, and the second assignment places the value 1 in the second position.

Figure 16.3

Array after initial values are stored

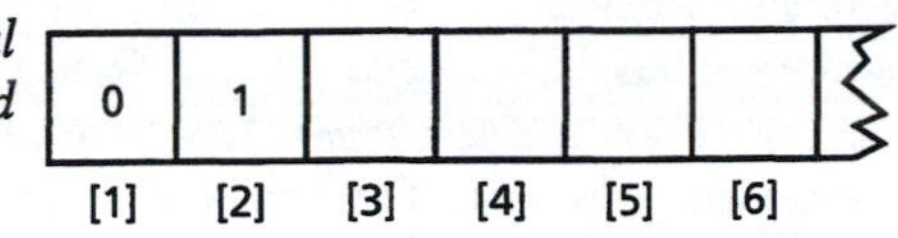

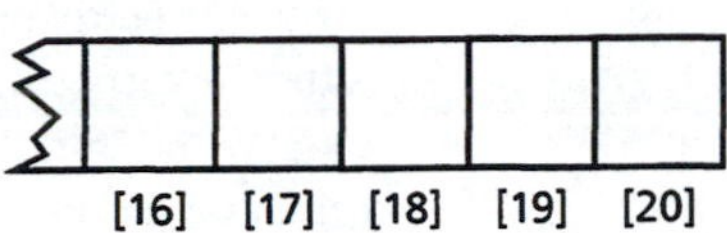

We can gain access to elements in arrays in one of two ways — *sequentially* or *randomly*. The preceding assignment statements are examples of random access. For example, `fib[2] := 1;` will place a value in the second element of an array without processing any information in array element 1. We could switch the order of the two assignment statements and achieve the same result. Random access simply means that we can refer to any element at any time and manipulate the elements in any order.

Sequential access means that we look at the elements in an array in the order that they are in the array. Very often, we want to use the elements in an array from the first element to the last. The lower and upper bounds of the array are ordinal types (integers or characters) — just like the lower and upper bounds specified in a FOR loop. When we gain sequential access to an array, we often want to repeat the same action for each element. Since we know how many elements are in the array, we can use a definite loop to initialize consecutive elements.

In the following code, we have completed the `Init` method by adding a FOR loop. Note that we also included a loop counter called `curNum` to loop through the elements in the sequence.

```
PROCEDURE FibSequence.Init;
VAR
  curNum: integer; { position in sequence being calculated }

BEGIN
{ Assign initial values. }
  fib[1] := 0;
  fib[2] := 1;

  { Calculate remainder of sequence. }
  FOR curNum := 3 TO MAXELEMENTS DO
    fib[curNum] := fib[curNum-1] + fib[curNum-2];
END; { Init }
```

In this method, the counter for the FOR loop is used to index successive locations in the array. The index value begins at 3. Now, the assignment statement makes references to three array elements. The left side of the assignment statement is `fib[curNum]`. On this first iteration through the loop, we know that `curNum` is 3, so the left side evaluates to `fib[3]`. Since `curNum` is an integer variable, we can use it as the subscript of the array.

The right side of the assignment statement can be evaluated similarly. The term `fib[curNum-1]` has an integer expression as the subscript. We first evaluate the expression; since `curNum` is 3, `curNum-1` is 2. Thus this term evaluates to `fib[2]`. Finally, the last term, `fib[curNum-2]`, is evaluated the same way; the expression `curNum-2` evaluates to 1. Thus the entire assignment statement evaluates to `fib[3]:= fib[2] + fib[1];`. As with all assignment statements, the expression on the right is evaluated first. We see that `fib[2]` (the second element in `fib`) is equal to 1, and `fib[1]` is equal to 0. Thus `fib[3]` gets the value 1 + 0, or 1. The array now looks like Figure 16.4.

Figure 16.4

Array at end of first iteration

fib

0	1	1				…					
[1]	[2]	[3]	[4]	[5]	[6]		[16]	[17]	[18]	[19]	[20]

In the next iteration of the loop, `curNum` is increased by 1, so `curNum` is now 4. This means that the statement in the loop body will assign `fib[4]` the value `fib[3] + fib[2]`. We saw that `fib[3]` received a value in the previous iteration, so the expression evaluates to 1 + 1, or 2, as seen in Figure 16.5.

Figure 16.5

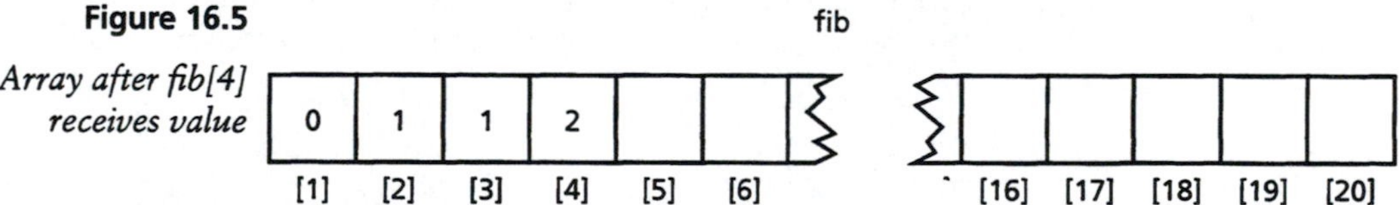

Array after fib[4] receives value

After that, `fib[5]` receives the sum of `fib[4]` and `fib[3]`. The execution continues until `fib[MAXELEMENTS]` receives the final value.

Notice that the array was filled one position at a time. In Figure 16.5, slots 5 through 20 hold undefined values. Even without having set all array elements, we can use elements of `fib` on the right side of assignment statements, as long as we refer only to those that already have received values. If we inadvertently use an index indicating an undefined value, the situation is identical to using any uninitialized atomic variable.

It is important to note the difference between an array such as `fib`, and an element of an array, such as `fib[curNum]`. While `fib` is an array, `fib[curNum]` is a single `integer`. `fib[curNum]` can be used in arithmetic expressions because it is an `integer`, whereas `fib` without a subscript cannot be used in any arithmetic expression because it is a collection of integers.

Individual elements have the data type following the `OF` in the array definition. Thus, in the following variation of our Fibonacci code, we see individual elements of the `fib` array passed to the `NextFib` procedure as parameters:

```
PROCEDURE FibSequence.NextFib(
        VAR nextFibNum    : integer;
        priorFib1,
        priorFib2         : integer);
BEGIN
  nextFibNum := priorFib1 + priorFib2;
END;

CONSTRUCTOR FibSequence.Init;
VAR
  curNum : integer;
BEGIN
  fib[1] := 0;
  fib[2] := 1;
  FOR curNum := 3 TO MAXELEMENTS DO
    NextFib(fib[curNum], fib[curNum - 1], fib[curNum -2]);
END;
```

In this example, `Init` calls the method `NextFib` and sends three elements of the `fib` array. Since the array's elements are of data type `integer`, they match the data type of the actual parameters `nextFibNum`, `priorFib1`, and `priorFib2`. It is important to note that we can use an array element as an actual parameter, even a `VAR` parameter, as long as its type matches the type of the corresponding formal parameter.

16.4 OUT-OF-BOUNDS ERRORS

The most common problem encountered when programming with arrays is the *out-of-bounds error.* This means that the current index value of the array is not within the range specified in the `TYPE` declaration. For example, if we have an array with a range `[3..20]` and the program tries to index the element number 21 or element number 2 during the program's execution, a runtime error will occur.

In some cases, you may want to test whether the index is in the valid range for the array. In the preceding example, we could use the condition

```
CONST
  UPLIM = 20;{ upper limit of array }
  LOWLIM = 3;{ lower limit of array }
  ...
```

```
BEGIN
   IF (current >= LOWLIM) AND (current <= UPLIM) THEN
      { code to process array element }
   ELSE
      { do something else }
END; { Method }
```

This code fragment assumes that `current` will be used as the index to an array. This code guarantees that an array element is not accessed if it is not within the range `3..20`.

16.5 MULTIDIMENSIONAL ARRAYS

All the arrays discussed so far have been diagrammed as a single horizontal column of storage locations. We also can diagram arrays as a single vertical column of storage locations, although not all collections of data can be represented as a single row or column. For example, to show the positions of pieces in a chess game, you would want to use a grid of two dimensions, where every square is denoted by both its row and its column. Arrays can be generalized to have two, three, or *n* dimensions. This section discusses two-dimensional arrays, but the ideas can be generalized to arrays of higher dimensions.

Suppose we want to represent the cities that Turbulent Airlines serves. Specifically, we want to be able to determine quickly whether there is a direct flight from Providence to Miami. With pencil and paper, we might list the flights, not in parallel columns, but in a grid, as in Figure 16.6. The columns and rows are the names of the cities with the rows representing the origin cities and the columns represent the destination cities. Each X in the grid represents a flight from one city to another. If a square has no X, there is no direct flight between the locations. For example, Figure 16.6 shows that there is a direct flight from Providence to Miami, but none from Miami to Providence.

Figure 16.6

Airline flights grid

		Destinations			
		Boston	San Francisco	Providence	Miami
Origins	Boston		X		X
	San Francisco	X		X	
	Providence		X		X
	Miami	X	X		

This grid is translated easily into a two-dimensional array, with each box in the grid an element in the array. Instead of labeling the rows and columns with city names, though, we use numeric subscripts. Like one-dimensional arrays, all of the elements in a multidimensional array must have the same type. In our airline example, each element can be represented as a `boolean`. The element is `true` if a direct flight exists; otherwise, the element is `false`. Thus we can show the same data represented in Figure 16.6 in the two-dimensional array in Figure 16.7.

Figure 16.7 *Boolean representation of flights grid*

Origins \ Destinations	[1]	[2]	[3]	[4]
[1]	false	true	false	true
[2]	true	false	true	false
[3]	false	true	false	true
[4]	true	true	false	false

When declaring a multidimensional array, we must indicate the range in each dimension, to allow OOPas to reserve enough space in memory for all the elements. To do this, we simply list the ranges, separated by commas, between the square brackets. The element in row 3, column 4 is `true`. Therefore, assuming that the rows are the origins and the columns are the destinations, this means a flight exists from city 3 to city 4.

```
CONST
  MAXELEMENTS = 100;{ total number of cities served }

TYPE
  ...
  CityElement = OBJECT
    CONSTRUCTOR Init(newName : string; newPos : GPPoint);
    FUNCTION GetName : string; { returns the name of the city }
    PROCEDURE GetPoint(VAR myPoint : GPPoint); { returns the
              city's position }
  PRIVATE
    name : string;
    position : GPPoint;
  END;

  CityList = ARRAY[1..MAXELEMENTS] OF CityElement;
  FlightMatrix = ARRAY[1..MAXELEMENTS, 1..MAXELEMENTS] OF boolean;
       { holds matrix of possible trips }
```

```
AirList = OBJECT
  CONSTRUCTOR Init;
  { other methods here }
PRIVATE
  cities: CityList;{ information about all cities }
  allFlights: FlightMatrix; {current flights from airline}
END;
```

In the preceding declarations, we have set up a data structure of booleans that will allow us to represent the flights.

In a one-dimensional array, we specify the array and a single subscript to reference any element. With a two-dimensional array, we have to specify two subscripts to gain access to an element; the first is the row subscript, and the second is the column subscript. These two subscripts are separated by a comma. Thus, if there is a flight from city 3 to city 4, we can use the following assignment:

```
allFlights[3,4] := true;
```

To specify that a particular flight exists, we could have a method called `SetFlight`. Let's say that the index of the rows and columns in `allFlights` corresponds to the elements in `cities`. For example, if the first element in `cities` is Seattle, that also should be the first element in the row and column in `allFlights`. We can loop through `cities` until we find the corresponding city:

```
FUNCTION AirList.GetLocation(cityToFind: string) : integer;
VAR
  location : integer;     { position of element in array }
  found    : boolean;     { indicates if city is found }
BEGIN
  location := 0;
  found := false;
  REPEAT
    location := location + 1;
    IF cities[location].GetName = cityToFind THEN
      found := true
  UNTIL found OR location >= MAXELEMENTS;

  IF NOT found THEN
    location := 0;
  GetLocation := location
END;
```

Using this method, we can create a method that, given the names of two cities and a boolean, will set (or unset) a direct flight from the first to the second:

```
PROCEDURE AirList.SetFlight(
      originCity          : string;                  { origin }
      destCity            : string;                  { destination }
      flightExists        : boolean);                { presence of flt }
VAR
  originLoc: integer;  { position of origin in list }
  destLoc: integer;    { position of dest in list }

BEGIN
   originLoc := GetLocation(originCity);
   destLoc := GetLocation(destCity);
   IF (originLoc > 0) AND (destLoc > 0) THEN
      allFlights[originLoc, destLoc] := flightExists;
END;
```

This method simply finds the locations of the origin and destination cities within the list of cities. Then, it sets the corresponding location in the `allFlights` array to the value of `flightExists`.

We can access sequentially the elements of a multidimensional array in pretty much the same way we access the elements of a one-dimensional array, except that we will use nested loops, as discussed in Section 12.2. The following method, for example, will draw a line from the origin to the destination city for each of the flights that are `true` in `allFlights`.

```
PROCEDURE AirList.ShowFlights(drawAreaLink: GPDrawingAreaAsn);
VAR
  curOrigin,              { current origin in list }
  curDest: integer;       { current dest in list }
  startPoint, endPoint : GPPoint; {where flight starts and ends }
  curLine: GPLine;        { line to connect points }

BEGIN
  curLine.Init;
  startPoint.Init;
  endPoint.Init;
  FOR curOrigin := 1 TO MAXELEMENTS DO
    FOR curDest := 1 TO MAXELEMENTS DO
      IF allFlights[curOrigin, curDest] THEN
        BEGIN
          cities[curOrigin].GetPoint(startPoint);
          curLine.SetStart(startPoint);
          cities[curDest].GetPoint(endPoint);
          curLine.SetEnd(endPoint);
          curLine.Draw(drawAreaLink);
        END;
END;
```

If you walk through this code, you will note that the method checks every element in `allFlights`. If the element is `true`, then a line is drawn from the origin's point to the destination's point. Note that we used two nested `FOR` loops, one for each dimension of the array. If we wanted to check all of the elements of a three-dimensional array, we would need three nested `FOR` loops.

The order of the indices is crucial. A reference to `allFlights[11, 4]` is not the same as a reference to `allFlights[4, 11]`. One statement refers to the 11th row and 4th column of the grid, the other to the 4th row and 11th column. Both statements are legal since both 4 and 11 are in the legal ranges.

Syntax Box 16.2

Declaring a two-dimensional array

Purpose:

To allow usage of arrays of more than one dimension.

Syntax:

```
TYPE
   <array type> = ARRAY[<range 1>, <range 2>, ..., <range n> ]
        OF <elem type> ;
   <class name> = OBJECT
     ...
   PRIVATE
     <array var> : <array type>;
   END;
```

Where:

<array type> , *<array var>*, *<class name>* are any legal variable identifiers.

Each of the ranges (*<range 1>*, *<range 2>*, . . . , *<range n>*) takes the form *<lower bound>* ..*<upper bound>*. Both *<lower bound>* and *<upper bound>* must be ordinal type constants. *<upper bound>* must also be greater than *<lower bound>*. *<lower bound>* and *<upper bound>* represent, respectively, the lower and upper bounds of a particular range.

<elem type> is the data type of each individual element in the array. This type can be any predefined type (see Appendix A) or any type declared in the program's `TYPE` declarations.

Usage:

The range of the array (*<lower bound>..<upper bound>*) says two things about the array: the number of subdivisions in one dimension of the array and the legal values of the indices to the array.

When referring to arrays, use the form:

```
<array name> [ <index 1>, <index 2>, . . . , <index n> ]
```

Each index must be in the range specified in the array declaration. For example, *<index 1>* must be between the upper and lower bounds of *<range 1>*. If any index is out of bounds, the program will halt.

The dimensions of a multidimensional array need not be specified with the same range; that is, the array need not be square. For example, suppose you want to declare a two-dimensional array to represent prices of theater seats. The theater has 20 rows with 35 seats in every row. The following declaration shows how this can be done:

```
CONST
  NumberOfRows = 20;{ number of rows in theater}
  SeatsPerRow = 35;{ number of seats in each row}

TYPE
  seatPriceArray = ARRAY[1..NumberOfRows, 1..SeatsPerRow] OF real;
    { holds price for each seat }
  TheaterPricing = OBJECT
    { Methods go here. }
  PRIVATE
    seating : SeatPriceArray;
  END;
```

The syntax for multidimensional arrays is described in Syntax Box 16.2.

Summary

This chapter looked at data structures called arrays. Arrays are used to handle a list of identical items that have the same purpose. Single elements in an array can be manipulated by identifying the name of the array and its subscripts, or indices. Elements in an array can be manipulated either through random access, where the order of access is sequential access, where the order of access is consecutive.

An array can be used as an instance variable of a class. Since the array instance variable is declared in the `PRIVATE` section of the class definition, all of the individual array elements also are considered private instance variables.

Finally, we can work with multidimensional arrays. These are used when each element in an array should have multiple indices. A common example of the two-dimensional array is a checkerboard, where every square is denoted by its row and its column. Again, these arrays hold identical elements and each element shares a common purpose in the program.

Exercises

Understanding Concepts

1. Can `integers` and `reals` be combined in the same array? Can objects of type `GPPushButton` and `GPToggleButton` be combined in the same array?

2. What is the difference between the following two declarations:

```
TYPE
  pointList = ARRAY[1..20] OF GPPoint;
TYPE
  pointCollection = OBJECT
    ...
    pointList: ARRAY[1..20] OF GPPoint;
  END;
```

3. What, if anything, is wrong with the following declarations?

```
TYPE
  List = OBJECT
    ...
    nums = ARRAY[5..1] OF integer;
    ...
  END;
TYPE
  List = OBJECT
    ...
    nums = ARRAY[-3..3] OF real;
    ...
  END;
PROCEDURE Grocery.Sort(VAR items: ARRAY[1..20] OF integer;
CONST
  size = 8
TYPE
  board = ARRAY[1..size][1..size] OF boolean;
FUNCTION Competition.Totals(num1, num2, num3): real):
            ARRAY[1..3] OF boolean;
CONST
  left = 15;
  right = 5;
TYPE
  extra = ARRAY[left..right] OF boolean;
TYPE
  Shape = OBJECT
    ...
  END;
  FigureAsn = @Figure;
  Figure = OBJECT
    ...
    shapeList = ARRAY[1..20] OF Shape;
  END;
  Picture = OBJECT
    ...
    figureList = ARRAY[1..20] OF FigureAsn;
  END;
```

```
TYPE
  dozen = ARRAY[1..6,7..12] OF integer;
```

4. What is wrong with the following code? (*Hint:* Consider the boundary conditions of the loop.)

```
CONST
  maxFlights = 100;
TYPE
  Flight = OBJECT
    CONSTRUCTOR Init(newNum: integer; newFrom, newTo: string);
    FUNCTION GetFlightNum: integer; { returns flight number }
  PRIVATE
    flightNum: integer; { flight number }
    origin, dest: string;  { beginning and ending of flight }
  END;
  flightArray = ARRAY[1..maxFlights] OF Flight;
  Airline = OBJECT
    ...
    FUNCTION FlightExists(key : integer): boolean;
  PRIVATE
    flightList: flightArray;
  END;
{ TRUE if the given key is already an existing flight number }
FUNCTION Airline.FlightExists(key: integer)  {value to find}
  : boolean;
VAR
  curFlight: integer;       { current position in array }
  found: boolean;  { indicates whether key is found }
BEGIN
  curFlight := 1;
  WHILE (curFlight <= maxFlights) AND
          (flightList[curFlight].GetFlightNum <> key) DO
    curElem := curElem + 1;
  IF curFlight > maxFlights THEN   { off end of array }
    found := FALSE
  ELSE
    found := TRUE;
  FlightExists := found
END;
```

Coding Problems

1. Given the declarations:

```
CONST
  edge = 8;
```

```
TYPE
   Square = OBJECT
      CONSTRUCTOR Init;
      PROCEDURE Draw;
   PRIVATE
      color: GPColor;
      position: GPRectangle;
   END;
   side = ARRAY[1..edge] OF Square;
   complete = ARRAY[1..edge] OF side;
   allIn1 = ARRAY[1..edge, 1..edge] OF Square;
   SquareCollection = OBJECT
      CONSTRUCTOR Init;
      PROCEDURE DrawAll;
   PRIVATE
      squareList1: complete;
      squareList2: allIn1;
   END;
```

Write the code for `SquareCollection.DrawAll`, assuming that its purpose is to send a `Draw` message to every `Square` in `squareList1`.

2. Rewrite the `SquareCollection.DrawAll` method, but use `squareList2` instead of `squareList1`.

3. Suppose you have an object called `Tournament` that contains an array of six team names (of type `string`). Write a method that prints all the games in a round-robin tournament (a tournament in which each team plays every other team exactly once).

4. Create an object called `Votes`. It should contain an array of 15 integers, where the first array slot contains the number of first place votes, the second array slot contains the number of second place votes, and so on. Write a function that tallies the votes by giving 15 points to each first place vote, 14 points for each second place, and so on.

Programming Problems

1. Write a program that asks the user to enter the monthly national production for a country over a twelve-month period. Then, depending on the user's choice, show the data as a bar chart or as a line graph.

2. Write a program that plays tic-tac-toe with the user. You can allow the user to go first or the program to go first. As an extension, think about playing a three-dimensional version of the game; the winner is the person who puts 3 X's or 3 O's in a row, column, or diagonal along any dimension.

3. Write a program that adds and multiplies 3×3 matrices. In case you've forgotten: When multiplying matrices A and B, the formula is as follows:

$$\begin{bmatrix} a_{11} & a_{12} & a_{13} \\ a_{21} & a_{22} & a_{23} \\ a_{31} & a_{32} & a_{33} \end{bmatrix} \begin{bmatrix} b_{11} & b_{12} & b_{13} \\ b_{21} & b_{22} & b_{23} \\ b_{31} & b_{32} & b_{33} \end{bmatrix} =$$

$$\begin{bmatrix} a_{11}b_{11} + a_{12}b_{21} + a_{13}b_{31} & a_{11}b_{12} + a_{12}b_{22} + a_{13}b_{32} & a_{11}b_{13} + a_{12}b_{23} + a_{13}b_{33} \\ a_{21}b_{11} + a_{22}b_{21} + a_{23}b_{31} & a_{21}b_{12} + a_{22}b_{22} + a_{23}b_{32} & a_{21}b_{13} + a_{22}b_{23} + a_{23}b_{33} \\ a_{31}b_{11} + a_{32}b_{21} + a_{33}b_{31} & a_{31}b_{12} + a_{32}b_{22} + a_{33}b_{32} & a_{31}b_{13} + a_{32}b_{23} + a_{33}b_{33} \end{bmatrix}$$

Notice the pattern in the entries on the right. Entry xy of AB follows:

$$\begin{bmatrix} a_{x1} & a_{x2} & a_{x3} \end{bmatrix} \begin{bmatrix} b_{1y} \\ b_{2y} \\ b_{3y} \end{bmatrix} = a_{x1}b_{1y} + a_{x2}b_{2y} + a_{x3}b_{3y}$$

Using a nested loop, evaluate this expression for each row-column pair.

4. Write a program to draw and number a crossword puzzle board. The program should start with a 12×12 grid. The user chooses the squares that should be black. When the user indicates that she is done, the program should number the crossword puzzle, starting at the first row and moving from left to right. Words begin immediately to the right and immediately below each black square. Words also begin in white squares that are on the top or left borders.

5. Write a program to play an arcade game like Space Invaders, Pac-Man, or Tetris. Some aspect of the game will be represented with an array. For example, the aliens in Space Invaders can be an array, the maze in Pac-Man can be an array, and the playing field in Tetris can be an array. Your array should probably be an array of links, so that, for example, You can have different kinds of aliens in the mass of attacking aliens in Space Invaders or different kinds of power pills in the maze in Pac-Man.

   Using links in this fashion, you should be able to add all sorts of "bells" and "whistles" to your game, such as many different kinds of aliens or power pills.

17

Sets

Like arrays, sets are collections of elements. Unlike arrays, however, the elements in sets are unordered. Typically, when working with sets, we want to use the entire collection at once, as opposed to looking consecutively at individual elements in an array. For example, an array can hold the value 'a' in position 1, 'b' in position 2, and so on, whereas a set variable can hold all the characters from 'a' to 'z' simultaneously, and treat them as a collective whole.

17.1 SET VARIABLES

OOPas places two restrictions on sets. First, all members of the set must be of the same data type. This data type is known as the set's *base type*. Second, there is an upper limit on the base type's *cardinality* — the number of members in the set's base type. In OOPas, the maximum cardinality is 256. Since there are 128 characters in the ASCII encoding, `char` is a legal base type. Enumerated types with fewer than 256 members are also legal base types (enumerated types were discussed in Chapter 11). `integer`, `real`, and `string`, however, are not legal base types, since they have more than 256 possible values. Instances of classes are not legal base types, because you can make as many instances as you want. Later in the book, we'll learn about data structures that we can use to build our own sets that don't have these restrictions. For now though, we'll use the sets provided by OOPas.

Declaring Set Variables

Declaring set variables is similar to declaring array variables, using the reserved word SET instead of ARRAY. We begin by defining a type. The following example defines a type that holds sets of characters:

```
TYPE
   charSet = SET OF char;        { can hold any number of chars }
```

The type name is `charSet`. Any variable of that type will hold a collection of `char` values. The type `charSet` can next be used as a data type in any parameter or variable list. Thus the following declaration reserves storage for four sets:

```
VAR
   letters,                 { set of letters of alphabet }
   digits,                  { set of numeric digits }
   punctuation,             { set of punc. used in OOPas }
   operators : charSet;     { set of operators used in OOPas }
```

Assigning to Set Variables

As usual, these declarations tell only what data types are involved; actual values must be assigned to the sets by explicit assignment. So, let's look at how we assign values to these sets. Suppose that we want punctuation to hold some of the punctuation symbols used in OOPas. In mathematical set notation (not OOPas), we could call the set *P* and use the following equation:

P = {‘.’, ‘;’, ‘:’, ‘[’, ‘]’, ‘{’, ‘}’, ‘^’, ‘’’ }

In OOPas, we can't use the curly brackets, since they are used to contain comments, so we need to use some other symbol to delimit the set — square brackets. We can assign all the set members to the set variable using one assignment statement:

```
punctuation := ['.', ';', ':', '[', '}', '{', '}', '^', ''''];
```

Note that all of the set members are assigned at once.

The ordering of members in the set is irrelevant; because members of a set are not used individually, but collectively, all the following assignment statements achieve the same result:

```
operators := ['+', '-', '*', '/', '=', '>', '<'];
operators := ['<', '+', '-', '/', '>', '=', '*'];
operators := ['-', '/', '=', '<', '>', '+', '*'];
```

A set cannot have more than one member of the same value. For example,

```
state := ['M', 'i', 's', 's', 'i', 's', 's', 'i', 'p', 'p', 'i'];
```

is the same as

```
state := ['M', 'i', 's', 'p'];
```

since all multiple values are ignored.

Set declaration syntax is summarized in Syntax Box 17.1. The syntax for set literals is described in Syntax Box 17.2.

Syntax Box 17.1

Set declarations

Purpose:

To create a set type.

Syntax:

```
TYPE
   <type name> = SET OF <base type>;
```

Where:

<type name> is any legal identifier.

<base type> is an ordinal type with no more than 256 possible values.

Usage:

The *<base type>* can be `char`, any enumerated type with 256 or fewer values in its range of representation, or a subrange of 256 or fewer values.

`integer` is not a legal base type, but subranges of integers, with 256 or fewer values, are legal.

Other versions of Pascal may allow a different maximum cardinality.

17.2 SUBRANGES

Sometimes it's useful to have a shorthand notation. Consider the following assignment:

```
letters := ['a', 'b', 'c', 'd', 'e', 'f', 'g', 'h', 'i', 'j', 'k',
            'l', 'm', 'n', 'o', 'p', 'q', 'r', 's', 't', 'u',
            'v', 'w', 'x', 'y', 'z'];
```

For a series of consecutive values, you can use a subrange. A subrange takes the form *<lower limit>.. <upper limit>*. The limits can be of any ordinal type, as is shown in the following examples:

```
6..12
'A'..'z'
Mon..Fri
```

Syntax Box 17.2

Set constants

Purpose:

To define members of a set.

Syntax:

```
[ <value 1>, <value 2>, . . . , <value n> ]
```

Where:

<value 1>, *<value 2>*, . . . , *<value n>* are values in the set's base type.

Usage:

Any of *<value 1>*, . . . , *<value n>* can be expressions (including constants or variables) that evaluate to the base type.

<value1>, . . . , *<value n>* should be distinct values. The second, third, fourth, . . . occurrences of the same value are ignored.

The constant notation can be used in places where set expressions are needed, as on the right side of an assignment symbol or in set operations.

The order of the values is irrelevant.

The empty set is denoted by the symbol [].

Subranges can be listed with the values.

The first subrange is the kind we've seen before — two integers represent the limits. The second subrange holds a list of characters consisting of all the characters in the collating sequence between the upper and lower limits. Thus `'A' .. 'z'` contains all characters with ASCII values between 65 and 122 — the uppercase letters, the lowercase letters, and the symbols [, \,], ^, _, and '. The third subrange uses values from an enumerated type called `Day` that lists the days of the week in order. This subrange includes all the values listed in the enumerated type between the designated limits.

Subranges can be used whenever you would use any other ordinal type. That is, any occurrence of the reserved word `char` can be replaced by a character subrange. For example, if you know that a particular variable will hold capital letters only, you needn't use the declaration

```
VAR
  cap : char;{ a single capital letter }
```

Instead, you can use the declaration

```
VAR
  cap : 'A'..'Z';{ a single capital letter }
```

Note that, unlike a set, which can hold multiple letters, the variable `cap` can hold only a single letter.

You also can declare subranges as types. The preceding declaration can be rewritten as follows:

```
TYPE
  upperRange = 'A'..'Z';{ range of capital letters }

VAR
  cap : upperRange;{ a single capital letter }
```

When dealing with sets, subranges are useful in two situations. First, you can use subranges when listing the members of a set. Thus the assignment for the set variable letters can be condensed to

```
letters := ['a' .. 'z'];
```

Subranges need not be the only thing in the set membership list. For example, the following declaration is valid:

```
consonants := ['b', 'c', 'd', 'f' .. 'h', 'j' ..'n', 'p' .. 't',
               'v' .. 'z'];
```

Subranges also can be used as a base type for a set. This is useful when you want to have sets of integers, since the type integer is not a valid base type. For example, the following code fragment creates a set type using the subrange `1..36` as a base type. Then a variable of that type is created and assigned a value.

```
TYPE
  lotteryNums = SET OF 1 .. 36;{ all available lottery numbers }

PROCEDURE Ticket.Winner;
VAR
  winningTicket : lotteryNums;{ winning combination }
BEGIN
  winningTicket := [1, 7, 10, 20, 21, 27];
  ...
END;
```

In set manipulations, the empty set is the set with no elements. No matter what its base type, any set variable can be assigned the empty set. The empty set is denoted by two square brackets as follows:

```
VAR
  myWinningNums : lotteryNums;    { winning nums I chose }
BEGIN
  myWinningNums := [];     { empty set }
  ...
```

17.3 SET OPERATIONS

In OOPas, we can combine sets in three ways. We can create a union of sets, find the intersection of sets, or determine the difference between sets. Imagine that two roommates, Chris and Terry, have found an apartment, but they need to find a third roommate. So how do they determine with whom to live? Chris is most compatible with folks born under Aries, Gemini, Virgo, or Pisces. Terry is compatible with sun signs Gemini, Scorpio, Aquarius, or Pisces. Figure 17.1 shows one representation of this information, with Chris's and Terry's compatible signs encircled. Notice that Chris and Terry are compatible with some of the same signs.

Figure 17.1

Sets of compatible signs

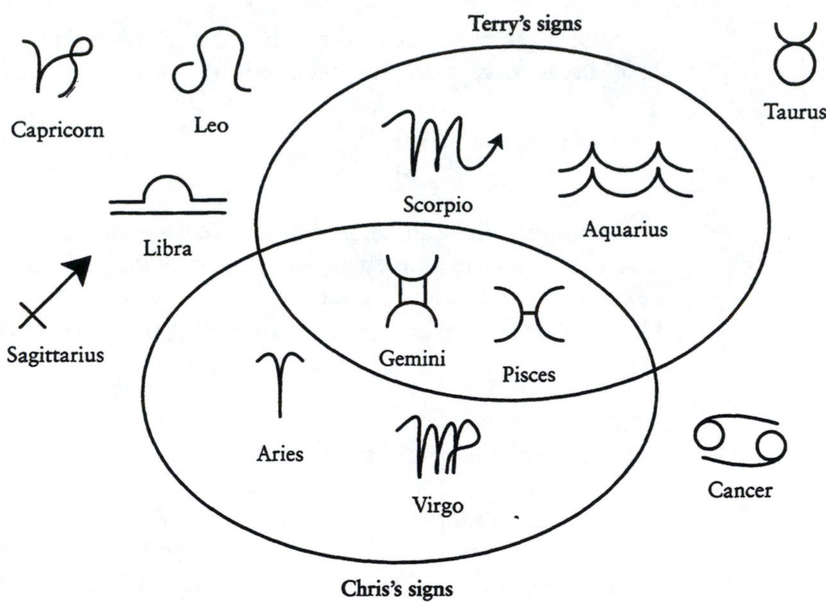

The information about the compatible signs can be represented in code, using the enumerated type `Signs`, as follows:

```
TYPE
  Signs = (Aries, Taurus, Gemini, Cancer, Leo, Virgo, Libra,
           Scorpio, Sagitarrius, Capricorn, Aquarius, Pisces);
  Compats = SET OF Signs; { holds a bunch of signs }

PROCEDURE Zodiac.Compatibility;
VAR
  chrisList,{ signs compatible with Chris }
  terryList : Compats;{ signs compatible with Terry }
```

```
BEGIN
   chrisList := [Aries, Gemini, Virgo, Pisces];
   terryList := [Gemini, Scorpio, Aquarius, Pisces];
   ...
```

We want to find those signs that are compatible with either of the roommates. This can be found by taking the union of the sets `chrisList` and `terryList`. If you have a `Compats` variable called `eitherOne`, you can use the following assignment:

```
eitherOne := chrisList + terryList;
```

The addition sign, when placed between sets, combines the members of both sets. Thus this assignment statement places the set `[Aries, Gemini, Virgo, Scorpio, Aquarius, Pisces]` in the variable `eitherOne`. `Gemini` and `Pisces` appear only once in the result, even though they are in both `chrisList` and `terryList`. In any set, no value can appear more than once.

The union of two sets contains all the members that are in one set or the other. We also can determine the intersection of two sets — the members that are in both sets. In OOPas, an intersection is represented by the asterisk (*). For example, to find the signs that are compatible with both Chris and Terry, we can create a `Compats` variable called `compatWithBoth` and use the assignment

```
compatWithBoth := chrisList * terryList;
```

This assignment places the set `[Gemini, Pisces]` in `compatWithBoth`, since `Gemini` and `Pisces` are in both `chrisList` and `terryList`. If the two sets had nothing in common, the empty set would have been assigned to `compatWithBoth`.

The third set operator lets you find the difference between two sets. Not surprisingly, this is represented with a minus sign (–). Differences often are used to define a set's complement, that is, to define one set as all of the members not in another set. For example, instead of listing the subranges of characters to define the set consonants in the last section, we could have used the following fragment:

```
TYPE
   letters = SET OF char;{ holds many characters}
PROCEDURE Alphabet.Complement;
VAR
   vowels, { small vowel characters }
   consonants : letters;{ small letters not in vowels }
BEGIN
   vowels := ['a', 'e', 'i', 'o', 'u'];
   consonants := ['a' .. 'z'] - vowels;
   ...
```

When OOPas finds the syntax *<set 1> - <set 2>*, it copies all the members of *<set 1>* into a temporary variable. OOPas then removes any member of *<set 2>* from the temporary variable, and the temporary variable is now the result. In the preceding fragment, `consonants` is the set of all letters between 'a' and 'z' that are not in the set `vowels`.

Not every member of the set on the right of the minus sign (*<set 2>*) has to be in the set on the left (*<set 1>*). Let's go back to the horoscope check. Suppose we create a variable `chrisAlone` of type `compats` and enter the statement

```
chrisAlone := chrisList - terryList;
```

When OOPas sees this statement, it begins by assigning `[Aries, Gemini, Virgo, Pisces]` to a temporary block of memory. Then, OOPas determines what values in that temporary block are also in `terryList` — `Gemini` and `Pisces`. The values `Scorpio` and `Aquarius` are ignored, since they are not in `chrisList`. The common values to both `chrisList` and `terryList` are removed, yielding a result of `[Aries, Virgo]`.

All of the set operators are described in Syntax Box 17.3.

Syntax Box 17.3

Set operations

Set Operations:

The following are binary operations that can be performed on sets to produce new sets:

Operation	**Syntax**	**Result**
Union	*<set 1> + <set 2>*	Set containing all values that are in either *<set 1>* or *<set 2>*
Intersection	*<set 1> * <set 2>*	Set containing all values that are in both *<set 1>* and *<set 2>*
Difference	*<set 1> - <set 2>*	Set containing all values in *<set 1>* not in *<set 2>*

In all cases, *<set 1>* and *<set 2>* must have the same base type. That is, if *<set 1>* is a `SET OF char`, then *<set 2>* must be, too.

Set operations have much in common with the arithmetic operations that use the same symbols. For example, intersection (`*`) takes precedence over union and difference (+ and –). Operations can be chained together in the same statement, and parentheses can be used to alter the order of operation. However, the operators must have sets on both sides, and the sets must have the same base type. For example,

```
myList := chrisList + Libra;
```

is not a valid statement, since the value `Libra` is not a set. To add the value `Libra` to `chrisList`, we must use set notation:

```
myList := chrisList + [Libra];
```

17.4 SET RELATIONSHIPS

Two set values can be compared, using five different comparison operators. You can determine whether two sets are equal by using an equals sign:

```
<set 1> = <set 2>
```

This expression is `true` if every member of *<set 1>* is in *<set 2>* and every member of *<set 2>* is in *<set 1>*. Since order does not matter in sets,

```
['a', 'e', 'i', 'o'] = ['o', 'a', 'i', 'e']
```

yields the result `true`. The not equals operator returns the opposite of the equals operator and is represented (as in the arithmetic and string comparisons) by the symbol <>.

Two other comparison operators determine whether one set is a subset of another. The expression

```
<set 1> <= <set 2>
```

is true if and only if every member of *<set 1>* is also in *<set 2>*. The following comparisons all yield `true`:

```
{1} ['a'] <= ['a' .. 'z']
{2} ['a', 'e', 'i', 'o'] <= ['a' .. 'z']
{3} ['k' .. 'n'] <= ['a' .. 'z']
{4} ['a' .. 'z'] <= ['a' .. 'z']
{5} [] <= ['a' .. 'z']
```

Comparison 1 is `true` because the member 'a' is in the range `'a' .. 'z'`. In comparisons 2 and 3, multiple members of the range `'a' .. 'z'` are listed on the left, but since each member on the left is in the set defined on the right, the comparisons yield `true`. Comparison 4 shows that a set is a subset of itself. Again, the same criterion is used: Each member of the set on the left is contained in the set on the right. Finally, as seen in comparison 5, the empty set is a subset of every set.

The notation `<set 1> >= <set 2>` yields `true` if *<set 1>* is a superset of *<set 2>*. A superset contains all the members of another set. Put another way, the notation `<set 1> >= <set 2>` asks if *<set 2>* is a subset of *<set 1>*.

The fifth set-comparison operator does not really compare sets. In fact, it determines whether a member is in a set, using the reserved word `IN`. The notation `<member> IN <set>` returns `true` if *<member>* is inside *<set>*. This comparison is legal only if *<member>* is a member of *<set>*'s base type. Thus you can have the following fragment:

```
TYPE
  letters : SET OF char;    { all possible characters }

VAR
  menuOptions : letters;    { set of all available options }
  userChoice : char;        { menu choice entered by user }

BEGIN
  menuOptions := ['D', 'Q', 'C', 'H'];
  { userChoice initialized here }
  IF userChoice IN menuOptions THEN
    BEGIN
      CASE userChoice OF
      ...
    END   { IF }
  ELSE
     ...
```

The variable `userChoice` is a single `char` value. In that `IF` statement, the code determines whether the character in `userChoice` is contained in the set of legal menu options. If it is, the appropriate action is performed; otherwise, an error message is printed.

`'D' IN menuOption` is a legal boolean expression, but `['D'] IN menuOption` is not, since `['D']` is a set, not a member. Also, the member to the left of the `IN` must be in the set's base type, even though you may not know whether the member will be in the set itself.

When the base type is a subrange, a slightly inconsistent set of rules applies. For example, the comparison that follows:

```
TYPE
  lotteryNums = SET OF 1..36; { all possible lottery nums }

VAR
  winner : lotteryNums;         { set of winning numbers }

BEGIN
  ...
  IF 45 IN winner THEN
    msgArea.SetText('Something''s wrong');
  ...
END
```

is legal even though `45` is not in the base type of `winners`. The base type of `winners`, for purposes of this comparison, is not the subrange `1..36`, but the type `integer`. The set-comparison operators are summarized in Syntax Box 17.4.

Syntax Box 17.4

Set-comparison operators

Set Comparison:

Name	Syntax	Is true when
Equality	`<set 1> = <set 2>`	All members of *<set 1>* are in *<set 2>* and all members of *<set 2>* are in *<set 1>*.
Inequality	`<set 1> <> <set 2>`	One set contains a member that is not in the other set.
Subset	`<set 1> <= <set 2>`	All members of *<set 1>* are in *<set 2>* or if *<set 1>* is the empty set.
Superset	`<set 1> >= <set 2>`	All members of *<set 2>* are in *<set 1>* or if *<set 2>* is the empty set.
Containment	`<member> IN <set>`	*<member>* is contained in *<set>*.

Summary

Set variables are used to hold a collection of values. All these values must be of the same data type (known as the base type), and no more than 256 of these values can exist in the base type.

Assignment statements can be used to assign a list of members to a set. You can use subrange notation — *<lower limit>* .. *<upper limit>* — as a shorthand for a series of consecutive values.

The three set operations are union, intersection, and difference. OOPas also provides five operations for comparing sets. You can determine whether one set is equal to another, is not equal to another, is a subset of another, is a superset of another, or contains a particular member.

Exercises

Understanding Concepts

1. Given the declarations

```
TYPE
  Profs = (Dull, Ok, Exciting);
  Dept = SET OF Profs;
```

```
University = OBJECT
  { methods here }
  introCourseTeachers: Dept;
END;
```

what are the possible values of `introCourseTeachers`?

2. When does *<set 1>* – *<set 2>* yield an empty set? What do we know about the maximum size of *<set 1>* – *<set 2>*?

Given the declarations

```
TYPE
    musicians = (Elvis, Platters, Fats, Supremes, Beatles,
            Stones, Dylan, Springsteen, Madonna, RunDMC,
            PearlJam);
VAR
    female, allArtists, fifties, solo, sixties, seventies: SET OF
            musicians;
```

and assignment statements:

```
female := [Supremes, Madonna];
allArtists := [Elvis..PearlJam];
fifties := [Elvis..Fats];
solo := [Elvis, Fats, Dylan, Springsteen, Madonna];
sixties := [Supremes..Dylan];
seventies := [Stones..Springsteen];
```

what do the following yield?

3. `allArtists - female`
4. `sixties * seventies`
5. `Elvis IN (allArtists - fifties)`
6. `sixties + seventies`
7. `(female * sixties) + (fifties - solo)`
8. `(fifties + sixties + seventies) = allArtists`
9. `Dylan IN (sixties - seventies)`
10. `female - solo`
11. `[] <=  allArtists`
12. `[Madonna] IN female`

Coding Problems

1. A set's cardinality is the number of elements in the set. Given the declaration:

```
TYPE
  voices = (Soprano, Alto, Tenor, Baritone, Bass);
  chorus = SET OF voices;

  SchoolMusicProgram = OBJECT
    ...
    FUNCTION GetNumVoices: integer;
    ...
    schoolChorus : chorus;
  END;
```

write the method `SchoolMusicProgram.GetNumVoices` that returns the cardinality of `schoolChorus`.

2. Refer to the declaration in Coding Problem 1, and write a function that initializes `schoolChorus` to three random elements from voices.

3. Write a function that accepts a parameter of type `lowerCase` (defined as follows):

```
TYPE
  lowerCase = SET OF 'a'..'z';
```

and returns the complement. The complement of set *A* is a set containing all of the elements in the base type that are not in *A*.

4. Given the sets

```
entrees = (fish, beef, chicken);
saladDressing = (oilVinegar, ranch, blueCheese);
```

Write a method that shows all combinations of salad dressings and entrees.

5. Write a method that takes two sets and draws the appropriate Venn diagram. If the sets have elements in common, they should be drawn in two overlapping ovals, where the common elements are shown in the intersection of the ovals (as in Figure 17.1). If there are no elements in the intersection, the sets should be drawn as distinct ovals.

Programming Problems

1. Figure 17.2 shows part of the Boston subway system (with some minor alterations). There are four subway lines; the points of intersection are stations where passengers can transfer from one line to another. The names of the lines (Blue, Green, Red, Orange) denote the ends of the lines in the diagram.

   Write a program that allows a user to choose an origin and a destination and prints directions, indicating which lines to take. For example, the program should tell a user who wants to get from Copley to Kendall to take the Green Line from Copley to Park, transfer to the Red Line, and take the Red Line from Park to Kendall.

2. Take a poll of some acquaintances. Record each person's name, astrological sign, shoe size, favorite type of music, and favorite type of fastener (paper clip, staples, glue, and the like). Then determine the most compatible pairs (those

with the most things in common and the closest shoe sizes) and the most incompatible pairs.

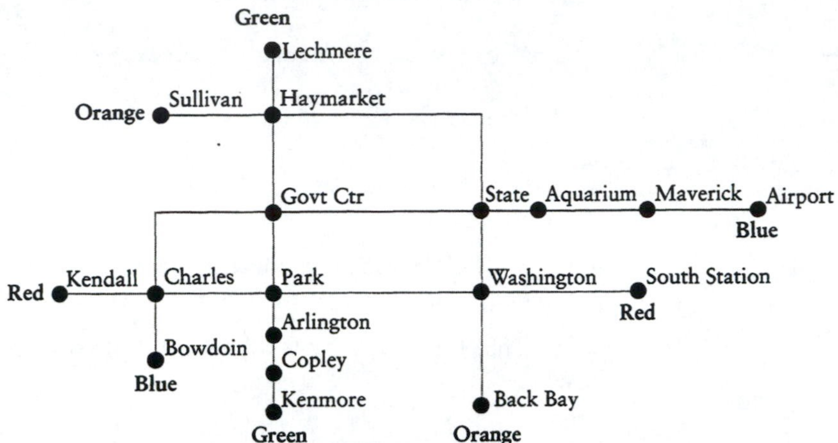

Figure 17.2 *The Boston subway system*

3. Write a program to help a chess player. Imagine that the user is playing black and is about to make a move. Given the positions of all the black and white pieces (perhaps from a file), determine all of the possible legal moves that the user can make.
4. Extend Programming Problem 3 by adding some intelligence. Remove from the set of legal moves all those that would put a black piece in danger of being captured (that is, if any white piece can reach a particular square on the next move, then no black piece should be moved to that particular square).
5. Modify the hangman game from Chapter 15's Programming Problem 2 to use sets to keep track of used and unused letters.
6. Write a program that deals from a standard deck of cards. Imagine that four players are playing five-card stud poker; that is, each player receives five cards. Deal one hand and display it on the screen, then deal a second hand without using any of the cards dealt in the first hand.

18 Parsing Strings

In Chapter 15, we began our discussion of strings. We looked at literal strings, string variables, and the string functions `Length`, `Copy`, and `Concat`. In this chapter, we will look at more advanced ways to manipulate strings: We're going to look at *parsing* strings — the process of programmatically analyzing a string and what it describes. We'll start with simple tasks done with functions provided by OOPas and finish by looking at some of the techniques used by OOPas itself to parse your programs.

As you might imagine, parsing is an extremely important topic in computer science, and as such, parsing can be quite complex.

The basic problem is one of pattern recognition. As we said in Chapter 1, computers use sequences of ones and zeros to represent numbers, characters, pictures, objects, or machine language instructions. A computer recognizes patterns of bits, representing the instructions, using hardware. The hardware was manufactured with a set of building block circuits to recognize various patterns of bits. Building a parser is assembling software building blocks that recognize various patterns of characters.

Before we describe parsing, we will describe some more of OOPas's character string manipulation functions. OOPas provides functions to convert strings to numbers (and vice versa) and to find and insert substrings.

18.1 CONVERSION

Strings are not integers. This means that `'100'` is not the same as `100`. The former is a `string` literal, and the latter is an `integer` literal. To display an `integer` in a `string` using an instance of `GPText`, you would make a `string` that has the digits of the number as its characters. Conversely, if you have a `string` whose characters happen to be a number, you have to process each character to figure out what the number is. This all sounds fairly complex, but fortunately, there are some *conversion functions* that convert from integers to strings and vice versa.

Converting from Integers to Strings

Suppose we want to calculate an area of a rectangle and output the result.[1] If we store the dimensions in variables called `length` and `width` and assign the result in a variable called `area`, we could use the following assignment statement:

```
area := length * width;
```

Now, we need to convert `area` to a `string` in order to pass it to the `SetName` method of `GPText`. The Pascal `Str` procedure converts an integer-valued numeric expression to a string; we then can take that string and store it in an instance of `GPText`. Suppose we know that we want to print the result starting at the pixel (100, 100). We can store this point and initialize an instance of `GPText` with that point. We then can use the conversion procedure `Str` to convert the `area` to a `string` and pass it to `SetName`. Finally, we can display the string on the screen.

```
PROCEDURE Rectangle.DisplayArea(
      newDrawingAreaLink: GPDrawingAreaAsn;
      length, width    : integer);
VAR
  area: integer;
  areaString: string;  { area represented as a string }
  areaText: GPText;    { GPText object to display area }
  outputPosition: GPPoint;
BEGIN
  areaText.Init;
  outputPosition.InitWithCoords(100, 100);
  areaString.SetStart(outputPosition);
  area := length * width;
  Str(area, areaString);
  areaText.SetText(areaString);
  areaText.Draw(newDrawingAreaLink)
END;
```

`Str` takes two parameters. The first is an expression that evaluates to an integer; the second is a string variable that will receive the converted string value. The result of the procedure `Str(area, areaString);` is that `areaString` receives the string representation of `area`. After `Str`, `areaString` contains the string `'100'`, which can then be used as a parameter in `areaText.SetText`. As Syntax Box 18.1 shows, `Str` is un-parsing: It is putting a value into a string. Next, we'll start looking at how we parse values from a string.

---

1. Procedural programmers using Pascal often use `Readln` and `Writeln` for input/output outside of the drawing area in a separate window. We will not be using this method of interaction. `Readln` and `Writeln` will be covered in Chapter 19.

Syntax Box 18.1

Str

Purpose:

To convert an integer or a real to a string.

Syntax:

`Str(<numeric expression>, <string var>);`

Where:

<numeric expression> is any expression that evaluates to an integer or real.

<string var> is a variable of type `string`.

Returns:

A `string` in *<string var>* that is the string representation of *<numeric expression>*.

Usage:

The procedure `Str` evaluates the expression and converts the result to a string. The result is returned in *<string var>*.

Converting from Strings to Integers

Let's start by considering the following literal string:

```
'25'
```

We might look at this string and think, "it's the number twenty-five." OOPas, however, cannot think in the same way. When it sees a sequence of characters inside apostrophes, it treats it as a literal-string, whether the string contains numbers or letters, spaces or symbols. Therefore OOPas can concatenate `'25'` to another string, but it can't treat it as an integer and do arithmetic on it. It is therefore very useful to be able to convert a string containing an integer to an integer itself. When we retrieve a string of characters from a user, we often want to extract the numeric part of the string.

In OOPas, the `Val` procedure converts a string to a number. Let's say that we were labeling houses on one side of the street. We could store the first value in a string called `houseName` as follows:

```
VAR
  houseName: string;
BEGIN
  houseName := '115 Waterman Avenue';
  ...
END;
```

Now, let's say we wanted to create the label for the neighbor's house. We'll assume for the moment that each house's number is two more than that of its neighbor. Using the `Val` procedure, we can retrieve a number from a string. First, though, we need to isolate the numeric part of the `houseName` string. That is, we need to remove all the characters from the string that are not part of the number we want to convert. In this case, we can establish a string variable to contain the house number; we'll call it `houseNumberString`. To isolate the number, we'll copy all of the characters up to the first blank. We can then use `Val` to convert the string to an integer.

```
VAR
  houseName: string;
  houseNumberString: string;
  houseNumber: integer;
  errorCode: integer;
BEGIN
  houseName := '115 Waterman Avenue';
  houseNumberString := Copy(houseName, 1, 3);
  Val(houseNumberString, houseNumber, errorCode);
  ...
END;
```

`Val` takes three parameters. The first is the string to convert. The second is the integer or real variable that will receive the conversion. In essence, this is the reverse of `Str`; the numeric variable receives the converted string value.

The third parameter is different from `Str`. `Val` expects an integer variable in this slot, which will receive an error code. If `Val` performs its conversion with no problem, it returns 0 in this parameter. If the conversion was unsuccessful, though, `errorCode` will receive the position of the first character in the string that cannot be converted to a number.

In our example statement, `houseNumberString` is `'115'`. Since there are no extra characters in the string, `houseNumber` retrieves the numeric value in the string (the integer value 115), and `errorCode` is assigned the value 0.

Suppose, though, we had sent the original string `houseName` as the first parameter to `Val`. In this case, `Val` would happily convert the first three characters, but it would get stuck when trying to convert the space after the `'5'`. Its reaction would be to send no value back to the second parameter, and to assign the value 4 to `errorCode`.

Once we have successfully converted a string to a number, we can perform any of the numeric operations on it. In this fragment, we find the number of the neighbor's house by adding 2. We can then generate the name of the next house on the street, using the `Str` procedure to convert the new number back to a string and concatenating to the street name.

Note that this simple example doesn't check the value of `errorCode`, because we know what string we are going to convert. In general, we would follow a `Val` statement with an `IF` statement or other test.

```
VAR
   houseName: string;
   houseNumberString: string;
   houseNumber: integer;
   errorCode: integer;
   neighborName: string;

BEGIN
   houseName := '115 Waterman Avenue';
   houseNumberString := Copy(houseName, 1, 3);
   Val(houseNumberString, houseNumber, errorCode);
   houseNumber := houseNumber + 2;
   Str(houseNumber, neighborName);
   neighborName:= Concat(neighborName, ' Waterman Avenue');
   ...
END;
```

The procedure `Val` is described in Syntax Box 18.2.

Syntax Box 18.2

Val

Purpose:

To convert a string to an integer or a real.

Syntax:

`Val(<string expression>, <numeric var>, <error code>);`

Where:

<string expression> is any expression that evaluates to a string.

<numeric var> is a variable of type `integer` or `real`.

<error code> is a variable of type `integer`.

Returns:

An `integer` or `real` in *<numeric var>* that is the numeric representation of *<string expression>*. *<error code>* returns 0 if the conversion is successful; otherwise, it returns the position in *<string expression>* where the conversion failed.

Usage:

The procedure `Val` evaluates the string expression, and attempts to convert the result to a number. If *<string expression>* contains any extraneous characters, the conversion will fail, and the error code will return the first position within the string that is not part of a number. If the string contains just a number, *<numeric var>* receives the value as a number, and *<error code>* is set to 0.

18.2 FINDING SUBSTRINGS

OOPas also provides functions to look at parts of strings. In programming problems, it is often useful to isolate single words in the sentence. For example, we could write a procedure to count how many sentences begin with the word 'The' or to determine how many people have 'III' as part of their names. Many word processors can tell you how many words you have in a particular document.

Let's start with a basic string processing operation — finding the first occurrence of a specific pattern (a substring) in a string. We can use the function `Pos` to find the first location of a specified pattern in a string.

Suppose we have a string variable called `entireName` that contains a person's first name, a blank, and the last name. (We are assuming that the first name does not contain a blank.) To parse the first and last names from `entireName`, we need to find where the first blank in the string exists. We'll use the `Pos` function to find the position of the first occurrence of the blank.

For example, suppose `entireName` contains the value `'Andy van Dam'`. To find the first blank, we can use the following assignment:

```
firstBlank := Pos(' ', entireName); { searching for single blank }
```

This statement finds the first occurrence of a string consisting of a single blank in `entireName`. In this case, the first blank appears in the fifth position, so `firstBlank` receives the integer value 5.

Even though the source string `entireName` contains more than one blank, the preceding call to `Pos` always returns the value of the first blank. A second call to the function (e.g., `secondBlank := Pos(' ', entireName);`) also returns the value 5 because the search for the pattern always begins at position 1. (Later we will see how to search for further occurrences of a pattern in a string.) If the pattern is not found in the source string, `Pos` returns the value 0. `Pos` is described in Syntax Box 18.3.

Inserting Substrings

Finally, OOPas has a procedure to insert strings in other strings. Suppose that a first and last name are stored in a single string variable. Then, because we want the name to look official, we decide to add the middle initial. We can use OOPas's `Insert` procedure to perform this task.

`Insert` inserts one string into another string at a specified position. In the name example, we found the end of the first name by searching for the first blank. At that position, we can insert the middle initial. The following code shows how:

Syntax Box 18.3

Pos

Purpose:

To indicate where a pattern can be found in a string.

Syntax:

```
Pos(<pattern>, <source>)
```

Where:

<pattern> and *<source>* are literal or variable `strings`. Each `string` can also be a string expression, meaning that it can contain any function that returns a `string`.

Returns:

An `integer`, indicating the position where *<pattern>* first appears in *<source>*.

Usage:

`Pos` begins at the start of *<source>* and searches for the first occurrence of the *<pattern>* string. If *<pattern>* is found, `Pos` returns the character position in *<source>* where *<pattern>* first occurs. If *<pattern>* is not found, `Pos` returns 0.

For example, if we have the assignment statement:

```
name := 'Jane Wang';
```

`Pos('Wan', name)` returns the value 6, `Pos('an', name)` returns the value 2 (the first occurrence), `Pos('xyz', name)` returns the value 0 (pattern not found in `string`), and `Pos('',name)` returns a garbage value (cannot search for a null `string`).

```
FUNCTION Person.NameWithInitial(initial : string) : string;
BEGIN
  Insert(initial, name, Pos(name, ' ') + 1);
  NameWithInitial := name
END;
```

Let's examine this fragment. If the value of `name` is `'Ely Greenfield'` and `initial` is `'S.'`, `Insert` makes a copy of the initial string appear at the position `Pos(name, ' ') + 1`, or `5`. This results in the following string being returned in `name`:

```
'Ely S. Greenfield'
```

`Insert` is described in Syntax Box 18.4.

Syntax Box 18.4

Insert

Purpose:

To insert a string inside another string at a specified position.

Syntax:

```
Insert(<str to insert>, <source str>, <position>);
```

Where:

<str to insert> is a literal or variable strings. It can also be a string expression, meaning that they can contain any function that returns a string. *<source str>* must be a variable — it is a `VAR` parameter.

<position> is an integer expression.

Usage:

`Insert` copies the contents of the string *<str to insert>* into *<source str>* at the position specified by *<position>*.

If *<position>* is less than 1, *<str to insert>* is concatenated to *<source str>* beginning at position 1. If *<position>* is greater than the length of *<source str>*, then *<str to insert>* is attached to the end of *<source str>*.

In the resulting string, the first character of *<str to insert>* occupies the position specified by *<position>*, and the length of the returned string is equal to `Length(`*<str to insert>*`) + Length(`*<source str>*`)`.

For example, if we have the assignment statements:

```
name := 'Edward Bielawa';
newPart := 'Mark ';
```

`Insert(newPart, name, 0)` places `'Mark Edward Bielawa'` in name, and `Insert(newPart, name, 20)` places `'Edward BielawaMark '` in name.

18.3 REGULAR EXPRESSIONS

String functions and procedures like `Pos` and `Insert` are fairly simple ways to manipulate strings. You could write them yourself without too much trouble. For each character in the source string, we can see whether the substring starting at that character matches the search pattern. For example, `Pos` could be implemented like this:

```
FUNCTION Pos(pattern, source: string): integer;
VAR
  tmpString: string;
  position: integer;
  patLength: integer;
```

```
BEGIN
  position := 0;
  patLength := Length(pattern);
  REPEAT
    position := position + 1;
    tmpString := Copy(source, position, patLength)
  UNTIL (tmpString = pattern) OR (position > Length(source));
  IF position > Length(source) THEN
    Pos := 0
  ELSE
    Pos := position
END;
```

In this code, we create a substring of the source string using the `Copy` function. We start by determining whether the pattern exists in the source string, starting at position 1. If not, we move to position 2, and so on. We continue until one of two things happens. If we find the pattern is in the source string, we exit and return the position where the pattern starts. If we advance the starting position *past* the end of the string (represented by `position > Length(source)`), the pattern has not been found, and we return the value 0. Recall that `Copy` beyond the end of the string simply returns the empty string. Looking past the end makes it easier to determine whether the pattern was not found or whether it was found at the end of the string.

This function isn't very complex, but it is extremely specialized — it tells only the position of one string, and it can find only exact matches.

A function like `Pos` isn't powerful enough to handle many of our string manipulation problems. Consider, for example, the problem of recognizing identifiers within a Pascal program. As we stated at the beginning of the book, the compiler is the software responsible for recognizing the legality of your Pascal code. It will generate an error message if you include an illegal identifier. But how does the compiler know whether an identifier is legal? We couldn't practically list all of the possible identifiers. Instead, the compiler uses a formula to recognize an identifier: It is a string that contains letters, numbers, and underscores and begins with a letter or underscore.

This problem of wanting to recognize strings that match a formula is not unusual. Programs routinely need to find any one of a number of possible substrings within a larger string. What we need to do is design an object that can indicate whether a particular string (such as an identifier you've used in a program) can be created by a formula.

These objects are called *regular expressions*, and they are used widely in various types of operating systems and application software. OOPas uses them internally to decide whether a string of characters is a reserved word or an integer literal or an identifier. File selection dialog boxes often use regular expressions as well when they use "wildcard characters" to specify a set of file names, such as `'*.txt'` for "all files whose names end in `'.txt'`."

We can think of a regular expression as generating a set of strings according to some formula. For example, our formula for an identifier tells us that we can create the set of all legal identifiers by starting with a letter or underscore, and then concatenating letters, numbers, and underscores. To determine whether a particular string matches a given regular expression, we try to create the string with the formula. If we can generate the string from the formula, we say that the regular expression *matches* the string.

A regular expression, then, consists of a formula and a method for matching. The formula can define a small set of strings (such as the set {`'IF'`, `'if'`, `'If'`, `'iF'`}) or a set with a potentially uncountable number of strings (such as the set of all strings that end in `'.txt'`). A formula can be a combination of other regular expressions (such as the set of all strings that begin with `'GP'` and end with `'Oval'`). The method for matching depends on the kind of formula used to define the regular expression's set of strings.

In the remainder of this section, we will examine different types of regular expressions and regular expression combinations. We want to write a program that can tell us whether different strings match particular regular expressions.

Being good object-oriented designers, we want to solve this problem with reusable code. Our solution will be to build generic regular expression objects that we can assemble in various ways. Putting different regular expressions together in different ways will provide us with a new aggregate object that searches for different particular strings. To create other regular expressions, we simply assemble familiar existing regular expressions in new ways. In the remainder of this section, we will examine different kinds of regular expression objects.

Let's first provide a minimal base class for regular expressions. From this class, we will create subclasses for different kinds of regular expressions. For the base class, there's really only one method we need — a function telling us whether this regular expression matches a particular string:

```
RegExpAsn = ^RegularExpression;
RegularExpression = OBJECT
  CONSTRUCTOR Init;
  FUNCTION Matches(source: string; VAR matchLength: integer):
             boolean; VIRTUAL;
END;
```

We also said that regular expressions contain formulas. We did not, however, define the formula in the base class because, as we will see, different subclasses will use different types of instance variables to store the components of the formula.

Let's examine the heading of the `Matches` method. The `source` parameter is the string we are testing to determine whether it is matched by the regular expression. The function returns a boolean, indicating whether there is a match. As we'll see in a moment, while a yes/no answer on a string match is useful, it will be even more useful to be able to match only part of a string, namely the beginning. So, in addition to returning a boolean, we return (using the `VAR` parameter `matchLength`) the number of characters of the string this regular expression matches. If `Matches` returns zero in `matchLength`, then the regular expression didn't match any characters in the string. If `Matches` returns another integer in `matchLength`, then the regular expression matched at least the initial part of the source string. We'll return to this concept shortly.

The base class is abstract, so we'll provide it with an empty constructor and a stub `Matches` method that says no passed strings match this regular expression by returning `FALSE` and assigning 0 to `matchLength`:

```
CONSTRUCTOR RegularExpression.Init;
BEGIN
END;

FUNCTION RegularExpression.Matches(
   source: string;
   VAR matchLength: integer): boolean;
BEGIN
   matchLength := 0;
   Matches := FALSE;
END;
```

Serial Composition

Let's start with a simple regular expression that generates and matches the set of all strings that start with a particular pattern. Each instance of this class can store a pattern as an instance variable. If the instance is passed a source string that begins with that pattern, then the match succeeds. Thus, if we define the pattern as `'19'`, then our `Matches` function should match `'1997'`, `'19:35'`, `'1984 by George Orwell'` and `'19'`. We can use the `Copy` function to determine whether the source begins with the pattern. We'll call this subclass `StringRegExp`, since our formula is simply a pattern string. We can define this subclass as follows:

```
StringRegExp = OBJECT (RegularExpression)
   CONSTRUCTOR Init(newRegExpPattern: string);
   FUNCTION Matches(source: string; VAR matchLength: integer):
              boolean; VIRTUAL;
PRIVATE
   regExpPattern: string;
END;

CONSTRUCTOR StringRegExp.Init(newRegExpPattern: string);
BEGIN
   INHERITED Init;
   regExpPattern := newRegExpPattern
END;
```

```
FUNCTION StringRegExp.Matches(
  source: string;
  VAR matchLength: integer): boolean;

BEGIN
  IF regExpPattern = Copy(source, 1, Length(regExpPattern)) THEN
    BEGIN
      matchLength := Length(regExpPattern);
      Matches := true;
    END
  ELSE
    BEGIN
      matchLength := 0;
      Matches := false;
    END
END;
```

As we mentioned earlier, we can build regular expressions from other regular expression building blocks. One way we can do this is with *serial composition*. A regular expression that is a serial composition has two subparts that are themselves regular expressions. The serial composition matches a string if the first subpart matches the beginning of the source string (known as the *head*) and the second subpart matches the remainder of the source string (known as the *tail*). Suppose we have a serial composition of two string regular expressions. If the first string regular expression matches `'19'` and the second matches `'84'`, our serial composition should match `'1984'`, `'1984-85'`, `'1984 by George Orwell'` but not `'8419'`, or `'19:84'`. Another way to put it is that this composition describes the set of strings that begin with `'1984'` — the concatenation of the two string regular expressions. (A string regular expression is itself a specific kind of serial composition: any string regular expression, such as `'19'`, is a composition of the characters `'1'` and `'9'`.)

To implement a simple kind of serial composition, we begin by storing the head and tail regular expressions as instance variables. Note that we are storing links to regular expressions. As we will see, the components of the serial composition need not be limited to the simple string regular expressions we just examined; the components could be, for example, other serial compositions. Using links as the instance variables allows us to use polymorphism to serially compose different subclasses of regular expressions.

```
SerialCompRegExp = OBJECT (RegularExpression)
  CONSTRUCTOR Init(newHeadRegExpLink, newTailRegExpLink :
            RegExpAsn);
  FUNCTION Matches(source: string; VAR matchLength: integer) :
            boolean; VIRTUAL;
PRIVATE
  headRegExpLink, tailRegExpLink: RegExpAsn;
END;
```

```
CONSTRUCTOR SerialCompRegExp.Init(newHeadRegExpLink,
                newTailRegExpLink: RegExpAsn);

BEGIN
   INHERITED Init;
   headRegExpLink := newHeadRegExpLink;
   tailRegExpLink := newTailRegExpLink;
END;
```

Now we can write the `Matches` method. Here, we begin by matching the head regular expression. If we have a match, we copy the tail of the string `source` before we try to match it against the tail regular expression. The idea is to match one regular expression *followed by* another. Thus, we don't want the tail regular expression to try to match the part of the string we already matched. The tail of the source is what we send to `tailRegExpLink^.Matches` to see whether the tail matches the tail regular expression.

```
FUNCTION SerialCompRegExp.Matches(
   source: string;
   VAR matchLength: integer): boolean;

VAR
   headMatchLength, tailMatchLength: integer;
   tailOfSource: string;

BEGIN
   headMatchLength := 0;
   tailMatchLength := 0;
   Matches := false; { set to true if BOTH reg exps match }
   IF headRegExpLink^.Matches(source, headMatchLength) THEN
      BEGIN
         tailOfSource := Copy(source, headMatchLength + 1,
                 Length(source));

         IF tailRegExpLink^.Matches(tailOfSource, tailMatchLength)
                 THEN
            Matches := true
      END
   matchLength := headMatchLength + tailMatchLength;
END;
```

Note that the calculation of `matchLength` proceeds regardless of whether the match succeeds. It is quite possible that knowing that a regular expression matched partway could be useful. For example, a compiler for OOPas might use the information that the string "THEM" matched three characters of THEN to suggest that the user has made a typographical error.

Parallel Composition

We said earlier that regular expressions are made from formulas. The string regular expression defines sets of strings that all have the same head. It is possible to make expressions that match strings that have a variety of heads.

For example, consider a regular expression that defines the set of strings that begin with a vowel. How could we determine whether a source string matches this regular expression? We can check the first character of the source string and see whether it is a member of the character set { 'a', 'e', 'i', 'o', 'u' }. If the first character is in the set, then we have a match.

The implementation of a character set-based regular expression follows. Notice that when an instance of this class is initialized, it receives a set of characters as its regular expression pattern. Then, when it receives a `Matches` message, it returns `true` if the source begins with *any* of the characters in the set.

```
CharSet = SET OF char;
CharSetRegExp = OBJECT (RegularExpression)
  CONSTRUCTOR Init(setToMatch : CharSet);
  FUNCTION Matches(source : string; VAR matchLength: integer) :
            boolean; VIRTUAL;
PRIVATE
  regExpPattern: CharSet;
END;

CONSTRUCTOR CharSetRegExp.Init(setToMatch: CharSet);
BEGIN
  INHERITED Init;
  regExpPattern := setToMatch
END;

FUNCTION CharSetRegExp.Matches(
  source: string;
  VAR matchLength: integer): boolean;
BEGIN
  matchLength := 0;
  Matches := false;
  IF (Length(source) > 0) THEN
    IF (source[1] IN regExpPattern) THEN
      BEGIN
        matchLength := 1;
        Matches := true
      END
END;
```

That was simple enough: If the first character is in the set, the regular expression matches with a length of one. Otherwise, the match fails. A character set regular expression is a simplification of the more general idea of *parallel composition*. A regular expression formed by parallel composition takes two regular expressions and matches a string if *either* regular expression matches the string. This is like placing the expressions side by side — either one offers a path to matching the string.

The difference between parallel and serial composition is that serial composition requires that the two regular expressions be matched in order, while parallel composition allows one of two regular expressions to be matched. If we create a parallel composition where the two regular expressions are the string regular expressions `'19'` and `'84'`, our new regular expression will match `'1997'` or `'84 = 7 x 12'` or any string that begins with `'19'` or `'84'`.

Now let's look at the code for general parallel composition looks like. The definition and constructor are very similar to serial composition. The difference is in the `Matches` method. The method tries to match the source to one regular expression; if that doesn't work, it tries to match the other.

```
ParallelCompRegExp = OBJECT (RegularExpression)
  CONSTRUCTOR Init(newOneRegExpLink, newOtherRegExpLink:
            RegExpAsn);
  FUNCTION Matches(source: string; VAR matchLength: integer):
            boolean; VIRTUAL;
PRIVATE
  oneRegExpLink, otherRegExpLink: RegExpAsn;
END;

CONSTRUCTOR ParallelCompRegExp.Init(
   newOneRegExpLink,
   newOtherRegExpLink : RegExpAsn);
BEGIN
  INHERITED Init;
  oneRegExpLink := newOneRegExpLink;
  otherRegExpLink := newOtherRegExpLink
END;

FUNCTION ParallelCompRegExp.Matches(
  source: string;
  VAR matchLength: integer): boolean;
VAR
  oneMatchLength, otherMatchLength: integer;
BEGIN
  IF oneRegExpLink^.Matches (source, oneMatchLength) THEN
    BEGIN
      matchLength := oneMatchLength;
      Matches := true
    END
```

```
        ELSE IF otherRegExpLink^.Matches(source, otherMatchLength) THEN
          BEGIN
            matchLength := otherMatchLength;
            Matches := true
          END
        ELSE
          BEGIN
            matchLength := 0;
            Matches := false
          END
    END;
```

Note that this form of parallel composition preferentially matches one regular expression. It doesn't check the second regular expression if the first one matched, even though the second might have been a better match (that is, might have matched more characters).

You might think about the distinction between parallel and serial compositions in two different ways. We've mentioned that regular expressions describe sets of strings. You could think of a parallel composition as a union of sets. That is, if we create a parallel composition of the string regular expressions `'19'` and `'84'`, then the resulting regular expression is the union of the set of strings matched by the regular expression `'19'` and the set of strings matched by the regular expression `'84'`. A serial composition is a cross-product of sets (i.e., the set of all pairs where the first element of the pair comes from one set while the second element comes from another set). Given our same two string regular expressions, the serial composition describes the set of strings matched by the regular expression `'19'` followed by the strings that start with `'84'`.

Another way to think of this distinction is to think about compositions in terms of boolean operators. A parallel composition is like the OR function (the set of strings matched by the regular expressions `'19'` OR `'84'`), and serial composition is like the AND function (the set of strings matched by the regular expression `'19'` AND whose tail is matched by the regular expression `'84'`). Note that the two parts of the AND expression are not talking about the same string; the first regular expression matches the head of the string, and the second matches the tail.

The Kleene Closure

We've seen that string regular expressions describe and match the set of the strings that begin with a particular pattern, and that character set regular expressions describe the set of strings that begin with any of a number of characters. Serial and parallel composition regular expressions are extensions of these ideas.

All of these regular expressions generate sets of strings that start with a pattern of a fixed size. There's a common class of regular expressions that cannot be defined by the subclasses we've seen thus far. As a simple example, consider the set of all strings that begin with any number of 'q' characters. This includes the strings that begin with 'q', 'qq', 'qqq', and so forth. This pattern doesn't have a predefined length; "any number" includes 0.

We need a kind of regular expression that is either recursive or iterative, in order to represent strings of arbitrary length in a very compact way. The *Kleene*[2] *closure*, also known as the *Kleene star* because it is often represented with an asterisk, is an operation that can be applied to a regular expression to produce a new regular expression that represents strings of arbitrary length. It was named for the mathematician S. C. Kleene, who first devised it. If we apply the Kleene closure to a regular expression, the result is a new regular expression that generates a set of strings that match any number of serial copies of the original expression, including no copies at all. Thus, if we take the simple string regular expression `'q'` and apply the Kleene closure, we are defining the set that includes the set that matches the string regular expression `'q'`, the set that matches the serial compositions of two 'q' string regular expressions (or `'qq'`), the set that matches the serial composition of three 'q' serial compositions (or `'qqq'`), and so on. This particular regular expression is often written as q*. (Note that the asterisk here represents the Kleene star, which is not the same as the * wildcard used in Windows to define a filename.)

The set *also* includes the serial composition of zero `'q'` string regular expressions, which means that any string that begins with the empty string is a match. Now, this might seem silly; *all* strings can be said to begin with the empty string. The Kleene closure is often used, however, as part of a serial composition, and thus we are using this regular expression to match part of a string. (We'll see an example in the next section.) Thus, we say that the regular expression q* = { '', 'q', 'qq', 'qqq', . . .}.

We can also apply the Kleene closure to more complex regular expressions. For example, if we have the parallel composition of the string regular expressions 'p' and 'q', and we apply the Kleene closure, we are then describing the set of strings of 0 or more copies of either 'p' or 'q', in any order: ('p' *or* 'q')* = { '', 'p', 'q', 'pq', 'qp', 'pp', 'qq', 'ppp', 'ppq', . . .}.

The class definition for a Kleene closure regular expression is straightforward. Our instance variables simply consist of a link to one other regular expression.

```
KleeneClosureRegExp = OBJECT (RegularExpression)
  CONSTRUCTOR Init(newRegExpLink: RegExpAsn);
  FUNCTION Matches(source: string; VAR matchLength: integer):
            boolean; VIRTUAL;
PRIVATE
  regExpLink: RegExpAsn; { the reg exp to "star" }
END;
```

2. Kleene is pronounced "Klee-nee" — with two syllables.

```
CONSTRUCTOR KleeneClosureRegExp.Init(
    newRegExpLink : RegExpAsn);
BEGIN
   INHERITED Init;
   regExpLink := newRegExpLink;
END;
```

The `Matches` method is a `WHILE` loop, since we'd like to handle the case where no copies of the repeated part of the regular expression match. This means that a Kleene closure regular expression *always* matches the beginning of the string, although it may match with a length of zero. Thus the function will always return `true`, but it might assign a value of 0 to `matchLength`.

```
FUNCTION KleeneClosureRegExp.Matches(
   source: string;
   VAR matchLength: integer): boolean;
VAR
   repeatMatchLength : integer;
BEGIN
   matchLength := 0;
   WHILE regExpLink^.Matches(source, repeatMatchLength) AND
      (repeatMatchLength <> 0) DO
      BEGIN
         matchLength := matchLength + repeatMatchLength;
         source := Copy(source, repeatMatchLength + 1,
                  Length(source) - repeatMatchLength);
      END;
   Matches := true
END;
```

The loop in this function begins by seeing whether the starred regular expression matches the string. If so, `matchLength` is increased, and the matched substring is removed from the source string. The loop then sees whether the regular expression matches the remainder of the source. The match is *greedy*, because it will match as much of the source as possible.

The regular expression might be any of the subclasses of `RegularExpression` — including `KleeneClosureRegExp`. In other words, the Kleene closure's regular expression could be a Kleene closure. Applying the Kleene closure to a Kleene closure produces the same regular expression (the proof is left as an exercise). As we said, it's entirely possible that when a Kleene closure regular expression is sent a `Matches` message, it could return `TRUE` but would be matching an empty string. If we continued with the loop, the `Copy` function wouldn't change the source string (since we would be removing an empty string). We would return to the top of the loop with the same source string we had before, and this would continue infinitely. Thus the loop condition includes a check to make sure that the length of the match returned by `Matches` is not 0.

Common Regular Expressions: Identifiers and Integers

As we said before, OOPas uses regular expressions as a convenient way to describe the various parts of its language, such as literals and identifiers.

Let's start with identifiers. As we said earlier, an identifier must start with a letter or an underscore. That's an easy regular expression, simply the parallel composition of all letters and the underscore character. This describes the first character in an identifier. The rest of an identifier consists of zero or more letters, underscores, or numbers. This is just the parallel composition of all alphanumeric characters and the underscore, with the Kleene closure applied to it.

```
IdentifierRegExp = OBJECT(SerialCompRegExp)
  CONSTRUCTOR Init;
  { matches already defined in superclass }
PRIVATE
  firstLetter, secondLetter : CharSetRegExp;
  tailOfId : KleeneClosureRegExp;
END;

CONSTRUCTOR IdentifierRegExp.Init;
BEGIN
  firstLetter.Init( ['A'..'Z', 'a'..'z', '_'] );
  secondLetter.Init( ['A'..'Z', 'a'..'z', '_', '0'..'9'] );
  tailOfId.Init( @secondLetter);
  INHERITED Init(@firstLetter, @tailOfId);
END;
```

Integer literals are similarly easy. They can be either positive, negative, or zero. Zero is easy: It's the string regular expression `'0'`. Positive literals start with one of the digits 1–9, since no leading zeros are allowed. They finish with any of the digits, repeated any number of times using a Kleene star. Negative numbers, then, are a serial composition: They start with a minus sign (which we can represent as the string regular expression `'-'`) and finish with a positive literal.

```
IntegerLiteralRegExp = OBJECT(ParallelCompRegExp)
  CONSTRUCTOR Init;
  { matches already defined in superclass }
PRIVATE
  zero, negative : StringRegExp;
  nonZeroDigit, anyDigit : CharSetRegExp;
  manyDigits : KleeneClosureRegExp;
  positiveNumber, negativeNumber : SerialCompRegExp;
  positiveOrNegative : ParallelCompRegExp;
END;
```

```
CONSTRUCTOR IntegerLiteralRegExp.Init;
BEGIN
  zero.Init('0');
  negative.Init('-');
  nonZeroDigit.Init(['1'..'9']);
  anyDigit.Init(['0'..'9']);
  manyDigits.Init(@anyDigit);
  positiveNumber.Init(@nonZeroDigit, @manyDigits);
  negativeNumber.Init(@negative, @positiveNumber);
  positiveOrNegative.Init(@negativeNumber, @positiveNumber);
  INHERITED Init(@zero, @positiveOrNegative)
END;
```

Floating point literals are more complex, since they include scientific notation. They are left as an exercise at the end of the chapter.

18.4 RECURSIVE PARSING

Regular expressions aren't powerful enough to handle everything that we might need to parse. For example, regular expressions can't handle nested parentheses. Nested arithmetic expressions are part of almost every modern programming language (including OOPas), so we need a more powerful technique to parse programming languages. Instead of building regular expression objects, we're going to build objects that are more powerful parsing rules.

Early on, in Chapter 1, we discussed the idea of a *grammar.* Fundamentally, a grammar is a set of rules describing a set of strings, much like a regular expression describes a set of strings. The grammar serves as a way to describe what strings are in the set (also called the *language*) and what strings are not. Strings in the language are said to be *parsed* by the grammar. Thus the grammar for OOPas describes all legal OOPas programs (in mathematical terms, it describes a finite but unbounded set). Grammars are at least as powerful as regular expressions in the sense that any set of strings matched by a regular expression can be described by a grammar. In fact, grammars are more powerful, since they can describe sets of strings that cannot be described by a regular expression, as we will see in a moment.

Grammars

A grammar is a set of rules. Grammar rules have two parts — a left-hand side and one or more right-hand sides. The left-hand side is simply the rule's name. Each right-hand side is a list of either *terminals* (also known as *tokens*) or names of rules (also known as *nonterminals*). We're going to start by using characters as terminals, but in general, we don't have to use them. We can use regular expressions instead. Then, we can use things like keywords and literals (whose regular expressions we developed in the previous section) as tokens in our grammar. This is what OOPas does to parse programs.

Let's start with a simple grammar. Many sentences in English can be constructed with a rule that says, "A sentence is a noun phrase followed by a verb phrase, followed by a period." This means that to construct a sentence, we could create a serial composition of three items: a noun phrase, a verb phrase, and a period. We can describe this rule as follows:

Rule	Replacement
Sentence	NounPhrase, VerbPhrase, '.'

In our notation, we use **or** to represent parallel composition, and commas to represent serial composition. In this case, the rule *Sentence* has two nonterminals (*NounPhrase* and *VerbPhrase*) and a terminal (the period).

To complete our sentence, we have to add some more rules. To make things simple, let's assume we have a list of verb phrases that are predefined. We could simply add this list as a rule, and extend the grammar as follows:

Rule	Replacement
Sentence	NounPhrase, VerbPhrase, '.'
VerbPhrase	'runs' **or** 'walks'

This means that when the rule *VerbPhrase* appears in *Sentence*, we can look up the right-hand side to find the appropriate replacement ('runs' or 'walks').

Suppose we wanted our noun phrases to be slightly more complicated. They could be an article ('A', 'An', or 'The') followed by a single noun (like 'dog' or 'cat'). First, we could define rules describing a noun and an article (leaving out 'An', since all our nouns start with consonants). Notice the spaces after the words that will handle the spaces between words in a sentence. Normally, we would list the spaces separately, but listing them together keeps this example simpler.

Rule	Replacement
Article	'A' **or** 'The'
Noun	'dog' **or** 'cat'

But how do we define the rule *NounPhrase* so it can handle an article followed by a noun? We combine the rules in the replacement as follows:

Rule	Replacement
Sentence	NounPhrase, VerbPhrase, '.'
NounPhrase	Article, Noun
Article	'A' **or** 'The'
Noun	'dog' **or** 'cat'
VerbPhrase	'runs' **or** 'walks'

This completes our grammar. We can compose very simple sentences using this set of rules, such as 'The dog runs.' and 'A cat walks.'.

Suppose we wanted to go in the other direction. Given a string, is it grammatical? To find out, we try to parse the string using the grammar's rules.

Let's say we wanted to parse the sentence 'A cat runs.' using the above grammar. A grammar has one rule identified as the starting rule; in this case, it is the rule *Sentence*. To parse a string using the grammar, we start with the string and the starting rule and see whether the right side matches the string. In this case, we see that the right side is *NounPhrase*, *VerbPhrase*, '.'.

So, how do we see whether a right side matches the source string? For each right-hand side, we go through its terminals and nonterminals in order. We start from the beginning of the source string and the beginning of the right side. If the right side begins with a terminal, we see whether the terminal is at the current position in the source string. If it is, we advance to the next position in the string and check the next part of the right side. If the right side begins with a nonterminal, we recursively evaluate the rule it names, starting at the current position in the string. If the evaluation succeeds, we continue.

Here, then, we are evaluating *NounPhrase*, *VerbPhrase*, '.'. The first item is the nonterminal *NounPhrase*, so we go to its replacement. We are now comparing our source string, 'A cat runs.' to the rule *Article*, *Noun*. We try the next section of *NounPhrase*'s replacement: *Article*, *Noun*. We are comparing our source string 'A cat runs.' We replace the nonterminal *Article* with 'A' or 'The' and discover that we can match the head of the source string with 'A'. Since the nonterminal *Article* has been matched, our *NounPhrase* rule says that we use *Noun* to match the remainder of our string ('cat runs.'). When we replace *Noun* (with 'dog' **or** 'cat'), we again find a match. Thus we have successfully parsed *NounPhrase*, and we can return to the original *Sentence* rule.

At this point, we go to the next section of the *Sentence* rule, which is *VerbPhrase*. We have already matched 'A cat', so we want *VerbPhrase* to match 'runs.'. We replace *VerbPhrase* with its right-hand side ('runs' or 'walks') and find a match. With this success, we return once more to the original *Sentence* rule.

The final part of the *Sentence* rule is a terminal: '.'. We have matched 'A cat runs' already, so the tail of our source string is '.'. Since the final part of the rule matches the tail of our string, we have successfully parsed the string and can call the sentence grammatical.

Grammars are more powerful than regular expressions. To prove that grammars are at least as powerful as regular expressions, we'll construct a simple grammar for each kind of regular expression. With that, we'll be able to make any sort of regular expression as a grammar simply by including rules of all the equivalent regular expression mechanisms, with the right-hand sides referring to the correct rules.

Serial and parallel composition are simple. As we have seen, serial composition is provided by having many components on the right-hand side (separated by commas), and parallel composition is provided by having more than one right-hand side (separated by **or**).

The Kleene closure derives from the fact that rules have names, allowing them to be recursive. Even though we implemented our `KleeneClosureRegExp` using a `WHILE` loop, we can use a recursive construct just as easily, since recursion and iteration are equivalent (as discussed in Chapter 13). So, the regular expression q^* (that is, the Kleene closure applied to the string regular expression `'q'`) can be specified with a grammar as follows:

Rule	Replacement
QString	'q', QString **or** nothing

Let's see how this would parse the string `'qqqq'`. According to the procedure described above, we begin with the starting rule and our string. In all of our grammar examples, the first rule listed is the starting rule. In this case, *QString* is also the only rule. We check the first right-hand side of *QString*. It starts with a terminal, the letter `'q'`. That matches the first character in our string, so we advance our position in the string one character, and check the second component of the right-hand side. The second component is the rule *QString*, so we start evaluating *QString* again. We do the same thing, matching the second `'q'` and recursively evaluating *QString*. This happens twice more, matching the third `'q'` and the fourth `'q'`. Our string is done, but we're still evaluating the rule *QString* (the fifth recursive use of it). This time, we can't match the first right-hand side: There's no `'q'` left in the string to match. So we try matching the second right-hand side; *nothing*. We always can match *nothing*, so the match succeeds. Since there are no more rules listed in that right-hand side, the parse is done and was successful.

Here's a grammar for integer literals, showing how a regular expression can be completely implemented in a grammar.

Rule	Replacement
Number	'0' **or** Negative **or** Positive
Positive	NonZero, Digits
Negative	'-', Positive
NonZero	'1' **or** '2' **or** '3' **or** '4' **or** '5' **or** '6' **or** '7' **or** '8' **or** '9'
Digits	Digit, Digits **or** nothing
Digit	'0' **or** NonZero

We've thus proven that grammars are at least as powerful as regular expressions. To prove that grammars are *more* powerful than regular expressions, let's do something with a grammar that we can't do with a regular expression — nested parentheses. We'd like our grammar to accept any string that has some number *n* of left parentheses, followed by a single 'q', followed by *n* right parentheses. Try as hard as we might, no regular expression can match that string. A grammar, however, does it quite simply:

Rule	Replacement
QStringNesting	'(', QStringNesting, ')' **or** 'q'

Parsing a string using this grammar proceeds much like the parse using the preceding *QString* grammar, except that the right parentheses are matched after each recursive application of the rule *QStringNesting*.

Tokens

So far, we've used characters as the tokens or terminals in our grammars. We don't have to use characters, as mentioned before. Using regular expressions as tokens is a widely used technique. Let's take our regular expressions for integers and identifiers and use them to build a simple grammar for fully parenthesized simple arithmetic expressions. (That is, the expression must have two parentheses for every plus sign.)

Rule	Replacement
ArithExpression	'(', ArithExpression, '+', ArithExpression, ')' **or** Value
Value	integer **or** identifier

Whereas our grammar for just integer literals was fairly complex, our grammar for arithmetic expressions is really quite simple and fairly easy to read. Most modern compilers for all sorts of programming languages are built using a combination of grammars and regular expressions.

Parsing Recursively

Having a grammar for a particular set of strings is useful, but not as useful as having an object that *parses* that grammar. We're going to use recursion to build parsers for the grammars we've been writing. The basic idea is simple: For each rule, we build an object that can determine whether a passed string matches one of the right-hand sides of the rule. To parse a right-hand side, we simply check that all terminals are matched in the passed string and recursively parse nonterminals. Eventually, we must come to a rule that is all terminals. If we don't, the grammar contains an infinite loop (see Section 14.3).

Once we've implemented all the rules, they can be collected in an object representing the grammar as a whole. Let's start with an abstract base class for a grammar. We won't include the code for either of the methods — both do nothing. Like the `RegularExpression` class we defined, we simply create an interface for the `Parses` method. It will take a source and return a boolean indicating whether the string can be parsed by the grammar's rules.

```
GrammarAsn = ^Grammar;
Grammar = OBJECT
  CONSTRUCTOR Init;
  FUNCTION Parses(source: string): boolean; VIRTUAL;
END;
```

The next class we need is an abstract class to represent a rule. This is a bit more complex, since a rule will generally parse only part of a string. To prevent having to copy substrings excessively, we're also going to let rules start parsing at an arbitrary point in the string (an extension you should be able to add to the regular expression objects presented earlier). These rules will indicate the position at which they completed their parse to make it easier for subsequent rules to pick up where a previous rule left off.

```
AbstractRule = OBJECT
   CONSTRUCTOR Init;
   FUNCTION Parses(
      source: string;
      startPos: integer;
      VAR endPos: integer) : boolean; VIRTUAL;
END;
```

Now, we can make subclasses of `AbstractRule` that implement the specific rules of our grammar. For this example, we're going to implement the grammar for simple arithmetic expressions we just saw. Let's start with the rule *Value*. It contains two regular expression objects, one for integer literals and one for identifiers, the two possible right-hand sides of *Value*. It doesn't invoke any other rules.

```
ValueRuleAsn = ^ValueRule;
ValueRule = OBJECT(AbstractRule)
   CONSTRUCTOR Init;
   FUNCTION Parses(
      source: string;
      startPos: integer;
      VAR endPos: integer) : boolean; VIRTUAL;
PRIVATE
   integerTerminal: IntegerLiteralRegExp;
   identifierTerminal: IdentifierRegExp;
END;
```

The `Parses` method is straightforward. If the string doesn't match an integer, then the rule checks whether the string matches an identifier. If it doesn't match either, then the parse fails.

```
FUNCTION ValueRule.Parses(
   source: string;
   startPos: integer;
   VAR endPos: integer): boolean;

VAR
   tempString : string;
   matchLength : integer;

BEGIN
   tempString := Copy(source, startPos, Length(source) - startPos);
```

```
  IF integerTerminal.Matches(tempString, matchLength) THEN
    BEGIN
      Parses := true;
      endPos := startPos + matchLength
    END
  ELSE IF identifierTerminal.Matches(tempString, matchLength) THEN
    BEGIN
      Parses := true;
      endPos := startPos + matchLength
    END
  ELSE
    Parses := false
END;
```

Now, we'll turn to the other rule. Since the rule *ArithExpression* refers to the rule *Value* in its right-hand side, our *ArithExpression* needs a pointer to the rule *Value*.

```
ArithExpressionRule = OBJECT(AbstractRule)
  CONSTRUCTOR Init(newValueRuleLink: ValueRuleAsn);
  FUNCTION Parses(
    source: string;
    startPos: integer;
    VAR endPos: integer) : boolean; VIRTUAL;
PRIVATE
  valueRuleLink: ValueRuleAsn;
END;
```

Now, we can implement the `Parses` method for `ArithExpressionRule`. This method initially looks complex, but the flow of control is not as complex as it first seems. Since *ArithExpression* has two alternative right-hand sides, we start with an `IF` statement to determine which right-hand side looks more like the one we have. One right-hand side (the `ELSE` part of our `IF` statement here) is simply a recursive call to parse the string as a *Value*. The other right-hand side is more complex, since its replacement has two recursive applications of the *ArithExpression* rule. It uses a series of `IF` statements to check whether successive parts of the string have parsed as expected. We can't use a boolean expression, because both sides of a `boolean` expression are evaluated. If the beginning of the string doesn't parse as expected, it makes no sense to try to parse the end of the string.

We have to keep track of two positions within the string. The `startPos` parameter indicates the beginning of the expression we are currently parsing. The `currEndPos` local variable changes over time and indicates the ending position of the current expression. As we parse each section of the expression, we move `currEndPos` to the end of the expression we've parsed thus far. If the parse succeeds, we return the number of characters in this expression and set the return value of the function to `TRUE`.

Note that the `IF` statements correspond to the serial composition of the rule. The first `IF` corresponds to parsing the left parenthesis. The second `IF` corresponds to the recursive application of the *ArithExpression* rule with a recursive `Parses` message. After a third `IF` parses the plus sign, another recursive application is found in the fourth `IF`. Finally, the fifth `IF` parses the closing parenthesis.

You should also note that this method matches the head of a string. If there are additional characters after the last right parenthesis, and everything has matched thus far, the `Parses` method will still return `true`.

```
CONSTRUCTOR ArithExpressionRule.Init(newValueRuleLink:
             ValueRuleAsn);
BEGIN
  valueRuleLink := newValueRuleLink;
END;

FUNCTION ArithExpressionRule.Parses(
      source: string;
      startPos: integer;
      VAR endPos : integer) : boolean;
VAR
  currEndPos : integer;   { end position of current expr }
BEGIN
  Parses := false;
  currEndPos := startPos;
  {Grammar rule: Expression can be
             '(',Expression,'+',Expression,')' }
  IF source[startPos] = '(' THEN
    BEGIN
      startPos := currEndPos + 1; { parsing complete up to (   }
      IF Parses(source, startPos, currEndPos) THEN
        BEGIN
          { parsing of first sub expr complete }
          IF source[currEndPos] = '+' THEN
            BEGIN
              startPos := currEndPos + 1; { parsed up to + }
              IF Parses(source, startPos, currEndPos) THEN
                BEGIN
                  { parsing of second sub expr complete }
                  IF source[currEndPos] = ')' THEN
                    BEGIN
                      { currEndPos currently points to ) }
                      endPos := currEndPos + 1;
                      Parses := true;
                    END
```

```
                    END
                END
            END
        END
    ELSE {Grammar rule: Expression can be just a value }
        Parses := valueRuleLink^.Parses(source, startPos, endPos)
END;
```

Note that in the preceding code fragment, we initialized the return value of the function to be `false`, so that we don't have to catch every possible way that the parse could fail.

All that remains is to collect our rules into a grammar. The method `Parses` for the grammar simply invokes the `Parses` method for the `ArithExpressionRule`. If the entire string is parsed, `Parses` will return `true`, and `parsedLength` will be one more than the length of the entire string (since `Parses` returns the position of the character following the parsed string).

```
ExpressionGrammar = OBJECT(Grammar)
  CONSTRUCTOR Init;
  FUNCTION Parses(source: string): boolean; VIRTUAL;
PRIVATE
  arithExpression: ArithExpressionRule;
  value: ValueRule;
END;

CONSTRUCTOR ExpressionGrammar.Init;
BEGIN
  value.Init;
  arithExpression.Init(@value)
END;

FUNCTION ExpressionGrammar.Parses(source: string): boolean;
VAR
  parsedLength: integer;  { # of characters in parsed string }
  parseResult: boolean;   { indicates if parse was successful }

BEGIN
  parseResult := arithExpression.Parses(source, 1, parsedLength);
  Parses := parseResult AND (parsedLength = (Length(source) + 1))
END;
```

Results of Parsing

Determining whether a string parses usually is not sufficient. In addition to parsing, the OOPas compiler generates machine code, the compiled version of your program.

Consider our simple arithmetic expression grammar for which we just implemented a parser. We might like to know the numerical value of the expressions we parsed. We can do this by passing along an additional `VAR` parameter — the integer value of the expression being parsed. Each rule can calculate this in its own way. For example, `ValueRule` can use the `Val` procedure to extract an `integer` value from strings that match integer literals. For strings that match identifier literals, we need to decide on reasonable semantics. We could decide that identifiers named variables or functions. These might be stored in a collection of name/value pairs, with the name corresponding to the actual identifier name and the value being the object representing a particular variable or arithmetic function. This is analogous to what the OOPas compiler does when it sees a variable in an expression — it looks for the variable's value in a list of name/value pairs. The value corresponds to a machine-code representation of the variable. The `VAR` section of a method identifies what name/value pairs might be found.

Of course, we would also want to do the actual arithmetic somewhere along the way. During our parsing, we might decide to evaluate subexpressions and add them together when we have reached a right parenthesis.

In general, parsing has a great number of capabilities beyond simply determining whether a string is parsed by a grammar. These capabilities include evaluating an expression, drawing pictures indicating the results of a parse, or even producing a complete executable machine language program.

Summary

In this chapter, we explored *parsing* — extracting information from a string of characters. Parsing can be quite complex, and this chapter serves as only a very basic introduction. However, the techniques are applicable in many situations, from simple word searches in a text editor to compiling an OOPas program.

We began with some built-in parsing functions, `Val` and `Str`, which convert a string to an integer and vice versa. We also examined some more general string functions. The `Pos` function allowed us to find particular substrings within a string. We also saw `Insert`, which copied a string with a new substring inserted at a particular position.

We then moved on to more advanced parsing techniques. We began with *regular expressions*, which can be used to describe sets of strings succinctly, even potentially infinite sets of strings. There are several kinds of basic regular expressions that can be assembled into more complex regular expressions, describing more complex sets of strings. The simplest regular expression is a single character — the set containing the one string with just that single character. Regular expressions can be composed serially, placing one after another, describing the set of strings that are the concatenations of the sets described by the composed regular expressions. Regular expressions also can be composed in a parallel fashion, describing the set that is the union of the sets described by the composed regular expressions. Finally, the Kleene closure can be applied to a regular expression, describing the set of all possible concatenations of any strings in the set described by the original regular expression.

Although powerful, regular expressions will not handle some very useful sets of strings, such as the set of all strings consisting of nested parentheses (e.g., "()", "(())", "((()))", "(((())))", etc.). A *grammar* can handle such sets easily. A grammar is a set of rules. Each rule has a name (its left-hand side) and some number of right-hand sides. Each right-hand side consists of an ordered list of terminals (such as characters) and nonterminals (names identifying other rules in the grammar). A string is parsed by the grammar if, beginning with one particular starting rule, each character in the string can be matched with a terminal in a single right-hand side. Nonterminals are handled by expanding them in place, matching their terminals in turn.

Regular expressions can be used in place of characters as terminals in a grammar, a technique used by OOPas to parse programs. Parsing a string using a grammar can be performed through a series of recursive messages, starting by sending a message to the start rule, indicating the string it is to parse. The start rule then forwards the `Parse` message on to appropriate other rules corresponding to the successive nonterminals on the right-hand side.

Exercises

Understanding Concepts

1. Use the `Val` procedure to retrieve the number from the string `'Beverly Hills, CA 90210'`.

2. Given the assignment statements `alpha := 'pizza';` and `beta := 'zapped';`, what is returned by the following:

```
Pos(alpha, 'za')
Pos('za', beta)
Pos('z', alpha)
Pos(alpha, beta)
Insert(beta, alpha, 3)
Insert(alpha, beta, 3)
Insert(alpha, beta, 18)
Insert(alpha, beta, Pos('za', alpha))
```

3. How could the code at the end of Section 18.1 be modified so that `houseNumberString` is assigned all of the characters up to the first blank of `houseName`?

4. Write out a grammar to define all real number literals.

5. Prove that applying a Kleene star twice has the same effect as applying it once. In other words, if r is a regular expression, prove that $r^{**} = r^{*}$.

6. Will the regular expression objects in this chapter match the regular expression a*a when given the string 'a'? The string 'aaaa'? Why or why not?

Coding Problems

1. Write a method that, when given a name in the form *<last>,<first>* returns a name in the form *<first> <last>* (with a space between *<first>* and *<last>*).

2. Write a function that, when given a string, returns the number of words in the string. A "word" is defined as one or more characters surrounded by blanks or punctuation. A set of characters at the beginning or end of the string also counts as a word.

3. Write a function to compress blanks — that is, a function that receives a string and eliminates any extra blanks. Thus, whenever the function finds two or more blanks in a row in the parameter it receives, the multiple blanks are replaced by a single blank. For example, if the function is sent `'   10 Downing   St.   '`, it should return `' 10 Downing St. '`.

4. We know a certain professor who uses a bizarre shorthand. When in a hurry, he writes messages by dropping all the vowels except those that appear at the beginning of a word. Thus the message "Please buzz office phone" becomes "Pls bzz offc phn". Write a method that takes a string and returns the shorthand version.

5. Write a method that accepts Roman numerals as input and prints the decimal equivalent.

6. Implement a regular expression object to recognize OOPas reserved words. A list of all reserved words is found in Appendix A. While we usually put reserved words in all caps, OOPas will accept any pattern of upper- and lowercase for a reserved word.

7. Implement a regular expression object to recognize floating-point literals. Don't forget about scientific notation.

8. Implement a regular expression object for negation of another regular expression. It should take a link to another regular expression and match exactly those strings that the passed regular expression does not match.

9. Implement a regular expression object for making a regular expression optional. It should take a pointer to another regular expression and always successfully match. The length of the match is either zero or the length of the match that would have occurred by just using the other regular expression.

10. Implement a regular expression object for accepting one or more occurrences of another regular expression. This is like a Kleene closure, except it does not accept zero occurrences of the given regular expression.

Programming Problems

1. Write a program that takes a date chosen by the user and outputs it in the form *<date>*, *<month> <day>*, *<year>* (such as "Friday, July 16, 1993"). The program should also indicate the date 90 days after the user's date.

2. Implement a calculator. The user should be able to enter an expression by selecting functions and operators using push buttons or menus. The expression should be shown as it is constructed using a `GPText` object. Whenever the expression is valid, the results should be displayed using another `GPText` object. Use the following grammar:

Rule	Replacement
ExpressionStart	real, ExpressionEnd **or** '(', ExpressionStart, ')' **or** Function
ExpressionEnd	'+', ExpressionStart **or** '-', ExpressionStart **or** '*', ExpressionStart **or** '/', ExpressionStart **or** nothing
Function	'sqrt(', ExpressionStart, ')' **or** 'sin(', ExpressionStart, ')' **or** 'cos(', ExpressionStart, ')'

All functions and operators should produce answers comparable with their OOPas counterparts (i.e., when responding to the "sin" rule, just call `sin` on the value returned by the *ExpressionStart* in the "sin" rule). Don't worry about associativity: Simply evaluate expressions in the order received. Note that the method handling *ExpressionEnd* will need to be passed the real in *ExpressionStart* representing the beginning of the expression in order to produce its result.

3. Implement a psychiatrist. The "patient" (or user) should be able to type in statements or questions (using dialog boxes) and the doctor should respond appropriately. For example, if the patient starts asking the doctor questions, the doctor should redirect the questions to the patient.

```
Patient: Do you like your work, Doctor?
Doctor: Let's talk about your work, not mine. How does your work
            make you feel?
Patient: It makes me feel sad.
Doctor: What about it makes you feel sad?
```

This exercise is based on an old computer game called "Eliza." Eliza was the doctor. By using very simple parsing of the user's statements, Eliza was quite convincing as a doctor. Many users demanded to talk to the doctor "face to face." You can recognize words like "you" and "yours" as being directed at the doctor. A few general questions, such as "How do you feel today?" along with some prompts used when the doctor can't figure out something to say, such as "Please continue," can provide a convincing "doctor."

19

Files

There are times when the user cannot be expected to enter all the input to a program at the keyboard. In Chapter 18, we discussed how to use string functions to find and replace parts of strings. Such a program could be used to correct spelling errors in a paper or an article. For example, you could search for each occurrence of a common error (such as "teh") and replace it with the correct spelling ("the"). It isn't practical to expect the user to retype an entire paper as input to the spelling correction program. Besides wanting the output to appear on the screen, the user would want to save the changed document somewhere on a disk.

Many applications make use of these capabilities. Scientific experiments run by a computer store results, and the IRS stores tax records. Large computers often process the data all at once, using *batch processing*. This chapter shows how to accommodate such needs by using file input and output (or *file I/O*, for short).

19.1 ABOUT FILES

A file is a collection of data that resides outside of the main memory in a computer, and its contents appear in main memory only when needed by the CPU. Usually, a file's contents are stored on some external storage device, such as a disk. We can think of the data in a file as characters, numbers, or graphic elements; internally, the data always are represented as a series of bits. Typically, the data are related in some way. For example, a file can hold a five-page paper, a company's budget, or a shopping list. In all cases, the computer sees a file as a sequence of ones and zeroes in a particular area of memory.

Files are used in an OOPas program for input and output. During a program's execution, a file can be used in one of three ways — as a read-only file or as a write-only file or as a read-write file. The contents of a read-only file can be used only as the input to a program; a write-only file can receive only output from a program; a read-write file can be used for both purposes.

A file consists of an ordered sequence of data items known as components. The number of components in a file is determined by how the file is used. Suppose a file contains the string '123 456'. Depending on how it is used, we can say that this file consists of seven characters, two integers, or a single string. The components of a file are numbered consecutively beginning at 0. When you are looking at a file's contents (you will see how to do this later in the chapter), the components are numbered from left to right and from top to bottom. In the last example, if the contents of the file are being used as integers, the integer 123 is component 0 and the integer 456 is component 1.

OOPas maintains a current file position for each file. The file position indicates from where the next input will come or where the next output will go. Components in files are accessed sequentially. For example, if you have a file that is being used for input, initially, the current file position is at component 0. After the first component is read, the current file position is set to 1. The next read from the file gets the second component and increments the current file position to 2. Figure 19.1 shows the elements of a file being accessed in order. Similarly, the first time you write a component to a file, the current file position moves to the end of the written component. The next write action puts an element immediately after the first component.

Figure 19.1

Sequential reading of components

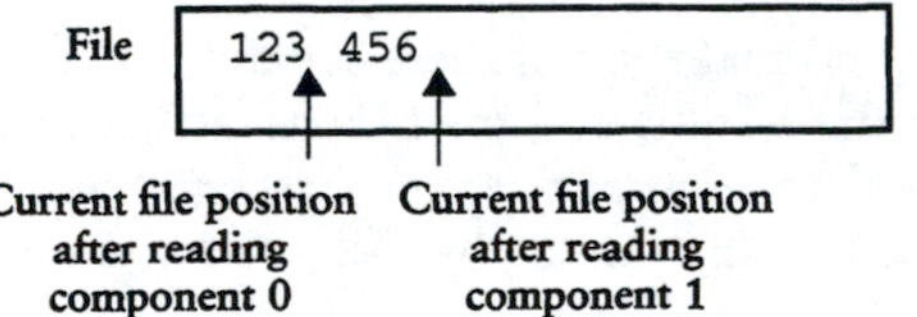

The next section examines the most common way to use files — for input. Files that contain all the input a program will receive often are called *data files*. We'll begin by seeing how you can make a file by hand using a text editor, then see how to manipulate that file programmatically.

19.2 CREATING DATA FILES

Suppose you are the sports editor for a school newspaper. Each day you publish a scoreboard that lists the previous day's results for each of the school's varsity teams. To keep track of what games are happening on which days, you decide to create computer files. In each file, you want to keep a list of one day's games — for example, the file `oct2.sch` contains all the games scheduled for October 2.

For each game, you need to record three things: the team that is playing (e.g., women's lacrosse, men's basketball), the opponent, and your school team's current record of wins and losses. The team and the opponent should be stored as strings; the record of wins and losses should appear as two integers. Note that we're describing the games in a file — we're not concerned about instance variables or objects yet. For reasons that will be explained later in the chapter, the strings should appear on separate lines. A sample data file looks like this:

```
Men's bowling
Bowling Green U.
38  16
Women's mountain climbing
Appalachian State U.
16   7
```

This file shows that the men's bowling team currently has a win–loss record of 38–16 and is playing Bowling Green U. On the same day, the women's mountain climbing team, with a record of 16–7, faces Appalachian State U.

To use a file in a program, you need a way of referring to it. As usual, you use variable declarations to create references. The data type `text` is used to refer to a file. The `text` data type does not mean that the file can hold only textual values. Integers, reals, booleans, or any other type of data that can be stored can be in the file. In each case, we need a way to read or write a textual version of the data.

A declaration of a `text` variable is not exactly like declarations of other variables. An `integer` variable declaration reserves space in memory for an `integer`; a `text` variable declaration does not reserve space for a file. Instead, an area called a *file buffer* is reserved in memory. Every reference to the `text` variable is a reference to the buffer. This buffer is filled by OOPas with the component at the current file position. Therefore the text variable does not refer to the entire file, but just to one component. In short, a buffer is a gateway between files and your programs.

Two file buffers, `input` and `output`, are predefined in OOPas. File buffers can be associated with devices — various pieces of hardware — as well as files. The predefined `text` variable `input` is associated with the keyboard, and `output` is associated with a special text-only window.

19.3 READING FROM FILES

Once we've made a `text` variable, we need to do three things with it:

1. *Associate a file with the* `text` *variable.* This function is analogous to initializing a pointer by assigning it an address or initializing an object by calling its constructor. We'll use special functions to do this, though, since `text` variables, like other built-in data types, are a part of Pascal designed before objects were added to the language.

2. *Read components from the file using the* `text` *variable.* Once the variable knows what file to read from, more special functions can be used to obtain the numbers and strings in the file.
3. *Tell the* `text` *variable we're done reading from the file.* This won't be crucial when reading data, but we will see that it is quite essential when writing data.

We'll deal with each of these topics in turn in this section.

Assigning a File to a Text Variable

Suppose you've declared a variable of type `text` called `games` to hold the file buffer. Before you can start reading from the file, you must open it. You've declared the variable games as a `text` type, and you want to use the file `oct2.sch` as input. The statements

```
Assign(games, 'oct2.sch');
Reset(games);
```

accomplishes this task.

An `Assign` statement does a number of things. Its two parameters are a `text` variable and a `string` representing the title of a file. When OOPas executes this statement, the `text` variable `games` is associated with the file `oct2.sch`. Then in the `Reset` statement, the file `oct2.sch` is opened as a read-write file. The current position for the file is set to component 0. Since you haven't read anything yet, the file buffer `games` is set to the top of the file and is now available as a gateway to the contents of `oct2.sch`. `Assign` and `Reset` are described in Syntax Box 19.1.

Reading Things from the File

You now can begin reading from the file using the `Read` and `Readln` statements. `Read` and `Readln` are special functions that behave like virtual functions, and take two parameters. A `text` variable, the first parameter, tells the function what file to read some data from. The second parameter is a `VAR` parameter of any built-in type, such as `real`, `integer`, `char`, or `string`. Depending on the type of the second parameter, `Read` and `Readln` perform various functions, much like what a message send does depends on the type of object it is sent to.

For example, a `Read` of an integer will scan the file from the current position, reading in digits until it encounters a character that can't be part of a number. The digits are then converted into the corresponding number, like using the `Val` function described in Section 18.1. `Read` and `Readln` are described in Syntax Box 19.2.

Syntax Box 19.1

Assign, Reset

Purpose:

`Assign` associates a file buffer with a file; `Reset` opens a file for use.

Syntax:

```
Assign(<file buffer>, <filename>);
Reset(<file buffer>);
```

Where:

<file buffer> is a variable of type `text`.

<filename> is a string expression.

Usage:

`Assign` associates *<file buffer>* with the file named in *<filename>*. The file specified by *<filename>* is opened by the `Reset` statement. After this statement, *<file buffer>* may be used as the first parameter in `Read` or `Readln` statements to read input from the file, or used as the first parameter to `Write` or `Writeln` to send output to the file.

The current file position is initialized to point to component 0 (the first component of the file).

It is crucial that the data sequence in a file match the program's input specifications. For example, if a program expects two strings followed by two integers, an error will result if the integers are placed before the strings. You also need to remember the semantics of the data. For example, in the school newspaper file, it is important that the first string is the home team and the second is the opponent. Although your program will not crash if the strings are out of order, you will get quite different results if the strings do not contain the correct data.

Each character you enter in a data file affects the input. Blank spaces are important when you are entering `char` or `string` type data. In addition, two special characters also are found in a data file. At the end of each line is an invisible marker called an *<eoln>* (end of line) marker, which is a character added to the data file each time you press *Return*. When you exit a file, an *<eof>* (end of file) character marker is placed after the final component in the file. You cannot see the *<eoln>* and *<eof>* markers, but they are a part of your data file. In the preceding example, the markers are placed as follows:

```
Men's bowling <eoln>
Bowling Green U. <eoln>
38 16 <eoln>
Women's mountain climbing <eoln>
Appalachian State U. <eoln>
  16  7 <eoln>
<eof>
```

Syntax Box 19.2

Read and Readln

Purpose:

To receive input from a data file.

Syntax:

```
Read( <file buf>, <var 1>, . . . , <var n> );
Readln( <file buf>, <var 1>, . . . , <var n> );
```

Where:

<file buf> is a variable of type `text`.

<var 1> . . . *<var n>* are variables of type `integer`, `real`, `char`, `string`, or any enumerated type.

Usage:

`Read` and `Readln` assign values to *<var 1>* ... *<var n>* by obtaining sequential components from the file associated with *<file buf>*. That is, *<var 1>* receives the component at the current file position, *<var 2>* receives the following component, and so on.

Blank spaces should be used to separate numeric data in a file. When reading numeric data, `Read` and `Readln` skip all blanks and *<eoln>* characters in the file until a number is found.

When any of *<var 1>* ... *<var n>* is a string variable, both `Read` and `Readln` assign all characters between the current file position and the next *<eoln>* marker to the variable. If the `string` is input with a `Read`, the current file position is then set to the *<eoln>* marker; if a `Readln` is used, the current file position moves to the beginning of the next line.

If `Read` or `Readln` attempts to assign the *<eoln>* marker to a `char` or `string` variable, the result can vary. You may not get an error when the input is made, but when you try to use the variable's contents (the *<eoln>* marker), the program may crash.

The file designated by *<file buf>* must have been opened with `Reset`.

If you left the insertion point after the 7 on the final line instead of pressing "Return," the final line markers would be placed as follows:

```
Appalachian State U. <eoln>
  16  7 <eof>
```

Whenever OOPas encounters a `Read` or `Readln`, it looks at the first parameter. If the parameter is a file buffer, input is received from that file. Otherwise, OOPas assumes that input is coming from the predefined file `input`, that is, the keyboard. The remainder of the `Read` and `Readln` statements are syntactically the same whether input comes from a file or from the keyboard.

A `Readln` statement reads data and then moves the current file position to the beginning of the next line in the file. When accepting numeric data, `Read` skips blanks and *<eoln>* characters to find the next number. Suppose you have the following lines in the data file `records.txt`:

```
92 68
90 70
```

If you use the statements

```
Assign(recBuf, 'records.txt');
Reset(recBuf);
Read(recBuf, wins);
Read(recBuf, losses);
Read(recBuf, wins2);
```

the variable `wins` receives the value 92 because the first `Read` will accept the first file component. The current file position then is set to the next component, so the result of `Read(recBuf,losses);` is that losses, as expected, receives the value 68. When the third `Read` is executed, OOPas skips the *<eoln>* character and assigns the next value (90) to `wins2`.

The statements

```
Assign(recBuf, 'records.txt');
Reset(recBuf);
Readln(recBuf, wins);
Read(recBuf, losses);
```

do something quite different.The parameter `wins` again receives the value 92. However, since you used a `Readln` to input the value, the current file position moves to the first component on the next line; thus, losses receives the value 90. The value 68 has been passed over because `Readln` moves the current file position to the next line. The statement `Read`, on the other hand, simply moves the current file position to the next component.

You can use `Readln` statements for the sole purpose of moving the current file position to the next line. For example, suppose you decide you need only the wins of each record (the first integer on each line). The following code first reads 92 into `wins`. The `Readln` statement then moves the current file position to the next line. The value 68 is skipped and the value 90 is input into `wins2`. Here, the line `Readln(recBuf, wins)` is broken into two parts: one to read the value and another to move the file position to the next line.

```
Assign(recBuf, 'records.txt');
Reset(recBuf);
Read(recBuf, wins);
Readln(recBuf);
Read(recBuf, wins2);
```

When reading strings from a data file, you always should use `Readln`. When reading a string from a data file, OOPas receives all the characters between the current file position and the next *<eoln>* marker. The current file position then will be at the *<eoln>* marker. If you use `Read` to input the string, the file position does not move to the next line. The next `Read` then will try to assign the *<eoln>* marker to a variable, and the result of such an action is unpredictable. The statement `Readln`, on the other hand, moves the file position to the next line, and the file is ready for the next input.

Closing the File

When you are finished reading or writing to a file, close the file by using the `Close` procedure. `Close` receives one parameter: a variable of type text. This command informs the operating system that the program will no longer be accessing the file. Syntax Box 19.3 describes `Close`.

Syntax Box 19.3
Close

Purpose:

To close a file.

Syntax:

```
Close(<file buffer>);
```

Where:

<file buffer> is a variable of type `text`.

Usage:

`Close` closes the file associated with *<file buffer>*. The file is stored on the disk designated when the file was opened.

<file buffer> must have been previously opened with `Reset` or `Rewrite`.

19.4 SENTINELS

In general, when we read data from a file, we don't know exactly how much data we're going to read. Typically, we don't read a single data value — we read a whole sequence of data values. This means we're going to use a loop to read our data. We might like to use a definite loop, and if our file starts with information about how much data is in the file, then we can use a definite loop. However, it isn't always convenient (or even possible) to start a file with some indication of how many data items are in the file.

In that case, we need to use an indefinite loop, because we don't know when we'll stop the loop. To figure out when the loop stops, we can use *sentinels*: markers in the file that indicate that the data are finished.

User-Defined Sentinels

Let's look again at the schedule example from Section 19.1. The number of games varies from day to day, so you need some method to designate the end of the data. Since each set of data begins with a string, you could use a string sentinel. If you use the sentinel `'STOP'`, then the data file would look like this:

```
Men's bowling
Bowling Green U.
38 16
Women's mountain climbing
Appalachian State U.
16  7
STOP
```

Since you don't know how many items are in the input, you can use an indefinite loop to read the data. The pseudocode for this procedure is:

```
Read first team
WHILE sentinel has not been read DO
   BEGIN
      Read opponent, wins, and losses
      { process data }
      Read next team
   END { WHILE }
```

Since the team and opponent names are strings, you should use `Readln` statements to get each of those items. We also know that the wins and losses will be on the same line, so you can use a `Readln` to read both pieces of data:

```
PROCEDURE TeamSchedule.ReadFromFile( filename : string );
VAR
  sched : text;
  sport, opponent : string;
  wins, losses : integer;

BEGIN
  Assign(sched, filename);
  Reset(sched);
  Readln(sched, sport); { Prepare for the WHILE loop. }
```

```
  WHILE Pos(sport, 'STOP') = 0 DO { WHILE sentinel isn't found...}
    BEGIN
      Readln(sched, opponent);
      Readln(sched, wins, losses);
      { process data }
      Readln(sched, sport);
    END { WHILE }
END;
```

The problem with string sentinels is that they are defined within the OOPas code, making it hard to find out what it is if the source of the program is unavailable. Usually the programmer and the creator of the data file are two different people. A data file creator who has no knowledge of programming may not know why the sentinel is important. The data file creator also may simply forget the sentinel at the end of the file. Suppose you try to run the preceding code on a data file that does not contain the 'STOP' sentinel. When the procedure tries to receive an input value after the *<eof>* marker, the program will crash with a run-time error.

Eof: The OOPas-Defined Sentinel

To avoid this situation, OOPas provides a function that detects every data file's built-in sentinel — the *<eof>* marker. The OOPas function `Eof` returns a `boolean` value (as described in Syntax Box 19.4). It returns `true` when the current file position has reached the *<eof>* marker in the file, that is, when the file position has moved beyond the last component in the file. At all other times, `Eof` returns `false`.

You can change the code for reading input from the schedule file so that the loop exits when the *<eof>* marker is found instead of the string sentinel. To do this, you need to change the exit condition of the loop to `WHILE NOT Eof(sched) DO`. You also can remove the `Readln` statement before the `WHILE` loop because a value for `sport` no longer is needed to test the exit condition. Now the first line of each set of input is read at the top of the loop.

When you run this code fragment using the data file `oct2.sch`, OOPas first associates the `text` variable with the file, then opens the file with the `Reset` command. Then OOPas reaches the condition of the `WHILE` loop. Since the current file position is at the top of the file and the file is not empty, `Eof(sched)` returns `false` and the loop condition is `true`. The loop is executed, and the information about the men's bowling match is entered. Flow of control then returns to the top of the loop. Since the current file position is still not at the *<eof>* marker, `Eof(sched)` returns `false` and the loop executes again. After the team, opponent, and record for the mountain climbing event are read, the loop condition is tested again. Now the current file position is at the *<eof>* marker, so the function `Eof(sched)` returns `true`. The loop condition `NOT Eof(sched)` is `false`, so the loop exits.

Syntax Box 19.4

Eof

Purpose:

To detect the end of a file.

Syntax:

```
Eof(<file buffer>)
```

Where:

<file buffer> is a variable of type `text`.

Returns:

A `boolean` value.

Usage:

`Eof` returns `true` if the current file position in the file associated with *<file buffer>* is at the file's *<eof>* marker. Otherwise, `Eof` returns `false`.

<file buffer> must have been used in a `Reset` or `Rewrite` statement prior to the call to `Eof`. When the file is initially opened, the value returned by `Eof` is `false`.

Using Eoln as a Sentinel

The *<eoln>* marker also can be used as a sentinel. Let's look at how graphics can be stored in a data file. A picture often is stored in a data file as a series of shapes. Each line of the data file contains a character representing a kind of shape and a series of coordinates. For example, the following data file represents a picture with two shapes:

```
L 0 0 200 200
R 35 35 70 70
```

This data file can be interpreted as a line (indicated by the "L") from (0, 0) to (200, 200) and a rectangle (indicated by the "R") with corners at (35, 35) and (70, 70). In both cases, we know that the shapes can be defined with four coordinates. But how could we specify a primitive with a varying number of coordinate pairs? A polygon, for example, can be specified by three or more coordinate pairs, but we don't want to be forced to use a separate character code for three-sided, four-sided, and *n*-sided polygons. If each primitive must be listed on a separate line, then we can use the *<eoln>* marker as a sentinel. OOPas has a `Eoln` function, described in Syntax Box 19.5, that is analogous to the `Eof` function. `Eoln` returns `true` when the current file position is at an *<eoln>* marker. When `Eoln` returns `true`, we need to use an empty `Readln` statement to move the current file position to the next line.

Syntax Box 19.5

Eoln

Purpose:

To detect the end of a line.

Syntax:

`Eoln(<file buffer>)`

Where:

<file buffer> is a variable of type `text`.

Returns:

A `boolean` value.

Usage:

`Eoln` returns `true` if the current file position in the file associated with *<file buffer>* is at an *<eoln>* marker. Otherwise, `Eoln` returns `false`.

<file buffer> must have been used in a `Reset` or `Rewrite` statement prior to the call to `Eoln`.

By using the `Eoln` function, we can use "P" at the beginning of each line to specify a polygon. The following constructor reads points until *<eoln>*:

```
CONSTRUCTOR Polygon.InitFromFile( VAR aFile : text );
VAR
  x, y : integer;
BEGIN
  WHILE NOT Eoln(aFile) DO
    BEGIN
      Read(aFile, x, y);
      AddPoint(x, y)
    END
END;
```

Similar constructors can read the data for other shapes. Now, using a `CASE` statement, we can read various kinds of primitives:

```
TYPE
  { Line, Rectangle, Polygon classes defined here }
PROCEDURE Drawing.ReadShape( VAR aFile: text);
VAR
  whatKind : char;
  newLine : Line;
  newRect : Rectangle;
  newPoly : Polygon;
```

```
BEGIN
   Read(aFile, whatKind);
   CASE whatKind OF
      'l', 'L' : newLine.InitFromFile(aFile);
      'r', 'R' : newRect.InitFromFile(aFile);
      'p', 'P' : newPoly.InitFromFile(aFile);
   END;
   { Do something with the shape now...}
END;
```

Note that we can't use polymorphism instead of this CASE statement. We don't know what object to create until we've read the letter from the file.

19.5 WRITING TO FILES

Let's complete the sports schedule example. For each game in the schedule, the user wants to output the result of the game as shown:

```
Bowling Green U. 3, Men's Bowling (38-17) 1
```

The winning team is listed on the left. The local team's record is updated and printed in parentheses.

You want to send the output to a file so that the newspaper's typesetting program can print the scoreboard automatically. To tell OOPas that you want to send output to a file, you can designate a file as write-only by using the `Rewrite` command. Like `Reset`, this command takes one parameter — a `text` variable that was previously associated with a file using an `Assign`. The current file position is set to component 0, so that writing will begin at the top of the file. `Rewrite` is described in Syntax Box 19.6.

Once a file has been opened with `Rewrite`, you can write to it with the `Write` and `Writeln` statements. The first parameter to `Write` or `Writeln` must be a `text` variable. `Write` and `Writeln` are analogous to `Read` and `Readln`, except, of course, they don't modify the values of the variables they are writing out. `Write` and `Writeln` are described in Syntax Box 19.7.

`Reset` and `Rewrite` can be used to change a file's status at any time. Be careful when switching a file's status from read-write to write-only. The `Reset` and `Rewrite` statements set the file position back to the top of the file. Changing a file to write-only with `Rewrite` overwrites the file's previous contents.

Syntax Box 19.6

Rewrite

Purpose:

To open a file for write-only access.

Syntax:

```
Rewrite(<file buffer>);
```

Where:

<file buffer> is a variable of type text.

Usage:

This statement opens the file associated with the *<file buffer>*. After this statement, *<file buffer>* can be used as the first parameter in `Write` or `Writeln` statements to send output to the file.

The current file position is set to component 0 (the first of the file).

<file buffer> must have been associated with a file using `Assign` prior to using this statement.

Syntax Box 19.7

Write and Writeln

Purpose:

To send output to a file.

Syntax:

```
Write( <file buf>, <exp 1>, ... , <exp n> );
Writeln( <file buf>, <exp 1>, ... , <exp n> );
```

Where:

<file buf> is a variable of type `text`.

<exp 1> ... *<exp n>* are expressions of any built-in atomic type.

Usage:

The textual representations of the expressions *<exp 1>* through *<exp n>* are sent to the file associated with *<file buf>*.

If no expressions follow *<file buf>* in a `Writeln` statement, a blank line appears in the file.

The current file position moves to the position immediately following the output printed by `Write` or `Writeln`.

`Writeln` adds an *<eoln>* marker after the output.

Summary

Files are used when we want to process a large amount of data. A file contains a set of related information and is stored on an external device. (In all likelihood, the only external devices you have been using are your disks. On other machines, files are stored on magnetic tapes and drums and digital disks.) Each piece of data in a file is called a component; components are numbered in a file starting at 0.

Files can be used in a program in one of three ways — read-only, write-only, and read-write. These terms designate whether the file is open for input, output, or both. Before a file can be used, it must first be opened. OOPas provides three statements for opening files — `Assign` to associate `text` variables with files, `Reset` to open files read-write, and `Rewrite` to open files write-only.

Once the data file has been created, you need a way of referring to it in the program. This is done by declaring a variable of type `text`. The `text` variable is a file buffer, which means it acts as a gateway between the file on the disk and the program.

`Text` variables, when used as the first parameter to `Read`, `Readln`, `Write`, or `Writeln` statements, allow input to come from or output to go to a specified file. When reading from a file, `Readln` differs from `Read` in that after each `Readln`, the current file position moves to the next line.

The *<eof>* and *<eoln>* markers can be used as sentinels. Pascal provides two functions (`Eof` and `Eoln`) that indicate when an end-of-line or end-of-file marker has been found. When the current file position is at an *<eoln>* marker, a `Readln` statement must be used to move the current file position to the next line. When the `Eof` function returns `TRUE`, no more data can be found in the file. Reading beyond the *<eof>* marker will cause your program to crash.

Exercises

Understanding Concepts

1. What are the differences among the commands `Assign`, `Reset`, and `Rewrite`?
2. Given the file:

```
555 1212
406 0531
```

   how many components are in this file if you treat them as integers? as components of type string?
3. In the file in Exercise 2, what is component number 0 if you read the contents as integers? as components of type string?
4. What does the file `Result.txt` contain after this fragment?

```
Assign(resText, 'Result.txt');
Rewrite(resText);
Writeln(resText, 'The first line');
Assign(resText, 'Result.txt');
Rewrite(resText);
Writeln(resText, 'The second line');
```

5. After the following code fragments, where is the current file position? (Assume that `inFile` has been declared as a `text` variable and `current` as a `char`.)

   a.
   ```
   Assign(inFile, 'Some.txt');
   Reset(inFile);
   WHILE NOT Eoln(inFile) DO
     Read(inFile, current);
   ```

   b.
   ```
   Assign(inFile, 'Some.txt');
   Reset(inFile);
   WHILE NOT Eof(inFile) DO
     BEGIN
       WHILE NOT Eoln(inFile) DO
         Read(inFile, current);
       Readln
     END; { while }
   ```

   c.
   ```
   Assign(inFile, 'Some.txt');
   Reset(inFile);
   WHILE NOT Eoln(inFile) DO
     Read(inFile, current);
   Readln(inFile);
   Rewrite(inFile);
   ```

6. What does the following code do? Comment it appropriately.

   ```
   PROGRAM Exercise;
   VAR
     inLine: string;
     file1, file2: text;

   BEGIN
     Assign(file1, 'First.txt');
     Reset(file1);
     Assign(file2, 'Second.txt');
     Reset(file2);

     WHILE NOT Eof(file1) DO
       BEGIN
         Readln(file1, inLine);
         Writeln(file2, inLine)
       END { WHILE }
   END. { Exercise }
   ```

Coding Problems

1. Write a method that concatenates two files. The user should specify two existing files. The contents of these files should then be output so that they can be read on the screen in the order specified.

2. Write a method that deletes the contents of a file. Allow the user to confirm that she really wants to delete the contents.

3. Write a method that allows the user to select any number of files and stores the names of those files in a new file called selections.

4. Write a method that, given a string and a file, prints all lines in the file that contain the specified string.

5. Write a method that compares two files and prints those lines that occur in both files.

6. Write a method that asks a user to enter his or her age, year of graduation, sex, astrological sign, the amount of cash in his or her wallet, and the number of films seen in the last month. Store the information in a file.

7. Modify the previous exercise so that the user also enters a unique ID number. Then write another procedure that, when given an ID number, allows the user to modify the associated information in the file.

8. Write a procedure that uses the file created in Coding Problem 7 and performs some statistical analysis. What is the average amount of cash held by the people in the file? Do seniors see more movies than sophomores? Are there an equal number of male Geminis and female Capricorns? Create your own inquiries into this database.

9. Assume that the block letters A to Z have been stored in files called `blockA.txt`, `blockB.txt`, . . . , `blockZ.txt`. Write a procedure that accepts a string as input and outputs the same string in block letters.

10. Document the code for the following object, and give the Exercise method a more appropriate name. What does the array most contain at the end of the Exercise method?

```
  TYPE
    mostList = ARRAY[0..9] OF integer;

    NumList = OBJECT
      CONSTRUCTOR Init;
      PROCEDURE Exercise;
    PRIVATE
      dataFile: text;
      most: mostList;
    END;

CONSTRUCTOR NumList.Init;
VAR
    ctr: integer;
```

```
BEGIN
  FOR ctr := 0 TO 9 DO
    most[ctr] := 0;
  Assign(dataFile, 'num.txt');
  Reset(dataFile)
END; { Init }
PROCEDURE NumList.Exercise;
VAR
  ctr: integer;
  key: integer;

BEGIN
  Readln(dataFile, key);
  WHILE NOT Eof(dataFile) DO
    BEGIN
      IF most[key mod 10] > key THEN
        most[key mod 10] := key;
      Readln(dataFile, key)
    END
END; { Exercise }
```

Programming Problems

1. Suppose you have two files called `College.txt` and `Grad.txt`. `College.txt` is a list of all undergraduate students; `Grad.txt` is a list of all graduate students. Both files contain names in the form *<last name>*, *<first name>*. Both files also contain one name per line, and both files are in alphabetical order. Write a program that creates a third file called `Univ.txt`. At the end of the program, `Univ.txt` should contain the merged contents of `College.txt` and `Grad.txt` in alphabetical order (this is known as a merge sort). For example, if `College.txt` contains

   ```
   Lofton, Hilary
   Baker, Chip
   ```

   and `Grad.txt` contains

   ```
   Smith, Phil H.
   McCormack, James
   Downes, Mary Ann
   ```

   then `Univ.txt` should end up with

   ```
   Baker, Chip
   Downes, Mary Ann
   Lofton, Hilary
   McCormack, James
   Smith, Phil H.
   ```

2. Create a program to check spelling. This program requires the use of two files — a document and a dictionary. The dictionary consists of a number of entries. Each entry is on two lines — the first line of the entry is the misspelled word,

and the second line of the entry is the correctly spelled word. For example, the dictionary could look like this:

```
TEH
THE
WNAT
WANT
...
```

Your program should work with one line of the document at a time. If the line contains any of the misspelled entries, replace it with the correct spelling. The final output should be a new file with all the correct spellings.

3. Add a Load Picture option to the paint program in Part I. When "Load Picture" is selected, the program should allow the user to choose a file. The file contains all the objects in a picture, and each line in the file contains the information about one object. Each line contains a character (representing the type of object), the position of the object, and, if necessary, the object itself. More specifically, the following formats can appear in the file:

   a. `T` *<horiz> <vert> <string>* — designates a text string. When this line is encountered in the file, <string> should be placed at (<horiz>, <vert>).
   b. `R` *<top> <left> <bottom> <right>* — designates a rectangle. This line should generate a framed rectangle with corners at (*<left>*, *<top>*) and (*<bottom>*, *<right>*).
   c. `O` *<top> <left> <bottom> <right>* — designates an oval. This command is similar to the Rectangle command, but a framed oval is drawn instead of a framed rectangle.
   d. `L` *<horiz1> <vert1> <horiz2> <vert2>* — designates a line. This command should generate a line starting at the point (*<horiz1>*, *<vert1>*) and ending at (*<horiz2>*, *<vert2>*).
   e. `P` *<x1> <y1> . . . <eoln>*— designates a pencil-scribble. It specifies a scribbly line passing through some number of points, starting with *<x1> <y1>*, and continuing through however many points are listed until the end of the line.

   Variation: Add a Start Saving option. This option allows the user to name a file. Then each of the other drawing commands (Line, Text, Rectangle, Oval) draws a shape on the screen and stores the appropriate information in a file, using the preceding formats.

4. Write a Mad Libs program. A Mad Lib is a story with certain words left out. These words are replaced by parts of speech in parentheses. For example, a Mad Lib could start like this:

```
A long, long time ago in a (noun) far, far, away, there lived
a (adjective) boy by the name of (name).
```

This story is in a file. The Mad Libs program should look through the file and ask the user to fill in words at the keyboard. For example, a program using the preceding file as input should first ask the user to enter a noun, followed by an adjective, followed by a name. The rest of the story is not revealed to the user until all the words have been filled. The entire story — with the user's entries replacing the parenthetical expressions — should be output in a new file.

5. Write a simple noninteractive word processing program. In the input file are two types of lines — text and commands. Commands have a period at the beginning of the line; text lines begin with any other character. Your program should copy text from an input file to an output file, one word at a time. In the output file, no line should contain more than 60 characters (including blanks). Words may not be split between lines. Along with text, the following commands can appear in the file, each command on its own line:

   .B — break a line. This means that the current file position should move to the beginning of the next line in the output file.

   .S — skip a line. A blank line should appear in the output file at this position.

   .P — start a new paragraph. The current file position moves to the beginning of the next line in the output file and then prints five spaces.

   .I <spaces> — indent the next lines a number of spaces. Whenever the current file position in the output file is moved to a new line, *<spaces>* number of spaces should be printed at the beginning of the line.

6. Write a program for a multiple-choice quiz. Each question in the quiz has four possible answers, and each answer is assigned a point value. The input comes from a file that could begin as follows:

```
Where do you feel most comfortable?
10 In open areas
20 In crowded elevators
30 In open areas in crowded elevators
40 Perched atop the Empire State Building
What makes you feel the most embarrassed?
...
```

   Each of the questions and possible answers should be displayed on the screen. The user should choose one option. The program should then determine the number of points for the user's option. A new question is then read from the file. The end of the questions is marked by the sentinel STOP.

   The user's point value for all of the questions is totaled. The total is used to print the final message. The final messages correspond to a scale listed after the STOP marking the end of the questions, as follows:

```
STOP
0 100 You like people at a distance.
110 200 You like to be intimate with people
210 300 You aren't sure what you like
310 400 You are King Kong
```
   <eof>

   Thus, if the user scores 250 points on the scale, he should see the message "You aren't sure what you like."

7. Write a program that tests a student's punctuation skills. The program uses two previously prepared files. One file, called `examples.txt`, contains one unpunctuated sentence per line. The other file, called `answers.txt`, is identical to `examples.txt` — except that each sentence has been punctuated. The program should display one sentence at a time from examples. The user responds by

indicating which words should be followed by punctuation, and what mark should follow the selected word. The user should continue to add punctuation until he enters a sentinel. At that point, the program should compare the student's sentence to the correct answer and inform the student of any mistakes.

8. Write an electronic date book that allows a user to store and retrieve dated messages. Your program should allow the user to do two things:
   a. Add messages. The user should be able to enter one-line messages. These messages should be placed in a file called `calendar.txt`. Each message should contain a date in *<month>/<day>* format, as the examples illustrate:
   ```
   9/20 Happy birthday to me.
   2/1 Finish Ground Hog's day shopping.
   ...
   ```
   b. Retrieve messages. When the user enters the current date, the program should output all the messages for today and for the next two days. For example, if the user indicates that today is 3/30, the program should print all messages for 3/30, 3/31, and 4/1.

9. You've learned that the picture on the monitor consists of a series of pixels; if you are using a monochrome monitor, they are colored black or white. To store a picture, you may indicate which pixels are black — you can then assume the remainder are white. Reducing this further, you can store a picture as a sequence of horizontal lines, listing only the starting and stopping points for each horizontal black line. This technique is known as run length encoding. The following is an example of such a file:
   ```
   19 5 18
   21 3 27 61 82
   ...
   ```
   In this file, the first number on each line is a vertical coordinate. Then, each line contains pairs of horizontal coordinates, representing starting and stopping points. These are the borders of the black areas of the picture. Thus, the above file indicates that pixels from (5, 19) to (18, 19), from (3, 21) to (27, 21), and from (61, 21) to (82, 21) should be black. Build a class that draws pictures based on such files.

10. Write a program that quizzes the user on world capitals. Create a file called `WrldCaps.txt`. The file consists of pairs of lines. The first line is a capital and the second is the nation:
    ```
    Ottawa
    Canada
    Manila
    Philippines
    ...
    ```
    The user should indicate whether she wants to see the capital and respond with the nation or vice versa. The user should get three guesses to match the answer before the program moves to the next capital–nation pair. When *<eof>* is reached, the program should tell the user how many times she correctly responded on the first, second, and third guess, and not at all.

Part IV

Data Structures

In this, the final part of the book, we will look at some specific systems. In the systems that we built earlier in the book, we implemented specifications of applications. The systems that we will examine in this section are much more generic than that. Rather than building specific application systems for end users, we will build generic systems for use by programmers.

We've always tried to make our object classes as useful as possible. We're simply taking that idea a little further. Instead of writing complete programs, we will focus on writing libraries that can be used by others to write complete programs.

All the systems we will be learning about are examples of *data structures*. Data structures are collections of instances linked together in various ways. Various data structures are characterized by differing patterns of links and different ways to add and remove instances to the collection.

Before we address data structures, we'll present the only new syntax of this part in Chapter 20, the special procedures `New` and `Dispose`. The procedure `New` lets you create stand-alone instances by providing a link to the new instance and invoking the instance's constructor. These instances live in an arbitrary place in memory and aren't instance variables or local variables of any other object. The procedure `Dispose` lets you get rid of them when you are done. We will use `New` to create the instances we'll place into our data structures.

Chapter 21 will investigate *stacks*. A stack is a simple data structure that keeps one instance on top of another. Like a stack of cafeteria plates in the real world, it is easy to place things on the top of the stack and easy to take things off the top of the stack.

Chapter 22 will examine *queues*. A queue is a data structure much like the queue (or line) you stand in at a movie theater. You get in line at the end. People at the beginning leave the line to enter the theater. Eventually, everyone goes into the theater in order.

Both stacks and queues provide a list of objects. Their principal differences lie in where new objects are added to the list and where old ones are removed. Chapter 23 will study this relationship more generally, looking at a *linked list*. The word "link" is not there by coincidence — since `New` provides a link to a new instance, all of these data structures use links extensively.

While various kinds of lists are extremely useful, not all things in the world are organized into lists. Thus Chapter 24 presents *trees*, structures that branch like real-world trees. Trees often are used to organize instances into hierarchies, such as the containment and inheritance hierarchies that we've seen.

Chapter 25 studies the overall efficiency of these systems. Using a system requires a certain amount of memory, as well as a certain amount of operations such as arithmetic and message sends. Well-designed systems use less memory and fewer operations than poorly designed systems. Analyzing the efficiency of computer programs is an entire field of study itself, so this chapter is only an introduction to this issue.

20 Memory Allocation

20.1 POINTERS

When building large programs, we would like to be able to model elements that aren't limited in size by some predetermined constant. For example, a simulation of an ecosystem might grow very large. Suppose the ecosystem is subarctic timberland. The simulation then might include rabbits that live in the underbrush and foxes that feed on the rabbits. The population of either the foxes or the rabbits might grow to an arbitrary size. If we tried to model the population of rabbits with an array, and the rabbits bred a great deal (as rabbits often do), the population of the rabbits might grow beyond the size of the array. Our simulation then would fail.

As it happens, the rabbit population won't grow without limit. As more rabbits are born, the foxes will find it easier to eat a rabbit. As a result of the greater availability of food, more foxes will be born and survive. The increased fox population soon will cause the rabbit population to decline. When it does, foxes will starve, and the fox population will decline as well. Neither the size of the fox population nor the size of the rabbit population will grow beyond a certain point. It might be tempting to think that this means we can model the two populations with arrays. The problem is that while a population won't grow too large, we really have no idea how big either population will be at its maximum size, and that may be the very information that we're trying to find out.

In general, when we build a very large program, we simply don't know beforehand how many instances it will need, so we can't use fixed-sized collections of objects like arrays or sets. However, we can use links, also known as *pointers*, to make arbitrarily large collections of objects. When we first saw pointers, in Chapter 5, we saw how to use the symbol @ to make a link to an existing object. If we're to build large collections, though, we'll have to make links to entirely new objects, objects that didn't exist before, rather than ones declared as instance variables or local variables. To make these links, we need to *allocate memory*.

20.2 POINTERS IN REAL LIFE

A link is first and foremost a design concept. When designing objects, we determine which objects need to talk to other objects, leading us to link these objects. We have been implementing links in OOPas using *pointers*, although we have continued to use the term "link" to make the correspondence between the design and the implementation apparent. A pointer is a variable that contains not an instance but rather *the address* of an instance that is stored somewhere in the computer's main memory. Thus it "points" to the value. This is exactly how we've been using links all along.

An example of pointers in real life is the card catalog system in a library. A card does not hold the contents of a book, but it does tell you the book's location (address) in the stacks. Thus each card can be considered a "pointer" to a certain piece of data. Figure 20.1 illustrates how the cards in a card catalog "point" to books.

Figure 20.1

Pointers in a library

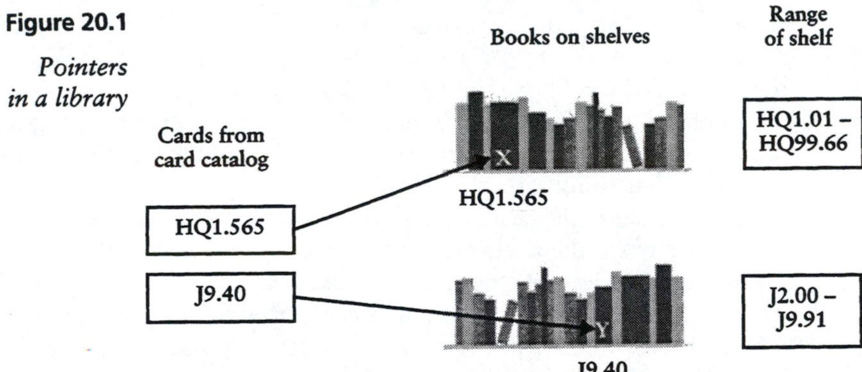

The advantages that computer scientists derive from their pointers are similar to those that librarians derive from their catalog systems. Librarians can arrange their cataloging system by changing the locations of cards in the card catalog, not the locations of all the books on the shelves. For instance, almost every library has two card catalogs — one organized by author and title and the other organized by subject. It's easy to have two sets of cards organized in different ways, but it would be impossible to have two complete sets of books organized in different ways.

If the library received a collection of rare books as a gift, it might put those books together in one safe place. It would still index, however, the books by author and subject and would file the cards for the rare books with those for the other books, even though the two sets of books would remain in separate parts of the library. In a similar way, pointers simplify data management. We made use of this capability in our paint program when we could change what interactor a drawing area used by changing a link (by changing a pointer).

Now, we will use pointers for large lists of instances, rather than the three or four instances we used in the paint program. We will be able to regroup our lists of instances without moving the instances. If we were using an array and wanted to reorganize the objects in the array, we would have to move the objects physically from one array slot to another, much as we would have to move books around on a shelf if we didn't have a card catalog.

20.3 POINTERS IN MEMORY

Let's review the syntax for links, making the correspondence between links and pointers clear. To define a pointer type, we must declare the type of data at which it will be pointing. In the following example `ThingAsn` has been declared as a type of pointer that points to instances of the class `Thing` and `newThingLink` is a pointer variable of that type:

```
TYPE
  ThingAsn = ^Thing;
  Thing = OBJECT
    { methods here }
  PRIVATE
    { private methods and instance variables here }
  END;
VAR
  newThing : Thing;
  newThingLink : ThingAsn;
```

Previously, we have given values to links (or, as we now know, pointers) by creating an instance and then assigning the instance's address (using the `@` operator) to the link, as in

```
newThing.Init;
newThingLink := @newThing;
```

The result here is shown in Figure 20.2. Our earlier object diagrams are a convenient abstraction; in reality, `newThingLink` is a memory address where the beginning of the `newThing` instance starts. Figure 20.2 shows that an instance of the `Thing` class starts at memory location `14B2` (memory locations usually are referred to in hexadecimal — base 16 — notation[1]). The `newThingLink` pointer, then, simply stores the value of that address. The advantage of point-

1. While binary notation had only two digits, 1 and 0, hexadecimal has 16. To identify digits above 9, we use letters. Thus the first 16 hexadecimal numbers are 0, 1, 2, 3, 4, 5, 6, 7, 8, 9, A, B, C, D, E, F.

ers is that we never have to deal with the actual memory addresses. We simply use the syntax provided for using links (such as @ and ^) and OOPas handles the actual addresses for us.

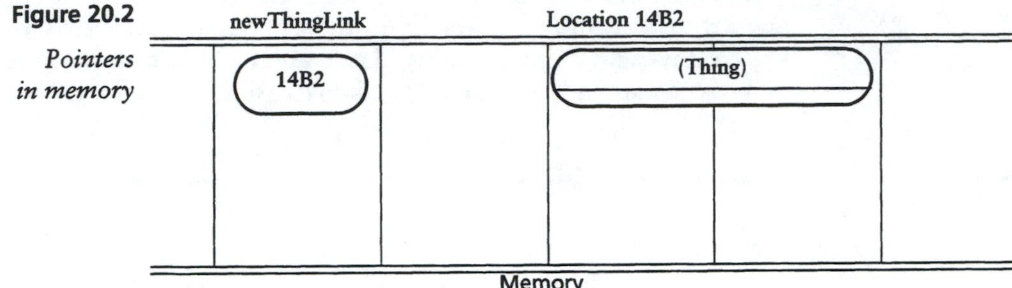

Figure 20.2 *Pointers in memory*

20.4 AN APPLICATION: UNDO

Let's write a drawing program that can draw a variety of shapes using tools selected from a palette of buttons, as in our paint program in Chapter 8. We'd like to add a new capability to our paint program — the ability to undo the last drawing action performed, or "Undo" for short.

When using a drawing program — or any program for that matter — you may find that you've made a mistake. You may choose the wrong endpoint for a corner accidentally or simply decide that you don't want the shape in your drawing. The Undo command allows you to correct mistakes by reversing the effect of the most recent command. Thus, when we want to Undo the drawing of a shape, we can erase the shape from the screen, as in Figure 20.3.

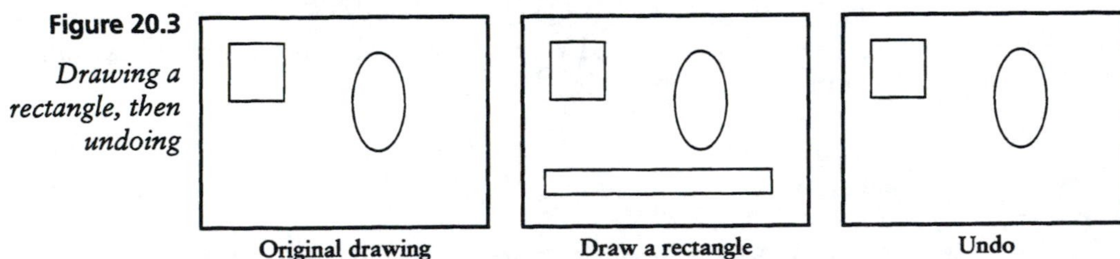

Figure 20.3 *Drawing a rectangle, then undoing*

Undo is probably the most valuable command in any interactive system. It allows the user to experiment without having to start over and protects her from mistakes. Let's describe what undo should do in a bit more detail.

Our paint program now will provide an "Undo" button. Whenever Undo is clicked, the last action the user performed will be reversed. Clicking Undo additional times will have no effect until something else is drawn.

Following our design rule of thumb, we can extract nouns from this specification. The one we're interested in right now is "the last action the user performed." This is a very generic concept — the user could have done any number of things, from clearing the entire drawing to drawing a long complex squiggly line.

So we'll use an abstract base class that models "actions performed in this application." Notice that the phrase "actions performed in this application" doesn't include any mention of painting. Thus, this action class will be general-purpose enough that we can use it in other applications as well, such as text editors and financial spreadsheets. In fact, keeping that generalization in mind, we'll model "editing actions" — drawing actions edit the canvas in our paint program, typing characters edit the text in a word processor, and selecting a new formula edits the matrix of rows and columns in a spreadsheet.

Our editing actions should be able to do two things — perform their action and reverse the effects. The Undo button will make use of reversal only. Before, a button (such as a Clear button) would send the messages we're now going to encapsulate in an action object. Thus the `Activate` method for buttons will simply send a `DoIt` message to an `Action`. Since these are editing actions, we'll put them in a unit called "EditActions," or "EA" for short:

```
EAActionAsn = ^EAAction;
EAAction = OBJECT
  CONSTRUCTOR Init;
  PROCEDURE DoIt; VIRTUAL;
  PROCEDURE UndoIt; VIRTUAL;
END;
```

The methods for this object are all quite simple — `EAAction` is an abstract class, so all of the virtual methods provide empty bodies. Since `EAAction` has no instance variables, the constructor doesn't need to initialize anything except the virtual methods themselves, which OOPas does automatically in the constructor. Hence all the methods of this class are simple `BEGIN/END` pairs.

```
CONSTRUCTOR EAAction.Init;
BEGIN
END;

PROCEDURE EAAction.DoIt;
BEGIN
END;

PROCEDURE EAAction.UndoIt;
BEGIN
END;
```

This concept of a general action as an instance is powerful and flexible. We will use actions only for undoing, although they also can be used for such tasks as building and executing macros or scripts or keeping a history of a program's execution.

Now, let's define a sample action — drawing (and erasing) a shape. Of course, this action object will have a link to a `GPShape` so that it can use polymorphism to draw any kind of shape. We can pass this link to the action in its constructor. We will also need a link to the drawing area the shape was drawn in. Finally, to keep our action general, we will need a link to a copy of the drawing style in effect when the action was performed, so that the action can be sure to `UndoIt` exactly what it performed when sent `DoIt`.

```
EADrawShapeAction = OBJECT(EAAction)
  CONSTRUCTOR Init(
      newShapeLink      : GPShapeAsn;
      newDALink         : GPDrawingAreaAsn);
  PROCEDURE DoIt; VIRTUAL;
  PROCEDURE UndoIt; VIRTUAL;
PRIVATE
  shapeLink : GPShapeAsn;
  drawingAreaLink : GPDrawingAreaAsn;
  styleLink : GPDrawingStyleAsn;
END;
```

We will leave constructing the action for later. Performing the action is fairly simple, consisting of two steps. First, the drawing style is copied from the drawing area in case the drawing area's style is modified between when this action is told `DoIt` and when it is told `UndoIt`. The `Copy` method is something we will look at in more detail shortly. Second, the shape is drawn:

```
PROCEDURE EADrawShapeAction.DoIt;
BEGIN
  styleLink := drawingAreaLink^.GetStyle;
  styleLink := styleLink^.Copy;
  shapeLink^.DrawWithStyle(drawingAreaLink, styleLink)
END;
```

Reversing the action for our paint program just means erasing the shape, which we will do by drawing the shape in white, the background color. This may not be exactly what we want, because it won't leave the drawing the way it was if the shape was drawn on top of other shapes (the other shapes will have parts erased as well). We will see how we can completely undo the drawing to its previous state in subsequent chapters.

```
PROCEDURE EADrawShapeAction.UndoIt;
VAR
  eraseColor : GPColor;
```

```
BEGIN
   eraseColor.InitAsWhite;
   styleLink^.SetDrawingForeground(eraseColor);
   shapeLink^.DrawWithStyle(drawingAreaLink, styleLink)
END;
```

Of course, we can create other sorts of actions, such as clearing a drawing area or choosing a tool or drawing color. These are left as exercises.

20.5 USING *NEW* TO MAKE OBJECTS

Each time the user draws a shape, an action is performed, specifically, a drawing action like the one we just defined. We can model "performing a drawing action" by creating an instance of `EADrawShapeAction`, then sending it the message `DoIt`. Since each action is something separate, we'd like to make a new one each time a shape is drawn.

To make a new drawing action when we need it, we will use the `New` statement to allocate memory. In a nutshell, `New` looks through the computer's unused memory until it finds a piece big enough to hold a new object. The procedure `New` then sets aside that piece of memory for the object and returns a pointer to it. This is called *dynamic memory allocation*, or simply memory allocation. In addition, `New` can call a constructor to initialize the object the memory holds.

The procedure `New` is a bit unusual. You can use it in three different ways. One syntax looks like a procedure, and another looks like a function that takes one parameter, but that "parameter" is the name of a type, something you can't use as a parameter. The third syntax looks like a function taking two arguments, one a type name and the other a call to a constructor (as if the constructor were a function, which it isn't).

The most common way to use `New` is to use the form that takes two parameters. We use this form because it is the only one that allows us to invoke a constructor for the instance that we are creating. The first parameter of this form of `New` is a *type*, specifically, the association corresponding to the instance to create. The legal types for this parameter are as follows:

1. The type of association declared for the link on the left side of the :=
2. An association to any subclass of that association's class.

Thus, if `newActionLink` is declared as a pointer of type `EAActionAsn`, we can use `EAActionAsn` as the first parameter to `New`. Because of polymorphism, we also could use an association to any subclass of `EAAction`, such as `EADrawShapeActionAsn`, as the first parameter.

The second parameter is a constructor. This is essentially the same as calling a function in a parameter list, except we don't expect to have anything returned. We simply name the constructor that we want to initialize the instance. Now, instances can have more than one constructor, but only one constructor can be called for any instance. For example, `GPPoint` has both an `Init` and an `InitWithCoords` constructor. For this reason, the `New` method requires us to indicate which constructor should be used to initialize the instance. If the constructor requires parameters, we can include those parameters as part of the `New` message. The syntax for `New` is described in Syntax Box 20.1, including the use of both parameters.

Syntax Box 20.1

New

Purpose:

To allocate space for an instance of a class.

Syntax:

```
New( <link> );
<link> := New(<association type>);
<link> := New(<association type>, <constructor name>);
```

Where:

<link> is a pointer to an instance.

<association type> is the type of link we want to create. If *<link>* is an instance of *<link association type>*, then *<association type>* can be the same as *<link association type>* or a subclass of *<link association type>*.

<constructor name> is the name of the constructor for the class to which *<association type>* links. If the constructor takes parameters, actual parameters should be listed in parentheses after the *<constructor name>*.

Usage:

In general, `New` allocates memory for an object of a particular type. If *<association type>* is present, it identifies the type of the object that `New` makes. If the type is not explicitly listed (as in the procedural form), the type of object to which the pointer variable *<link>* points indicates what type of object `New` will create. If the constructor is listed (including parameters), that constructor will be called (with any passed parameters) to initialize the object. Otherwise, no constructor is called.

The function forms of `New` then return a pointer to that instance, which is assigned to *<link>*. The procedure form of `New` treats its parameter as a `VAR` parameter, assigning the pointer variable the pointer to the newly created instance.

If you will want a link to one of the subclasses, you should declare *<link>* to be a link to an instance of the superclass of those subclasses.

Versions of `New` that do not take a constructor can allocate memory for built-in types as well, such as `integer` and `real`.

Let's use `New` to make a new drawing action at the right time. First, we need a button the user can click on to undo an action.

```
EAUndoButtonAsn = ^EAUndoButton;
EAUndoButton = OBJECT(GPPushButton)
  CONSTRUCTOR Init(containerLink: GPManagerAsn);
  PROCEDURE Activate; VIRTUAL;
  PROCEDURE LastActionWas( newLastActionLink : EAActionAsn );
PRIVATE
  lastActionLink : EAActionAsn;
END;
```

The link `lastActionLink` will be initialized to `NIL`. So, when the user clicks on the button, causing the `Run` method to call `Activate`, the button should call the `UndoIt` method of `lastActionLink`, but only if the link isn't `NIL`. The `LastActionWas` method simply sets the `lastActionLink` pointer.

```
PROCEDURE EAUndoButton.Activate;
BEGIN
  IF lastActionLink <> NIL THEN
    lastActionLink^.UndoIt
END;
```

Now, we need to extend the interactor we built in Chapter 8 so that it builds an action when the shape has been drawn by the user. To do this, we'll of course need a link to the Undo button:

```
EAUndoableRubberbandInteractor = OBJECT(PRubberbandInteractor)
  { This stores the button link and calls INHERITED Init. }
  CONSTRUCTOR Init(
      newUndoBtnLink   : EAUndoButtonAsn;
      newTargetLink    : GPDrawingAreaAsn;
      newShapeLink     : PRubberShapeAsn);
  PROCEDURE ButtonUp( point : GPPoint ); VIRTUAL;
PRIVATE
  undoButtonLink : EAUndoButtonAsn;
END;
```

We only need to redefine the method `ButtonUp`, because it needs to make an action and give it to the undo button. Since we still need to handle the last point the user entered as before, we will also call `INHERITED ButtonUp`:

```
PROCEDURE EAUndoableRubberbandInteractor.ButtonUp(point: GPPoint);
VAR
  lastActionLink : EAActionAsn;
BEGIN
  INHERITED ButtonUp(point);
```

```
    lastActionLink := New(EADrawShapeActionAsn, Init(shapeLink,
              targetLink);
    lastActionLink^.DoIt; { Perform the action. }
    undoButtonLink^.LastActionWas(lastActionLink)
  END;
```

20.6 GETTING RID OF OLD OBJECTS

When we allocate some memory, we could throw it out when we're done with it. This practice is wasteful, however, given that we can recycle the memory and reuse it for some other purpose, such as a different object.

We used constructors to build our objects, and we used the `New` function to have a place to build them. Now, we'll use *destructors* to tear them down when we're done with them, and we'll use `Dispose` to recycle the memory used to hold them.

Dispose: Releasing the Memory

Suppose we've just drawn a rectangle, giving an action to the Undo button. If we draw a second rectangle, the Undo button receives a new action. The old one is no longer necessary. If `LastActionWas` simply assigns the `lastActionLink` pointer to be the pointer to the new action, the pointer to the old action no longer is stored anywhere. We can't get to the old action anymore. But, if we discard the pointer to an instance, not only can't we gain access to the information in the instance, but OOPas can't use the space it occupies in memory. Since we don't need the information, it is a good idea to free up the memory so that OOpas can later recycle it, using a `Dispose` statement that is the inverse of the `New` statement. You supply the `Dispose` statement with the address of the object you no longer need to use, and it frees up that block of memory so it can be used again. The `Dispose` procedure is described in Syntax Box 20.2.

Destructors: Cleaning Up After the Object

When you dispose of one object, it might have other objects it would like to dispose of itself. A *destructor* is a special method we can use to handle this situation. The destructor is complementary to the constructor: The constructor builds the object, while the destructor demolishes it.

For example, the constructor for `EADrawShapeAction` is given a link to the shape. If the constructor assigns that link to the instance variable `shapeLink`, what happens if the shape itself is edited by some other object, such as an instance of `PRubberbandInteractor` (which may be, as we saw earlier, what

Syntax Box 20.2

Dispose

Purpose:

To free unused storage.

Syntax:

```
Dispose(<link>);
Dispose(<link>, <destructor name>);
```

Where:

<link> is a pointer to any instance or type.

<destructor name> is the name of the destructor for the object.

Usage:

The `Dispose` procedure is used to release a block of memory. When you are finished with an instance that you are accessing via a link, the `Dispose` procedure tells OOPas that the memory is no longer needed and allows OOPas to recycle those memory locations in a later `New`.

If the *<destructor name>* is included, the destructor is called before the memory is released.

made the action in the first place)? If the action is told to undo itself, it inadvertently will undo the drawing of the new shape rather than the original shape it was supposed to undo. Thus the constructor calls the virtual method `Copy`, which is defined for all kinds of `GPShape`. This method allocates memory for a shape using `New`, filling in all the appropriate instance variables. We also used `Copy` for the drawing style in `DoIt`. Now the action will undo the shape exactly as it was.

```
CONSTRUCTOR EADrawShapeAction.Init(
       newShapeLink : GPShapeAsn;
       newDALink : GPDrawingAreaAsn );
BEGIN
  INHERITED Init;
  shapeLink := newShapeLink^.Copy;
  drawingAreaLink := newDALink;
  styleLink := NIL; { Don't set this until we DoIt. }
END;
```

But what will happen when we `Dispose` of this drawing action? We've told OOPas that it can reuse the memory for the action itself. Given that we've destroyed the action, however, we have no way to access `shapeLink`, and thus we have another object "lost in space" whose memory has been wasted. The same thing happens if this action receives the message `DoIt` — it will have copied the drawing style as well.

In addition to procedures, functions, and constructors, OOPas provides one other method type called the *destructor.* If the constructor does something, the destructor should undo it. In our case, it would `Dispose` of the copy of the object. So let's add a destructor to our `EADrawShapeAction` — we'll add it to `EAAction`, as well, since we can dispose of any action.

```
EAActionAsn = ^EAAction;
EAAction = OBJECT
  CONSTRUCTOR Init;
  DESTRUCTOR Done; VIRTUAL;
  PROCEDURE DoIt; VIRTUAL;
  PROCEDURE UndoIt; VIRTUAL;
END;

EADrawShapeAction = OBJECT(EAAction)
  CONSTRUCTOR Init(newShapeLink : GPShapeAsn; newDALink :
              GPDrawingAreaAsn);
  DESTRUCTOR Done; VIRTUAL;
  PROCEDURE DoIt; VIRTUAL;
  PROCEDURE UndoIt; VIRTUAL;
PRIVATE
  shapeLink : GPShapeAsn;
  drawingAreaLink : GPDrawingAreaAsn;
  styleLink : GPDrawingStyleAsn;
END;
```

Note that we simply need to use the keyword `DESTRUCTOR`, just as we used `CONSTRUCTOR` when identifying the constructor in a class definition or method definition, as described in Syntax Box 20.3. The action's destructor itself simply calls `Dispose` on the shape link.

```
DESTRUCTOR EADrawShapeAction.Done;
BEGIN
  Dispose(shapeLink, Done);
  IF styleLink <> NIL THEN {i.e., if the action was told DoIt }
    Dispose(styleLink, Done);
  INHERITED Done
END;
```

Note that the call to `Dispose` calls the shape's destructor as well, as described in Syntax Box 20.2. Further note that this destructor also calls its superclass's destructor, so the superclass can dispose of objects it may have allocated.

Destructors almost always should be `VIRTUAL`. Consider what would happen if you had a pointer to `EAAction` and `Disposed` it, calling `Done` in the process. Remember how OOPas determines what method to call for virtual methods versus nonvirtual methods. A virtual method calls the instance's ver-

Syntax Box 20.3
DESTRUCTOR

Purpose:

To destroy an object when it is no longer needed.

Syntax:

```
DESTRUCTOR <destructor name>; VIRTUAL;
```

Where:

<destructor name> is the name of the destructor for the object.

Usage:

The destructor is used to destroy an object when it no longer is needed. Typically, it will `Dispose` of memory that the object allocated itself.

A destructor can be virtual, and almost always should be, allowing a pointer to the superclass to be `Disposed` properly.

sion of a method, whereas a nonvirtual method calls the version defined by the class named in the association type (see Section 6.3). If `Done` wasn't virtual, then we'd be back in the same boat as when we had no destructor — `EAAction.Done` would be called, not `EADrawShapeAction.Done`, and the copied shape would not be disposed of properly. Thus the only time a destructor should not be virtual is when it is defined for a class that has no virtual methods (a situation that is extremely rare).

Summary

In this chapter, we discussed pointers. Pointers, which we have been calling links for most of this book, point to locations in the computer's memory. By reorganizing a list of pointers, we can reorganize our objects without having to move the objects themselves.

Previously, we have used pointers only to point to objects that existed somewhere else. Using `New`, we were able to allocate a piece of memory to hold a completely new object. This procedure provides a pointer to the newly created object. Also, `New` provides a way to call the constructor for the object, letting it be constructed in the correct way.

When done with an object we created with `New`, we should `Dispose` of it. This tells OOPas that the memory that was being used before now is available to be used by some other object. A destructor can clean up for an object, disposing of any memory it may have allocated when it was created. The `Dispose` procedure is provided in a form that allows the destructor to be called, much as `New` exists in a form allowing the constructor to be called.

Exercises

Understanding Concepts

1. Explain some of the problems that can occur if you do not use `Dispose`.
2. What's wrong with the following code sample? If an instance of `Exercise` is created as a local variable, how many objects will it try to make?

```
ExerciseAsn = ^Exercise;
Exercise = OBJECT
  CONSTRUCTOR Init;
PRIVATE
  nextExercise : ExerciseAsn;
END;
CONSTRUCTOR Exercise.Init;
BEGIN
  nextExercise := New(ExerciseAsn, Init)
END;
```

3. Suppose `myItem` is an instance of an object that begins at memory location 2000 and is 8 bytes long. If we have the assignment statement `myItemLink := @myItem;` what does `myItemLink` contain?
4. Suppose `firstItem` and `secondItem` are instances of the same class and that `myItemLink` is declared as a link to an instance of that class. Show what happens in memory with the following sequence:

```
myItemLink := @firstItem;
myItemLink := @secondItem;
```

5. What are the differences among each of the three versions of `New`?
6. Describe the difference between `DESTRUCTOR` methods and the `Dispose` procedure.
7. Why should destructors be virtual?

Coding Problems

1. Modify the paint program of Chapter 7 by allowing the user to revert back to the last color chosen. (That is, a "Last Color" button should automatically select the color used prior to the current color.)
2. Extend Coding Problem 1 by writing actions for other user actions in the paint program in Chapter 8, such as clearing the drawing area, selecting a tool, or any other actions you may have added in other exercises. Obviously, exiting the program need not be done using an action — it can't be undone.
3. Write the `EAUndoButton.LastActionWas` method, so that it properly disposes of an action at the right time. In addition, make sure that an action can't be

undone more than once — if an action is undone by the user's clicking on the button, dispose of the action. Note that disposing of an object does not make the pointer to that object `NIL` — you must assign the pointer `NIL` yourself.

Use the following definition for Coding Problems 4–6:

```
TYPE
  ThingAsn = ^Thing;
  Thing = OBJECT
    CONSTRUCTOR Init(newName: string);
    ...
  END;
VAR
  thingLink : ThingAsn;
```

4. Allocate memory for a new instance of `Thing` using the `New` procedure.
5. Allocate memory for a new instance of `Thing` using the two different forms of the `New` function.
6. Define an array of 20 elements, where each element is a `ThingAsn`. Then, allocate memory for each element in the array.
7. Write a method that merges two sorted arrays. The method should receive two parameters, each containing an array with ten sorted integers. The method should create a new array of 20 elements, including all of the elements of the two parameter arrays in sorted order.

Programming Problems

1. An extension of the "feel free to experiment" idea is to revert Undo commands with Redo commands. Redo commands undo undone actions. In other words, a Redo restores the data to its state before the Undo. Implement a push button that redoes the last action that was undone. You will need to provide a slightly different Undo button, since it won't dispose of an action at the same time as an Undo button that doesn't need to be able to redo an action. Make sure you call `Dispose` at all the right places.
2. Extend the paint program from Chapter 8 with an Undo button. You may want to use the code defined in Section 13.3.
3. Extend the paint program by allowing a user to reposition the last object drawn. The user should be able to click on a new location and see the object in that new place.
4. Modify the Aquarium program (last seen in Chapter 8), so that when a fish or a shark hits a wall (the edge of the aquarium), it reverses direction.
5. Create a grid of 200×200 squares. Color one of the corners red and the opposite corner blue. These two corners will be the starts of two paths. In alternating turns, extend each path, choosing one of the blank squares adjacent to the

end of the current path and filling it with the current color (this newly filled square now is considered the end of the current path). Note that a path cannot be extended onto paths of either color. The program ends when one color is blocked, when there are no more blank squares adjacent to the end of the path.

6. Modify Programming Problem 5 by having the computer always choose the blank square that is farthest from the end of the other path.

7. Modify the previous problem by allowing the user to select which direction the path should go. (You may want to allow the user to control one color, or allow two users to control both colors.)

8. Extend the paint program of Programming Problem 2 to provide ten "levels" of undo. The user should be able to undo the last ten actions and redo any actions that have been undone. You will want to use an array of ten links to instances of `EAAction` to provide ten levels of undo. Be careful to set these links to `NIL` when necessary. You will also want to use `MOD` to specify which link in the array corresponds to the current action. This will make it easier to handle the eleventh action uniformly.

21

Stacks

21.1 USING LINKS TO MAKE COLLECTIONS

Let's continue with the example we began with in Chapter 20. We started with what is called single-level undo, meaning we could undo only the most recent drawing action. Sometimes we'd like to be able to undo an arbitrary number of operations, a feature sometimes called *unlimited undo*. One way we could provide multiple undoable actions is by using an array of pointers to actions.

Arrays wouldn't allow unlimited undo, however, because we would have to declare the size of the array when writing the program. Further, if we ran out of indices in the array, we couldn't enlarge the array during the program's execution. We would have to change the array bounds and recompile the program, which of course doesn't help the user that ran out of array indices.

However, we've just learned how to create new objects by employing currently unused memory in the computer. Using this feature, we can make collections of objects (in particular, a collection of undoable actions) of arbitrary size. Like the chain of elephants in Figure 21.1, each holding the next one's tail, any one object can point to another, a technique we saw way back in Chapter 5. If one object points to another, that second object can point to a third, and on and on. Our chain of elephants, or objects, can go on for as long as we'd like.

Figure 21.1 *One elephant holds the next one by the tail.*

The next few chapters deal with this idea and the different collections of objects we can build by connecting objects in different ways. The first collection we'll look at is called a *stack*.

21.2 STACKS: A DESCRIPTION

A *stack* is a data structure for storing lists of instances. Elements in the stack are processed in LIFO — last in, first out — order. The stack works like a stack of plates in a cafeteria. Consider a cafeteria line: Each person passing the plates takes the top one off the stack. As people finish eating and dishes are washed, a kitchen worker comes along and places several clean plates on top of the stack, burying the plate that was on top. The last plate put on top will be the first plate removed, hence the plates are put on the stack in LIFO order.

This brief description shows us the two behaviors stacks provide, *push* and *pop*. When a new element is placed on the top of the stack, we say it has been pushed on the stack. Figure 21.2 shows how a plate is pushed on a stack. Elements also may be lifted off the top of the stack, as shown in Figure 21.3. When an item is removed, we say it has been *popped* from the stack.

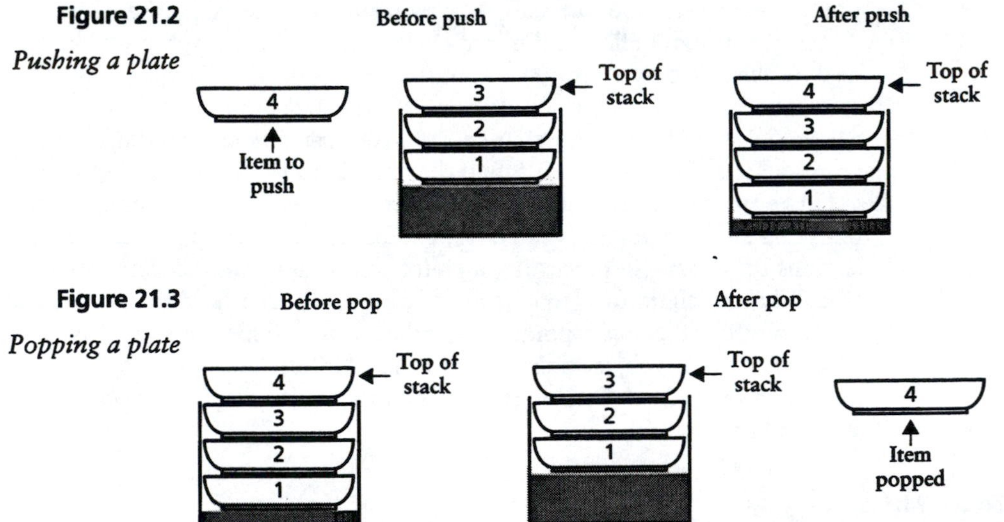

Figure 21.2 *Pushing a plate*

Figure 21.3 *Popping a plate*

The most important point to remember about stacks is that we can gain access to only one element at any time. We can pop only the top element off the stack; we can push elements only onto the top of the stack. We cannot gain access to any elements in the middle or on the bottom of the stack. The processes of pushing and popping are useful when you want to enter elements in one order and access them in reverse order.

21.3 AN APPLICATION: UNLIMITED UNDO

To implement a simple Undo command, we must keep track of the order in which actions are performed. The last drawing command to be executed is the first to be undone, so we can keep track of the actions in a stack. As each action is executed, we can push the action onto the stack, and each time the Undo command is selected, we can pop an action off the stack.

When the program begins, the program window appears, including the palettes of tools and the drawing area. Let's say that the user first chooses to draw a rectangle. She drags out her rectangle, and when she releases the button, an instance of `EADrawRectangleAction` is pushed onto the stack of drawing commands. At this point, the screen and stack look like Figure 21.4. (In the diagrams, we use letters to label the shapes.) Now, let's say that the user decides to drawn an oval, followed by another rectangle. The program asks the user for the endpoints of each shape, draws the shape on the screen, and pushes the information on the stack. We now have three shapes on the screen and three commands in the stack, as shown in Figure 21.5.

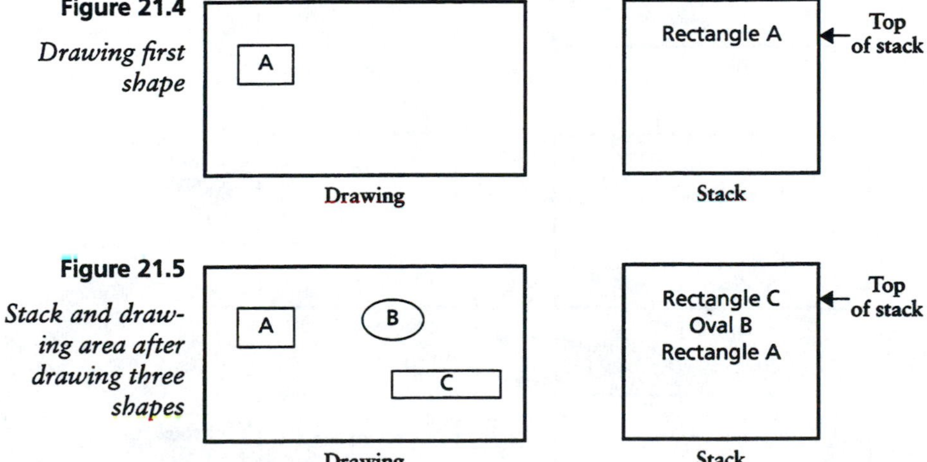

Figure 21.4 *Drawing first shape*

Figure 21.5 *Stack and drawing area after drawing three shapes*

Looking at the screen, the user decides that she doesn't want that last rectangle. To remove it, she chooses the Undo button. We then pop the most recently drawn shape — rectangle C. We erase that rectangle from the screen, as seen in Figure 21.6. Then, the user decides to draw an oval. After she draws the oval, the shape is pushed on the stack (see Figure 21.7).

Now, the user decides that she wants to start all over again. Our undo button allows her to undo all the shapes to the beginning. When the user first picks undo, the shape at the top of the stack (oval D) is popped and erased from the screen (Figure 21.8). When the user next chooses Undo, the program pops oval B, since that shape has moved to the top of the stack (Figure 21.9).

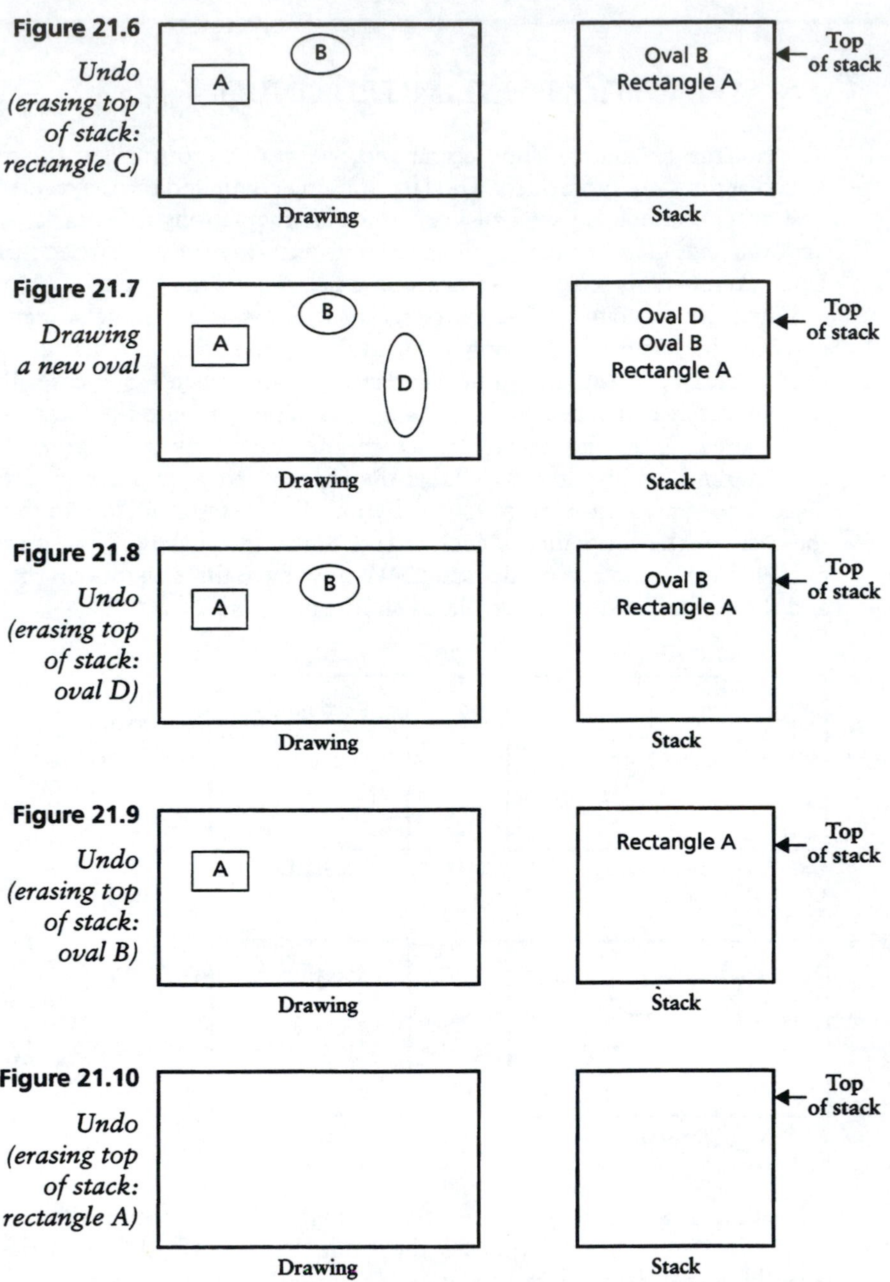

Figure 21.6 *Undo (erasing top of stack: rectangle C)*

Figure 21.7 *Drawing a new oval*

Figure 21.8 *Undo (erasing top of stack: oval D)*

Figure 21.9 *Undo (erasing top of stack: oval B)*

Figure 21.10 *Undo (erasing top of stack: rectangle A)*

The next Undo removes the remaining shape from the screen (Figure 21.10). If the user chooses Undo yet again, nothing should happen on the screen, since the stack is empty.

21.4 STACKS: DEFINING THE CLASS

We also can think about stacks as a collection of elements. Since we're implementing undo, the elements we're collecting in our stack are actions like `EADrawShapeAction` we used in Chapter 20. We have identified four operations that the stack should be able to perform:

CLASS: Stack
CONSTRUCTOR Init;
  Initialize the stack
PROCEDURE Push(<*element to be pushed onto stack*>);
  Adds <*element to be pushed*> to the top of the stack
FUNCTION Pop: <*element removed from stack*>;
  Removes the top of the stack and returns the <*element*>
FUNCTION Empty : boolean;
  Returns true if the stack is empty, false otherwise

This is the basic interface to our stack. We will provide one class that has exactly these methods. Because this class is only the interface to the stack, we still need the stack's implementation. First, we need the elements we wish our stack to contain; in this case, they are instances of `EAAction`. However, things that are pushed in a stack know things that instances of `EAAction` don't know. For example, a pushed element knows what is underneath it in the stack. We will make new classes called *nodes* to provide this functionality. A node will have two links, one to whatever node is underneath it, and another to the element it "contains" (using links to model containment in order to take advantage of polymorphism). Thus, we have three kinds of objects — the interface to the stack, the implementation nodes, and the contained elements. This design is shown in Figure 21.11.

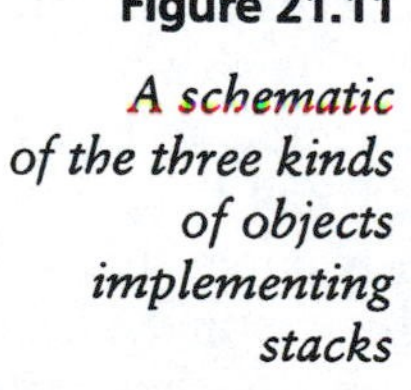

Figure 21.11
A schematic of the three kinds of objects implementing stacks

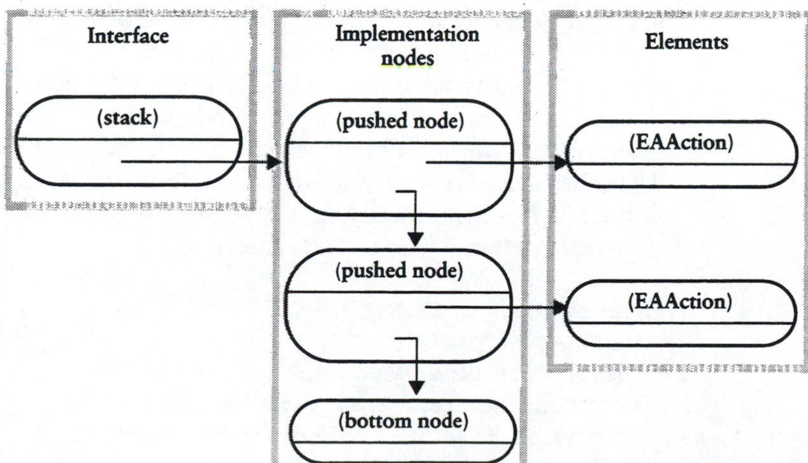

There are two kinds of nodes in the stack. The first type of node in a stack is the bottom of the stack. If we try to take off the bottom of the stack, we will fail because the stack is empty. The second type of node is a pushed node. Each pushed node will have a pointer to the node *beneath* it, as well as a pointer to the element that it contains. Hence, we can implement a class for stacks of `EAActions` as follows:

```
EAStackNodeAsn = ^EAStackNode;
EAStack = OBJECT
  CONSTRUCTOR Init;
  DESTRUCTOR Done; VIRTUAL;
  PROCEDURE Push(newPALink: EAActionAsn); VIRTUAL;
  FUNCTION Pop: EAActionAsn; VIRTUAL;
  FUNCTION Empty: boolean; VIRTUAL;
PRIVATE
  topLink : EAStackNodeAsn;
END;
```

The `EAStackNode` class is a base class for the bottom of the stack and for pushed items. The stack itself is just a pointer to whatever happens to be the top item (or node) of the stack. Notice that most of the stack's methods are virtual. This is a generic stack of actions, though not abstract. The methods `Push`, `Pop`, and `Empty` will all behave appropriately. Thus we'll make an undo stack by subclassing from this one, redefining `Pop` to do what it does in this one (by calling `INHERITED Pop`), as well as calling the `Undo` method of the action. We'll just as easily be able to make a redo stack that redoes actions that were undone earlier: Items popped off the undo stack can be pushed onto the redo stack. Popping something from the redo stack will `Do` the action and return it to the undo stack.

But first, let's look at the nodes of our stack — the bottom node and pushed nodes. We should provide a base class for them, as we just mentioned, but first we must decide exactly what a generic node of the stack needs to do. Since we've already decided that we can implement a stack by having something in the stack point to whatever is underneath it, we'll need to be able to find out the next node underneath any given node of the stack. We'll call this method `NextNode` and we will have it return a pointer to whatever is under the node. The other thing we'll need to do with a node of a stack (besides make it and destroy it) is retrieve the action it is storing. We'll do this with a method called `GetAction`, returning an `EAActionAsn`:

```
EAStackNode = OBJECT
  CONSTRUCTOR Init;
  DESTRUCTOR Done; VIRTUAL;
  FUNCTION NextNode : EAStackNodeAsn; VIRTUAL;
  FUNCTION GetAction : EAActionAsn; VIRTUAL;
PRIVATE
END;
```

All these methods are pure virtual functions, so we won't write them down here (though you can find them in the software distribution). Instead, we'll move on to describing the subclasses of `EAStackNode`.

The first one we'll define will be the bottom of the stack. The class description is simple: It simply is a repeat of the class description for the base class, since the bottom of the stack needs no instance variables:

```
EAStackBottomNode = OBJECT(EAStackNode)
   CONSTRUCTOR Init;
   DESTRUCTOR Done; VIRTUAL;
   FUNCTION NextNode : EAStackNodeAsn; VIRTUAL;
   FUNCTION GetAction : EAActionAsn; VIRTUAL;
PRIVATE
END;
```

The methods `Init` and `Done` are simple — they call their `INHERITED` versions. The `NextNode` and `GetAction` methods are also both quite simple — they both return `NIL`. The method `NextNode` returns `NIL` because, by definition, there is nothing underneath the stack. The method `GetAction` returns `NIL` because the bottom of the stack is like the bottom of the stack of plates — there's no plate there and thus no action on the bottom of our undo stack. The complete methods can be found in the software distribution as well.

The class for pushed nodes is a bit more interesting. The constructor now takes two parameters — a pointer to the action that this node contains, and a pointer to whatever node is underneath this pushed node (the "next" node). `EAPushedActionNode` thus has two instance variables to hold these pointers. The `NextNode` and `GetAction` methods simply return the relevant pointers.

```
EAPushedActionNode = OBJECT(EAStackNode)
   CONSTRUCTOR Init(
        newPALink          : EAActionAsn;
        newNextLink        : EAStackNodeAsn);
   DESTRUCTOR Done; VIRTUAL;
   FUNCTION NextNode : EAStackNodeAsn; VIRTUAL;
   FUNCTION GetAction : EAActionAsn; VIRTUAL;
PRIVATE
  pushedActionLink : EAActionAsn;
  nextLink : EAStackNodeAsn;
END;

CONSTRUCTOR EAPushedActionNode.Init(
        newPALink          : EAActionAsn;
        newNextLink        : EAStacknodeAsn );
BEGIN
  pushedActionLink := newPALink;
  nextLink := newNextLink
END;
```

```
DESTRUCTOR EAPushedActionNode.Done;
BEGIN
  INHERITED Done
END;

FUNCTION EAPushedActionNode.NextNode : EAStackNodeAsn;
BEGIN
  NextNode := nextLink
END;

FUNCTION EAPushedActionNode.GetAction : EAActionAsn;
BEGIN
  GetAction := pushedActionLink
END;
```

Though it might not seem like it, these extremely simple classes provide enough machinery for us to implement the interface provided by our `EAStack` class. Now we'll examine each of the methods we need to define for our stack.

21.5 INITIALIZING THE STACK

When created, the stack should be empty. Thus we need to create the bottom of the stack and make sure the pointer in `EAStack` for the top of the stack points to this new instance of `EAStackBottomNode`, as in this method:

```
CONSTRUCTOR EAStack.Init;
BEGIN
  topLink := New(EAStackBottomNodeAsn; Init)
END;
```

The result of this code is the simple stack shown in Figure 21.12.

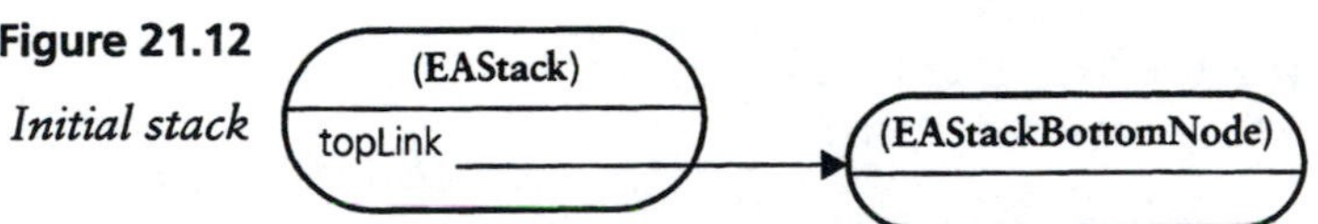

Figure 21.12 *Initial stack*

21.6 PUSHING AN ELEMENT ON THE STACK

Let's suppose that an empty stack is sent the message `Push`. The stack and the parameter to `Push` are shown in Figure 21.13. The method `Push` now must make a new `EAPushedActionNode`, telling it what is underneath it and what the action should be. The action is simply the action passed as `newPALink`. Whatever is currently on top right now will be underneath the new pushed action. Pushing a new action means we need to have a new top of the stack.

Figure 21.13

Beginning a call to EAStack.Push

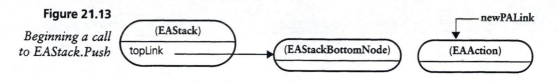

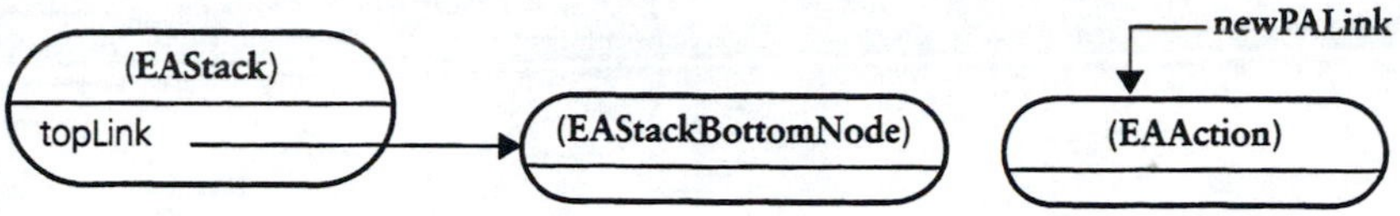

```
PROCEDURE EAStack.Push( newPALink : EAActionAsn );
BEGIN
  topLink := New(EAPushedActionNodeAsn, Init(newPALink, topLink))
END;
```

The call to `New` creates a new `EAPushedActionNode`, as shown in Figure 21.14. The assignment of the return from `New` resets the top of the stack to point to the pushed action, as seen in Figure 21.15. Another push, with a new action, produces the stack seen in Figure 21.16.

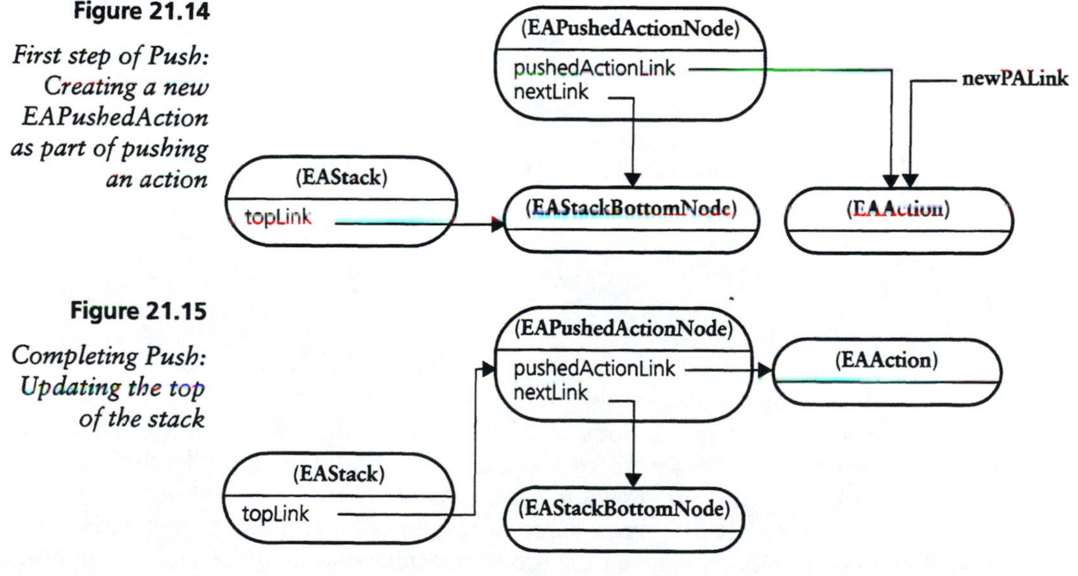

Figure 21.14

First step of Push: Creating a new EAPushedAction as part of pushing an action

Figure 21.15

Completing Push: Updating the top of the stack

21.7 POPPING AN ELEMENT FROM THE STACK

Popping an element off of the top of the stack involves taking whatever is at the top, getting whatever node is underneath it (the `NextNode`), and making

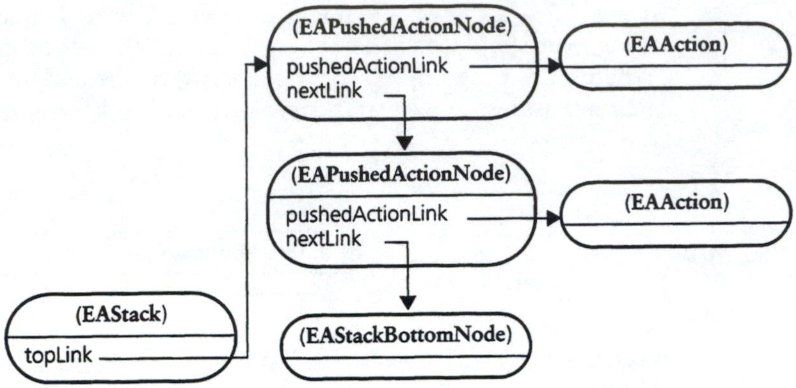

Figure 21.16

A stack with two actions pushed on it

this lower node the new top of the stack. We do have to be careful to check for the bottom of the stack and do nothing if we try to `Pop` the bottom.

```
FUNCTION EAStack.Pop : EAActionAsn;
VAR
  newTopLink : EAStackNodeAsn;
BEGIN
  newTopLink := topLink^.NextNode;
  IF newTopLink <> NIL THEN
    BEGIN
      Pop := topLink^.GetAction;
      Dispose(topLink, Done);
      topLink := newTopLink
    END
  ELSE
    Pop := NIL
END;
```

Using our stack of two items from Figure 21.16, let's look at the steps of this method. First, we ask the top of the stack for whatever node is underneath it. If there is nothing underneath it, the stack is empty and `NIL` is returned. In our case, there is a node underneath the top node; the stack along with `newTopLink` is shown in Figure 21.17.

We then set the return value of the function to point to the action in the `EAPushedActionLink` on the top of the stack and then `Dispose` of the pushed action. The last step is to set the real top of the stack to point at the new top. These steps are illustrated in Figure 21.18. The final resulting stack is the same as the stack in Figure 21.15.

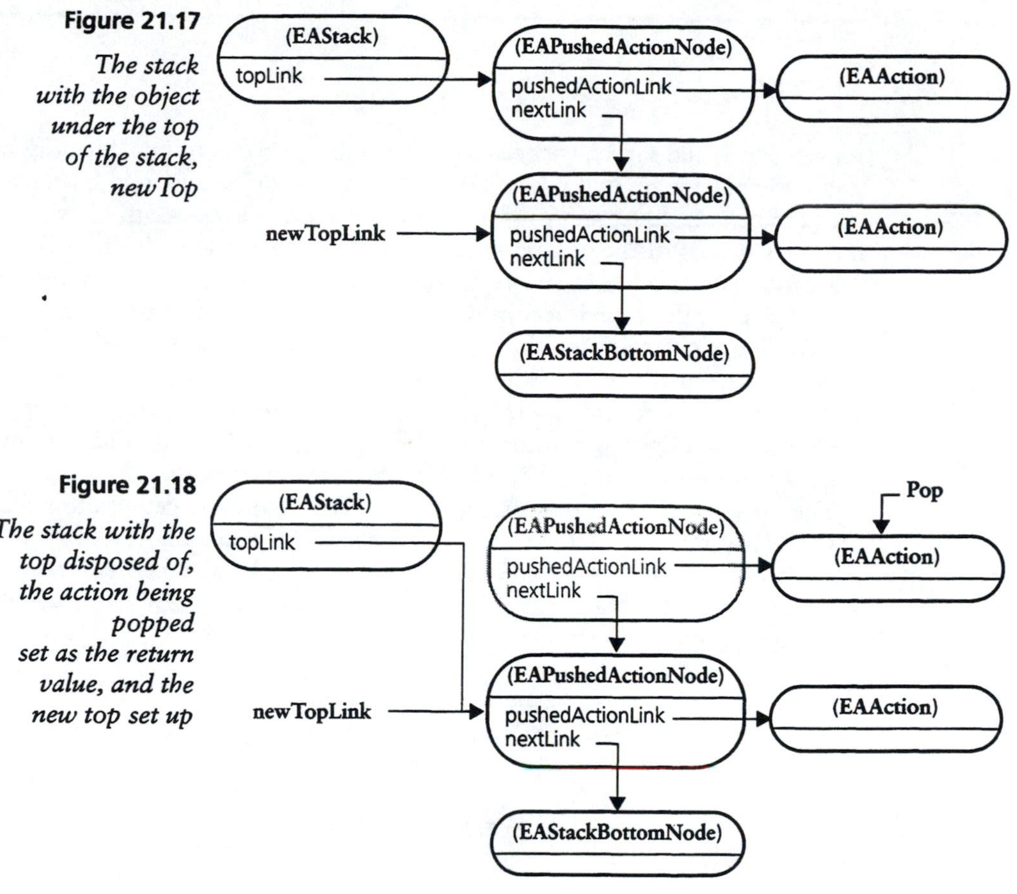

Figure 21.17 *The stack with the object under the top of the stack, newTop*

Figure 21.18 *The stack with the top disposed of, the action being popped set as the return value, and the new top set up*

21.8 CHECKING WHETHER A STACK IS EMPTY

Sometimes, it is useful to know whether there is anything in a stack. The `Empty` method is performed simply by seeing whether there is anything under the top of the stack. If not, then `top` actually is pointing to an instance of `EAStackBottom`, meaning that the stack itself is empty.

```
FUNCTION EAStack.Empty : boolean;
BEGIN
  Empty := topLink^.Nextnode = NIL
END;
```

21.9 MAKING AN UNDO STACK

As we mentioned earlier, we need to do something special to implement unlimited undo. There are two possibilities: We could provide an Undo button that uses the generic stack and calls `Undo` on any actions it pops off, or we could make a subclass of the generic stack of actions, causing `Pop` also to call `Undo`. To some extent, this is a subtle design decision, depending on exactly what results you'd like to produce. In this case, it might be better to use the latter design. We might want multiple ways for the user to perform undo — either selecting it from a menu, clicking on a button in a panel, or even hitting a special key on the keyboard (some keyboards even have keys labeled "Undo"). If the stack of actions were inside a button, it would be harder to have a menu item, a panel button, and a key all share the same undo stack.

The only thing we need to change is `Pop`. Thus our class definition includes only the `Pop` method — all the others are the same, including the constructor and destructor. The method `Pop` itself is simple: It calls the inherited version of `Pop` and then calls undo on the return value, unless the return value was `NIL`, meaning the stack was empty:

```
EAUndoStack = OBJECT(EAStack)
  FUNCTION Pop : EAActionAsn; VIRTUAL;
END;

FUNCTION EAUndoStack.Pop : EAActionAsn;
VAR
  tempActionLink : EAActionAsn;
BEGIN
  tempActionLink := INHERITED Pop;
  IF tempActionLink <> NIL THEN
    tempActionLink^.Undo;
  Pop := tempActionLink
END;
```

You might ask why `Pop` doesn't destroy the action. It looks like we've done everything with it that we want to do. Besides the fact that `Pop` still needs to return something useful, we can use this stack in other ways to provide greater capabilities. A similar class can provide a "redo stack" — actions that are undone are pushed onto the redo stack. Popping off of the redo stack calls the action's `Do` method and returns the action to the undo stack.

Summary

In this chapter, we learned about stacks. A stack is a collection of objects that can be added and removed in a LIFO — last-in, first-out — order, like plates in a physical stack. We built a stack of actions to implement unlimited undo.

A stack supports four basic operations:

1. Initialization: The stack is constructed. Initially, a stack has no elements in it. This is known as an empty stack.
2. Pushing an element onto the stack: An element is added to the top of the stack. This may be performed repeatedly.
3. Popping an element from the stack: An element is removed from the top of the stack. If the stack is empty, this operation fails. A number of pushes followed by an equal number of pops always results in the same stack.
4. Determining emptiness: A boolean indicating whether or not the stack is empty.

Stacks are simple, yet quite powerful despite their simplicity. They are the first way we have learned to make an arbitrary sized collection of objects.

Exercises

Understanding Concepts

1. Could a stack be implemented with an array? How? Why are stacks usually implemented using pointers?
2. If it is possible, show how you can push the data 1, 2, 3, 4 (in order) on a stack and pop them in the order 2, 3, 1, 4 from a single stack.
3. Why is it not possible, using the input 1, 2, 3, 4, to manipulate a single stack (with pushes and pops) so that they can be popped in the order 3, 1, 4, 2?
4. In the following sequence, the command `Push <x>` adds the datum *<x>* to a stack; `Pop` pops an item and outputs it. What is the resulting output?

```
Push A, Pop, Push B, Push C, Pop, Push D, Pop, Push E, Pop, Pop
```

Programming Problems

1. Add a push button to the paint program of Chapter 8 that undoes painting actions. Use the undo stack. Don't forget to augment the interactors to place actions on the undo stack.
2. Unlimited undo has a potential drawback — the stack can grow so large that the computer runs out of memory. Implement a stack that has a `Flush` method. `Flush` should pop every action on the stack, without undoing any of them. Each action should be discarded; the stack should be left empty. Provide a button in the user interface to flush the undo stack.

3. Modify the last program by adding a Redo button. This option is an undo of an undo. For example, if the user draws an oval and chooses Undo, the oval disappears. If the user then chooses Redo, the oval reappears. Redo can reverse the actions only of the Undo commands following the last action (an action being defined, in this case, as a Draw or Delete command). This means that if the user draws four shapes and then chooses Undo three times, Redo can be chosen three times. However, if the user draws four shapes, chooses Undo three times and then draws another shape, Redo has no effect because there is no Undo following the last action. There should be unlimited levels of redo, just as there are unlimited levels of undo. The flush button also should flush the redo stack.

4. Modify the Calculator program of Chapter 9, Programming Problem 3, by adding buttons for left and right parentheses. (*Hint*: Keep a stack of running totals. Left and right parentheses should correspond to a push and pop, respectively.)

5. Write a program to deal cards. The program should generate a stack of all 52 cards. Then, it should ask the user how many players are in the hand, and how many cards each gets. The program should show all of the cards that each player gets. (You may start by representing each card as a simple text, like 9H for nine of hearts and JC for jack of clubs. For the more aesthetically inclined, you might think about how you might draw the cards in some way.)

6. Write a program to simulate the following scenario. Suppose you have eight blocks, numbered from 1 to 8. The number 1 block is smaller than the number 2 block, which is smaller than the number 3 block, and so on, up to the number 8 block. The computer should make stacks of blocks. It should pick one of the blocks at random and begin a stack that we'll call Stack A. Then, it should pick any of the other blocks at random. If it is smaller than the block at the top of Stack A, it should be placed on Stack A. Otherwise, it should create a new Stack B. For each block, the program looks through the stacks, starting with A. If the current block is smaller than the block on top of the stack, the block is placed on the stack. Otherwise, the program looks at the next stack. If the block is not smaller than the block on top of any stack, a new stack is created. The program should show the stacks and indicate how many stacks are created. (If you run the simulation 100 times, what is the average number of stacks that are created?)

7. Modify the blocks in Programming Problem 6 as follows. Suppose there is a 10 percent chance that after a block is placed, a two-year-old appears and knocks over exactly one of the stacks. The blocks from that stack are then put back in the pile of blocks that can be chosen. (You may also want to have multiple sets of blocks; that is, say, four sets of blocks where each set has 8 blocks numbered from 1 to 8.)

22

Queues

22.1 REAL-LIFE QUEUES

An example of a *queue* is a line of people, one after the other, like the line that forms at the ticket counters at movie theaters. The first person in line is the first one to get into the movie. The people in a line get tickets in a first-come, first-served order. Unlike stacks, queues work on a FIFO — first in, first out — basis.

By looking at a group of people in an orderly line, we can establish some of the characteristics of queues. Knowing those characteristics, we can model them in OOPas. We then will be able to build queues of any length, containing many sorts of objects, just as we built stacks in Chapter 21. As we did for stacks, we will implement three kinds of objects — the interface, the nodes that implement that interface, and the elements that the queue contains.

The first thing we can see about a queue is that it has three kinds of nodes — the beginning, the middle, and the end. Elements are added to a queue at the end and taken out of the queue at the beginning. Any number of things can be in the middle of the line. The beginning of the line is called the *head* of the queue, and the end is called the *tail* of the queue.

A Brief Description of Queues

This brief description of queues also provides us with an overview of the operations we can perform on queues. We can add an item to the queue, an operation called *enqueueing* and depicted in Figure 22.1 as a person gets into the queue from the end. Taking an item from the beginning of the queue is called *dequeueing*, as is illustrated in Figure 22.2.

We then can say we have the following operations:

Figure 22.1

Enqueueing: Adding an item to the end of the queue

Before enqueueing

1 2 3 4

Head of queue Tail of queue Person to add

After enqueueing

1 2 3 4

Head of queue Tail of queue

Figure 22.2

Dequeueing: Removing something from the beginning of the queue

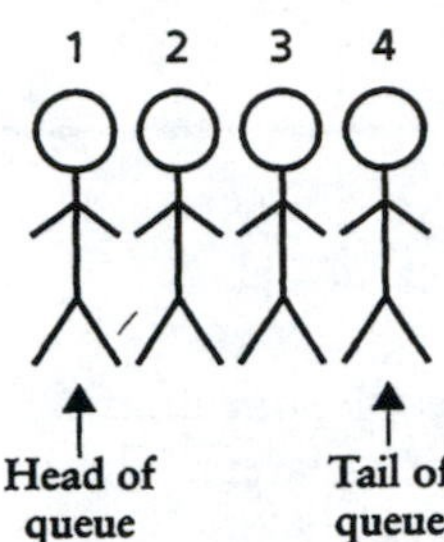

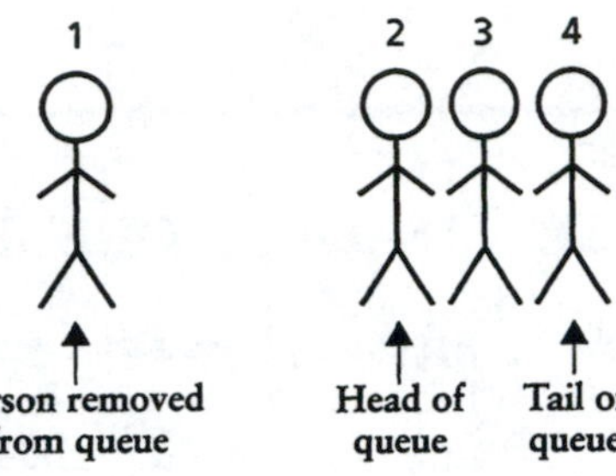

CLASS: Queue
CONSTRUCTOR Init;
  Initializes a queue
FUNCTION Empty: boolean;
  Returns true if the queue is empty, false otherwise
PROCEDURE Enqueue(*<element to add>*);
  Adds the *<element to add>* to the tail of the queue
PROCEDURE Dequeue: *<element returned>*;
  Removes the element at the head of the queue and returns it

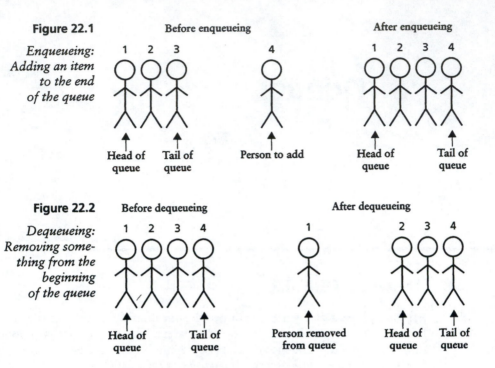

There is a lot of similarity between the basic operations of a stack and a queue. Both have a behavior to add an element (one was called push, while the other is called dequeue), and both have a behavior to remove an element (pop and dequeue). Both also know whether or not they are empty.

We could generalize the stack and the queue to reflect this similarity. Our generalization could be called a "collection," and we'd rename the push, pop, enqueue, and dequeue methods appropriately and provide a suitable constructor and a method to check for emptiness:

Collection
CONSTRUCTOR Init;
PROCEDURE AddElement(*<element to add>*); VIRTUAL;
FUNCTION RemoveElement : *<element returned>*; VIRTUAL;
FUNCTION Empty : boolean; VIRTUAL;

Stack (subclass of Collection)
CONSTRUCTOR Init;
PROCEDURE AddElement(<*element to add*>); VIRTUAL;
FUNCTION RemoveElement : <*element returned*>; VIRTUAL;
FUNCTION Empty : boolean; VIRTUAL;

Queue (subclass of Collection)
CONSTRUCTOR Init;
PROCEDURE AddElement(<*element to add*>); VIRTUAL;
FUNCTION RemoveElement : <*element returned*>; VIRTUAL;
FUNCTION Empty : boolean; VIRTUAL;

We won't generalize our two classes in this way, however, for two reasons. First, our stack was a stack of actions, whereas our queue is a queue of moviegoers. Since we can't change the types of any parameters when we redefine a virtual method, we couldn't build the classes this way. We could make a more specific collection, however, such as a "Collection of Actions" and create two subclasses — "Stack of Actions" and "Queue of Actions." This has been left as an exercise. Second, we'd like to use different names for the first two subclasses, to emphasize how these classes behave differently.

Implementing Queues: An Overview

Handling the head of the queue is easy. Essentially, we can look at the head of the queue as the top of a stack. We can dequeue an item using code that resembles the code we used to pop an item off a stack. We enqueue an item differently, however. With a stack, we added items in the same place we removed them. With a queue, we need to add items at the other end.

When we implemented our stack, the bottom of the stack had no members. We could implement the bottom this way because the bottom of the stack never needed to send a message to another object — the bottom was self-contained. However, the tail of our queue must be able to add an item, and so it needs to tell whatever is the last item in the queue what the new last item in the queue should be. This will ensure that the head of the queue always will be able to find the next item to dequeue after dequeueing any item. We can see a schematic of this in Figure 22.3.

This leads us to conclude that an empty queue is modeled by two instances — the head and the tail, each pointing to each other. This also implies that both the head and the tail are nodes, since they both need to point to queued items and to each other (unlike a stack, where the top was simply a link in the interface class `EAStack` and the bottom never pointed to the top). This is diagrammed in Figure 22.4.

We must be alert for one special case of enqueueing and dequeueing: dequeueing the last item in the queue. The head will point to the tail, since the head always points to the next item after anything is dequeued. But the queue

Figure 22.3

The tail needs to tell the last item about the new end of the queue so that the old end of the queue can point to the new end of the queue.

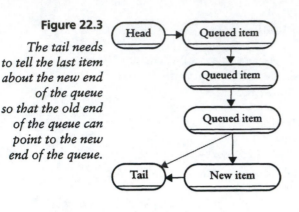

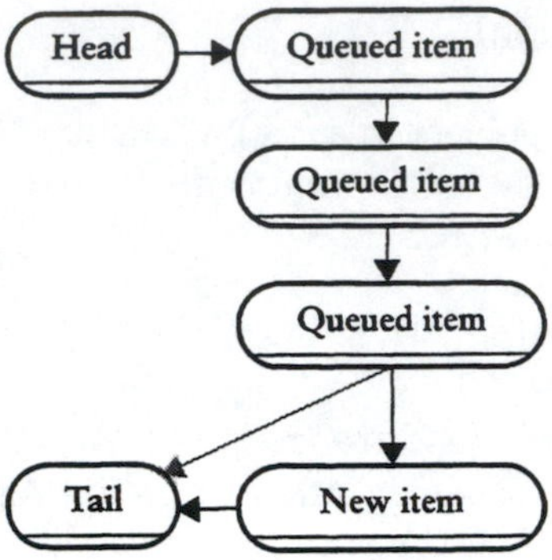

Figure 22.4

An empty queue consists of a head pointing to a tail and vice versa.

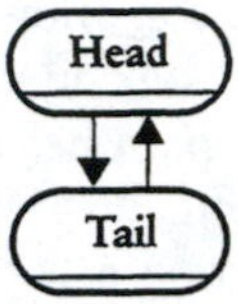

is now empty. Whenever the queue becomes empty, the tail must point to the head instead of the node it was pointing to. This is illustrated in Figure 22.5.

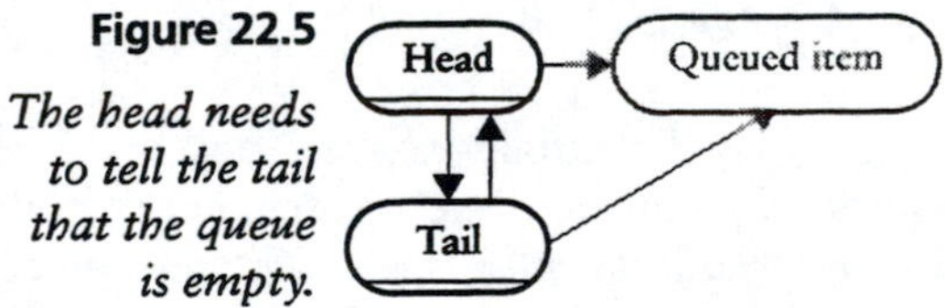

Figure 22.5

The head needs to tell the tail that the queue is empty.

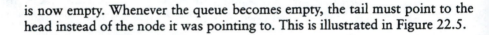

Since the head doesn't know how long the queue is, we can handle this situation by having the head send a message to the new leading item whenever something is dequeued. We'll call this message `NowAtHead`. A queued item simply will ignore this message, but the tail of the queue will use it to note that it needs to point to a different node.

22.2 THE PARTS OF THE QUEUE

From the diagrams in the last section, and from the description of what the queue and the nodes contain and need to be able to do, we can develop our class declarations. We'll start with the elements we'll contain in the queue. Sticking with our movie-goer example, we'll make a queue of people waiting to get into a theater. Since this is a small example, we'll keep the people simple: They'll be able to draw themselves. Since this is a queue of movie-goers waiting to get into a theater, we'll call the unit these classes are in `MovieQueue`, or `MQ` for short.

```
UNIT MovieQueue;
USES GraphicsPackage;
INTERFACE
TYPE
  MQMovieGoerAsn = ^MQMovieGoer;

  MQMovieGoer = OBJECT
    CONSTRUCTOR Init;
    PROCEDURE Draw(drawingAreaLink: GPDrawingAreaAsn); VIRTUAL;
  END;
```

Having pseudocoded our interface in Section 22.1 and described our elements, we need to describe the different kinds of nodes in our queue. We'll start with a base class. Following the pattern of our stack classes, we'll have methods to get the next node (which is essentially the same as for the stack) and to get the movie-goer in the queue (which corresponds to getting the action from a stack node). We'll also need a method to tell a node in the queue that it has a different node following it (for when a node is at the end and a new node is enqueued behind it), and a method to tell an item that it has gotten to the head of the queue (to handle the case where the last node is dequeued, as mentioned earlier). This `MQQueueNode` class is a pure virtual class, so we won't bother to show the implementations of all the methods. As always, they can be found in the software distribution.

```
MQQueueNodeAsn = ^MQQueueNode;
MQQueueNode = OBJECT
  CONSTRUCTOR    Init;
  DESTRUCTOR     Done; VIRTUAL;
  PROCEDURE      NewNextNode(newNextLink:MQQueueNodeAsn);VIRTUAL;
  PROCEDURE      NowAtHead(headLink : MQQueueNodeAsn); VIRTUAL;
  FUNCTION       GetNextNode : MQQueueNodeAsn; VIRTUAL;
  FUNCTION       GetMovieGoer : MQMovieGoerAsn; VIRTUAL;
END;
```

Now, we need objects for the specific kinds of nodes of a queue. Starting with the head, it will contain one pointer to the first node in the queue that contains an element (or the tail if there is no such node). It also will provide a method to dequeue an item. Since an empty queue consists merely of the head and the tail, the head itself can't provide a movie-goer. Thus the head doesn't override the method `GetMovieGoer`. Similarly, the head never moves to the head of the queue, so is never told that it is `NowAtHead`.

```
MQHeadNode = OBJECT (MQQueueNode)
  CONSTRUCTOR     Init;
  DESTRUCTOR      Done;                         VIRTUAL;
  FUNCTION        Dequeue : MQMovieGoerAsn;     VIRTUAL;
  PROCEDURE       NewNextNode(newNextLink:MQQueueNodeAsn);VIRTUAL;
  FUNCTION        GetNextNode : MQQueueNodeAsn; VIRTUAL;
PRIVATE
  nextLink : MQQueueNodeAsn;
END;
```

Note that technically this violates our definition of an abstract class — this class (and others in this queue) will have empty virtual methods, but we will be constructing instances of them. In this case, however, our methods truly do nothing. Thus the class, although seemingly abstract, actually is concrete.

We now need an object to hold the movie-goers in the queue. We'll call these nodes "internal" nodes. The class MQInternalNode will have two pointers, one to the next node and one to the movie-goer, much like the class EAPushedActionNode in the previous chapter. The constructor takes pointers to the next node and to the movie-goer as parameters. Instances of the class ignore the message NowAtHead, so the default (abstract) implementation of that virtual method is sufficient, but all the other methods defined by MQQueueNode will be overridden.

```
MQInternalNode = OBJECT (MQQueueNode)
  CONSTRUCTOR     Init(
      newMovieGoerLink : MQMovieGoerAsn;
      newNextLink      : MQQueueNodeAsn );
  DESTRUCTOR Done;  VIRTUAL;
  PROCEDURE       NewNextNode(newNextLink:MQQueueNodeAsn);VIRTUAL;
  FUNCTION        GetNextNode : MQQueueNodeAsn; VIRTUAL;
  FUNCTION        GetMovieGoer : MQMovieGoerAsn; VIRTUAL;
PRIVATE
  movieGoerLink : MQMovieGoerAsn;
  nextLink      : MQQueueNodeAsn;
END;
```

We also need a kind of node for the end of the queue. It needs to provide a method to enqueue a new movie-goer. It also needs to provide an overriding method NowAtHead. Its only instance variable will be a link to the last MQInternalNode in the queue, or else the head if the queue is empty.

```
MQTailNode = OBJECT (MQQueueNode)
  CONSTRUCTOR     Init(newAheadOfMeLink : MQQueueNodeAsn);
  DESTRUCTOR      Done; VIRTUAL;
  PROCEDURE       Enqueue(newMGLink : MQMovieGoerAsn); VIRTUAL;
  PROCEDURE       NowAtHead(newPrevLink : MQQueueNodeAsn);VIRTUAL;
```

```
PRIVATE
  prevLink        : MQQueueNodeAsn;
END;
```

Finally, we can provide a class definition for the queue itself, the interface object. The queue will have two methods: `Enqueue` and `DeQueue`. It also will have two instance variables corresponding to the head and the tail of the queue. Notice that these are instance variables, not links as they were in the stack. We will see why in the next section.

```
MQQueue = OBJECT
  CONSTRUCTOR     Init;
  DESTRUCTOR      Done; VIRTUAL;
  PROCEDURE       Enqueue(newMGLink : MQMovieGoerAsn); VIRTUAL;
  FUNCTION        Dequeue : MQMovieGoerAsn; VIRTUAL;
PRIVATE
  head : MQHeadNode;
  tail : MQTailNode;
END;
```

22.3 INITIALIZING THE QUEUE

We'll begin implementing methods by considering how we initialize the queue. Figure 22.4 showed that the initial queue contains a head node and a tail node. Each of these nodes has a link that points at the other. Therefore, when we send the `Init` messages to `head` and `tail`, we pass each node a link to the other as a parameter. Thus we can rewrite the pseudocode as follows:

MQQueue.Init
Purpose: Initializes the queue
  Initializes the head node sending a link to the tail
  Initializes the tail node sending a link to the head

MQHeadNode.Init
Purpose: Initializes the head node
  Set nextLink instance variable to new tail node

MQTailNode.Init
Purpose: Initializes the tail node
  Set prevLink instance variable to point to the head

Notice that each node needs a link to the other. If the tail were pointed to by a link and thus initialized with `New`, we wouldn't know what link to pass to the head until we had constructed the tail, but we can't construct the tail without a link to a head. However, `@` applied to an instance variable will return the same address whether or not the object has been constructed, because construction doesn't move the object in memory. Thus we use instance variables.

We can then put these methods together with the following code:

```
CONSTRUCTOR MQQueue.Init;
BEGIN
  head.Init(@tail);
  tail.Init(@head)
END;

CONSTRUCTOR MQHeadNode.Init(newNextLink: MQQueueNodeAsn);
BEGIN
  INHERITED Init;
  nextLink := newNextLink
END;

CONSTRUCTOR MQTailNode.Init(newPrevLink: MQQueueNodeAsn);
BEGIN
  INHERITED Init;
  prevLink := newPrevLink
END;
```

Let's walk through this code. When we begin, the `MQQueue` node receives the `Init` message. Its first statement is to send an `Init` message, passing a link to the yet uninitialized `tail`, as shown in Figure 22.6.

Figure 22.6

Queue instance creating new head node

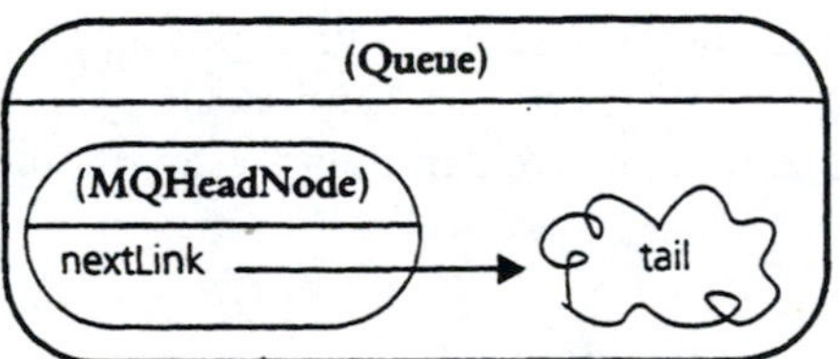

Now we send an `Init` message to the `tail` instance, passing it a link to the `head` instance variable. The initialized queue appears as it does in Figure 22.7

Figure 22.7

Queue instance creating new tail node

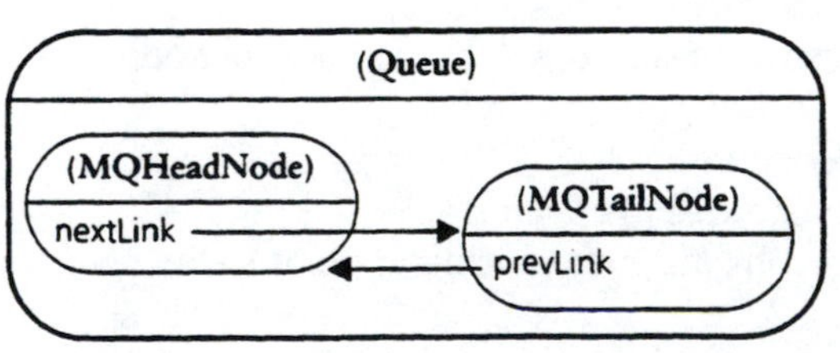

22.4 ENQUEUE

Enqueueing is the point at which we will use the `prevLink` pointer in the tail node. We want to add a new node to the end of the list, and this node must be inserted just before the tail node.

We also need to connect the previous node to the new node. This means that we have to set the `nextLink` instance variable of the previous node to the new node. The easiest way to do this is to establish a `NewNextNode` method for the nodes; then, we can set the `nextLink` instance variable of the previous node by sending it a `NewNextNode` message. Finally, we can make the new node the previous node of the tail by setting the `prevLink` instance variable:

MQQueue.Enqueue
Purpose: Adds an element to the queue
Pseudocode:
  Send an enqueue message to the tail node

MQTailNode.Enqueue
Purpose: Adds a node to the end of the list
Pseudocode:
  Creates and initializes a new internal node; call it newWaiter
  Tell prevLink's node that there is a new person behind her — newWaiter
  Set prevLink to newWaiter

MQInternalNode.Init
Purpose: Initializes the internal node
Pseudocode:
  Set movieGoerLink to passed parameter
  Set nextLink to passed parameter

We can now rewrite this pseudocode as actual code.

```
PROCEDURE MQQueue.Enqueue(newMGLink : MQMovieGoerAsn);
BEGIN
  tail.Enqueue(newMGLink);
END;

PROCEDURE MQTailNode.Enqueue(newMGLink: MQMovieGoerAsn);
VAR
  newWaiterLink: MQQueueNodeAsn;
BEGIN
  newWaiterLink :=New(MQInternalNodeAsn, Init(newMGLink,@self));
  prevLink^.newNextNode(newWaiterLink);
  prevLink := newWaiterLink;
END;
```

```
CONSTRUCTOR MQInternalNode.Init(
        newMGLink          : MQMovieGoerAsn;
        newNextLink        : MQQueueNodeAsn);
BEGIN
  INHERITED Init;
  nextLink := newNextLink;
  movieGoerLink := newMGLink
END;
```

Now, we'll walk through the process of enqueueing a node to the initial queue. We can begin with the situation shown in Figure 22.7; we have a head node and a tail node, each connected to the other. Let's say that newMovieGoerLink points to an element we'll call "Ralph." At the point shown in Figure 22.8, the Queue is about to send an Enqueue message to the tail node, with newMovieGoerLink as a parameter.

Figure 22.8 *Queue at beginning of Enqueue*

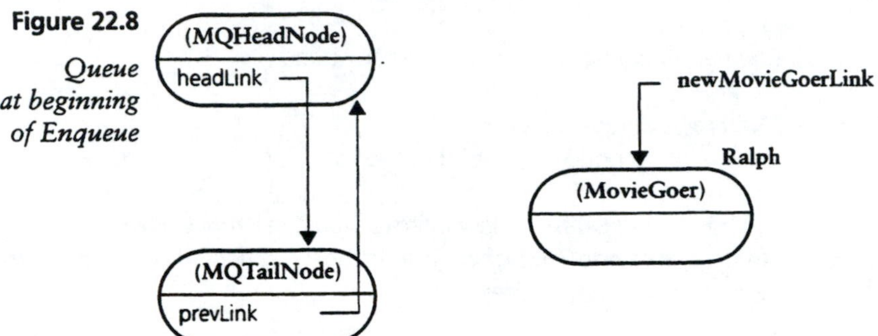

The method MQTailNode.Enqueue begins with the statement

```
newWaiterLink := New(MQInternalNodeAsn, Init(newMGLink, @self));
```

This means that we create a new internal node, and in so doing, we also construct it, using the message Init(newMGLink, @self). That is, the new node should set its nextLink instance variable link to the address of the message sender, self — which in this case is the tail node. Thus we create a new internal node, and set its two links as shown in Figure 22.9. The local variable newWaiterLink is set to the link that New returns.

The next statement in the MQTailNode.Enqueue code is

```
prevLink^.NewNextNode(newWaiterLink);
```

We haven't seen a NewNextNode method before. The method simply assigns a value to the nextLink instance variable. The class MQTailNode doesn't have a nextLink node, so we define its NewNextNode to do nothing. Both classes MQHeadNode and MQInternalNode want to set their nextLink or headLink

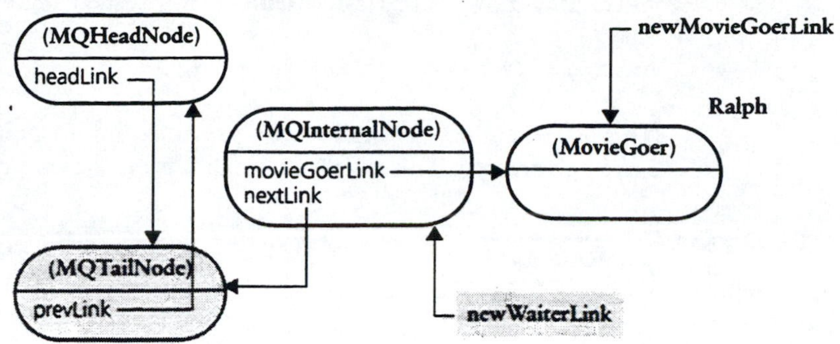

Figure 22.9 *Tail.Enqueue: A new node is created and linked to element and tail.*

instance variables to the parameter, so we define their `NewNextNode` methods to do just that:

```
PROCEDURE MQQueueNode.NewNextNode(newNextLink : MQQueueNodeAsn);
BEGIN
END;

PROCEDURE MQHeadNode.NewNextNode(newNextLink : MQQueueNodeAsn);
BEGIN
  nextLink := newNextLink;
END;

PROCEDURE MQInternalNode.NewNextNode(newNextLink: MQQueueNodeAsn);
BEGIN
  nextLink := newNextLink;
END;
```

The `NewNextNode` message is sent to the node that is previous to the tail node. This node can be a head node or an internal node (in this case it is the head), thus the similar behavior in `NewNextNode` for both classes. Figure 22.10 shows the links in the queue after the internal node has been built and the head has been told what its `NewNextNode` is.

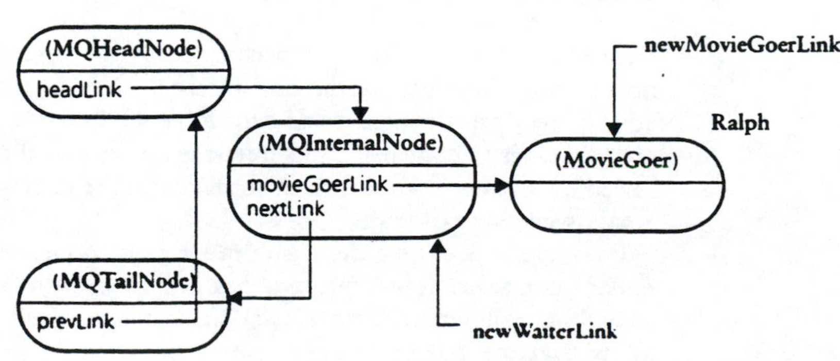

Figure 22.10 *Tail.Enqueue: Result of sending NewNextNode message to tail node's previous node*

We now move to the last statement of the `Enqueue` method:

```
prevLink := newWaiterLink;
```

This statement sets the tail node's previous link to point at the new node we have just created. This results in the situation shown in Figure 22.11.

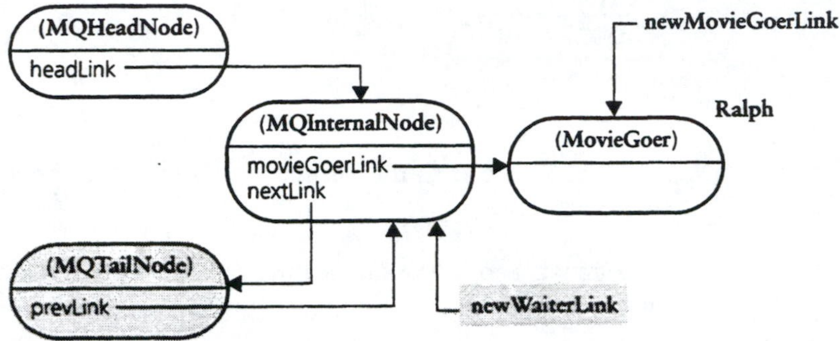

Figure 22.11 *Tail.Enqueue: Result of setting tail node's previous link to the new internal node*

Now, we have the correct queue. The head node points to the first internal node; the tail points to the last internal node (which, in this case, is the same as the first). The new node is linked into the list; the `NewNextNode` method was used to link the prior node (here, the head node) to the new node.

The `Queue` class sent an `Enqueue` method to the `MQTailNode`; the `MQTailNode` sent an `Init` message to the new node, and then sent a `NewNextNode` message to the last item in the list, telling it a new item is now to be last. In a queue, the tail node (for this method) is always responsible for enqueueing.

Hand simulate this code by enqueueing a couple of elements. Remember the `MQTailNode`'s `prevLink` always should point to the last node to be inserted (or the `MQHeadNode` if the list is empty).

22.5 DEQUEUE

Dequeueing from the queue is performed by the head of the queue. The head node simply can remove the first internal node in the list, unless the list is empty. How can the head node determine whether the queue is empty? There are two cases to consider. If the queue is not empty, then the head node is followed by an internal node. In the other case, the queue is empty, and the head is followed by a tail node.

If the queue is empty, there isn't much to be done, since we can't dequeue a movie-goer, so we'll just return `NIL`. But how can the head figure out whether something follows it? We can't ask an instance to tell us its class, but we do know that the tail of the queue isn't followed by anything. Thus `MQTailNode.GetNextNode` returns `NIL`. So if the head asks the instance pointed to by its `nextLink` for the next node, that next node will be `NIL` if the list is empty, and not `NIL` otherwise.

If the list is not empty, the head must ask the internal node pointed to by its `head` link to provide the movie-goer it stores. The head then can `dispose` of the internal nodeand return the movie-goer.

We can develop the pseudocode as follows:

MQQueue.Dequeue: MQMovieGoerAsn;
Purpose: *Dequeue* removes the element at the head of the queue and returns it
Pseudocode:

```
Send Dequeue message to head node
```

MQHeadNode.Dequeue: MQMovieGoerAsn;
Purpose: Removes a node at the front of the list
Pseudocode:

```
Get the first node's next node
IF the first node has a next node THEN
    Get the movie-goer link of the first node (to return it)
    Dispose current first node
    Set nextLink to point to old first node's next node
ELSE
    Return NIL { The queue is empty. }
```

And now we can provide the actual code for this pseudocode.

```
FUNCTION MQQueue.Dequeue: MQMovieGoerAsn;
BEGIN
  Dequeue := head.Dequeue;
END;

FUNCTION MQHeadNode.Dequeue: MQMovieGoerAsn;
VAR
  newNextLink : MQQueueNodeAsn;
BEGIN
  newNextLink := nextLink^.GetNextNode;
  IF newNextLink <> NIL THEN
    BEGIN
      Dequeue := nextLink^.GetMovieGoer;
      Dispose(nextLink, Done);
      nextLink := newNextLink;
      nextLink^.NowAtHead(@self)
    END
  ELSE
    Dequeue := NIL
END;
```

Let's consider the two possibilities: that the queue contains an element t delete, and that it does not. Let's start by dequeueing the first element in th list shown in Figure 22.12.

Figure 22.12

At beginning of Dequeue

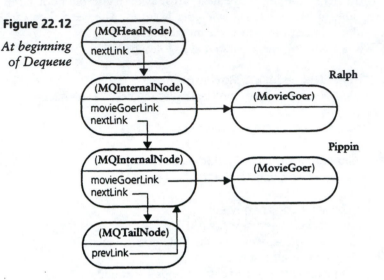

The code begins with a `Dequeue` message sent from the `Queue` to the hea node. The first line of `MQHeadNode.Dequeue` is

```
newNextLink:= nextLink^.GetNextNode;
```

Figure 22.13 shows how this line places a link to the node following the fir internal node in the local variable `newNextLink`.

Figure 22.13

Assignment in MQInternal-Node.Dequeue

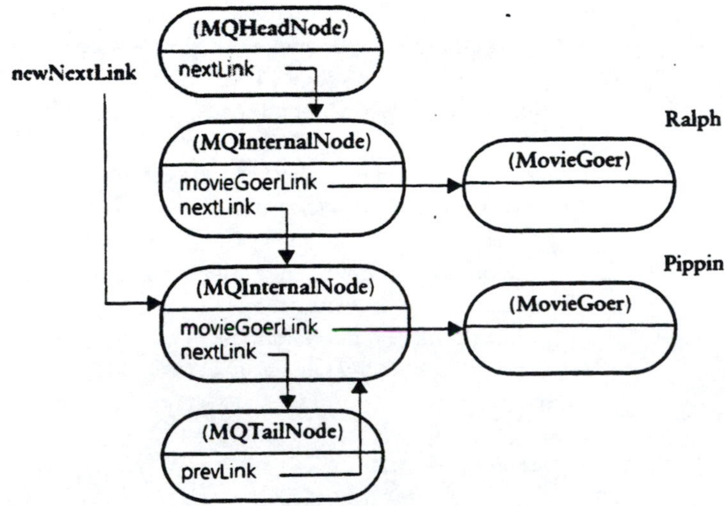

The function returns the first node's `nextLink` instance variable. This assigns a value to `newNextLink`. So, inside `MQHeadNode.Dequeue`, the `newNextLink` variable now points to the node after the node we want to dequeue.

The next line in `MQHeadNode.Dequeue` checks whether `newNextLink` is `NIL`. If we look at Figure 22.13, we see that the `nextLink` instance variable points to the node linked to the "Ralph" element, so the `newHead` local variable points to the node linked to the "Pippin" element. Thus the condition `newNextLink <> NIL` is `true`. This means we execute the following code:

```
Dequeue := nextLink^.MovieGoer;
Dispose(nextLink, Done);
nextLink := newNextLink;
nextLink^.NowAtHead(@self)
```

The first line stores a link to the movie-goer to be returned. (Note the use of the function name to store the return value until the end of the method.) The second line disposes the node pointed to by `nextLink` (see Figure 22.14).

Figure 22.14

Disposing internal node

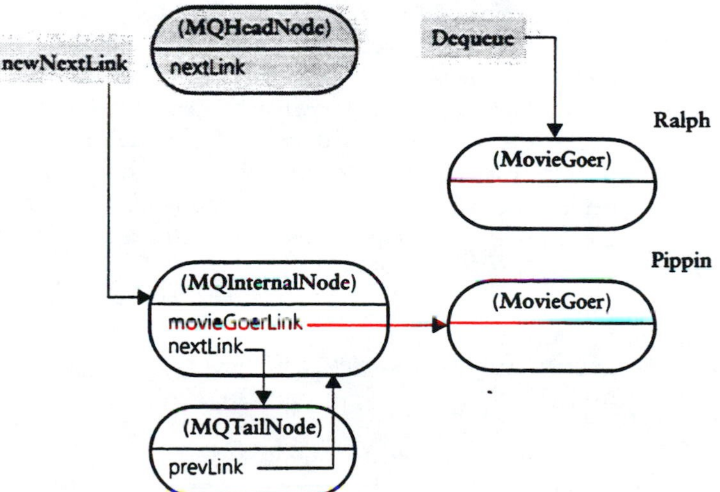

We complete the process by setting the head node's `nextLink` instance variable to the value of `newNextLink`. The queue now is reconnected and contains one fewer node, as shown in Figure 22.15. We conclude by telling the new head of the list that it is `NowAtHead` (which does nothing in this case).

Now, let's consider what happens when we send a `Dequeue` message to an empty queue. As before, the head node starts things off and sends `GetNextNode` to its `nextLink`. In an empty queue, this will also be the tail.

When `GetNextNode` returns `NIL`, the `MQHeadNode.Dequeue` method assigns `newNextLink`:

```
newNextLink := nextLink^.GetNextNode;
```

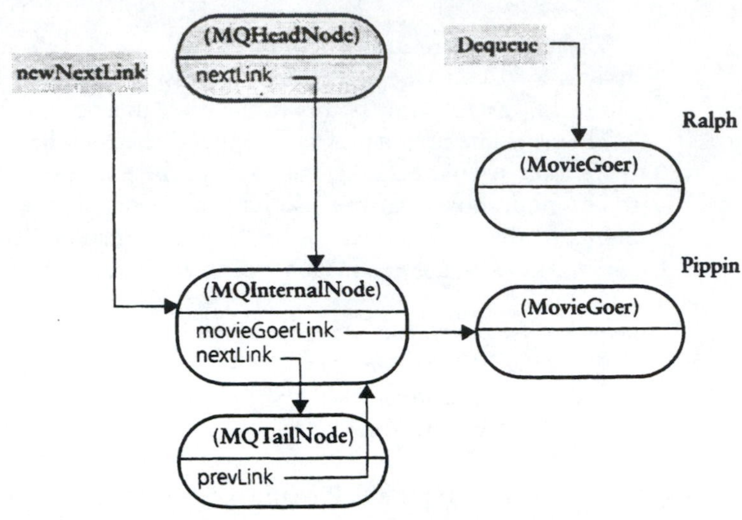

Figure 22.15 *Setting node to follow head*

Otherwise, we reach the comparison `IF newNextLink <> NIL THEN`. Here, we see that `nextLink` points to the tail node. Thus `newNextLink` is `NIL`. Since the condition is `false`, the `BEGIN/END` block is skipped and no deletion takes place. The `MQHeadNode.Dequeue` method returns `NIL`, so `MQQueue.Dequeue` returns `NIL` as well.

As a last step, consider what happens when a single internal node is in the queue and it is dequeued. The head node's `nextLink` instance variable will point to the tail, and the tail will be sent the message `NowAtHead`. As we noted before, the tail node uses this method to ensure that it points to the head when the list is empty. Thus it defines `NowAtHead` as follows:

```
PROCEDURE MQTailNode.NowAtHead( newPrevLink : MQQueueNodeAsn );
BEGIN
  prevLink := newPrevLink
END;
```

Summary

In this chapter, we learned about queues, a data structure that stores objects in a first-in, first-out order, like a line to enter a theater.

Queues support three basic operations:

1. Initialization: The queue is constructed with no objects waiting in it.
2. Enqueue: An item is added to the end of the queue.
3. Dequeue: An item is removed from the beginning of the queue.

A queue can be built using three different kinds of objects. The first represents the beginning of the queue. Usually called the head of the queue, it typically contains a single link to the next item to be removed by dequeueing. The second kind of object represents the items waiting in the queue. In our implementation, each item waiting in the queue had a link to the item behind it. The third kind of object of course provides the end of the queue, also known as the tail. It contains a link to the last item that was enqueued. When items are enqueued, the tail informs the last item enqueued that a new item now follows it.

Like stacks, queues are useful collections of objects that can grow in size without limit.

Exercises

Understanding Concepts

1. What is the difference between how information is stored on a stack and how it is stored in a queue?
2. Explain the differences between the nodes of a stack and of a queue.
3. If it is possible, show how to enqueue the data 1, 2, 3, 4 (in order) on a single queue and dequeue them in the order 2, 3, 1, 4.
4. Describe all possible ways in which you can dequeue the data that are enqueued 1, 2, 3, 4.
5. In the following sequence, the command `Enqueue <x>` adds the datum <x> to a queue; the command `Dequeue` removes an item from the queue and prints it. What does the sequence output?

```
Enqueue A, Dequeue, Enqueue B, Enqueue C, Dequeue, Enqueue D,
Dequeue, Dequeue, Enqueue E, Dequeue, Dequeue
```

6. Describe three situations in which you might use a queue and three in which you might use a stack.

Coding Exercise

1. Write an `Empty` method for queues analogous to a stack's `Empty` method.

Programming Problems

1. Write a program that simulates the activity at a supermarket. At any given moment, there is a 3 in 10 chance that someone will get in any one of the five cashiers' lines. Each customer in line has between 1 and 50 items (your program should determine this by using a random number generator). A cashier takes 10 seconds to ring up each item; when finished, the cashier needs 1 minute to get the cash from the customer and make change. (We won't worry about the bagging.) Write a program that shows the activity at 1-minute intervals for an hour.

2. Write a program that tests memorization skills. Your program should divide a square into four rectangular areas. Then, it should randomly choose one of the four areas and highlight it for a few seconds. The user then has to indicate which area the computer highlighted by clicking on that area. If the user is correct, the program should choose a second area at random; the user should see the first area highlighted again, followed by the second area. The user should respond by clicking the two areas in order. The program should give the user longer and longer sequences, adding one area each time. Thus, if we number the areas 1, 2, 3, and 4, the user might first see area 1 highlighted; if the user clicks on area 1, then she might see area 1 followed by area 3; if the user responds by clicking on 1 and 3 in order, then she might see area 1 followed by area 3 followed by area 2. The process repeats until the user correctly remembers a sequence of 16 areas or makes a mistake. In the latter case, the program should display the correct sequence.

3. In music, there are 12 names for tones. In order, these are C, C# (pronounced C-sharp), D, D#, E, F, F#, G, G#, A, A#, and B. Each tone in this list is a half-step above the previous tone. Write a program that accepts a tone name as input and outputs the major scale that begins at that note. A major scale consists of 8 tones, with the first tone being the note chosen by the user. Each tone is one step (i.e., two half-steps) above the previous tone, *except* that the fourth tone is one half-step above the third tone, and the eighth tone is one half-step above the seventh tone. Thus the major scale that begins at D is D, E, F#, G, A, B, C#, D.

4. Write a program to shuffle a deck of cards and allow the user to play solitaire. In this game, seven piles of cards are dealt face down (one card in the first pile, two in the second, and so on). The top cards on each pile is placed face up. These piles are called the tableaus.

   You can build on the top cards of the tableaus. Cards are placed in descending order and alternating colors. For example, a black queen can be played on a red king. All the face-up cards on one tableau can be moved to build on another tableau. Whenever a face-down card becomes the top of the pile, it is turned over. The cards not initially in the tableau are the hand. Cards are dealt, three at a time, from the hand to a pile called the talon. The card at the top of the talon can be played on any of the tableaus, and the subsequently exposed cards can also be played. The top card on the talon or on any of the tableaus can also be placed on one of the four foundations. These are built up, starting with the ace, in ascending order and in suit.

   In your program, the user should be able to quit at any time; if the user doesn't quit, the game ends when all of the cards are on the foundations.

5. Implement the collection of actions described in Section 22.1. Reimplement the stack of actions from Chapter 21 as a subclass of this collection class, and implement a queue of actions as a subclass of the collection class. Use the stack to provide undo and redo capabilities to the paint program. Use the queue to record all user actions in order — each action is enqueued as it is performed. Add a redraw button to the paint program's interface that clears the drawing area and then redraws the drawing by dequeuing each action and sending it the `DoIt` message.

23

Linked Lists

Storage in arrays is static, not dynamic. In other words, the number of array slots is fixed and cannot change during the execution of your program. When you define your array variable, you tell OOPas how many storage positions you'll need. If your list turns out to be longer than that, you're out of luck.

Moving information around in arrays also can cause problems. Suppose we have kept an array of students in alphabetical order, and a new student enrolls. To put the new student's name in the array in the correct order, we must find the right spot in which to insert the new student and then move every piece of information in the array after that spot over one slot in the array, starting with the last slot. Figure 23.1 shows how the information in an array would have to be manipulated.

Figure 23.1

Inserting in a sorted array

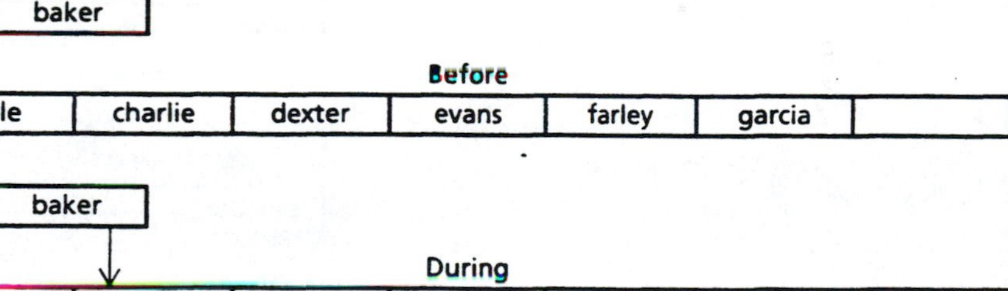

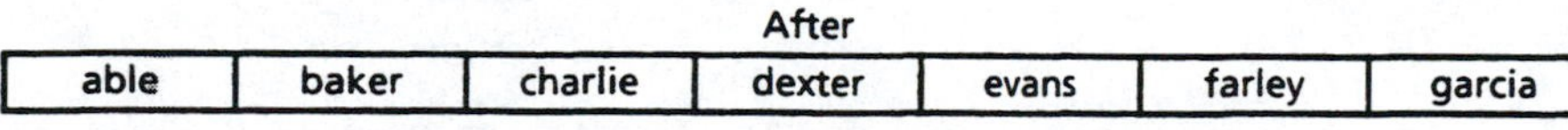

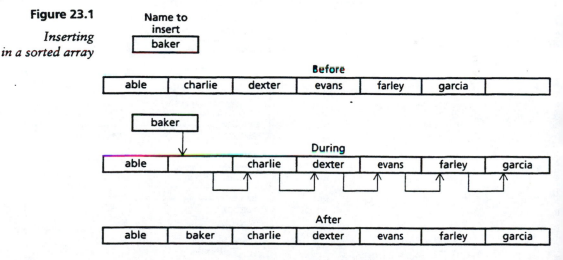

Deletion from arrays is also a problem. Every time a student leaves the class, we would have to perform the same type of manipulation that we did with insertion. Otherwise, we'd have a "hole" in the data. We'd have to check whether each slot contains an "actual" value or a deleted value; furthermore, we couldn't recycle the slot where the deleted element's name used to be. With large amounts of data, these consecutive data moves are inefficient, and we'd like to avoid them.

Although stacks and queues change their size to adapt to the number of elements that must be stored, they won't work for this problem either. We want to insert or remove a student at a particular place, not just at the beginning or the end of the list. To do this, we will build a *linked list*.

23.1 NODES

As we did for stacks and queues, our linked list will have three kinds of objects: the interface, the nodes that implement that interface, and the elements stored in the list. The differences among stacks, queues, and linked lists arise in the differences between the nodes and how they work together.

Figure 23.2 is a diagram of a linked list. The list contains links to elements. Defining an element, so that we are discussing a particular list, will be helpful.

Figure 23.2

A linked list

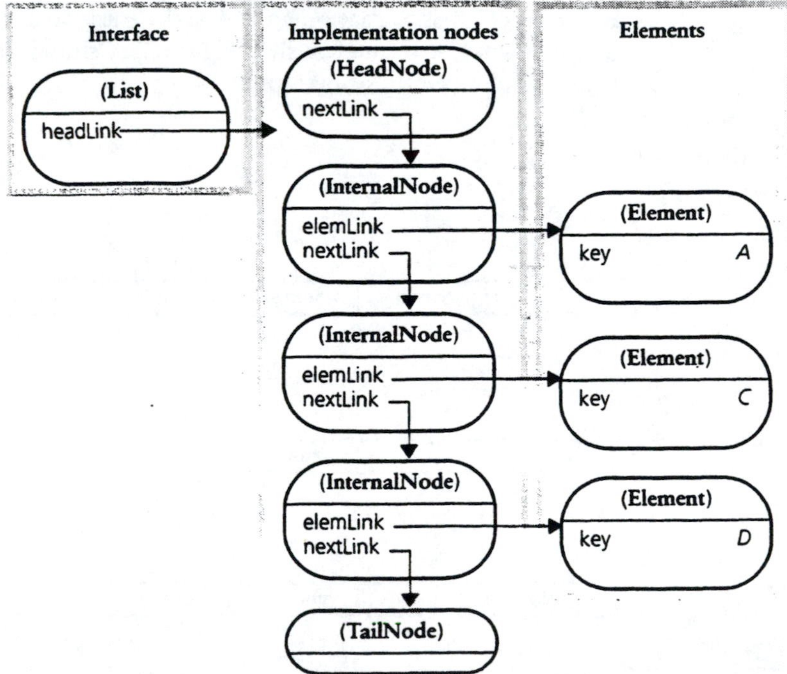

Suppose we wanted to develop a variation of our shape-drawing program from Chapter 8. Remember that our earlier program drew squiggles, rectangles, and lines in a drawing area. It's often useful to maintain a sorted list of shapes. Some drawing applications provide "layers" with different shapes drawn in different layers. These programs typically allow the user to move a shape toward the "back" or toward the "front"— implying that shapes in the back should be drawn before shapes in the front.

Rather than continue development of our paint program (leaving that for exercises), we will build a linked list that can serve as a simple rolodex or database. We'll focus on the fact that such systems often maintain their elements in sorted order. Adding a new element must be performed at some particular place in the collection that is almost never the beginning or the end. Thus we can't use a stack or a queue.

Let's start by defining an `Element` that contains a `key` instance variable as the string (or name) that maintains the sorted order. Each element will be placed in the collection based on the alphabetic ordering of its key. We can define the `Element` class as follows:

```
Element = OBJECT
   CONSTRUCTOR Init(newKey: string);
   FUNCTION GetKey: string;
   PROCEDURE Draw(canvasLink : GPDrawingAreaAsn); VIRTUAL;
PRIVATE
   key: string;
END;
```

The nodes in our list each contain a link to an element. Why do we use a link rather than the element itself? So that we can generalize our list for different kinds of elements, exploiting polymorphism. Notice the `VIRTUAL` method `Draw`, which we will use to allow entries in our rolodex to display themselves in some interesting fashion.

Like a queue, a linked list contains three kinds of nodes. The *head node* marks the beginning of the list; a *tail node* marks the end of the list. Neither the head node nor the tail node contains any information; they simply provide the markers for the beginning and end of the list. All of the nodes in the middle are called *internal nodes*.

Let's consider the OOPas class definition for these nodes. We'll use our definition of the `Element` class, and we'll create a superclass called `Node`. As mentioned before, the internal nodes are where the actual information is maintained. Thus the `InternalNode` definition contains an instance variable that is a link to the element.

```
TYPE
   ElementAsn = ^Element;
   NodeAsn = ^Node;
   HeadNodeAsn = ^HeadNode;
   InternalNodeAsn = ^InternalNode;
   TailNodeAsn = ^TailNode;
```

```
Element = OBJECT
   CONSTRUCTOR Init(newKey: string);
   FUNCTION GetKey: string;
   PROCEDURE Draw(canvasLink : GPDrawingAreaAsn); VIRTUAL;
PRIVATE
   key: string;
END;

Node = OBJECT
   { methods here }
PRIVATE
END;

HeadNode = OBJECT (Node)
   { methods here }
PRIVATE
   nextLink: NodeAsn;
END;

InternalNode = OBJECT (Node)
   { methods here }
PRIVATE
   elemLink: ElementAsn;
   nextLink: NodeAsn;
END;

TailNode = OBJECT (Node)
   { methods here, no instance variables }
END;
```

The head node and internal node also have an additional instance variable called `nextLink`, much like the nodes in stacks and queues. Note that unlike queues, the tail node does not have a link to the previous node. We will insert a new node at a particular position by starting from the beginning of the list and searching for the correct node at which to insert the new node.

23.2 LIST OPERATIONS

Let's define our list interface class at this time. The stack and the queue both had methods to add items (`Push` and `Enqueue`) and to remove items (`Pop` and `Dequeue`). Our list will have two corresponding methods, `Insert` and `Delete`. In addition, we will need to determine whether an `Element` is in the list, so our list will also have a `Search` method. Finally, we will want to perform some sort of action for every element in the list, such as printing every card in our rolodex. The method `MakeIterator` will perform this function.

```
IteratorAsn = ^Iterator;
List = OBJECT
  CONSTRUCTOR Init;
  PROCEDURE Insert(newElementLink: ElementAsn); VIRTUAL;
  FUNCTION Delete(keyToDelete: string): ElementAsn; VIRTUAL;
  FUNCTION Search(keyToFind: string): ElementAsn; VIRTUAL;
  FUNCTION MakeIterator : IteratorAsn;
PRIVATE
  headLink : NodeAsn
END;
```

Our list contains only a link to the head node. Since nodes contain a link to their neighbors, the head node contains a link to the first internal node, which contains a link to the second internal node, and so on, until the last internal node, which contains a link to the tail node. This is quite similar to the pattern we saw in stacks and queues. Notice, though, that we don't need to contain the head or the tail this time, since the tail does not link to the previous node.

In the next sections, we will describe each of the list's methods.

23.3 INITIALIZING THE LIST

When we initialize the list, we want to create the situation shown in Figure 23.3. Note that unlike the queue we saw in Chapter 22, the list doesn't need to send messages to both the head and the tail — inserting will always start at the beginning, as we shall see shortly.

Figure 23.3
Initial linked list

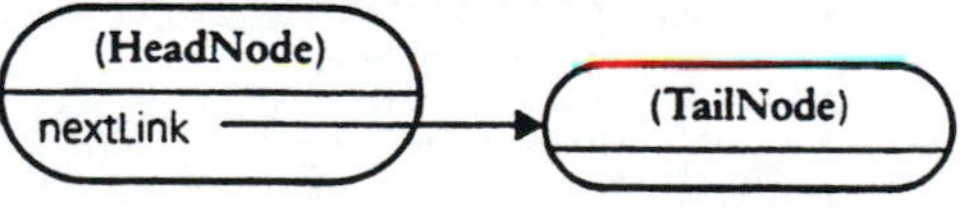

Here, we have a head node containing a link to a tail node. We can use `New` to initialize the `headLink` instance variable of the list:

```
CONSTRUCTOR List.Init;
BEGIN
  headLink := New(HeadNodeAsn, Init);
END;
```

The statement in this constructor creates a link to an instance of `HeadNode`, using the `HeadNode`'s constructor `Init`. Let's look at `HeadNode.Init`:

```
CONSTRUCTOR HeadNode.Init;
BEGIN
  nextLink := New(TailNodeAsn, Init);
END;
```

This constructor initializes the `nextLink` instance variable. It uses the `New` function, this time to create a link to an instance of `TailNode`. The tail node, we saw earlier, contains no instance variables, so its constructor is an empty shell.

```
CONSTRUCTOR TailNode.Init;
BEGIN
END;
```

The initialization shows a theme we will see throughout the methods of the list. The `List` class sends a message to the head of the list. The head node, in turn, sends a message to the next node in the list — in this initial case, the tail.

23.4 SEARCHING FOR A NODE

Let's assume we have a list already — specifically, the list in Figure 23.4.

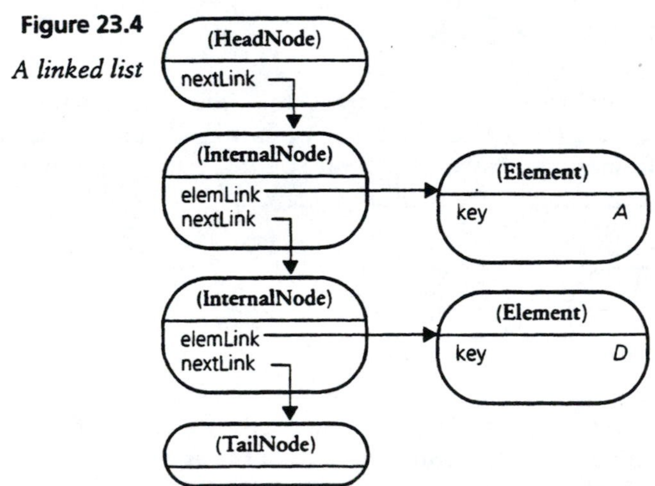

Figure 23.4
A linked list

While *we* can see the entire list in Figure 23.4, each *node* knows only about the next node in the list. So, if the `List` is asked to search for, say, the element with a `key` instance variable equal to 'D', it begins by asking the only node it knows about (the head node) if it contains the link to the 'D' element. We'll call this message `SearchNode`.

The head node's response to this message is to say, "Since I don't contain a link to any element, I certainly don't have the link to the 'D' element. But that doesn't mean the 'D' element isn't in the list. I'll send a `SearchNode` message to the next node."

In Figure 23.4, the next node happens to be an internal node, which has one of three reactions to a `SearchNode` message. The first is, "The `key` in the element I link to is the same as the key you're looking for. Therefore the key to find is in the list." The second is, "I contain a link to an element whose `key` is greater than the key we want to find. That means you must have passed the place where the `key` should be (since the keys are kept in order). So, I can say for certain that the key is not in the list." The third possibility is, "I contain a link to an element whose `key` is less than the key we want to find. I'll pass the `SearchNode` message to the next node in the list and see how it responds."

In our example, the head node sends the message to the node whose `elemLink` instance variable links to an element with a `key` of 'A'. We are looking for the key of 'D', so the node responds with the third case — sending a `SearchNode` message to the next node in the list.

When this next node receives the message, it also has three choices because it is an internal node. This node, though, contains an `elemLink` that links to an element with a `key` of 'D'. Eureka! We've found it! The node can say for certain that the 'D' node is in the list and return a pointer to the node's element. This pointer is returned to the previous node — the node that sent this node the `SearchNode` message. The previous node returns this link to its own previous node, and so on back to the head of the list, where the head node returns the pointer to the `List` class.

Now, suppose we were looking for a key that wasn't in the list, like 'E'. We'd want each node in the list to send a `SearchNode` to the next node. If the tail node receives the `SearchNode` message, that means that all of the internal nodes passed on the message to their next node. The tail node knows that this has to stop here; there are no more nodes after the tail, so the tail node has to return the news that the element is not contained in the list.

So, how do we write this message-passing strategy in OOPas? The best way to think about it is to look at one node at a time. We start with the list as a whole. The `List` has a `Search` method that returns an element link (or `NIL` if no element is found), the result of sending a `SearchNode` message to the head of the list.

```
FUNCTION List.Search(keyToFind: string): ElementAsn;
BEGIN
   Search := headLink^.SearchNode(keyToFind);
END;
```

So, we need to code the `SearchNode` method for the head node. We know, though, that the head node cannot contain the key we want, since only internal nodes contain data. The head node will send a `SearchNode` message to the next node in the list:

```
FUNCTION HeadNode.SearchNode(keyToFind: string): ElementAsn;
BEGIN
  SearchNode := nextLink^.SearchNode(keyToFind);
END;
```

When the internal node receives the message, it compares its key to the key to find. If there's a match, the node can return the link to its element and pass that all the way back up the list. If the key in the current node's element is greater than the key to find, then the key to find is not in the list. If the key to find doesn't match this particular node, the `SearchNode` message is sent to the next node.

```
FUNCTION InternalNode.SearchNode(keyToFind: string): ElementAsn;
VAR
  resultLink : ElementAsn;          { result of search }
BEGIN
  IF (elemLink^.GetKey = keyToFind) THEN
    resultLink := elemLink
  ELSE IF (elemLink^.GetKey > keyToFind) THEN
    resultLink := NIL
  ELSE
    resultLink := nextLink^.SearchNode(keyToFind);
  SearchNode := resultLink;
END;
```

If we reach the tail node and the node has not been found, we know that the search is unsuccessful and that we should return `NIL`.

```
FUNCTION TailNode.SearchNode(keyToFind: string): ElementAsn;
BEGIN
  SearchNode := NIL;
END;
```

Let's walk through this code. Let's again assume we are searching for the node containing a link to the element 'D'.

The `List.Search` method begins by sending a `SearchNode` message to the head node, as shown in Figure 23.5. The gray node indicates the currently active node. The head node responds to the message with the statement:

```
SearchNode := nextLink^.SearchNode(keyToFind);
```

This sends a `SearchNode` message to the next node in the list, as shown in Figure 23.6. The head node now will wait until the next node's `SearchNode` message returns something.

Now, the first internal node contains a link to the element 'A'. When we look at the code for `InternalNode.SearchNode`, we see that the action taken depends on the key of the element whose link is contained by the node; that is

Figure 23.5

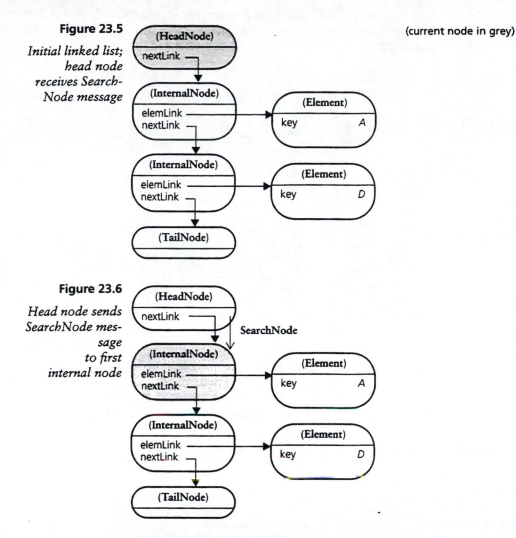

Initial linked list; head node receives Search-Node message

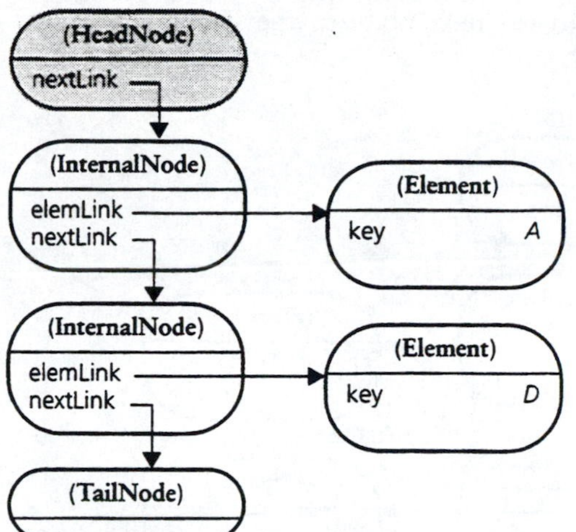

Figure 23.6

Head node sends SearchNode message to first internal node

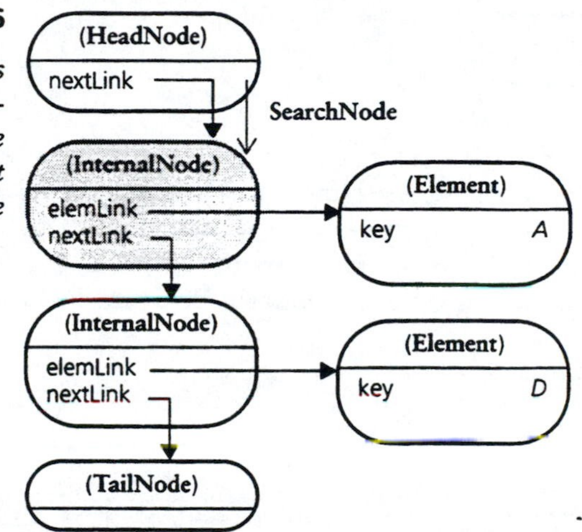

the action is dependent on whether the key is equal, greater than, or less than the key to find. The block of code for `InternalNode.SearchNode` depends on an `IF-THEN-ELSE IF` conditional:

```
IF (elemLink^.GetKey = keyToFind) THEN
  resultLink := elemLink
ELSE IF (elemLink^.GetKey > keyToFind) THEN
  resultLink := NIL
ELSE
  resultLink := nextLink^.SearchNode(keyToFind);
```

If `elemLink^.GetKey` — the key of the element our link points to — is the same as the key to find, then `elemLink` is the link we want. If the key from our element is greater than the key to find, then the key to find cannot be in the list and we return `NIL`. If neither of these things is true, then this node can send a message to the next node in the list and wait for its answer, as shown in Figure 23.7.

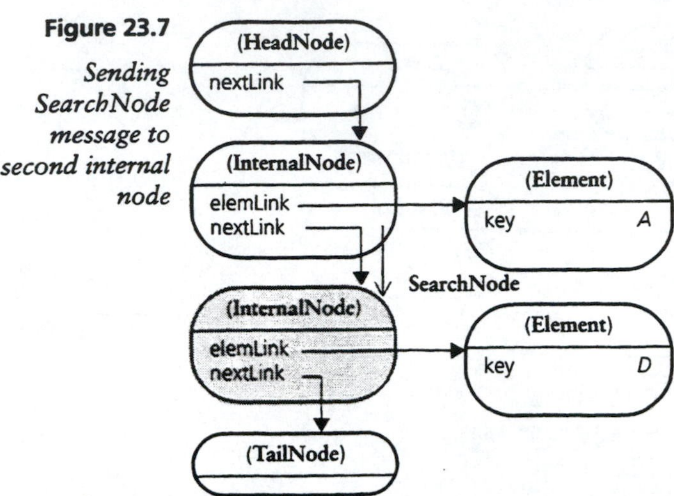

Figure 23.7 *Sending SearchNode message to second internal node*

It turns out the next node is another internal node, so it uses the same `InternalNode.SearchNode` method. This time, `elemLink^.GetKey` yields a key that is the same as the key we want to find ('D'). This means that the first part of the condition is `true`, so the result is the link to the 'D' element (Figure 23.8). That variable `resultLink` is returned to the preceding node.

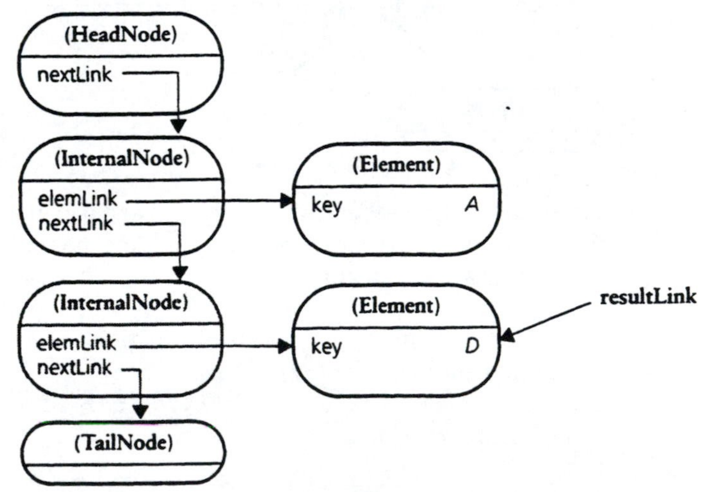

Figure 23.8 *Setting value of resultLink local variable in second internal node*

The previous node now receives the returned link from the `SearchNode` message it sent in this statement in its own invocation of `SearchNode`:

```
resultLink := nextLink^.SearchNode(keyToFind);
```

The instance that `nextLink` links to returned a link to its element. So, the `resultLink` local variable is set to the link (Figure 23.9).

Figure 23.9

First internal node receives value returned by second internal node

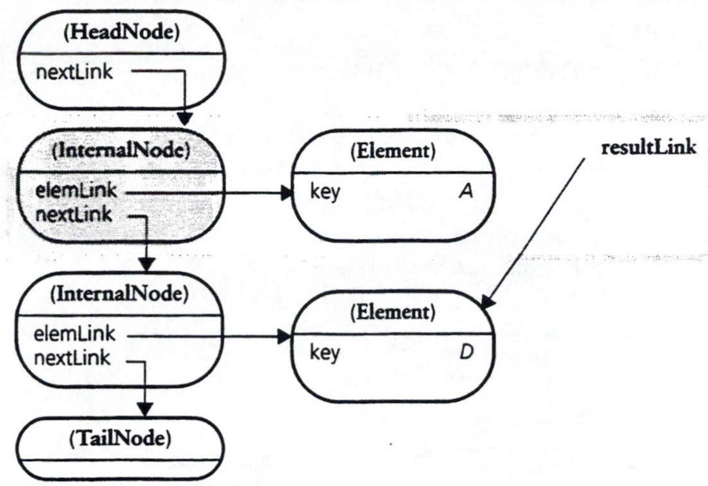

We are now done with the first internal node, and the value of result is returned to `HeadNode.SearchNode`. The return value of the single statement in this method is the value received from the first node in the list (Figure 23.10).

Figure 23.10

Head node receives value from first internal node

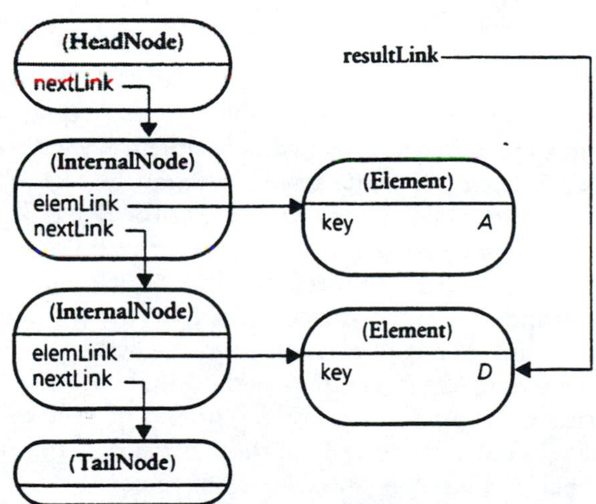

In short, we sent messages from one node to the next until we had a definitive answer. Then, a link to the element we wanted or a `NIL` was sent back as the result of the message sent to each node in turn, until `HeadNode` received the response that it could send back to `List`.

If we had searched for any value greater than 'D', the last internal node would have sent a `SearchNode` message to the tail node. The tail node, knowing it is the end of the list, sets the return value to `NIL`, and that value is carried back to the head of the list.

23.5 ADDING A NODE

The pattern of sending a message from one node to the next is also useful in inserting and deleting a node. Let's consider how we insert a node in the list, starting with building a list from scratch. This means that we could begin with an initialized list and insert an element with a key of 'A'. We want to achieve the result shown in Figure 23.11.

Figure 23.11 *After first insertion*

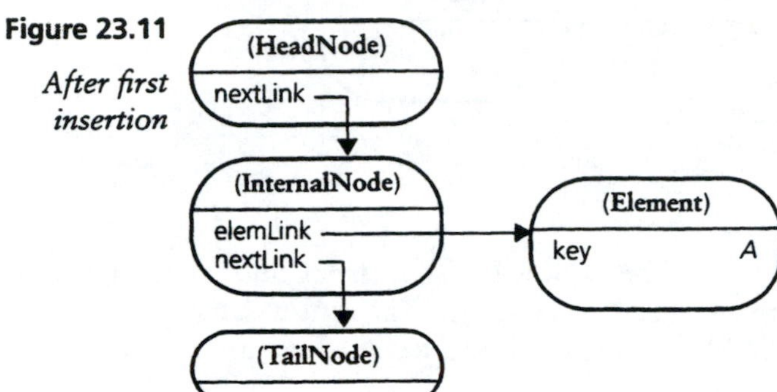

In this figure, we created a new internal node. We set the `nextLink` instance variable of the head node to link to the new node, and we set the new internal node's `nextLink` instance variable to link to the tail node and its `elemLink` to point to its element. Now, what happens when we insert the second node?

We achieve the same results we had in Figure 23.4. Here, the new node (containing a link to the element with 'D') is linked to the tail node. The node's predecessor is the internal node containing the link to the 'A' element. Again, we have to connect two links (the `next` instance variable of the new node, and the `next` instance variable of the previous node — the one containing the link to the 'A' element — in the list).

We would like to create a method that will work for insertion, whether that occurs at the beginning, middle, or end of the list; our strategy for inserting a node should work for any of these situations. In general, then, we want to find the place to insert — then, we want to connect the new node to its neighbors.

So consider a situation where our list contains 'A', 'B', 'P', and 'R' and that our `Insert` method is given a link to a new element whose key is 'Q'. We send a message to the head node to insert the element, and its response is, "I don't know where this node goes in the list, but it has to be somewhere after me."

So, the head node passes the new element to its `nextLink` successor. Note that this is a form of recursion — the current node can't perform the task of inserting, so it forwards the message to another node.

This next internal node, the one for 'A', then examines the new element. 'A' is less than 'Q', so this internal node has the same response as the head node — the new element goes somewhere after this place in the list, and the new element is passed to the next internal node.

Eventually, an "add node" message is sent to the node whose element contains the key 'P'. This node's response, as its predecessors has been, is to send the message to the next node in the list.

Next, the "add node" message is sent to the node whose element contains the 'R' key. Here, we get a different response. Since the key is greater than the element we want to insert, this internal node says, "This new node has to come before me."

Thus the `InsertNode` messages are recursively sent from one node to the next until a node sees that the element should come *before* itself. This node does the insertion and creates the new node. In our example, this means that the 'R' node will have responsibility for creating a new node. We have to execute three steps. First, the 'R' node creates a new node, which is initialized with the `elemLink` instance variable set to the passed in link to the 'Q' element.

We also can set the `nextLink` instance variable of the new node for 'Q' to its successor — the 'R' node that sent the message to create the node. This means that two links now point to the node containing a link to the 'R' element.

Now, the new node is connected to its successor in the list. But what happens to the link before the new node? How can we tell the node with a link to the 'P' element that it has a new successor in the list?

The answer here is the return value of the recursive message send. We can return, to each node, a link to its successor. Thus the 'R' node was sent an "add node" message from the 'P' node; if we make the "add node" message a function, we can have the 'R' node's `InsertNode` function return a link to the new successor back to the 'P' node. The 'P' node will store this link in its own `nextLink` instance variable. The new node is now completely in the list; it is connected to its predecessor and its successor in the list. Nodes that didn't create a new node will simply return a link to `@self`, keeping the list the way it was before the insertion.

Let's look at the code here, and then walk through it. The `List` wants to send a message to the head node to insert the new element. It expects to receive back from `InsertNode` a link to a node, the node at the head of the list. As with the `Init` method, we start with a message sent to the `headLink` instance variable that will insert a node.

```
PROCEDURE List.Insert(newElemLink: ElementAsn);
BEGIN
  headLink := headLink^.InsertNode(newElemLink);
END;
```

Now, let's consider each of the nodes, and how it will handle the `InsertNode` message. The head node sends the `InsertNode` message to the `nextLink`, then returns a link to itself to the `List`, since it is always the first node in the list:

```
FUNCTION HeadNode.InsertNode(newElemLink: ElementAsn): NodeAsn;
BEGIN
  nextLink := nextLink^.InsertNode(newElemLink);
  InsertNode := @self
END;
```

Now let's look at the `InternalNode`. First, consider its constructor:

```
CONSTRUCTOR InternalNode.Init(
      newElemLink: ElementAsn;
      newNextLink: NodeAsn);
BEGIN
  elemLink := newElemLink;
  nextLink := newNextLink
END;
```

The internal node checks whether it should add the element. If not, it sends the message `InsertNode` to the next node in the list and returns a link to itself. If it should insert the new element before the current internal node, the method creates a new internal node and returns a link to that new node.

```
FUNCTION InternalNode.InsertNode(newElemLink:ElementAsn): NodeAsn
VAR
  linkToReturn: NodeAsn;
BEGIN
  IF (elemLink^.GetKey < newElemLink^.GetKey) THEN
    BEGIN
      nextLink := nextLink^.InsertNode(newElemLink);
      linkToReturn := @self;
    END
  ELSE
    linkToReturn := New(InternalNodeAsn,Init(newElemLink,@self))
  InsertNode := linkToReturn;
END;
```

If the `TailNode` receives the `InsertNode` message, the new element must go at the end of the list. Thus this method creates a new internal node, then returns it, using the same call to `New` as was used by the internal node:

```
FUNCTION TailNode.InsertNode(newElemLink: ElementAsn): NodeAsn;
BEGIN
  InsertNode := New(InternalNodeAsn, Init(newElemLink, @self));
END;
```

Let's walk through the insertion of a new element, whose key is 'C', in the list in Figure 23.4.

Our code begins with `List.Insert` receiving a link to an element. It executes the one statement of the method:

```
headLink := headLink^.InsertNode(newElemLink);
```

The `Insert` method sends a message to the head of the list, telling it to add the node (Figure 23.12). Thus we move to the `InsertNode` method for the `HeadNode` class. The first statement of this function is

```
nextLink := nextLink^.InsertNode(newElemLink);
```

This is an assignment statement; as we've seen before, we perform the operation on the right-hand side of the `:=` and assign the value to the variable on the left. What operation do we perform? The right side says to send an `InsertNode` message to the instance that `nextLink` links to, as in Figure 23.13.

Figure 23.12

Beginning of insertion of 'C'

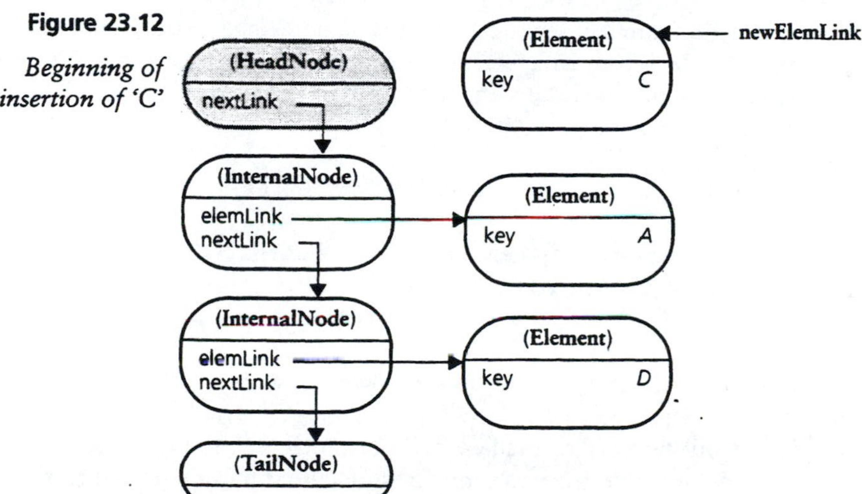

The `nextLink` of the head node links to the first internal node, so we look at the method `InternalNode.InsertNode`. This code begins with a comparison:

```
IF (elemLink^.GetKey < newElemLink^.GetKey) THEN
```

Simply put, we are comparing the current key to the new key. The instance variable `elemLink` links to the element containing 'A'. The parameter `newElemLink` is the passed-in link to the new element; its key is 'C'. 'A' < 'C' is `true`, so we execute the code within this `BEGIN/END` block. The first statement is the same as the statement we saw in the head node:

Figure 23.13

Head node sending InsertNode message to first internal node

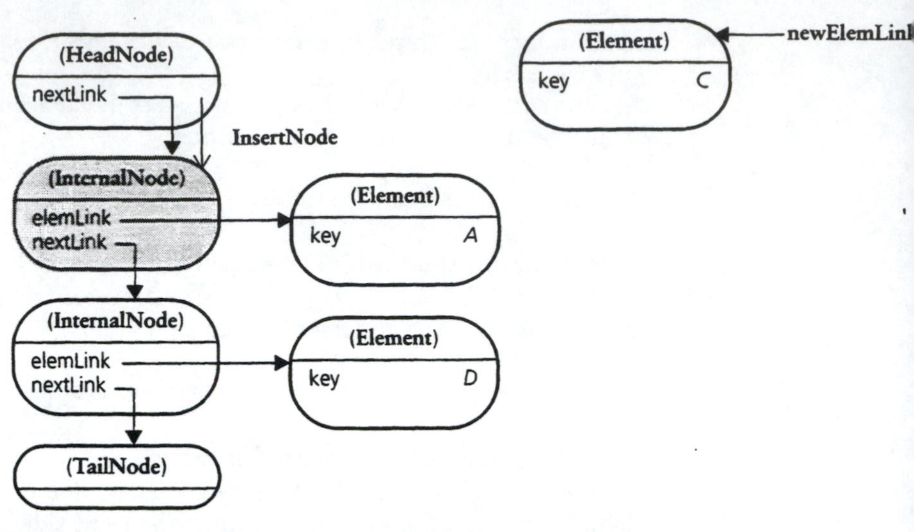


```
nextLink := nextLink^.InsertNode(newElemLink);
```

This function call sends an `InsertNode` message to the next node in the list as shown in Figure 23.14. The next node also happens to be an internal node so this instance uses the same method (`InternalNode.InsertNode`). We begin again with the comparison:

```
IF (elemLink^.GetKey < newElemLink^.GetKey) THEN
```

This time, however, `elemLink^.GetKey` returns 'D' and `newElemLink^.GetKey` returns 'C'. The comparison 'D' < 'C' is `false`, so we move to the code following the `ELSE`:

```
linkToReturn:= New(InternalNodeAsn, Init(newElemLink, @self));
```

Here's our first use of the `New` function in the `InsertNode` sequence. We want to point `linkToReturn` to something. The first parameter tell us that it will be a link of type `InternalNodeAsn`. OOPas allocates memory for a new instance of `InternalNode` and executes the specified constructor. We now have the situation shown in Figure 23.15.

Now, let's carefully consider the parameter passing here. The `Init` message is sent with two actual parameters: `newElemLink` and `@self`. The header of the `InternalNode.Init` method looks like this:

```
CONSTRUCTOR InternalNode.Init(
        newElemLink: ElementAsn;
        newNextLink: NodeAsn);
```

The formal parameter `newElemLink` receives the value of the actual parameter also called `newElemLink` — nothing unusual there. The second parameter is

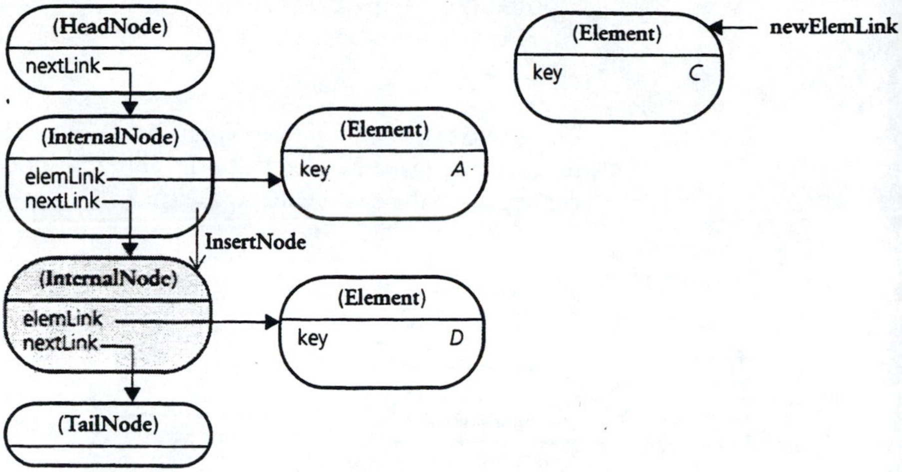

Figure 23.14

InsertNode message sent to second internal node

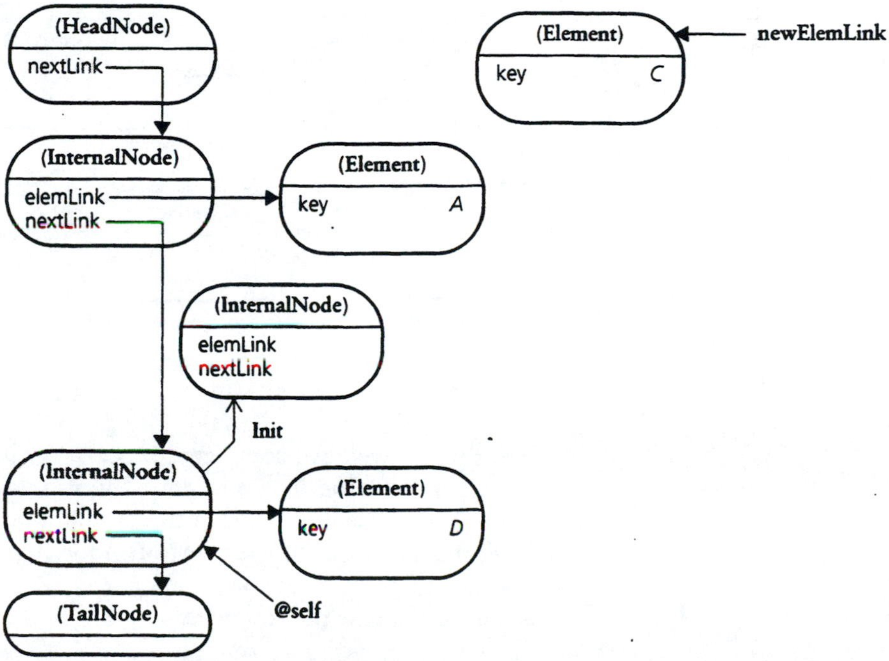

Figure 23.15

Creation of new internal node

worth investigating. The formal parameter is `newNextLink`; its corresponding actual parameter is `@self`. The `self`, in this case, refers to the internal node with the link to the 'D' element. Thus `@self` is a link to the node that sent the `Init` message. Essentially, the node that sent the message will be the node that follows the new node in the list.

Now, we can make the assignments to establish the values of the new node's instance variables.

```
BEGIN
   elemLink := newElemLink;
   nextLink := newNextLink
END;
```

These two statements simply assign links. The link `nextLink` is now connected to the same place as `nextNode`, D's internal node, and the `elemLink` is now connected to the new element. Figure 23.16 shows the new situation.

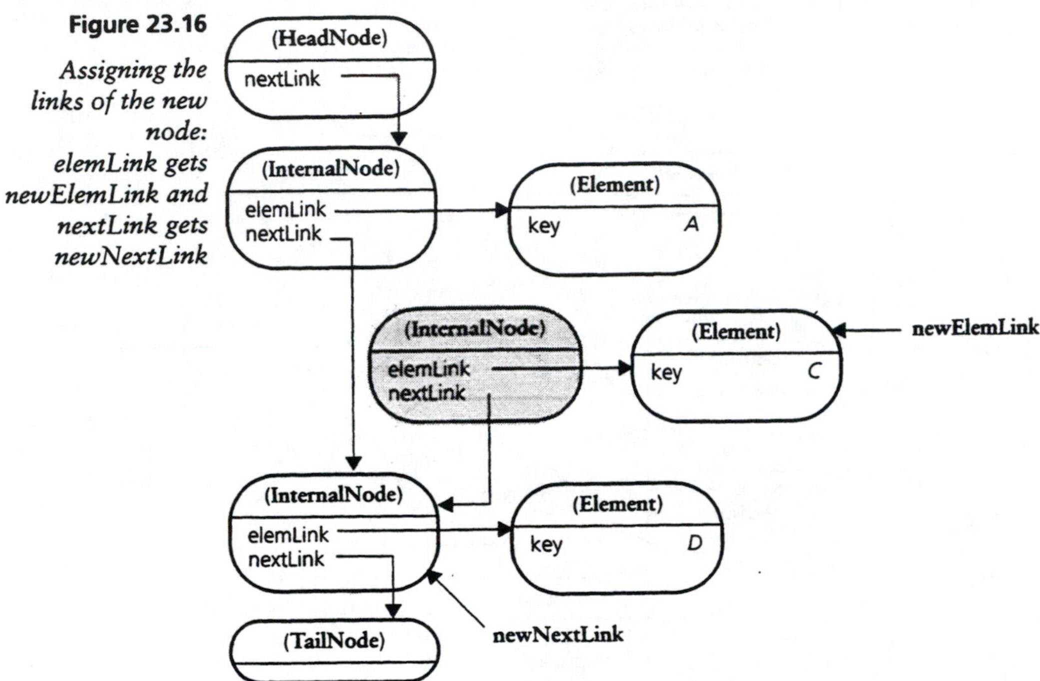

Figure 23.16 *Assigning the links of the new node: elemLink gets newElemLink and nextLink gets newNextLink*

At this point, we have completed most of the job. We have a new node that contains a link to the new element. The `nextLink` instance variable of that node is linked to the next node in the list alphabetically. Now what we have to do is set the `nextLink` of the previous node (the one containing a link to the 'A' element) to point to the new node.

Let's look again at the statement

```
linkToReturn:= New(InternalNodeAsn, Init(newElemLink, @self));
```

The variable `linkToReturn` is set to the value that `New` will return. Since it receives the result of `New`, it is now pointing to the node we just created. (Note that parameter `newNextLink` disappeared when the `Init` method finished.)

The final statement of D's activation of the `InternalNode.InsertNode` method sets `InsertNode` to return the value of `linkToReturn`. So, D's node having responded to its method, returns the value of `nodeLinkToReturn` to the instance that sent the `InsertNode` message — A's node.

D's node received the `InsertNode` message from A's node as part of this statement:

```
nextLink := nextLink^.InsertNode(newElemLink);
```

Thus the result of the `InsertNode` method — the link to the new node — is assigned to the `nextLink` instance variable of A's node. This means that we have linked the new node into the list (Figure 23.17).

Figure 23.17

Returning link to new node back to previous neighbor

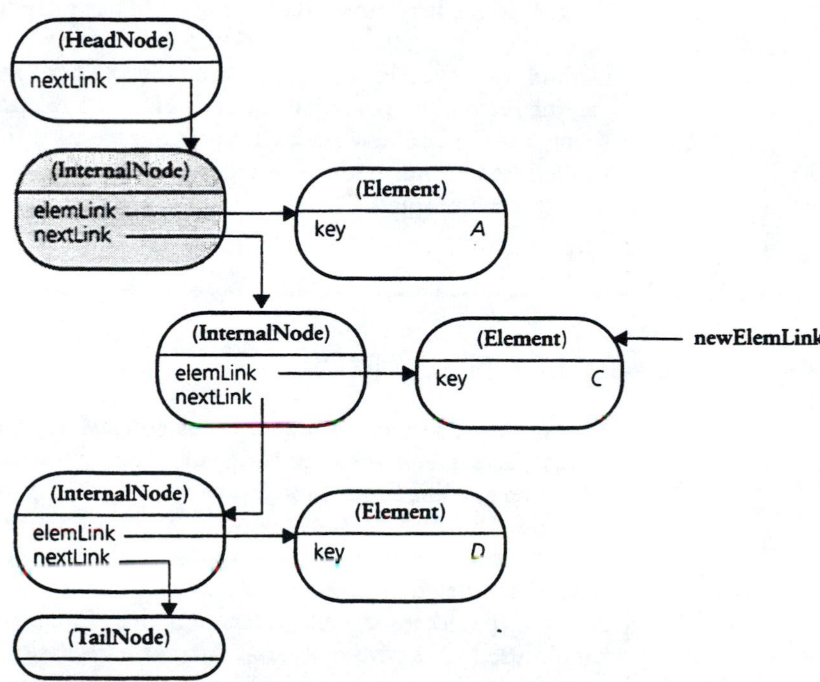

We are still in the middle of the `InternalNode.InsertNode` method for the node containing the 'A' element. After the recursive call, we now reach the statement

```
linkToReturn := @self;
```

This means that we should send back a link to the current node. Again, this is the key point in the algorithm. In other words, if we have made an insertion in the list, prior to the current node, `InternalNode.InsertNode` will return a link to the new node. If not, it will return a link to itself.

The result is that each instance will return a link to a successor to its predecessor node. In one case, that link will be a new node. In the other cases, the node will return a link to itself.

Now, we have completed this internal node's InsertNode method, and we return to the HeadNode.InsertNode method. The nextLink instance variable is assigned to the returned value — which in this case is the same as what nextLink pointed to beforehand. The link to the head node itself is passed back to the List.Insert method.

You may wonder why HeadNode.InsertNode is a function, since we would never, with this algorithm, change the value of the head node. We need the InsertNode methods of the InternalNode and TailNode classes to be functions, so they can return the successor. Because HeadNode inherits from the same superclass as InternalNode and TailNode, they have the same interface for each method. Thus HeadNode's InsertNode method is a function, too.

Now, if our new element contained a key that had been greater than all of the keys in the list, successive nodes would have kept passing InsertNode messages until a message reached the tail node. The TailNode.InsertNode method, however, knows that if the message had been passed that far in the list, the node must belong at the end. Thus the TailNode.InsertNode method simply creates the new node, links it, and passes a link to the new node back to the last internal node. The recursion unwinds as before, and the order of the list is maintained.

23.6 DELETING A NODE

Deleting a node from a linked list is somewhat similar to inserting a node: each node sends a message to its successor until the appropriate node says "That's me!" This time, though, we want to send a message to delete the node from the list.

Each node will pass along a message called DelNode to its next node until the node to delete is found. That node will return its nextLink to its predecessor. The predecessor will understand this returned link as the new link it should use for its own nextLink. Then, the recursion will unwind all the way.

As for insertion, each internal node will return a link to what its predecessor should use as its nextLink. When inserting, the node that figured out that the new element should be contained in its previous node returned a link to a new node rather than a link to itself. Now, for deletion, the node that figures out it should be deleted returns its own nextLink rather than a link to itself. For example, in Figure 23.18, B's node is deleted. This means that the nextLink instance variable of A's node is now a link to C's node.

Our strategy, then, is to have each node ask its next node if it is the node to be deleted, using the DelNode message. If the next node is the node to delete, it returns a link to the following node in the list; if it isn't the node to delete, it returns a link to itself. The return value of DelNode is compared to the node's nextLink. The deletion takes place when the returned value from DelNode is not the same as the original link.

Figure 23.18 *Rearranging links after deleting B's node*

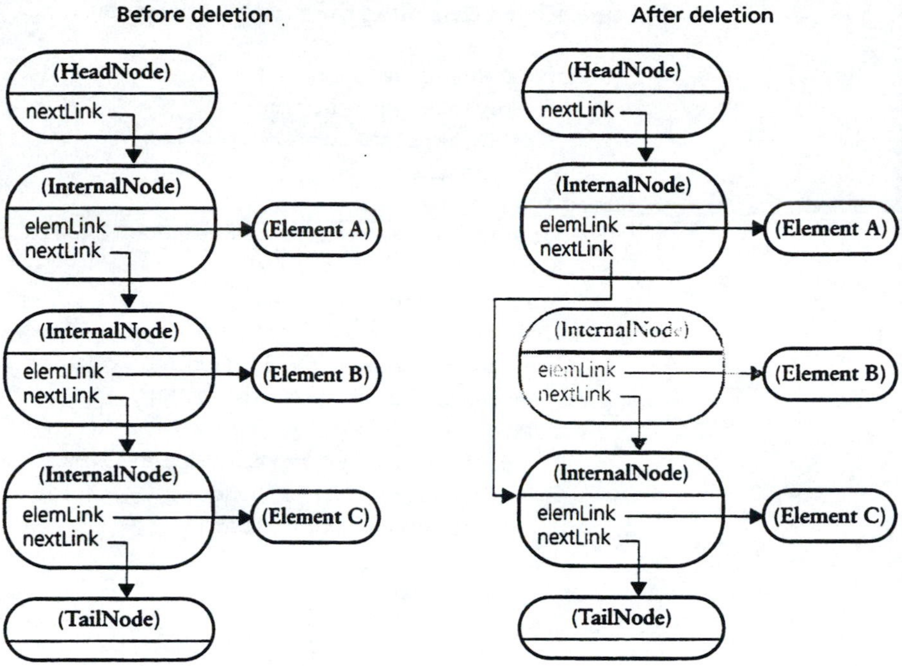

Before deletion | After deletion

We will also want to return a link to the element we have deleted; as pointed out in Chapter 22, we may want to delete an element from one list and add it to another. We'll use a variable parameter to return the deleted element. (Note that this is one of the rare times where we will use a variable parameter in a function.)

The code that gets us started is the `Delete` function:

```
FUNCTION List.Delete(keyToDelete: string): ElementAsn;
VAR
  delElemLink: ElementAsn; { link to deleted element }
BEGIN
  headLink := headLink^.DelNode(keyToDelete, delElemLink);
  Delete := delElemLink;
END;
```

The list asks the head node to delete the element from the list and send back the link to the deleted element in the `VAR` parameter. Then, `Delete` will return that deleted element's link to whatever method asked the list to perform the deletion.

Let's turn to the code that defines how the nodes handle the `DelNode` message. The `HeadNode` passes the `DelNode` message to the next node. `DelNode` will return a link to the successor (possibly a new successor) of the current node. If `DelNode` returns the same value as the current `nextLink` instance variable, the successor remains the same; that is, it is not deleted. Otherwise, we store the link to its successor in the nextLink instance variable. We also return a link to the deleted element in the variable parameter.

```
FUNCTION HeadNode.DelNode(
        keyToDelete: string;
        VAR delElemLink: ElementAsn)
        : NodeAsn;
VAR
  newNextLink: NodeAsn; { node that should be next in list }
BEGIN
  { get successor }
  newNextLink := nextLink^.DelNode(keyToDelete, delElemLink);
  { If new successor is different, replace nextLink inst. var. }
  IF newNextLink <> nextLink THEN
    BEGIN
      delElemLink := nextLink^.GetElemLink; {return deld element}
      Dispose(nextLink, Done);
      nextLink := newNextLink;
    END;
  DelNode := @self
END;
```

The DelNode message is sent by the previous node in the list to the current node. The method returns a link to either itself or its own next node to the previous node. That is, if the current node is the node to delete, the DelNode method will return a link to the next node in the list. If the current node is not the node to delete, the node will pass the DelNode message to the next node in the list and then return a link to itself. In the second case, this method determines whether the link returned from passing the DelNode message is the same as the current nextLink instance variable. If the return is different, that means that the neighbor should be deleted and the current node should adjust its nextLink instance variable accordingly, using the link returned from the DelNode method.

```
FUNCTION InternalNode.DelNode(
        keyToDelete: string;
        VAR delElemLink: elementAsn)
        : NodeAsn;
VAR
  newNextLink: NodeAsn; { node that should be next in list }
  nodeLinkToReturn: NodeAsn; { link to new neighbor in list }

BEGIN
  { If this is the node to delete, return the next node in list. }
  IF elemLink^.GetKey = keyToDelete THEN
    nodeLinkToReturn := nextLink
```

```
    ELSE
      BEGIN
        { Get new neighbor. }
        newNextLink := nextLink^.DelNode(keyToDelete, delElemLink);
        { If new neighbor differs, replace nextLink inst. var. }
        IF newNextLink <> nextLink THEN
          BEGIN
            delElemLink := nextLink^.GetElemLink;
            Dispose(nextLink, Done);
            nextLink := newNextLink;
          END;
        { Return current node. }
        nodeLinkToReturn := @self;
      END;
  DelNode := nodeLinkToReturn
END;
```

The DelNode method potentially changes the successor of a node. However, the TailNode does not have a successor, so it can always return itself.

```
FUNCTION TailNode.DelNode(
        keyToDelete: string;
        VAR delElemLink: elementAsn)
        : NodeAsn;
BEGIN
  delElemLink := NIL; { The element to delete was not found. }
  DelNode := @self;
END;
```

Let's start again with our list from the last section, but this time we'll delete the 'C' node from the list. This means that the head node is sent the DelNode message with the key 'C'. As with insertion, HeadNode.DelNode begins with a recursive call:

```
newNextLink := nextLink^.DelNode(keyToDelete);
```

This means that we pass the DelNode message to the first internal node. Now, we move to the code of InternalNode.DelNode. This method begins with a comparison:

```
IF (elemLink^.GetKey = keyToDelete) THEN
```

In this case, elemLink links to an instance with 'A', and the keyToDelete is 'C', so we move on to the ELSE clause. The ELSE clause begins with another recursive call:

```
newNextLink := nextLink^.DelNode(keyToDelete);
```

So we now move to the second internal node. This is also an instance of `InternalNode`, so we use the `InternalNode.DelNode` method. We begin with the comparison, and this time the keys match. The `THEN` clause says:

```
nodeLinkToReturn := nextLink
```

Thus the node that the `next` instance variable points to (the 'D' node) is returned. Where is this link returned? To the instance that sent the message — in this case, A's node. The result is assigned to a variable called `newNextLink`. When we return to that first internal node, we have the situation as shown in Figure 23.19. The next line in the `DelNode` method (for the node containing the 'A' element), now that we have finished the recursive call, is a comparison:

```
IF newNextLink <> nextLink THEN
```

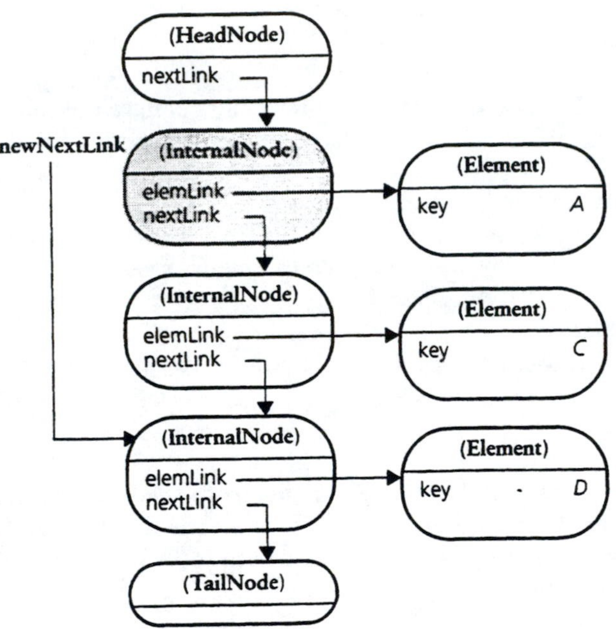

Figure 23.19 *Deletion: newNextLink receives the link returned by the deleted node*

When we compare these two links, we see that they do not point to the same instance. `newNextLink` points to a node with a link to the 'D' element, and `nextLink` points to a node with a link to the 'C' element. Thus we execute the `BEGIN/END` block after the `IF`.

The following block performs the deletion:

```
BEGIN
  delElemLink := nextLink^.GetElemLink;
  Dispose(nextLink, Done);
  nextLink := newNextLink;
END;
```

We'll assume that we can define a `GetElemLink` for the `Node` classes that returns the link to the element (or `NIL` in the case of the head and tail nodes). Here, we place the link to the element of the deleted node in the formal parameter `delElemLink` (assuming another instance wants it; it is that instance's responsibility to dispose of the element when it is done).

The next statement disposes the node that `nextLink` links to. This way, we can allow the memory to be recycled. Except for the link to the element, there is no trace of the internal node.

The problem now is that the list is no longer connected. In the code, we see that an assignment statement takes care of this for us — the `nextLink` instance variable is linked to the same instance as the `newNextLink` variable. This reconnects the list, as shown in Figure 23.20.

Figure 23.20

Relinking a list when a node has been deleted

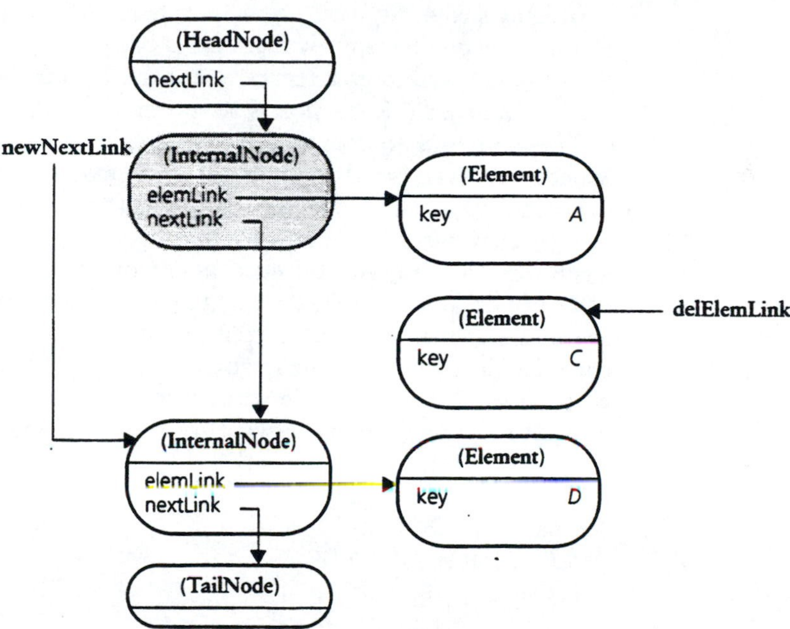

To complete the function, `InternalNode.DelNode` returns the address to the current node. This link is sent back to the assignment statement in `HeadNode.DelNode`. The `newNextLink` variable in this method is now pointing to the first internal node.

We are at the point in `HeadNode.DelNode` where we make the comparison:

```
IF newNextLink <> nextLink THEN
```

In this case, the comparison is false because both `newNextLink` and `nextLink` are links to the same node. This means we skip the `IF` clause and go to the next statement, which simply returns the head node to the instance that sent the initial message.

The `TailNode.DelNode` method plays the same role that `TailNode.InsertNode` did for the insertion. If the tail node receives the `DelNode` message, that means that the node was not found in the list. The tail node sends itself back to the node that sent it the `DelNode` message. Then, each instance will return itself to its predecessor, and the list will be unchanged. Because the node is not found, the tail node also sets the `delElemLink` parameter to `NIL`.

23.7 ITERATORS

So far, we have examined internal manipulations of the list. But what if we just want to walk through the list, accessing each item? For example, each element knows to draw itself, though each may draw differently using polymorphism. How could we draw them all in order?

We could take either a recursive approach, like we did with `Search`, or an iterative approach. Recursion is simple and elegant, but once started, a recursive method runs to completion — we can't do half of a recursive method. Suppose we want to draw half the elements, then do something else, then draw the other half; our recursive method won't serve our purposes. In another example, we might have two lists, and we'd like to pair up the elements from one list with the elements of another.

We can do all of these tasks using arrays indexed by an integer variable, but as we said at the beginning of this chapter, arrays have serious limitations of data manipulation. Thus we're going to extend the idea of an indexed list, but we'll use our linked lists instead of arrays and an object instead of an integer. First, let's consider what we want to do by writing some pseudocode to display the elements in a list:

```
Get first node
WHILE NOT at end of list DO
   BEGIN
      Draw this node's element
      Get next node in list
   END
```

What we are doing is going through the list, one node at a time. For each node, we determine whether we are at the end of the list. If not, we draw the element linked to by this node and move on to the next node. How can we handle the concept of "this node"?

We can create something called an *iterator*, an object that contains a link to "this node." Thus an iterator is something like the index in a `FOR` loop; it keeps track of where we are in a list, and knows when we have reached the end of the list. Iterators have the following methods, all of which we have seen in the preceding pseudocode:

- `Init` — sets the iterator to the head of the list
- `Advance` — moves the iterator to the next item in the list
- `EndOfList` — returns `true` if the iterator is at the end of the list
- `GetCurrentElement` — retrieves the element from the current node

From this list comes a general class definition of an iterator:

```
Iterator = OBJECT
  CONSTRUCTOR Init;
  PROCEDURE Advance; VIRTUAL;
  FUNCTION EndOfList: boolean; VIRTUAL;
  FUNCTION GetCurrentElement: ElementAsn; VIRTUAL;
PRIVATE
END;
```

This iterator is generic — in particular, it doesn't indicate what kind of list it iterates over. For instance, if it contained an integer instance variable, it could iterate over an array. Rather than make the preceeding iterator more specific, we'll create a more specific subclass that will work with our particular linked list implementation. So, let's create a subclass called `NodeIterator`.

```
NodeIteratorAsn = ^NodeIterator;
NodeIterator = OBJECT (Iterator)
  CONSTRUCTOR Init( newCurNodeLink: NodeAsn);
  PROCEDURE Advance; VIRTUAL;
  FUNCTION EndOfList: boolean; VIRTUAL;
  FUNCTION GetCurrentElement: ElementAsn; VIRTUAL;
PRIVATE
  curNodeLink: NodeAsn;
END;
```

The subclass contains an instance variable called `curNodeLink`. This variable is the index and will indicate our current position in the list. In an array implementation, this instance variable might be an integer.

We also need to define the constructor; the iterator has to be initialized with the head of the list. The iterator has to receive that information, in this case, from the `List`. It's very common for lists to contain a method called `MakeIterator`, to initialize an iterator based on the particular implementation. Thus we can create a new iterator for our list by using the following code:

```
FUNCTION List.MakeIterator: IteratorAsn;
BEGIN
   MakeIterator := New(NodeIteratorAsn, Init(headLink));
END;
```

This one-line constructor simply creates a new link to an iterator and initializes that iterator with the head of the list.

Now, with this information, we can code our pseudocode for displaying all of the elements in a list. Suppose we had a drawing program and wanted to "refresh" the screen, that is, to ask the program to redraw all of the shapes in a list, in order. If we assume that we have a program in which we can add `GPButtons`, we can create a button called `RefreshButton`, and its `Activate` method should walk through the list of shapes. (We'll assume the `RefreshButton` class has the customary link to the drawing area in an instance variable called `drawAreaLink`.) The code follows from our earlier pseudocode. The `Activate` method of the `RefreshButton` draws all the shapes in the list `shapesLink`, an instance variable. Note that we don't care how the list is stored; all we need to know is that we have an iterator and, from that iterator, can retrieve the next element in the list, then send a message to that element.

```
PROCEDURE RefreshButton.Activate;
VAR
  drawIteratorLink : IteratorAsn; { link to current node }
  curElemLink : ElementAsn; { current element in list }
BEGIN
  drawAreaLink^.Clear(backgroundColor); { bg color set elsewhere }
  drawIteratorLink:= shapesLink^.MakeIterator;
  drawIteratorLink^.Advance;
  WHILE NOT drawIteratorLink^.EndOfList DO
    BEGIN
      curElemLink := drawIteratorLink^.GetCurrentElement;
      curElemLink^.Draw(drawAreaLink);
      drawIteratorLink^.Advance;
    END
END;
```

Let's step through the code. The first statement, `drawIteratorLink := shapesLink^.MakeIterator;`, initializes the iterator. The next statement, `drawIteratorLink^.Advance`, moves the iterator to the first piece of information. Then, we enter the loop. The condition `drawIteratorLink^.EndOfList` sends a message to the iterator to determine whether we are at the end of the list. Within the loop, we retrieve the element whose link is contained within the current position in the list; then we send a `Draw` method to that element. Finally, we move to the next position in the list. It's important to note that this code does not mention anything specifically about nodes. This code will work if the list is an array or a linked list.

So, let's turn to the actual implementation of the `NodeIterator` methods. The `NodeIterator` class contains a single instance variable, indicating the position within the list. Thus the three methods (besides the constructor) that do anything rely on the link to the current node to do most of the work. The `Init` method starts at the beginning of the list; then the iterator's `Advance` method moves the iterator to the next node in the list. We can return the element link contained within the node with the `GetCurrentElement` method. The `EndOfList` method returns `true` if the current node is the end of the list.

```
CONSTRUCTOR NodeIterator.Init(headOfList: NodeAsn);
BEGIN
   curNodeLink := headOfList;
END;

PROCEDURE NodeIterator.Advance;
BEGIN
   curNodeLink := curNodeLink^.GetNextLink;
END;

FUNCTION NodeIterator.GetCurrentElement: ElementAsn;
BEGIN
   GetCurrentElement := curNodeLink^.GetElemLink;
END;

FUNCTION NodeIterator.EndOfList: boolean;
BEGIN
   EndOfList := curNodeLink^.EndOfList;
END;
```

Each of these methods is fairly straightforward. The `Init` message sets the current node to be the beginning of the list; the others simply pass the message on to the current node.

This implies, then, that we have to create some new methods for the nodes: `GetNextLink`, `GetElemLink` and `EndOfList`. The first two are standard `Get` methods: We simply return the appropriate instance variable. In our list, the tail node does not have a `nextLink` instance variable, and both the head and the tail node lack a link to an element. In both of those cases, we can use `NIL` instead of retrieving the "real" valuc.

```
FUNCTION HeadNode.GetNextLink : NodeAsn;
BEGIN
   GetNextLink := nextLink;
END;

FUNCTION InternalNode.GetNextLink : NodeAsn;
BEGIN
   GetNextLink := nextLink;
END;

FUNCTION TailNode.GetNextLink: NodeAsn;
BEGIN
  GetNextLink := NIL;
END;
```

The `GetElemLink` function returns the link to the element. There is none in the head node, so the function returns `NIL`, as it does for the tail.

```
FUNCTION HeadNode.GetElemLink: ElementAsn;
BEGIN
  GetElemLink := NIL;
END;

FUNCTION InternalNode.GetElemLink: ElementAsn;
BEGIN
  GetElemLink := elemLink;
END;

FUNCTION TailNode.GetElemLink: ElementAsn;
BEGIN
  GetElemLink := NIL;
END;
```

We also must define `EndOfList` methods. These boolean methods are eas to define; `EndOfList` is `TRUE` for the tail node, and `FALSE` for the head an internal nodes.

```
FUNCTION HeadNode.EndOfList: boolean;
BEGIN
  EndOfList := false;
END;

FUNCTION InternalNode.EndOfList: boolean;
BEGIN
  EndOfList := false;
END;

FUNCTION TailNode.EndOfList: boolean;
BEGIN
  EndOfList := TRUE;
END;
```

With these methods in place, we can walk through the list to perform ju about any action on the elements. The general strategy is shown in th `RefreshButton.Activate` method; all we have to do is change the statemen so we send the `Draw` method to whatever action we would like to do to the lis

23.8 BOUNDARY CONDITIONS

Ideally, whenever you write a program, you would like to check all the poss ble conditions. This is best done by hand simulation. Our insertion and del tion walk-throughs show how a linked list program should be hand simulate

When you insert and delete from a linked list, however, some special conditions may arise that must be checked.

These problems usually occur at the beginning and end of your list manipulation. Thus, when you hand simulate your code and pseudocode, check the boundary conditions. First, determine that the linked list is initialized correctly, then check what happens when you insert the first node into the list.

Once your program passes the initial test, examine what happens when it tries to delete the last node in the list. You also may want to see what happens when the list has only one node and your program wants to delete it.

Finally, check a typical case. Make a list with three or four nodes and see what happens when you insert a node into the middle of the list. Is the correct spot for insertion found? After the insertion, are all the pointers pointing to nodes in the correct order? What happens if you insert at the end of the list? After answering these questions, you may want to do the same for the code that deletes nodes from your linked list.

Summary

This chapter looked at a method for manipulating linked lists. Linked lists are more powerful than arrays, and allow you to create programs that use only as much memory as necessary. Instead of declaring a maximum size array, you can use linked lists that are as long (or short) as you want.

Linked lists are used in place of arrays when we don't know how many elements we will have in our list. Arrays require us to declare how many elements we will need at compile time; linked lists let us allocate memory for each new instance as we need it at run time. In addition, arrays require a great deal of data movement for maintaining a sorted list.

In OOPas, we have implemented a linked list using three kinds of nodes — a head node, an internal node, and a tail node. The internal nodes hold the data; the head and tail nodes mark the ends of the list.

To insert, delete, and search for a node, we use the same general recursive algorithm. We send a message to the head node, which passes it to the first internal node. If the first internal node can handle the message, it does so; otherwise, it sends the message to the second internal node. When a node is found that can do the right thing (insert, delete, or end the search), it performs its action and sends a value or a message to the instance that send it the message. That instance sends the message back toward the head. The instances unwind the recursion until the head node makes the final response.

We also can access the elements of a linked list sequentially using an iterator. An iterator is a "current" node that we can manipulate. We can set it to the beginning, tell it to advance, and determine whether we are at the end of the list. If we're not at the end, we can perform an action on the current node's element.

Exercises

Understanding Concepts

1. What are the differences between a linked list and an array in terms of accessing information? inserting information? deleting information?
2. Which class of `Node` (head node, internal node, tail node) handles insertion in a linked list? deletion in a linked list? How does this differ from stacks or queues?
3. Suppose that after Section 23.5, we inserted another node with the same key 'C'. Where would it go in the list?
4. What would happen if we `Insert` while using an `Iterator`? What would happen if we `Delete` while using an `Iterator`?

Coding Problems

1. Write a method for the `List` class that takes an `integer` called `num` as a parameter and returns a link to the `num`th node in the list.
2. Write a method that reverses the order of the nodes within the list.

Programming Problems

1. Modify the aquarium program to allow any number of fish, sharks, and plants to exist in the aquarium. Within a "turn," each creature in the aquarium should respond to the current situation (fish moving away from sharks, sharks moving toward fish and eating fish if they occupy the same space). At the end of a turn, the program should generate a random number to determine whether creatures should be added to or deleted from the aquarium. (There should be a 5 percent chance of adding a creature, and a 5 percent chance that one will be deleted.) The number of turns is up to you.
2. Modify the paint program by turning it into a draw program. The user should be able to draw rectangles, ovals, or lines and delete any object on the screen. If an object is deleted, the screen is refreshed; that is, the drawing area is cleared and all the remaining objects are redrawn in the order in which they were created.
3. Modify the draw program from Programming Problem 2 by adding segmentation, or grouping of objects. The user should be able to select a rectangular area of the screen. All objects that are totally inside of that area become a single group. The group is treated as a single unit that can be moved or deleted.
4. Write a program that maintains a registrar's database. The program should read a list of courses (no more than 20) from a file. Then the user should be able to ask the program to do the following:

   a. Add a particular student to a course

b. Print the list of students in a particular course in alphabetical order
c. Print the list of courses in which a particular student is registered
d. Indicate whether a particular student is registered for a particular course
e. Quit the program, which saves the contents of the database in a file

The program may get this information from a graphical interface or from a set of keyboard commands.

5. Write a program that is a polynomial calculator. Suppose that we allow a polynomial to be written as a string — `'3x7 - 4x3 + 1'` represents $3x^7 - 4x^3 + 1$. The program should be able to take two polynomials, and depending on the user's choice, add or multiply them. An additional function should allow the program to evaluate a polynomial for a particular value of x.

6. Write a program that simulates commands in the language LOGO. In that language, a triangular cursor (known as a turtle) starts in the center of the screen, facing the top of the screen. The turtle has a current position and direction. The turtle and the screen can then be controlled with the following commands:

FORWARD <*x*> — moves the turtle <*x*> pixels in the current direction. If the pen is down, a line is also drawn.

BACK <*x*> — moves the turtle <*x*> pixels in the reverse of the current direction (but doesn't change the turtle's direction). If the pen is down, a line is also drawn.

LEFT <*x*> and RIGHT <*x*> — changes the turtle's current direction by <*x*> degrees to the left or right. This occurs whether or not the pen is up.

PEN UP and PEN DOWN — When the program begins the pen is down, meaning that each FORWARD and BACK command has a visible result. PEN UP means that future FORWARD and BACK commands still change the current position but do not show any visible result. PEN DOWN reverses the effect of PEN UP.

TO <*procedure name*>
<*statements*>
END

The TO and END commands are the brackets of a procedure. The TO command gives the name of the procedure and indicates where it begins. This is followed by a series of PEN, FORWARD, BACK, LEFT, RIGHT, or previously declared procedure statements. END denotes the end of the procedure, after which the <*procedure name*> can be used simply by stating <*procedure name*> as a statement.

The following program produces two right triangles, where the turtle's starting position is the lower left corner of the right triangle (Figure 23.21).

```
TO TRIANGLE
   FORWARD 50
   RIGHT 135
   FORWARD 70
   RIGHT 135
   FORWARD 50
END
```

```
TRIANGLE
PEN UP
FORWARD 100
RIGHT 90
PEN DOWN
TRIANGLE
```

Figure 23.21

The results of a simple LOGO program

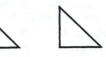

7. Modify Programming Problem 6 by allowing the user to enter the commands from a menu rather than from the keyboard. How would you represent each of the commands using mouse clicks? What do you need the keyboard to do?

8. Write a program to play the card game Crazy Eights. Deal eight cards to the user and eight to the computer. The remaining cards are the stack. The top card of the stack is revealed and becomes the top of the discard pile. The user then discards a card that matches the discard pile's suit OR number. For example, if the discard pile is headed by the jack of clubs, the user can discard any jack or any club. The computer then should discard a card matching the suit or number of the card played by the user. Play alternates between the computer and the user.

   Eights are wild — they match any number and can be played on any turn. When a player discards an 8, that player gets to announce a new suit, which the other player must match on the next turn. A player who cannot make a play must draw cards from the stack until a play is possible. If the stack runs out of cards, all the cards in the discard pile except the top card are shuffled and become the new stack. A player wins by running out of cards.

24

Trees

Your friend Pippin says to you, "I'm thinking of a number between 1 and 1000. I want you to guess what that number is. If you guess wrong, I will tell you whether my number is greater or less than your guess. How many guesses do you need to identify my number?"

The trick to minimizing the number of guesses is realizing that each response of "greater" or "less" eliminates many of the numbers. For example, if you guess 750 and Pippin says "greater," you've eliminated three quarters of the numbers, but if Pippin says "less than," you've eliminated only one quarter of the possibilities. You would like to ensure that you never eliminate fewer possibilities than you could have. You can do this if you always eliminate half of the remaining possibilities.

Thus your first guess should be the halfway point — 500. No matter how your friend Pippin responds, half of the numbers are eliminated. Let's say she answers with "less than." You now know that the number is between 1 and 499. Again you choose the halfway point and guess 250. (Similarly, if Pippin says "greater than" to your first guess of 500, your second guess should be 750.) No matter how your friend responds to your second guess, you have 250 possibilities left. The third guess should again split the possibilities in half, leaving 125 choices. Continuing in this manner, you can leave, in succession, 63, 32, 16, 8, 4, 2, and 1 possibilities. Thus you can close in on a single number between 1 and 1000 in 10 guesses. This method of halving the possibilities successively is known as *binary search,* or *bisection.*

The guesses can be diagrammed as shown in Figure 24.1. In the diagram, each guess, starting at the root "500," has two numbers below it. The number on the left is the next guess if you receive a "less than," and the number on the right is the next guess if you receive a "greater than." So, if your second guess is 750 and you are told "less than," your third guess should be 625.

In the diagram, each number appears only once; and only one set of questions leads to any single number. Each answer can be either "greater than" or "less than" — two choices — so a sequence of ten answers lets you identify

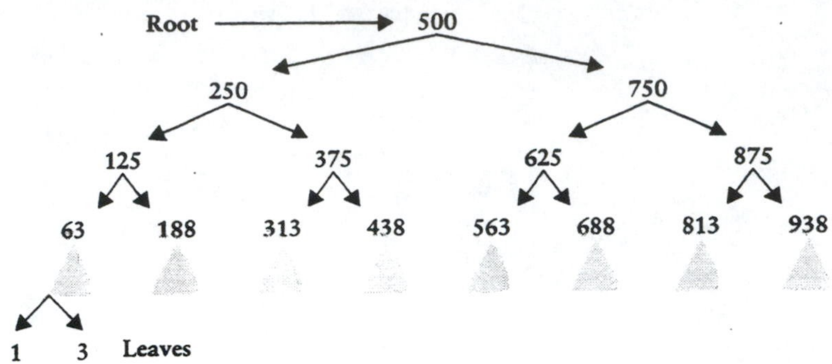

Figure 24.1 *Binary search being used to guess a number*

2^{10} possibilities. Thus any number from 1 to 1000 can be found in ten (or fewer) steps, because 2 to the power of 10 is 1024, which is greater than 1000.

The structure shown is a collection called a *binary tree*. Following our pattern from other collections, each part of the tree is called a *node*. The top node in the tree is called the *root*, and any node that is at the bottom of a path is called a *leaf*. The relationship between consecutive nodes often is expressed in familial terms. For example, in our tree, 250 is the *parent* node of 125 and 375; 125 is the *left child* and 375 is the *right child* of 250.

The root node traditionally is drawn at the top of the tree. Trees are used for storing large sets of data and are particularly useful when we want to access any individual node randomly. Suppose we wanted to store the names and phone numbers of all the people in the Topeka phone book. Imagine what would happen if we put them in linear (sequential) order, so that the first element in the data structure holds 'Aaron' and the last element holds 'Zyman.'

We have seen two data structures to solve this problem — arrays and linear linked lists. When we have to find a particular name in the phone book, the array is clearly the better choice, since by using a subscript, we can access any name in the array more directly than by using a recursive search to move from one node to the next. We even can do a binary search on a sorted array by halving the array index at each iteration.

With a linked list, searching takes more time, because we have to start at the beginning and may have to look at 40,000 names (Aaron, Abbott, Abercrombie, . . .) before finding what we want. On the other hand, to insert a name in the array in alphabetical order, we may have to move thousands of entries; in a linked list, a new element can easily be inserted by having the previous node change a link to point to the new element.

We'd like a collection that lets us perform a binary search while still allowing simple insertion. The binary tree meets this requirement, whereas both arrays and linear linked lists fall short on one requirement or the other. The difference in search speeds can be quite significant — binary search for an ordered array or binary tree takes, on average, $\log_2 n$ for n entries, and sequential search in an unordered array or linked list takes, on average, $n/2$.

24.1 BUILDING A BINARY TREE

As in other collections we have examined, such as stacks, queues, and linked lists, our implementation of trees consists of three overall parts:

1. *An interface:* A single instance that has the basic behaviors we wish our tree to have, namely, insertion, deletion, searching, and traversal.
2. *Implementation nodes:* Many instances that comprise the data structure itself. Unlike the nodes in previous chapters, the nodes in this chapter will have two links to other nodes to provide a branching structure to our tree.
3. *Elements:* The actual instances that the tree "contains." We think of the tree as containing these instances, even though links to the elements are used to provide polymorphism.

We make one assumption when building our first binary tree: No item should appear more than once. Thus our trees can also act as sets, which, unlike the built-in sets of Chapter 17, can contain any kinds of elements and be as large as necessary. Given this assumption, we can build a binary tree from the root up — or down, depending on your point of view. Say we decide to list all the things in a closet. We'll put them in the tree as we pull them out of the closet.

First, we find a bunch of nails. The term 'NAILS' will be the root of our tree (Figure 24.2).

Figure 24.2 *Adding the first element to a binary tree*

NAILS

Next, we find a koala bear. Additions always are made at the bottom of the tree, so the second addition is always a child of the root. In this case, 'KOALA' is a child of 'NAILS'. But on which side? We follow the convention that places "greater" items on the right and "lesser" ones on the left. Since the string 'KOALA' is alphabetically less than the string 'NAILS', it belongs on the left, as in Figure 24.3.

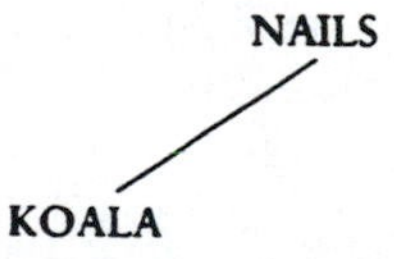

Figure 24.3 *Adding a second element to a binary tree*

```
      NAILS
      /
KOALA
```

Going back to the closet, we find a fishbowl. To determine where the new node belongs in the tree, we start at the root. Since 'FISHBOWL' < 'NAILS', we move to the left. We cannot insert 'FISHBOWL' as the left child of 'NAILS', however, because 'KOALA' is already in that location. Since the desired location is occupied, we compare what we want to add to what is occupying the space. Here, we compare 'KOALA' to 'FISHBOWL'. Since 'KOALA' > 'FISHBOWL', we move to the right. Nothing is currently at the right of 'KOALA', so we insert 'FISHBOWL' in that location, as in Figure 24.4.

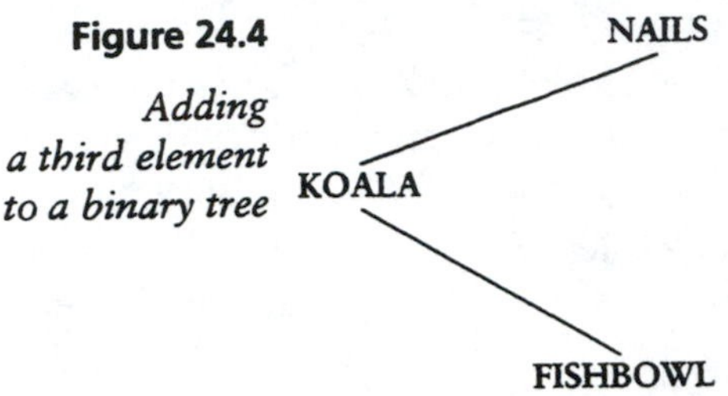

Figure 24.4 *Adding a third element to a binary tree*

The next item we find is a saxophone. We've now developed a general strategy. We start at the root and compare the new item to the current node. If it is less than the current node, we move to the left; otherwise, we move to the right. We see whether a node currently exists in that location. If one does, we again move to the left or right. Otherwise, we create a new node and attach it to the bottom of the tree. Thus, to insert 'SAXOPHONE', we compare the item to 'NAILS'. Since 'SAXOPHONE' > 'NAILS', we move to the right. Nothing is on the right of 'NAILS', so we can insert 'SAXOPHONE' there, as in Figure 24.5.

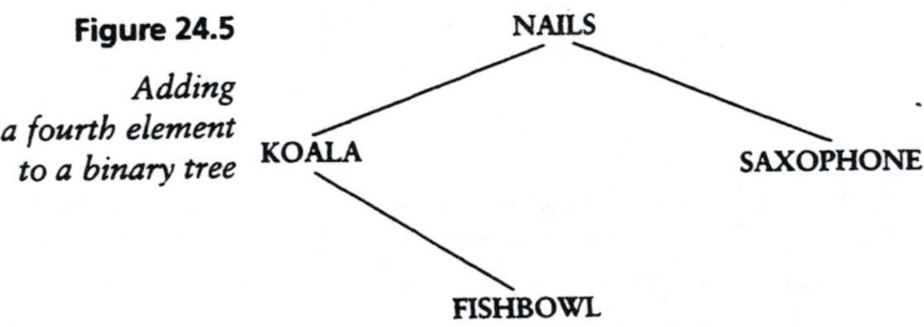

Figure 24.5 *Adding a fourth element to a binary tree*

Notice that, unlike a linear structure, the order of the input determines the shape of the tree. For example, if the input had the order 'KOALA', 'NAILS', 'SAXOPHONE', 'FISHBOWL', the tree would look like Figure 24.6. And if the input was in the sorted order 'SAXOPHONE', 'NAILS', 'KOALA', 'FISHBOWL', the tree would look like Figure 24.7.

A structure like that in Figure 24.7, which has the unfortunate name *degenerate tree*, is nothing more than a linked list down the left side of the tree. Because the items came from the input in sorted order, each element became the left child of the previous addition. In Figure 24.5 and Figure 24.6, how-

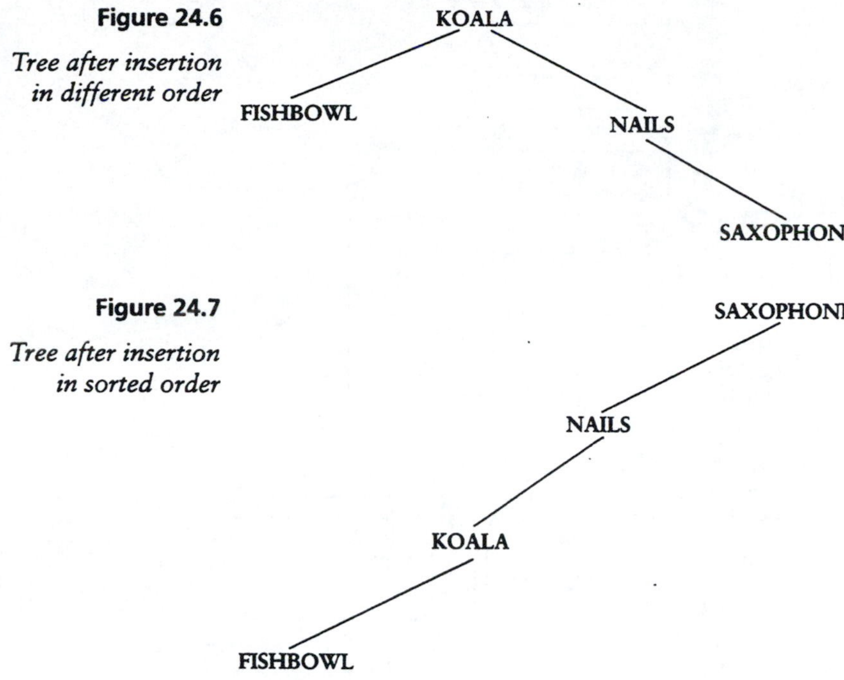

Figure 24.6

Tree after insertion in different order

Figure 24.7

Tree after insertion in sorted order

ever, the trees have about the same number of nodes on both sides and so are called *balanced* trees. The diagram of the 1000 numbers in Figure 24.1 is thus a perfectly balanced tree — all the leaf nodes are either 9 or 10 links away from the root. Most binary trees are somewhere between the perfect balance of Figure 24.1 and the degenerate tree of Figure 24.7. If the input appears for the most part in random order, the tree will be for the most part balanced.

Note that a balanced tree is more efficient than a degenerate one, because its maximum *height*— that is, the number of nodes between the root and the furthest leaf — is as small as possible.

24.2 INTERFACE OF A BINARY TREE

Now let's consider the implementation of a binary tree. It's probably easiest to look at a binary tree with all of the connected pointers, shown in Figure 24.8.

Figure 24.8 looks imposing, but let's take it one part at a time. At the top of the tree is the root; this node, as we have seen in head nodes earlier, simply contains a link to the first node in the tree. Then, the tree contains four internal nodes, each with three links. One of them links to the element, and the other links, labeled `leftLink` and `rightLink`, link to the "children" or "subtrees" of the node. These `leftLink` and `rightLink` instance variables link either to another internal node, or at the bottom of the tree, to leaf nodes. The

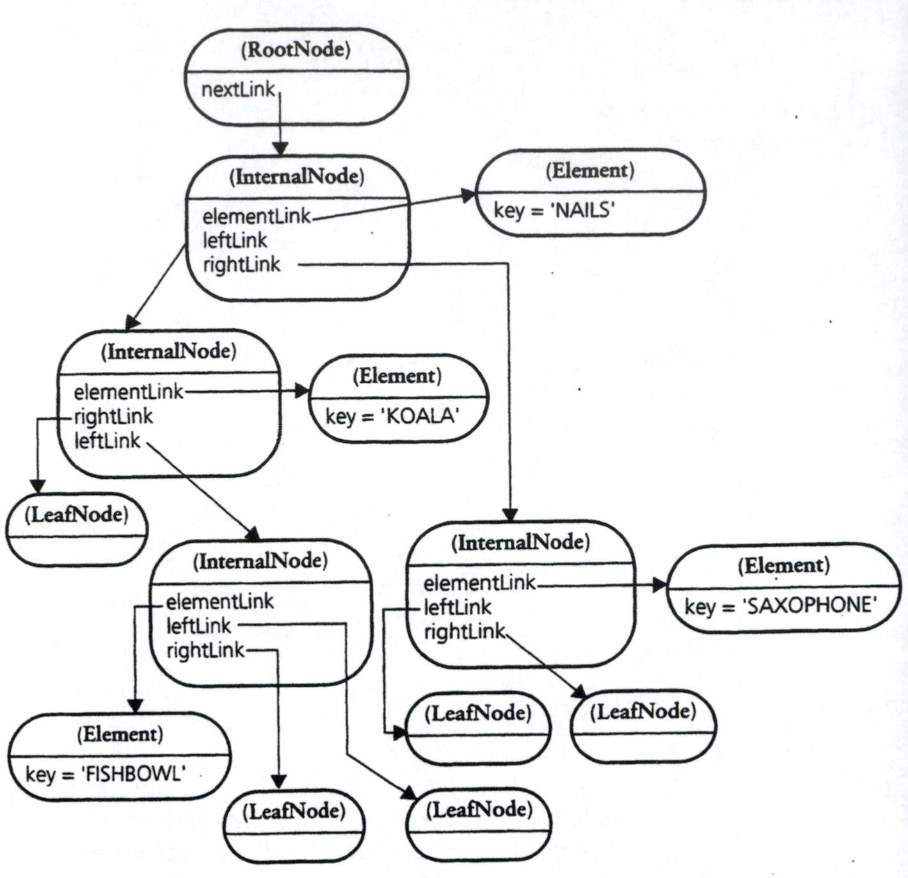

Figure 24.8

An instance diagram showing a binary tree

leaf nodes are like the tail nodes in Chapters 22 and 23, except that a tree has many leaf nodes (as opposed to the one tail node in a linked list and queue). Note that the change from an internal node in a queue or list to an internal node in a tree requires only a single additional link.

To enhance our visual depiction, we will use a shortcut (just for this chapter). We'll draw the element that `elemLink` points to inside the internal node as shown in Figure 24.9.

Now, let's look at the type declarations for each of these kinds of nodes. As before, we begin with an `Element`, which we assume contains a `key` instance variable (keeping in mind that we can exploit polymorphism by using links).

```
ElementAsn = ^Element;
Element = OBJECT
  CONSTRUCTOR Init(newKey: string);
  FUNCTION GetKey: string;
  PROCEDURE Draw; VIRTUAL;
PRIVATE
  key: string; { unique identifier }
END;
```

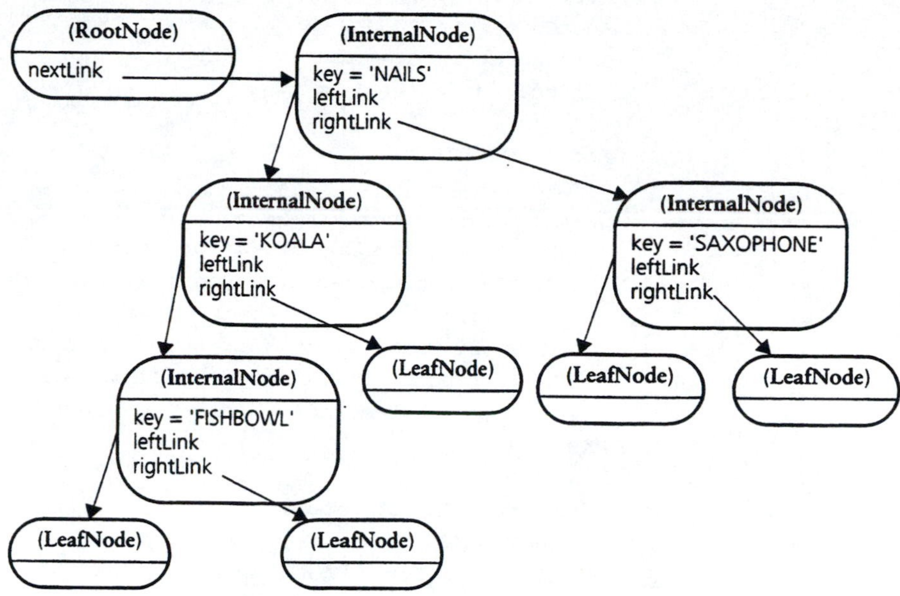

Figure 24.9 *A tree redrawn showing elements drawn contained in nodes*

Next, we need to consider what we want to do with the tree as a whole. In this chapter, we will examine five operations:

1. Initialization: Constructing an empty tree
2. Searching: Finding an element in the tree, given a key
3. Inserting: Adding an element to the tree
4. Deleting: Removing an element from the tree
5. Traversing the tree: Performing some action at each node

We'll define these methods for the tree as follows:

```
TreeActionAsn = ^TreeAction;
Tree = OBJECT
  CONSTRUCTOR Init;
  FUNCTION Search(keyToFind: string): ElementAsn; VIRTUAL;
  PROCEDURE Insert(newElemLink: ElementAsn); VIRTUAL;
  FUNCTION Delete(keyToRemove : string) : ElementAsn; VIRTUAL;
  PROCEDURE Traverse(actionLink : TreeActionAsn); VIRTUAL;
PRIVATE
  rootLink : NodeAsn;
END;
```

The tree's one private instance variable is a link to the root of the tree. As with the linked lists, stacks, and queues, we'll employ smart nodes to handle the different tree functions. The tree shown in Figure 24.9 has three kinds of nodes — a head node, internal nodes (that contain the data), and leaf nodes. We can define the interface as follows:

```
NodeAsn = ^Node;
RootNodeAsn = ^RootNode;
InternalNodeAsn = ^InternalNode;
LeafNodeAsn = ^LeafNode;

Node = OBJECT
  CONSTRUCTOR Init;
  DESTRUCTOR Done; VIRTUAL;
  FUNCTION SearchNode(keyToFind: string): ElementAsn; VIRTUAL;
  FUNCTION AddSubtree(keyToAdd : string;
      subtreeLink : NodeAsn): NodeAsn; VIRTUAL;
  PROCEDURE TraverseNode(actionLink : TreeActionAsn); VIRTUAL;
  FUNCTION DeleteNode(keyToFind : string;
      VAR delElemLink : ElementAsn) : NodeAsn; VIRTUAL;
END;

RootNode = OBJECT (Node)
  CONSTRUCTOR Init;
  DESTRUCTOR Done; VIRTUAL;
  FUNCTION SearchNode(keyToFind: string): ElementAsn; VIRTUAL;
  FUNCTION AddSubtree(keyToAdd : string;
      subtreeLink : NodeAsn): NodeAsn; VIRTUAL;
  PROCEDURE TraverseNode(actionLink : TreeActionAsn); VIRTUAL;
  FUNCTION DeleteNode(keyToFind : string;
      VAR delElemLink  : ElementAsn) : NodeAsn; VIRTUAL;
PRIVATE
  nextLink : NodeAsn; { first node in tree }
END;

InternalNode = OBJECT (Node)
  CONSTRUCTOR Init(
      newElemLink: ElementAsn;
      newLeftLink, newRightLink: NodeAsn);
  DESTRUCTOR Done; VIRTUAL;
  FUNCTION SearchNode(keyToFind: string): ElementAsn; VIRTUAL;
  FUNCTION AddSubtree(keyToAdd : string;
      subtreeLink : NodeAsn): NodeAsn; VIRTUAL;
  PROCEDURE TraverseNode(actionLink : TreeActionAsn); VIRTUAL;
  FUNCTION DeleteNode(keyToFind : string;
      VAR delElemLink  : ElementAsn) : NodeAsn; VIRTUAL;
PRIVATE
  elemLink: ElementAsn; { link to data }
  leftLink,   { link to left subtree }
  rightLink : NodeAsn; { link to right subtree }
END;
```

```
LeafNode = OBJECT (Node)
  CONSTRUCTOR Init;
  DESTRUCTOR Done; VIRTUAL;
  FUNCTION SearchNode(keyToFind: string): ElementAsn; VIRTUAL;
  FUNCTION AddSubtree(keyToAdd : string;
      subtreeLink : NodeAsn): NodeAsn; VIRTUAL;
  PROCEDURE TraverseNode(actionLink : TreeActionAsn); VIRTUAL;
  FUNCTION DeleteNode(keyToFind : string;
      VAR delElemLink : ElementAsn) : NodeAsn; VIRTUAL;
END;
```

In the following sections, we'll define the code for each of the methods. At this time, we also can define a class for the `TreeAction`, which is much like the `EAAction` class we used in Chapter 21:

```
TreeAction = OBJECT
  CONSTRUCTOR Init;
  DESTRUCTOR Done; VIRTUAL;
  PROCEDURE DoIt(elementLink : ElementAsn); VIRTUAL;
END;
```

We will see how the virtual method `DoIt` is employed by a tree in Section 24.6.

24.3 INITIALIZING THE TREE

We'll begin by initializing the data structure. In this case, an empty tree is very similar to the empty linked list — it contains a root node and a leaf node, and the root simply points to the leaf, as shown in Figure 24.10.

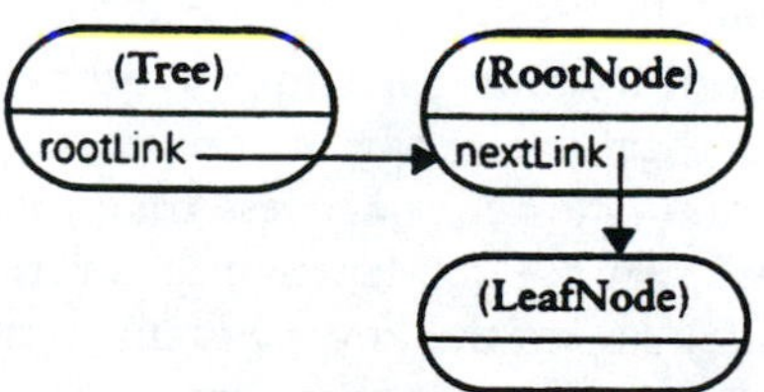

Figure 24.10
Initial binary tree

The code for initializing the tree uses three very simple methods:

```
CONSTRUCTOR Tree.Init;
BEGIN
  rootLink := New(RootNodeAsn, Init);
END;
```

```
CONSTRUCTOR RootNode.Init;
BEGIN
  INHERITED Init;
  nextLink := New(LeafNodeAsn, Init);
END;

{ LeafNode has no instance variables of its own. }
CONSTRUCTOR LeafNode.Init;
BEGIN
  INHERITED Init;
END;
```

The `Tree.Init` method uses the `New` procedure to create a new root, an stores a link to that root in `rootLink`. In turn, the `RootNode.Init` method use the `New` procedure to create a new leaf and stores a link to that leaf in `next Link`. This gives us the result shown in Figure 24.10.

24.4 SEARCHING FOR A NODE IN THE TREE

The root and leaf nodes of a tree are simply placeholders. When we initializ the tree, it does not have any data. Before we look at adding a node, let's loo at the easier function of searching for a node. The `Search` code will help us t build the `Insert` code in the next section.

The algorithm for searching within a tree is similar to that for search withi a linked list. In the linked list, we began at the head node and passed a me sage to the next node. If the next node was the node with the element to fin we returned a link to its element; otherwise, we sent a message to the ne node in the list (recursively). The search stopped when we found the elemen or when we found an element that was greater than the key we wanted to fin or when we reached the end of the list.

In a tree, we essentially do the same thing. We begin at the root, and mo through the nodes until we find either the element or a leaf. The advantage using a binary tree is that we can narrow the search. From any given node, a nodes to the left contain keys that are less than the current key; all nodes the right contain keys that are greater than the current key. Thus we can con pare the current node's key to the key we want to find and send a message the left or to the right according to that comparison. In pseudocode terms, v have the following:

Tree.Search(keyToFind: string)
Purpose: Finds an element in the tree
Pseudocode:
    Send SearchNode message to root node

RootNode.SearchNode(keyToFind: string)
Purpose: Finds an element in the tree
Returns : a link to the current element
Pseudocode:
  Send SearchNode message to next node

InternalNode.SearchNode(keyToFind: string)
Purpose: Finds an element in the tree
Returns: A link to the current element
Pseudocode:
  Get key from elemLink's element; store in currentKey
  IF currentKey = keyToFind THEN
    SearchNode is true (key has been found); return current element
  ELSE IF currentKey > keyToFind THEN
    Send SearchNode message to left node
  ELSE
    Send SearchNode message to right node

LeafNode.SearchNode(keyToFind: string)
Purpose: Finds an element in the tree
Pseudocode:
  SearchNode is false (if a leaf is reached, key is not in tree); return NIL

From here, we can develop the code for these methods:

```
FUNCTION Tree.Search(keyToFind: string): ElementAsn;
BEGIN
  Search := rootLink^.SearchNode(keyToFind);
END;

FUNCTION RootNode.SearchNode(keyToFind: string): ElementAsn;
BEGIN
  SearchNode := nextLink^.SearchNode(keyToFind);
END;

FUNCTION InternalNode.SearchNode(keyToFind: string) : ElementAsn;
VAR
  currentKey: string;{ key in node's element }
BEGIN
  currentKey := elemLink^.GetKey;
  IF (currentKey = keyToFind) THEN { we've found it! }
    SearchNode := elemLink
  ELSE IF (currentKey > keyToFind) THEN
    SearchNode := leftLink^.SearchNode(keyToFind)
  ELSE { currentKey < keyToFind }
    SearchNode := rightLink^.SearchNode(keyToFind)
END;
```

```
FUNCTION LeafNode.SearchNode(keyToFind: string) : ElementAsn;
BEGIN
  SearchNode := NIL;
END;
```

Let's walk through the code. We'll assume we are beginning with the tree shown in Figure 24.9. Let's search for the 'FISHBOWL'. We begin with `Tree.Search` sending a `SearchNode` message to the `rootLink`. The root node then executes its one statement,

```
Search := nextLink^.SearchNode(keyToFind);
```

sending a `SearchNode` message to the node `nextLink`. We thus have a message sent as shown in Figure 24.11.

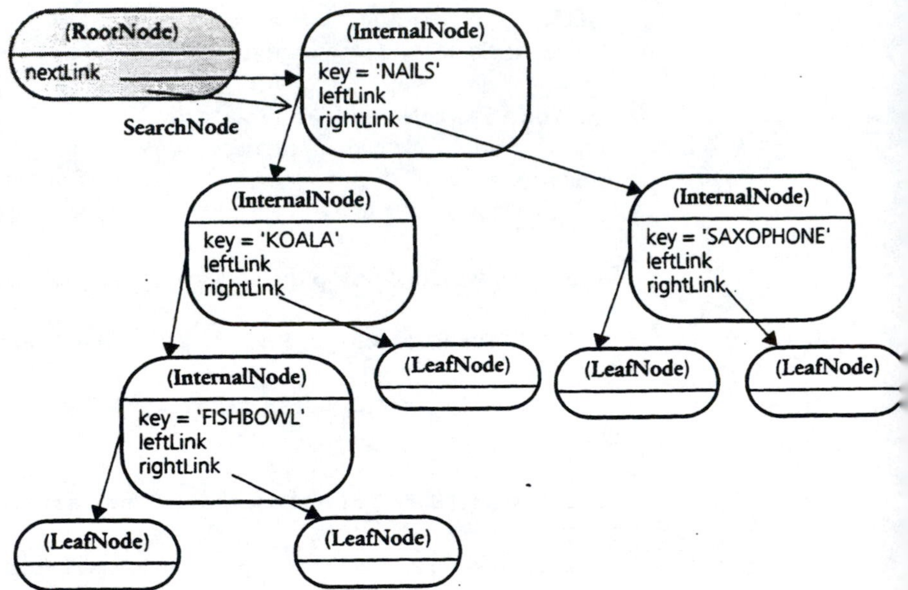

Figure 24.11 *SearchNode message for FISHBOWL being sent to first internal node*

We now execute the `InternalNode.Search` method. We begin by retrieving the key from the element; here the `currentKey` local variable is set to 'NAILS'. Then, we compare the `currentKey` ('NAILS') to the `keyToFind` ('FISHBOWL'). Since `currentKey > keyToFind`, we perform the associated code:

```
ELSE IF (currentKey > keyToFind) THEN
  Search := leftLink^.SearchNode(keyToFind)
```

This means that we send a `SearchNode` message to the instance that `left` links to, as shown in Figure 24.12.

Now, we use the same method, but this time using the instance of `InternalNode` whose `elemLink` links to an element with the key 'KOALA'. Agai

Figure 24.12

Sending SearchNode for FISHBOWL to the left subtree

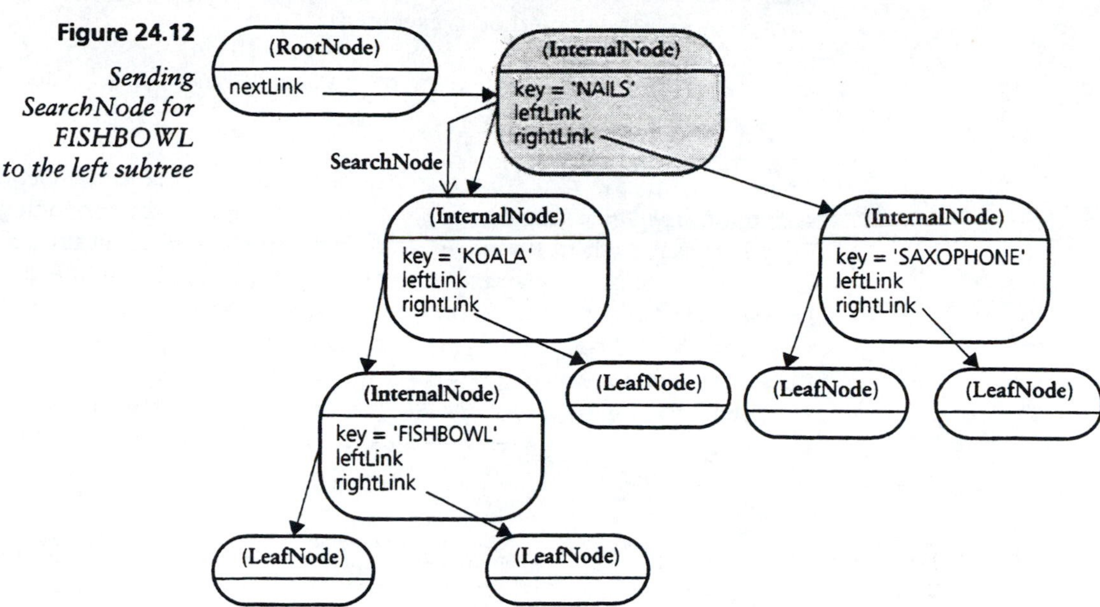

we retrieve the key and compare it to the key we are seeking. Here, we see that the `currentKey` is 'KOALA' and the `keyToFind` is 'FISHBOWL'. Since 'KOALA' > 'FISHBOWL', we send the `SearchNode` message to the left child, as shown in Figure 24.13.

Figure 24.13

Sending SearchNode for FISHBOWL to the left again

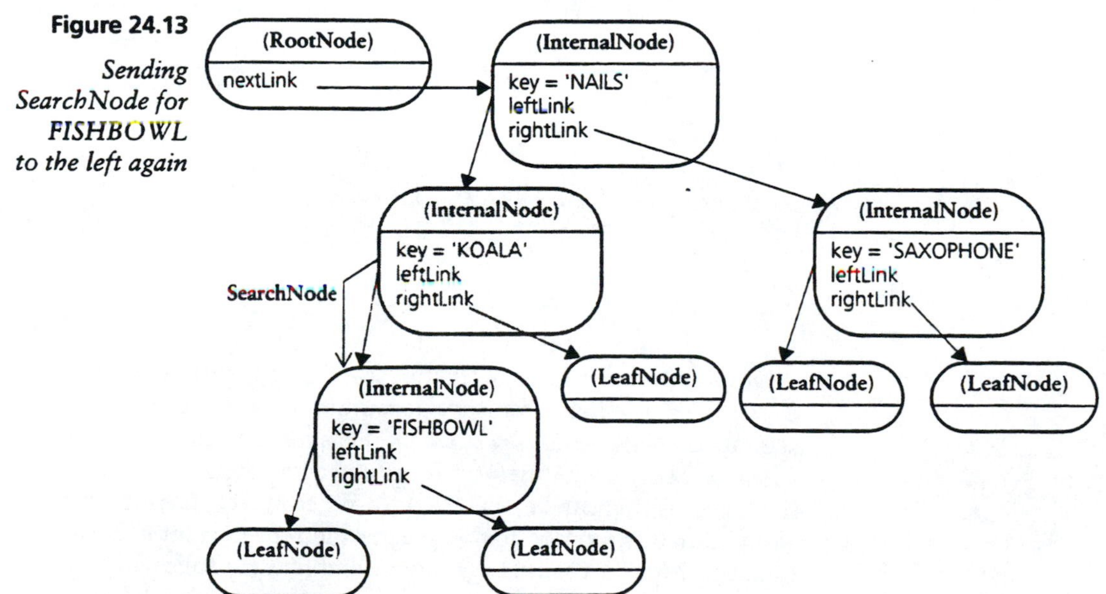

Now we are at the node at which the `elemLink` instance variable links to an element whose key is 'FISHBOWL'. We have reached a point at which `cur-`

rentKey and keyToFind are equal. This means that the first part of the InternalNode.SearchNode method is executed:

```
IF (currentKey = keyToFind) THEN { We've found it! }
  SearchNode := elemLink
```

This statement says that we return the value of elemLink to the instance that sent the SearchNode message. Thus, a link to the element containing 'FISHBOWL' is sent back to the previous node in the tree, which in turn, sends the link to its previous node and all the way up the line, as shown in Figure 24.14, Figure 24.15, and Figure 24.16. This process is similar to the one we used when searching through a linked list in Chapter 23 except that this search uses the IF-THEN statement to perform a binary search, making it more efficient. (Although the figure shows the SearchNode function returning a link to an internal node, this really is shorthand for the link to the element linked to by the internal node.)

Figure 24.14

Result of SearchNode for FISHBOWL being returned to 'KOALA' internal node

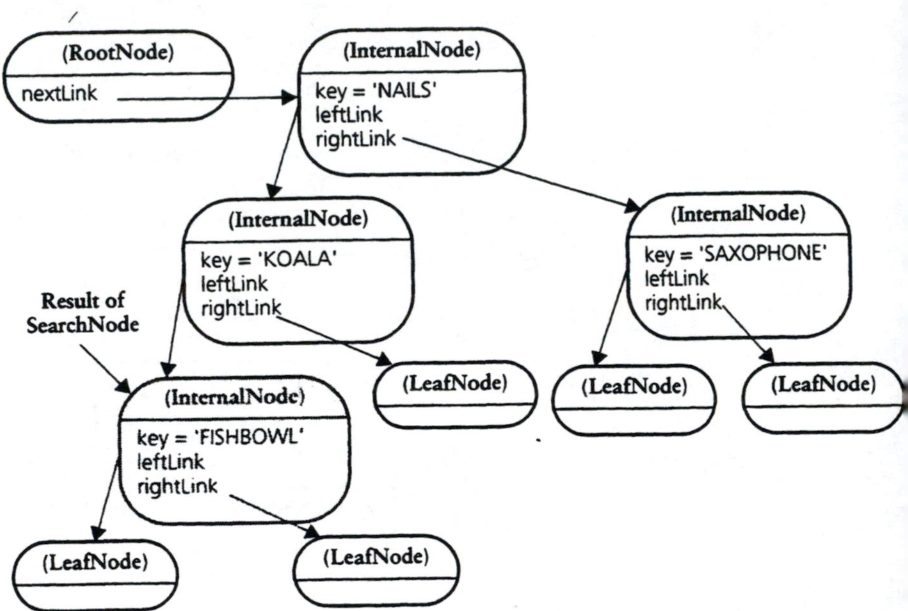

Now, let's try an unsuccessful search, say, searching for 'RADIATOR' Beginning at the top, a message goes from Tree.Search to RootNode.SearchNode to InternalNode.SearchNode. Let's jump to the point where the InternalNode.SearchNode method is executed for the node where elemLink link to an element whose key is 'NAILS'. We compare 'NAILS' and 'RADIATOR and find that the key to find is greater than the current key. We go to the ELS clause of InternalNode.SearchNode and find the following:

```
ELSE { currentKey < keyToFind }
  SearchNode := right^.SearchNode(keyToFind)
```

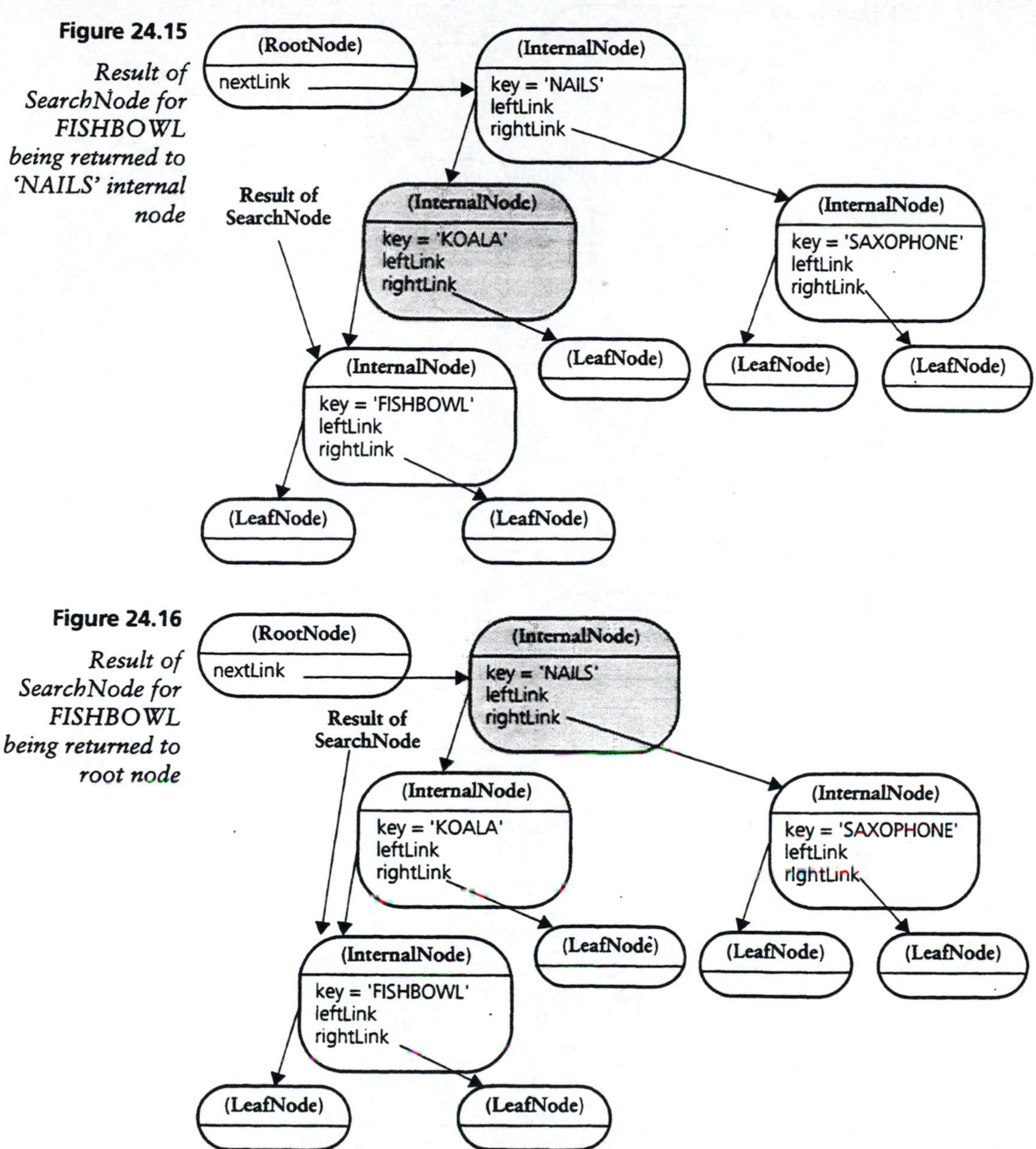

Figure 24.15 *Result of SearchNode for FISHBOWL being returned to 'NAILS' internal node*

Figure 24.16 *Result of SearchNode for FISHBOWL being returned to root node*

This means we send the `SearchNode` message to the child on the right, as shown in Figure 24.17.

It turns out that the node on the right is also an instance of `InternalNode`. We compare 'SAXOPHONE' and 'RADIATOR' and determine that we should send a `SearchNode` message to the node on the left, as shown in Figure 24.18.

Figure 24.17 *Sending SearchNode for RADIATOR to the right child*

Figure 24.18 *Sending SearchNode for RADIATOR to the left*

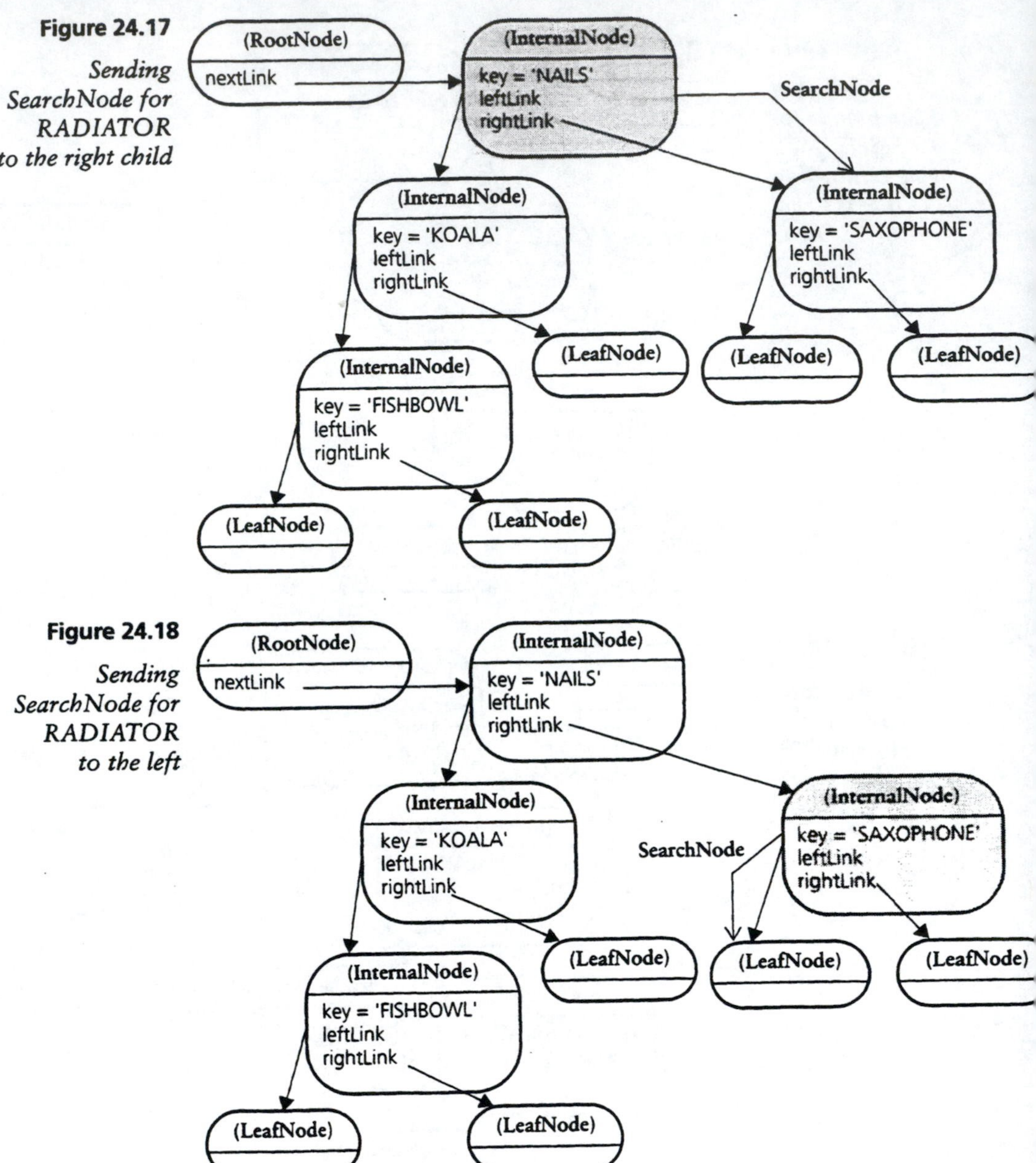

The current node is now a `LeafNode`, meaning that we need to execute the method `LeafNode.SearchNode`:

```
FUNCTION LeafNode.SearchNode(keyToFind: string) : ElementAsn;
BEGIN
  SearchNode := NIL;
END;
```

This very short method says that the value we should return is a `NIL`. The returned value is sent up the tree, just as it was in our successful search, until the instance that called `RootNode.SearchNode` knows that the key 'RADIATOR' is not currently in the list.

24.5 ADDING A NODE IN THE TREE

When we add a node to a binary tree, we always add the node at a leaf. Our algorithm, simply put, is to search for the key in the tree. If the key is not in the tree, the search will end at a leaf. At this leaf, the new node should be inserted.

Suppose we were adding 'PIANO' to our tree. If we traverse the tree, we see that 'PIANO' > 'NAILS', so we move to the right of 'NAILS'; we then see that 'PIANO' < 'SAXOPHONE', so we move to the left of 'SAXOPHONE'. We are now at a leaf node, and we need to make an insertion, as shown in Figure 24.19.

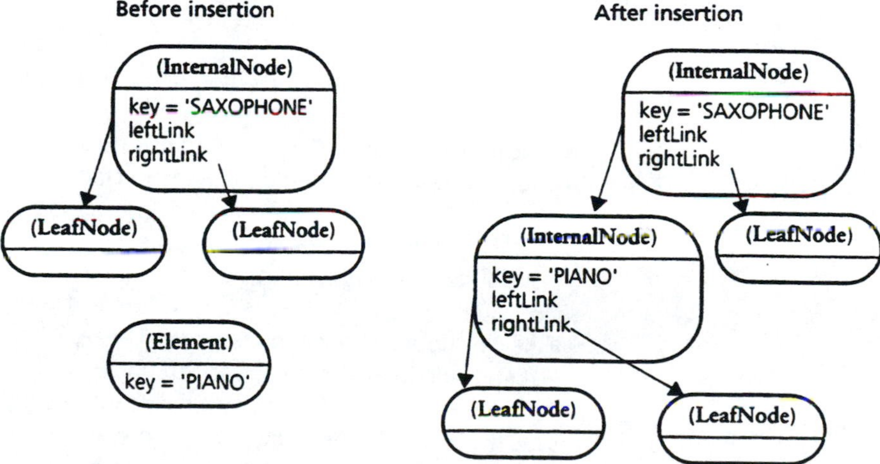

Figure 24.19 *Inserting a node at a leaf*

The leaf is replaced by an internal node with two leaf children. Thus we will use the method `AddSubtree` to pass an internal node with two leaves down the tree until the correct leaf to replace is found. We also will use `AddSubtree` when deleting a node, as we shall see in Section 24.7.

To show how we insert, we begin by showing how we initialize a new internal node. The internal node has three instance variables — an element and a left and right link. As with linked lists, queues, and stacks, we'll assume each of these things are given to us as parameters in the method to initialize the new internal node:

```
CONSTRUCTOR InternalNode.Init(
      newElemLink          : ElementAsn;
      newLeftLink, newRightLink: NodeAsn);
BEGIN
  INHERITED Init;
  elemLink := newElemLink;
  leftLink := newLeftLink;
  rightLink := newRightLink;
END;
```

So, whose responsibility is it to initialize the internal node? Since we know we want to pass an internal node down the tree to the correct leaf, the `Tree` can create the internal node and pass it to its root node.

When the messages unwind back up the tree, each node should be receiving back a link to its child node, which will be different above the new internal node. In that case, whatever node received the new node should `Dispose` of the old one that it had.

If we find that an element is already in the tree, that node can return a link to itself to its parent node. This allows the recursion to stop but doesn't change any of the values within the tree. The pseudocode is as follows:

Tree.Insert(newElemLink: ElementAsn)
Purpose: Adds an element to the tree
Pseudocode:
    Send AddSubtree to root, passing a new InternalNode

RootNode.AddSubtree(keyToAdd : string; subtree : NodeAsn)
Pseudocode: send AddSubtree message to child

InternalNode.AddSubtree(keyToAdd:string; subtree: NodeAsn)
Purpose: Replaces a leaf with an entire subtree .
Pseudocode:

```
IF key in subtree < key in my element THEN
    Send AddSubtree message to left node
    Dispose of my old left subtree if AddSubtree gives me a new one back
ELSE IF key in subtree > key in my element THEN
    Send AddSubtree message to right node
    Dispose of my old right subtree if AddSubtree gives me a new one back
Return self
```

LeafNode.AddSubtree(keyToAdd : string; subtree : NodeAsn)
Purpose: Replace myself with the passed subtree
Pseudocode:
    Return subtree

From here, we can develop the code for these methods:

```
PROCEDURE Tree.Insert(newElemLink: ElementAsn);
BEGIN
  rootLink := rootLink^.AddSubtree(newElemLink^.GetKey,
    New(InternalNodeAsn, Init(newElemLink,
      New(LeafNodeAsn, Init),
      New(LeafNodeAsn, Init))));
END;

FUNCTION RootNode.AddSubtree(keyToAdd : string;
             subtreeLink : NodeAsn) : NodeAsn;
VAR tempLink : NodeAsn;
BEGIN
  tempLink := nextLink^.AddSubtree(keyToAdd, subtreeLink);
  IF tempLink <> nextLink THEN
    BEGIN
      Dispose(nextLink, Done);
      nextLink := tempLink
    END;
  AddSubtree := @self
END;

FUNCTION InternalNode.AddSubtree(keyToAdd : string;
             subtreeLink : NodeAsn): NodeAsn;
VAR    myKey : string;          tempLink : NodeAsn;
BEGIN
  myKey := elemLink^.GetKey;
  IF keyToAdd < myKey THEN
    BEGIN
      tempLink := leftLink^.AddSubtree(keyToAdd, subtreeLink);
      IF tempLink <> leftLink THEN
        BEGIN
          Dispose(leftLink, Done);
          leftLink := tempLink
        END
    END
  ELSE IF keyToAdd > myKey THEN
    BEGIN
      tempLink := rightLink^.AddSubtree(keyToAdd, subtreeLink);
      IF tempLink <> rightLink THEN
        BEGIN
          Dispose(rightLink, Done);
          rightLink := tempLink
        END
    END;
  AddSubtree := @self
END;
```

```
FUNCTION LeafNode.AddSubtree(keyToAdd : string;
              subtreeLink : NodeAsn ): NodeAsn;
BEGIN
  AddSubtree := subtreeLink
END;
```

Let's then look at the details of how we add a subtree. Let's say that our new element contains the key 'PIANO'. We begin with the situation shown in Figure 24.20; the root node receives the `AddSubtree` message and immediately sends it to its `nextLink`.

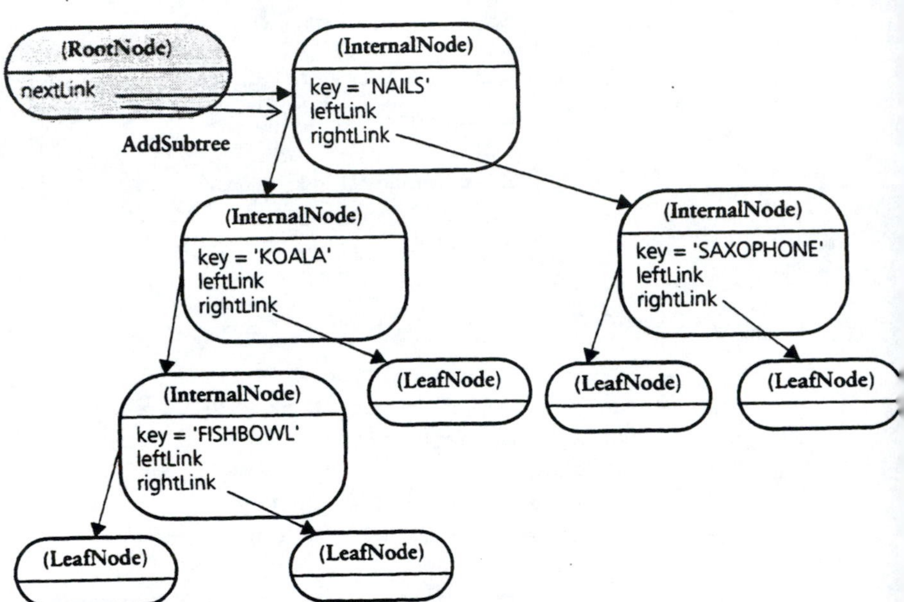

Figure 24.20 *Root node sends AddSubtree on to the first internal node*

We execute the `InternalNode.AddSubtree` method, retrieving the value of the `key` instance variable ('NAILS') and placing it in `myKey`. Then we make a comparison using the following block:

```
IF keyToAdd < myKey THEN
  BEGIN
    tempLink := leftLink^.AddSubtree(keyToAdd, subtreeLink);
    IF tempLink <> leftLink THEN
      BEGIN
        Dispose(leftLink, Done);
        leftLink := tempLink
      END
  END
ELSE IF keyToAdd > myKey THEN
  BEGIN
    tempLink := rightLink^.AddSubtree(keyToAdd, subtreeLink);
```

```
        IF tempLink <> rightLink THEN
          BEGIN
            Dispose(rightLink, Done);
            rightLink := tempLink
          END
      END;
```

We are making the comparison `keyToAdd < myKey`, meaning that we are comparing 'NAILS' and 'PIANO'. The comparison is `false`, so we move to the `ELSE IF` block, and send an `AddSubtree` message to the `rightLink` instance variable (Figure 24.21).

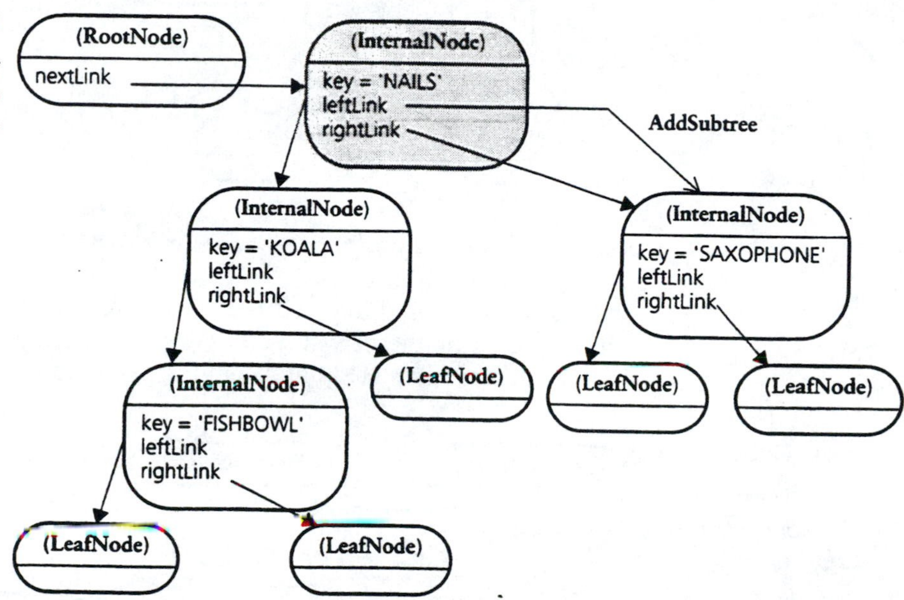

Figure 24.21 *Sending AddSubtree to the right subtree*

Now, we execute `InternalNode.AddSubtree` again, this time comparing 'SAXOPHONE' and 'PIANO'. The key ('SAXOPHONE') is greater than the key we want to insert, so we send an `AddSubtree` message to the left child (Figure 24.22).

We now have found the leaf that we need to replace with the subtree we've been passing along. The leaf node responds to the `AddSubtree` message by simply returning the subtree:

```
AddSubtree := subtreeLink
```

The `LeafNode.AddSubtree` method is finished. The method is a function, so let's see what it returns — a link to the subtree replacing the leaf. Thus the node whose `elemLink` connects to the 'SAXOPHONE' element receives the new internal node to complete the assignment:

Figure 24.22

Sending AddSubtree to the left child

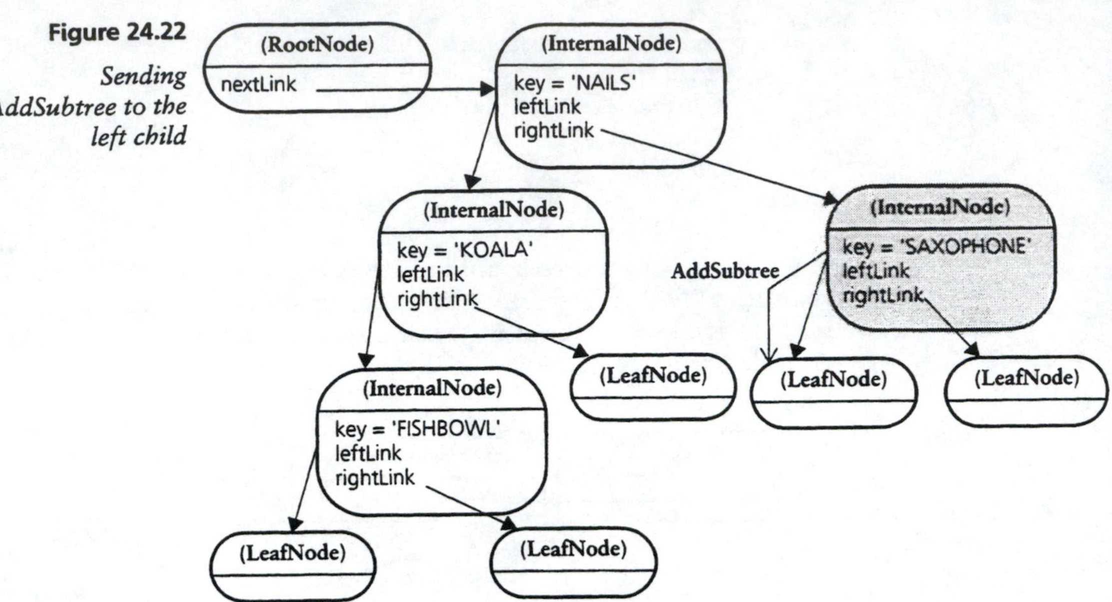


```
tempLink := leftLink^.AddSubtree(keyToAdd, subtreeLink);
```

Thus `tempLink` is different from `leftLink`, and `leftLink` is disposed of, being replaced by the new subtree. We can rearrange the diagram and show the tree with its completed links as in Figure 24.23.

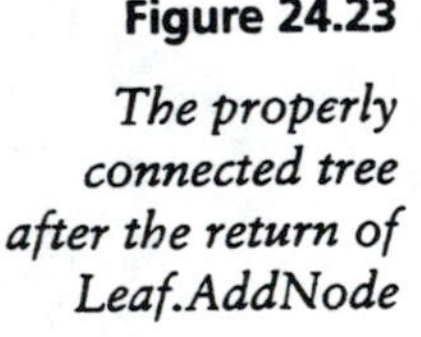

Figure 24.23

The properly connected tree after the return of Leaf.AddNode

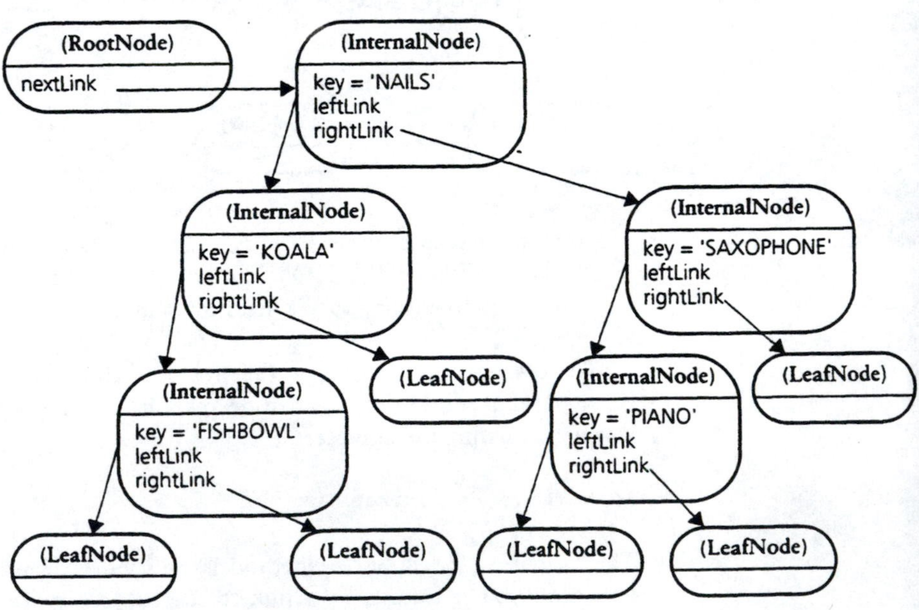

As the messages unwind up the tree, each node will receive its current child. That is, when `InternalNode.AddSubtree` is done for the node whose element contains 'SAXOPHONE', it will return itself to its parent. (All internal nodes previously in the tree will return themselves, since insertion only displaces a leaf.) Figure 24.23 shows the tree in its final state.

24.6 TRAVERSING TREES

We have seen how to add a node and find a node in a tree. Each operation has dealt with a random access of a single item. Now we consider how to access each node sequentially.

Although they may not appear so at first glance, the tree's nodes are in alphabetical order — every move to the left is a move toward the beginning of the order. Thus if we start at the root and go as far to the left as we can, we find that the left-most internal node will have an element whose key is first alphabetically. Similarly, the node all the way at the right has a link to the element whose key is at the bottom of the list. As a rule, nodes whose keys are less than the given node's element will be to the left; nodes whose keys are greater than the key of the given node's element will be to the right.

We'd like to walk through each node in the tree in alphabetical order, performing some action at each node. The action we perform will be some subclass of `TreeAction`. For example, we can `Draw` an `Element`, so we might make a subclass called `DrawElementAction`:

```
DrawElementAction = OBJECT (TreeAction)
  CONSTRUCTOR Init;
  DESTRUCTOR Done; VIRTUAL;
  PROCEDURE DoIt( elementLink : ElementAsn ); VIRTUAL;
END;

PROCEDURE DrawElementAction.DoIt( elementLink : ElementAsn );
BEGIN
  elementLink^.Draw;
END;
```

We've left out the definitions of the constructor and the destructor. They simply call the inherited constructor and destructor.

Now, how can we use an action? While searching and inserting recursively followed one subtree, traversing will follow *both* subtrees, much as drawing a graphical tree made two recursive message sends back in Section 13.1.

```
FUNCTION Tree.Delete(keyToRemove : string) : ElementAsn;
VAR tempLink : ElementAsn;
BEGIN
  tempLink := NIL;
  rootLink := rootLink^.DeleteNode(keyToRemove, tempLink);
  Delete := tempLink
END;

FUNCTION Root.DeleteNode(keyToRemove : string;
      VAR delElemLink : ElementAsn ) : NodeAsn;
VAR tempLink : NodeAsn;
BEGIN
  tempLink := nextLink^.DeleteNode(keyToRemove, delElemLink);
  IF tempLink <> nextLink THEN
    BEGIN
      Dispose (nextLink, Done);
      nextLink := tempLink
    END
  DeleteNode := @self;
END;

FUNCTION InternalNode.Delete(keyToRemove : string;
      VAR delElemLink : ElementAsn ) : NodeAsn;
VAR myKey : string; tempLink : NodeAsn;
BEGIN
  myKey := elemLink^.GetKey;
  If myKey > keyToRemove THEN
    BEGIN
      tempLink := leftLink^.DeleteNode(keyToRemove, delElemLink);
      IF tempLink <> leftLink THEN
        BEGIN
          Dispose(leftLink, Done);
          leftLink := tempLink
        END;
      DeleteNode := @self
    END
  ELSE IF myKey < keyToRemove THEN
    BEGIN
      tempLink := rightLink^.DeleteNode(keyToRemove, delElemLink);
      IF tempLink <> rightLink THEN
        BEGIN
          Dispose(rightLink, Done);
          rightLink := tempLink
        END;
      DeleteNode := @self
    END
```

```
      ELSE
         BEGIN
            delElemLink := elemLink;
            leftLink^.AddSubtree(keyToFind, rightLink);
            DeleteNode := leftLink
         END
   END;

   FUNCTION Leaf.DeleteNode(keyToRemove : string;
            VAR delElemLink  : ElementAsn ) : NodeAsn;
   BEGIN
      delElemLink := NIL; { Node to delete was not found. }
      DeleteNode := @self;
   END;
```

Summary

The binary tree is a data structure that is used to store large amounts of data. Its items are not stored in sequential order, but are placed in the tree in the order in which they are entered. Thus the order in which elements are input affects the way the tree is built.

Elements always are added at the bottom of the tree. To find the place to add the item, start at the root and compare this item to add to the root's contents. If the item is less than the contents of the root, move to the left child. Otherwise, move to the right child. Then, compare the item to add to the child's contents. Again, depending on the comparison, move to the left or the right. Eventually this path takes you to a leaf of the tree, where you can add the item.

Searching for a key item follows the same algorithm as adding items. Start at the root and move to the left or right, depending on how the contents of the current node compare to the key. Searches in balanced binary trees are more efficient than searches in linear lists. For a list of n items, a search in a binary tree requires looking at approximately $\log_2 n$ items, and a search in a linear list requires looking at approximately $n/2$ items. A degenerate tree, however, can use as much time as a linear list.

We can also traverse a tree, meaning that we can perform an action on each individual element in the tree. Using recursion to draw every element, first draw everything to the left of an internal node recursively, then draw the node's element, and then draw everything to the right of the internal node recursively.

Finally, we can delete an element in the tree. To do this, find the node containing the element using a recursive search. Then, replace the deleted node with its left subtree. The right subtree can be inserted at a suitable leaf in the left subtree using a normal insert.

Exercises

Understanding Concepts

1. The traversal presented in Section 24.6 is called in-order traversal. Reordering the three statements in `InternalNode.Traverse` will change the order in which actions on the elements in the tree are performed. Explain the differences among the six possible orders of traversing the left subtree, traversing the right subtree, and performing the action on the current node.
2. Show the binary tree that results when the following names are added in the given order to an empty tree:

   `chicken, alligator, cat, cow, bee, cattle`
3. Show the binary tree that results from entering the names from Exercise 2 in reverse order.
4. How would you arrange the list from Exercise 2 so that the tree was degenerate — that is, it was equivalent to a linked list?
5. In the example tree in Figure 24.23, what nodes are visited when the tree searches for 'SAXOPHONE'? for 'MOOSE'?
6. What happens when the tree is asked to insert a name that is already present in the tree?
7. How does the tree algorithm ensure that nodes are always added at the bottom of the tree?
8. If a linear list has 35 items, what is the worst case for a search; that is, what is the maximum number of comparisons necessary to find a particular key in the list? What is the average case? What are the worst and average cases for 35 items in a balanced binary tree?

Coding Problems

1. Provide the `Tree` class with traversal methods that traverse the elements in each of the six possible orders discussed in Understanding Concepts 1.
2. Write a method that determines the length of the longest path from the root to a leaf.
3. Write a method that prints every other name in a sorted list stored in a binary tree.
4. Modify the tree to accept a secondary key. That is, the keys might be a last name and a first name; if the last name of two keys is the same, then the sort order is determined by the first name.

5. Write an iterator that will traverse a tree. The `Tree` will need a `MakeIterator` method, and the nodes will need methods to provide the "next" node and to provide their element.

Programming Problems

1. Write a program that accepts seven inputs and outputs the number 0 through 9. The inputs correspond to the LCD components used to make numerals appear on a digital clock.

2. Write a program that accepts a Morse code sequence of dots and dashes and prints the corresponding letters. Letters are separated by spaces in the input.

A	*-	J	*---	S	***
B	-***	K	-*-	T	-
C	-*-*	L	*-**	U	**-
D	-**	M	--	V	***-
E	*	N	-*	W	*--
F	**-*	O	---	X	-**-
G	--*	P	*--*	Y	-*--
H	****	Q	--*-	Z	--**
I	**	R	*-*		

3. Write a program in which the computer plays tic-tac-toe with the user. Before making a move, the program should consider the user's next two possible moves and choose for itself the move that has the best chance of yielding a win. (This algorithm uses a tree, but not necessarily a binary one.)

4. Pascal's triangle (which has nothing to do with the language Pascal, except that they were named after the same person) is shown in Figure 24.24. Each value in the triangle is found by adding the two values above it in the triangle. (Note that the triangle differs from a binary tree because many nodes share children.) Write a program that accepts a number from 1 to 10 and outputs that row in Pascal's triangle.

Figure 24.24

Pascal's triangle

```
                    1
                 1     1
              1     2     1
           1     3     3     1
        1     4     6     4     1
     1     5    10    10     5     1
```

5. Create a taxonomy of things in the universe using a binary tree. Each nonleaf node contains a yes or no question; the leaf nodes contain things in the universe. After a few things have been added, the tree is as shown in Figure 24.25. Allow the user to insert items in the taxonomy. For each new item, the user should answer yes or no to the questions in the path. When the program reaches a leaf, the user should enter a new question that differentiates the new

item from the leaf. For example, the following user-program dialog inserts the item Silo in the tree. (U is user, P is program.)

Figure 24.25

A taxonomy of things

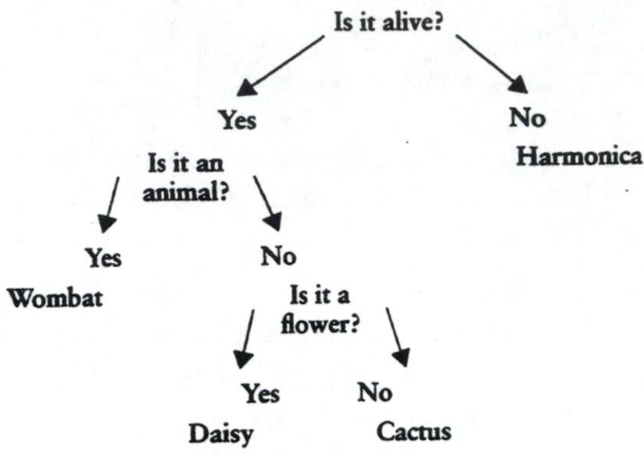


```
P: What is the item to insert?
U: Silo
P: Is it alive?
U: NO
P: You have described a Silo. What question differentiates a
           Silo from a Harmonica?
U: Does it play music?
P: Is Harmonica a YES or NO response to this question?
U: YES
```

Use appropriate GP dialog classes to ask questions of the user. In this case, the resulting tree appears below in Figure 24.26. Note that the addition to the tree is not strictly at the leaf.

Figure 24.26

A taxonomy of things with Silo added

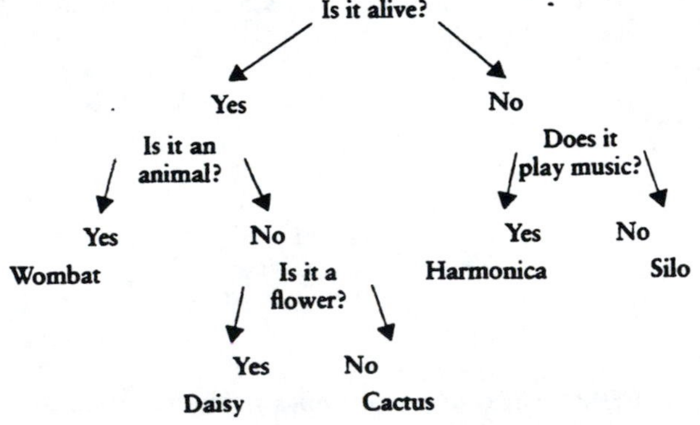

25

Analysis of Program Efficiency

25.1 MAKING A PROGRAM RUN WELL

When you design and build a computer program or purchase an oven, your first task is to make sure that it works correctly. If it doesn't work, it isn't useful. But once your program (or oven) is working correctly, you can ask yourself, "Does it work *well*?" You can ask yourself whether your oven heats efficiently, or whehter it costs more in electricity or gas to run it than it could.

It is relatively easy to figure out how efficient an oven is. By studying how much it costs to run the oven and comparing that cost to the results of the oven's cooking, we can calculate its efficiency and compare that efficiency to the efficiency of other ovens. But how do we do this with a computer program? We have to first figure out what the cost in running a computer program is.

If resources are limited, they tend to be valuable. Two computer resources are scarce — space and time. Space refers to places to store things: files, memory, disks. These are all hardware (or, in the case of files, stored on hardware), and there can only be so much of any of them. Adding more space to a computer costs money, because you have to buy memory chips or new disks. By time, we mean that entity that no one ever seems to have enough of. Providing more time for a computer to work on a problem costs money as well, either in the form of hardware by buying a faster computer or in the form of salaries for the people using the computer.

A program can be inefficient in its use of either space or time. A program that is extremely inefficient in space might run out of space and not be able to run at all. If the program uses up all the memory in the computer and still needs more, the program will crash, just as it would if it tried to divide by zero. A program that is inefficient in time can't run out of time in the same way — it won't crash if it takes too long. But a program that takes too long to provide an answer might provide an answer after it would have been useful.

Consider a program calculating the flight path of the space shuttle. If the program takes too long, the space shuttle will have landed, or worse, crashed, before the answer is produced.

In this chapter, we'll learn about ways to study the efficiency of computer programs. As it happens, the analysis of both space and time usage has a lot in common. The mathematics used to study one are useful for studying the other as well. We'll begin with the basic ideas behind measuring how much space or time a computer program takes to perform its job.

25.2 ANALYZING AND IMPROVING A PROGRAM THROUGH OBSERVATION

The easiest way to determine how efficiently a program is performing is to measure its performance. It usually isn't sufficient to simply time the program from start to stop — that may tell you that a program runs too slowly, but it doesn't provide any information on how to make the program run faster. Rather than simply knowing how long a program takes, we would like to know how long different *parts* of the program take to perform their own tasks.

Most programming environments (Borland Pascal included) provide a tool called a *profiler* that lets you measure your program's performance in this manner. A profiler creates a *profile* from one execution of the program. The profile consists of a list of your program's methods. For each method in the list, the profile lists how often the method was used, and how much time was spent in the method.

This kind of information helps determine what parts of your program are the performance bottlenecks — where your program spends the most time. The answers may surprise you. Most programs spend more than 80 percent of their time executing only 20 percent of their code. For some programs, especially scientific and engineering applications, this ratio of time to code is even more extreme, with more than 90 percent of the time spent in only an extremely small part of the code.

Once you have this information, what can you do with it? Four techniques frequently are used to help speed up code. The first is trivial — most compilers support options describing how code is compiled. Some options produce faster code than others, although the compiler usually has to work harder to produce faster code. Thus these options are usually turned off when developing code and turned on later. The second technique is called *inlining*, which attempts to make code faster by reorganizing it. The third technique, *caching*, attempts to avoid redoing operations that have been done before. Finally, the fourth option is the most drastic — *reimplementing* the slow part of the program completely.

We will address the last three techniques by seeing how they can be applied to some sample code. We will look at a simple task — adding one point to a hundred other points:

```
...
FOR i := 1 TO 100 DO
  BEGIN
    points[i].Add(aPoint)
  END;
...
```

For the compilation options available for your compiler, see your manual.

Inlining

Sending a message takes a small amount of time. Each message send must create a new activation (as discussed in Chapter 13), and this creation takes time. Sending lots of messages thus can add up to a significant amount of time. A well-designed object-oriented program usually sends a great deal of messages — everything that happens in the program happens as a result of a message send.

How can we fix this problem? Clearly, we need to send fewer messages. But our program still needs to do the same amount of work. So each message must do more work. We can rewrite one method that sends many messages by copying the code from the methods that will respond to those messages into the method that would have sent those messages. For example, consider this procedure to add a `GPPoint` to a `GPPoint`:

```
PROCEDURE GPPoint.Add(point : GPPoint);
BEGIN
  x := x + point.GetX;
  y := y + point.GetY;
END;
```

We can make this code perform slightly better by replacing the message sends `point.GetX` and `point.GetY` with the code those methods perform. They each simply return the `x` and `y` instance variables of the point. So, our new `Add` method looks like this:

```
PROCEDURE GPPoint.Add(point : GPPoint);
BEGIN
  x := x + point.x;
  y := y + point.y;
END;
```

This code is faster because it takes less time to get an integer value (using `point.x`) than it does to send a message (using `point.GetX`). We can inline in other places as well. For example, consider our loop of adding a hundred points. We could replace the message send `Add` with the corresponding code:

```
...
FOR i := 1 TO 100 DO
  BEGIN
    { equivalent to points[i].Add(aPoint) }
    points[i].x := points[i].x + aPoint.x;
    points[i].y := points[i].y + aPoint.y;
  END;
...
```

This code points out the big problem with inlining — it breaks encapsulation and prevents the use of polymorphism. First, we break encapsulation by accessing instance variables directly rather than through a message. Indeed, inlining like this is not even possible unless instance variables are not declared `PRIVATE`. Not declaring instance variables to be `PRIVATE` makes code hard to modify, since changing one piece of code (e.g., changing the names of the instance variables for points) requires rewriting other parts of the program.

Second, instead of allowing for the possibility that different points `Add` in different ways, inlining forces all points to `Add` in the same way, because the code for `Add` simply is written in where it will be used.

Caching

The second technique, caching, simply is storing a computed instance or value if it will be needed again. For example, instead of sending the same message twice, send it once and store the result in a temporary variable, such as a local variable, and then use that variable where you would have used a message send. For example, consider our loop:

```
VAR
  tempX, tempY : integer;
BEGIN
...
  tempX := aPoint.GetX;
  tempY := aPoint.GetY;
  FOR i := 1 TO 100 DO
    points[i].SetCoords(points[i].GetX + tempX,
              points[i].GetY + tempY)
END;
...
```

Unlike inlining, caching doesn't break encapsulation or prevent polymorphism, but it can change the meaning of a program. If a message send has *side effects*, such as drawing something on the screen, it may not be possible to use caching. Thus caching is useful mostly for storing the results of purely arithmetic calculations.

Caching has a minor drawback, however: It tends to make code more complex and harder to understand.

Reimplementing Entirely

The final possibility is simply to rewrite the slow part of a program completely. In some cases, you can use a different process or collection of objects that is inherently more efficient. The remainder of this chapter discusses that possibility, examining helpful mathematical tools that you can use to decide how to design a system more efficiently.

The most extreme form of reimplementing a slow part of the program is to write that part directly in *assembly language* rather than in OOPas. We haven't mentioned this term since Chapter 1, when we discussed machine code. Assembly language is one step above machine code and, as such, is extremely difficult to use and very low level. However, you can almost always make a program faster by using assembly language. Programming in assembly language is so difficult that almost no one does it, and these days, it is used only for code where speed is absolutely essential. Some of these places include key parts of the operating system, time-critical applications such as software for the space shuttle, and video games.

25.3 ANALYZING A PROGRAM THROUGH MATHEMATICS

Computers come in all sorts of different shapes and sizes, each with different intrinsic abilities. While a small laptop with a high-performance CPU might run a single application faster than a large desktop computer, the desktop computer might be able to run many different systems simultaneously. Comparing the speed of the system on the laptop to the speed of many systems on a desktop computer using a stopwatch doesn't tell us much about how well any of the systems involved perform.

Compare this situation to our earlier example of an oven baking bread. Let's suppose we want bake some number of loaves of bread. A small, hot oven might bake a single loaf quickly. A large, cooler oven might take more time to bake single loaf, because it is cooler, but might bake a great many loaves more quickly, because of its greater size. Depending on exactly how many loaves we're baking, we might conclude the small oven is faster, and thus more efficient, or that the large oven is faster, and thus more efficient. Clearly, both can't be more efficient than the other.

In both cases, we'd like to separate the abilities of the machine (either the computer or the oven) from the inherent difficulty of what the machine is doing. We don't necessarily care about the absolute stopwatch performance of the machines. For example, both kinds of ovens are baking loaves essentially the same way. One may bake ten at a time, and the other may bake one at a time. Both follow the same procedure: heat a loaf for some amount of time.

So how do we analyze the performance of a system if we don't time it with a stopwatch? We instead follow a sequence of four steps:

1. Determine the size of the job: How many objects does a system have to handle or examine in order to produce the answer desired?
2. Determine the size of the solution: How many objects comprise the solution the system must produce?
3. Determine the relationship between the size of the job and the size of the solution: How much space and time does it take to produce the desired output objects from the provided input objects?
4. Simplify the relationship: Is the relationship expressed in the simplest form possible?

Step 1: Determine the Size of the Job

The idea of ignoring the actual time it takes to perform a task is a crucial aspect of analyzing the performance of a computer program. Baking bread doesn't get faster when a manufacturer releases a new model of oven, but running a computer program does get faster when a new model of computer is released. Thus, to determine whether a program is performing well, a quantitative measure of the time or space required is less useful than a qualitative measure of complexity of the program's task.

The first step to understanding this complexity is to figure out the size of the job we are asking the system to do. If we are baking bread, we ask, "How many loaves?" If we are trying to find an element in a tree, we ask, "How big is the tree?" If we are trying to draw a line, we ask, "How long is the line?" We will usually call the amount of work n.

Step 2: Determine the Size of the Solution

The next step is to figure out how big the desired result is. If our system is a financial calculator, our desired results may be a single number. If our system is a paint program, our desired results may be a complete image. If our system is a database of personnel records, the desired results could be quite large.

Just as we examined the starting situation of our problem, we need to examine the ending situation.

Step 3: Relate the Size of the Job to the Size of the Program

We now need to determine how much work the system needs to do. To avoid the stopwatch problem, we would like to express this work as a function of the size of the job. We can analyze either how much time a system requires or how much space a system requires. In either case, we want a qualitative, not a quantitative, measure.

Thus, instead of noting that a particular oven can bake three loaves of bread in 55 minutes, we'll make the more general statement that the time it takes any oven to bake n loaves of bread is proportional to the number n. We will use a notational abbreviation, called "Big-O" notation, saying that baking loaves of bread takes $O(n)$ time, or "order n" time.

Mathematically speaking, a function $f(n)$ is $O(g(n))$ for some function $g(n)$ if you can find two numbers c and n_0 such that the following situation is true:

$$0 \le f(n) \le cg(n)$$

whenever $n \ge n_0$. In other words, $f(n)$ is growing less rapidly than $g(n)$. So to say a process is $O(n)$ time is to say that, as long as n is big enough, the process takes time proportional to n.

But how do we figure out the function $g(n)$ to use to describe a process? To measure the time required to perform a particular job, we ask ourselves how many messages need to be sent to perform the job. Consider popping one element off the top of a stack. In this case, the size of our problem is the size of the stack. But popping an element off the top of a stack looks only at the top of the stack. Popping an element is thus $O(1)$ in time, meaning it takes some small number of operations to perform, and the number doesn't depend on the size of the problem. Finding a particular element in a linked list is $O(n)$ in time. Our list is of length n. The element may be the first element, but it may also be the last, and we would have to walk through all n elements in order to find the one we want.

To measure the space required to perform a particular job, we ask ourselves how many objects it takes to perform the job. For example, adding n sequential numbers is $O(1)$ in space, since we only need to store the sum — we don't need to store each number. A linked list is $O(n)$ in space, since it requires approximately n objects to store n elements.

In general, when analyzing a program, we concentrate on large jobs, not small ones. Large jobs are the ones where efficiency matters most — a small job takes a small amount of time, no matter how the job is performed. A program in regular use solving real-world problems invariably will be used for larger and larger jobs. For example, $0.5n^2$ seems to be better than $3n$ when $n = 2$, but the situation will be reversed as n gets larger and larger.

Focusing on large jobs also allows us to ignore implementation details of the program. For example, suppose a programmer named Sonia used three statements when she could have used one. While the part of the program that uses those three statements might run three times slower, it won't matter so much if Sonia's program uses $O(n)$ time and the program we're comparing hers to uses $O(n^3)$ time. On big problems, Sonia's program will still perform better.

Finally, using large jobs makes it easier to discount differences in hardware. For example, any program will run faster on a faster computer. We'd hate for our analysis to suggest that one program was faster when that program simply was being run on a faster computer.

A Mathematical Aside: Constants, Logarithms, Polynomials, and Exponentials

When using Big-O notation, we want to express the relationship between the size of our starting configuration and the size of our ending configuration as a function. What sort of functions are we likely to use? We use four broad categories of functions: constants, logarithms, polynomials, and exponentials.

Let's use n as our variable. Constant functions are ones that don't depend on the value of n. For example, returning the first item in a list is a constant-time operation — it doesn't matter how long the list (the starting situation) happens to be. Logarithmic functions use the logarithm of some number. By way of review, the logarithm of n in base 2 is the number x such that $2^x = n$. Polynomials of n are familiar functions like n raised to some constant power. For example, the area of a circle, given its radius, is a polynomial: $4\pi r^2$. Finally, exponentials are functions where some constant number is raised to the power n.

As n gets extremely large, it can be hard to tell which category of function will have greater or lesser values. A graph of various functions is shown in Figure 25.1.

However, a special kind of graph, called a *log-log graph*, makes the differences apparent. A log-log graph has increments along its axes representing successive *powers* rather than successive numbers. Each step on the graph thus multiplies the number represented, rather than adding to the number represented as in a regular graph. Figure 25.2 shows a log-log graph of the same functions in Figure 25.1. Each step on the graph represents successive powers of 10. The differences are now quite pronounced: Polynomials now show up as straight lines, and exponentials clearly curve up and away from them. Similarly, logarithms are always less than the polynomials. Thus, as n gets large exponentials grow fastest, followed by polynomials, then logarithms, then constants.

Step 4: Producing the Simplest Answer Possible

When we write an expression in Big-O notation, we are looking at a function of n as n gets extremely large. Since exponentials are always greater than

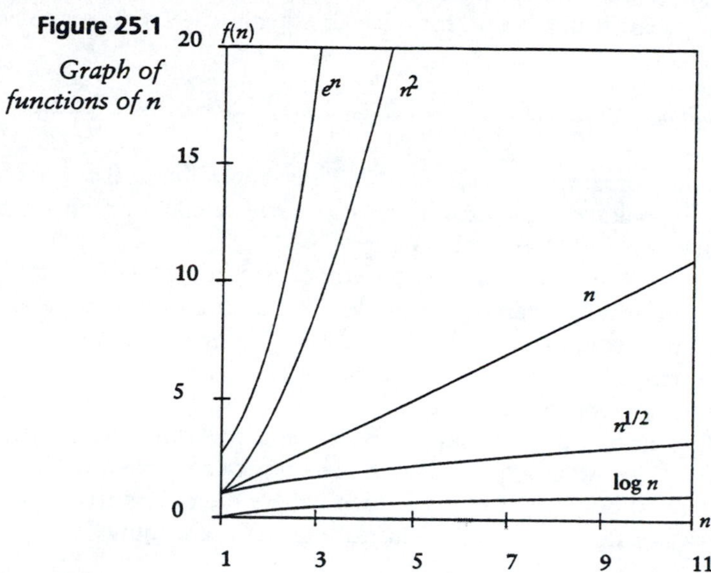

Figure 25.1 *Graph of functions of n*

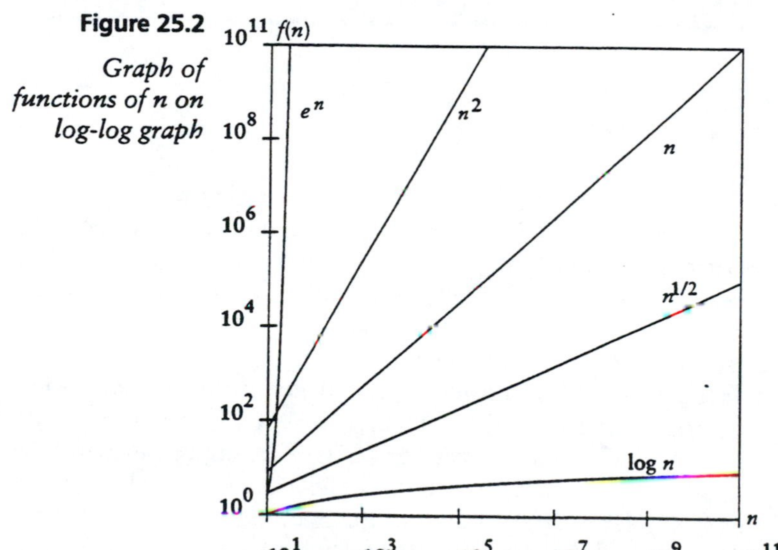

Figure 25.2 *Graph of functions of n on log-log graph*

polynomials as n gets large, an exponential function plus a polynomial will look more and more like a pure exponential the bigger n gets. Similarly, a polynomial plus a logarithm will look more like a polynomial the bigger n gets, and a logarithm plus a constant will look like a logarithm.

We can make the further observation that the same kinds of relationships hold when functions are multiplied by a constant. More interestingly, as n gets large, constant factors do not matter at all. Thus $100000n$ looks more like n the bigger n gets.

Thus, in a list of seven items, we have to look at an average of 4 items during any search. In general, for a list of n items, the average is calculated as follows:

$$\frac{1+2+\cdots+(n-2)+(n-1)+n}{n} = \frac{n\times(n+1)}{2}\times\frac{1}{n} = \frac{(n+1)}{2}$$

We approximate $(n + 1)/2$ as $n/2$. Thus, for a linear list, an average searc requires looking at about $n/2$ items, or $O(n)$, while for a binary tree, a searc requires looking at about log n.

For small sets of data, this difference is minimal. For example, with eigh items, a linear-list search requires looking at 8/2, or 4 items, and a binary-tre search requires looking at log 8, or 3 items. When data sets are large, howeve the difference is substantial. For example, with 128 items, a linear searc requires looking at about 128/2, or 64 items, and a binary search require looking at log 128, or 7 items. Because of this difference, a binary search i more *efficient* than a linear search. The binary algorithm is faster for the ave age case, although in the worst case (where the binary tree is degenerate), th binary tree algorithm and the linear algorithm are equivalent.

25.5 AN EXAMPLE: THE TRAVELING SALES REPRESENTATIVE PROBLEM

Consider Jane, who travels from city to city, trying to sell paper airplanes each city. Jane would like to spend as little time traveling as possible. After a travel time is time that isn't spent selling. Given a list of cities and the travelir time between each pair of cities, Jane would like to know the shortest way visit all of the cities. This problem is historically called the Traveling Sal Representative Problem, or TSP for short.

At first glance, TSP seems like a straightforward problem to solve. If Jane touring only a small number of cities, it is a straightforward problem. F example, if Jane needs to visit the cities Washington, Providence, and Pa Alto, there are 6 different orders she could visit them in, as seen Figure 25.4. Only 3 are shown in the figure, since the other 3 are simply the reverse order. As we can see, the worst route to take is from Providence Palo Alto to Washington. Visiting Providence and Washington first and th visiting Palo Alto means you fly coast to coast only once, rather than twice.

What's So Hard?

Unfortunately, as Jane tries to travel to more and more cities, she will find increasingly hard to find the best route. While there were 3 routes to consic with 3 cities, with 4 cities there are 12 routes, as seen in Figure 25.5. With

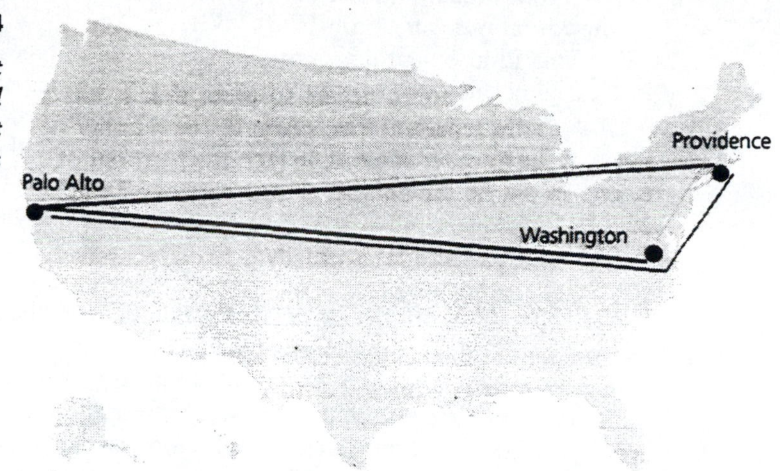

Figure 25.4

Three different ways to travel to three different cities

cities there are 60 routes! Adding one city seems to greatly increase the number of different routes.

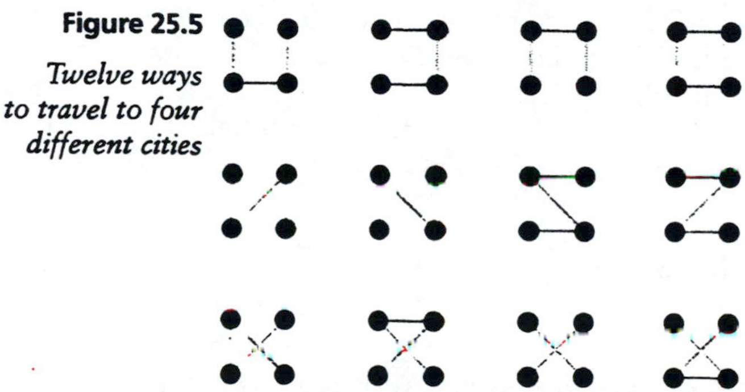

Figure 25.5

Twelve ways to travel to four different cities

But how many different routes does each city add? When there were 4 cities, there were 9 more routes than when there were 3 cities. Adding another city didn't add 9 more routes — it added 48 new routes! It doesn't look like adding one city adds some constant number of new routes, so let's take a look at the number of routes per city and see whether we can detect a pattern. When analyzing a system's complexity, looking at small examples is often a good place to start. We'll start with two cities, in which case there's only one route that visits both of them. Since we're interested in the length of the route, we don't care which direction we traverse the route.

Number of cities:	2	3	4	5	6	7
Number of routes:	1	3	12	60	360	2520

A pattern to the number of routes is now quite apparent. Each time we add a new city, we multiply the previous number of routes by the *total* number of cities. For example, with 2 cities, we have 1 route. With 3 cities, we multiply that total number of routes (1) by the total number of cities (3), to obtain th new total number of routes (3).

This kind of pattern occurs so often that it has a name: *factorial*. In ou traveling sales representative example, the number of routes is almost the fa torial of the number of cities. In fact, the factorial of 2 is 2, the factorial of 3 6, and so on. So the number of routes is one-half the factorial of the numb of cities.

The function factorial is usually defined recursively as follows:

$$n! = n((n-1)!)$$

In concrete terms, the factorial of a number n is the number of different wa you can arrange n things in a row. In our example, we were arranging the c ies in different possible orders we could travel to them. We had only half many arrangements because we were interested in length only, and going fro Washington to Providence to Palo Alto is the same distance as going fro Palo Alto to Providence to Washington (the reverse order).

The factorial function grows extremely fast, faster than any polynomi For example, consider x^2. At $x = 2$, it is 4, and at $x = 3$, it is 9. Factori meanwhile, has values of 2 and 6. So far, it looks like factorial isn't winnin but factorial increased by six in one step, while the quadratic functi increased by 5. At $x = 4$, the quadratic function is 16, but factorial h zoomed ahead, with a value of 24. By $x = 5$, the quadratic function, at 25, eating factorial's dust, as factorial is way out at 120. Any polynomial will p form as badly. For low values of x, the polynomial will seem to be winnin but before too long, factorial will pull ahead.

NP-Completeness

TSP is widely considered to be exactly solvable only for problems with a ve small number of cities. Although it is possible to guess at a good answer larger numbers of cities, coming up with the *shortest* route, rather than sim a route shorter than some others, can take a prohibitively long time.

The problem is that adding one city means we have to consider an ev growing number of additional routes. If it took a computer 2 seconds to fi the shortest route among 10 cities, it would take 22 seconds to find the sho est route among 11 cities. The computer has 11 times as many routes to c sider. Twelve cities would take 264 seconds, or about 4.5 minutes. Thirt cities would thus take 3432 seconds, or nearly an hour. By the time reached fifteen cities, the same computer would take over 200 *days*. Sevent cities would take almost 150 *years*.

Clearly, Jane isn't about to wait 150 years for the ideal schedule for a gr tour of 17 cities. While it is easy to write a program to figure out the best to the program takes too long to provide its answer to be of any real use.

TSP is an example of a large category of programs that, in general, thought to be impractical to solve because there is no known polynomial-t solution to any problems in the category. Only exponential-time solutions known, and researchers in the field generally believe no polynomial-time solution exists, though to date no one has proved this assertion. This category of programs is called *NP*, which stands for "nondeterministic polynomial time." What does this phrase mean? "Nondeterministic" comes from guessing an answer. "Polynomial time" comes from verifying that guess in polynomial time. Thus a problem is NP if you can omnisciently guess the correct answer and then prove that the answer is correct in polynomial time.

Another category of problems is called P. It is the category of "deterministic polynomial time" problems. It is thus the set of problems for which we have a polynomial time way to find the answer. Any problem that is in P is also in NP, because if we had a polynomial time way to find the answer, it would also serve as a way to verify a guess in polynomial time. The thorniest category of problems we will discuss in this book is the NP-complete problems. A problem is said to be *NP-complete* if it is as hard as the hardest problems in *NP*. TSP is an NP-complete problem. No one knows for sure if NP-complete problems are inherently harder than all P problems. If NP-complete problems are not harder than P problems, then all NP problems can be solved in polynomial time. This field of analysis is still open research.

Note that we've defined NP-complete in terms of the running time of a program that solves a particular problem. What about the space usage of a program? Of course, a program can require an exponential amount of space as well — a trivial example of such a program would be one that stored all possible routes of the traveling sales representative problem. A program that uses exponential space necessarily runs in exponential time because space usage is never asymptotically less than time usage — a program has to construct all the objects it creates, so constructing an exponential number of objects takes an exponential amount of time.

What If Your Problem Is NP-Complete?

What can you do if analysis of your system indicates that your system runs in exponential time? The easiest thing to do is to not perform any large tasks using the program. This of course is not a terribly helpful solution.

Instead, you can try to apply *heuristics*. A heuristic is an educated guess, rather than a demonstrably correct answer. For example, we could provide a good answer to the traveling sales representative problem by always traveling to the closest city. We pick one city at random for the sales representative to start in and then choose the closest city as the next city to travel to. From the remaining cities, we always choose the closest one. We build a route incrementally, repeatedly adding the closest city until no more cities remain.

Sometimes, this will produce a correct answer. It will for the travel routes in Figure 25.4. Suppose, however, our sales representative had to visit Chicago as well. If our heuristic happens to choose Chicago as the first city, then the closest city is Providence, followed by Washington, then Palo Alto. But, as we can see in Figure 25.6, this produces a route that backtracks — Providence to Washington to Chicago to Palo Alto is a better route.

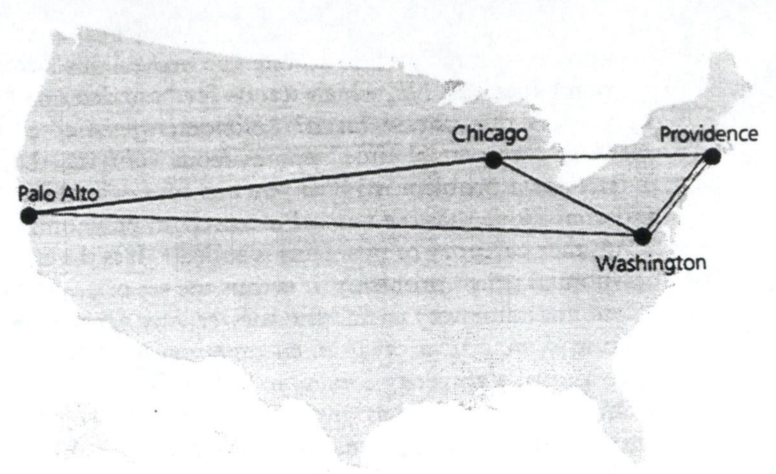

Figure 25.6

A poor route across the country and a good route across the country

This doesn't mean that we shouldn't use this heuristic — an okay answer i better than no answer at all. In fact, we can often provide a heuristic answe for NP-complete problems in the same manner. We can choose some startin point and incrementally build the answer, always choosing the smallest incre ment. This process is called the *greedy algorithm*, because it greedily takes th best incremental value, although, as we have seen, greed doesn't always pa off.

25.6 AN EXAMPLE: DOES A PROGRAM TERMINATE?

The traveling sales representative problem is a difficult one to solve, but pro lems exist that are in general impossible to solve. Such unsolvable problen are often called uncomputable, or *Turing*-uncomputable, named for the con puter scientist Alan Turing, who devised a mathematical model of a comput — and then proved that there were problems it could not solve.

What kind of problem could be so fiendishly complex that a comput couldn't solve it? As it happens, it is quite simple to express:

Given a computer program in a particular language, when run, will the pr gram ever stop?

This problem is usually called the *halting problem*. At first glance, this loo like it should be easy to solve. Certainly, we've always written programs th stopped eventually. However, remember the situations we examined Section 14.3 where loops or recursion never ended.

The crux of the problem is that we can't figure out whether a program w stop without running it or doing some sort of analysis that is at least as co plex as running the program in the first place, such as simulating the progra

Suppose the program has a loop in it. Although we might be able to identify some simple cases (such as `REPEAT ... UNTIL TRUE` or `REPEAT ... UNTIL FALSE`), the exit condition for the loop could be extremely complex, relying on the values of variables set within the body of the loop. Since those values depend on the execution of the program, we can't determine the values without actually running the program.

Once we have to run the program in order to determine the answer, we're stuck. If the program does stop, we'll know the answer to our question the instant the program stops. But if we don't get an answer right away, we have no way of determining if the program will never stop or if it simply hasn't stopped *yet*.

This is a simple example of the set of problems that computers cannot be guaranteed to answer. These go beyond questions of Big-O efficiency. It is no longer a question of how quickly do we get an answer but a question of whether we will get an answer at all.

25.7 DESIGNING EFFICIENT SYSTEMS

When we aren't dealing with a program that is uncomputable, we can try to provide a design for our system that runs as well as possible. This is a harder design task than simply designing something that works. We now wish to design something that works well.

We can provide two guidelines for tackling this problem. First, it pays to have a complete understanding of what you are trying to build. Second, you usually can't have it all, and you will be forced to make trade-offs. Make the trade-offs that make sense for your particular application.

Understand What Is Being Built

Having a complete understanding of the system you are designing is simply a strengthening of the specification and analysis phases of design first discussed in Chapter 1 and elaborated in Chapter 8. We said those phases were important then, and we're saying it again now. You can't build a good design without a good understanding of what you're trying to design. The way to attain that understanding is through careful and thorough specification and analysis.

The mathematical tools we described in this chapter can help in your analysis — knowing the asymptotic behavior of a system can provide a profound understanding of the interrelations of the objects in the system. These tools can also help you identify the parts of your system that are either extremely difficult to perform or perhaps even impossible. Identifying these parts early on gives you a jump-start on trying to simplify or limit your problem so that it isn't as complex or find good heuristics so that at least you can get a moderately good answer.

Trade-Offs

This sort of analysis is also the first step to identifying trade-offs you can make in your design. Usually it is not possible to make both efficient use of space and efficient use of time. By analyzing your system, you not only determine what parts of the system are the most inefficient, you also determine the parts of the system where efficiency is most important.

For example, large databases need efficient use of space, because space is what they're most likely to deplete as users add more and more information to the database. In contrast, a compiler needs efficient use of time, to avoid wast ing the programmer's time. Computers used for developing programs usually are equipped with a great deal of memory and disk space, because compiler so routinely use so much memory. But the extra memory is worth less than th time it takes to pay a programmer to sit and wait for a slow compiler.

Thus analyze both the space and time usage of your systems. For some situ ations, it makes sense to use a little more memory in order to save a calcula tion for use later. In other situations, it makes more sense to recompute value, rather than using the memory required to store it. These are trade-off only you can decide on and only after you have carefully considered the sys tem and how it will be used. Remember the surprising rule that program spend 80 percent of their time in 20 percent of their code. Without analysis you will most likely spend time speeding up parts of your program that don affect the overall efficiency of your program as a whole.

As always, the first step is to get the program working. If it doesn't work, doesn't matter how efficient it is.

Summary

In this chapter, we introduced more advanced and mathematical forms of analys of computer programs. We began with a sequence of four steps:

1. Determine the size of the starting situation.
2. Determine the size of the result.
3. Relate the size of the starting situation to the size of the result.
4. Simplify this relationship as much as possible.

To address these steps, we examined Big-O notation, which relates the size the result to the size of the starting situation when the starting situation extremely large.

As an example of using these tools, we investigated the efficiency of trees vers linked lists for problems such as searching and insertion. Trees usually perfor better than linked lists, although some kinds of extremely unbalanced trees a essentially linked lists and thus perform no better.

We next examined the traveling sales representative problem. The task is to fi the shortest way to travel to every city in a set of n cities. We demonstrated th the obvious solution to this problem takes an exponential amount of time. Pro lems like this are known as NP-complete problems, and it is believed that no polynomial-time solution exists for them.

As a final example, we examined the halting problem. The task here is simply to determine whether a given program will halt. In general, it is impossible to solve this problem — a computer must effectively run the program in order to provide an answer, but we don't know if the program will stop. A program that halts provides an immediate "yes," but a computer that is still working may yet provide a "yes" answer, but in general can never provide a "no" answer — it must run the program, but if the program doesn't stop, the computer can't provide an answer.

Using these tools and these examples, we presented two rules of thumb for designing efficient systems. First, provide a complete specification and analyze it thoroughly. Second, make trade-offs where necessary, but always emphasize the aspect — time or space — where efficiency will matter most.

Exercises

Understanding Concepts

1. Consider the method that draws a straight line in Chapter 12. Describe the time required to execute that method in big-O notation.
2. Consider the method that draws a rectangle in Chapter 12. Describe the time required to execute that method in big-O notation.
3. Does removing an element from a queue depend on the amount of data? How about from a stack? a linked list?
4. Place the following in order, from least to most complex:

   a. $O(n)$ b. $O(\log n)$ c. $O(n^2)$ d. $O(n \log n)$ e. $O(n^3)$
5. If an algorithm requires exactly $3n^2 + 2n + 3$ time, why do we simplify it as $O(n^2)$?
6. Describe the space-time trade-off between keeping a sorted list in an array and in a linked list.
7. Why is a binary tree search considered more efficient than a search in a linked list? Does this hold in the "worst case" of a binary tree?
8. Why is the traveling sales representative problem considered NP-complete?
9. What is the difference between an NP-complete and an uncomputable problem?

Appendix A

Reserved Words

Borland Pascal, like any programming language, reserves a set of words for particular purposes. This appendix summarizes these words by category. In all categories, case is irrelevant: upper- and lowercase characters in the word produce the same result (e.g., `integer` is equivalent to `INTEGER` and `Integer`). In this book, however, we have conventions for when we use uppercase characters that we will note in each section.

RESERVED WORDS

Reserved words are symbols that you cannot use as an identifier (i.e., they cannot be used as variable, method, constant, type, or other kind of identifier). The words in the following list appear in CAPITAL LETTERS in our programs. (A few of these words are defined as directives, rather than reserved words, in Borland Pascal, meaning that they may not give you an error message if you use them as an identifier but may cause other run-time errors. The words `TRUE` and `FALSE` are constants, rather than reserved words, but are so commonly used that you should also avoid using them as identifier names.)

```
ABSOLUTE
AND
ARRAY
ASM
ASSEMBLER
BEGIN
CASE
CONST
CONSTRUCTOR
DESTRUCTOR
DIV
DO
DOWNTO
ELSE
END
EXPORT
EXPORTS
EXTERNAL
FALSE
FAR
FILE
FOR
FORWARD
FUNCTION
GOTO
IF
IMPLEMENTATION
IN
INDEX
INHERITED
INLINE
INTERFACE
INTERRUPT
LABEL
LIBRARY
MOD
NEAR
NIL
NOT
OBJECT
OF
OR
PACKED
PRIVATE
PROCEDURE
PROGRAM
PUBLIC
RECORD
REPEAT
RESIDENT
SELF
SET
SHL
SHR
STRING
THEN
TO
TRUE
TYPE
UNIT
UNTIL
USES
VAR
VIRTUAL
WHILE
WITH
XOR
```

PREDEFINED DATA TYPES

The following words are predefined data types. These words can be used on the right of colons in variable or parameter declarations.

Boolean	Double	PChar	String
Byte	Extended	Pointer	Text
ByteBool	Integer	Real	Word
Char	LongBool	Shortint	WordBool
Comp	Longint	Single	

PREDEFINED PROCEDURE AND FUNCTION IDENTIFIERS

The following words are predefined as procedures and functions in the standard units used with Borland Pascal and thus should not be used as identifiers in your programs. Other versions of Pascal use most of these functions, but it is best to check with your software manual to determine which are available.

Abs	Erase	Low	Round
Addr	Exclude	MaxAvail	RunError
Append	Exit	MemAvail	SPtr
Arctan	Exp	MkDir	SSeg
Assign	FilePos	Move	Seek
Assigned	FileSize	New	SeekEof
BlockRead	FillChar	Odd	SeekEoln
BlockWrite	Flush	Ofs	Seg
Break	Frac	Ord	SetTextBuf
CSeg	FreeMem	ParamCount	Sin
ChDir	GetDir	ParamStr	SizeOf
Chr	GetMem	Pi	Sqr
Close	Halt	Pos	Sqrt
Concat	Hi	Pred	Str
Continue	High	Ptr	Succ
Copy	IOResult	Random	Swap
Cos	Inc	Randomize	Trunc
DSeg	Include	Read	Truncate
Dec	Insert	Readln	TypeOf
Delete	Int	Rename	UpCase
Dispose	Length	Reset	Val
Eof	Ln	Rewrite	Write
Eoln	Lo	RmDir	Writeln

Appendix B

Borland Pascal Procedures and Functions

This appendix lists the predefined functions and procedures and their purposes. For each function, the following notation is used:

```
<result type> := <function name>(<parameter list>);
```

This notation does *not* imply that functions must be used in assignment statements; functions can be nested inside expressions or passed as parameters.

The `<result type>` and parameter types use the following codes:

```
i       integer
r       real
n       numeric (integer or real)
s       string
c       character
b       boolean
o       ordinal type (integer, character, boolean, or enumerated)
p       pointer (or link)
t       text (file variable)
```

Thus the notation in the first function in the following list means that the function `Abs` takes a parameter of type `integer` and returns a value of type `integer`.

ARITHMETIC FUNCTIONS

```
i := Abs(i);              { absolute value }
r := Abs(r);

b := Odd(i);              { returns TRUE if i is odd, FALSE other-
                          wise}

i := Sqr(i);              { square of a number }
r := Sqr(r);

r := Sqrt(r);             { square root of a number }

r := Sin(n);              { returns sine of angle n where n is in
                          radians }
```

```
r := Cos(n);               { returns cosine of angle n where n is in radians }
r := Arctan(n);            { returns arctangent of angle n where n is in radians }
r := Exp(n);               { returns e to the n power }
r := Ln(n);                { returns natural log of n }
r := Frac(r);              { returns fractional part of r }
i := Int(r);               { returns integer part of r }
i := Round(r);             { rounds r to the closest integer }
i := Trunc(r);             { returns greatest integer that is less than r }
r := Pi;                   { returns pi }
i := Random(i);            { returns a random number between 0 and i }
Randomize;                 { initializes the built-in random generator with a random value }
```

ORDINAL FUNCTIONS

```
i := Ord(o);               { returns ordinality of o ; if o is a character, Ord returns ASCII value of o }
c := Chr(i);               { returns character with ASCII value of i ; i should be between 0 and 127}
o := Succ(o);              { returns successor of o }
o := Pred(o);              { returns predecessor of o }
o := High(o);              { returns highest value in o's range }
o := Low(o);               { returns lowest value in o's range }
Dec(o);                    { decrements the value of o }
Inc(o);                    { increments the value of o }
```

MEMORY MANIPULATION

```
New(p);                    { allocates memory for an instance of the type p is defined to point to }
p := New(<type of p>);     { allocates memory as New procedure does }
```

p := New(<type of p>, <constructor> (<parameter list>));	{ allocates memory as New does and calls <constructor> of the new instance with <parameter list> }
Dispose(p);	{ frees memory pointed to by p }
Dispose(p, <destructor>);	{ frees memory pointed to by p after calling the named destructor on the instance }

FILE MANIPULATION

Reset(t);	{ opens an existing file }
Rewrite(t);	{ opens a new file for write-only}
Close(t);	{ closes an open file }
b := Eof(t);	{ returns TRUE if file pointer is at end-of-file marker }
b := Eoln(t);	{ returns TRUE if file pointer is at end-of-line marker }
Assign(t, s);	{ assigns a text variable value to t, associating it with the file indicated by the string s }
Rename(t, s);	{ assigns s as the new file name of the file associated with t }
Erase(t);	{ erases the file associated with t }
Read(t, <var1>, <var2>, ..., <var n>);	{ reads input from file }
Readln(t, <var1>, <var2>, ..., <var n>);	{ reads input from file; moves file position to next line }

WRITING TO FILES

In the following statements, <exp> denotes an expression — that is, a constant, variable, function, or combination thereof. Each expression can be followed by formatting as follows:

```
<exp> : <field width>
```

Expressions of type real can be formatted as follows:

```
<exp> : <field width> : <precision>

Write(t, <exp1>,            { writes output to file  }
<exp2>, ..., <exp n>);
Writeln(t, <exp1>,          { writes output to file and skips to next
<exp2>, ..., <exp n>);      line }
```

STRING FUNCTIONS

```
s := Concat(<str 1>,        { returns concatenation of 2 strings}
<str 2>);
s := Copy(<source --        { returns substring of <source>, starting
s>, <start -- i>,           at position <start> and continuing for
<num chars -- i>)           <num chars> }
i := Length(s);             { returns length of s}
i := Pos(<pattern --        { returns position where <pattern> is
s>, <source -- s>);         found in <source> }
s := Insert(<str to         { returns <original str> with <str to
include -- s>,              include> inserted in the string starting
<original str -- s>,        at <position> }
<position -- i>);
Str(n, s);                  { returns in s the string representation of
                            the number n }
Val(s, n, <error            { returns in n the numeric representation
code -- i>);                of the string s; if s correctly represents
                            a number, returns 0 in <error code>; other-
                            wise, another integer appears in <error
                            code> }
```

Appendix C

ASCII Chart

	0	16	32	48	64	80	96	112
0	NUL	DLE	SPACE	0	@	P	‘	p
1	SOH	DC1	!	1	A	Q	a	q
2	STX	DC2	“	2	B	R	b	r
3	EXT	DC3	#	3	C	S	c	s
4	EOT	DC4	$	4	D	T	d	t
5	ENQ	NAK	%	5	E	U	e	u
6	ACK	SYC	&	6	F	V	f	v
7	BEL	ETB	‘	7	G	W	g	w
8	BS	CAN	(	8	H	X	h	x
9	HT	EM	)	9	I	Y	i	y
10	LF	SUB	*	:	J	Z	j	z
11	VT	ESC	+	;	K	[	k	{
12	FF	FS	,	<	L	\	l	|
13	CR	GS	-	=	M	]	m	}
14	SO	RS	.	>	N	^	n	~
15	SI	US	/	?	O	_	o	DEL

The decimal representation of any character is found by adding the row and the column numbers (e.g., the representation of G is 64 + 7, or 71).

NUL stands for the null character (represented by 0); SP stands for the space character (represented by 32).

Characters 0 through 31 and character 127 (DEL) are nonprinting “control codes,” which are used by the computer and display to perform various functions but which are of no concern for string representations.

Appendix D

Graphics Package (GP) Library

This appendix describes the GP classes mentioned in the text, in addition to other interesting features of GP. Please also refer to the GP documentation that accompanies your software. The preface indicates how you may obtain your free copy of GP from the Internet.[1]

GP CLASS INHERITANCE

Figures D.1 through D.6 illustrate the inheritance hierarchy of the GP classes.

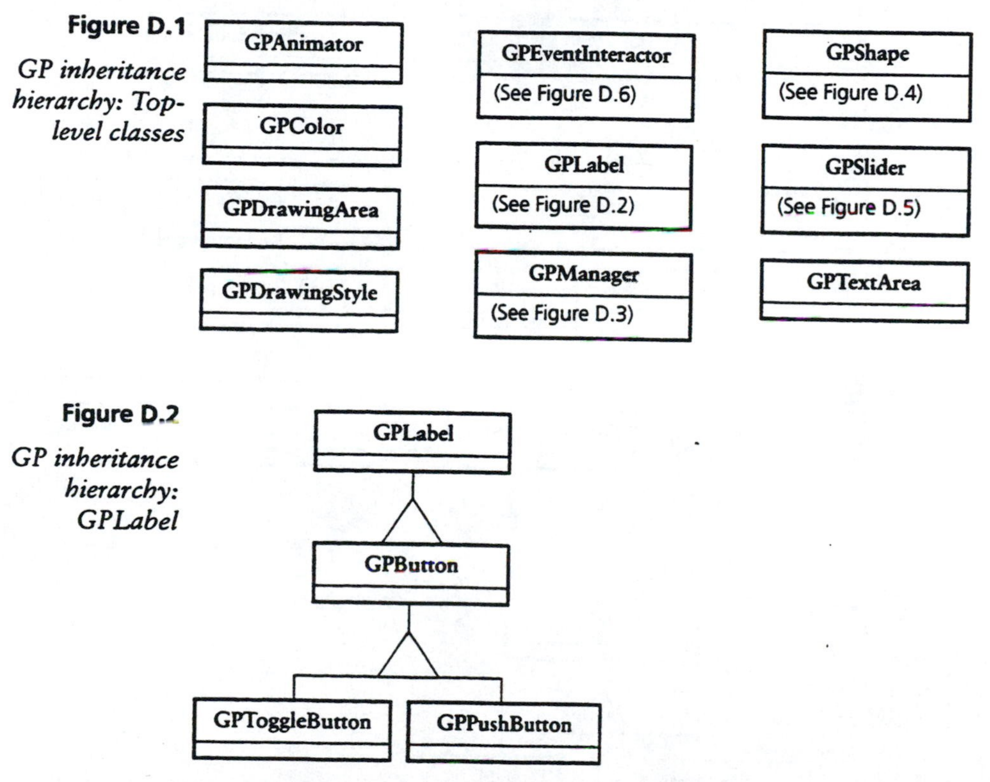

Figure D.1 *GP inheritance hierarchy: Top-level classes*

Figure D.2 *GP inheritance hierarchy: GPLabel*

1. The Graphics Package (GP) library for Borland Pascal was written by Rafael R. Ruiz, based on a previous implementation by Brook Conner and Robert Duvall. The documentation in this appendix is based on documentation written by Brian M. McDonald.

Figure D.3

GP inheritance hierarchy: GPManager

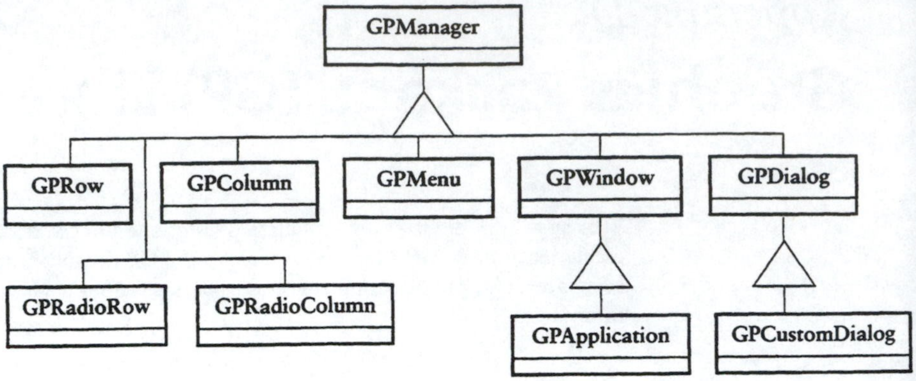

GPManager
GPRow
GPColumn
GPMenu
GPWindow
GPDialog
GPRadioRow
GPRadioColumn
GPApplication
GPCustomDialog

Figure D.4

GP inheritance hierarchy: GPShape

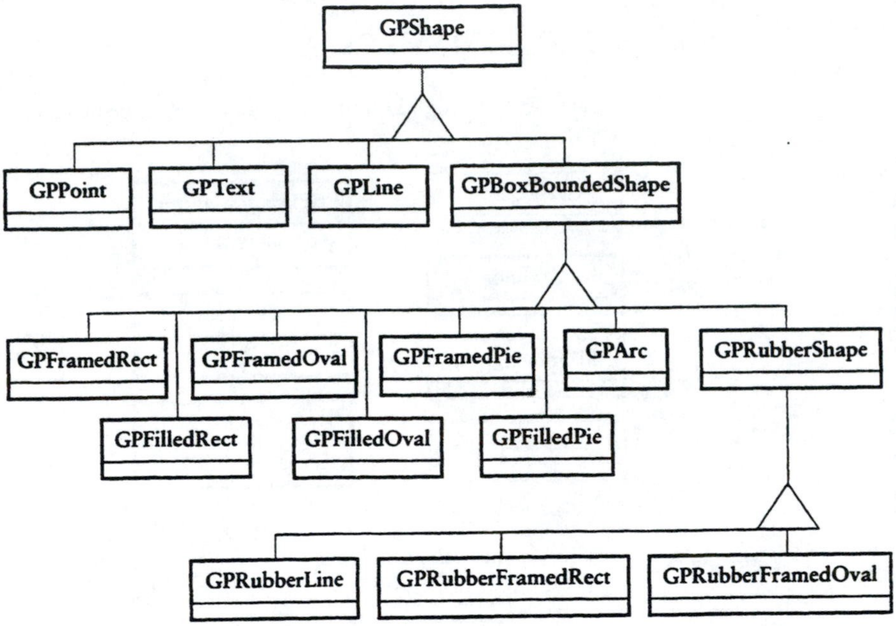

GPShape
GPPoint
GPText
GPLine
GPBoxBoundedShape
GPFramedRect
GPFramedOval
GPFramedPie
GPArc
GPRubberShape
GPFilledRect
GPFilledOval
GPFilledPie
GPRubberLine
GPRubberFramedRect
GPRubberFramedOval

Figure D.5

GP inheritance hierarchy: GPSlider

GPSlider
GPIntSlider
GPRealSlider

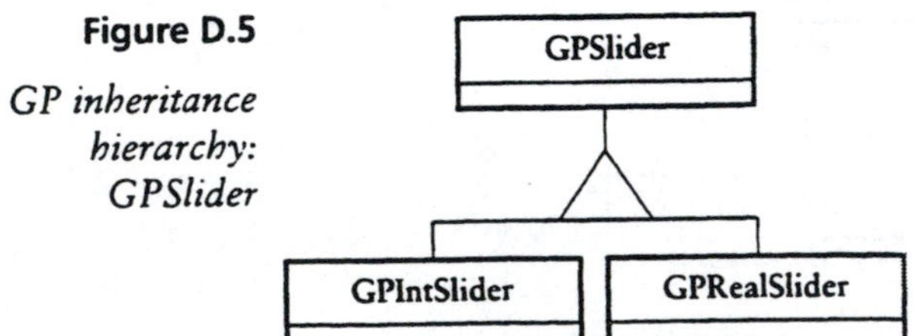

Figure D.6
GP inheritance hierarchy: GPInteractor

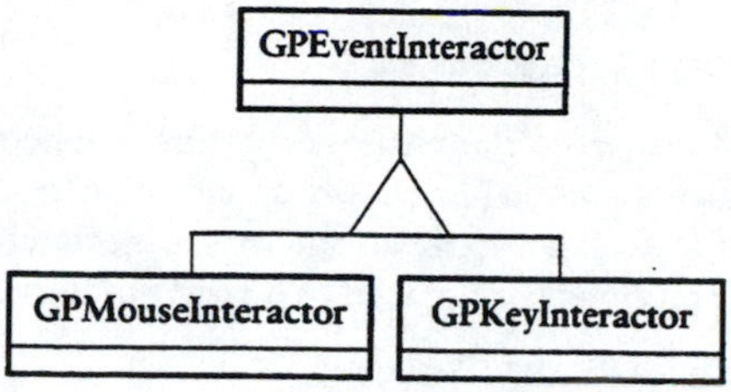

GP CLASS DESCRIPTIONS

The remainder of this appendix describes each class in GP in alphabetical order.

GPAnimator

Unit `GPAnimatorUnit`

Association `GPAnimatorAsn`

Description This class repeatedly calls its `Action` method. The `Start`, `Step`, and `Stop` methods provide control over this process. The `SetInterval` method controls the interval between each call to the `Action` method. The smaller the interval, the more often `Action` will be called.

Public Interface `CONSTRUCTOR Init;`
Initializes the `GPAnimator`.

`DESTRUCTOR Destroy; VIRTUAL;`
Destroys the `GPAnimator`.

`PROCEDURE Start; VIRTUAL;`
Starts the calling of the `Action` method, if not already active.

`PROCEDURE Step; VIRTUAL;`
Calls the `Action` method once, then calls `Stop`.

`PROCEDURE Stop; VIRTUAL;`
Stops the calling of the `Action` method, if already active.

`PROCEDURE SetInterval(milliseconds: integer);`
Sets the time interval between calls to the `Action` method. The `milliseconds` parameter specifies number of milliseconds. The default interval is 100 milliseconds.

`PROCEDURE Action; VIRTUAL;`
Method that is repeatedly called. This method should be redefined in subclasses. Note: no other `GPAnimator` method should be called from within `Action`.

Inherits from None

Subclasses None

GPApplication *Unit* `GPApplicationUnit`

Association `GPApplicationAsn`

Description Manager of the entire program. Each program that uses GP must have a `GPApplication` object. This object provides the main window for the application. Any objects contained by a `GPApplication` object are placed in a row, similar to a `GPRow`.

Public Interface

`CONSTRUCTOR Init;`
Initializes a `GPApplication`. The title of the main window is set to "GPApp".

`CONSTRUCTOR InitWithName (appName: string);`
Initializes a `GPApplication`. The title of the main window is set to `appName`.

`DESTRUCTOR Destroy; VIRTUAL;`
Destroys a `GPApplication`.

`PROCEDURE Run;`
Displays the `GPApplication` window and any graphical GP objects it contains and processes events until the `Quit` method is called. This method should only be called once in a program.

`PROCEDURE Quit;`
Halts the execution of the program.

Inherits from `GPWindow`, `GPManager`

Subclasses None

GPArc *Unit* `GPShapesUnit`

Association `GPArcAsn`

Description An arc is part of the boundary of a framed oval. The oval is defined by the bounding box (see `GPBoxBoundedShape`). The start and end angles are defined in degrees, with 0° and 360° both to the right of the oval. Thus an arc representing the bottom left quarter of a filled oval should start at 180° and end at 270°.

Public Interface

`CONSTRUCTOR Init;`
Initializes a `GPArc` with (0,0) for both corners and 0 as its angles.

```
CONSTRUCTOR InitWithPoints (topLeft, bottomRight:
  GPPoint; startAngle, endAngle: integer);
```
Initializes a `GPArc` with top left and bottom right points, start and end angles.

```
CONSTRUCTOR InitWithSize (topLeft: GPPoint; width,
  height: integer; startAngle, endAngle: integer);
```
Initializes a `GPArc` with top left corner and dimensions, start and end angles.

GPArc (cont.) *Public Interface*

```
CONSTRUCTOR InitWithCoords (leftX, topY, rightX,
  bottomY: integer; startAngle, endAngle: integer);
```

Initializes a GPArc with coordinates, start and end angles.

```
DESTRUCTOR Destroy; VIRTUAL;
```

Destroys a `GPArc`.

```
PROCEDURE SetStartAngle (startAngle: integer);
```

Modifies the start angle.

```
FUNCTION GetStartAngle: integer;
```

Returns the current start angle.

```
PROCEDURE SetEndAngle (endAngle: integer);
```

Modifies the end angle.

```
FUNCTION GetEndAngle: integer;
```

Returns the current end angle.

```
PROCEDURE Copy: GPShapeAsn; VIRTUAL;
```

Produces a copy of the `GPArc`.

```
PROCEDURE CopyAsGPArc: GPArcAsn;
```

Produces a copy of the `GPArc`.

```
FUNCTION Equal(other : GPArc): Boolean;
```

Returns `TRUE` if the coordinates of `other` are the same as this instance's.

Inherits from `GPBoxBoundedShape`, `GPShape`

Subclasses None

GPBoxBounded-Shape

Unit `GPShapesUnit`

Association `GPBoxBoundedShapeAsn`

Description An abstract base class for shapes that are bounded by a rectangle defined by two opposite corners. This class does not have a graphical representation and does nothing when `Draw` is called.

Public Interface

```
CONSTRUCTOR Init;
```

Initializes a `GPBoxBoundedShape` with (0, 0) for both corners.

```
CONSTRUCTOR InitWithPoints (topLeft, bottomRight:
  GPPoint);
```

Initializes a `GPBoxBoundedShape` with corners `topLeft` and `bottomRight`.

```
CONSTRUCTOR InitWithSize (topLeft: GPPoint; width,
  height: integer);
```

Initializes a `GPBoxBoundedShape` with top left corner and dimensions.

GPBox-Bounded-Shape (cont.)

Public Interface (continued)

```
CONSTRUCTOR InitWithCoords (leftX, topY, rightX,
   bottomY: integer);
```
Initializes a GPBoxBoundedShape with coordinates.

```
DESTRUCTOR Destroy; VIRTUAL;
```
Destroys a GPBoxBoundedShape.

```
PROCEDURE SetTopLeft(topLeft: GPPoint); VIRTUAL;
```
Modifies the top left corner.

```
PROCEDURE GetTopLeft (VAR topLeft: GPPoint);
```
Returns the current top left corner.

```
PROCEDURE SetBottomRight (bottomRight: GPPoint);
```
Modifies the bottom right corner.

```
PROCEDURE GetBottomRight (VAR bottomRight: GPPoint);
```
Returns the current bottom right corner.

```
PROCEDURE SetPoints (topLeft, bottomRight: GPPoint);
```
Modifies both corners.

```
PROCEDURE GetPoints (VAR topLeft, bottomRight:
   GPPoint);
```
Returns both corners.

```
PROCEDURE SetCoords (leftX, topY, rightX, bottomY :
   integer);
```
Modifies the current coordinates.

```
PROCEDURE GetCoords (leftX, topY, rightX, bottomY :
   integer);
```
Returns the current coordinates.

```
FUNCTION GetHeight: integer;
```
Returns the current height.

```
FUNCTION GetWidth: integer;
```
Returns the current width.

Inherits from GPShape

Subclasses GPArc, GPFilledOval, GPFramedOval, GPFilledPie, GPFramed-Pie, GPFilledRect, GPFramedRect, GPRubberShape, GPRubber-Line, GPRubberFramedRect, GPRubberFramedOval

GPButton

Unit GPButtonUnit

Association GPButtonAsn

Description An abstract base class representing a labeled area of a window that can be clicked on to produce user-defined behavior. This class should never be instantiated directly.

GPButton (cont.)

Public Interface

`CONSTRUCTOR Init;`
Initializes a `GPButton`.

`DESTRUCTOR Destroy; VIRTUAL;`
Destroys a `GPButton`.

`PROCEDURE Activate; VIRTUAL;`
Defines the action that should occur when a button is pressed. This method should be redefined in subclasses.

Inherits from `GPLabel`

Subclasses `GPPushButton`, `GPToggleButton`

GPColor

Unit `GPColorUnit`

Association `GPColorAsn`

Description A color for use with other `GP` objects. Colors are made of red, green, and blue components.

Public Interface

`CONSTRUCTOR InitWithRGB (r, g, b: integer);`
Initializes a `GPColor` with red, green, and blue values. Each value must be between 0 and 255.

`CONSTRUCTOR InitAs (name : string);`
Initializes a `GPColor` with the named color. If no such color with that name exists, it uses the color with the closest matching name.

`CONSTRUCTOR InitAsRed;`
Initializes a `GPColor` as red.

`CONSTRUCTOR InitAsOrange;`
Initializes a `GPColor` as orange.

`CONSTRUCTOR InitAsYellow;`
Initializes a `GPColor` as yellow.

`CONSTRUCTOR InitAsGreen;`
Initializes a `GPColor` as green.

`CONSTRUCTOR InitAsBlue;`
Initializes a `GPColor` as blue.

`CONSTRUCTOR InitAsPurple;`
Initializes a `GPColor` as purple.

`CONSTRUCTOR InitAsBlack;`
Initializes a `GPColor` as black.

`CONSTRUCTOR InitAsWhite;`
Initializes a `GPColor` as white.

`DESTRUCTOR Destroy;`
Destroys a `GPColor`.

GPColor (cont.) *Public Interface (continued)*

`FUNCTION Equal(other: GPColor): boolean;`
Returns `TRUE` if `other` parameter has the same red, green, blue values as this instance; otherwise returns `FALSE`.

`FUNCTION GetName: string;`
Returns the name of the color. If the color has no name, the string returned is made up of the color's red, green, and blue color values.

`PROCEDURE GetRGB (VAR r, g, b: integer);`
Sets the parameters equal to the red, green, and blue color values, respectively.

`FUNCTION GetR: integer;`
Returns the red value of the `GPColor`.

`FUNCTION GetG: integer;`
Returns the green value of the `GPColor`.

`FUNCTION GetB: integer;`
Returns the blue value of the `GPColor`.

`PROCEDURE ChangeRGBTo (r, g, b: integer);`
Changes the `GPColor` to specified red, green, and blue values. Each value must be between 0 and 255.

`PROCEDURE ChangeTo (name : string);`
Changes the `GPColor` to the named color. If no such color with that name exists, it uses the color with the closest matching name.

`PROCEDURE ChangeToRed;`
Changes the `GPColor` to red.

`PROCEDURE ChangeToOrange;`
Changes the `GPColor` to orange.

`PROCEDURE ChangeToYellow;`
Changes the `GPColor` to yellow.

`PROCEDURE ChangeToGreen;`
Changes the `GPColor` to green.

`PROCEDURE ChangeToBlue;`
Changes the `GPColor` to blue.

`PROCEDURE ChangeToPurple;`
Changes the `GPColor` to purple.

`PROCEDURE ChangeToBlack;`
Changes the `GPColor` to black.

`PROCEDURE ChangeToWhite;`
Changes the `GPColor` to white.

Inherits from None

Subclasses None

GPColumn

Unit `GPManagerUnit`

Association `GPColumnAsn`

Description A simple manager that arranges the objects it contains in a vertical column. Objects that are added to the column appear below objects already in the column. See `GPManager` for an explanation on how managers are used.

Public Interface `CONSTRUCTOR Init (containerLink: GPManagerAsn);`
Initializes a `GPColumn`.

`DESTRUCTOR Destroy; VIRTUAL;`
Destroys a `GPColumn`.

Inherits from `GPManager`

Subclasses None

GPCustom-Dialog

Unit `GPDialogUnit`

Association `GPCustomDialogAsn`

Description A `GPCustomDialog` is equivalent to a `GPWindow` except that dialogs should be used when a window will be on the screen for a short amount of time. Dialogs have a different graphical representation than `GPWindows`.

Public Interface `CONSTRUCTOR InitWithName(dialogName:string);`
Initializes a `GPCustomDialog`.

`DESTRUCTOR Destroy; VIRTUAL;`
Destroys a `GPCustomDialog`.

`PROCEDURE Show; VIRTUAL;`
Causes the `GPCustomDialog` to appear on the screen.

`PROCEDURE Hide; VIRTUAL;`
Causes the `GPCustomDialog` to disappear from the screen.

Inherits from `GPDialog`, `GPManager`

Subclasses None

GPDialog

Unit `GPDialogUnit`

Association `GPDialogAsn`

Description This is an abstract base class and should never be instantiated. Dialogs are windows that appear on the screen for short periods of time. Their graphical representation is different from that of a `GPWindow` (and its subclasses).

Public Interface `CONSTRUCTOR Init;`
Initializes a `GPDialog`.

`DESTRUCTOR Destroy; VIRTUAL;`
Destroys a `GPDialog`.

Inherits from `GPManager`

Subclasses `GPCustomDialog`

GPDrawingArea

Unit `GPDAreaUnit`

Association `GPDrawingAreaAsn`

Description An area on the screen that can be drawn on by using `GPShapes`. A `GPDrawingArea` contains a default `GPDrawingStyle` used for all drawing. Methods for this class allow the user to get a link to this `GPDrawingStyle` and make changes to it, give the `GPDrawingArea` a link to a different `GPDrawingStyle` to use, or make a copy of the current `GPDrawingStyle` (contained by the `GPDrawingArea`).

Public Interface

```
CONSTRUCTOR Init (containerLink: GPManagerAsn);
```
Initializes a `GPDrawingArea` (with default size 300 pixels square).

```
CONSTRUCTOR InitWithSize (containerLink:
  GPManagerAsn; width, height: integer);
```
Initializes a `GPDrawingArea` with given width and height (in pixels).

```
DESTRUCTOR Destroy; VIRTUAL;
```
Destroys a `GPDrawingArea`.

```
PROCEDURE SetDrawingStyle (style:
  GPDrawingStyleAsn);
```
Sets the drawing style to be used when drawing objects.

```
FUNCTION GetDrawingStyle: GPDrawingStyleAsn;
```
Returns a link to the current drawing style.

```
PROCEDURE CopyDrawingStyle (VAR style:
  GPDrawingStyle);
```
Returns in `style` a copy of the current drawing style.

```
PROCEDURE AddInteractor (interactorLink:
  GPMouseInteractorAsn);
```
Adds a mouse interactor to the drawing area.

```
PROCEDURE RemoveInteractor (interactorLink:
  GPMouseInteractorAsn);
```
Removes a mouse interactor from the drawing area.

```
PROCEDURE SetHeight (height: integer);
```
Sets the height of the drawing area.

```
PROCEDURE SetWidth (width: integer);
```
Sets the width of the drawing area.

GPDrawingArea (cont.)

Public Interface (continued)

```
PROCEDURE Clear (color : GPColor);
```
Clears the `GPDrawingArea` using `color` as the background color.

```
FUNCTION ColorAtMatches (x, y : integer; color:
   GPColor): Boolean;
```
Returns `TRUE` if the color at location specified by `pt` matches `color`.

Inherits from None

Subclasses None

GPDrawingStyle

Unit `GPDStyleUnit`

Association `GPDrawingStyleAsn`

Description The style in which objects are drawn. This includes the color, the width and style of lines, and the drawing mode.

Public Interface

```
CONSTRUCTOR Init;
```
Initializes a drawing style.

```
CONSTRUCTOR InitCopy(src: GPDrawingStyle);
```
Initializes a new drawing style, copying the style elements of `src`.

```
DESTRUCTOR Destroy;
```
Destroys a `GPDrawingStyle`.

```
FUNCTION Copy: GPDrawingStyleAsn;
```
Returns a new drawing style, copying the style elements of this drawing style.

```
PROCEDURE SetDrawingForeground (foreground:GPColor);
```
Sets the foreground color of objects to be drawn with this drawing style.

```
PROCEDURE GetDrawingForeground (VAR foreground:
   GPColor);
```
Returns the current drawing foreground color.

```
PROCEDURE SetDrawingMode (mode: GPDrawingMode);
```
Sets the mode of object to be drawn with this drawing style. There are two predefined values of `GPDrawingMode`. When `GPxor` is sent as the parameter to mode, it means that drawing will be done using pixel-XOR. That is, when a new shape (call it shape 1) is drawn and it overlaps an existing shape (shape 2), the overlap is drawn in a color that is a combination of shape 1's and shape 2's colors. In `GPcopy` mode, when shape 1 is drawn, all of shape 1's area, including the overlap with any other shape, is drawn in shape 1's color.

```
FUNCTION GetDrawingMode: GPDrawingMode;
```
Returns the current drawing mode (`GPxor` or `GPcopy`).

GPDrawingStyle (cont.)

Public Interface (continued)

`PROCEDURE SetLineStyle (style: GPLineStyle);`
Sets the line style of objects to be drawn with this drawing style. There are five predefined values of `GPLineStyle`: `PS_SOLID`, `PS_DASH`, `PS_DOT`, `PS_DASHDOT`, and `PS_DASHDOTDOT`.

`FUNCTION GetLineStyle: GPLineStyle;`
Returns the current line style.

`PROCEDURE SetLineWidth (width: integer);`
Sets the line width of objects to be drawn with this drawing style.

`FUNCTION GetLineWidth: integer;`
Returns the current line width.

Inherits from None

Subclasses None

GPEvent-Interactor

Unit `GPInteractorUnit`

Association `GPEventInteractorAsn`

Description A superclass for all interactors that handle events from Windows.

Public Interface

`CONSTRUCTOR Init;`
Initializes a `GPEventInteractor`.

`DESTRUCTOR Destroy; VIRTUAL;`
Destroys a `GPEventInteractor`.

Inherits from None

Subclasses `GPKeyInteractor`, `GPMouseInteractor`

GPFilledOval

Unit `GPShapesUnit`

Association `GPFilledOvalAsn`

Description A filled oval. The oval is circumscribed within the bounding box (see `GPBoxBoundedShape`).

Public Interface

`CONSTRUCTOR Init;`
Initializes a `GPFilledOval`with (0, 0) for both corners.

```
CONSTRUCTOR InitWithPoints (topLeft, bottomRight:
   GPPoint);
```
Initializes a `GPFilledOval`with corners `topLeft` and `bottom-Right`.

```
CONSTRUCTOR InitWithSize (topLeft: GPPoint; width,
   height: integer);
```
Initializes a `GPFilledOval` with top left corner and dimensions.

GPFilledOval (cont.)

Public Interface (continued)

`CONSTRUCTOR InitWithCoords (leftX, topY, rightX, bottomY: integer);`
Initializes a `GPFilledOval` with its coordinates.

`DESTRUCTOR Destroy; VIRTUAL;`
Destroys a `GPFilledOval`.

`PROCEDURE Copy: GPShapeAsn; VIRTUAL;`
Produces a copy of the `GPFilledOval`.

`PROCEDURE CopyAsGPFilledOval: GPFilledOvalAsn;`
Produces a copy of the `GPFilledOval`.

`FUNCTION Equal(other : GPFilledOval): Boolean;`
Returns `TRUE` if the coordinates of `other` are the same as this instance's.

Inherits from `GPBoxBoundedShape`, `GPShape`

Subclasses None

GPFilledPie

Unit `GPShapesUnit`

Association `GPFilledPieAsn`

Description A filled pie piece, which is a section of a filled oval. The oval is defined by a bounding box (see `GPBoxBoundedShape`). The start and end angles are defined in degrees, with 0° and 360° both to the right of the oval. Thus the bottom left quarter of a filled pie should start at 180° and end at 270°.

Public Interface

`CONSTRUCTOR Init;`
Initializes a `GPFilledPie` with (0, 0) for both corners and 0° as its angles.

`CONSTRUCTOR InitWithPoints (topLeft, bottomRight: GPPoint; startAngle, endAngle: integer);`
Initializes a `GPFilledPie` with top left and bottom right points, start and end angles.

`CONSTRUCTOR InitWithSize (topLeft: GPPoint; width, height: integer; startAngle, endAngle: integer);`
Initializes a `GPFilledPie` with top left corner and dimensions, start and end angles.

`CONSTRUCTOR InitWithCoords (leftX, topY, rightX, bottomY: integer; startAngle, endAngle: integer);`
Initializes a `GPFilledPie` with coordinates, start and end angles.

`DESTRUCTOR Destroy; VIRTUAL;`
Destroys a `GPFilledPie`.

`PROCEDURE SetStartAngle (startAngle: integer);`
Modifies the start angle.

GPFilledPie (cont.) *Public Interface (continued)*

`FUNCTION GetStartAngle: integer;`
Returns the current start angle.

`PROCEDURE SetEndAngle (endAngle: integer);`
Modifies the end angle.

`FUNCTION GetEndAngle: integer;`
Returns the current end angle.

`PROCEDURE Copy: GPShapeAsn; VIRTUAL;`
Produces a copy of the `GPFilledPie`.

`PROCEDURE CopyAsGPFilledPie: GPFilledPieAsn;`
Produces a copy of the `GPFilledPie`.

`FUNCTION Equal(other : GPFilledPie): Boolean;`
Returns `TRUE` if the coordinates of `other` are the same as this instance's.

Inherits from None

Subclasses None

GPFilledRect *Unit* `GPShapesUnit`

Association `GPFilledRectAsn`

Description A filled rectangle.

Public Interface

`CONSTRUCTOR Init;`
Initializes a `GPFilledRect` with (0, 0) for both corners.

```
CONSTRUCTOR InitWithPoints (topLeft, bottomRight:
  GPPoint);
```
Initializes a `GPFilledRect` with corners `topLeft` and `bottomRight`.

```
CONSTRUCTOR InitWithSize (topLeft: GPPoint; width,
  height: integer);
```
Initializes a `GPFilledRect` with top left corner and dimensions.

```
CONSTRUCTOR InitWithCoords (leftX, topY, rightX,
  bottomY: integer);
```
Initializes a `GPFilledRect` with coordinates.

`DESTRUCTOR Destroy; VIRTUAL;`
Destroys a `GPFilledRect`.

`PROCEDURE Copy: GPShapeAsn; VIRTUAL;`
Produce a copy of the `GPFilledRect`.

`PROCEDURE CopyAsGPFilledRect: GPFilledRectAsn;`
Produce a copy of the `GPFilledRect`.

GPFilledRect (cont.)

Public Interface (continued)

`FUNCTION Equal(other : GPFilledRect): Boolean;`
Returns `TRUE` if the coordinates of `other` are the same as this instance's.

Inherits from `GPBoxBoundedShape`

Subclasses None

GPFramedOval

Unit `GPShapesUnit`

Association `GPFramedOvalAsn`

Description A framed oval. The oval is circumscribed within the bounding box (see `GPBoxBoundedShape`).

Public Interface

`CONSTRUCTOR Init;`
Initializes a `GPFramedOval` with (0, 0) for both corners.

```
CONSTRUCTOR InitWithPoints (topLeft, bottomRight:
  GPPoint);
```
Initializes a `GPFramedOval` with corners `topLeft` and `bottom-Right`.

```
CONSTRUCTOR InitWithSize (topLeft: GPPoint; width,
  height: integer);
```
Initializes a `GPFramedOval` with top left corner and dimensions.

```
CONSTRUCTOR InitWithCoords (leftX, topY, rightX,
  bottomY: integer);
```
Initializes a `GPFramedOval` with coordinates.

`DESTRUCTOR Destroy; VIRTUAL;`
Destroys a `GPFramedOval`.

`PROCEDURE Copy: GPShapeAsn; VIRTUAL;`
Produces a copy of the `GPFramedOval`.

`PROCEDURE CopyAsGPFramedOval: GPFramedOvalAsn;`
Produces a copy of the `GPFramedOval`.

`FUNCTION Equal(other : GPFramedOval): Boolean;`
Returns `TRUE` if the coordinates of `other` are the same as this instance's.

Inherits from `GPBoxBoundedShape`, `GPShape`

Subclasses None

GPFramedPie

Unit `GPShapesUnit`

Association `GPFramedPieAsn`

GPFramedPie (cont.)

Description

A framed pie piece, which is a section of a framed oval. The oval is defined by the bounding box (see `GPBoxBoundedShape`). The start and end angles are defined in degrees, with 0° and 360° both at the right of the oval. Thus a pie piece representing the bottom left quarter of a filled oval should start at 180° and end at 270°.

Public Interface

```
CCONSTRUCTOR Init;
```

Initializes a `GPFramedPie` with (0, 0) for both corners and 0 as its angles.

```
CONSTRUCTOR InitWithPoints (topLeft, bottomRight:
  GPPoint; startAngle, endAngle: integer);
```

Initializes a `GPFramedPie` with top left and bottom right points, start and end angles.

```
CONSTRUCTOR InitWithSize (topLeft: GPPoint; width,
  height: integer; startAngle, endAngle: integer);
```

Initializes a `GPFramedPie` with top left corner and dimensions, start and end angles.

```
CONSTRUCTOR InitWithCoords (leftX, topY, rightX,
  bottomY: integer; startAngle, endAngle: integer);
```

Initializes a `GPFramedPie` with coordinates, start and end angles.

```
DESTRUCTOR Destroy; VIRTUAL;
```

Destroys a `GPFramedPie`.

```
PROCEDURE SetStartAngle (startAngle: integer);
```

Modifies the start angle.

```
FUNCTION GetStartAngle: integer;
```

Returns the current start angle.

```
PROCEDURE SetEndAngle (endAngle: integer);
```

Modifies the end angle.

```
FUNCTION GetEndAngle: integer;
```

Returns the current end angle.

```
PROCEDURE Copy: GPShapeAsn; VIRTUAL;
```

Produces a copy of the `GPFramedPie`.

```
PROCEDURE CopyAsGPFramedPie: GPFramedPieAsn;
```

Produces a copy of the `GPFramedPie`.

```
FUNCTION Equal(other : GPFramedPie): Boolean;
```

Returns `TRUE` if the coordinates of `other` are the same as this instance's.

Inherits from `GPBoxBoundedShape`, `GPShape`

Subclasses None

GPFramedRect

Unit `GPShapesUnit`

Association `GPFramedRectAsn`

Description A framed rectangle

Public Interface

`CONSTRUCTOR Init;`
Initializes a `GPFramedRect` with (0, 0) for both corners.

```
CONSTRUCTOR InitWithPoints (topLeft, bottomRight:
  GPPoint);
```
Initializes a `GPFramedRect` with corners `topLeft` and `bottomRight`.

```
CONSTRUCTOR InitWithSize (topLeft: GPPoint; width,
  height: integer);
```
Initializes a `GPFramedRect` with top left corner and dimensions, start and end angles.

```
CONSTRUCTOR InitWithCoords (leftX, topY, rightX,
  bottomY: integer);
```
Initializes a `GPFramedRect` with coordinates, start and end angles.

`DESTRUCTOR Destroy; VIRTUAL;`
Destroys a `GPFramedRect`.

`PROCEDURE Copy: GPShapeAsn; VIRTUAL;`
Produces a copy of the `GPFramedRect`.

`PROCEDURE CopyAsGPFramedRect: GPFramedRectAsn;`
Produces a copy of the `GPFramedRect`.

`FUNCTION Equal(other : GPFramedRect): Boolean;`
Returns `TRUE` if the coordinates of `other` are the same as this instance's.

Inherits from `GPBoxBoundedShape, GPShape`

Subclasses None

GPIntSlider

Unit `GPSliderUnit`

Association `GPIntSliderAsn`

Description Displays a numeric value with upper and lower bounds, and allows the user to change that value interactively using a slider mechanism similar to that of a scroll bar. This slider is used for integer values. To use, you should make a subclass and redefine the `IntValue` method.

Public Interface

`CONSTRUCTOR Init (containerLink: GPManagerAsn);`
Initializes a `GPIntSlider`.

`DESTRUCTOR Destroy; VIRTUAL;`
Destroys a `GPIntSlider`.

GPIntSlider (cont.)

Public Interface (continued)

`PROCEDURE ValueChanged; VIRTUAL;`
Defines behavior to occur when value in slider is changed. In this class, an `IntValue` message will be sent.

`PROCEDURE SetMaximum (max: integer);`
Modifies the upper bound.

`PROCEDURE SetMinimum (min: integer);`
Modifies the lower bound.

`PROCEDURE SetInterval (num: integer);`
Sets the distance to move the slider when the user moves it by a multiple increment (clicking on the scroll bar in between the arrows and the thumb).

`PROCEDURE SetValue (num: integer);`
Sets the current value of the slider.

`FUNCTION GetValue: integer;`
Returns the value of the slider.

`PROCEDURE IntValue (value: integer); VIRTUAL;`
Defines behavior to occur when value in slider is changed. The parameter value is the value defined by the position on the scroll bar. For example, if the thumb is halfway between the two ends, and the minimum and maximum are set to 0 and 100, `value` will receive 50. This method will be executed whenever the slider is moved.

Inherits from `GPSlider`

Subclasses None

GPKeyInteractor

Unit `GPInteractorUnit`

Association `GPKeyInteractorAsn`

Description This class defines behavior for certain keys. Using a `GPKeyInteractor` and a `GPTextArea` simultaneously is not suggested. Lowercase letters are not supported.

Public Interface

`CONSTRUCTOR Init (key: char);`
Initializes a `GPKeyInteractor` for `key`.

`DESTRUCTOR Destroy; VIRTUAL;`
Destroys a `GPKeyInteractor`.

`FUNCTION GetKey: char;`
Gets the key represented by the key interactor.

`PROCEDURE KeyPress; VIRTUAL;`
Method called when the specified key is pressed down. This method should be redefined in a subclass.

GPKeyInteractor (cont.)

Public Interface (continued)

`PROCEDURE KeyRelease;VIRTUAL;`
Method called when the specified key is released. This method should be redefined in a subclass.

Inherits from `GPEventInteractor`

Subclasses None

GPLabel

Unit `GPButtonUnit`

Association `GPLabelAsn`

Description A labeled area in a window. The text is centered inside a rectangle designated by the label's height and width. The difference between this class and `GPText` is that `GPLabel` can be placed inside `GPManagers` and `GPText` is drawn in a `GPDrawingArea`.

Public Interface

`CONSTRUCTOR Init (containerLink: GPManagerAsn);`
Initializes a `GPLabel`.

`DESTRUCTOR Destroy; VIRTUAL;`
Destroys a `GPLabel`.

`PROCEDURE SetName (name: string);`
Clears the label and resets the string displayed by it.

`PROCEDURE SetWidth (width: integer);`
Establishes the width of the rectangle where the label appears.

`PROCEDURE SetHeight (height: integer);`
Establishes the height of the rectangle where the label appears.

`PROCEDURE SetNameWithInt (num: integer);`
Establishes the width of the rectangle where the label appears.

`PROCEDURE SetNameWithReal (num: real);`
Establishes the width of the rectangle where the label appears.

Inherits from None

Subclasses `GPButton`, `GPPushButton`, `GPToggleButton`

GPLine

Unit `GPShapesUnit`

Association `GPLineAsn`

Description A line connecting two points.

Public Interface

`CONSTRUCTOR Init;`
Initializes a `GPLine` (with endpoints (0, 0) and (0, 0)).

```
CONSTRUCTOR InitWithCoords (startX, startY, endX,
   endY: integer);
```
Initializes a `GPLine` with the given coordinates.

GPLine (cont.) *Public Interface (continued)*

```
CONSTRUCTOR InitWithPoints (startPt, endPt:
   GPPoint);
```
Initializes a GPLine with the given endpoints.

```
DESTRUCTOR Destroy; VIRTUAL;
```
Destroys a GPLine.

```
PROCEDURE SetStart(startPt : GPPoint);
```
Set the start point of the GPLine.

```
PROCEDURE GetStart(VAR startPt : GPPoint);
```
Get the start point of the GPLine.

```
PROCEDURE SetEnd(endPt : GPPoint);
```
Set the endpoint of the GPLine.

```
PROCEDURE GetEnd(VAR endPt : GPPoint);
```
Get the endpoint of the GPLine.

```
PROCEDURE SetCoords(startX, startY, endX, endY:
   integer);
```
Set the coordinates of the GPLine.

```
PROCEDURE SetCoords(startX, startY, endX, endY:
   integer);
```
Get the coordinates of the GPLine.

```
PROCEDURE Copy: GPShapeAsn; VIRTUAL;
```
Produce a copy of the GPLine.

```
PROCEDURE CopyAsGPLine: GPLineAsn;
```
Produce a copy of the GPLine.

```
FUNCTION Equal(other : GPLine): Boolean;
```
Returns TRUE if the coordinates of other are the same as this instance's.

Inherits from GPShape

Subclasses None

GPManager *Unit* GPManagerUnit

Association GPManagerAsn

Description Manager objects help us to control the placement and sizing of other objects in our application. All graphical interface GP objects take a link to their container (manager), the object that will contain them, as a parameter in their constructors. Managers can also contain or be contained by other managers. GPManager is an abstract superclass for a number of subclasses. You should never instantiate a GPManager; its functionality is inherited by each of its subclasses.

Public Interface `CONSTRUCTOR Init;`
Initializes a `GPManager`.

`DESTRUCTOR Destroy; VIRTUAL;`
Destroys a `GPManager`.

Inherits from None

Subclasses `GPColumn, GPDialog, GPMenu, GPRadioColumn, GPRadioRow, GPRow, GPWindow`

GPMenu

Unit `GPMenuUnit`

Association `GPMenuAsn`

Description A simple button manager that acts like a pull-down menu. It organizes its contained objects from top to bottom like a `GPColumn`. `GPButtons` and `GPLabels` should be the only kind of `GP` objects put inside of `GPMenus`.

Public Interface `CONSTRUCTOR Init (containerLink: GPWindowAsn);`
Initializes a `GPMenu`.

`DESTRUCTOR Destroy; VIRTUAL;`
Destroys a `GPMenu`.

`PROCEDURE SetName (name: string);`
Sets the displayed name of the `GPMenu`.

Inherits from `GPManager`

Subclasses None

GPMouse-Interactor

Unit `GPInteractorUnit`

Association `GPMouseInteractorAsn`

Description This class attaches behavior so that the program responds when the user uses the mouse. It must be installed on a `GPDrawingArea` using the `InstallInteractor` method.

Public Interface `CONSTRUCTOR Init;`
Initializes a `GPMouseInteractor`.

`DESTRUCTOR Destroy; VIRTUAL;`
Destroys a `GPMouseInteractor`.

`PROCEDURE ButtonDown (pt: GPPoint); VIRTUAL;`
Called when one of the mouse buttons is pressed down. `pt` is set to the position on the screen where the mouse pointer is located.

`PROCEDURE ButtonUp (pt: GPPoint); VIRTUAL;`
Called when one of the mouse buttons is released from the down position. `pt` is set to the position on the screen where the mouse pointer is located.

GPMouse-Interactor (cont.)

Public Interface (continued)

PROCEDURE ButtonMotion (pt: GPPoint); VIRTUAL;
Called when the mouse is moving while one of the mouse buttons being held down. pt is set to the position on the screen where th mouse pointer is located.

PROCEDURE MouseMotion(pt: GPPoint); VIRTUAL;
Called when the mouse is moving, regardless of the status of t mouse button. pt is set to the position on the screen where the mou pointer is located.

Inherits from GPEventInteractor

Subclasses None

GPPoint

Unit GPShapesUnit

Association GPPointAsn

Description A single pixel on the screen. Note that the coordinate system pla the point (0, 0) in the top left corner of the window.

Public Interface

CONSTRUCTOR Init;
Initializes a GPPoint with (0, 0).

CONSTRUCTOR InitWithCoords (x, y: integer);
Initializes a GPPoint with a location.

CONSTRUCTOR InitWithPoint (pt: GPPoint);
Initializes a GPPoint with the values of another GPPoint.

DESTRUCTOR Destroy; VIRTUAL;
Destroys a GPPoint.

FUNCTION GetX: integer;
Returns the value of the *x*-coordinate.

PROCEDURE SetX (x: integer);
Sets the value of the *x*-coordinate.

FUNCTION GetY: integer;
Returns the value of the *y*-coordinate.

PROCEDURE SetY (y: integer);
Sets the value of the *y*-coordinate.

PROCEDURE SetCoords (x, y: integer);
Sets the values of the *x*- and *y*-coordinates to the correspon parameters.

PROCEDURE GetCoords (VAR x, y: integer);
Returns the value of the *x*-coordinate and the *y*-coordinate in respective parameters.

PROCEDURE Copy: GPShapeAsn; VIRTUAL;
Produces a copy of the GPPoint.

GPPoint (cont.)

Public Interface (continued)

`PROCEDURE CopyAsGPPoint: GPPointAsn;`
Produces a copy of the `GPPoint`.

`FUNCTION Equal(other : GPPoint): Boolean;`
Returns `TRUE` if the coordinates of `other` are the same as this instance's.

Inherits from `GPShape`

Subclasses None

GPPushButton

Unit `GPButtonUnit`

Association `GPPushButtonAsn`

Description A button that performs an action when pressed. The `Activate` method (inherited virtually from `GPButton`) is where that action is defined.

Public Interface

`CONSTRUCTOR Init (containerLink: GPManagerAsn);`
Initializes a `GPPushButton`.

`DESTRUCTOR Destroy; VIRTUAL;`
Destroys a `GPPushButton`.

Inherits from `GPButton`, `GPLabel`

Subclasses None

GPRadioColumn

Unit `GPManagerUnit`

Association `GPRadioColumnAsn`

Description A simple manager that arranges the objects it contains in a vertical column. Objects that are added to the column appear below objects already in the column. All `GPRadio` managers are meant to contain only `GPToggleButtons`. `GPRadio` managers maintain that only one `GPToggleButton` is ever "on". Each time a `GPToggleButton` is pressed, a `GPRadio` manager calls the `DeActivate` method of the current `GPToggleButton` and then calls the `Activate` method of the `GPToggleButton` that was just pressed. Therefore, the radio manager turns a button "off" before turning the one pressed "on".

Public Interface

`CONSTRUCTOR Init (containerLink: GPManagerAsn);`
Initializes a `GPRadioColumn`.

`DESTRUCTOR Destroy; VIRTUAL;`
Destroys a `GPRadioColumn`.

Inherits from `GPManager`

Subclasses None

GPRadioRow

Unit GPManagerUnit

Association GPRadioRowAsn

Description A simple manager that arranges the objects it contains in a vertica row. Objects that are added to the row appear below objects alread in the row. All `GPRadio` managers are meant to contain only `GPTog gleButtons`. `GPRadio` managers maintain that only one `GPTog gleButton` is ever "on". Each time a `GPToggleButton` is pressed, `GPRadio` manager calls the `DeActivate` method of the currer `GPToggleButton` and then calls the `Activate` method of th `GPToggleButton` that was just pressed. Therefore, the radio mar ager turns a button "off" before turning the one pressed "on".

Public Interface

```
CONSTRUCTOR Init (containerLink: GPManagerAsn);
```
Initializes a `GPRadioRow`.

```
DESTRUCTOR Destroy; VIRTUAL;
```
Destroys a `GPRadioRow`.

Inherits from GPManager

Subclasses None

GPRealSlider

Unit GPSliderUnit

Association GPRealSliderAsn

Description Displays a numeric value with upper and lower bounds and allo the user to change that value interactively using a slider mechani similar to that of a scroll bar. This slider is used for real values. use, you should make a subclass and redefine the `RealVal` method.

Public Interface

```
CONSTRUCTOR Init (containerLink: GPManagerAsn);
```
Initializes a `GPRealSlider`.

```
DESTRUCTOR Destroy; VIRTUAL;
```
Destroys a `GPRealSlider`.

```
PROCEDURE ValueChanged; VIRTUAL;
```
Defines behavior to occur when value in slider is changed. In class, a `RealValue` message will be sent. This method should no redefined.

```
PROCEDURE SetMaximum (max: real);
```
Modifies the upper bound.

```
PROCEDURE SetMinimum (min: real);
```
Modifies the lower bound.

```
PROCEDURE SetInterval (num: real);
```
Sets the distance to move the slider when the user moves it by a r tiple increment (clicking on the scroll bar in between the arrows the thumb).

GPRealSlider (cont.)

Public Interface (continued)

`PROCEDURE SetValue (num: real);`
Sets the current value of the slider.

`FUNCTION GetValue: real;`
Returns the value of the slider.

`PROCEDURE RealValue (value: real); VIRTUAL;`
Defines behavior to occur when value in slider is changed. The parameter value is the value defined by the position of the scroll bar. For example, if the thumb is halfway between the two ends, and the minimum and maximum are respectively set to 0.0 and 100.0, `value` will receive 50.0. This method should be redefined. It will be called whenever the slider is moved.

Inherits from `GPSlider`

Subclasses None

GPRow

Unit `GPManagerUnit`

Association `GPRowAsn`

Description A simple manager that arranges the objects it contains in a horizontal row. Objects that are added to the row appear to the right of objects already in the row. See `GPManager` for an explanation on how managers are used.

Public Interface

`CONSTRUCTOR Init (containerLink: GPManagerAsn);`
Initializes a `GPRow`.

`DESTRUCTOR Destroy; VIRTUAL;`
Destroys a `GPRow`.

Inherits from `GPManager`

Subclasses None

GPRubber-FramedOval

Unit `GPRubberShapesUnit`

Association `GPRubberFramedOvalAsn`

Description A framed oval that can "rubberband," drawing and erasing itself to allow the user to resize the shape before it is permanently drawn.

Public Interface

`CONSTRUCTOR Init;`
Initializes a `GPRubberFramedOval` (with a bounding box with both corners set to (0, 0)).

`CONSTRUCTOR InitWithPoints (start, finish: GPPoint);`
Initializes a `GPRubberFramedOval` with the given bounding box locations.

`DESTRUCTOR Destroy; VIRTUAL;`
Destroys a `GPRubberFramedOval`.

GPRubber-FramedOval (cont.)

Publc Interface (continued)
`PROCEDURE Copy: GPShapeAsn; VIRTUAL;`
Produce a copy of the `GPRubberFramedOval`.

Inherits from `GPRubberShape`, `GPBoxBoundedShape`, `GPShape`

Subclasses None

GPRubber-FramedRect

Unit `GPRubberShapesUnit`

Association `GPRubberFramedRectAsn`

Description A framed rectangle that can "rubberband," drawing and erasin itself to allow the user to resize the shape before it is permanent drawn.

Public Interface
`CONSTRUCTOR Init;`
Initializes a `GPRubberFramedRect` (with corners (0, 0), (0, 0)).

`CONSTRUCTOR InitWithPoints (start, finish: GPPoint)`
Initializes a `GPRubberFramedRect` with given (`start` and `finis` locations.

`DESTRUCTOR Destroy; VIRTUAL;`
Destroys a `GPRubberFramedRect`.

`PROCEDURE Copy: GPShapeAsn; VIRTUAL;`
Produces a copy of the `GPRubberFramedRect`.

Inherits from `GPRubberShape`, `GPBoxBoundedShape`, `GPShape`

Subclasses None

GPRubberLine

Unit `GPRubberShapesUnit`

Association `GPRubberLineAsn`

Description A line that can "rubberband," drawing and erasing itself to allow user to resize the shape before it is permanently drawn.

Public Interface
`CONSTRUCTOR Init;`
Initializes a `GPRubberLine` (with endpoints (0, 0), (0, 0)).

`CONSTRUCTOR InitWithPoints (start, finish: GPPoint`
Initializes a `GPRubberLine` with the given endpoints.

`DESTRUCTOR Destroy; VIRTUAL;`
Destroys a `GPRubberLine`.

`PROCEDURE Copy: GPShapeAsn; VIRTUAL;`
Produces a copy of the `GPRubberLine`.

Inherits from `GPRubberShape`, `GPBoxBoundedShape`, `GPShape`

Subclasses None

GPRubberShape *Unit* `GPRubberShapesUnit`

Association `GPRubberShapeAsn`

Description A shape that "rubberbands," drawing and erasing itself to allow the user to resize the shape before it is permanently drawn.

Public Interface `CONSTRUCTOR Init;`
Initializes the `GPRubberShape` (with the bounding box's corner coordinates set to (0, 0)).

`CONSTRUCTOR InitWithPoints (start, finish: GPPoint);`
Initializes the `GPRubberShape` with the given locations.

`DESTRUCTOR Destroy; VIRTUAL;`
Destroys the `GPRubberShape`.

`PROCEDURE StartDraw (target: GPDrawingAreaAsn);`
Starts the drawing process by drawing the shape in its initial location.

`PROCEDURE Draw (target: GPDrawingAreaAsn);`
Erases the shape from its old location and draws it in its new location.

`PROCEDURE FinishDraw (target: GPDrawingAreaAsn);`
Draws the line in its final location, and sets the shape to be reused later.

`PROCEDURE Copy: GPRubberShapeAsn; VIRTUAL;`
Produces a copy of the `GPRubberShape`.

Inherits from `GPBoxBoundedShape`, `GPShape`

Subclasses `GPRubberFramedOval`, `GPRubberFramedRect`, `GPRubberLine`

GPShape *Unit* `GPShapesUnit`

Association `GPShapeAsn`

Description A generic shape base class. This class should not be instantiated directly.

Public Interface `CONSTRUCTOR Init;`
Initializes a `GPShape`.

`DESTRUCTOR Destroy; VIRTUAL;`
Destroys a `GPShape`.

`PROCEDURE Draw (targetLink: GPDrawingAreaAsn);`
Draws the `GPShape` in a `GPDrawingArea`.

GPShape (cont.)

Public Interface (continued)

`PROCEDURE DrawWithStyle (targetLink: GPDrawingAreaAsn; styleLink:GPDrawingStyleAsn);`
Draws the `GPShape` in a `GPDrawingArea` using a `GPDrawingStyle`.

`PROCEDURE Copy: GPShapeAsn; VIRTUAL;`
Produces a copy of the `GPShape`.

Inherits from None

Subclasses `GPBoxBoundedShape`, `GPLine`, `GPPoint`, `GPText`

GPSlider

Unit `GPSliderUnit`

Association `GPSliderAsn`

Description Displays a numeric value with upper and lower bounds and allows the user to change that value interactively using a slider mechanism similar to that of a scroll bar. This class should not be instantiated directly.

Public Interface

`CONSTRUCTOR Init (containerLink: GPManagerAsn);`
Initializes a `GPSlider`.

`DESTRUCTOR Destroy; VIRTUAL;`
Destroys a `GPSlider`.

`PROCEDURE ValueChanged; VIRTUAL;`
Defines behavior to occur when value in slider is changed.

`PROCEDURE SetHeight (num: integer);`
Sets the height of the scale (in pixels).

`PROCEDURE SetWidth (num: integer);`
Sets the width of the scale (in pixels).

`PROCEDURE MakeHorizontal;`
Sets the slider's orientation to horizontal.

`PROCEDURE MakeVertical;`
Sets the slider's orientation to vertical.

`PROCEDURE ShowVal;`
Displays the value of the slider.

`PROCEDURE HideVal;`
Hides the value of the slider.

Inherits from None

Subclasses `GPIntSlider`, `GPRealSlider`

GPText

Unit `GPShapesUnit`

Association `GPTextAsn`

GPText (cont.)

Description

Text that can be drawn on a `GPDrawingArea`. The text is saved as a single string.

Public Interface

```
CONSTRUCTOR Init(initText: string);
```
Initializes `GPText` with given text at location (0, 0).

```
CONSTRUCTOR InitWithCoords (initText: string;
   x,y:integer);
```
Initializes `GPText` with given text at set coordinates.

```
CONSTRUCTOR InitWithPoint (initText: string; pt:
   GPPoint);
```
Initializes `GPText` with a location.

```
DESTRUCTOR Destroy; VIRTUAL;
```
Destroys a `GPText`.

```
PROCEDURE SetString (newText: string);
```
Modifies the `GPText`'s string.

```
FUNCTION GetString: string;
```
Returns the `GPText`'s string.

```
FUNCTION GetX: integer;
```
Returns the value of the *x*-coordinate.

```
PROCEDURE SetX (x: integer);
```
Sets the value of the *x*-coordinate to `x`.

```
FUNCTION GetY: integer;
```
Returns the value of the *y*-coordinate.

```
PROCEDURE SetY (y: integer);
```
Sets the value of the *y*-coordinate to `y`.

```
PROCEDURE SetCoords (x, y: integer);
```
Sets the values of the *x*- and *y*-coordinates to the corresponding parameters.

```
PROCEDURE GetCoords (VAR x, y: integer);
```
Returns the value of the *x*-coordinate in the first parameter and gets the value of the *y*-coordinate and puts it in the second parameter.

```
PROCEDURE Copy: GPShapeAsn; VIRTUAL;
```
Produces a copy of the `GPText`.

```
PROCEDURE CopyAsGPText: GPTextAsn;
```
Produces a copy of the `GPText`.

```
FUNCTION Equal(other : GPText): Boolean;
```
Returns `TRUE` if the coordinates of `other` are the same as this instance's.

Inherits from `GPShape`

Subclasses None

GPTextArea

Unit `GPTextAreaUnit`

Association `GPTextAreaAsn`

Description A text area that allows the user to manipulate text.

Public Interface

`CONSTRUCTOR Init (containerLink: GPManagerAsn);`
Initializes the `GPTextArea`.

`DESTRUCTOR Destroy; VIRTUAL;`
Destroys the `GPTextArea`.

`PROCEDURE TextChanged (newText: string); VIRTUAL;`
This method is automatically called after the text in the `GPTextArea` is modified by the user and the enter key is pressed. It is virtual and can be redefined in subclasses.

`PROCEDURE Clear;`
Clears the `GPTextArea` of all text.

`PROCEDURE SetText (text: string);`
Sets the text in the `GPTextArea` to `text`.

`FUNCTION GetText: string;`
Returns the text that is in the `GPTextArea`.

`PROCEDURE AppendText (text: string);`
Appends `text` to the end of the text in the `GPTextArea`.

`PROCEDURE InsertText (text: string; pos: integer);`
Inserts `text` into the text in the `GPTextArea` at the desired location.

`PROCEDURE MakeEditable;`
Allows the user to modify the text in the `GPTextArea`.

`PROCEDURE MakeUnEditable;`
Prevents the user from modifying the text in the `GPTextArea`.

`PROCEDURE SetWidth (width: integer);`
Establishes the width (in pixels) of the text area.

`PROCEDURE SetHeight (height: integer);`
Establishes the height (in pixels) of the text area.

Inherits from None

Subclasses None

GPToggleButton

Unit `GPButtonUnit`

Association `GPToggleButtonAsn`

GPToggleButton (cont.)

Description

An area of a window that can be seen and clicked on to produce an action with an "on" and "off" state. The `Activate` method (inherited virtually from `GPButton`) defines the behavior when switching to the "on" state. The `DeActivate` method (defined virtually here) defines the behavior for switching to the "off" state.

Public Interface

`CONSTRUCTOR Init (containerLink: GPManagerAsn);`
Initializes the `GPToggleButton`.

`DESTRUCTOR Destroy; VIRTUAL;`
Destroys the `GPToggleButton`.

`PROCEDURE SetButton;`
Activates the button visually. This method will also call the `Activate` method.

`PROCEDURE UnSetButton;`
Deactivates the button visually. This method will also call the `DeActivate` method.

`PROCEDURE DeActivate; VIRTUAL;`
This method is called when the button is deactivated. Like the `Activate` method, it is virtual and should be redefined in a subclass.

Inherits from

`GPButton`, `GPLabel`

Subclasses

None

GPWindow

Unit

`GPWindowUnit`

Association

`GPWindowAsn`

Description

A rectangular area on the screen that can contain other GP objects. Use this class when your application will have more than one window that will be on the screen for the life of the application.

Public Interface

`CONSTRUCTOR InitWithName (windowName: string);`
Initializes a `GPWindow`.

`DESTRUCTOR Destroy; VIRTUAL;`
Destroys the `GPWindow`.

`PROCEDURE Show; VIRTUAL;`
Makes the window appear on the screen.

`PROCEDURE Hide; VIRTUAL;`
Removes the window from the screen.

Inherits from

`GPManager`

Subclasses

`GPApplication`

Index